TEACHER'S HANDBOOK

Contextualized Language Instruction

Fourth Edition

Judith L. Shrum

Virginia Polytechnic Institute and State University

Eileen W. Glisan

Indiana University of Pennsylvania

HEINLE
CENGAGE Learning

Australia • Brazil • Japan • Korea • Mexico • Singapore • Spain • United Kingdom • United States

Teacher's Handbook: Contextualized Language Instruction, Fourth Edition
Judith L. Shrum, Eileen W. Glisan

Publisher: Beth Kramer

Executive Editor: Lara Semones

Associate Development Editor:
Catharine Thomson

Editorial Assistant: María Colina

Media Editor: Laurel Miller

Marketing Manager: MJ Prinaris

Marketing Coordinator: Janine Enos

Marketing Communications Manager:
Stacey Purviance

Content Project Manager: Tiffany Kayes

Senior Art Director: Linda Jurras

Print Buyer: Susan Carroll

Senior Rights Acquisition Account Manager:
Katie Huha

Text Researcher: Sarah D'Stair

Production Service/Compositor:
Pre-Press PMG

Text Designer: Pre-Press PMG

Photo Manager: Leitha Etheridge-Sims

Photo Researcher: Joshua Brown

Cover Designer: Wing Ngan

For product information and technology assistance, contact us at
Cengage Learning Customer & Sales Support, 1-800-354-9706

For permission to use material from this text or product,
submit all requests online at **www.cengage.com/permissions.**
Further permissions questions can be emailed to
permissionrequest@cengage.com.

Library of Congress Control Number: 2009934070

ISBN-13: 978-1-4130-3321-2

ISBN-10: 1-4130-3321-0

Heinle
20 Channel Center Street
Boston, MA 02210
USA

Cengage Learning is a leading provider of customized learning solutions with office locations around the globe, including Singapore, the United Kingdom, Australia, Mexico, Brazil, and Japan. Locate your local office at:
international.cengage.com/region

Cengage Learning products are represented in Canada by
Nelson Education, Ltd.

For your course and learning solutions, visit **www.cengage.com.**

Purchase any of our products at your local college store or at our preferred online store **www.cengagebrain.com.**

Printed in United States
4 5 6 7 8   16 15 14 13 12

Contents

Acknowledgments

In this fourth edition, the sources of our inspiration continue to be the students and colleagues with whom we work: language learners, beginning teachers, peers, and experts. We have also found inspiration in recent changes in the visibility of our field. Key national endeavors, such as the development of standards for students and teachers, have continued to serve as a catalyst for moving language education forward in the U.S. Recognizing the importance of these initiatives, we have again represented real case study experiences against the backdrop of the changes in our profession, always saluting those teachers who daily commit their intellect and energy to the work of language instruction.

Words cannot adequately express our gratitude to Dr. Richard Donato for his expert guidance as our consultant and primary reviewer for this edition. We thank Rick for the many hours he devoted to reading and critiquing the drafts of each chapter, pointing us to additional sources of information, and acting as a sounding board for our ideas. We are most appreciative of his encouragement, positive feedback, sympathetic listening, patience, and never-ending willingness to take time out of his busy schedule to assist us in various ways.

In addition, we sincerely thank our principal reviewers:

Luisa C. Pérez, Emporia State University
C. Brian Barnett, Indiana University-Bloomington
Jing Luo, Bloomsburg University
Peter A. Schultz, Kennesaw State University
Valery Prill, Lipscomb University
Catherine M. Barrette, Wayne State University
Jay Siskin, Cabrillo College
Stacey Katz, University of Utah

Benjamin Rifkin, Temple University
Claudia Fernández, DePaul University
Reika Ebert, Murray State University
Markus Muller, California State University, Long Beach
Anne Nerenz, Eastern Michigan University
Flore Zéphir, University of Missouri – Columbia

Colleagues at our respective universities and teachers and students with whom we have worked also played an important role as we wrote the book and tested concepts, providing a classroom laboratory, some of the materials, as well as reasons for reflection. We hope that they will recognize themselves in the Teach and Reflect sections, in the Discuss and Reflect case studies, and on the Web site.

As always, we are pleased that the book is published by Heinle, Cengage Learning and the great team of editors, under the leadership of P. J. Boardman as Editor-in-Chief, Beth Kramer as Publisher, and Lara Semones as Executive Editor.

Finally, we wish to thank those dear to our hearts for their continuing support of our efforts. Judith thanks her Mom, Elaine Shrum, for lifelong encouragement, support, and understanding; and John for passing up horseback riding time to allow for writing time. Eileen thanks her family—Roy, Nina, and Alex—for their support and patience during the many months of the writing process. She also owes much gratitude to her friend and proofreader par excellence, Anne Ribar, for her expert proofreading of page proofs for the text.

Preface

*T*eacher's Handbook was designed with the philosophy that the purpose of language use is to convey meaning in a variety of contexts. The central theme of the text is the contextualization of language instruction. Language that is introduced and taught in meaningful contexts enables the learner to acquire competency in using language for real-world communicative purposes. Integrated language instruction allows learners to approach the learning task by combining their ability to create interpretive, interpersonal, and presentational communication with their knowledge of culture and their background knowledge.

The *Standards for Foreign Language Learning in the 21st Century (SFLL)* (National Standards in Foreign Language Education Project [NSFLEP], 2006) focus on context and content, prompting the question: What should students know and be able to do with another language? Each chapter of *Teacher's Handbook* assists language professionals as they develop a contextualized approach to language instruction that is based on meaningful language use, real-world communication, interaction among language learners, and learning of new information. The teaching examples and case studies offer a broad perspective of diverse circumstances taken from real settings in elementary schools, middle/intermediate/junior high schools, high schools, and post-secondary settings. Further, the teaching examples are offered for various languages to show that the principles underlying contextualized instruction are constant for the many age groups represented and the languages taught.

The philosophy of *Teacher's Handbook* is that professionals in language teaching benefit from an openness to new ideas, research findings, and an ever-expanding and emerging repertoire of practices that evolve as we discover more about teaching and learning foreign languages in today's classrooms. This philosophy is grounded in the sociocultural environment of each individual school and classroom, recognizing the idiosyncratic influences of that environment and the roles teachers and learners perform. *Teacher's Handbook* is not simply a compendium of research on second language acquisition and foreign language teaching. Rather, its purpose is to synthesize the wealth of research for teachers, help them to understand it, and identify its implications for classroom practice. Current research undergirds *Teacher's Handbook* and serves as the backdrop for the suggestions for planning, teaching, and assessment. Since research and practice are dynamic in nature, teachers are encouraged to continuously seek new research that occurs beyond this edition and to use their own classrooms as laboratories for trying out the strategies presented here.

WHAT'S NEW IN THE FOURTH EDITION?

We have remained true to our initial aim of creating a book for beginning as well as experienced teachers that they would use for reference beyond the methods course or the workshop in which they encountered it. We hoped it would find a place among the books on each teacher's desk, and that it would be well-worn with dog-eared pages. In each new edition we bring contemporary research-based views of language teaching, incorporating the wide-ranging developments in our field. While the basic pedagogical support within the structure of *Teacher's Handbook* has been maintained in the fourth edition, there are five significant changes:

1. **Post-Secondary Icons.** Although the third edition incorporated several topics of interest to graduate students, GTAs, and post-secondary faculty, we have expanded the range and number of instances in which we address language teaching at the post-secondary level. Additional applications suitable for that level appear in all sections of each chapter, that is, in the Teach and Reflect, the Discuss and Reflect, and the View and Reflect sections. These instances are now marked with a mortar board that serves as a post-secondary icon.

2. **New Techno Focus.** With the explosion of technological possibilities for the foreign language classroom, we have provided a brief "Techno Focus" in each chapter of this edition of *Teacher's Handbook,* showing how teachers use technology in their classrooms. Just as a single course in technology can prepare teachers to integrate technology only in a very limited way, we believe that featuring only one chapter that deals with this topic is a narrow approach to such an important topic (Kassen, Lavine, Murphy-Judy, & Peters, 2007). Instead, we have integrated the discussion of technology throughout each chapter to prompt teachers to contemplate its integration with each of the chapter's topics involving planning, instruction, and assessment. The Techno Focus appears in the Teach and Reflect and the Discuss and Reflect sections. Additional uses of technology appear in the View and Reflect sections on the *Teacher's Handbook* Web site. The Techno Focus sections deal with blogging, the Web, YouTube, cell phones, iPods and MP3 players, and other tools, as shown in the following table.

TECHNO FOCUS TOPIC	CHAPTER IN *TEACHER'S HANDBOOK*	SECTION
Using online music, lyrics, photos, and language practice to teach authentic songs	1	Discuss and Reflect
Podcasting	2	Teach and Reflect and View and Reflect
Content-based instruction module	3	Discuss and Reflect
Planning for a story-based lesson using comic strips	4	Discuss and Reflect
E-chat with experienced teacher	5	Teach and Reflect
Blogging	6	Teach and Reflect
Coordinating authentic online material with a textbook	7	Teach and Reflect
Using cell phones	8	Discuss and Reflect
Video journal of literary film	9	Teach and Reflect
i–Movies	10	Teach and Reflect
Online testing	11	Teach and Reflect
Creating a WebQuest and evaluating Web sites. Since this is the chapter on technology, many sections focus on classroom uses, e.g., photography, Activboard®, ACTFL Talk Radio, and others.	12	Teach and Reflect and the View and Reflect segments on the *Teacher's Handbook* Web site

3. **New Themes.** Several new themes have been introduced in the Conceptual Orientation: Language Policy and Language Education Policy, research on brain-based learning, sheltered and dual language instruction, genre-based writing, and Dynamic Assessment. The fourth edition features more in-depth and updated coverage on topics introduced in the third edition, notably, recasts and error correction, staying in the target language, teacher-to-student and student-to-student interaction, teaching grammar, intercultural communication, teaching writing, and differentiated instruction. The focus on sociocultural theory, a key element in all editions of *Teacher's Handbook*, continues to receive full treatment throughout each chapter of the fourth edition.

4. **New Aspects of Implementation Sections.** The Teach and Reflect and Discuss and Reflect sections of each chapter are designed to put knowledge into practice. In addition, in the Preliminary Chapter, implementation of knowledge takes the shape of an Investigate and Reflect section, and in Chapter 1 this section is called Observe and Reflect. Although the Teach and Reflect and Discuss and Reflect sections typically contain two "episodes" within each section, several chapters contain additional Teach and Reflect episodes designed to appeal to post-secondary instructors. Discuss and Reflect sections contain case studies; sometimes the research findings are supported and sometimes the real circumstances of the classroom indicate the need for further research. More teacher-developed materials appear in these sections, as in the "Survivor" game in the case study in Chapter 8. Each chapter contains one Case Study in the Discuss and Reflect section of the book, with additional case studies on the *Teacher's Handbook* Web site. Case studies have been revised or replaced with new, more engaging and illustrative cases. The section entitled "To prepare the case," which was formerly in the book, now appears on the *Teacher's Handbook* Web site. Additional case studies also appear on the *Teacher's Handbook* Web site. It bears reiterating that all case studies were inspired by real classroom scenarios, real teachers and other professionals, and real students, and as such they reflect the reality of today's foreign language classrooms. In the Teach and Reflect and the Discuss and Reflect sections, the ACTFL/NCATE Standards are now accompanied by the TESOL/NCATE Standards. Furthermore, the numerical listings of the standards now include the full statement of each standard to facilitate association of the task or item with the standard it addresses. In addition, we have preserved the View and Reflect implementation section on the *Teacher's Handbook* Web site. Here, one to three video segments appear for each of the 12 chapters of the book. All of these video selections show teaching practices in real classrooms, many of which are part of the WGBH and Annenberg/CPB project "Teaching Foreign Languages K–12: A Library of Classroom Practices."

5. **Expanded Web Site.** For each of the chapter sections, new resources appear on the *Teacher's Handbook* Web site at www.cengagebrain.com. Numerous links to Web sites created by teachers, as well as other online resources, are provided. For example, the Web site contains a video of a kindergarten class on a children's story about chicken pox, content-based units designed by the Center for Advanced Language Proficiency Education and Research (CALPERS), Linguafolios, teacher-designed WebQuests, and rubrics. Each of these resources is integrated with the appropriate chapter in the book, where an icon appears signaling that important information and extension materials can be found on the Web.

WHAT STRENGTHS OF THE PREVIOUS EDITIONS HAVE BEEN MAINTAINED?

Teacher's Handbook is designed especially for the teacher who is about to start his/her career teaching foreign languages at the K–12 levels. In addition, professionals in higher education can make practical use of the book's suggestions with regard to standards for student learning, teacher performance, and program effectiveness. *Teacher's Handbook* is also suited for accomplished and experienced teachers who are searching for an update in current theory and practice, for those who are returning to the classroom after an absence from teaching, and for those who are seeking national board certification. Faculty members responsible for the accreditation/program review process in foreign language teacher education will also find the book useful in designing tasks to meet ACTFL/NCATE and TESOL/NCATE standards.

This text aims to enable foreign language teachers to use current theories about learning and teaching as a basis for reflection and practice. Teachers are active decision makers who use opportunities to apply theory by observing classroom interaction, designing and teaching their own lessons, and making appropriate decisions in a wide variety of situations. We believe that preparing to be language teachers is not a matter of learning knowledge and skills but rather it is about becoming "educators who contribute deliberately and critically to the discourses and practices that constitute schools and society" (Willett & Miller, 2004, p. 53). As developing foreign language teachers reflect upon their teaching and make decisions, they draw from many sources: competence in the second language and culture; knowledge of how the curriculum is designed and implemented; application of subject knowledge to actual teaching; application of research findings to classroom teaching; understanding of the power that technology can have in a fully articulated language program; clinical experience; and knowledge of the means by which teaching effectiveness is examined within the school context (Glisan, 2001, 2006). Accordingly, *Teacher's Handbook* presents theoretical findings concerning key aspects of language teaching, as well as observational episodes, micro-teaching situations, and case studies, in order to assist beginning teachers as they develop their teaching approaches and to guide experienced teachers as they update their theoretical knowledge and teaching practices.

Teacher's Handbook assists teachers as they begin their journey toward accomplished teaching by basing their learning, teaching, and reflecting on the five propositions established by the National Board for Professional Teaching Standards (NBPTS):

- Teachers are committed to students and their learning.
- Teachers know the subjects they teach and how to teach those subjects to students.
- Teachers are responsible for managing and monitoring student learning.
- Teachers think systematically about their practice and learn from experience.
- Teachers are members of learning communities (NBPTS, 2009).

The philosophy of *Teacher's Handbook* reflects Freeman's interpretist view of teaching founded in the daily operation of thinking and acting in context, i.e., "knowing [...] Freeman, 1996, p. 98). In addition, the text adopts the view that knowledge [...] lly constructed (Freeman, 2004). The teacher's sense of self is cen[...] nstruction, and his/her authority and expertise are shared in the [...] of knowledge among peers (Baxter Magolda, 2001). Teachers learn [...] worlds (e.g., their subject matter, their classroom context, and the peo[...] use these interpretations to act and react appropriately and effectively.

Knowing how to teach does not simply involve knowing how to do things in the classroom. Rather, it involves a cognitive dimension that connects thought with activity. This contextual know-how is acquired over time and its interpretations bring about effective classroom practice (Freeman, 1996).

Accordingly, novice and experienced teachers using *Teacher's Handbook* will find structured and open-ended opportunities to observe classroom teaching and to plan and conduct micro-teaching lessons, all in light of the theory and information discussed in each chapter. A variety of case studies for K–16 describe the reality of actual teachers and learners, sometimes in support of current research findings, sometimes adding puzzling contradictions to current research, but always enriching the interpretive experience of teaching and reflecting. Related activities provide interesting opportunities to investigate and discuss effective classroom practice. Indeed, novice and experienced teachers can strengthen their individual approaches to teaching by observing, investigating, discussing ideas, teaching, and then relating these activities to one another.

In sum, according to Cochran-Smith (2004), teacher quality is "one of the most, if not the most, significant factor in students' achievement and educational improvement" (p. 3). It is our sincere hope that *Teacher's Handbook* impacts the quality of foreign language teachers so that language learners have successful experiences in our classrooms and are encouraged to pursue lifelong learning about other languages and cultures.

SUGGESTIONS FOR USING *TEACHER'S HANDBOOK*

We have received a substantial amount of feedback from reviewers and users of *Teacher's Handbook* that has shed light on the many ways in which the text is being used. The following is a description of the key uses of the text, with selected quotes from *Handbook* users, whose names will be kept anonymous:

- *The primary methodology textbook in a methods course:* "I have two types of classes I use this text with: One is the FL methodology course, composed of undergraduates who are education majors, usually 5–8 students . . . who are getting ready to do their student teaching and graduate the following semester; and the other is made up of graduate students who are getting ready to start being FL Graduate Teaching Assistants in our department at the university and who are mixed with middle/high school FL teachers taking this as a refresher course."

- *One of several texts for preparation in ESL and World Languages:* "We use the text as one of several course texts for our initial licensure program in ESL and World Languages. It is the main source of reading that relates specifically to World Languages. . . . It is used in an integrated program that spans four courses over two semesters."

- *The primary methodology textbook divided for use in two courses:* "I teach two methods courses, Introduction to Teaching FLs and Methods of Teaching FLs. . . . I have used Chapters 1, 2, part of 3, and 10 in the first course, along with study of the *Standards for Foreign Language Learning in the 21st Century (SFLL)* (NSFLEP, 2006) (generic and language-specific) and the proficiency levels, plus some work on teaching culture (Chapter 5), teaching pronunciation, and presenting vocabulary in context. In the second course I have used Chapters 4, 5, 6, 7, 8, and 11."

- *The methodology textbook for endorsement programs, bilingual education programs, and independent studies:* "I use it . . . in my . . . upper-level interdisciplinary program, Bilingual Education and Teaching. . . . The program is preparatory for teaching careers and provides endorsement credits in foreign language and bilingual teaching. . . . I also use it extensively as the methodology textbook when working with students conducting independent studies on foreign language teaching in the elementary grades."

- *The methodology textbook for a special topics course:* When asked for a description of *Teacher's Handbook* for a colleague, one reviewer stated: "A very complete textbook that provides students (or whomever its audience) with up to date theory and empirical research on instructed second language acquisition, and guides them on how to apply all this information to their classroom practices. The textbook provides in a clear and accessible way the information that language teachers need in order to teach better. The case studies and the tasks are relevant and realistic; they help students reflect and become critical research readers and practitioners. The textbook also provides a wealth of additional information to support the student in his/her learning. It is a textbook that all language teachers should have and consult frequently."

As indicated by the above sampling of quotes by *Teacher's Handbook* users, the flexible nature of the text offers the possibility of multiple uses to serve the unique purposes and demands of specific instructional settings. In addition to the uses listed above, the text serves as a reference book and is also used as a textbook in conjunction with field experiences, including student teaching or teaching internships. As one reviewer commented: "The 4th edition of the *Teacher's Handbook* is clear, complete, and yet concise. The references at the end of each chapter and the extensive material available on the web site give enough information to build a more than satisfactory understanding of the topics raised in the text itself . . . presenting these materials through the web allows the text's initial presentation of the ideas to be clear and concise enough for undergraduates to grasp them."

The features of the fourth edition of *Teacher's Handbook*, including the expanded Web site, inclusion of additional topics, and applicability to more languages and levels, will undoubtedly offer methodology instructors even more possibilities for its use.

ORGANIZATION OF *TEACHER'S HANDBOOK*

Teacher's Handbook consists of 12 chapters plus a Preliminary Chapter. The first chapters present topics of a more general nature, and later chapters proceed to more specific technique-oriented issues. The Preliminary Chapter provides an introduction to the profession of language teaching. This chapter helps teachers (1) to become familiar with the professional organizations and their resources, (2) to understand the expectations of their performance in schools, and (3) to understand how language policy and language educational policy function in contemporary U.S. society. Chapter 1 explores the role of contextualized input, output, and interaction in the language learning process, including a presentation of key theoretical frameworks that focus on the importance of meaning and learner engagement in acquiring language. In Chapter 1, the Observe and Reflect section helps teachers think about language learning and teaching as natural processes occurring in an environment outside of the classroom. Chapter 2 examines an integrative approach to language instruction in which language is presented and taught in meaningful contexts, consistent with the *Standards for Foreign Language Learning in the 21st Century (SFLL)* (NSFLEP, 2006). An overview of the standards framework presented in this chapter is followed by specific ways to match activities and materials to the standards in subsequent chapters. In Chapter 3, teachers learn how to organize content and plan for integrated instruction by means of long- and short-r[...] standards-based goals. Suggestions are offered for using aut[...] organize instruction and to engage students in the learning pro[...]

Special attention is given in Chapters 4 and 5 to foreign/se[...] at elementary and middle school levels of instruction. The unique [...] tional characteristics of learners at these two levels respond best to pa[...] and strategies. An approach utilized with older adolescents, for examp[...] propriate for young children. However, as will be highlighted throughou[...] many techniques can be adapted for use across instructional levels. The i[...] Chapters 4 and 5 is introduced in terms of the interaction between learning an[...] developmental stages, the possible effects of maturity on language learning, and [...] sequent implications for teaching. Teachers explore the cognitive and maturational [...] ences between the elementary and middle school child and the adolescent learner[...] develop lessons appropriate to these cognitive levels. Ways of connecting learning acro[...] disciplines and grade levels are explored as the Connections goal area is addressed in[...] Chapter 4. In Chapter 5, the Cultures and the Comparisons goal areas are explored in terms of the products–practices–perspectives framework.

Chapters 6 through 9 offer many opportunities for teachers to focus instruction on the three modes of the Communication Standard, all within real language contexts and at various levels of instruction. Chapter 6 presents ideas for developing interpretive communication through the use of authentic input and building of interpretation strategies. In Chapter 7, teachers explore an approach for contextualizing grammar instruction through the use of dialogic story-based teaching using the PACE model. In Chapter 8, teachers learn strategies for helping students to develop oral and written interpersonal communication through meaningful contexts and opportunities for classroom interaction. Chapter 9 presents ideas for helping students develop oral/multimedia and written presentational communication through practices such as writing across the curriculum, process-oriented writing, and use of presentational software.

Chapter 10 presents ideas on how teachers might handle the diverse needs of their students that affect classroom language learning, such as learning styles, multiple intelligences, and learning disabilities. Addressing the Communities goal area, teachers explore strategies for helping students who are from a variety of cultural, ethnic, and racial backgrounds, and those who have been labeled as "at risk" or "gifted," to use language to connect with target-language communities through service learning or differentiated instruction. In Chapter 11, teachers explore many alternatives for assessing learner progress, including authentic assessment, portfolios, rubrics, and other contextualized test formats and techniques that go beyond paper-and-pencil tests, including ways to empower learners through assessment. Chapter 12 provides models and insights into the ways in which teachers can use technology to connect their students with target language communities, while addressing the national technology standards established by the International Society on Technology Education (ISTE, 2007, 2008).

Chapter Organization

Each chapter of *Teacher's Handbook* is organized into three sections:

1. **Conceptual Orientation.** This section grounds teaching practices in a valid body of research and theoretical knowledge. It briefly describes the theoretical principles underlying the language learning observation, teaching tasks, and case studies presented later in the chapter. The section is a summary of what is known about topics in

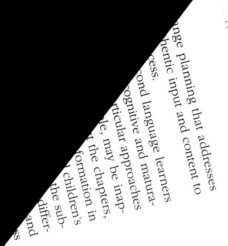

...d includes references to the original research sources for addi-
...r review.

...ions: Investigate and Reflect, Observe and Reflect, Teach

...tigate and Reflect (Preliminary Chapter), Observe and Reflect
...nd Reflect (all subsequent chapters) sections highlight practi-
...how to teach. In some cases, additional episodes appear on
...Web site. The Preliminary Chapter contains Web-based tasks
...e Web sites of their professional organizations. Chapter 1
...ns, and subsequent chapters contain two to four teaching
...or micro-teaching situation integrates the theoretical ori-
...hers an opportunity to implement pedagogically sound
...e environment of a methods class. These micro-teaching
...or experienced teachers attempting to learn new tech-
...llowing each teaching or observation situation will help
...iques into personal teaching approaches. In each Web
...fourth implementation section called View and Reflect, which
...pportunities to view one to three video clips of teaching scenarios and ana-
...yze them in terms of the information explored in the corresponding text chapter.

3. **Discuss and Reflect.** This section provides a case study presenting non-fictitious
situations actually experienced by foreign language teachers at various levels of instruction. Additional case studies appear on the *Teacher's Handbook* Web site. The
case studies offer teachers the opportunity to link the theoretically grounded practices
explored in the first two sections of each chapter with the reality of teaching circumstances. Every day, foreign language teachers face challenges like those presented in
the case studies—challenges that may arise out of mismatches among teaching goals,
learner preparedness, and academic tasks, or out of institutional goals that are inconsistent with teaching goals.

The Discuss and Reflect section includes two types of cases, based on real-life classroom scenarios: those that present teaching situations that support the theoretical bases
featured in the chapter and those that present problematic teaching situations that are inconsistent with the theory and rationale of the chapter. The cases provide the information
necessary to enable teachers to read the case and the referenced materials and to prepare
a resolution of the case for class discussion. Often the cases include many details about
teachers and/or teaching situations so that readers might decide which details contribute
the most to resolving the case.

How to Use the Case Studies

We have been inspired by Cochran-Smith's (1999) view that "the teacher is an intellectual
who generates knowledge, that teaching is a process of co-constructing knowledge and
curriculum with students, and that the most promising ways of learning about teaching
across the professional lifespan are based on inquiry within communities rather than
training for individuals" (pp. 114–115). The case study approach was recommended by
the Task Force on Teaching as a Profession (Carnegie Corporation, 1986). Cases are created for purposes of discussion and seek to elicit active analysis by users with different
perspectives.

A case has been defined as a descriptive document, presented in narrative form,
that is based on a real-life situation or event. Case studies are used to "gain an in-depth
understanding of the situation and meaning for those involved. The interest is in process

rather than outcome, in context rather than a specific variable, in discovery rather than confirmation" (Merriam, 2001, p. 19). Cases are not problems, though they may include problems and problem solving. In a case study, the real conditions, complexity, and coping behavior of the participants are described. As Stake (2000) points out, the "utility of [the] case research to practitioners . . . is in its extension of experience" (p. 449). Case study for teaching purposes selects the major elements of a case for illustrative discussion and debate among students (Merriam, p. 19). A case study "focuses attention on a single entity, usually as it exists in its naturally occurring environment," and provides the basis for three levels of analysis and reflection (Johnson, 1992, p. 75). First, readers are given maximum guidance as they reflect upon the situations and attempt to analyze them. In the first several chapters of *Teacher's Handbook*, teachers are given a list of alternatives that represent plausible solutions to the problem or challenge presented in the teaching situation. The class discussion of each alternative assists readers in developing their own approaches to the case. In some chapters, additional information is presented, as in Chapter 8, where teachers provide a description of their "Survivor" game, which serves as a catalyst for keeping instruction in the target language.

Second, *Teacher's Handbook* users are encouraged to collaborate with their peers and the instructor as they discuss the alternatives and/or the development of their approaches to the situations. Sharing ideas within the classroom greatly facilitates the problem-solving process and empowers teachers in the decision-making process. In the **To prepare the case** section on the *Teacher's Handbook* Web site, teachers are encouraged to consult other referenced works for additional information that will assist them in formulating sound approaches to the case development. *Teacher's Handbook* users may choose from among the suggested references or consult others recommended by their instructor.

Third, as readers become increasingly familiar with case study exploration, they are asked to assume greater responsibility for developing their own solutions to the problems and challenges presented in the cases on the basis of the information provided in the chapter, the class discussions, and the previously acquired knowledge and experience. Instructors might encourage online discussions, or completion of a professional diary or journal to include students' reflections on the cases. Thus, the entire process leads teachers to develop their problem-solving abilities while preparing them to reflect on their teaching and classroom experiences, which are familiar and yet not completely understood.

As the case studies are designed to evoke discussion, one way to use them is to follow a jigsaw pattern, as outlined in Chapter 8, placing students in expert and novice roles and rotating them around the class, thus allowing for discussion of two or more case studies in an efficient manner.

In conclusion, we hope you will enjoy using *Teacher's Handbook* and we welcome your feedback on the fourth edition.

REFERENCES

American Council on the Teaching of Foreign Languages (ACTFL) (2002). *ACTFL/NCATE program standards for the preparation of foreign language teachers*. Yonkers, NY: Author.

Baxter Magolda, M. B. (2001). *Making their own way*. Sterling, VA: Stylus.

Carnegie Corporation. (1986). *A nation prepared: Teachers for the 21st century*. New York: Carnegie Corporation.

Cochran-Smith, M. (1999). Learning to teach for social justice. In G. A. Griffith (Ed.), *The education of teachers: Ninety-eighth Yearbook of the National Society for the Study of Education* (pp. 114–144). Chicago, IL: University of Chicago Press.

Cochran-Smith, M. (2004). Taking stock in 2004: Teacher education in dangerous times. *Journal of Teacher Education, 55*(1), 3–7.

Freeman, D. (1996). Redefining the relationship between research and what teachers know. In K. M. Bailey & D. Nunan (Eds.), *Voices from the language classroom: Qualitative research in second language education* (pp. 88–115). Cambridge, UK: Cambridge University Press.

Freeman, D. (2004). Language, sociocultural theory, and L2 teacher education: Examining the technology of subject matter and the architecture of instruction. In M. R. Hawkins (Ed.), *Language learning and teacher education* (pp. 169–197). Clevedon, England: Multilingual Matters, Ltd.

Glisan, E. W. (2001). Reframing teacher education within the context of quality, standards, supply, and demand. In R. Z. Lavine (Ed.), *Beyond the boundaries: Changing contexts in language learning* (pp. 165–200). Boston: McGraw-Hill.

Glisan, E. W. (2006). Today's pre-service foreign language teachers: New expectations, new realities for teacher preparation programs. In D. McAlpine & S. Dhonau (Eds.), *Responding to a new vision for teacher development.* 2006 Report of the Central States Conference on the Teaching of Foreign Languages (pp. 11–40). Eau Claire, WI: Crown Prints.

Glisan, E. W., & Phillips, J. K. (1998). Making the standards happen: A new vision for foreign language teacher preparation. *ACTFL Newsletter, 10*(4), 7–8, 13–14.

International Society for Technology Education (ISTE)/ National Educational Technology Standards Project. (2007). *National Educational Technology Standards for Students* (NETS-S). Retrieved September 22, 2008, from http://www.iste.org/AM/Template.cfm?Section=NETS.

International Society for Technology Education (ISTE)/ National Educational Technology Standards Project. (2008). *National Educational Technology Standards for Teachers* (NETS-T). Retrieved September 22, 2008, from http://www.iste.org/AM/Template. cfm?Section=NETS.

Interstate New Teacher Assessment and Support Consortium. (2002, June). *Model standards for licensing beginning foreign language teachers: A resource for state dialogue.* Washington, DC: Council of Chief State School Officers.

Johnson, D. M. (1992). *Approaches to research in second language learning.* White Plains, NY: Longman.

Kassen, M. A., Lavine, R. Z., Murphy-Judy, K., & Peters, M. (Eds.). (2007). *Preparing and developing technology-proficient L2 teachers.* CALICO Monograph Series Volume 6. San Marcos, TX: The Computer Assisted Language Instruction Consortium.

Merriam, S. B. (2001). *Qualitative research and case study applications in education.* San Francisco: Jossey-Bass.

National Board for Professional Teaching Standards (NBPTS). (2001, 2008). *World languages other than English standard*s. Arlington, VA: Author.

National Standards in Foreign Language Education Project (NSFLEP). (2006). *Standards for foreign language learning in the 21st century (SFLL).* Lawrence, KS: Allen Press.

National Board for Professional Teaching Standards (NBPTS). (2009). *The five core propositions.* Retrieved February 21, 2009, from http://www.nbpts.org/ the_standards/the_five_core_propositions.

Stake, R. E. (2000). Case studies. In N. K. Denzin & Y. S. Lincoln (Eds.), *The handbook of qualitative research* (2nd ed.) (pp. 435–454). Thousand Oaks, CA: Sage Publications.

Teachers of English to Speakers of Other Languages (TESOL). (2006). *PreK–12 English language proficiency standards.* Alexandria, VA: Author.

Willett, J., & Miller, S. (2004). Transforming the discourses of teaching and learning: Rippling waters and shifting sands. In M. R. Hawkins (Ed.), *Language learning and teacher education* (pp. 52–88). Clevedon, UK: Multilingual Matters, Ltd.

Preliminary Chapter: Becoming Familiar with the Profession and Expectations for Language Teachers

This preliminary chapter introduces the foreign language profession by describing its structure or "architecture" and by presenting expectations for teachers in terms of standards that have been developed for teacher candidates, beginning teachers, and accomplished teachers of foreign languages. As you explore this chapter, you will want to visit the *Teacher's Handbook* Web site, where indicated, in order to access the links to professional organizations and standards documents. At the end of the chapter, you will be asked to complete a series of tasks in which you will consult these Web sites to find specific information about the organizations, conferences, and teacher standards.

In this chapter, you will be introduced to:

- key national membership organizations important to the profession
- national language-specific organizations
- organizations that provide valuable professional resources and support

- regional language conferences
- your state language association
- key professional journals
- the continuum of foreign language teacher standards: NCATE, INTASC, NBPTS, TESOL, ISTE
- language policy and language education policy

Investigate and Reflect: Learning About Your National Language-Specific Organization and Your State Language Association; Learning About Your Regional Language Conference; Familiarizing Yourself With Foreign Language Resources; Comparing Teacher Standards Across the Career Continuum; Language Policy and Language Education Policy

In recent years, the foreign language field has made great strides in achieving a level of professional status that enables us to play an increasingly more prominent role in educational and legislative circles. Professional organizations have collaborated with one another as never before in order to set professional goals, establish policies, and offer their constituents valuable support and assistance.[1] These were pivotal steps as the foreign language education profession came together to articulate its expectations for language teachers in terms of standards for teacher candidates, beginning teachers, and accomplished teachers.

ARCHITECTURE OF THE PROFESSION[2]

The foreign language profession has been shaped by the contributions of many organizations, conferences, resources, and journals that constitute the architecture of our profession. Below is a summary of the key components of our architecture, summarized

www.cengagebrain.com

from that which appears on the Web site for each organization. On the *Teacher's Handbook* Web site, you will find links to each of these sites, where you can acquire additional information and updates. You will notice throughout the chapter the use of a number of acronyms. Consult the *Teacher's Handbook* Web site for a list of key acronyms as you become familiar with the architecture of the profession.

Key National Membership Organizations

MLA.   Founded in 1883, the Modern Language Association (MLA) promotes the study and teaching of language and literature and offers opportunities for its members to share their scholarly literary findings and teaching experiences with colleagues. Comprised of over 30,000 members in 100 countries, MLA hosts an annual convention and other meetings, works with related organizations, and maintains one of the finest publishing programs in the humanities. Its involvement with foreign language teaching and learning specifically is evidenced by its role in the creation of other key organizations.

ACTFL.   The national umbrella organization for the foreign language teaching profession is the American Council on the Teaching of Foreign Languages (ACTFL), founded in 1967 by the leadership of the MLA to address issues of teacher preparation, language instruction, and curriculum development. At that time, MLA turned its focus to the promotion of foreign language study and the development of tests for use in colleges, universities, and secondary schools (Hancock & Scebold, 2000).

ACTFL is the only national organization dedicated to the improvement and expansion of the teaching and learning of all languages at all levels of instruction. The mission of ACTFL is to promote and foster the study of foreign languages and cultures as an integral component of American education and society. It is an individual membership organization of currently more than 12,000 language educators and administrators from elementary school through graduate levels of education, as well as government and industry. The organization focuses on issues that are critical to the growth of the profession as well as the individual teacher. ACTFL publishes (1) the refereed journal *Foreign Language Annals*, which publishes research and theoretical articles on language learning and/or teaching and research-based classroom practices relevant to the concerns of language professionals at all levels of instruction; and (2) the magazine *The Language Educator,* which includes reports on ACTFL's activities, news and information of national and international interest to foreign language educators, teaching ideas, and resources. In addition to sponsoring an annual conference, the organization offers many professional development workshops and publications for its members dealing with a wide range of topics, such as oral proficiency testing, standards-based instruction and curriculum development, and integrated performance assessment. Since 1992, ACTFL has also maintained a language testing office, Language Testing International (LTI), which provides standardized, valid, language-proficiency assessments conducted by certified testers.

State Language Associations.   Under ACTFL's umbrella are the state language associations. To obtain information about your state association, see the *Teacher's Handbook* Web site for a link to foreign language state associations.

Also working in collaboration with ACTFL are the national language-specific organizations, which include:

- American Association of Teachers of Arabic (AATA)
- American Association of Teachers of French (AATF)
- American Association of Teachers of German (AATG)
- American Association of Teachers of Italian (AATI)

- American Association of Teachers of Slavic and East European Languages (AATSEEL)
- American Association of Teachers of Spanish and Portuguese (AATSP)
- American Classical League (ACL)
- American Council of Teachers of Russian (ACTR)
- Chinese Language Association of Secondary-Elementary Schools (CLASS) and Chinese Language Teachers Association (CLTA)
- National Council of Japanese Language Teachers (NCJLT) and Association of Teachers of Japanese (ATJ)
- American Association of Teachers of Korean (AATK)
- American Association of Teachers of Turkic Languages (AATTL)
- African Languages Teachers Association (ALTA)
- Council of Teachers of Southeast Asian Languages (COTSEAL)
- North American Association for Celtic Language Teachers (NAACLT)
- International Association of Teachers of Czech (formerly the North American Association of Teachers of Czech) (IATC-NAATC)
- National Association of Professors of Hebrew (NAPH)
- Norwegian Teachers Association of North America (NORTANA)
- South Asian Language Teachers Association (SALTA)

Some of these associations also have local chapters within the states.

See the *Teacher's Handbook* Web site for descriptions of additional professional organizations.

TESOL. TESOL—Teachers of English to Speakers of Other Languages—is an acronym that refers to the field itself and to the professional association.[3] The field of teaching English to speakers of other languages is a professional endeavor that requires specialized training. TESOL differs from teaching English to native speakers of English, since its primary focus is on teaching non-natives to communicate in English and understand cultural practices of English-speaking communities. English as a second language (ESL) educators teach in countries where English is the dominant language, such as Australia, Canada, England, and the United States. English as a foreign language (EFL) educators teach in countries where English is spoken only as a foreign language, such as Japan and Saudi Arabia.

In English-speaking countries, ESL teachers work with immigrants and refugees at all levels of the education system, including pre-K through adult education in community colleges and community-based programs. In higher education settings, they work with international students in intensive and semi-intensive English language programs. There has been an increasing interest in the specialized area of English for specific purposes (ESP), which focuses on language skills required for academic fields (e.g., engineering, medicine, computer science) as well as business and vocational fields, and in the area of English for Academic Purposes (EAP), which prepares students to use English in their academic pursuits.

Founded in 1966, TESOL is headquartered in Alexandria, Virginia, and has approximately 11,500 members in over 120 countries. Its mission is to ensure excellence in English language instruction to speakers of other languages. TESOL has more than 100 affiliated organizations worldwide that represent 47,000 TESOL professionals, and its annual convention attracts 7,000–10,000 participants. TESOL values professionalism in language education; individual language rights; accessible, high-quality education collaboration in a global community; interaction of research and reflective practice for educational improvement; and respect for diversity and multiculturalism. TESOL publishes a professional refereed journal, *TESOL Quarterly*, committed to bridging theory and practice, and a practical magazine, *Essential Teacher*, which offers guidance for teachers and administrators in varied ESL and EFL workplaces.

Key Professional Journals

The following are some prominent journals in the fields of second language acquisition and/or foreign language teaching that you will find helpful as you engage in the assignments presented in *Teacher's Handbook* and as you continue your professional development as a language teacher. Many of these journals are published by national associations. You will undoubtedly encounter other journals, particularly those that relate to the teaching of your specific language.

www.cengagebrain.com

The Canadian Modern Language Review
Die Unterrichtspraxis
Foreign Language Annals/
    Language Educator
French Review
Hispania
English Language Teaching Journal

Language Learning
Learning Languages
The Modern Language Journal
Studies in Second Language Acquisition
TESOL Quarterly/Essential Teacher
Language Teaching

Regional Language Conferences

The foreign language profession also has regional conferences, whose mission is to conduct a yearly conference and other professional development opportunities for language teachers in the region:

- Central States Conference on the Teaching of Foreign Languages (CSCTFL)
- Northeast Conference on the Teaching of Foreign Languages (NECTFL)
- Pacific Northwest Council for Languages (PNCFL) (meets in conjunction with a member state's annual meeting)
- Southern Conference on Language Teaching (SCOLT)
- Southwest Conference on Language Teaching (SWCOLT)

As a language teacher, you should become familiar with ACTFL and/or TESOL, your national language-specific organization, your state language association, your regional language conference, and other resources that can assist you in your teaching and professional development. Your local geographical area should also have foreign language collaboratives, local chapters of the national language-specific organizations, and other language groups that offer opportunities for professional development and networking with fellow professionals.

EXPECTATIONS FOR LANGUAGE TEACHERS: A CONTINUUM OF TEACHER STANDARDS

Since 2002, our profession has had an articulated set of expectations for language teachers at three key points across their teaching career paths: teacher preparation (National Council for Accreditation of Teacher Education—NCATE), initial teacher licensure (Interstate New Teacher Assessment and Support Consortium—INTASC), and advanced professional certification (the National Board for Professional Teaching Standards—NBPTS). Of the three agencies responsible for standards, NCATE is the agency that accredits colleges and universities and approves or "recognizes" their teacher preparation programs (i.e., in foreign language teacher preparation); colleges and universities decide whether they will seek NCATE accreditation. INTASC provides a set of voluntary standards to states that they may use to make decisions regarding continuing teacher licensure. NBPTS creates standards for experienced teachers who individually and voluntarily seek National Board certification in an effort to bring recognition to themselves as models of best practices in language instruction. These standards offer the framework for a professional development continuum—"a seamless system that takes teachers from the entry level to the accomplished level over time and acknowledges that a teacher is never really finished learning and developing as a professional" (Glisan & Phillips, 1998, p. 8; Glisan, 2001).

In October 2002, NCATE approved the *ACTFL/NCATE Program Standards for the Preparation of Foreign Language Teachers*, which had been developed over a two-year period by ACTFL and the National Foreign Language Standards Collaborative, with review, feedback, and approval by the foreign language profession at large. These standards describe the knowledge, skills, and dispositions necessary for teacher candidates who are completing foreign language teacher preparation programs and earning teacher certification. NCATE is recognized by the U.S. Department of Education and the Council for Higher Education as an accrediting body for schools, colleges, and departments of education. NCATE determines which colleges of education meet rigorous national standards in preparing teachers and other classroom specialists. Foreign language teacher preparation programs seeking NCATE review and national recognition must submit program reports that address the new ACTFL/NCATE standards and provide candidate performance evidence that illustrates attainment of the standards.

In October 2001, NCATE approved the *TESOL/NCATE Standards for the Recognition of Initial Programs in P–12 ESL Teacher Education*, designed by TESOL and updated in 2003 and 2008. These standards address the need for consistency throughout the United States in how teachers are prepared to teach ESL to children in pre-K–12 schools.

Simultaneous with the development of the ACTFL/NCATE Standards, INTASC, with support from ACTFL, developed its *Model Licensing Standards for Beginning Foreign Language Teachers* (INTASC, 2002). INTASC was created in 1987 by the Council of Chief State School Officers (CCSSO) to improve collaboration among the states as they assessed teachers for initial licensure and as they prepared and inducted new teachers into the profession. The model standards were designed to be compatible with the ACTFL/NCATE standards for teacher preparation programs as well as with the advanced certification standards of the National Board for Professional Teaching Standards. This effort is another step toward creating a coherent approach to licensing teachers based upon shared views among the states and within the profession of what constitutes professional teaching.

The NBPTS released its *World Languages Other Than English Standards* in 2001, with an update in 2008, which describe what accomplished teachers should know and be able to do. NBPTS hopes to raise awareness of the expertise of accomplished teachers of world languages and create greater professional respect and opportunity for the teaching community as a whole. With the NBPTS standards in place, the language profession has an articulated set of expectations for teachers from completion of a teacher preparation program to state licensing to the accomplished level. In sum, NCATE standards are used by teacher preparation programs in colleges and universities, INTASC standards are used by states in the licensure process, and NBPTS standards are voluntarily used by individual teachers.

The International Society for Technology in Education (ISTE) updated and released *National Educational Technology Standards for Students* (2007) and *Teachers* (2008), addressing what students and teachers should know and be able to do with technology in education. The technology standards are also available for administrators and other school personnel. The technology standards for teachers and students (NETS-S and NETS-T), as well as the *TESOL Technology Standards* (2007), will be fully treated in Chapter 12. See the *Teacher's Handbook* Web site for links to these four sets of standards documents.

LANGUAGE POLICY AND LANGUAGE EDUCATION POLICY

As a language teacher, you may have read about or heard comments about language policy and language education policy in the United States. Language policy (LP) "concerns the decisions that people make about languages and their use in society in a given nation or nation state" (Shohamy, 2003, p. 279). According to Spolsky (2004), language policy has three components: language practice, language belief, and language management. Language practice refers to what members of a speech community do with language; that is, when to speak or keep silent, what to say, what tone or inflection to use to say it, and to whom to speak. Language beliefs are common understandings held by members of a speech community, for example, that some languages are more useful, expressive, or beautiful than others. Language management occurs when people or governments attempt to control which language(s) are spoken in their homes, schools, or other locations (Spolsky, 2006). Parents who encourage their children to speak a language that will enable them to be more successful in their environment are also practicing language management. Governmental decisions about language management can be made in the form of legislation or through collaborative agreements. An example of a collaborative agreement between the scientific, legislative, and educational communities is *The Common European Framework of Reference for Languages* (CEFR), produced by the Council of Europe and the European Union. The CEFR recognizes stages of language proficiency in over 30 languages for citizens of Europe (Council of Europe, 2001).

One aspect of management of language policies relates to which languages are taught, at what age they are taught, for how long, by whom and for whom, and using which materials (Shohamy, 2003, p. 279). These are referred to as language education policies (LEPs) because they concern the contexts in homes and educational settings where citizens learn or acquire languages, including native, or "mother tongue," languages or second or foreign languages.[4] In the United States, linguistic variety is extensive. The MLA Language Map reveals 343 different languages spoken, organized by county or zip code.[5] Since September 11, 2001, several governmental and educational agencies have focused attention on the nation's capacity to communicate in languages other than English. As part of the Year of Languages organized by ACTFL, a blueprint for action on language education emerged from a policy summit held and organized by ACTFL on January 10–11, 2005 (Müller, 2006). This document suggests partnerships among business, government, and education to recognize the need for prioritizing language education and for providing funding to increase capacity in knowledge and use of languages.

As you will see from the K–16 student standards in Chapter 2, the language teaching profession in the United States believes that language learning should be for all learners, should embrace multiple languages, and should encompass long sequences of language study/experiences. Nevertheless, there is yet a discussion among scholars and the general public as to whether or not the United States should adopt a national language, which language it should be, whether policies should be put in place at the national or state level for language learning in schools, how articulation should occur across educational agencies in elementary schools through college, and even who the stakeholders and decision makers are or should be. Since these are topics of discussion in the language education field and elsewhere, you should become informed of the stance of your professional organization, as well as some of the counter arguments. In addition, you should read what the professional journals have to say in various fora that have been organized on these topics. See Task Five on page 8.

INVESTIGATE AND REFLECT ·

The following tasks ask you to use the Internet to find additional information concerning professional organizations, conferences, and resources, and to explore the various sets of foreign language teacher standards. Respond to the tasks from the standpoint of the level you teach or intend to teach (e.g., elementary school, secondary, post-secondary).

TASK ONE
Learning About Your National Language-Specific Organization and Your State Language Association

Go to the *Teacher's Handbook* Web site and access the links to the Web sites of (1) your national language-specific organization (e.g., AATF, ACL, ATJ, TESOL) and (2) your state language association. Find the following information:

1. What is the mission (the goals) of each organization?
2. How do you join each organization? What is the cost of joining and what are the member benefits (e.g., publications received, discounts on conference attendance)?
3. Describe the professional development opportunities and/or other major events that each organization will sponsor in the near future (e.g., conferences, summer institutes).
4. How might your professional growth be affected by your membership and participation in one or more of these associations?

TASK TWO
Learning About Your Regional Language Conference

Go to the *Teacher's Handbook* Web site and access the link to the Web site of the regional conference in which your state is included. Your state might be included within two conferences. Find the following information:

1. What is the name of your regional conference(s) and where are the headquarters?
2. When and where will the upcoming conference be held?
3. What services and/or resources does the conference offer to teachers (e.g., publications, teaching materials, job announcements)?
4. How might your attendance at this regional conference enable you to gain a broader perspective of the foreign language profession?

TASK THREE
Familiarizing Yourself With Foreign Language Resources

Go to the *Teacher's Handbook* Web site and visit the Web site of one of the resources listed in the chapter that most interests you (JNCL-NCLIS, CAL, one of the national language resource centers, FLTEACH, etc.). List three to five ways in which this resource can provide valuable assistance to foreign language teachers. Your instructor may ask you to share this information with fellow classmates.

TASK FOUR
Comparing Teacher Standards Across the Career Continuum

Go to the *Teacher's Handbook* Web site and access the links to the Web sites for the following three sets of foreign language teacher standards: ACTFL/NCATE or TESOL/NCATE, INTASC, NBPTS. Then find the foreign language/ESL teacher standards for the state in which you reside. You can probably access these standards through the Web site for your state organization. Compare these sets of standards in the following areas of teacher performance as you complete the tasks below:

- level of oral proficiency
- cultural understanding
- instructional strategies
- implementation of performance-based assessments
- professionalism

1. Compare and describe the similarities and differences between the state standards and the ACTFL/NCATE standards in each of the areas above.
2. Cross-reference the description of level of language proficiency found in the ACTFL/NCATE standards and the NBPTS standards with the *ACTFL Proficiency Guidelines for Speaking (1999)* and the *ACTFL Proficiency Guidelines for Writing* (2001).
3. Using the rubrics found in the ACTFL/NCATE or the TESOL/NCATE standards, trace how your teacher preparation program has prepared or will prepare you for your teaching career:
   a. Identify where in your program the following standards are addressed: ACTFL/NCATE Standards 1 (Language, Linguistics, Comparisons) and 2 (Cultures, Literatures, Cross-Disciplinary Concepts) or TESOL/NCATE Domains 1 (Language) and 2 (Culture) (i.e., courses and/or experiences).
   b. Choose any two of the ACTFL/NCATE or TESOL/NCATE standards and do a brief self-assessment—i.e., to what extent do you meet these standards?
   c. What are some ways in which you as an individual might meet some of these standards? Your instructor might have you work in small groups on this assignment.

TASK FIVE
Language Policy and Language Education Policy

The tasks below are designed to help you become familiar with the issues related to language policy and language education policy; your instructor may assign several of these tasks for you to complete.

1. Go to http://www.actfl.org, click on "About ACTFL" and then on the "Position Statements" link. Or go to http://www.tesol.org, click on "News" and then on "Position Statements." What is ACTFL's position on "General Principles of Language Learning (May 2006)"? What is TESOL's position on "English-only legislation in the United States (June 2005)"?
2. *The Modern Language Journal* has dedicated the "Perspectives" section (Byrnes, 2003a, b; 2008) of the journal on three occasions to discussion about language policy and language education policy in the U.S. Similarly, the *TESOL Quarterly* dedicated special issues to language, race, policies, power, and identity and to language policies and practice, in locations such as the U.S., Quebec, Djibouti, and Cuba. Read two articles from the list below. Then, using the position statements from your professional organization that you found in question 1 above, write a two-page personal "white paper" in which you define your own perspectives on LP and/or LEP.

   - *TESOL Quarterly, 41*(3), September 2007, Special Issue: Language policies and TESOL: Perspectives from practice.
   - *TESOL Quarterly, 40*(3), September 2006: several articles on issues of race, language policy, educational policy, power, and identity in TESOL.
   - *The Modern Language Journal, 87*(2), Summer 2003. In the "Perspectives" forum, a key article by Shohamy explores the relationships between LPs and LEPs and their implications for language study. Four scholars react and respond to the Shohamy article.

- *The Modern Language Journal, 87*(4), Winter 2003. In the "Perspectives" forum, a key article by Phillips identifies the issues of language education policy (LEP) and the formal as well as the implied policies that affect language education. She also identifies the role of the national standards on school reform for learners, teachers, and institutions that prepare teachers. Four scholars contribute their views in the remainder of the forum.
- *The Modern Language Journal, 91*(2), Summer 2007. In the "Perspectives" forum, co-editors Blake and Kramsch identify the issues of national language educational policy (LEP) that emerged from a national summit on National Language Educational Policy, held at the University of California, Berkeley, in October 2005. This key article, as well as the reactions and responses, focuses on three questions: What should be the goals of language education in the United States?; What has been the effect today of existing language policies and professional initiatives?; How do we get to where we want to go in language education as a nation?

3. In Spring 2004, the Modern Language Association appointed an ad hoc committee on foreign languages, chaired by Mary Louise Pratt, former president of the MLA, to examine the language crisis that occurred as a result of the tragic events of September 11, 2001, and to consider the effects of the crisis on the teaching of foreign languages in colleges and universities. The committee's work resulted in the publication of the document, "Foreign Languages and Higher Education: New Structures for a Changed World," released to the public in May 2007, which recommended that the language major in higher education be designed to produce educated speakers who have deep translingual and transcultural competence (TTC) and that foreign language departments and programs be redesigned in order to meet the new expectations of today's language major. In Summer 2008, *The Modern Language Journal, 92*(2) dedicated a special forum in its "Perspectives" section to the transformation of college or university foreign language departments. Read the document produced by the committee at http://www.mla.org/flreport. Then read "Perspectives" (Byrnes, 2008, 287–292) in which Mary Louise Pratt and her committee describe the issues related to transformation of college and university language departments and teaching for TTC. Then read two of the ten responses/reactions by scholars in the "commentaries" section beginning on p. 292. Complete the tasks below.
   a. Identify ways in which FL departments in higher education should be transformed (pp. 288–289).
   b. Identify the five additional priorities made by the committee and the supporting or critical positions of the responding authors.
4. Read Müller's (2006) summary of the ACTFL's Policy Summit. List five ways in which your professional life as a teacher of languages will be affected by the objectives outlined on pp. 46–47.

REFERENCES

American Council on the Teaching of Foreign Languages. (1999). *ACTFL proficiency guidelines—Speaking.* Yonkers, NY: Author.

American Council on the Teaching of Foreign Languages. (2001). *ACTFL proficiency guidelines—Writing.* Yonkers, NY: Author.

American Council on the Teaching of Foreign Languages (2002, October). *ACTFL/NCATE program standards for the preparation of foreign language teachers.* Yonkers, NY: Author.

August, D., & Hakuta, K. (Eds.). (1997). *Improving schooling for language-minority children: A research agenda.* Washington, DC: National Academy Press.

Blake, R., & Kramsch, C. (Eds.). (2007). Perspectives. *The Modern Language Journal, 91*, 247–283.

Byrnes, H. (Ed.). (2003). Perspectives. *The Modern Language Journal, 87*, 277–296.

Byrnes, H. (Ed.). (2003). Perspectives. *The Modern Language Journal, 87*, 578–597.

Byrnes, H. (Ed.). (2008). Perspectives. *The Modern Language Journal, 92*, 284–312.

Council of Europe. (2001). *Common European Framework of Reference for Languages*. Cambridge, UK: Cambridge University Press.

Glisan, E. W. (2001). Reframing teacher education within the context of quality, standards, supply, and demand. In R. Z. Lavine (Ed.), *Beyond the boundaries: Changing contexts in language learning* (pp.165–200). Boston: McGraw-Hill.

Glisan, E. W., & Phillips, J. K. (1998). Making the standards happen: A new vision for foreign language teacher preparation. *ACTFL Newsletter, 10* (4), 7–8, 13–14.

Hancock, C. R., & Scebold, C. E. (2000). Defining moments in foreign and second-language education during the last half of the twentieth century. In D. W. Birckbichler & R. M. Terry (Eds.), *Reflecting on the past to shape the future* (pp. 1–17). Lincolnwood, IL: National Textbook Company.

International Society for Technology in Education. (2007). *National Educational Technology Standards for Students*. Washington, DC: Author.

International Society for Technology in Education. (2008). *National Educational Technology Standards for Teachers*. Washington, DC: Author.

Interstate New Teacher Assessment and Support Consortium (2002, June). *Model standards for licensing beginning foreign language teachers: A resource for state dialogue*. Washington, DC: Council of Chief State School Officers.

Modern Language Association (MLA). (2007). Foreign languages and higher education: New structures for a changed world. Retrieved May 27, 2008, from http://www.mla.org/flreport.

Müller, K. (2006). A blueprint for action on language education. In A. L. Heining-Boynton (Ed.), *2005–2015: Realizing our vision of languages for all* (pp. 39–54). Upper Saddle River, NJ: Pearson Education, Inc.

National Board for Professional Teaching Standards. (2001, 2008). *World languages other than English standards*. Arlington, VA: Author.

Shohamy, E. (2003). The issue: Implications of language education policies for language study in schools and universities. *The Modern Language Journal, 87,* 278–286.

Spolsky, B. (2006). Does the US need a language policy or is English enough? Language policies in the US and beyond. In A. L. Heining-Boynton (Ed.), *2005–2015: Realizing our vision of languages for all* (pp. 15–38). Upper Saddle River, NJ: Pearson Education, Inc.

Spolsky, B. (2004). *Language policy*. Cambridge, UK: Cambridge University Press.

Teachers of English to Speakers of Other Languages. (2001). *TESOL/NCATE standards for P–12 teacher education programs*. Arlington, VA: Author.

Teachers of English to Speakers of Other Languages. (2003). *TESOL/NCATE Standards for the Accreditation of Initial Programs in P–12 ESL Teacher Education*. Arlington, VA: Author.

Teachers of English to Speakers of Other Languages. (2007). *TESOL technology standards for teachers and students*. Arlington, VA: Author.

Teachers of English to Speakers of Other Languages. (2007). Special Issue: Language policies and TESOL: Perspectives from practice. *TESOL Quarterly, 41*(3).

Wallinger, L. M., & Scebold, C. E. (2000). A future shaped by a united voice. In R. M. Terry (Ed.), *Agents of change in a changing age* (pp. 211–236). Lincolnwood, IL: National Textbook Company.

NOTES

1. On the *Teacher's Handbook* Web site, see the link to the New Visions in Action (NVA) Project, a national endeavor begun in 1998 by the National K–12 Foreign Language Resource Center (NFLRC) at Iowa State University and the American Council on the Teaching of Foreign Languages (ACTFL). It is a project involving Pre-K–16 foreign language educators from every state in a collaborative effort to identify and implement the actions necessary to improve the education system so that it can achieve the goal of language proficiency for all students.

2. The inspiration for this section came from the Foreign Language Methods online course developed by ACTFL/ Weber State University in Ogden, UT, in 2003, with a grant from the U.S. Department of Education. This section is an expanded version of the original Module 2, Theme IV of the online course.

3. Professional preparation in TESOL is available throughout the world for native speakers of English and those whose first language is not English.

4. The term *language-minority students* refers to individuals from homes where a language other than English is actively used and who therefore have had an opportunity to develop some level of proficiency in a language other than English. A language-minority student may be of limited English proficiency, bilingual, or essentially monolingual in English (August & Hakuta, 1997, p. 15).

5. See the MLA Language Map at http://www.mla.org/census_main.

CHAPTER 1

Understanding the Role of Contextualized Input, Output, and Interaction in Language Learning

Over the years, teachers, researchers, and theorists have attempted to answer the questions "How do people learn languages?" and "What does it mean to know a language?" Our understanding of language learning continues to develop as new research findings in the field of second language acquisition (SLA) tell us more about this process and about how we can more effectively facilitate foreign language learning in settings within and beyond the classroom. Chapter 1 presents a discussion of key theoretical positions that attempt to explain the role of contextualized input, output, and interaction in the language learning process. In reflecting current dialogue in the field of SLA, a framework based on sociocultural theory is posited in an effort to acknowledge that language-learning processes are as much social as they are cognitive. Since only key ideas concerning these theoretical frameworks are provided here, you may want to consult the references included at the end of the chapter in order to explore them in further detail. In Chapter 2, you will see that many of these theoretical underpinnings have served as the foundation for the development of specific approaches and methods of language teaching; see Appendix 2.1 on the *Teacher's Handbook* Web site for the chronological development of language teaching.

www.cengagebrain.com

In this chapter, you will learn about:

- Universal Grammar
- competence vs. performance
- communicative competence
- Krashen's Input Hypothesis
- acquisition vs. learning
- input processing
- variability in performance
- Interlanguage Theory
- Long's Interaction Hypothesis

- negotiation of meaning
- Swain's Output Hypothesis
- sociocultural theory
- Vygotsky's Zone of Proximal Development
- scaffolding
- mediation
- language play
- interactional competence
- affect and motivation

CONCEPTUAL ORIENTATION

Since the 1970s, research in SLA has offered the field of language teaching valuable insights into the nature of language learning (Dulay & Burt, 1977; Ellis, 1997; Gass, 1979; Gass, Lee, & Roots, 2007; Hall, 1997, 1999; Krashen, 1982; Schulz, 1991; VanPatten & Cadierno, 1993). Although SLA research continues to evolve over time and does not always result in universal consensus by researchers, it continues to provide (1) a theoretical basis that can help language instructors shape their classroom practices and (2) a venue through which the profession can engage in healthy debate about how learners acquire language. By studying SLA research, teachers are able to examine critically the principles upon which they base foreign language instruction. In your reading of the research, you will often encounter the term *foreign language learning* (FLL) used to refer to formal classroom instruction outside of the geographical region where it is commonly spoken, and *second language acquisition* (SLA) used to refer to acquiring another language within one of the regions where the language is commonly spoken. However, in our discussion, we will use the term *language learning* to refer to the process of learning a language other than the native language in either a natural or classroom setting. The term *target language* (TL) is used to refer to the language of instruction in the classroom. The term *L1* refers to the first or native language and the term *L2* refers to the second language or TL or foreign language (FL) being studied.

A great deal of early SLA research examined how individual language learners use their intellect to acquire a second language within experimental settings and classrooms—i.e., acqusition as a *cognitive process* that occurs in the individual's brain (Chomsky, 1968; Corder, 1973). More recent SLA research conducted in settings within and beyond classrooms (e.g., study abroad, in TL communities) has studied how language use and social interaction bring about acquisition—i.e., acquisition as a *social process* that occurs during interaction with others (Firth & Wagner, 1997, 2007; Hall, 1997; Swain & Deters, 2007). In the third edition of *Teacher's Handbook,* we divided the research themes into two categories: those that view language learning as an individual achievement and those that view language learning as a collaborative achievement within a community of learners. This distinction continues to be a useful one in helping teachers to understand language acquisition both from a cognitive and social point of view and, further, it provides a lens through which the evolution of research and thinking in the field can be examined. As you will see, each explanation of language learning generates research, new theories emerge to explain what previous theories inadequately explained, and each perspective often occurs in response to a previous one. Furthermore, each theoretical framework has implications for classroom instruction, which are suggested here after each theoretical description. As you explore this chapter, you might consider which frameworks you find to be most helpful in your classroom observations and teaching experiences.

Language Learning as an Individual (Cognitive) Achievement

From Behaviorism to Cognitive Psychology: Communicative Competence

In the 1940s and 1950s, a behaviorist view of language learning held that people learn through habit formation by repeatedly associating a stimulus with a response; imitation, practice, and positive reinforcement were thought to be key components of learning a language (Skinner, 1957). Cognitive theorists, on the other hand, believed that this explanation did not account for the ways in which humans use thought to process language. Chomsky (1965), for instance, observed that children use elements of language they know to say something they have never heard before. Chomsky proposed that humans are born with an innate "language acquisition device" (LAD) that enables them to process language. He posited that the LAD contained abstract principles of language that are universal to all languages, referred to as *Universal Grammar* (Chomsky; Ellis, 1985). When children pay attention to features of the language they hear, the LAD is activated; it triggers and selects the innate rules specific to the language they hear. For example, children who say "I falled down" are overgeneralizing a grammatical rule about formation of past tenses even though they have not heard that irregular form used by family, friends, and others around them; they are creating language based on what they already know. (An asterisk at the beginning of a sentence indicates that the sentence is ungrammatical.) This creative use of language based on meaningful input led Chomsky to distinguish between *competence* and *performance*. Chomsky viewed *competence* as the intuitive knowledge of rules of grammar and syntax and of how the linguistic system of a language operates. *Performance*, he thought, is the individual's ability to produce language. In this view, language production results from the creative application of a learned set of linguistic rules.

Chomsky, however, was not concerned with the context in which language is learned or used. His views are considered "innatist" or "nativist" because they explain language learning capacity as being "hard-wired" into the human brain at birth. Foundational to later research was Chomsky's notion that when children hear large amounts of language as input, they acquire language as a result of their innate ability to discover a language's underlying system of rules, not because they repeat and imitate language they hear. According to this nativist perspective, children do not acquire language rules that are outside of the boundaries of the Universal Grammar (White, 1996, 2003).[1] An implication of Chomsky's theory for language instruction is that knowing a language is more than just stringing words together, but rather knowing how language works as a system.

A Broader Notion of Communicative Competence: The Importance of Context

Chomsky's definition of competence was expanded to a broader notion of "communicative competence," or the ability to function in a communicative setting by using not only grammatical knowledge but also gestures and intonation, strategies for making oneself understood, and risk-taking in attempting communication (Bachman, 1990; Campbell & Wales, 1970; Canale & Swain, 1980; Hymes, 1972; Savignon, 1972). This expanded notion of competence was based upon communication within a meaningful context. The most recent model of communicative competence (Celce-Murcia, Dörnyei, & Thurrell, 1995), shown in Figure 1.1, defines the core of the concept as *discourse competence*, which refers to the way in which language elements, such as words and phrases, are arranged into utterances in order to express a coherent idea on a particular topic. Discourse competence is surrounded by sociocultural, linguistic, and actional competence. *Sociocultural*

FIGURE 1.1 Communicative Competence

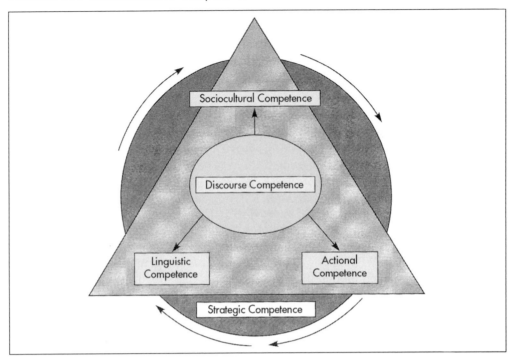

Source: From "Communicative competence: A pedagogically motivated model with content specifications," by M. Celce-Murcia, Z. Dörnyei, and S. Thurrell, 1995, *Issues in Applied Linguistics, 6,* p. 10. Reprinted by permission.

competence is knowledge about context, stylistic appropriateness, nonverbal factors, and cultural background knowledge; *linguistic competence* is the ability to make meaning when using form such as morphology, syntax, vocabulary, and spelling; and *actional competence* is the ability to match linguistic form with the speaker's intent. These components are sustained by *strategic competence*, a set of skills that enable people to communicate and compensate for deficiencies in the other competencies. For example, think of what happens when you walk into a party. Your knowledge of sociocultural competence tells you how to greet others already present in that setting with the appropriate greeting, including the most acceptable words, gestures, and body language. Actional competence helps you determine how to greet a friend you see across the room, how to ask about where another friend is, and how to express thanks for being invited to the party. Linguistic competence helps you to relate what happened to you on the way to the party by using correct tense and aspect to form past narration. Discourse competence enables you to combine multiple utterances as you talk about yourself to a new friend you meet, by using connector words such as *therefore* and *in addition*. In case you have a temporary mental block on the name of someone who greets you at the door, your strategic competence will enable you to utter a suitable greeting to buy time until you remember the name or someone else notices your discomfort and gives you the name.

An implication of communicative competence for language teachers is that students need more than grammatical or linguistic knowledge to function in a communicative setting. Of great importance, they need to be able to make meaning using grammatical forms. Also, they need knowledge of the various sociocultural factors that affect communication, knowledge of how to use language to express their ideas and intent, and knowledge of strategies for how to communicate with others and compensate for deficiencies in the other competencies.

The Role of Input

Krashen's Input Hypothesis.   Building on some of the innatist views of language learning proposed in Chomsky's work on acquisition, Krashen (1982) proposed further explanations of how language is acquired in his widely known albeit somewhat controversial *Monitor Model*:

1. **The acquisition-learning hypothesis:** *Acquisition* is defined as a subconscious "picking up" of rules characteristic of the L1 acquisition process. *Learning,* by contrast, is a conscious focus on knowing and applying rules. Acquisition, not learning, leads to spontaneous, unplanned communication.
2. **The monitor hypothesis:** The conscious knowledge of rules prompts the internal "monitor" that checks, edits, and polishes language output and is used only when the language user has sufficient time, attends to linguistic form, and knows the rule being applied.
3. **The natural order hypothesis:** Learners acquire the rules of a language in a predictable sequence, in a way that is independent of the order in which rules may have been taught. Studies have shown that learners experience similar stages in development of linguistic structures in spite of their first languages (see, for example, VanPatten, 1993).
4. **The input hypothesis:** Acquisition occurs only when learners receive an optimal quantity of comprehensible input that is interesting, a little beyond their current level of competence ($i + 1$), and not grammatically sequenced, but understandable using background knowledge, context, and other extralinguistic cues such as gestures and intonation. Note that the "i" refers to the current competence of the learner; the "1" represents the next level of competence that is a little beyond where the learner is now (Krashen).
5. **The affective filter hypothesis:** Language acquisition must take place in an environment where learners are "off the defensive" and the affective filter (anxiety) is low in order for the input to be noticed and reflected upon by the learner (Krashen).

Krashen's perspectives are intuitively appealing to teachers and have been influential in terms of the strong implications for classroom instruction. Among these implications are that the language classroom should provide comprehensible input at the $i + 1$ level, in a low-anxiety environment in which learners are not required to speak until they are ready to do so; input should be interesting, relevant, and not grammatically sequenced; and error correction should be minimal in the classroom since it is not useful when the goal is acquisition.

An area of language instruction that developed significantly as a result of Krashen's theory of acquisition and comprehensible input is the teaching of vocabulary. Historically, vocabulary in textbooks was presented in lists of words in the target language followed by their native language equivalents, as in the following list related to the destruction and conservation of the environment:

la contaminación	pollution
el desperdicio	waste
desarrollar	to develop
construir	to construct
los recursos naturales	natural resources
proteger	to protect
reciclar	to recycle

This approach suggests to learners that vocabulary acquisition is a matter of memorizing target language equivalents of native language words (Lee & VanPatten, 2003). Our understanding of L1 acquisition and input illustrates that children acquire vocabulary as a result of attending to large quantities of meaningful input and by interacting with the concrete objects referred to in the input. For example, children acquire the word "milk" by hearing their caretakers say "Here's your milk" and grasping a cup of milk handed to them; or by accidentally spilling their milk on the floor and hearing someone say "Oops, you spilled your milk!"; or by watching a caretaker select a brand of milk for purchase in the grocery store. A similar process occurs in second language acquisition of vocabulary when learners are given opportunities to make connections between form (i.e., the language they hear) and meaning (i.e., the concrete objects referred to in the input)—Terrell (1986) refers to this process as *binding*:

> *Binding* is the term I propose to describe the cognitive and affective mental process of linking a meaning to a form. The concept of binding is what language teachers refer to when they insist that a new word ultimately be associated directly with its meaning and not with a translation (p. 214; as cited in Lee & VanPatten, 2003, p. 39).

Binding can be facilitated during vocabulary acquisition by presenting vocabulary in meaningful groups (e.g., physical descriptions, clothing, weather), providing meaningful input in presenting vocabulary, using visuals and objects so that students can match the TL description to the concrete referents, and engaging students in demonstrating comprehension and acquisition of vocabulary before actually asking them to produce it orally or in written form. (A more detailed discussion of activities that lead to vocabulary acquisition can be found in Chapter 4.) Textbooks increasingly have moved toward using visuals to present vocabulary in order to facilitate binding, as in the example in Figure 1.2 of the destruction and conservation of the environment; compare this type of presentation to the vocabulary list you saw above.

Krashen's claims have been strongly criticized by various researchers on the grounds that (1) his theories have not been empirically tested in language learning environments; (2) concepts such as *comprehensible input* and the learning-acquisition distinction are not clearly defined or testable; and (3) his model presents far too simplistic a view of the acquisition process (Lightbown, 2004; McLaughlin, 1987; Munsell & Carr, 1981). Furthermore, use of the *acquisition-rich environment* diminishes the role of the learner in the foreign language classroom by highlighting the role of the teacher as the source of comprehensible input and by failing to recognize the function of learner-to-learner talk

FIGURE 1.2 Visual Representation of Vocabulary to Facilitate Acquisition

Source: From *Plazas: Lugar de Encuentros* (p. 356), by R. Hershberger, S. Navey-Davis, and A. Borrás, 2nd ed. Boston: Heinle & Heinle. From *Contextos: Spanish for Communication* (p. 25), by B. Freed and B. W. Bauer. Copyright © 2005 Heinle/Arts & Sciences, a part of Cengage Learning, Inc. Reproduced with permission. www.cengage.com/permissions.

(Platt & Brooks, 1994). Few would deny that Krashen's model sparked a great deal of thought and discussion in the profession regarding the role of input in language learning and prompted many language teachers to provide more comprehensible TL input in their classrooms. Nevertheless, many of his claims paint an unclear picture of the role of classroom instruction in language learning and remain to be empirically tested.

Input Processing.   One application and extension of Krashen's input theory is the focus on how learners actually process input to "connect grammatical forms with their meanings" (VanPatten, 2004, p. 5). Building on Krashen's views on input, some researchers suggested that when input is simplified and tailored to the level of the learner, learners are able to make connections between form and meaning and thus convert input to intake. *Intake* is language that is comprehended and used by learners to develop a linguistic system that they then use to produce *output* in the language. VanPatten and Cadierno (1993) argue that beginning language learners need structured input activities that enable them to focus on meaning while they pay attention to form before they can use the language to produce output. Research across languages and with a variety of grammatical structures has indicated that instructional strategies that incorporate input are successful in helping learners build linguistic systems (Buck, 2000; Cheng, 2002; Farley, 2003; Wong & VanPatten, 2003).

This line of research on how learners process input led to an instructional approach called "processing instruction" (VanPatten, 2004), which is not a theory of acquisition but rather a set of principles about how languages are learned and taught, based on a primary tenet that learners pay attention to meaning before they pay attention to grammatical form. For example, one principle is that "learners process input for meaning before they process it for form"; i.e., they attempt to understand the meaning of the message before they process grammatical structures (Lee & VanPatten, 2003, p. 139). A second related principle is that "learners process content words in the input before anything else"; that is, they search for the words that offer the most clues to content, such as nouns, verbs, and adjectives (Lee & VanPatten, p. 139).[2] Processing instruction has also been called *attention-oriented instruction* (Doughty, 2003), based on the concept of the *Noticing Hypothesis*, which proposes that "SLA is largely driven by what learners pay attention to and notice in target language input and what they understand the significance of noticed input to be" (Schmidt, 2001; as cited in Doughty, p. 288).

In processing instruction, learners process the form or structure by means of activities that contain structured input, "input that is manipulated in particular ways to push learners to become dependent on form and structure to get meaning" (Lee & VanPatten, 2003, p. 142). Figure 1.3 illustrates a series of three structured-input activities in which students must attend to grammatical structure (past-tense endings) to obtain meaning and then use the new structure in order to complete a communicative task. These activities are preceded by a brief explanation by the teacher of how past-tense endings work (Lee & VanPatten). Note that processing instruction begins with comprehension-based activities and moves to production later, as the example in Figure 1.3 illustrates. Key implications of input processing theory for foreign language instruction are (1) in order to make sense of grammatical forms and be able to use them in communication, learners need to be engaged in attending to meaningful input, and (2) mechanical grammar practice is not beneficial for language acquisition (Wong & VanPatten, 2003).

Variability in Performance.   Krashen's claim that only acquisition, and not learning, leads to spontaneous communication has been criticized by researchers because it fails to account for ways in which learners use both automatic and controlled processing in communicative situations. Krashen's model also fails to account for the fact that what learners can do with language often varies within a single learner, over time, within contexts, and

FIGURE 1.3 Structured Input Activities

Activity A. Listening for Time Reference

Listen to each sentence. Indicate whether the action occurred last week or is part of a set of actions oriented toward the present.

(Sentences read by instructor or heard on tape)

1. John talked on the phone.
2. Mary helped her mother.
3. Robert studies for two hours.
4. Sam watched T.V.
5. Lori visits her parents.

Learners might then be given sentences and told to match each to a particular adverbial.

Activity B. Matching

Once again, listen to each sentence. Select the appropriate time-related adverbials that can be added to the sentence you hear.

Model: *(you hear)* John deposited money in the bank.

　　　　(you select from)

a. last Monday
b. right now
c. later this week

(you say) Last Monday

Further activities could be developed that involve what the learners themselves did or didn't do at a particular time.

Activity C. Did You Do It, Too?

Listen to the speaker make a statement. Indicate whether you did that same thing last night.

Model: *(you hear)* I studied for a test.

　　　　(you say)　Me too.

　　　　or　　　　I didn't.

Note that, in each of these activities, only the verb ending encodes tense in the input sentence. Lexical items and discourse that would indicate a time frame are not present, thereby encouraging learners to attend to the grammatical markers for tense. Thus we have *structured* the input so that grammatical form carries meaning and learners must attend to the form in order to complete the task.

Source: From *Making Communicative Language Teaching Happen* (p. 143), by J. F. Lee and B. VanPatten. Copyright © 2003 by The McGraw-Hill Companies. Reprinted by permission.

across different learners. In attempts to explain how and why performance varies, some researchers (Bialystok, 1981, 1982; Ellis, 1997; McLaughlin, Rossman, & McLeod, 1983; Tarone, 1983) posited that learners use automatic processes and controlled processes in a variety of combinations in their production and comprehension of the target language. When engaged in a conversation task, for example, the learner may activate automatic, unanalyzed processing as shown in this example:

Speaker 1: Hi.

Speaker 2: Hi, how are you?

Speaker 1: Fine, and you?

Speaker 2: Fine. (Gass & Selinker, 1994, p. 154)

The elements of language in this conversation become so automatized, i.e., used automatically, that we may answer "Fine" even before the question is asked. Controlled processing becomes automatic processing when learners practice regularly and what they practice becomes part of long-term memory. However, sometimes learners may be able to begin language processing with an automatized lexical item, i.e., word or expression. For instance, beginning learners on the first day of language class can ask classmates their names in Spanish without consciously thinking through the use of reflexive verbs, simply by using a lexical item of "¿Cómo te llamas?" which quickly becomes used as an automatized item. When the teacher instructs them that they must address a visiting adult guest in the classroom using the form "¿Cómo se llama?" they do so using controlled processing because they now have to consciously think about how to modify what they already know in order to use the correct phrase. In addition, Ellis (2005) asserts that only implicit or unconscious knowledge is at the basis of unplanned communicative performance; that is, when learners communicate spontaneously, they draw upon grammatical rules that have been acquired, and therefore, they do not have to consciously access and think about this knowledge. Some research also suggests that the more automatic the learner's access to language stored in long-term memory, the more fluent the language use, since the learner is able to direct more attention to the meaning of the message and production (Segalowitz, 2003). According to Ellis (1994), use of controlled and automatic processes accounts for (1) the individual variation in the language of a second language learner as different types of knowledge and processes are activated in different communicative contexts, and (2) variation in language use across language learners.

Lightbown (1985) also proposes some explanations to account for variations in learners' production of language. For example, in certain situations, learners might use a given structure that is error-free and consistent with the target language, while in subsequent situations, such as after new material has been presented, they might use the same structure with errors. Errors may arise for a variety of reasons: the learner is tired, the communicative situation is too demanding, or the new learning leads to restructuring of existing linguistic knowledge. In the face of these circumstances, the learner "makes the very error that he or she had so recently appeared to have learned to overcome" (Segalowitz, 2003, p. 397). Then, learners use the form correctly again, having presumably restructured their understanding of the original structure plus the new material. This is called *U-shaped behavior* because of the way it is typically mapped, as illustrated in Figure 1.4. The source of U-shaped behavior is overgeneralization of language rules (see next section) and creation of rules for the language system. In this sense, when a student says, "*I eated*," this is a positive sign of progress toward working out the language system and

FIGURE 1.4 U-Shaped Behavior

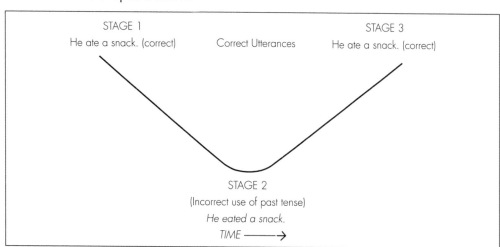

Source: Adapted from Gass & Selinker, 1994, p. 159.

differentiating, in this case, certain patterns for regular and irregular past tense verbs in English; it is not considered to be a misapplication of rules.

 Learners use automatic processes and controlled processes in a variety of combinations in their production and comprehension of the target language.

Research in the area of variability in performance is significant for language teachers because it indicates that an individual's performance will vary over time and that performance varies from one individual learner to the next. In addition, the evidence convincingly indicates that the ability to verbalize a language rule does not signify that the language learner can use it in communication (Lightbown, 1985).

 The ability to verbalize a language rule does not signify that the language learner can use it in communication.

Interlanguage Theory. The variability in language performance that you explored in the previous section is also evident in the learner's use of the target language at any point in time. Selinker (1974) defines the developing "language of the learner" as *interlanguage*. Interlanguages are systematic and dynamic, "continually evolving as learners receive more input and revise their hypotheses about the second language" (Lightbown & Spada, 2006, p. 80). It is an individual linguistic system created by second language learners as a result of five cognitive processes: (1) interference from the native language; (2) effect of instruction, e.g., an instructional approach, rules provided by the teacher, classroom activities; (3) overgeneralization of target language rules, such as application of rules to contexts where they do not apply; (4) strategies involved in second language learning, such as rote memorization, use of formal rules, and guessing in context; and (5) strategies involved in second language communication, such as circumlocution, use of gestures, and appeal for assistance from a conversational partner (Selinker). Current theories of L2 acquisition maintain that learners modify their interlanguage only when they integrate into their long-term memories the input that they hear or read; that is, they construct new hypotheses in order to incorporate the noticed features into the interlanguage system (Ellis, 1997; Gass, 1988).

Selinker's Interlanguage Theory helps us to understand what happens in the mind of the learner. An implication for foreign language teachers is that a learner's use of the target language reflects a system in development and therefore has errors that occur as a natural part of the acquisition process. As teachers provide good models of TL input and engage learners in attending to that input, learners alter their interlanguage to incorporate new and/or more accurate features of native speaker language.

Up to this point, you have examined the role of input in the language acquisition process and ways in which language performance is variable. As you will see in the next section, there are several ways in which input can be modified and converted to intake.

Role of Modified Input, Interaction, and Output

Long's Interaction Hypothesis. According to Long (1983), input comes to the individual from a variety of sources, including others. Individuals make their input "comprehensible" in three ways:

- by simplifying the input, i.e., using familiar structures and vocabulary;
- by using linguistic and extralinguistic features, i.e., familiar structures, background knowledge, gestures; and
- by modifying the interactional structure of the conversation.

This third element is the basis of Long's (1981) Interaction Hypothesis, which accounts for ways in which input is modified and contributes to comprehension and acquisition. Long (1983, 1996) maintains that speakers make changes in their language as they interact or "negotiate meaning" with each other. *Negotiation of meaning* has been characterized as "exchanges between learners and their interlocutors as they attempt to resolve communication breakdown and to work toward mutual comprehension" (Pica, Holliday, Lewis, & Morgenthaler, 1989, p. 65). Speakers negotiate meaning to avoid conversational trouble or to revise language when trouble occurs. Through negotiation of meaning, interactions (i.e., between native and non native speakers or between nonnative speakers) are changed and redirected, leading to greater comprehensibility. Further, these negotiations can lead to language development by the learner (Long, 1996). That is, by working toward comprehension, language input is made available for intake, cognitive inspection, and thus acquisition. The following exchange illustrates how a nonnative speaker recognizes a new lexical item as a result of negotiating the meaning of the phrase *reading glasses*:

NS: there's a pair of reading glasses above the plant.

NNS: a what?

NS: glasses—reading glasses to see the newspaper?

NNS: glassi?

NS: you wear them to see with, if you can't see. Reading glasses.

NNS: ahh ahh, glasses to read—you say, reading glasses

NS: yeah.

(Mackey, 1999; as cited in Gass, 2003, p. 235)

What exactly does it mean to negotiate meaning?[3] Just as in a business negotiation, two parties must participate by challenging, asking questions, and changing their positions. Merely conceding is not full negotiation. In the classroom this means that both parties in a teacher-student and student-student interaction must seek clarification, check comprehension, and request confirmation that they have understood or are being understood by the other. This process is often difficult to achieve in the classroom, given the traditional roles between teachers and students. Since students are often hesitant to question or counter-question the teacher, negotiation of meaning may not occur often. Although teachers often work to provide comprehensible input through a variety of techniques (visuals, simplified input, mime, etc.), this process does not necessarily inspire or lead to the negotiation of meaning. For this type of interaction to occur, both interlocutors must have equal rights in asking for clarification and adjusting what they say.[4] Thus Long's theory implies that learners cannot simply listen to input, but that they must be active conversational participants who interact and negotiate the type of input they receive in order to acquire language.

As you have now seen, interaction also plays a role as the cognitive processes of learners interact with the input to which they pay attention. Input can become implicit, or automatic language, when learners notice specific features of it, compare these features to those of their own output, and integrate the features into their own developing language system (Gass & Selinker, 1994; White, 1987).

 Learners must be active conversational participants who interact and negotiate with the type of input they receive in order to acquire language.

Swain's Output Hypothesis.   Krashen (1982) maintains that input is both a necessary and sufficient condition for language acquisition; that is, nothing else is needed for acquisition to occur. Swain (1985, 1995) maintains that input is a necessary but insufficient condition for language development. She argues that learners also need opportunities to produce output. Simply stated, learners need to speak the language to achieve higher levels of language competence. Swain's ideas derived largely from observing immersion students who, after several years of comprehensible input in immersion programs in Canada, did not show signs of language growth, specifically in the area of grammatical accuracy and sociolinguistic appropriateness. According to Swain (1995), *output*, or speaking the language for the purpose of communicating one's ideas, facilitates acquisition, as it (1) helps learners to discover that there is a gap between what they want to say and what they are able to say, (2) provides a way for learners to try out new rules and modify them accordingly, and (3) helps learners to actively reflect on what they know about the target language system. During speaking tasks, learners engage in what Swain refers to as *pushed output*, which allows them to move from what they want to say (e.g., the vocabulary they need) to how they say it (e.g., the grammar and syntax to make their meanings clear and appropriate to the context). (See Chapters 8 and 9 for a discussion of Swain's [2000] work regarding output and the use of *collaborative dialogue*.)

Additionally, by repeatedly using the target language in natural communicative situations and focusing on their output, learners eventually develop automaticity and move from analyzing what they want to say to being able to say it with ease. According to Ellis (1997), the use of linguistic knowledge becomes automatic only when learners make use of interlanguage knowledge under real conditions of communication. An example of this process occurs in a conversation in which a student who is narrating a story in the past states: "*Realicé . . . no, no 'realicé' . . . me di cuento . . . ¿cuento? . . . cuenta, me di cuenta de que no tenía la. . . ¿aplicación? . . . no sé (laugh). . .*" (E. Glisan, advisory Oral Proficiency Interview, May 13, 2008) [Translation: "I brought about . . . , no, not 'I brought about' . . . I realized (puts wrong ending on the noun), I realized that I didn't have the application?. . . I don't know (laugh) . . . "] In this example, the student uses two false cognates. First, he initially uses the verb *realizar,* which resembles the English "to realize" but is not the correct verb for the context; he remembers the expression *darse cuenta de que* but questions whether it should be *cuento* or *cuenta* and then decides on *cuenta*; second, he uses a false cognate *aplicación* and questions whether this is correct; he says *no sé* to signal that he's unsure about the word he needs; he hypothesizes about a correct form based on what he already knows about cognates (*aplicación*); by laughing he shows that he is not sure of this invention and invites modification from his more capable listener; ultimately, the student succeeds in making the tale understandable to his listener. By talking through the difficulty, the student makes the story comprehensible, hypothesizes about the correct structure, attempts to apply what is already known, and reflects on the forms of language being used. Thus, as learners create output in the target language, focus on form naturally arises.

The implication of Swain's theory is that teachers need to provide opportunities for output that is meaningful, purposeful, and motivational so that students can consolidate what they know about the language and discover what they need to learn. Teachers need to provide age-appropriate and interesting topics that students can explore in discussion and collaborative writing tasks that will produce output that leads students to reflect on the forms they are using, on the appropriateness of their language, and on ways to express what they want to say using what they have learned (R. Donato, personal communication, February 25, 2004). Output activities are also an effective way to improve the use of specific communication strategies, such as circumlocution (Scullen & Jourdain, 2000). After collaborative tasks are completed, teachers may also find it useful to discuss with students how they communicated "in order to clear up unresolved language problems that the collaborative dialogues . . . revealed" (Lapkin, Swain, & Smith, 2002, p. 498). Finally, teachers should recognize that the struggles they may observe in their students as they produce output are actually a sign that learning is taking place right before their eyes (R. Donato, personal communication, June 13, 2008).

? What factors influence an individual's ability to acquire language?

You have now learned about the cognitive factors that are involved in language acquisition, as well as how input, interaction, and output play a role in acquisition as an individual achievement. What the individual learner does cognitively to acquire language is only part of the story. Firth and Wagner's (1997) seminal article served as a catalyst for much debate in the field concerning the question of whether SLA should be reconceptualized in order to acknowledge the role of language use in social contexts as contributing to acquisition. The argument continues between researchers who believe that language acquisition is an individual cognitive process that occurs in the mind of the learner and those who view acquisition as a social process through which learners acquire a TL by using it in social interaction (Lafford, 2007).[5] However, of importance to foreign language teachers is that the SLA community is increasingly recognizing the pivotal role of language use in social interaction in facilitating language acquisition. This viewpoint that social interaction is the key to second language acquisition is the foundation of *Teacher's Handbook* and will be defined and explored in the following section of this chapter. This concept will also be examined and exemplified in further detail throughout the themes presented in each chapter.

Language Learning as a Collaborative (Social) Achievement

The ability to acquire and develop a new language through input, output, and interaction is one of the goals of classroom language instruction. Much of the research explored in the previous sections focuses on how L2 input is negotiated by individual learners by means of their own cognition and made more comprehensible. Although these studies acknowledge the importance of collaborative interaction in the learning process, their focus on negotiation of L2 input offers an incomplete picture of learners' interaction in an L2 classroom setting (Antón & DiCamilla, 1998). The cognitivist and interactionist views have been challenged by researchers examining the nature of sociocultural theory. According to sociocultural theory, our linguistic, cognitive, and social development as members of a community is socioculturally constructed (Vygotsky, 1978; Wertsch, 1991; Wertsch & Bivens, 1992). As Wertsch states, our development "is inherently linked to the cultural, institutional and historical settings in which it occurs" (1994, p. 203). In this view, learning and development are as much social processes as cognitive processes, and occasions for instruction and learning are situated in the discursive interactions between experts and novices (Appel & Lantolf, 1994; Brooks, 1990; Lantolf, 1994; Rogoff, 1990; Wells, 1998).

 Occasions for instruction and learning are situated in the discursive interactions between experts and novices.

Sociocultural Theory: Vygotsky's Zone of Proximal Development

Sociocultural theory, which appeared in the field in the 1990s, maintains that language learning is a social process rather than one that occurs within the individual and is based largely on the work of Vygotsky, a developmental psychologist, who highlighted the role of social interaction in learning and development (1978, 1986). Vygotsky's views on learning and development in children differ markedly from those of Piaget, for whom a child's cognitive development and maturity at least in part determine how he or she uses language. According to Piaget (1979), learning does not affect the course of development since maturation precedes learning. In this framework, the learner must be cognitively and developmentally ready to handle certain learning tasks. In Vygotsky's (1978) view, however, learning precedes and contributes to development, and the learner's language performance **with others** exceeds what the learner is able to do **alone**. The learner brings two levels of development to the learning task: an *actual developmental level*, representing what the learner can do without assistance, and a *potential developmental level*, representing what the learner can do with the assistance of adults or more capable peers. Through interaction with others, the learner progresses from the "potential developmental level" to the "actual developmental level." In other words, what learners can do with assistance today, they will be able to do on their own tomorrow or at some future point in time. Vygotsky defined the learner's Zone of Proximal Development (ZPD) as "the distance between the actual developmental level as determined by independent problem solving and the level of potential development as determined through problem solving under adult guidance or in collaboration with more capable peers" (p. 86). It is important to understand that "the ZPD is not a physical place situated in time and space" (Lantolf, 2000, p. 17), but rather it is a metaphor for observing how social interaction and guided assistance are internalized by learners and contribute to language development. Further, it is not understood to be a transmission of information from an expert to a novice through social interaction. Instead, it is about people working together to "co-construct contexts in which expertise emerges as a feature of the group" (Lantolf, p. 17). Thus, the ZPD results in opportunities for individuals to develop their cognitive abilities by collaborating with others.[6]

Figure 1.5 illustrates the continuous cycle of assistance in the Zone of Proximal Development, as it occurs in the task of co-constructing a puzzle with a novice. In Session 1, or the first attempt at building a puzzle, the novice recognizes the straight edges of the perimeter and is able to put those pieces of the puzzle together alone, without assistance from the expert. When engaging in this task, the novice is demonstrating his/her actual developmental level. With assistance from the expert, the novice puts together pieces of the puzzle that are within the puzzle but still close to the perimeter. In performing this set of tasks, the novice is working at his/her potential developmental level; he or she is able to perform the task, but only with expert assistance. Soon the novice will be able to perform this set of tasks without assistance, hence the term *potential developmental level*. Where the learner can achieve no performance with assistance, no ZPD is created. Session 2 represents some future point in time (perhaps moments, weeks, or months later) when the novice can put more of the puzzle together on his/her own and needs assistance for only some of the puzzle. In other words, the potential developmental level of Session 1 becomes the actual developmental level of Session 2, illustrating the iterative nature of performance and assistance. In both sessions, the ZPD is depicted in the areas marked by assisted performance. Note that the ZPD gets smaller in Session 2, which is a sign of development and learning and indicates that the novice can now complete more tasks alone. In order to discover the ZPD of the novice, the expert or more capable peer enters into dialogic negotiation with the novice and offers help that is graduated, i.e., tailored to the level of the novice, and contingent, i.e., given only when needed and

FIGURE 1.5 The Continuous Cycle of Assistance in the Zone of Proximal Development

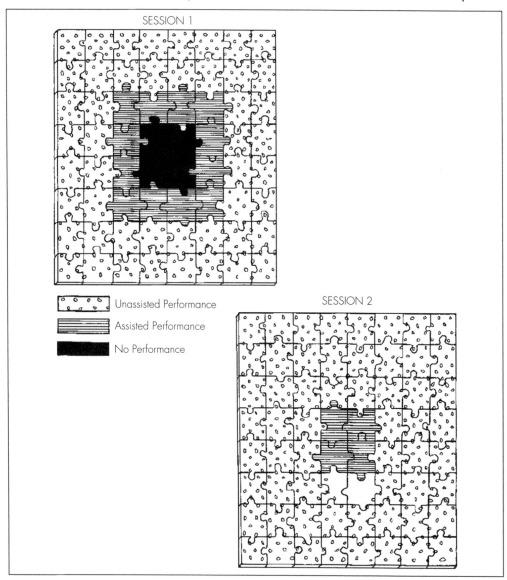

SESSION 1

Unassisted Performance

Assisted Performance

No Performance

SESSION 2

Source: From "Exploring language and cognitive development within the Zone of Proximal Development," by B. Adair-Hauck, 1995. Paper presented at the University of Pittsburgh. Used by permission of the author.

then withdrawn when the novice is able to function independently (Aljaafreh & Lantolf, 1994). The following is an example of a dialogue that might occur between an expert and a novice as they complete the task depicted in Figure 1.5, Session 1:

Expert: Let's use the picture on the box to help us put the puzzle together. Why don't we find the straight-edge pieces first?

Novice: OK. I can make the outside with the straight pieces by myself [unassisted performance].

Expert: Great, now we have the frame. Let's try to find the pieces that have the same color. Can you find the blue and white pieces?

Novice: Here are some, but I don't know how they go together.

Expert: That's OK. We'll do it together. Can we find pieces that have similar shapes?

Novice: Does this one go in this way?

Expert: Here . . . maybe if you turn it around, it'll fit. There, you got it! [assisted performance] [Let's try the other pieces that look the same].

 What learners can do with assistance today, they will be able to do on their own tomorrow or at some future point in time.

Scaffolding in the ZPD.   The language of the expert or more knowledgeable peers serves as directives and moves the learner through his or her ZPD to the point where the learner is able to perform a task alone (Aljaafreh & Lantolf, 1994; Vygotsky, 1978). The interaction between the expert and novice in a problem-solving task is called *scaffolding* (Duffy & Roehler, 1986; Wood, Bruner, & Ross, 1976). In scaffolding, the expert's help is determined by what the novice is doing, and is structured so that irrelevant aspects of the task do not interfere with the learner's range of ability. The expert provides the novice with scaffolded help by enlisting the learner's interest in the task; simplifying the task; keeping the learner motivated and in pursuit of the goal; highlighting certain relevant features and pointing out discrepancies between what has been produced and the ideal solution; reducing stress and frustration during problem solving; and modeling an idealized form of the act to be performed by completing the act or by explicating the learner's partial solution (Wood et al., p. 98). The Vygotskyan concept of the ZPD suggests that language learning occurs when the learner receives appropriate types of assistance from the expert, e.g., teacher. In order to provide scaffolded assistance, it is important that the teacher know where students are in terms of their language development. Furthermore, the teacher's role is (1) to recognize that assistance is contingent on what the novice is doing, not on what the expert thinks should be done, and (2) to know when to turn the task over to the novice for solo performance (R. Donato, personal communication, February 15, 2004; McCormick & Donato, 2000; VanLier, 1996). Appendix 1.1 on the *Teacher's Handbook* Web site lists the types of language-promoting assistance that reflect scaffolded help (Scarcella & Oxford, 1992).

Transformation in the ZPD.   The ZPD occurs in interactive activity where novices and experts work together to solve problems and, in the process, transform their individual knowledge of the task and understanding of each other (Newman & Holtzman, 1993). Working in the ZPD produces learning, which is reciprocal, and not just unidirectional from expert to novice. Wells (1999) points out that the results of this kind of ZPD activity enable learners to participate easily in similar communicative events and learn from them, such as when they speak with native speakers of the TL. In addition, by collaborating on a problem or task, the novice and expert transform their relationship and understanding of each other and of the task at hand.

When discussed in the context of the foreign language classroom, some view activity in the ZPD as limited to instruction on language content, such as a grammatical structure. The ZPD can be conceived of more broadly, as pointed out by Kinginger (2002), and applied to all aspects of foreign language instruction and learning, including developing discourse competence and pragmatic and cultural appropriateness. For instance, in a setting where a teacher and a small group of students are helping each other to write and edit an e-mail letter to a school in Madrid, one student might suggest "You mentioned that you went to a football game, and that your team won by an extra point at the end of the game. Will the reader understand what an extra point is in American football?" The student who wrote the letter might say, "Do you think I need to explain a little about American football?" The assistance the first student provides could then lead the teacher to another suggestion, such as, "Your audience in Madrid may not be familiar with American football since they play soccer. Let me check with their teacher in Madrid and get back to you." By working in the ZPD, this teacher and his/her learners provide mutual assistance and co-construct cultural knowledge that is available for present and future learning events. Perhaps in the future and because of this assistance, the concept of "audience" and the need to make cultural references clear will re-emerge for these students as an important aspect of the writing process. Moreover, as students make suggestions for what they want to say, they set their own learning agenda. Thus within the ZPD, teachers are informed of areas of interest to the learners and language and cultural knowledge they want to know.

When individuals work in the ZPD, scaffolding often arises. Scaffolded interactions occur when the expert, e.g., the teacher or a more knowledgeable peer, reduces the frustration level of the task. In the case of the collective e-mail letter writing, the teacher provides suggestions and tools in the form of information about the audience to reduce student frustration in trying to provide necessary details in the letter. Scaffolding also suggests that the expert identifies critical features of the task (e.g., considering the audience when writing a letter and not assuming that football is played the same way everywhere in the world). During scaffolded interactions in the ZPD, the teacher is transformed from one who provides solutions to one who facilitates the learners' search for solutions. The teacher also gains from the interaction by observing how his/her assistance is used by the students, how his/her help leads them to a potential level of development, and where his/her students might be in their letter writing ability in the future. Empirical evidence also supports the function of the ZPD as an activity through which social patterns of interaction and mutual assistance can result in learning (Donato, 1994; Ohta, 1995; Swain & Lapkin, 1998). It is important to note that the ZPD is an activity that is at the same time the tool for learning language and the result of using language with others. It is not just a tool for a result, but rather tool *and* result; e.g., a teacher uses the tool of a story and engages students in short retelling or writing, which results in the creation of the ZPD where he or she may provide scaffolding. Language use creates a ZPD so that learning can happen; this learning may be decided upon by the learners (i.e., not just by curricular objectives) and involve what they need to know in order to accomplish the activities in which they are engaged. The ZPD, therefore, is a powerful concept that offers a different view from that of the typical "delivery of instruction" model of language teaching. Donato points out that the concept of the ZPD and sociocultural aspects of interactions in second language classrooms have been largely ignored, but that they offer a rich source of understanding about how a language can be learned by learners who are actively using it in collaborative interaction.

i + 1 is not ZPD.   The concepts of *i* + 1 and the ZPD are intuitively appealing to teachers and are often viewed as the same concept. They are indeed very different concepts and offer differing explanations for language learning. The *i* + 1 is primarily a cognitive view that holds that language learning makes use of innate knowledge within the mind of a learner, who functions primarily as an individual in processing comprehensible input (Atkinson, 2002; Dunn & Lantolf, 1998; Pennycook, 1997). By contrast, the ZPD posits that language learning is an activity that happens through interaction and collaboration in social settings while the learner responds to those around him/her. It is an "outside-in" (Shore, 1996) process in which learners use the language with the support of others while simultaneously learning it. The *i* + 1 is about language and input. The ZPD is about working together, participating in a community and obtaining the assistance needed to enable continued participation in that community. Thus, the ZPD is not just a tool for using and learning about language but also arises as a result of using language in meaningful and purposeful ways with others (McCafferty, 2002; Newman & Holtzman,

1993). When teachers and learners work in the ZPD, language learning cannot be separated from language use (Kinginger, 2001).

Mediation in the ZPD.   Within a sociocultural perspective, learners use tools as a means of mediating between themselves and the world, as a way of assisting and supporting their learning and making sense of the world around them, including the language classroom. Mediational tools can take the form of the textbook, visuals, classroom discourse patterns, opportunities for interaction in the second language, direct instruction, or teacher assistance (Donato & McCormick, 1994). One type of mediational tool is the portfolio, which students can construct to reflect on language, to clarify and set goals, to select effective strategies to enhance performance, and to provide concrete evidence of strategy use (Donato & McCormick). Mediational tools assist learning, are both social and cultural, and may be determined by a variety of factors, such as distribution of educational resources. For example, in one school setting, every student might have a wireless computer, while in another setting computers may be largely inaccessible to students, e.g., there may be two computers sitting in the back of the classroom. Additionally, based largely on the instructional practices of the teacher, some students may feel that they can't learn the language unless they are given specific types of tools such as vocabulary lists and verb conjugations. In other classes, students may be more willing to use tools such as authentic documents to mediate their learning if they are provided with occasions to do so. The attitudes toward using mediational tools are often the result of social and school learning practices, since students are socialized into certain forms of mediation as a way to learn, into how to use tools to learn, and even into believing that certain types of tools contribute to learning in a valuable way.

In addition to all of the mediational tools discussed above, it is important to recognize that language itself is also an important mediational tool. Classroom discourse (i.e., classroom conversational episodes) can mediate language development by facilitating a range of communicative and cognitive functions of talk (Donato, 2000; Tharp & Gallimore, 1991). See Chapter 8 for a discussion of one such type of mediational tool called "instructional conversations." Further, collaboration allows students to use language to mediate their language learning because in collaboration students use language to reflect on the language they are learning. It is not uncommon to hear students hypothesize about a certain way to say something in the target language when they work together on producing the language for projects, presentations, or interpersonal communication tasks. For example, learners may try out alternate ways of saying a phrase or sentence *(Un piscine? Une piscine? Or Il est allé a l'école? Il a allé a l'école?)*. Here language itself is a tool for reflecting on the language being learned. Additionally, as one learner speaks aloud alternate forms, other learners are signaled to provide assistance. Donato's (1994) study revealed the use of this type of verbal mediation by learners of L2 French, who negotiated linguistic forms with one another in small-group work. Although no individual possessed complete knowledge of the forms produced, through their mutual assistance and collective problem solving, the group was able to correctly construct utterances for their later presentation to the class. Thus learners can successfully acquire language through their verbalizations, which act as a way of scaffolding each other.

Sociocultural theory also maintains that learning is facilitated by the learner's use of *self-talk*, which serves as a mediational tool (Ellis, 1997). According to Vygotsky (1986), one of the mediational tools used by children is speech for the self, or *private speech*, a type of thinking aloud that helps to structure and clarify a task to be done or a problem to be solved. For example, Vygotsky cites the following example of private speech used by a child during play activity to overcome a cognitive difficulty: (Child speaking to himself/herself) "Where's the pencil? I need a blue pencil. Never mind, I'll draw with the red one and wet it with water; it will become dark and look like blue" (Vygotsky, p. 30).

Private speech is the convergence of thought and language, which acts as "an instrument of thought in the proper sense–in seeking and planning the solution of a problem" (Vygotsky, p. 31). Adults use private speech, sometimes in the form of whispering to the self in second language learning, as they attempt to make sense of a task or reveal that they suddenly understand or have mastered a source of difficulty with some aspect of the task (Antón & DiCamilla, 1998; Brooks, Donato, & McGlone, 1997; Frawley & Lantolf, 1985; McCafferty, 1994). Smith (1996) found that learners use private speech to make sense of grammatical structures and explanations and that this private speech is often marked by repetitions, hesitations, and incomprehensible utterances. Of importance here is that teachers can most effectively deal with students' private speech by playing the role of a patient and understanding listener, not by reacting like a "lifeguard ready to dive in as soon as the student goes under" as soon as private speech emerges (Smith, as cited in Donato, 2000, p. 31).

Lantolf (1997) proposes that one of the functions of private speech is *language play*, the mediational tool by which learners experiment with those grammatical, phonological, and lexical features of the language being acquired. Children, for example, compare their old and new knowledge of the language by modifying language structures through strategies such as completions and substitutions, by imitating and transforming what others say, and by repeating their own utterances (Kuczaj, 1983). Language play involves producing L2 forms to be used later in public, talking out loud to oneself, and repeating L2 sounds (Lantolf). Children imitate parts of new utterances that are either within or slightly beyond their current level of linguistic competence. During this imitation, children also play with the language, changing it slightly or experimenting with its words. For Vygotsky, language play creates a zone of proximal development in which the child "always behaves beyond his average age, above his daily behavior" (Vygotsky, 1978, p. 102).

Some studies suggest that adolescent and adult language learners mediate learning through *mental rehearsal*, a form of language play, through activities such as mental correction of errors, silent repetition, mental practice of grammatical rules, and taking notes (de Guerrero, 1994; Reiss, 1985). Although there has been little research in the area of language play by adult learners, some evidence suggests that those who engage in these activities are more successful language learners (Ramsey, 1980) and that the value of language play in the acquisition process may decrease as the learner's proficiency in the language increases (Lantolf, 1997; Parr & Krashen, 1986). An interesting finding in Lantolf's 1997 study of the use of language play by university students studying Spanish is that learners tended to engage in language play most frequently after more meaningful activities, such as conversations, and less so after mechanical tasks, such as grammar study and pattern drills. For foreign language instruction, language play may be activated through meaningful activities and may facilitate the language learning process. In this perspective, language play is rehearsal of private speech and thus, it is part of the cognitive work of language learning. Thus, private speech, mental rehearsal, and language play foster flexibility and change within the interlanguage system of the learner, resulting in its growth and development.

 As students acquire language, why does language play decrease?

This view of language play as rehearsal contrasts with the view of language play as fun or self-amusement known as *ludic play* (Broner & Tarone, 2001; Cook, 2000). Fun, defined as "an experience of positive affect often associated with laughter" (Broner & Tarone, p. 364), can be play with language form, including sounds, rhyme, rhythm, song, etc. It can also be play with meaning, combining semantic elements to create words that do not exist. In this sense, ludic play is not transactional or interactional since its primary function is to amuse oneself and have fun (Cook). Tarone (2000) points out that children often play with language they know or are learning for enjoyment and self-entertainment. Of importance to language teachers is that, when students invent words, create songs, or write graffiti on their notebooks in the language, they are engaging in ludic play, and are mediating learning as a result of reflecting upon language, exploring the language, and learning it. This process is very common in L1 language development. Thus, ludic language play may contribute to the growth and development of the learner's interlanguage (Broner & Tarone, 2001).

 Private speech, mental rehearsal, and language play foster flexibility and change within the interlanguage system of the learner, resulting in its growth and development. ▪

It is important to remember that sociocultural (i.e., Vygotskyan) theory differs from the Interaction Hypothesis because of the different emphasis placed on internal cognitive processes. Whereas the Interaction Hypothesis offers learners the input they need to activate internal processes, sociocultural theory maintains that "Speaking and writing mediate thinking, which means that people can gain control over their mental processes as a consequence of internalizing what others say to them and what they say to others" (Lightbown & Spada, 2006, p. 47). Interactional and cognitive models have also placed a great deal of emphasis on the elevated role of native speakers and have portrayed non-native speakers to be their subordinates (Firth & Wagner, 1997, 2007). Sociocultural research, however, has rejected the notion that language learners are deficient communicators striving to reach the level of an idealized native speaker, but rather sees them as learners who succeed at communication by using every competency and strategy they have at their disposal (Firth & Wagner, 1997, 2007).[7] A new attitude toward learners and what they do, rather than what they do not do, derives from the perspective of the learner as creatively managing language resources rather than struggling to find a strategy to compensate for a gap in knowledge.

You have seen how sociocultural theory provides the impetus for language teachers to develop a classroom setting in which learners collaborate with each other, receive scaffolded help from the teacher, work within their ZPDs, use mediational tools in order to make sense of the target language and progress in their language development, and creatively manage language resources they have at their disposal. Through a sociocultural approach to classroom instruction, teachers will become more familiar with the language levels of their students and consequently will be able to provide more effective support for their language development.

Interactional Competence

As seen in the previous section, sociocultural theory focuses on the social nature of language learning and development and the role of learners' interaction in the classroom setting. Within this framework, Mehan (1979) stresses the importance of "interactional competence," which includes the ability to manage discussions in relevant ways. Hall (1995) expanded on Krashen's $i + 1$ concept by illustrating that input is a necessary but insufficient condition for acquisition to occur; that is, input must also occur within meaningful contexts and be situated within real communication. Hall points out the significance of interactive practices, "recurring episodes of purposeful, goal-directed talk," in the establishment and maintenance of a community (p. 38). Providing interactive classroom environments that help facilitate the development of learners' interactional competence in the TL involves more than the use of simplified syntax, repetition, and clarification requests (Hall, p. 56). Examples of interactive practices within the classroom community are how teachers lead discussions about texts, how they introduce or practice

vocabulary, and how they promote pair/group work. Com [...]
practices requires the development of interactional comp[...]
ers participate in "real" conversations. Characteristics of "r[...]
adapted from Hall, are:

- Opening utterances establish the topic and frame [...]
  was your vacation?"
- Ellipsis—that is, not repeating information tha[...]
  the distinction between new and old informatio[...]
  continues, already established information is g[...]
  in response to a question such as "When do [...]
  give the short answer "Ten o'clock," rather tha[...]
  class today at ten o'clock."
- Related lexical items occur in topic-specific discourse and are [...]
  their common referent. The meaning of new words is figured out by using [...]
  rounding topically oriented words to help narrow the possible meaning choices
  (Clark, 1992; Halliday, 1994). For example, in a discussion about hunting, related
  lexical items might include these expressions: to go hunting, to shoot, gun, trap,
  deer, bears, turkeys, tracks, animal protectionists.
- Expressive reactions are made: "Oh my! I don't believe it!"; questions that advance
  the topic are asked: "What do you mean by that?"; explanations or extensions, or a
  transition to a new topic are made: "By the way, I wanted to ask you. . ."

Hall (1995, 2004) has used *conversation analysis* (CA) as a technique for analyzing and understanding classroom interactional patterns as revealed in episodes of actual
classroom discourse.[8] In her 1995 study, Hall examined the nature of topic development
and management of communication in classroom interactive practices that claimed to
focus on speaking in a high school first-year Spanish classroom. She recorded classroom conversational exchanges between teacher and students and analyzed them for
the characteristics of opening utterances, use of ellipses, and use of related lexical items.
She found that the typical conversational exchanges that the teacher considered to be
communicative showed little evidence of a real conversational topic, opening utterances,
related lexical items, ellipses, or reactions. A major implication of Hall's study is that
learners need truly interactive environments in the classroom if they are to develop the
ability to interact effectively outside the classroom with other speakers of the target language. See Case Study 1 for examples of real-life utterances.

 How does language learning occur as a result of collaboration with others?

The Role of Affect and Motivation

Other variables that may influence the degree of success in learning another language
are those pertaining to affect, such as motivation, anxiety, personality, and attitude. The
Affective Filter Hypothesis, as first proposed by Dulay and Burt (1977), relates these affective factors to the second language acquisition process. Also, as seen earlier, Krashen
(1982) maintains that acquisition can occur only in the presence of certain affective conditions: the learner is motivated, self-confident, and has a low level of anxiety.

According to Dörnyei and Skehan, "motivation concerns the direction and magnitude
of human behavior, or more specifically (i) the choice of a particular action, (ii) the persistence with it, and (iii) the effort expended on it" (2003, p. 614). Motivation has been

...ied as the most influential factor in successfully learning a new language (Masgoret & ...dner, 2003). However, it is also one of the most complex issues in SLA research.

Motivation of Individual Learners

There are many sources that motivate an individual to succeed in language learning, and it is difficult to match specific motivational factors to success. Gardner (1985) identifies two kinds of motivation: (1) *instrumental*, e.g., learning a language to get a better job or to fulfill an academic requirement; and (2) *integrative*, e.g., learning a language to fit in with people who speak the language natively. According to Gardner (2001), the focus on creating "real bonds of communication with another people" is what sets integrative motivation apart from other motivational factors (as cited in MacIntyre, 2007, p. 566). In his summary of motivational research, MacIntyre asserts that "the major motivation to learn another language is to develop a communicative relationship with people from another cultural group" (p. 566). The research points to the likelihood that instrumental and integrative motivation are interrelated; that is, that they may operate in concert or that one may lead to the other (Gardner & MacIntyre, 1993). Shaaban and Ghaith (2000) found that integratively motivated students worked harder if they have a positive attitude about language outcomes in EFL. A study on integrative motivation at the post-secondary level revealed that students with higher integrative motivation tended to receive higher oral proficiency ratings and expressed a greater desire to continue their study of Spanish (Hernández, 2006). The author suggests that language teachers can enhance the integrative motivation of their students by providing opportunities for interaction with authentic materials (including multimedia) and with members of the TL community (Hernández).

Gardner's paradigm was expanded by Oxford and Shearin (1994) to acknowledge the role of other motivational factors, resulting in a socioeducational model that includes such elements as relevance of course goals to the learner, personal beliefs about success or failure, the ability of the learner to provide self-reward and self-evaluation, the nature of the teacher's feedback and assistance to the learner, and instructional features of the course; other studies have suggested similar factors (Crookes & Schmidt, 1991; Ely, 1986; Tremblay & Gardner, 1995). Furthermore, Dörnyei (1994) maintains that language learners are often motivated by the classroom experience itself: (1) course-specific factors, such as the degree to which the teaching method, materials, and learning tasks are interesting and engaging; (2) teacher-specific factors, such as the teacher's personality, teaching style, and relationship to students; and (3) group-specific factors, such as the dynamics of the learning group (p. 277). Motivation encourages greater effort from language learners and usually leads to greater success in terms of language proficiency (Gardner, 1985), maintenance of language skills over time (Tucker, Hamayan, & Genesee, 1976), and identification with members of the target language community (Goldberg & Noels, 2006).

Some researchers studied aspects of motivation known as *orientations* using a questionnaire developed by Clément and Kruidenier (1983). Among the orientations identified were integrative, instrumental, travel, friendship, knowledge, identification, sociocultural, media, whether or not the language was a requirement, ethnic heritage related, and school related (Ely, 1986; Sung & Padilla, 1998; Yang, 2003). For instance, among learners whose goal for language study was to fulfill a requirement, Reiss (1985) and Gillette (1990) found an absence of language play.

Dörnyei (2001) proposed a "process model of learning motivation in the L2 classroom," which depicts motivation as a dynamic process that changes over time and consists of three phases. In the pre-actional phase, "choice motivation" refers to setting goals and launching one's study of L2 and is influenced by factors such as attitudes towards the L2 and expectancy of success. The actional phase features "executive motivation" and deals with carrying out the tasks required to maintain motivation; this phase is affected by factors such as the quality of the learning experience, one's sense of autonomy, and the classroom reward-and-goal structure. In the post-actional stage, "motivational retrospection" enables the learner to reflect on his or her learning experience, assess the outcomes, and determine future goals; this phase is influenced by self-concept beliefs and feedback and praise received (Dörnyei & Skehan, 2003, p. 619).[9] In another model called "expectancy-value theory," researchers have linked motivation to one's expectancy to succeed and the value that the individual associates with success in a given task (Eccles & Wigfield, 1995; Mori & Gobel, 2006). Following this line of research, Mori and Gobel found that female students of EFL were more integratively motivated than their male peers, using both the expectancy-value theory and models suggested by Gardner and his associates.

Some research examined the motivational factors among specific native-language groups. For instance, Yang (2003) showed that East Asian students in the United States were integratively motivated, that they were more interested in developing communication skills in listening and speaking than in reading and writing, and that female students were more integratively motivated than male students.

Personality or cognitive styles also affect language learning; these factors include the willingness to take risks, openness to social interactions, and attitude toward the target language and target language users (Wong-Fillmore, 1985; Young, 1990). Motivation and attitudes are often related to anxiety, apprehension, or fear about the language learning experience. In some cases, language activities such as speaking in front of a group can create performance anxiety, especially in the case of learners who do not enjoy interacting with others spontaneously or learners whose oral-aural skills are weaker than their visual skills (Scarcella & Oxford, 1992). Anxiety often stems from the traditional social structure of the classroom, in which the powerful teacher-centered atmosphere may inhibit interaction, or from the feeling that the learning experience is irrelevant or a waste of time (Scarcella & Oxford). Gregersen and Horwitz (2002) found that anxious learners attempted to avoid errors and were disturbed at having made them. Gregersen (2003) found that anxious learners made more errors, self-repaired and resorted to their native language more often, recognized fewer errors in a stimulated recall situation, and overestimated the number of errors they made (p. 29). Nonanxious learners, on the other hand, used their errors to learn and to communicate better.[10]

Motivation of Learners Within Tasks

The motivation of individuals, either alone or in composite groups, has been the traditional focus of motivational research. Some scholars have studied performance on tasks as a way to explore the effects of motivation. Wen's 1997 study illustrated that expectations of the learning task and of one's own ability play a significant role in motivation and learning: When learners think that learning experiences will lead to certain meaningful results, they exert more effort. Motivation has an effect on how and when students use language learning strategies and the degree to which they take responsibility for their own progress (Oxford & Nyikos, 1989).[11] Dörnyei and Kormos (2000) also used a task-based framework to study motivation. They examined how learners addressed certain tasks and related their findings to the students' attitudes toward the L2 class, toward specific tasks, and toward achievement in the course. Findings showed that motivational factors have a significant impact on the learner's engagement in a task. Students with high positive attitude toward a task were more engaged in the task and produced more language. Also, students with a low attitude toward a task still performed well if they had a positive attitude toward the course in general.

For the beginning teacher, it is important to recognize that motivational factors play an important but complex role in language learning and performance in a language classroom. Figure 1.6 illustrates ten suggestions for how teachers can motivate language

FIGURE 1.6 Dörnyei and Csizér's Ten Commandments for Motivating Language Learners

1. Set a personal example with your own behavior.

→ Dörnyei and Csizér recommended that teachers prepare for lessons, be committed and motivated themselves, behave naturally, and be sensitive and accepting.

2. Create a pleasant, relaxed atmosphere in the classroom.

→ Teachers should bring in humor, laughter and smiles, do fun things in class, and have game-like competitions, Dörnyei and Csizér wrote.

3. Present the tasks properly.

→ To present tasks properly, Dörnyei and Csizér recommended that teachers give clear directions, provide guidance about how to do the task, and state the purpose and utility of every task.

4. Develop a good relationship with the learners.

→ This is a well-known principle that Dörnyei and Csizér let stand for itself—basically, they say to make the students want to please you.

5. Increase the learner's linguistic self-confidence.

→ Dörnyei and Csizér said to make sure students experience success regularly. Teachers should also constantly encourage them, demystify mistakes (they are natural), and select tasks that do not exceed the learner's competence.

6. Make the language classes interesting.

→ Dörnyei and Csizér recommended that teachers select interesting, challenging, and a variety of tasks and supplementary materials, vary the tasks; build on students' interests rather than tests or grades as the learning impetus, and raise curiosity by introducing unexpected and exotic elements.

7. Promote learner autonomy.

→ Dörnyei and Csizér asked teachers to encourage creative and imaginative ideas, encourage questions, and share responsibility by having students help organize the learning. They should also involve students in choosing the materials, they wrote.

8. Personalize the learning process.

→ Teacher should, Dörnyei and Csizér wrote, try to fill the tasks with personal content that is relevant to the students.

9. Increase the learners, goal-orientedness.

→ Dörnyei and Csizér wrote that teachers can do this by helping the students develop realistic expectations about their learning and by helping them set up several specific learning goals. They suggested that teachers do a needs analysis with the students, and help students design individual study plans.

10. Familiarize learners with the target language culture.

→ To do this, Dörnyei and Csizér wrote that teachers should use authentic materials, occasionally invite native speakers to the classroom, and help establish penpals for the learners.

Note: This is a summary of Tables 4 and 5 in the "Ten Commandments for Motivating Language Learners," which appear in Dörnyei and Csizér, 1998, pages 215–223.

Source: From "Promoting motivation in the foreign language classroom," by P. Winke, 2005, *CLEAR News* 9(2), p. 6. Reprinted by permission of CLEAR News, Michigan State University.

learners by creating a supportive and engaging environment that is goal-oriented and personalized to the interests of learners.

 Motivational factors play an important but complex role in language learning and performance in a language classroom.

 What are some considerations you need to keep in mind about the motivation of your students?

Implications of the Research for Classroom Teaching

Throughout this chapter, you have explored key research findings and their important implications for classroom language instruction. *Teacher's Handbook* supports a sociocultural view of language instruction, whereby learners have ample opportunities to interact

WRITE about Universal Body Language
+ gestures
+?

meaningfully with others. Within this type of instructional framework, there is NO room for mechanical practice that is devoid of meaning. Accordingly, throughout the rest of this text, you will learn more about the importance of providing the following elements in the foreign language classroom:

- comprehensible input in the target language that is directed toward a larger communicative goal or topic;
- an interactive environment that models and presents a variety of social, linguistic, and cognitive tools for structuring and interpreting participation in talk;
- opportunities for learners to negotiate meaning in the target language, with assistance from the teacher and one another;
- opportunities for learners to interact communicatively with one another in the target language;
- conversations and tasks that are purposeful and meaningful to the learner and that parallel real-life situations in which they might expect to use their language skills (Met, 2004, p. 86);
- explicit instruction in strategies that facilitate language awareness, learner autonomy, and making meaning when interpreting the foreign language (Met; Pica, 2002);
- a nonthreatening environment that encourages self-expression;
- opportunities for learners to work within their ZPDs in order to develop their language and transform their knowledge; and
- opportunities for language learners to participate in setting the agenda for what they learn.

www.cengagebrain.com

This chapter will serve as the foundation for the topics that follow in *Teacher's Handbook*. In Appendix 1.2 on the *Teacher's Handbook* Web site, you will find a list of "Best Practices for World Language Instruction," designed by the Pittsburgh (PA) Public Schools to identify for teachers and administrators effective instructional practices that reflect current SLA theories. It is included here to illustrate how school districts are implementing many of the practices that are presented in this text.

In some of the activities that appear in the Observe and Reflect, Teach and Reflect, and Discuss and Reflect sections, it is suggested that you observe a foreign language classroom. Appendix 1.3 on the *Teacher's Handbook* Web site contains a list of "etiquette guidelines" for observing a language classroom as a guest visitor; you may find it helpful to review these guidelines prior to making your first observation.

Pg5

Network SRC9449 @ clpm

OBSERVE AND REFLECT ·

The following two activities will enable you to examine elements of language learning that occur in classrooms and in other settings.

NCATE_____

EPISODE ONE
Observing a Child Interacting in His/Her Native Language (L1)

ACTFL/NCATE[12] 3.a. Understanding Language Acquisition and Creating a Supportive Classroom

TESOL/NCATE 1.a. Describing Language and 1.b. Language Acquisition and Development

Observe a small child between the ages of two and a half and three years old who is interacting with one or more persons (parent, older siblings, etc.) in his/her native language. Observe for at least one hour, paying particular attention to the child's use of language. Use the Observation Guide to analyze the conversation.

Alternative Observation of a Child Interacting in His/Her Native Language (L1)

If you cannot observe a small child using his/her native language, use the following transcription of a 3-year-old boy named Alex talking to his mother in their native language after he returns home from preschool. Use the Observation Guide to help analyze the script as you read it.

Mother: Hi Alex! How was your day at preschool?

Alex: Good.

Mother: What did you do at preschool today?

Alex: Eated a snack.

Mother: You ate a snack? Great! What did you eat?

Alex: Cupcakes with M&Ms. It was Steven's birthday. We singed "Happy Birthday."

Mother: Really?

Alex: Yep.

Mother: Did you do anything else for Steven's birthday?

Alex: Oh, we broke a...a...pin...uh...you know...with a big stick.

Mother: What did you break?

Alex: A big thing. It had candy in it and went all over the floor. Can't remember what you call it...A pin...

Mother: Oh, you mean a piñata.

Alex: Yeah, a piñata. It looked like a big fish with feathers.

Mother: I'll bet that was fun, Alex.

Alex: Yep. I got a lot of candy!

Source: ACTFL / Weber State University, 2003, Foreign Language Methods Online course

NCATE

EPISODE TWO
Observing a Beginning Language (L2) Class

ACTFL/NCATE 3.a. Understanding Language Acquisition and Creating a Supportive Classroom

TESOL/NCATE 1.a. Describing Language and 1.b. Language Acquisition and Development

Now observe a beginning language learning classroom in an elementary or secondary school, or college/university setting. Refer to the questions presented in the Observation Guide below as you observe the students interacting in the foreign language. Then answer the questions in the guide.

OBSERVATION GUIDE
The Language of Interaction

novice = child or classroom learner
expert = caretaker, older individual, teacher

1. Why are the expert and novice speaking? What is the topic of conversation?
2. When does the novice participate in the conversation? To answer questions? To ask questions? To provide additional information? How would you characterize the nature of the novice's talk?
3. When does the expert speak? To offer information? To ask questions? What kinds of questions does the expert ask? How would you characterize the nature of the expert's talk?

4. How does the expert react to what the novice says?
5. How does the expert help the novice when the novice has trouble expressing an idea? Do you see examples of explicit talk about the language?
6. What happens when the expert and novice do not understand each other?
7. What kind of language errors do you notice?
8. What does the expert do when the novice makes a language mistake?
9. What types of assistance does the expert offer to the novice?
10. What are some examples of language play or mental rehearsal used by the novice?

As you reflect upon the classroom you visited in Episode Two (or upon any other observation you made), describe the role of input, output, meaningful social interaction, and collaboration in light of the theoretical frameworks presented in this chapter. Describe the similarities and differences between the observations you did in Episodes One and Two.

www.cengagebrain.com

Also see the *Teacher's Handbook* Web site for a link to a video of a kindergarten immersion French class for examples of emerging language use.

DISCUSS AND REFLECT ·

www.cengagebrain.com

See the *Teacher's Handbook* Web site for additional case studies:
Case Study Two: Using Songs to Engage Learners
Case Study Three: Conducting a Cooperative Learning Task

NCATE_____

CASE STUDY ONE
Creating Real Conversational Models

ACTFL/NCATE 3.a. Understanding Language Acquisition and Creating a Supportive Classroom; 3.b. Developing Instructional Practices That Reflect Language Outcomes and Learner Diversity; 4.b. Integrating Standards in Instruction

TESOL/NCATE 1.b. Language Acquisition and Development and 2.a. Cultural Groups and Identity

Mr. Noonen has been teaching Spanish and French for over fifteen years in an urban middle school. He is very active in local, regional, and state organizations devoted to the teaching of foreign languages. His peers, both native and nonnative speakers of Spanish, consider him to be very proficient in his knowledge of and ability to use Spanish. He is committed to providing a Spanish language environment in which his students have many opportunities to develop their ability to use the language. He uses Spanish almost exclusively in his teaching.

Dr. Lindford, professor of the foreign language teaching methods class at a local university, decided to send three Spanish Education majors to observe Mr. Noonen's class so that they could observe interactive practice labeled by the teacher as "practicing speaking" and identified by him as being significant to his goal of preparing his students for participation in "natural conversation" in Spanish (Hall, 1995, p. 43). Students were instructed to script several brief episodes of conversation between Mr. Noonen and his students. They would then analyze these scripted episodes for characteristics of real conversational models.

The next week students returned to the methods class with the scripts, one of which appears below (Hall). Students reported that the teacher began the lesson by playing a tape of songs by Gloria Estefan, and after about 30 seconds, he began the questioning that appears in the script below. [Note: The ↓ arrow indicates a falling intonation and the ↑ arrow indicates a rising intonation. Ellipses (...) indicate pauses or interruptions in the discussion. Colons (:::) indicate an elongated vowel. The teacher asks questions and various students in the class respond.]

1 Teacher: Es música ↓ no ↑ música ↓ no ↑
2 Julio: no
3 T: es música ↓ es música ↓ es música ↓
4 T: ahora señor te gusta ↑ te gusta la música ↑
5 Julio: no me gusta ↓
6 T: no me gusta ↓
7 Julio: no me gusta ↓
8 T: no me gusta la música ↓ te gusta la música ↑
9 T: no me gusta la música ↓ te gusta la música ↑
10 Several Ss: I do sí sí yeah sí
11 Rafael: aw man where you goin ↓
12 T: sí me gusta la música ↓ te gusta la música ↑
13 Andrea: sí ↓
[...]
31 T: [loudly] es música de Gloria Estefan ↓
32 Several Ss: [unintelligible talk]
33 [T writes on board]
34 Rafael: If you'd speak English I'd understand
35 T: sí Gloria Estefan...Pon Poncherelo te gusta Gloria Estefan ↑
36 Ponch: sí ↓
37 T: sí ↓
38 Julio: who's Gloria Estefan ↑
39 Ponch: me sí gusta
40 T: sí ↓ me gusta me gusta Gloria Estefan...sí ↓ me gusta Gloria Estefan
41 Rafael: Oh, that's the person who was singing that song...that's the person who was singing that song
[...]
Santiago: hey can we listen to some Spanish rap called the Spanish [unintelligible]
62 T: perdón ↑
63 Santiago: (repeats the name [unintelligible])
64 T: te gusta ↑
65 Santiago: yeah [unintelligible talk]
66 T: ah bueno fantástico tienes la cinta ↑
67 Santiago: yeah
68 T: sí ↑ la cinta es es la (goes to get cassette tape) aquí (holds up tape)
69 T: la cinta clase la cinta
70 Ss: la cinta
71 T: sí:::sí la cinta tienes la cinta de::: [unintelligible]
72 T: tú tienes la cinta ↑ la cinta ↑
73 Male S: where'd you get it
74 Rafael: where'd you get it
75 Laura: do you have it on tape
76 Julio: do you have it on tape
77 Rafael: do you have it on tape
78 Santiago: I don't have it on tape I saw it in a store
79 Santiago: I saw it in a store
80 T: o::::h cómpramelo ↓ eh ↑
81 T: ok bueno fantástico ↓

Ask yourself these questions:

1. What purpose or objective do you think the teacher has in mind for conducting this conversational exchange? Is his objective achieved?
2. How can you tell that there is no larger topical issue or goal to which the conversation is directed?
3. Explain why this exchange does not reflect a "real conversation" as described by Hall in this chapter.
4. What do the responses of the students indicate about the degree to which they understand the conversation and/or are motivated to engage in discussion?
5. What does the teacher attempt to do with his talk about "la cinta" in lines 68–72? How would you characterize what happens in lines 73–79?

To prepare for class discussion:

1. Analyze the script presented above for characteristics of a real conversational model using the criteria suggested by Hall (1995): opening utterance, ellipsis, use of related lexical items, and reactions.
2. Now analyze the script to find uses of L1 and L2. Who uses each language and for what purpose(s)?
3. What larger conversational topic might the teacher develop on the basis of the authentic Gloria Estefan music? Look at the full description of the TESOL/NCATE standards suggested for this Case Study. For an ESL or an EFL class, how might such a discussion of authentic music from any of the cultures represented in the class fit into a content-area lesson?
4. What types of language-promoting assistance, as presented in Appendix 1.1 on the *Teacher's Handbook* Web site, might the teacher have used to encourage students to speak and engage in conversation?
5. Teachers often require students to respond to questions in complete sentences so that they can practice various grammatical points and new vocabulary. As we saw in the script above, this teacher's goal caused problems in the conversational exchange. Students need to be able to talk in sentence form, yet a question-answer format does not always lend itself to responses in complete sentences without making the conversation seem unnatural. What type of activity might you design that would more naturally elicit a discussion of likes and dislikes in the language you teach? Try to elicit sentence-length utterances.

TECHNO FOCUS: In this Case Study, you have seen how a teacher attempts to use a song for discussion. Now you will see how a college professor engaged her learners with authentic materials from the Dominican Republic using music, lyrics, photos, and language-practice exercises. She instructed students to do the following: Go to http://www.colby.edu/~bknelson/SLC/ojala/index.html. Click on *la canción* to listen to the song entitled *Ojalá que llueva café* by Juan Luis Guerra. Click on the underlined vocabulary words to see images and explanations of new words. Follow the links on the word *Ojalá* to see how Arabic culture influenced the Spanish-speaking world. Click on *galería de fotos* to see images of the homeland of the singer. Click on *ejercicios* to analyze the song and send your analysis to the professor. Click on *repaso de vocabulario en Ojalá* to check your understanding of the new words. Click on several of the grammatical exercises to explore formation and use of the subjunctive. Click on *Global Forum on the World's Future* to write a short essay on your fears and hopes for the future of the world using noun clauses and the present subjunctive. Click on *traducción* to see a translation of the lyrics for the song."

Reflect on the activities that learners were asked to do by answering the following questions:

1. How do you think learners might work in their ZPDs using this song as presented in this Web page?

2. How might learners be engaged in meaningful interaction with one another as they explore this song and complete the various activities?

3. What role do you think authentic materials like these will play in learner motivation?

4. The Multimedia Educational Resource for Learning and Online Teaching (MERLOT) awarded this page its "Editor's choice" medallion in 2002 and named it a "MERLOT classic." Go to MERLOT's main page at http://www.merlot.org, click on "World Languages" and explore other items in the collection.

REFERENCES

ACTFL/Weber State University. (2003). Foreign Language Methods online. Course Module 4 Introduction. Ogden, UT. Funded by the U.S. Department of Education.

Adair-Hauck, B. (1995). Exploring language and cognitive development within the Zone of Proximal Development. Paper presented at the University of Pittsburgh.

Aljaafreh, A., & Lantolf, J. P. (1994). Negative feedback as regulation and second language learning in the zone of proximal development. *The Modern Language Journal, 78,* 465–483.

Antón, M., & DiCamilla, F. (1998). Socio-cognitive functions of L1 collaborative interaction in the L2 classroom. *The Canadian Modern Language Review, 54,* 314–342.

Appel, G., & Lantolf, J. P. (1994). Speaking as mediation: A study of L1 and L2 text recall tasks. *The Modern Language Journal, 78,* 437–452.

Atkinson, D. (2002). Toward a sociocognitive approach to second language acquisition. *The Modern Language Journal, 86,* 525–545.

Bachman, L. F. (1990). *Fundamental considerations in language testing.* Oxford, UK: Oxford University Press.

Bialystok, E. (1981). Some evidence for the integrity and interaction of two knowledge sources. In R. W. Andersen (Ed.), *New dimensions in second language acquisition research* (pp. 62–74). Rowley, MA: Newbury House.

Bialystok, E. (1982). On the relationship between knowing and using forms. *Applied Linguistics, 3,* 181–206.

Block, D. (2007). The rise of identity in SLA Research, Post Firth and Wagner (1997). *The Modern Language Journal, 91,* Focus Issue, 863–876.

Broner, M. A., & Tarone, E. E. (2001). Language play in a fifth-grade Spanish immersion classroom. *The Modern Language Journal, 85,* 363–379.

Brooks, F. B. (1990). Foreign language learning: A social interaction perspective. In B. VanPatten & J. F. Lee (Eds.), *Second language acquisition-foreign language learning* (pp. 153–169). Clevedon, UK: Multilingual Matters.

Brooks, F. B., Donato, R., & McGlone, V. (1997). When are they going to say "it" right? Understanding learner talk during pair-work activity. *Foreign Language Annals, 30,* 524–541.

Buck, M. (2000). Procesamiento del lenguaje y adquisición de una segunda lengua. Un estudio de la adquisición de un punto gramatical en inglés por hispanohablantes. Unpublished doctoral dissertation, Universidad Autónoma de México, Mexico City.

Campbell, R., & Wales, R. (1970). The study of language acquisition. In J. Lyons (Ed.), *New horizons in linguistics* (pp. 242–260). Harmondsworth, UK: Penguin.

Canale, M., & Swain, M. (1980). Theoretical bases of communicative approaches to second language teaching and testing. *Applied Linguistics, 1,* 1–47.

Celce-Murcia, M., Dörnyei, Z., & Thurrell, S. (1995). Communicative competence: A pedagogically motivated model with content specifications. *Issues in Applied Linguistics, 6,* 5–35.

Cheng, A. (2002). The effects of processing instruction on the acquisition of ser and estar. *Hispania, 85,* 308–323.

Chomsky, N. (1965). *Aspects of the theory of syntax.* Cambridge, MA: MIT Press.

Chomsky, N. (1968). *Language and mind.* New York: Harcourt, Brace, Jovanovich.

Clark, H. (1992). *Arenas of language use.* Chicago: University of Chicago Press.

Clément, R., & Kruidenier, B. G. (1983). Orientations in second language acquisition: I. The effects of ethnicity, milieu, and target language on their emergence. *Language Learning, 33,* 273–291.

Cook, G. (2000). *Language play, language learning.* Oxford, UK: Oxford University Press.

Corder, S. P. (1973). *Introducing applied linguistics.* Harmondsworth, UK: Penguin.

Crookes, R., & Schmidt, R. (1991). Motivation: Reopening the research agenda. *Language Learning, 41,* 469–512.

de Guerrero, M. C. M. (1994). Form and function of inner speech in adult second language learning. In J. P. Lantolf & G. Appel (Eds.), *Vygotskian approaches to second language research* (pp. 83–115). Norwood, NJ: Ablex.

Dewey, J. (1938). *Experience and education.* New York: Macmillan.

Donato, R. (1994). Collective scaffolding. In J. Lantolf & G. Appel (Eds.), *Vygotskyan approaches to second language acquisition research* (pp. 33–56). Norwood, NJ: Ablex.

Donato, R. (2000). Sociocultural contributions to understanding the foreign and second language classroom. In J. P. Lantolf (Ed.), *Sociocultural theory and second language learning* (pp. 27–50). Oxford, UK: Oxford University Press.

Donato, R. (2004). Aspects of collaboration in pedagogical discourse. In M. McGroarty (Ed.), *Annual Review of Applied Linguistics (vol. 24), Advances in language pedagogy* (pp. 284–302). West Nyack, NY: Cambridge University Press.

Donato, R., & McCormick, D. (1994). A sociocultural perspective on language learning strategies: The role of mediation. *The Modern Language Journal, 78,* 453–464.

Dörnyei, Z. (1994). Motivation and motivating in the foreign language classroom. *The Modern Language Journal, 78,* 273–284.

Dörnyei, Z. (2001). *Teaching and researching motivation.* Harlow: Longman.

Dörnyei, Z., & Csizér, K. (1998). Ten commandments for motivating language learners: Results of an empirical study. *Language Teaching Research, 2*(3), 203–229.

Dörnyei, Z., & Kormos, J. (2000). The role of individual and social variables in oral task performance. *Language Teacher Research, 4,* 275–300.

Dörnyei, Z., & Skehan, P. (2003). Individual differences in second language learning. In C. J. Doughty & M. H. Long (Eds.), *The handbook of second language acquisition* (pp. 589–630). Oxford, UK: Blackwell Publishing Ltd.

Doughty, C. J. (2003). Instructed SLA: Constraints, compensation, and enhancement. In C. J. Doughty & M. H. Long (Eds.), *The handbook of second language acquisition* (pp. 256–310). Oxford, UK: Blackwell Publishing Ltd.

Duffy, G. G., & Roehler, L. R. (1986). The subtleties of instructional mediation. *Educational Leadership, 43,* 23–27.

Dulay, H., & Burt, M. (1977). Remarks on creativity in language acquisition. In M. Burt, H. Dulay, & M. Finnochiaro (Eds.), *Viewpoints on English as a second language* (pp. 95–126). New York: Regents.

Dunn, W., & Lantolf, J. P. (1998). Vygotsky's zone of proximal development and Krashen's *i*+1: Incommensurable constructs, incommensurable theories. *Language Learning, 48,* 411–442.

Eccles, J. S., & Wigfield, A. (1995). In the mind of the actor: The structure of adolescents' achievement task values and expectancy-related beliefs. *Personality and Social Psychology Bulletin, 21,* 215–225.

Ellis, R. (1985). *Understanding second language acquisition.* Oxford, UK: Oxford University Press.

Ellis, R. (1994). *The study of second language acquisition.* Oxford, UK: Oxford University Press.

Ellis, R. (1997*). SLA research and language teaching.* Oxford, UK: Oxford University Press.

Ellis, R. (2005). Measuring implicit and explicit knowledge of a second language. *Studies in Second Language Acquisition, 27,* 141–172.

Ely, C. M. (1986). Language learning motivation: A descriptive and causal analysis. *The Modern Language Journal, 70,* 28–35.

Farley, A. P. (2003). Authentic processing instruction and the Spanish subjunctive. *Hispania, 84,* 289–299.

Firth, A., & Wagner, J. (1997). On discourse, communication, and (some) fundamental concepts in SLA research. *The Modern Language Journal, 82,* 91–94.

Firth, A., & Wagner, J. (2007). Second/Foreign language learning as a social accomplishment: Elaborations on a reconceptualized SLA. *The Modern Language Journal, 91,* Focus Issue, 800–819.

Frawley, W., & Lantolf, J. P. (1985). Second-language discourse: A Vygotskyan perspective. *Applied Linguistics, 6,* 19–44.

Gardner, R. C. (1985). Social psychology and second language learning: The role of attitudes and motivation. London, Ontario, Canada: Edward Arnold.

Gardner, R. C. (2001). *Integrative motivation: Past, present, and future.* Paper presented at the Distinguished Lecturer Series, Temple University Japan, Tokyo, and Osaka. Retrieved July 5, 2008, from http://publish.uwo.ca/~gardner/GardnerPublicLecture1.pdf.

Gardner, R. C., & MacIntyre, P. (1993). A student's contributions to second-language learning. Part II: Affective variables. *Language Teaching, 26,* 1–11.

Gass, S. (1979). Language transfer and universal grammatical relations. *Language Learning, 29,* 327–344.

Gass, S. (1988). Integrating research areas: A framework for second language studies. *Applied Linguistics, 9,* 198–217.

Gass, S. (2003). Input and interaction. In C. J. Doughty & M. H. Long (Eds.), *The handbook of second language acquisition* (pp. 224–255). Oxford, UK: Blackwell Publishing Ltd.

Gass, S., Lee, J., & Roots, R. (2007). Firth and Wagner (1997): New ideas or a new articulation? *The Modern Language Journal, 91,* Focus Issue, 788–799.

Gass, S., & Selinker, L. (1994). *Second language acquisition.* Hillsdale, NJ: Lawrence Erlbaum.

Gillette, B. (1990). *Beyond learning strategies: A whole-person approach to second language acquisition.* Unpublished doctoral dissertation, University of Delaware, Newark, DE.

Goldberg, E., & Noels, K. A. (2006). Motivation, ethnic identity, and post-secondary education language choices of graduates of intensive French language programs. *The Canadian Modern Language Review, 62,* 423–447.

Gregersen, T. S. (2003). To err is human: A reminder to teachers of language-anxious students. *Foreign Language Annals, 36,* 25–32.

Gregersen, T. S., & Horwitz, E. K. (2002). Language learning and perfectionism: Anxious and non-anxious language learners' reactions to their own oral performance. *The Modern Language Journal, 86,* 562–570.

Hall, J. K. (1995). "Aw, man, where we goin'?": Classroom interaction and the development of L2 interactional competence. *Issues in Applied Linguistics, 6,* 37–62.

Hall, J. K. (1997). A consideration of SLA as a theory of practice: A response to Firth and Wagner. *The Modern Language Journal, 81,* 301–306.

Hall, J. K. (1999). The communication standards. In J. K. Phillips & R. M. Terry. *Foreign language standards: Linking research, theories, and practices* (pp. 15–56). Lincolnwood, IL: NTC/Contemporary Publishing Group.

Hall, J. K. (2004). Language learning as an interactional achievement. *The Modern Language Journal, 88,* 607–612.

Halliday, M. A. K. (1994). *An introduction to functional grammar.* London, Ontario, Canada: Edward Arnold.

Hernández, T. (2006). Integrative motivation as a predictor of success in the intermediate foreign language classroom. *Foreign Language Annals, 39,* 605–617.

Hershberger, R., Navey-Davis, S., & Borrás A., G. (2005). *Plazas: Lugar de encuentros* (2nd ed.). Boston: Thomson Heinle.

Hymes, D. (1972). On communicative competence. In J. P. Pride & J. Holmes (Eds.), *Sociolinguistics* (pp. 269–293). Harmondsworth, UK: Penguin.

Kinginger, C. (2001). *i* +1 ≠ ZPD. *Foreign Language Annals, 34,* 417–425.

Kinginger, C. (2002). Defining the zone of proximal development in U.S. foreign language education. *Applied Linguistics, 23,* 240–261.

Krashen, S. (1982). Principles and practice in second language acquisition. Oxford, UK: Pergamon Press.

Kuczaj, S. A., II. (1983). *Crib speech and language play.* New York: Springer-Verlag.

Lafford, B. A. (2007). Second language acquisition reconceptualized? The impact of Firth and Wagner (1997). *The Modern Language Journal, 91,* Focus Issue, 735–756.

Lantolf, J. P. (1994). Sociocultural theory and second language learning. *The Modern Language Journal, 78,* 418–420.

Lantolf, J. P. (1997). The function of language play in the acquisition of L2 Spanish. In W. R. Glass & A. T. Pérez-Leroux (Eds.), *Contemporary perspectives on the acquisition of Spanish* (pp. 3–24). Somerville, MA: Cascadilla Press.

Lantolf, J. P. (2000). Introducing sociocultural theory. In J. P. Lantolf (Ed.), *Sociocultural theory and second language learning* (pp. 1–26). Oxford, UK: Oxford University Press.

Lapkin, S., Swain, M., & Smith, M. (2002). Reformulation and the learning of French pronominal verbs in a Canadian French immersion context. *The Modern Language Journal, 86,* 485–507.

Larsen-Freeman, D. (2007). Reflecting on the cognitive-social debate in second language acquisition. *The Modern Language Journal, 91,* Focus Issue, 773–787.

Lee, J. F., & VanPatten, B. (2003). *Making communicative language teaching happen.* San Francisco: McGraw-Hill.

Lightbown, P. (1985). Great expectations: Second-language acquisition research and classroom teaching. *Applied Linguistics, 6,* 173–189.

Lightbown, P. (2004). Commentary: What to teach? How to Teach? In B. VanPatten (Ed.), *Processing instruction* (pp. 65–78). Mahwah, NJ: Erlbaum.

Lightbown, P., & Spada, N. (2006). *How languages are learned* (3rd ed.). Oxford, UK: Oxford University Press.

Long, M. H. (1981). Input, interaction and second language acquisition. In H. Winitz (Ed.), *Native language and foreign language acquisition* (pp. 259–278). Annals of the New York Academy of Sciences 379. New York: Academy of Sciences.

Long, M. H. (1983). Native speaker/non-native speaker conversation in the second language classroom. In M. A. Clarke & J. Handscomb (Eds.), *On TESOL '82: Pacific perspectives on language learning and teaching* (pp. 207–225). Washington, DC: TESOL.

Long, M. (1996). The role of the linguistic environment in second language acquisition. In W. Ritchie & T. Bhatia (Eds.), *Handbook of Second Language Acquisition* (pp. 413–468). New York: Academic Press.

MacIntyre, P. D. (2007). Willingness to communicate in the second language: Understanding the decision to speak as a volitional process. *The Modern Language Journal, 91,* 564–576.

Mackey, A. (1999). Input, interaction and second language development. *Studies in Second Language Acquisition, 21,* 557–581.

Masgoret, A.-M., & Gardner, R. C. (2003). Attitudes, motivation, and second language learning: A meta-analysis of studies conducted by Gardner and Associates. *Language Learning, 53,* 123–163.

McCafferty, S. G. (1994). Adult second language learners' use of private speech: A review of studies. *The Modern Language Journal, 78,* 421–436.

McCafferty, S. G. (2002). Gesture and creating zones of proximal development for second language learning. *The Modern Language Journal, 86,* 192–203.

McCormick, D. E., & Donato, R. (2000). Teacher questions as scaffolded assistance in an ESL classroom. In J. K. Hall & L. Verplaetse (Eds.), *Second and foreign language learning through classroom interaction* (pp. 183–201). Mahwah, NJ: Lawrence Erlbaum and Associates.

McLaughlin, B. (1987). *Theories of second-language learning.* London, Ontario, Canada: Edward Arnold.

McLaughlin, B., Rossman, T., & McLeod, B. (1983). Second language learning: An information processing perspective. *Language Learning, 33,* 135–158.

Mehan, H. (1979). What time is it, Denise: Asking known information questions in classroom discourse. *Theory Into Practice, 28*(4), 285–294.

Met, M. (2004). Foreign language. In Cawelti, G. (Ed.), *Handbook of research on improving student achievement* (pp. 86–87). Arlington, VA: Educational Research Service.

Mori, S., & Gobel, P. (2006). Motivation and gender in the Japanese EFL classroom. *System, 34*, 194–210.

Munsell, P., & Carr, T. (1981). Monitoring the monitor: A review of second-language acquisition and second language learning. *Language Learning, 31*, 493–502.

Newman, F., & Holtzman, L. (1993). *Lev Vygotsky: Revolutionary scientist*. New York: Routledge.

Ohta, A. S. (1995). Applying sociocultural theory to an analysis of learner discourse: Learner-learner collaborative interaction in the zone of proximal development. *Issues in Applied Linguistics, 6*, 93–122.

Oxford, R., & Nyikos, M. (1989). Variables affecting choice of language learning strategies by university students. *The Modern Language Journal, 73*, 291–300.

Oxford, R., & Shearin, J. (1994). Language learning motivation: Expanding the theoretical framework. *The Modern Language Journal, 78*, 12–28.

Parr, P. C., & Krashen, S. D. (1986). Involuntary rehearsal of second language in beginning and advanced performers. *System, 14*, 275–278.

Pennycook, A. (1997). Cultural alternatives and autonomy. In P. Benson & P. Voller (Eds.), *Autonomy and independence in language learning* (pp. 35–53). London: Longman.

Piaget, J. (1979). *The development of thought*. New York: Viking.

Pica, T. (2002). Subject-matter content: How does it assist the interactional and linguistic needs of classroom language learners? *The Modern Language Journal, 86*, 1–19.

Pica, T., Holliday, L., Lewis, N., & Morgenthaler, L. (1989). Comprehensible output as an outcome of linguistic demands on the learner. *Studies in Second Language Acquisition, 11*, 63–90.

Platt, E., & Brooks, F. B. (1994). The "acquisition-rich environment" revisited. *The Modern Language Journal, 78*, 497–511.

Ramsey, R. (1980). Learning-learning approach styles of adult multilinguals and successful language learners. *Annals of the New York Academy of Sciences, 345*, 73–96.

Reiss, M. (1985). The "good" language learner: Another look. *The Canadian Modern Language Review, 41*, 511–523.

Rogoff, B. (1990). Apprenticeship in thinking, cognitive development in social context. New York: Oxford University Press.

Sacks, H., Schegloff, E. A., & Jefferson, G. (1974). A simplest systematics for the organisation of turn-taking for conversation. *Language, 50*, 696–735.

Savignon, S. J. (1972). *Communicative competence: An experiment in foreign language teaching*. Philadelphia: Center for Curriculum Development.

Scarcella, R. C., & Oxford, R. L. (1992). *The tapestry of language learning*. Boston: Heinle & Heinle.

Schmidt, R. W. (2001). Attention. In P. Robinson (Ed.), *Cognition and second language instruction* (pp. 3–32). Cambridge: Cambridge University Press.

Schulz, R. A. (1991). Second language acquisition theories and teaching practice: How do they fit? *The Modern Language Journal, 5*, 17–26.

Scullen, M. E., & Jourdain, S. (2000). The effect of explicit training on successful circumlocution: A classroom study. In J. F. Lee & A. Valdman (Eds.), *Form and meaning: Multiple perspectives* (pp. 231–253). Boston: Heinle & Heinle.

Segalowitz, N. (2003). Automaticity and second languages. In C. J. Doughty & M. H. Long (Eds.), *The handbook of second language acquisition* (pp. 382–408). Oxford, UK: Blackwell Publishing Ltd.

Selinker, L. (1974). Interlanguage. In J. H. Schumann & N. Stenson (Eds.), *New frontiers in second-language learning* (pp. 114–136). Rowley, MA: Newbury House.

Shaaban, K. A., & Ghaith, G. (2000). Student motivation to learn English as a foreign language. *Foreign Language Annals, 33*, 632–644.

Shore, B. (1996). Culture in mind: Cognition, culture, and the problem of meaning. New York: Oxford University Press.

Skinner, B. F. (1957). *Verbal behavior*. New York: Appleton-Century-Crofts.

Smith, J. (1996). A seven-minute slice of chaos or I'm puzzling through now. Unpublished research report, University of Pittsburgh, Pittsburgh, PA.

Sung, H., & Padilla, A. M. (1998). Student motivation, parental attitudes, and involvement in the learning of Asian languages in elementary and secondary schools. *The Modern Language Journal, 82*, 205–216.

Swain, M. (1985). Communicative competence: Some roles of comprehensible input and comprehensible output in its development. In S. Gass & C. Madden (Eds.), *Input in second language acquisition* (pp. 235–253). Rowley, MA: Newbury House.

Swain, M. (1995). Three functions of output in second language learning. In G. Cook & B. Seidlhofer (Eds.), *Principle and practice in applied linguistics: Studies in honour of H. G. Widdowson* (pp. 125–144). Oxford, UK: Oxford University Press.

Swain, M. (2000). The output hypothesis and beyond: Mediating acquisition through collaborative dialogue. In J. P. Lantolf (Ed.), *Sociocultural theory and second language acquisition* (pp. 97–114). Oxford, UK: Oxford University Press.

Swain, M., & Deters, P. (2007). "New" mainstream SLA theory: Expanded and enriched. *The Modern Language Journal, 91*, Focus Issue, 820–836.

Swain, M., & Lapkin, S. (1998). Interaction and second language learning: Two adolescent French immersion students working together. *The Modern Language Journal, 82*, 320–337.

Tarone, E. (1983). On the variability of interlanguage systems. *Applied Linguistics, 4,* 142–163.

Tarone, E. (2000). Getting serious about language play: Language play, interlanguage variation, and SLA. In B. Swierzbin, F. Morris, M. Anderson, C. Klee, & E. Tarone (Eds.), *Interaction of social and cognitive forces in SLA: Proceedings of the 1999 Second Language Research Forum* (pp. 31–53). Somerville, MA: Cascadilla Press.

Terrell, T. D. (1986). Acquisition in the natural approach: The binding/access framework. *The Modern Language Journal, 70,* 213–227.

Tharp, R. G., & Gallimore, R. (1991). *The instructional conversation: Teaching and learning in social activity.* Santa Cruz, CA: The National Center for Research on Cultural Diversity and Second Language Learning.

Tremblay, P. F., & Gardner, R. C. (1995). Expanding the motivation construct in language learning. *The Modern Language Journal, 79,* 505–518.

Tucker, G. R., Hamayan, E., & Genesee, F. H. (1976). Affective, cognitive, and social factors in second language acquisition. *The Canadian Modern Language Review, 32,* 214–226.

VanLier, L. (1996). *Interaction in the language classroom.* New York: Longman.

VanPatten, B. (1993). Grammar teaching for the acquisition-rich classroom. *Foreign Language Annals, 26,* 435–450.

VanPatten. B. (Ed.). (2004). *Processing instruction.* Mahwah, NJ: Erlbaum.

VanPatten, B., & Cadierno, T. (1993). Input processing and second language acquisition: A role for instruction. *The Modern Language Journal, 77,* 45–57.

Vygotsky, L. S. (1978). Mind in society: The development of higher psychological processes. Cambridge, MA: Harvard University Press.

Vygotsky, L. S. (1986). *Thought and language.* Cambridge, MA: MIT Press.

Wells, G. (1998). Using L1 to master L2: A response to Antón and DiCamilla's "Socio-cognitive functions of L1 collaborative interaction in the L2 classroom." *The Canadian Modern Language Review, 54,* 343–353.

Wells, G. (1999). Dialogic inquiry: Toward a sociocultural practice and theory of education. Cambridge, UK: Cambridge University Press.

Wen, X. (1997). Motivation and language learning with students of Chinese. *Foreign Language Annals, 30,* 235–251.

Wertsch, J. V. (1991). *Voices of the mind: A sociocultural approach to mediated action.* Cambridge, MA: Harvard University Press.

Wertsch, J. V. (1994). The primacy of mediated action in sociocultural studies. *Mind, Culture, and Activity, 1,* 202–208.

Wertsch, J. V., & Bivens, J. (1992). The social origins of individual mental functioning: Alternatives and perspectives. *Quarterly Newsletter of the Laboratory of Comparative Human Cognition, 14,* 35–44.

White, L. (1987). Against comprehensible input: The input hypothesis and the development of second language competence. *Applied Linguistics, 12,* 121–134.

White, L. (1996). Universal Grammar and second language acquisition: Current trends and new directions. In W. Ritchie & T. Bhatia (Eds.), *Handbook of second language acquisition* (pp. 85-120). New York: Academic Press.

White, L. (2003). *Second language acquisition and Universal Grammar.* Cambridge, MA: Cambridge University Press.

Winke, P. M. (2005). Promoting motivation in the foreign language classroom. *CLEAR News, 9*(2), 2005, 1, 3–6.

Wong, W., & VanPatten, B. (2003). The evidence is IN: Drills are OUT. *Foreign Language Annals, 36,* 403–424.

Wong-Fillmore, L. (1985). Second language learning in children: A proposed model. Proceedings of Conference on Issues in English Language Development for Minority Language Education. Arlington, VA, July 24. (ERIC Document Reproduction Service No. ED273149)

Wood, D., Bruner, J. S., & Ross, G. (1976). The role of tutoring in problem solving. *Journal of Child Psychology and Psychiatry, 17,* 89–100.

Yang, J. S. R. (2003). Motivational orientations and selected learner variables of East Asian language learners in the United States. *Foreign Language Annals, 36,* 44–56.

Young, D. J. (1990). An investigation of students' perspectives on anxiety and speaking. *Foreign Language Annals, 23,* 539–553.

NOTES

1. For example, children would not use a word order that was not characteristic of the language being acquired.

2. See VanPatten (2004) for a full description of the principles of Processing Instruction and Lee and VanPatten (2003) for a listing (p. 139). For examples of structured input activities, see pp. 142–146 of Lee and VanPatten (2003).

3. Thanks to Dr. Rick Donato, University of Pittsburgh, for the insights here concerning negotiation of meaning. If students learn explicitly through instruction or implicitly through a teacher model and understand that their signals of noncomprehension are welcomed and are good for language learning, then classrooms can provide the context for negotiation of meaning. If learners are merely passive receivers of comprehensible input, or the beneficiaries of teacher reformulations, then we cannot claim that the classroom is providing opportunities for students to negotiate meaning.

4. Refer to Chapter 8 for a discussion of how learners use various types of "talk" during pair-work activities in order to understand the tasks more fully and ultimately to complete them more successfully.

5. At the time of the writing of the fourth edition of *Teacher's Handbook,* the "cognitive-social" debate was presented in an entire issue of *The Modern Language Journal,* Volume 91 Focus Issue, 2007. For more details on this SLA discussion, the reader is encouraged to access the articles in this special focus issue, especially the Larsen-Freeman article (pp. 773–787).

6. Sociocultural theory and the concept of the ZPD are also related to "constructivism," a theory of knowledge acquisition that portrays learners as constructing their own knowledge on the basis of personal experiences and interactions (Dewey, 1938; Firth & Wagner, 2007).

7. See Block (2007) for his recent discussion of the issue of "identity" of the language learner.

8. For early work on CA, see Sacks, Schegloff, and Jefferson (1974).

9. See Dörnyei (1994) for a list of thirty strategies for motivating L2 learners according to language level, learner level, course content and activities, teacher-specific factors, and group-specific factors. Also see Dörnyei (2001) for innovative methods and techniques for motivating learners across his process-oriented model.

10. See Chapter 8 for a more extended discussion of error correction and repair.

11. See Chapter 10 for a discussion of learning strategies.

12. The NCATE icon indicates that a teacher education program might use these activities to address the ACTFL/NCATE or the TESOL/NCATE standards.

Contextualizing Language Instruction to Address Goals of the Standards for Foreign Language Learning

In this chapter, you will learn about:

- the chronological development of language teaching
- context
- proficiency
- *Standards for Foreign Language Learning in the 21st Century* (philosophy, development, goal areas, content standard, progress indicator, learning scenario)

- *PreK–12 English Language Proficiency Standards*
- bottom-up/top-down approaches to teaching
- textbook evaluation

Teach and Reflect: Developing a Learning Scenario; Contextualizing the Teaching of a Past Tense Grammar Point; Using the Standards at the Post-Secondary Level

Discuss and Reflect: Teachers Talking Textbooks

CONCEPTUAL ORIENTATION

Foreign language instruction in the U.S. evolved historically from an emphasis on reading and writing in the 18th and 19th centuries to a focus on using languages for real-life, interactive purposes in the 21st century. Approaches to language instruction have been influenced by research in psychology, linguistics, and, more recently, in second language acquisition (SLA), as you saw in Chapter 1. In the past several decades, language instruction in the U.S. has also been significantly influenced by (1) the concept of assessing and teaching for language proficiency and (2) student standards published at the national level for foreign languages and English as a Second Language, both of which have served as an impetus for *contextualized* language instruction. It is the position of *Teacher's Handbook* that the current goal of communicative language teaching can only be realized if instruction occurs within meaningful contexts. As pointed out in the *Teacher's Handbook* Preface, *context* refers to the "interrelated conditions in which something exists or occurs" (Merriam-Webster, 2003, p. 270). We might think of it as those events or circumstances that come before or after or surround a communication between or among people. Context includes the setting, topic, situation, purpose, actors, roles, cultural assumptions, goals, and motivation that are involved in the communication. It consists of all the features of the world outside the classroom that allow people to use and interpret language (R. Donato, personal communication, June 13, 2008). For our purposes as language teachers, *context* refers to the degree to which meaning and situations from the world outside the classroom are present in an instructional approach, method, or classroom activity, thus engaging learners in constructing meaning and in using L2 to communicate and acquire new information.

For decades, elementary school teachers have been teaching foreign language within the context of academic subject areas, e.g., mathematics, geography, science, and through techniques such as storytelling, games, and role playing. However, at secondary and post-secondary levels of instruction, linguistic form has traditionally been separated from context, such as academic content and culture, as students in higher language levels become cognitively able to analyze linguistic forms. Furthermore, earlier methods of language instruction, as illustrated in Appendix 2.1, advocated teaching language via the separate skills of listening, speaking, reading, or writing, and some suggested a discrete-point approach to the teaching of grammar, which focused on the learning of isolated grammar rules. Unfortunately, many teachers are still influenced by outdated methods and allow their instruction to be driven by a textbook that is organized around a grammatical syllabus and devoid of stimulating content. Fortunately, the implementation of student standards, the vision of language learning as a subject area that can be related to other disciplines and to the world at large, current research that advocates a sociocultural approach to language learning and teaching, and the advances in modern technology continue to serve as catalysts in placing context and meaning into the forefront of language teaching. In this chapter, you will see the history of the profession unfold, and you will explore how methods, perspectives about language learning, assessment, and standards have led to a new view of language learning as meaningful, purposeful, and accomplished through *contextualized* practice.

A Historical View of Context in Foreign Language Instruction

Appendix 2.1 presents a chart that illustrates the chronological development of language teaching in terms of key time periods when particular approaches and/or methods were used. You may find it helpful to review the chart, explore the role of context in each method, and associate the theories you learned in Chapter 1 with these approaches.

This section presents a brief discussion of the key methods featured in Appendix 2.1, in terms of their impact on the development of foreign language teaching. The earliest method, used in the teaching of Latin and Greek, was the Grammar-Translation (G-T) method, which focused on translation of printed texts, learning of grammatical rules, and memorization of bilingual word lists. Context played no role in this teaching method, except to help explain the translation. The Direct Method appeared in reaction to G-T and its emphasis was on teaching speaking through visuals, exclusive use of the Target Language (TL), and inductive teaching in which students subconsciously "pick up" grammar rules and guess meaning within context. The Audiolingual Method (ALM), which brought a new emphasis to listening and speaking, advocated teaching the oral skills by means of stimulus-response learning: repetition, dialogue memorization, and manipulation of grammatical pattern drills (Lado, 1964). Therefore, speaking in the ALM mode usually meant repeating after the teacher, reciting a memorized dialogue, or responding to a mechanical drill, as in the following example of a person-number substitution drill taken from a 1969 French I ALM textbook, with English translations in parentheses:

Teacher: Vous travaillez tout le temps.	(You [plural] work all the time.)
Nous. . .	(We. . .)
Student: Nous travaillons tout le temps.	(We work all the time.)
Teacher: Je. . .	(I. . .)
Student: Je travaille tout le temps.	(I work all the time.)
Teacher: Michel. . .	(Michel. . .)
Student: Michel travaille tout le temps.	(Michel works all the time.)
Teacher: Ils. . .	(They. . .)
Student: Ils travaillent tout le temps.	(They work all the time.)
(Ray & Lutz, 1969, p. 15)	

You will notice the lack of context in such a drill—there is little apparent meaning nor a situation in the world outside the classroom where one would interact in this way. Since the language was presented in dialogues, drills typically used in the ALM method deceptively appeared to be contextualized. In actuality, students can complete a mechanical drill successfully by simply following the pattern, without even knowing the meaning of what is being said. With the ALM method, unfortunately, learners were seldom exposed to meaningful, contextualized input and were unable to transfer the memorized material into spontaneous communication. Of importance, however, is that the ALM methodology dominated language teaching in the 1950s and 1960s, primarily because large numbers of pre- and in-service teachers were trained and re-trained in summer institutes funded by the *National Defense Education Act (NDEA)* (Hadley, 2001). Many teachers today still use ALM-based teaching strategies.

The cognitive approaches, first proposed in the 1960s, promoted more meaningful language use and creativity (Ausubel, 1968). This cognitive view was based largely on Chomsky's (1965) claims that an individual's linguistic knowledge does not reflect conditioned behavior but rather the ability to create an infinite number of novel responses. In this theoretical framework, learners must understand the rules of the language before they can be expected to perform or use the language. However, although the cognitive approaches advocate *creative* language practice, usually related to varied contexts, there is often little time left for communicative language use in real-world contexts due to extensive discussion about grammar rules in either a deductive or an inductive mode and mechanical practice.

 How did Chomsky define "competence" and "performance"? See Chapter 1.

 How did Canale and Swain (1980) expand upon the definition of communicative competence? See Chapter 1.

In the 1970s, greater attention was given to developing a more communicative approach to teaching language, focusing on the needs of learners and on the nature of communication in realistic settings outside the classroom. In a commentary on the work of the 1970s, Savignon supported the communicative approach, stating that "the development of the learner's communicative abilities is seen to depend not so much on the time they spend rehearsing grammatical patterns as on the opportunities they are given to interpret, to express, and to negotiate meaning in real-life situations" (Savignon, 1997, p. xi). She further suggested the development of a communicative approach that includes appealing topics, a functional treatment of grammar, and emphasis on communication rather than on formal accuracy in the beginning stages.

Several methods for teaching language that were developed since the late 1970s reflect many of Savignon's ideas for a communicative approach. The Natural Approach, a modern-day version of the Direct Method, was Terrell's (1982) attempt to operational-ize Krashen's theories in the classroom. Anchored in the philosophy that L2 learning occurs in the same way as L1 acquisition, the Natural Approach stresses the importance of authentic language input in real-world contexts, comprehension before production, and self-expression early on, and de-emphasizes the need for grammatical perfection in the beginning stages of language learning. Based on the same philosophy, the Total Physical Response Method (TPR) by Asher, Kusudo, and de la Torre (1974) uses activi-ties directed at the learner's kinesthetic-sensory system, i.e., body movements. Learners initially hear commands in the foreign language, respond physically to the commands, e.g., run, jump, turn around, walk to the door, and later produce the commands orally and in writing. TPR is based on the way in which children acquire vocabulary naturally in their native language. This method, which is often used as one instructional strat-egy for teaching vocabulary, has been shown to be very effective in enabling learners to acquire large amounts of concrete vocabulary and retain them over time (Asher, Kusudo, & de la Torre, 1974).[1] You will learn more about TPR and the teaching of vocabulary in Chapter 4.

Among the various humanistic or affective approaches to language instruction that place a top priority on the emotions, or the affect, of the learner are the Silent Way (Gattegno, 1976), Community Language Learning (Curran, 1976), and Suggestopedia (Lozanov, 1978). In many affective approaches, learners determine the content of what they are learning and are encouraged to express themselves from the start, with the teacher's support.

 How is *context* defined in *Teacher's Handbook?*

The Role of Context in Proficiency-Oriented Instruction

The definitions of communicative competence of the 1970s prompted new insights into the various aspects of language ability that needed to be developed in order for an individual to know a language well enough to use it. Early approaches to language instruction failed to specify levels of competence so that learners' prog-ress could be measured or program goals could be articulated. Furthermore, there was a growing realization in the profession that perhaps rather than searching for one perfect method, we needed an "organizing principle" about the nature of language proficiency that could facilitate the development of goals and objectives of language teaching (Higgs, 1984).

With World War II came the realization that the United States needed a citizenry who could communicate with people from other countries. Consequently, by the end of the 1970s, it was clear that a nationally recognized procedure for assessing language proficiency was needed, as was some consensus on defining proficiency goals for sec-ond language programs. This need for goals and assessment in the area of foreign languages was later brought to the public's attention by Senator Paul Simon of Illinois and other legislators, whose efforts led to the creation of the President's Commission on Foreign Language and International Studies in 1978, with the support of President Jimmy Carter. In 1979, the Commission published the report *Strength Through Wisdom*, which recommended that the profession develop foreign language proficiency tests to assess language learning and teaching in the United States. This report, together with recommendations by the Modern Language Association–American Council on Language Studies (MLA–ACLS) Task Force and the work of the Educational Testing Service (ETS), initiated a project whereby a proficiency scale and oral interview procedure developed in the 1950s by the Foreign Service Institute (FSI) of the U.S. Department of State would be adapted for use in academic contexts. In what came to be known as the Common Yardstick Project of the 1970s, ETS cooperated with organizations in Great Britain and Germany, representatives of the U.S. government, and business and academic groups to adapt the government FSI scale, currently known as the Interagency Language Roundtable (ILR) scale, and interview procedure for academic use (Liskin-Gasparro, 1984). This work, which was continued in 1981 by the American Council on the Teaching of Foreign Languages (ACTFL), in consultation with MLA, ETS, and other professional organizations, ultimately led to the development of the *ACTFL Provisional Proficiency Guidelines* (ACTFL, 1982).

These guidelines define what language users should be able to do with the language in speaking, listening, reading, and writing, at various levels of performance. These guidelines, which marked a shift from a focus on methodology to a focus on outcomes and assessment, continue to have a great impact on language instruction. Although neither a curricular outline nor a prescribed syllabus or sequence of instruction in and of themselves, the guidelines have implications for instructional strategies, the setting of performance expectations, and performance-based assessment (see Chapters 3, 8, and 11). See Appendix 2.2 for a historical overview of the development of the proficiency concept and Appendix 2.3 (both are on the *Teacher's Handbook* Web site) for the guidelines themselves. See the *Teacher's Handbook* Web site for the link to the speaking guidelines (ACTFL, 1999) the writing guidelines (ACTFL, 2001) and listening and reading guidelines. See the *Teacher's Handbook* Web site for the link to video clips of various teaching methods described above (Bateman & Lago, 2007).

www.cengagebrain.com

It is worth noting at this point the parallel between the response of the federal government to World War II and its similar response to the tragic events of September 11, 2001, in terms of the sudden importance given to language study in the U.S. In times of national crisis, as in World Wars I and II, the U.S. recognizes the need to communicate better in multiple languages. Since the bombing of the World Trade Centers in New York City on September 11, 2001, language learning has received much attention from governmental agencies. The Secretaries of the Departments of State, Education, and Defense, as well as the Director of National Intelligence, have been directed to provide funding in order to increase the capacity of U.S. citizens to communicate with speakers of languages other than English. In 2006, President George W. Bush announced the National Security Language Initiative (NSLI), intended to dramatically increase the number of Americans learning critically needed foreign languages such as Arabic, Chinese, Russian, Hindi, Farsi, and others through new and expanded programs from kindergarten through university and into the workforce. NSLI has three broad goals:

- expand the number of Americans mastering critical need languages and start at a younger age;
- increase the number of advanced-level speakers of foreign languages, with an emphasis on critical needs languages; and
- increase the number of foreign language teachers and the resources for them (Powell & Lowenkron, 2006).

The proficiency framework assesses language ability in terms of four interrelated criteria: (1) **global tasks or functions**: linguistic tasks, such as asking for information, narrating and describing past events, and expressing opinions; (2) **contexts/content areas:** the sets of circumstances, linguistic or situational, in which these tasks are performed and the topics that relate to these contexts (e.g., context—in a restaurant in Mexico; content—ordering a meal); (3) the **accuracy** with which the tasks are performed: the grammar, vocabulary, pronunciation, fluency, sociolinguistic appropriateness or acceptability of what is being said within a certain setting, and the use of appropriate strategies for discourse management; and (4) the **oral text type** that results from the performance of the tasks: discrete words and phrases, sentences, paragraphs, or extended discourse (Swender, 1999, p. 2). Language practice that is *contextualized* and reflects real-world use forms the foundation for an approach that seeks to develop proficiency.[2]

 The proficiency framework assesses language ability in terms of global tasks or functions, contexts/content areas, accuracy, and oral text type.

An Introduction to the Standards for Foreign Language Learning in the 21ˢᵗ Century (*SFLL*)

The Developmental Process

An interest in standards in the academic disciplines was sparked by an initiative of the George H. W. Bush administration and was continued under the Goals 2000 initiative of the Clinton administration. The visionary Goals 2000 (1994) described the competence that all students should demonstrate in challenging subject matter in grades four, eight, and twelve in seven subject areas, including foreign language. With its inclusion in Goals 2000, foreign language was recognized as part of the K–12 core curriculum in the United States (Phillips & Lafayette, 1996).

The National Standards in Foreign Language Education Project (NSFLEP, 1996) was a collaborative effort of ACTFL, the American Association of Teachers of French (AATF), the American Association of Teachers of German (AATG), and the American Association of Teachers of Spanish and Portuguese (AATSP). The standards framework was drafted by an eleven-member task force that represented a variety of languages, levels of instruction, program models, and geographic regions. The task force shared each phase of its work with the profession as a whole, disseminating the drafts and seeking written comments, which were then considered as subsequent revisions were made. The final draft, called *Standards for Foreign Language Learning: Preparing for the 21ˢᵗ Century* 1999, was published in 1996 and made available to members of the profession. It was expanded and renamed *Standards for Foreign Language Learning in the 21ˢᵗ Century* (1999), to include standards for the post-secondary level (K–16) as well as language-specific versions of the standards and learning scenarios created by the professional organizations in Chinese, classical languages, French, German, Italian, Japanese, Portuguese, Russian, and Spanish. In 2006 a third edition was issued, containing standards for Arabic. The vast majority of states have developed student standards based entirely or in large part on the national standards, abbreviated as *SFLL* in this text.

 To what degree are the foreign language student standards in your state based upon the *Standards for Foreign Language Learning in the 21ˢᵗ Century (SFLL)?* Consult the *Teacher's Handbook* Web site of your state language association or your state department of education to access your state's foreign language student standards.

Organizing Principles: Philosophy, Goal Areas, Standards

The work on proficiency during the past two decades has placed the profession in an excellent position to define what students should know and be able to do with a foreign language they learn. Although influenced by the proficiency guidelines, the standards do not represent communication as four separate skill areas of listening, speaking, reading, and writing. Standards define the central role of foreign language in the learning experiences of all learners, and they have the potential for a lasting impact in the future by placing content (i.e., gaining access to information in a range of areas of inquiry and human activity) as the central focus for instruction (NSFLEP, 2006). The NSFLEP task force developed a Statement of Philosophy, shown in Appendix 2.4 on the *Teacher's Handbook* Web site, which describes key assumptions leading to five goal areas that reflect a rationale for foreign language education. These goals are known as the "Five Cs of foreign language education": Communication, Cultures, Connections, Comparisons, Communities.

 The Five Cs of foreign language education are Communication, Cultures, Connections, Comparisons, Communities.

As Figure 2.1 illustrates, these five goals interconnect to suggest the richness of human language; no one goal can be separated from the other, nor is any one goal more important than another. Each goal area contains two to three content standards that describe the knowledge and abilities that all students should acquire by the end of their high school education in order to achieve the goals. Figure 2.2 illustrates the five goals and 11 standards. Each goal area and standards, as they relate to topics in *Teacher's Handbook*, will be explored in depth in subsequent chapters. The research base, theories, and instructional models related to each goal area will also be presented.

FIGURE 2.1 The Five Cs of Foreign Language Education

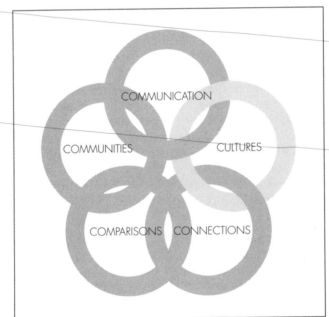

Source: From *Standards for Foreign Language Learning in the 21st Century, 1999* (p. 32). Used by permission of the American Council of the Teaching of Foreign Languages.

FIGURE 2.2 Standards for Foreign Language Learning

STANDARDS FOR FOREIGN LANGUAGE LEARNING

COMMUNICATION
Communicate in Languages Other Than English

Standard 1.1: Students engage in conversations, provide and obtain information, express feelings and emotions, and exchange opinions.

Standard 1.2: Students understand and interpret written and spoken language on a variety of topics.

Standard 1.3: Students present information, concepts, and ideas to an audience of listeners or readers on a variety of topics.

CULTURES
Gain Knowledge and Understanding of Other Cultures

Standard 2.1: Students demonstrate an understanding of the relationship between the practices and perspectives of the culture studied.

Standard 2.2: Students demonstrate an understanding of the relationship between the products and perspectives of the culture studied.

CONNECTIONS
Connect with Other Disciplines and Acquire Information

Standard 3.1: Students reinforce and further their knowledge of other disciplines through the foreign language.

Standard 3.2: Students acquire information and recognize the distinctive viewpoints that are only available through the foreign language and its cultures.

COMPARISONS
Develop Insight into the Nature of Language and Culture

Standard 4.1: Students demonstrate understanding of the nature of language through comparisons of the language studied and their own.

Standard 4.2: Students demonstrate understanding of the concept of culture through comparisons of the cultures studied and their own.

COMMUNITIES
Participate in Multilingual Communities at Home and Around the World

Standard 5.1: Students use the language both within and beyond the school setting.

Standard 5.2: Students show evidence of becoming life-long learners by using the language for personal enjoyment and enrichment.

Source: From *Standards for Foreign Language Learning in the 21st Century, 1999* (p. 9). Used by permission of the American Council of the Teaching of Foreign Languages.

 Content standard = What students should know and be able to do

It is important to note that these 11 standards are *content standards*, which describe what students should know and be able to do. They are not *performance standards*, which address the issue of how well students demonstrate competency in subject matter (e.g., a state's program exit standard). Individual states and school districts are responsible for determining performance standards for their students and for answering the question, "How good is good enough?" However, in order to assist states and districts in this task, the standards document includes sample progress indicators for grades 4, 8, and 12 that define student progress in meeting the standards but are not themselves standards. They are appropriate for many languages, can be realistically achieved at some level by all students, provide many instructional possibilities, are assessable in numerous ways, and are designed for use by states and districts to establish acceptable performance levels for their students. The following is an example of these progress indicators:

Goal area: Cultures—Gain knowledge and understanding of other cultures

Standard 2.1: Students demonstrate an understanding of the relationship between the practices and perspectives of the cultures studied.

Sample progress indicators:

Grade 4: Students use appropriate gestures and oral expressions for greetings, leave takings, and common classroom interactions.

Grade 8: Students observe, analyze, and discuss patterns of behavior typical of their peer group.

Grade 12: Students identify, examine, and discuss connections between cultural perspectives and socially approved behavioral patterns. (NSFLEP, 2006, pp. 50–51)

 Sample progress indicator = Defines student progress in meeting standards

To assist teachers in addressing the standards in their classroom instruction, the standards document includes various examples of learning scenarios, each of which is a series of learner-centered activities based on a specific theme or unit of instruction and integrated so that one activity is the basis for the subsequent activity (e.g., a listening activity provides the content for a small-group discussion). See **Teach and Reflect**, **Episode One** of this chapter for a sample learning scenario.

 Learning scenario = Series of learner-centered activities based on a specific theme and integrated so that one activity is the basis for the next

In order to address expectations of what learners should be able to do in terms of both proficiency and key areas of the standards, ACTFL published its *ACTFL Performance Guidelines for K–12 Learners* (ACTFL, 1998). The guidelines take into account the various sequences of language instruction that typically exist in American schools and outline language performance expectations, depending on the length and nature of students' learning experiences. These guidelines describe language performance evidenced by K–12 students at the benchmarks of language development labeled Novice Range, Intermediate Range, and Pre-advanced Range. See Appendix 2.5 on the *Teacher's Handbook* Web site for sample descriptors. Each of these learner ranges defines the following areas of student performance within the three modes of communication (Interpersonal, Interpretive, Presentational):

- Comprehensibility: How well are they understood?
- Comprehension: How well do they understand?
- Language Control: How accurate is their language?
- Vocabulary Use: How extensive and applicable is their vocabulary?
- Communication Strategies: How do they maintain communication?
- Cultural Awareness: How is their cultural understanding reflected in their communication?

The language performance descriptions featured in these guidelines are designed to help teachers understand how well students demonstrate language ability at various points along the language learning continuum, according to the length and nature of their language learning experiences (ACTFL, 1998).

Focus on Context: The "Weave" of Curricular Elements

The *Standards for Foreign Language Learning in the 21st Century* (NSFLEP, 2006) broaden the definition of the content of the language curriculum. Figure 2.3 depicts the elements that should be "woven" into language learning: language system, cultural traits and concepts, communication strategies, critical thinking skills, and learning strategies. In addition, other subject areas and technology are also important elements in a standards-driven curriculum.

The language system goes beyond grammar rules and vocabulary; it also includes sociolinguistic elements of gestures and other forms of nonverbal communication, discourse style, and "learning what to say to whom and when" (p. 33). In addition to being able to use the language system, learners must be able to identify key cultural concepts that will facilitate sensitive and meaningful interaction. Communication strategies such as circumlocution, guessing intelligently, making hypotheses, asking for clarification, and making inferences will empower learners in their attempts to interact. In learning a foreign language, students use critical thinking skills as they apply their existing knowledge to new tasks, incorporate new knowledge, and identify and analyze issues in order to arrive at informed decisions and to propose solutions to problems. In assuming greater responsibility for their own learning, students use learning strategies such as organizing their learning, previewing new tasks, summarizing, using questioning strategies, and inferring information from a text. By exploring interesting and challenging content and topics, students can enhance their learning of the language while expanding their knowledge of other subject areas. Additionally, increased access to a wide range of forms of technology, such as the World Wide Web,

FIGURE 2.3 The *Weave* of Curricular Elements

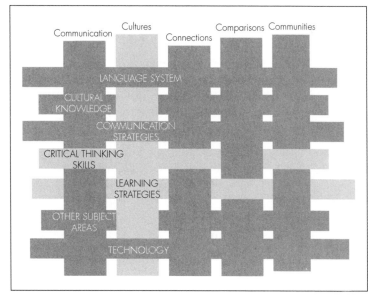

Source: From *Standards for Foreign Language Learning in the 21st Century, 1999* (p. 33). Used by permission of the American Council of the Teaching of Foreign Languages.

e-mail, CD-ROMs, and interactive video, will enable learners to use their linguistic skills to establish interactions with peers and to learn about the contemporary culture of the target country.

PRE K–12 ENGLISH LANGUAGE PROFICIENCY STANDARDS

In 1997, Teachers of English to Speakers of Other Languages (TESOL) published *ESL Standards for Pre-K–12 Students*, informed in part by the work that was then underway to develop foreign language standards. In 2006, the standards were revised to further define the second goal area in the content areas of language arts, math, science, and social studies. Some English language learners (ELLs) in U.S. schools are recent immigrants, others are seeking refuge from political unrest in their homelands, and others are in the United States with their families for professional reasons.[3] Their levels of education vary as does their language proficiency in English. You may find some English language learners in your foreign language classes.

The ESL Standards are undergirded by these important perspectives:

- language as communication;
- language learning through meaningful and significant use;
- the individual and societal value of bi- and multilingualism;
- the role of ESOL students' native languages in their English language and general academic development; and
- cultural, social, and cognitive processes in language and academic development; assessment that respects language and cultural diversity (TESOL, 2006, p. 2).

The *PreK–12 English Language Proficiency Standards* (TESOL, 2006) delineate what ELLs should know and be able to do with English, including how to communicate in socially and culturally appropriate ways and how to achieve academically in all content areas: language arts, mathematics, science, and social studies.

Supported by a federal grant, the World-Class Instructional Design and Assessment (WIDA) formed a consortium of 19 member states to provide teachers with a resource and assessment guide (WIDA, 2007). Using topics developed in the TESOL (2006) standards, WIDA also offers rubrics and a K–12 English language proficiency test called Assessing Comprehension and Communication in English State to State (ACCESS) for ELLs® and a placement test called the WIDA ACCESS Placement Test (W-APT)®. Performance on the tests is organized by standards and by grade-level clusters: preK–K; 1–3, 4–5, 6–8, and 9–12. Within grade levels, English language proficiency is described as entering, beginning, developing, expanding, bridging, and reaching. Each cluster's goals, standards, and proficiency levels are aligned within strands of model performance indicators, "can do" descriptors, and performance definitions that reflect the language learning domains of listening, speaking, reading, and writing. Content topics, such as *points of view* or *life cycles*, drawn from national and state content standards in ESL, provide spiraling and repeated exposure throughout the curriculum. This way of organizing the material allows for multiple entry points into the language education program, helps build foundational knowledge, and shows how sophistication of language use develops as students progress through the grades. Examples of student writing samples are also provided.

See the *Teacher's Handbook* Web site for links to the Foreign Language and the ESL Standards.

Using the Standards Framework to "Contextualize" the Curriculum

The authors of the *Standards for Foreign Language Learning in the 21st Century* (NSFLEP, 2006) caution educators of what the standards are NOT intended to be:

- They do not describe the current state of foreign language education in this country nor do they describe what is being accomplished by the majority of foreign language students.
- They are not a curriculum guide inasmuch as they do not prescribe specific course content nor a recommended scope and sequence.
- They do not represent a stand-alone document, but should be used with state and local frameworks and standards to determine the best approaches and responsible expectations for students (p. 28).

For what purposes are the standards intended to be used? Since they describe the ideal best practices, the standards provide a gauge against which to measure improvement in foreign language education. They are visionary in describing what language learners should be able to attain as a result of foreign language study. In addition, the standards support the ideal of extended sequences of language study and suggest the kinds of content and curricular experiences that will enable learners to attain the standards. Finally, the document has the potential to inform and influence teachers, parents, administrators, and others to ensure that all students have opportunities to acquire the knowledge and skills necessary to enable them to function successfully in our multicultural society.

According to Met (2000), the standards built upon a number of instructional practices that were previously found to be effective in realizing communicative and proficiency-based learner goals. However, the standards have also introduced instructional implications that are new for the majority of foreign language teachers. Figure 2.4 illustrates the areas of current classroom practice and the ways in which the standards can provide direction in refining these areas, as teachers work to address them in curricular design, instruction, and assessment. Note the emphasis on the notion of *contextualized* language practice. The initial release of the standards in 1996 spawned studies that examined the standards through the lens of both current research and classroom practice. See, for example, Phillips (1997); other studies will be explored with the presentation of each standards goal area in subsequent chapters. In addition, having knowledge of the standards has become practically synonymous with being a current foreign language professional. For example, Allen (2002) found that teachers who held beliefs and/or knowledge consistent with the standards were those who were members of ACTFL or members of two or more professional organizations. Additionally, the standards have become a key component in the pre-professional and continuing professional development of foreign language teachers (Cooper, 2004; Dhonau, McAlpine, & Shrum, 2007). See the *Teacher's Handbook* Web site for published debates about standards and their effect on our profession.

The standards framework and implications, as discussed in the previous section, present various possibilities to language teachers as they strive to strengthen their curricula and instruction. The specific ways in which the standards may be embraced by teachers depend largely on teachers' philosophies of and approaches to language instruction. The methods of instruction presented earlier in this chapter can be categorized into one of two broader approaches to language teaching, based on the teacher's theoretical understanding of how learners best learn a second language: the bottom-up approach and top-down approach. The standards framework has something to offer to each of these approaches in view of the role of context that can be brought to the learning experience. Furthermore, the standards have implications for the selection and use of foreign

FIGURE 2.4 Standards: Where We Are Now and Where the Standards Take Us

WHERE WE ARE NOW (adapted from Met, 2000, p. 52)	WHERE THE STANDARDS TAKE US (Shrum & Glisan, 2008, original material)
Concept of proficiency in listening, speaking, reading, writing	Communication in three modes to mirror real communication and to emphasize the purpose of communication
Student pair and group work	Tasks that provide opportunities for students to negotiate meaning, engage in language play, and develop interactional competence (e.g., ability to manage discussions)
Oral teacher-to-student exchanges that are communicative in nature	Purposeful goal-directed talk that is intellectually meaningful and stimulating (i.e., encourages students to ask questions, expand on their talk, take multiple turns in conversations)
Grammar as a component of communication rather than an end itself	Grammar that serves communication needs
Use of authentic[4] materials and commercially produced materials organized around communicative topics or situations	A central focus on the development of interpretation skills, which are pivotal to acquiring new information, cultural knowledge, and connections to other disciplines and target-language communities
Classroom activities that are meaningful and purposeful	A central role for inquiry-based activities, such as cultural investigations, authentic text exploration, and research- and technology-based projects—previously considered unit add-ons or supplemental
Classroom environment that focuses on meaningful communication	Classroom environment that fosters a sociocultural community of learners engaged in meaning making and acquiring knowledge through the foreign language
Integration of various aspects of culture into language learning	Approach to culture that emphasizes a constructivist approach to exploring the connection of cultural products and practices to their philosophical perspectives, enabling learners to develop more relevant cultural insights into the target culture and their own
Ways of measuring student learning that focus on performance, on knowledge in use	Performance assessments that are integrated with instruction and learning, go beyond paper-and-pencil test formats, and have an expanded role in determining student progress in meeting the standards

language textbooks, which may influence the teacher's approach and which, unfortunately, still often drive the curriculum and content of instruction.

The Traditional Bottom-Up Approach: Skill-Based Approaches

Historically, foreign languages have been taught in the U.S. by means of a bottom-up approach: Students analyze and learn grammar rules and vocabulary, and then later practice using them in communication. Rivers (1983) used the terms *skill getting* and *skill using* to characterize this dichotomy. *Skill getting* refers to the type of practice that helps students learn grammatical structures, while in *skill using*, students use the learned structures in communicative activities designed to focus their attention on meaningful interaction. A decade earlier, Paulston (1972) classified three categories of drills: (1) mechanical—complete control of the response and only one correct way of responding; (2) meaningful—still control of the response, may be more than one way to respond, learner must understand the stimulus; and (3) communicative—learner provides new information, no right or wrong response except in terms of grammatical correctness.[5]

Despite the emphasis on more meaningful and communicative activities in recent years, decontextualized mechanical practice has remained pervasive over the course of decades in the language approaches used by teachers. However, the usefulness of rote practice for the language learner has repeatedly been called into question, particularly in light of the key role that meaning-making and social interaction play in language acquisition, as shown in Chapter 1. A study that examined the utility of mechanical drills boldly concluded that these exercises "are not beneficial for foreign language acquisition or the development of fluency and should be discarded from instructional practice" (Wong & VanPatten, 2003, p. 403). See Chapter 7 for additional discussion of the focus on form vs. focus on meaning controversy and the teaching of grammar. Further, according to Allen (2007), "the theories of language learning that underpin the standards for FL learning do not promote a skill getting/skill using approach" (p. 44).

It should be noted that students require copious amounts of practice in using the target language, but this practice must be meaningful and engaging for students. In *Teacher's Handbook*, whenever we advocate practice, we are referring only to practice that has meaning and is purposeful.

 What theories from Chapter 1 support the key role of meaning-making and social interaction in facilitating language acquisition?

For teachers who prefer to use an approach that is primarily bottom-up, the *SFLL* can help them to incorporate more engaging content. While maintaining a familiar sequence of instruction that is often organized around the textbook, the teacher might:

- include additional information, practice, and activities related to the standards as each chapter or unit is explored (e.g., for practice of numbers, students listen to and interpret an authentic radio advertisement announcing a sale at a local department store);
- incorporate an increasing number of *synthesis* activities that integrate more than one mode of communication and address a particular goal area/standard (e.g., students send an e-mail message to a key pal abroad in order to find out information about peers in the target country);
- limit the number of mechanical, decontextualized textbook exercises and replace or revise them to bring meaning to the tasks as well as opportunities for student interaction and negotiation of meaning; and
- use some resources beyond the text to accommodate the gaps in context (e.g., video, Internet, visuals, stories).[6]

A Top-Down Approach

A top-down approach to language instruction resists reducing language to word lists, verb conjugations, discrete grammar points, or isolated linguistic elements (Adair-Hauck & Cumo-Johanssen, 1997). In this approach, learners are presented with a "whole" text (e.g., story, poem, song, tape-recorded listening selection), are guided through comprehending its main ideas, explore these ideas through interaction with others, and then focus on specific details and/or linguistic structures (e.g., vocabulary, grammar). Learners manipulate language to communicate thoughts using higher-level skills (e.g., relating knowledge from several areas, using known ideas to create new ones, generalizing from facts, predicting, drawing conclusions) before attending to discrete language structures with the use of lower-level skills (e.g., recognizing, identifying, recalling, explaining, observing, interpreting). By means of information gap activities and joint problem solving with the teacher and classmates, learners negotiate meaning and demonstrate performance before competence; that is, they participate in a more complex task than they are capable of completing without assistance (Rogoff, 1990). You will learn in a later chapter the specific implications of this approach for the teaching of grammar.

The purpose of top-down learning is to give the student a clear and whole picture of how the words and structures they must learn are contained in a context that makes these elements meaningful through the overall message. This, in turn, allows for strategic guessing, similar to the process one uses to identify unfamiliar elements in L1. In this type of learning, meaning is constructed from the whole and does not represent a linear process.[7] An example of this kind of human learning in another field is the way in which novice golfers might approach playing golf for the first time. They may have observed other golfers on the golf course or watched golf tournaments on television. Consequently, they may use this background knowledge to approach the sport in a top-down fashion initially by just grasping their golf clubs and swinging to see if they can even hit the ball. They may keep practicing by trying out different strategies and imitating what they see fellow golfers do. In this way, novice golfers get a feel for what it is like to play golf—i.e., the focus is on the "whole picture" of golfing. However, novice golfers may revert to a bottom-up approach if, for example, they want to improve their golf swing. They may take private golf lessons to focus on the way to properly grip the clubs, align themselves with the ball, and swing correctly. This bottom-up approach involves a linear, step-by-step process of focusing on one aspect of the golf game at a time.

The purpose of top-down learning is to give the student a clear and whole picture of how the words and structures they must learn are contained in a context that makes these elements meaningful through the overall message.

How does one implement a top-down approach? Within the thematic unit being taught, the teacher might present a *text* to the class for the purpose of helping learners understand its meaning while discussing it. This text can be a story, an authentic taped conversation or short reading, a piece of *realia* (an object from the target culture such as a postcard, a letter, an invitation, etc.), or any verbal input given by the teacher. For example, in a chapter dealing with travel, learners might (1) listen to a public service announcement that gives advice to travelers, (2) read an advertisement for taking a cruise, or (3) listen to their teacher tell a story about a family vacation. If the vocabulary and grammar have been appropriately matched to the theme, then these initial authentic contexts contain examples of structures and words used naturally. In a Spanish version of the contexts given above, appropriate grammatical structures might include the future tense, the prepositions *por* and *para*, and the subjunctive used with adverbial expressions.

As students attend to the initial context, they are given tasks for demonstrating understanding of main ideas and/or particular details, such as selecting the main idea from a list of alternatives, creating a possible title for the text, responding to true-false statements, and finding specific pieces of information. The teacher leads the class in discussion for the purpose of relating new information to previously learned information, for heightening understanding of the text, or, in the case of a story, for recreating the text. While the text may contain new vocabulary and grammatical structures, students cope with the unknown by negotiating meaning with the teacher by asking questions, requesting clarification, and gleaning meaning from the context itself. Through exploration of the text, students indirectly learn vocabulary and grammar that can later become the focus of more directed and personalized practice. Students may actively use grammatical forms that are contained in the text prior to actually being taught the forms explicitly. Students can also use technology to access additional authentic sources of information in order to explore cultural products, practices, and perspectives related to the theme. Within a top-down approach, the *Standards for Foreign Language Learning in the 21st Century* (NSFLEP, 2006) can serve as the organizing principle, focusing on meaningful and motivating content through which students develop language abilities, rather than allowing a textbook or teacher-controlled grammatical content to drive the curriculum (Sandrock, 2000). Thus a standards-based unit/chapter plan that is top-down in nature might feature the following sequence of learner activity:

Level of instruction: intermediate high school/college Spanish
Context: Travel
Language functions: Making travel plans, getting a hotel room, discussing means of transportation, investigating a *parador* (historical site such as a castle or convent turned into a place to stay overnight) on the Internet, communicating with a key pal by e-mail, understanding main ideas of authentic conversations dealing with lodging and travel arrangements, interpreting an authentic travel advertisement, interacting in role play situations dealing with travel.

1. Students listen to an authentic conversation between an airline employee and a traveler. Students explore main ideas through discussion and check-off lists. They acquire and practice using new vocabulary from the conversation through TPR activities, role play, and contextual guessing.

2. Students read an authentic advertisement on vacation packages. They explore main ideas and offer their opinions.

3. Students listen to the teacher introduce the concept of a *parador* while looking at a map of Spain and finding areas in which *paradores* are located. Students read an authentic article from a travel magazine that presents three types of *paradores*. The reading includes pictures, symbols that illustrate the amenities included in each *parador*, and a key to understanding the symbols. Working in groups, students read about one of the *paradores* and interpret the symbols. Each group presents its *parador* to the class by describing its location on the map, type of construction, rooms, and amenities.

4. Students listen to an authentic conversation between a hotel clerk and a guest. They explore main ideas and some details and use this as a context for discussion and role play.

5. Students engage in discovery learning and co-construct the form and meaning of new grammatical structures (future tense, *por/para*, present subjunctive with adverbial clauses) that were seeded in the initial authentic oral and printed texts. They complete several PACE grammar lessons (more on this in Chapter 7) and co-construct grammatical structures. Grammar is practiced in context by means of guided and open-ended activities and self-expression.

6. Students find other *paradores* on the Internet and acquire additional information about historical sites, geography, and travel.

7. Students communicate with key pals in Spain via e-mail in order to acquire information about daily life that would be important to know as a traveler. Once they receive responses from their key pals, they discuss cultural comparisons with their classmates.

8. Students are assessed on their ability to make travel plans through tasks such as:

- an oral role play situation in which they interact with a hotel clerk or airline employee;
- reading a written text found on the Internet that deals with a *parador* and summarizing key points about it, including whether or not they might want to stay there on a trip; and
- responding by e-mail to a Spanish-speaking key pal, in which they discuss suggestions for travelers and explore cultural products, practices, and perspectives that would be important information for someone traveling to a Spanish-speaking country.[8]

Although more research is needed on top-down processing and instruction, there is some evidence to indicate that students of a top-down or whole-language approach may be able to acquire language at a higher and more successful rate than through the traditional bottom-up approach (Adair-Hauck & Cumo-Johanssen, 1997). One of the reasons for this may be that a bottom-up approach often allows little time in the unit for contextualized practice, since most of the time is spent analyzing small segments of language. *Teacher's Handbook* believes that top-down instruction holds much promise in promoting a sociocultural and standards-based approach to language instruction.

Curricular Models

Earlier in this chapter you read about the influence of the *SFLL* on curricula. Other influences on curricula sometimes result in a curricular model, e.g., Junior Great Books, Reading is Fundamental, the Learner-Centered Curriculum, or your college's core curriculum. In each of these models, the curriculum is based on some valued principle, goal, or context. Advanced Placement® (AP) and International Baccalaureate (IB) are two curricular models that have particular appeal to language learners. Since 1955, Advanced Placement has provided a series of high school courses in math, science, languages, social studies, and other subjects, which prepare students in the United States and Canada to take AP tests and earn college credits provided they attain the qualifying scores (About AP, 2008). Founded in 1968, IB is a program designed to assist learners in 2,363 primary, middle, and secondary schools all over the world. It provides consistency for learners who spend their schooling years in a variety of countries and enables school administrators to evaluate student performance on a consistent basis. Available in English, French, or Spanish, IB courses may also count for college credit, depending on a student's score on the IB test (Quality education, 2008). In subsequent chapters of the *Teacher's Handbook* you will learn more about how the *SFLL* provide context for a variety of curricular models, including AP and IB. See the *Teacher's Handbook* Web site for further details and links for AP and IB.

www.cengagebrain.com

The Role of the Foreign Language Textbook

Historically, the foreign language textbook has been at the center of the foreign language curriculum, used by teachers—especially those who use a bottom-up approach—as the framework for organizing instruction and the primary source of exercises and activities. The student standards and the goal of contextualizing language instruction prompt several observations concerning the role of the language textbook. On the one hand, more attention to context is evident in some textbook series published in the last several years, since many of them have begun to integrate connections to other disciplines, exploration of cultural perspectives, and interaction with target-language communities. On the other hand, despite the wealth of research in second language learning that supports the notion that language learners require opportunities for meaningful interaction (see Chapter 1), foreign language textbooks have continued to depend heavily on bottom-up, drill, and form-focused activities that lack context or meaning (Aski, 2003, 2005). This finding has been corroborated by studies that have examined textbooks in French (Lally, 1998), Italian (Aski), Japanese (Takenoya, 1995), and Spanish (Frantzen, 1998).

Foreign language publishers have pointed out that, despite the major initiatives undertaken by the profession (e.g., proficiency and standards) to develop national *policies*, the world of *practice* has reflected less change in materials and teaching than the field realizes (Dorwick & Glass, 2003). In their experience, what changes most notably in textbooks are the prefaces and names of *features*, usually in response to the latest trends or policies. An example of this kind of change can be seen in current textbooks, in which icons or marginal notes indicate to instructors how a given activity addresses one of the Five Cs, or how to modify or extend an activity to address additional elements of the Five Cs. Respondents in Bragger and Rice's (2000) study reported that materials change slowly due to factors such as the conservative nature of the profession, resistance to or fear of change, the teacher/publisher tension, lack of time to make changes, and budgets. Aski (2003) echoes the view of Dorwick and Glass when she concludes that textbook publishers only produce the materials requested by their audience—foreign language instructors—and that the change will occur only when instructors embrace SLA research and indicate a preference for materials that reflect this research.[9] This view is confirmed in Allen's (2007) recent study concerning teachers' beliefs on implementing curricular change, in which she concludes that providing teachers with textbooks that introduce innovation does not necessarily lead to change in teaching practices. According to Allen (2007), teachers will only embrace new ideas if these ideas are consonant with their own beliefs about how students learn a foreign language in the classroom setting.

In his review of textbook exercise formats, Walz (1989) found that, in the mid- to late-1980s, textbook authors and publishers responded to the focus on communicative language teaching by *contextualizing* mechanical or skill-getting exercises in a wide variety of ways, such as by (1) connecting exercise sentences with the same situation or theme; (2) providing a context for the exercise in the form of information concerning people, activities, or descriptions; and (3) combining cultural aspects with language practice within the exercise. Note that this discussion of context is different from the definition given at the beginning of the chapter. As noted by both Frantzen (1998) and Walz (1989), textbook authors have different ideas about what contextualization of an exercise means. "Contextualization, especially with respect to mechanical drills, does not seem to be the same as creating a context, which is the topic and situation of a communicative act that are necessary for understanding" (Walz, 1989, p. 162). Frantzen cautions that the contextualization of mechanical drills may trick students and teachers into believing that meaningful discourse is being fostered. Further, textbook exercises and activities designed to be done by students in pairs may appear to be interactive; however, they often result in little if any interpersonal communication taking place if both students know what the other is to say and there is no real information gap that serves as the catalyst for negotiation of meaning.

Although textbooks form a backbone of instructional materials for foreign language classes, dependence on the textbook is not likely to lead to addressing of SLA research and student standards in classroom practice. Chaffee (1992) defined the *coverage model* as situations where the textbook defines the content of a course and teachers view their role as *covering* the textbook. *Coverage* has also been defined as "An approach in which students march through a textbook, page by page (or teachers through lecture notes) in a valiant attempt to traverse all the factual material within a prescribed time. . . . Coverage is a negative term . . . because when content is "covered" the student is led through unending facts, ideas, and readings with little or no sense of the overarching ideas, issues, and learning goals that might inform study" (Wiggins & McTighe, 2005, p. 16). See Case Study one for a view of teachers' concerns about covering the textbook. Allen (2002) found that this is an area in which teachers may benefit from redefining their programs according to national standards so that the textbook is viewed as one of many tools for instruction rather than the primary focus.

Unfortunately, many school districts use the same textbook series for seven to ten years or even longer. Teachers who seek to address the *Standards for Foreign Language Learning in the 21st Century* may be faced with using an old textbook that is filled with drills and/or decontextualized exercises. In this case, teachers might consider adapting the more promising exercises by:

- attaching a real-world context, such as a situational or cultural one, that students must understand in order to communicate (Frantzen, 1998);
- providing opportunities in the exercises for students to acquire new information, such as from other disciplines;
- eliminating fictitious characters and personalizing the exercises to the lives of students; and
- allowing for divergent responses rather than one correct answer.

See **Case Study One** in this chapter for sample textbook exercises.

Teachers in a position to select a new textbook should consider the degree to which the textbook is aligned with the Five Cs and standards as well as with proficiency and current SLA research implications for foreign language teaching. In a standards-based language curriculum that focuses on the development of real-world communication, the components of a textbook that are labeled "supplementary materials" are often just as important as, or even more important than, the textbook itself, for they provide contextual, visual, cultural, and interdisciplinary support that is at the heart of meaningful, contextualized language instruction. Figure 2.5 presents sample criteria that teachers might use as they evaluate and select new language textbooks.

In summary, the *Standards for Foreign Language Learning in the 21st Century* (NSFLEP, 2006) offer a description of what language learners should be able to attain as a result of foreign language study, a framework for contextualizing language instruction, and a gauge against which to measure improvement in foreign language learning. The *SFLL* can also assist teachers in self-assessing the effectiveness of their curricular design, unit and lesson plans, and materials, as well as in measuring improvement in their teaching practices. Additionally, the standards present a future research agenda and challenges as we find new ways to provide language learning experiences that meaningfully relate to real-world communication, the interests of learners, the content of other disciplines, and target culture communities.

FIGURE 2.5 Textbook Evaluation Criteria

Rate each criterion on the following scale: 3 = Excellent   2 = Satisfactory   1 = Poor

1. Features an organization based on relevant and interesting topics and cultural contexts
2. Provides activities in which students talk to each other, share information and opinions, ask personalized questions, and express feelings and ideas
3. Provides tasks in which students must negotiate meaning with one another
4. Provides authentic oral input (audiotapes, videotapes, CD-ROM programs) that has engaging content and tasks
5. Provides authentic printed texts (newspaper/magazine articles, ads, poems, short stories) that have engaging content and tasks
6. Suggests strategies for comprehending and interpreting oral and written texts
7. Includes pre-listening/pre-viewing/pre-reading tasks
8. Includes tasks in which students speak and write to an audience of listeners/readers (i.e., process-oriented tasks)
9. Provides contextualized and meaningful activities that relate to a larger communicative goal
10. Presents clear, concise grammar explanations that are necessary for communication
11. Presents vocabulary thematically, in context, and with the use of visuals and authentic realia
12. Provides for integrated practice of the three modes of communication
13. Presents an accurate view of the cultures in which the target language is spoken
14. Includes visuals for presenting vocabulary and illustrating authentic cultural aspects (overhead transparencies, visuals, PPT slides, realia)
15. Provides opportunities for students to discover and explore the products of the culture and their relationship to cultural perspectives
16. Provides opportunities for students to discover and explore the practices of the culture and their relationship to cultural perspectives
17. Provides opportunities for students to use the target language to learn about other subject areas
18. Engages students in using the target language to acquire new information on topics of interest
19. Provides opportunities for students to compare key features of the native and target languages in interesting ways
20. Provides opportunities for students to compare products, practices, and perspectives of the native culture and target cultures in interesting ways
21. Includes activities in which students use the target language with peers in other communities and target language regions (e-mail, World Wide Web, interactive video, field trips)
22. Provides opportunities for students to select authentic texts to explore for enjoyment and learning
23. Provides contextualized, performance-based achievement tests with scoring rubrics[10]
24. Suggests strategies for assessing student progress in attaining standards
25. Integrates technology effectively into instruction (audiotapes, videotapes, interactive video, CD-ROM, World Wide Web, e-mail, online chatrooms)

The evaluator/teacher may choose to add additional criteria of importance to specific language programs.

Source: Shrum & Glisan, 2005, original material; revised 2008.

TEACH AND REFLECT ·

NCATE_____

EPISODE ONE
Developing a Learning Scenario

ACTFL/NCATE 4.a. Understanding and integrating standards in planning

TESOL/NCATE 3.a. Planning for Standards-Based ESL and Content Instruction

Part One: Read the following learning scenario (NSFLEP, 2006, p. 231) and then identify which goal areas and standards are addressed and how you can tell.

A Roman Election

Mrs. Robinson's eighth grade Latin students at Harbor Day School in Corona del Mar stage an election while they are studying the Roman Republican Period. Students read a variety of original and adapted texts on the topic, including passages from Cicero, Catullus, and Pompeian campaign graffiti.

Students discuss thoroughly the Roman political system, how elections were held, and what political campaigns were like. Students then prepare to reenact the election of 63 B.C. Cicero presided over this election, and one of the two consular seats was hotly contested by the lawyer Sulpicius and the general Murena. Students discuss the different personalities and qualifications of these two men and the general state of affairs in the Roman world, and they compare them to modern American elections, campaigns, and candidates.

Students receive instruction on Latin commands, greetings, questions, and responses. Simple sentence constructions are reviewed. Then every student receives a personal "voter profile" with name, occupation, family background, ties to candidates, and other pertinent information. Two students, chosen by the teacher to portray the candidates, write campaign speeches and learn how to respond in character to questions from the voters. The remaining students work in groups to produce Latin campaign posters to decorate the room and hall on election day. Latin slogans are checked for historical and linguistic accuracy. Election events can last one to three hours (longer versions include Roman lunch and victory games sponsored by the winner). Students dress in Roman attire, a student playing the role of Cicero conducts the opening ceremonies.

After the candidates are introduced, they give their speeches, answer questions from the voters, give rebuttals, and mill among voters for a little handshaking. Finally, after all voters file past the voting boxes and cast their tokens, Cicero congratulates the winner who is acclaimed by the "voters."

Part Two: Choose one of the following themes and develop a learning scenario for the foreign language you teach. Remember to build the scenario around an interesting context and to integrate at least two of the modes of communication and culture. Identify the standards addressed in the scenario and address at least one standard in each of three goal areas. How much class time do you think it might take to complete this scenario?

Suggested themes: Education, celebrations, work and leisure time, life in the city, health and medicine, the environment, fine arts, tourism

You might want to keep this learning scenario for **Teach and Reflect** activities in later chapters.

www.cengagebrain.com

TECHNO FOCUS: The following is a description of a session presented at the ACTFL 2007 Annual Convention and World Languages Expo. On the *Teacher's Handbook* Web site, look at the handout and the PowerPoint presentation prepared by Drs. Lomicka and Lord in Appendices 2.6 and 2.7. Then answer the questions listed here below the description:

Podcasting Projects for Language Classes: What, When, Why and How

This session describes two different podcast projects with unique linguistic and cultural goals. The rationale, design, and implementation of these projects are provided. Participants will learn where and how to find target language podcasts, how to create their own podcasts, and how to integrate podcast projects into their courses. Presenters: Lara Lomicka, Associate Professor of French and Linguistics at the University of South Carolina; Gillian Lord, Associate Professor of Spanish and Linguistics at the University of Florida.

1. What is a podcast?
2. What are the two projects described in this podcast?
3. Which foreign language and ESL standards does the Study Abroad project address?
4. What type of podcast might you develop to integrate with the scenario you designed in Part Two above?
5. What are some considerations to keep in mind as you develop a podcast project?
6. How might you assess a podcast project?

More on Podcasting: Go to the View and Reflect section of this chapter on the *Teacher's Handbook* Web site and look at Activity B to see how faculty members at the secondary and post-secondary levels incorporate podcasts.

NCATE

EPISODE TWO
Contextualizing the Teaching of a Past Tense Grammar Point

ACTFL/NCATE 3.a. Understanding Language Acquisition and Creating a Supportive Environment; 4.a. Understanding and Integrating Standards in Planning; 4.c. Selecting and Designing Instructional Materials

TESOL/NCATE 3.a. Planning for Standards-Based ESL and Content Instruction

You are beginning a new unit/chapter that introduces a past tense in your target language. Unfortunately, your textbook is outdated and organized around grammar points with little contextual support. Vocabulary is included for news events (e.g., earthquake, fire, flood, robbery). Your task, as you plan, is the following:

1. Find a context in which the past tense can logically be studied (e.g., school, work, current events, diversion, travel). You might build on the theme of the given vocabulary.
2. Identify what you would like students to be able to do by the end of the unit/chapter in terms of language functions (e.g., tell a personalized story, relate a news event, report on the results of an interview with a classmate). Be sure to address the integration of modes and the culture paradigm.
3. Describe a possible authentic oral text (e.g., news report, talk show segment, conversation) and a possible authentic printed text (e.g., newspaper or magazine article, short story) that you might find to present in this unit in a top-down fashion, keeping in mind your unit theme, the language level, and the interest level of your students. Your instructor may ask you to actually select these texts. How would students explore these texts?
4. What other vocabulary and grammar would you need to integrate into this unit in addition to the past tense, given the theme and your language functions?

NCATE

EPISODE THREE
Using the Standards at the Post-Secondary Level

ACTFL/NCATE 4.a. Understanding And Integrating Standards In Planning; 4.b. Integrating Standards In Instruction; 6.b. Knowing the Value of Foreign Language Learning

TESOL/NCATE 3.a. Planning for Standards-Based ESL and Content Instruction; and 5.b. Professional Development, Partnerships and Advocacy

If you are preparing to teach or are already teaching at the post-secondary level (beyond K–12), this task is designed to engage you in reflecting upon the implications of the standards for foreign language program development, instruction, and assessment at the college and university levels. First, access and read Dorothy James's white paper: "The Impact on Higher Education of *Standards for Foreign Language Learning: Preparing for the 21st Century*" (1998) (to access the paper, go to the ACTFL Web site [http://www.actfl.org], click on "Publications," "Resources," "Download Library," and then on James's paper). Second, read the MLA Report (2007), "Foreign Languages and Higher Education: New Structures for a Changed World," released to the public in May 2007 (http://www.mla.org/flreport); you may have already read this document in the Preliminary Chapter of this book. Compare these two papers and then respond to the following:

1. Explain Paul Sandrock's statement that is cited in the James white paper: "Curriculum really bubbles up: it does not get directed from the highest level down." Then relate this statement to the "Continuing Priorities" section of the MLA document.
2. According to James, the publication of the standards "signals the end of business as usual in departments of national languages and literature in our colleges and universities." Give several examples to explain what this statement means. How does the MLA report continue where this statement ends?
3. Explain several reasons why the standards might not be fully embraced at the higher education levels.
4. In what areas do you envision the standards having a positive impact at the post-secondary level?[11]

DISCUSS AND REFLECT ·

See the *Teacher's Handbook* Web site for additional case studies:
Case Study Two: Developing a Top-Down ESL Lesson
Case Study Three: Textbook Evaluation: A Look at the Use of Context in Exercises

www.cengagebrain.com

NC&TE_____

CASE STUDY ONE
Teachers Talking Textbooks

ACTFL/NCATE 4.a. Understanding and integrating standards in planning

TESOL/NCATE 3.a. Planning for Standards-Based ESL and Content Instruction; 5.a. ESL Research and History

Foreign language teachers in the Squiresville School District are in the process of selecting new first- and second-year high school textbooks for next year. In a preliminary meeting before they look at any sample textbooks, the teachers brainstorm what they would like to see in a textbook. Since they sometimes agree and sometimes disagree, they decide to attempt an objective standards-based analysis of the sample books by using the Textbook Evaluation Criteria in Figure 2.5. The teachers want to see how the foreign language standards appear in the book, how material is presented to students, how students are led to engage with it, and then how they will use the book for communication with students. Most, but not all, of the teachers are experienced and familiar with the foreign language standards. Ms. Cooper took notes during the meeting; below are her summaries of the teachers' comments, all made *before* analyzing the text.

Comments prior to examining the sample text:

Mr. Gentry wants to see that communication is the primary goal for the chapter; he will look for communicative functions in the table of contents and in the presentation of grammar and vocabulary as it appears in the exercises. He wants to be sure that the tasks that students are asked to do in the exercises give them some opportunities to practice form, but will ultimately lead to more practice in the three modes of communication. He wants to be sure the exercises enable students to interact with one another, native speakers of the language, and with him. He recently attended a workshop on technology use in the foreign language classroom and he wants some help in providing online or other activities students can do to practice outside of class.

Mrs. Tiglia, a native speaker from Peru, is concerned that students typically don't have enough exposure to the culture of the target countries so that they can understand the communities in which people live and use the target language. She will look for interesting visual appeal of authentic photos and text integrated with listening and reading materials so that the three Ps are readily accessible in the textbook. She is also concerned that the vocabulary and exercises help students understand the communities of people who speak the target language.

Ms. Hofmeister and her student teacher have been working with the social studies teacher on ways to connect what students study in language and social studies classes. They regularly use authentic articles in their classes and are eager to see how the textbook presents these materials.

Mr. Bell wants to make sure that the textbook is "doable"—that is, whether there are options to accomplish the Five Cs, add some of his own materials, and still "cover" the book.

Ask yourself these questions:

1. Which of the Five Cs do the teachers' comments address?
2. Which items in Figure 2.5 **Textbook Evaluation Criteria** do the teachers address in their comments?
3. Which research implications presented in Chapter 1 support what the teachers are looking for in a textbook? In your opinion, what other research implications have they not considered?
4. Mr. Bell's comment appears to be anchored in standards-based instruction but he still refers to a trditional *coverage* model. What might be the influences that result in this carryover belief, and how might he more fully show his commitment to standards-based teaching?

To prepare for class discussion:

1. Regardless of whether you are preparing to teach elementary, secondary, or post-secondary foreign language, find a textbook for a first- or second-year class for the language you are preparing to teach. Using Figure 2.5 **Textbook Evaluation Criteria**, describe your textbook's effectiveness in addressing current research implications and the *SFLL.*
2. Use the same textbook from the previous task and analyze the speaking exercises in one chapter. Classify each exercise according to Paulston's categorization of drills presented earlier in this chapter. What percentage of exercises are *mechanical? Meaningful? Communicative?* Describe the extent to which you feel that these exercises reflect meaningful communication, a larger goal-oriented topic, and interactional competence as discussed in Chapter 1.

REFERENCES

About AP. Retrieved June 7, 2008, from http://www.collegeboard.com/student/testing/ap/about.html.

Adair-Hauck, B., & Cumo-Johanssen, P. (1997). Communication goal: Meaning making through a whole language approach. In J. K. Phillips (Ed.), *Collaborations: Meeting new goals, new realities, Northeast Conference Reports* (pp. 35–96). Lincolnwood, IL: NTC/Contemporary Publishing Group.

Allen, L. Q. (2002). Teachers' pedagogical beliefs and the standards for foreign language learning. *Foreign Language Annals, 35,* 518–529.

Allen, L. Q. (2007). The impact of teacher's beliefs on implementing curricular changes. In H. J. Siskin (Ed.), *From thought to action: Exploring beliefs and outcomes in the foreign language program* (pp. 30–47). AAUSC volume. Boston: Thomson Heinle.

American Council on the Teaching of Foreign Languages (ACTFL). *ACTFL performance guidelines for K–12 learners*. (1998). Yonkers, NY: Author.

American Council on the Teaching of Foreign Languages (ACTFL). *ACTFL provisional proficiency guidelines*. (1982). Hastings-on-Hudson, NY: Author.

American Council on the Teaching of Foreign Languages (ACTFL). *ACTFL proficiency guidelines—Speaking*. (1999). Yonkers, NY: Author.

American Council on the Teaching of Foreign Languages (ACTFL). *ACTFL proficiency guidelines—Writing*. (2001). Yonkers, NY: Author.

Asher, J., Kusudo, J., & de la Torre, R. (1974). Learning a second language through commands: The second field test. *The Modern Language Journal, 58,* 24–32.

Aski, J. M. (2003). Foreign language textbook activities: Keeping pace with second language acquisition research. *Foreign Language Annals, 36,* 57–65.

Aski, J. M. (2005). Alternatives to mechanical drills for the early stages of language practice in foreign language textbooks. *Foreign Language Annals, 38,* 333–343.

Ausubel, D. (1968). *Educational psychology: A cognitive view*. New York: Holt, Rinehart and Winston.

Bateman, B., & Lago, B. (2007). *Methods of language teaching*. Provo, UT: Brigham Young University.

Bragger, J. D., & Rice, D. B. (2000). Foreign language materials: Yesterday, today, and tomorrow. In R. M. Terry (Ed.), *Agents of change in a changing age* (pp. 107–140). Lincolnwood, IL: National Textbook Company.

Canale, M., & Swain, M. (1980). Theoretical bases of communicative approaches to second language teaching and testing. *Applied Linguistics, 1,* 1–47.

Chaffee, J. (1992). Teaching critical thinking across the curriculum. In C. A. Barnes (Ed.), *Critical thinking: Educational imperative* (pp. 25–35). San Francisco: Jossey-Bass.

Chomsky, N. (1965). *Aspects of the theory of syntax*. Cambridge, MA: MIT Press.

Cooper, T. (2004). How foreign language teachers in Georgia evaluate their professional preparation: A call for action. *Foreign Language Annals, 37,* 37–48.

Curran, C. (1976). *Counseling-learning in second languages*. Apple River, IL: Apple River Press.

Dhonau, S., McAlpine, D. C., & Shrum, J. L. (2007, November). *Incorporating new trends in today's foreign language methods course*. Paper presented at the meeting of the American Council on the Teaching of Foreign Languages, San Antonio, TX.

Dorwick, T., & Glass, W. R. (2003). Language education policies: One publisher's perspective. *The Modern Language Journal, 87,* 592–594.

Frantzen, D. (1998). Focusing on form while conveying a cultural message. *Hispania, 81,* 134–145.

Galloway, V. (1998). Constructing cultural realities: "Facts" and frameworks of association. In J. Harper, M. Lively, & M. Williams (Eds.), *The coming of age of the profession* (pp. 129–140). Boston: Heinle & Heinle.

Gattegno, C. (1976). The common sense of foreign language teaching. New York: Educational Solutions.

Glisan, E. W. (1986). Total physical response: A technique for teaching all skills in Spanish. *Foreign Language Annals, 19,* 419–427.

Glisan, E. W. (1999). The impact of standards on higher education: For more than just the sake of "continuity." *ADFL Bulletin, 31,* 75–78.

Glisan, E. W., & Phillips, J. K. (1998). Making the standards happen: A new vision for foreign language teacher preparation. *ACTFL Newsletter, X*(4), 7–8, 13–14.

Goals 2000: World-class education for every child. (1994). Washington, DC: U.S. Government Printing Office.

Hadley, A. O. (2001). *Teaching language in context* (2nd ed.). Boston: Heinle & Heinle.

Higgs, T. V. (Ed.). (1984). *Teaching for proficiency: The organizing principle*. The ACTFL Foreign Language Education Series. Lincolnwood, IL: NTC/Contemporary Publishing Group.

James, D. (1998, Fall). The impact on higher education of standards for foreign language learning: Preparing for the 21st century. *ACTFL Newsletter,* 11–14.

Lado, R. (1964). *Language teaching*. New York: McGraw-Hill.

Lally, C. (1998). Back to the future: A look at present textbooks and past recommendations. *Foreign Language Annals, 31,* 307–314.

Liskin-Gasparro, J. E. (1984). The ACTFL Proficiency Guidelines: A historical perspective. In T. V. Higgs (Ed.), *Teaching for proficiency: The organizing principle*. The ACTFL Foreign Language Education Series (pp. 11–42). Lincolnwood, IL: NTC/Contemporary Publishing Group.

Lozanov, G. (1978). *Suggestology and outlines of suggestopedy*. New York: Gordon and Breach.

Merriam-Webster, Inc. (2003). *Merriam-Webster's collegiate dictionary* (11th ed). Springfield, MA: Author.

Met, M. (2000). Instruction: Linking curriculum and assessment to the standards. In G. Guntermann (Ed.), *Teaching Spanish with the Five C's: A blueprint for success* (pp. 49–69). Fort Worth, TX: Harcourt College.

Modern Language Association (MLA). (2007). Foreign languages and higher education: New structures for a changed world. Retrieved May 28, 2008, from http://www.mla.org/flreport.

National Standards in Foreign Language Education Project (NSFLEP). (1996). *Standards for foreign language learning: Preparing for the 21st century (SFLL)*. Lawrence, KS: Allen Press.

National Standards in Foreign Language Education Project (NSFLEP). (1999). *Standards for foreign language learning in the 21st century (SFLL)*. Lawrence, KS: Allen Press.

National Standards in Foreign Language Education Project (NSFLEP). (2006). *Standards for foreign language learning in the 21st century (SFLL)*. Lawrence, KS: Allen Press.

Paulston, C. B. (1972). Structural pattern drills: A classification. In H. Allen & R. Campell (Eds.), *Teaching English as a second language* (pp. 129–138). New York: McGraw-Hill.

Paulston, C. B., & Bruder, M. N. (1976). *Teaching English as a second language: Techniques and procedures.* Cambridge, MA: Winthrop.

Phillips, J. (Ed.). (1997). *Collaborations: Meeting new goals, new realities.* Lincolnwood, IL: National Textbook Company.

Phillips, J. K., & Lafayette, R. C. (1996). Reactions to the catalyst: Implications for our professional structure. In R. C. Lafayette (Ed.), *National standards: A catalyst for reform* (pp. 197–209). Foreign Language Education Series. Lincolnwood, IL: National Textbook Company.

Powell, D., & Lowenkron, B. (2006). President Bush brings languages front and center: National Security Language Initiative (NSLI). Washington, DC: U.S. Department of State.

Quality education for a better world. IB Programmes. Retrieved June 7, 2008, from http://www.ibo.org.

Ray, M., & Lutz, K. B. (1969). *A-LM French: Level One.* New York: Harcourt, Brace & World.

Rivers, W. (1983). *Communicating naturally in a second language.* Chicago, IL: University of Chicago Press.

Rogoff, B. (1990). *Apprenticeship in thinking.* New York: Oxford University Press.

Sandrock, P. (2000). Creating a standards-based curriculum. In G. Guntermann (Ed.), *Teaching Spanish with the Five C's: A blueprint for success* (volume 2). Orlando, FL: Harcourt, AATSP.

Savignon, S. J. (1997). *Communicative competence: Theory and practice.* New York: McGraw-Hill.

Strength through wisdom: A critique of U.S. capability. (1979). A report to the President from the President's Commission on Foreign Languages and International Studies. Washington, DC: U.S. Government Printing Office.

Swender, E. (1999). *ACTFL oral proficiency interview tester training manual.* Yonkers, NY: American Council on the Teaching of Foreign Languages.

Takenoya, M. (1995). Acquisition or pragmatic rules: The gap between what the language textbooks present and how learners perform. In M. A. Haggstrom, L. Z. Morgan, & J. A. Wieczorek (Eds.), *The foreign language classroom: Bridging theory and practice* (pp. 149–164). New York: Garland.

Teachers of English to Speakers of Other Languages (TESOL). (1997). *ESL standards for pre-K–12 students.* Alexandria, VA: Author.

Teachers of English to Speakers of Other Languages (TESOL). (2006). *PreK–12 English language proficiency standards.* Alexandria, VA: Author.

Terrell, T. (1982). The natural approach to language teaching: An update. *The Modern Language Journal, 66,* 121–132.

Walz, J. (1989). Context and contextualized language practice in foreign language teaching. *The Modern Language Journal, 73,* 160–168.

Wiggins, G., & McTighe, J. (2005). *Understanding by design.* Alexandria, VA: Association for Supervision and Curriculum Development.

Wong, W., & VanPatten, B. (2003). The evidence is IN: Drills are OUT. *Foreign Language Annals, 36,* 403–423.

World-Class Instructional Design and Assessment (WIDA). (2007). *Understanding the WIDA English language proficiency standards: A resource guide.* Madison, WI: University of Wisconsin System.

NOTES

1. For additional ideas for using TPR as a strategy in teaching all skills, see Glisan (1986).

2. The ACTFL Proficiency Scale will be described in detail in Chapter 8, and the oral proficiency interview procedure will be presented in Chapter 11.

3. The acronym *ESL* is used to refer to the field of English as a second language and the standards themselves. Those students who are learning English are called English language learners (ELLs). The *ESL Standards* (TESOL, 1997, 2006) also use the term *English-to-Speakers-of-Other-Languages* (ESOL) students. The term *LEP* (Limited English Proficient) is used in most federal legislation.

4. *Authentic materials* are "those written and oral communications produced *by* members of a language and culture group *for* members of the same language and culture group" (Galloway, 1998, p. 133). See Chapter 3 for a more detailed discussion.

5. Examples of drill types (Paulston & Bruder, 1976, p. 8, 18, 42):

1. Mechanical single slot substitution drill: Negative modal

Repeat:	T: I might not go to class today.	
Substitute:	go shopping	S: I might not go shopping today.
	do the laundry	S: I might not do the laundry today.
	finish the lesson, etc.	

2. Meaningful:
   T: Which boy is in   S: The thin boy with
   your class?   long sideburns.
                               S: The handsome boy
                               with black hair.

3. Communicative:
   T: Describe the weather   S: It's beautiful.
   in your country.   S: It's wonderful.

6. These ideas were adapted from the four options for implementing the *SFLL*, developed by Tom Welch, Jessamine County Public Schools, Kentucky.

7. Thanks to an anonymous reviewer for this explanation of top-down learning.

8. For an in-depth description of a standards-based daily lesson based on travel plans featuring these student activities, see Glisan and Phillips (1998).

9. See Bragger and Rice (2000), pp. 127–128, for a description of what the classroom and materials of the future might look like.

10. See Chapter 11 for an explanation of performance-based assessment and rubrics.

11. Read Glisan (1999) for other ideas concerning ways in which the *SFLL* can impact post-secondary language instruction.

Organizing Content and Planning for Integrated Language Instruction

In this chapter, you will learn about:

- the current paradigm for instructional planning
- brain-based research findings and instructional planning
- Bloom's Revised Taxonomy of Thinking
- L2 input and teacher talk
- classroom discourse: IRE vs. IRF
- Oller's Episode Hypothesis

- unauthentic, authentic, semiscripted oral texts
- content-based instruction (CBI)
- backward-design planning
- state frameworks
- thematic unit planning
- lesson objectives
- anticipatory set
- advance organizers

Teach and Reflect: Planning for Instruction: Writing Daily Lesson Objectives, Creating a Daily Lesson Plan, and Designing a Unit of Instruction; Developing a Content-Based Level 5 Foreign Language Class; Comparing State Framework and Curriculum Documents; Exploring Options for CBI at the Post-Secondary Level

Discuss and Reflect: Analyzing the Use of Content and Context in a Japanese Lesson

CONCEPTUAL ORIENTATION

In Chapter 2, you learned about how the *Standards for Foreign Language Learning in the 21st Century (SFLL)* (National Standards in Foreign Language Education Project [NSFLEP], 2006) have provided a framework for integrating language and content into instruction. *Integrating* instruction means combining and blending aspects of instruction that have historically been taught as separate aspects of language learning. A standards-based approach requires abandoning the traditional notions of language teaching as developing the four discrete skills of listening, speaking, reading, and writing. Instead, it emphasizes that language learning and practice involve the integration of modes of communication with meaningful content, such as that based on culture and connections with other disciplines. In this chapter, you will explore further this concept of integrated language instruction in terms of (1) integration of the three modes of communication, (2) integration of oral and printed (cultural) texts, and (3) integration of content and language.

You also saw in Chapter 2 that Goals 2000 (1994) provided a broad-based structure of goals that prompted states and local school districts to rethink and redesign curricula in ways pertinent to their local situations. Figure 3.1 depicts the relationship between the national, state, and local systems. The set of documents at each level informs the others: "standards" at the national level provide the basis for "frameworks" at the state level, for "district curricula" at the school district level, and for "lesson/unit plans" at the classroom level. More states are using the *SFLL* as the basis for the creation of state frameworks or standards, and school districts are using state frameworks to specify curricular goals and objectives.

Beginning teachers usually receive a written foreign language curriculum guide that outlines the content students are expected to learn by the end of the year while remaining consistent with the general purposes described for the entire school system and for the statewide framework. Curriculum guides are generally optional, although some states monitor their implementation more than others. Historically, curriculum guides have been nothing more than a list of the textbook's table of contents, consisting of a series of grammar points and sometimes including vocabulary themes such as weather expressions, numbers, kinship terms, and so on. However, curriculum design has changed over the past decade to reflect the content standards students should achieve at each level of instruction. Teachers regularly use curriculum guides as they organize the content of the year-long course into unit and daily lesson plans.

FIGURE 3.1 The Relationships Among National, State, and Local Standards Documents

NATIONAL STANDARDS	STATE FRAMEWORK	DISTRICT CURRICULUM	LESSON/UNIT PLAN
Goals	Goals for Instruction	Local Goals for Instruction	Specific Objectives for Learning
Standards	Standards Content Unit types Structure of content	Content Unit specifics Suggested units and sequence Methods Resources	Content Lesson specifics Unit topics and lessons Procedures Teaching/learning resources for unit lessons
Sample Progress Indicators	Recommended assessment procedures	Specific assessment techniques	Specific objectives and assessments

Source: From *Standards for Foreign Language Learning in the 21st Century, 1999* (p. 28). Used by permission of the American Council of the Teaching of Foreign Languages.

In this chapter, we will use the following terms as they relate to organizing content and planning for instruction:

- *Goal:* An aim or purpose of instruction, often stated in broad terms, as in the five goal areas of the *SFLL*; for example, "to gain knowledge of another culture."
- *Objective:* What the learner will be able to do with the language as a result of instruction, defined in terms of observable behavior; for example, "The learner will be able to invite a friend to go to a social event"; sometimes the term *outcome* is used to refer to an objective.
- *Framework:* State document that describes goals and standards to be met by language programs.

Current Paradigm for Instructional Planning

In the third edition of *Teacher's Handbook,* we introduced a new paradigm for instructional planning and discussed a paradigm shift that was beginning to occur as a result of second language acquisition (SLA) research and the publication of the *SFLL.* Although many teachers have embraced the current paradigm, we believe that the field is still in transition as research makes its way into classroom practices. Figure 3.2 illustrates the old and current paradigms in instructional planning. Objectives are designed to reflect what students should know and be able to do with the language rather than the table of contents in the textbook. Interdisciplinary content and culture are no longer ancillary but rather the core of standards-driven curricula. The three modes of communication are integrated into lesson design by means of tasks that relate to larger communicative goals or topics and build on one another. The learner is given more responsibility for learning and is encouraged to use the foreign language to acquire new knowledge about topics of personal interest. The teacher assumes the role of a facilitator who guides instruction without being the sole source or expert transmitter of knowledge. This approach helps to dispel what Lee and VanPatten (2003) refer to as the "Atlas Complex," through which the teacher provides all information and students merely receive it.

Planning in the current paradigm assumes (1) the use of a wide variety of materials and tools that extend beyond the capabilities of a textbook and (2) ongoing assessment of student progress toward addressing the standards through strategies such as completion of real-world tasks, exploration of content, and self-assessment.

 The current paradigm for planning assumes the use of a variety of materials beyond the textbook and ongoing performance assessments of student progress toward meeting the standards.

Planning for Student Learning and the Development of Thinking Skills

Before considering planning issues that are of unique concern to teachers of foreign languages, this section will present information regarding brain-based principles of classroom learning and the development of thinking skills, which teachers should keep in mind as they plan instruction.

FIGURE 3.2 Paradigm Shift in Instructional Planning

	OLD PARADIGM	**CURRENT PARADIGM**
Objectives	Stated in terms of grammatical knowledge as provided in textbook	Stated in terms of what learners should know and be able to do with the language
Content/Culture	Content limited to bits and pieces of cultural information included in textbook; connections to other disciplines absent	Interdisciplinary and cultural connections; integration of cultural and academic content; culture explored by means of products, practices, and perspectives
Skills	Practice of individual skills: listening, speaking, reading, and writing	Integrated practice of three modes of communication, which build on one another; tasks situated within larger communicative goals or topics
The Learner	Mostly passive and learns the material presented by the teacher	Actively engaged in learning and constructing meaning; interacts with others who speak the TL; has opportunities to explore his/her own interests
The Teacher	The center of instruction and the audience for learners; students work to impress the teacher	Facilitates instruction and guides student learning; designs opportunities for interactive learning; provides feedback and assistance; not the only audience for student work (includes peers and community also)
Materials	Textbook as primary material	Textbook as one of many tools; others include authentic materials (tape recordings, videos, magazines, short stories, folklore), World Wide Web, visuals, realia
Assessment	Purpose to evaluate student achievement; focus on discrete-point grammar items, often out of context; primarily paper-and-pencil testing; learners provide one right answer	Purpose to assess progress in meeting standards, provide feedback to students, and improve instruction; assessments include open-ended formats; assessment strategies include integration of modes for meaningful purposes, exploration of content, completion of real-world tasks, self-assessment by learners

Source: Adapted from Bragger & Rice, 1998.

Implications of Brain-Based Research for Student Learning

In the 1990s, researchers began to investigate and disseminate new information about how the brain functions and what implications these findings hold for classroom learning and teaching (Armstrong, Kennedy, & Coggins, 2002). These findings have more recently been applied to learning a second language (Kennedy, 2006). While a detailed neurological description of this research is beyond the scope of *Teacher's Handbook,* it is important to note here that brain-based studies have confirmed the following principles of learning, which Sousa suggests teachers keep in mind in planning for instruction:

- Learning engages the entire person (cognitive, affective, and psychomotor domains);
- The human brain seeks patterns in its search for meaning;
- Emotions affect all aspects of learning, retention, and recall;
- Past experience always affects new learning;
- The brain's working memory has a limited capacity;
- Lecture usually results in the lowest degree of retention;
- Rehearsal is essential for retention;
- Practice [alone] does not make perfect; and
- Each brain is unique. (2006, p. 274).

 Which SLA theories from Chapter 1 can you relate to some of these principles of learning?

Brain-based investigations have revealed that the factors of time, stimulation, repetition, novelty, and motivation are key in laying the foundation for learning and that learning is directly affected by students' emotional and physical well-being (Jensen, 1998). These ideas reflect many of the concepts presented in Chapter 1 related to the importance of language learners having a low level of anxiety and a high level of motivation in order to be successful in acquiring language. Regardless of the age at which language study is begun, a critical variable is time on task. Indeed, studies at the Foreign Service Institute and those conducted in secondary and post-secondary settings revealed that it takes hundreds of hours of contact time to achieve a survival level of proficiency in languages such as French and Spanish and two to three times longer for languages such as Arabic, Chinese, Japanese, and Korean (Liskin-Gasparro, 1982; see other studies and discussion presented in Chapter 8). Thus, long sequences of language study respond to the call for the maximum amount of time on task in order to bring about language acquisition.

Whether in infancy or in childhood, language processing involves many senses and an enriched environment (e.g., comprehensible Target Language (TL) input, oral interaction, movement, feedback) that promotes neuronal development (Kennedy, 2006). Also, due to time limits of the learner's working memory, creating lessons in 15- to 20-minute components may lead to greater student interest and retention (Sousa, 2006). An interesting phenomenon is the *primacy-recency effect,* which explains that, during a learning episode, learners remember best that which comes first, second best that which comes last, and least that which comes just past the middle, or during downtime (Sousa). Implications for classroom planning are that teachers should teach the new material first, use the downtime to have students engage in practice or discussion with one another, conduct closure during the last part of the lesson, and avoid using the precious first and last segments of a lesson for classroom management tasks such as collecting homework or taking attendance (Sousa). Further, the brain stores information based on functionality and meaningfulness, confirming the need for language teachers to design lessons that feature meaningful topics and communicative goals. Repetition is necessary but, in order to be effective, it requires *novelty* in instructional design (Kennedy); that is, rote repetition is much less effective than is repetition that is built into a communicative task in a natural way. Language teachers can integrate novelty into their teaching through the use of humor, movement of students in an activity, multisensory instruction (e.g., visuals, technology), quiz games developed by students to test one another, and playing music at certain times in the classroom (Sousa).

The pivotal role of emotions cannot be stressed enough: Learners use their emotions to focus their attention and to identify what is important to learn, and this attention drives learning and memory (Cahill & McGaugh, 1998; Sousa, 2006). Emotions can be related to the classroom climate, as we have seen with the impact of the anxiety filter and a sociocultural approach to learning. However, emotions can also pertain to how students respond to the learning content or task; for example, students often have more of an emotional investment when they are engaged in simulations, role-playing, journal writing, and real-world experiences than when they perform mundane or mechanical tasks. Teachers can foster the association of positive emotions with learning when they use humor in the lesson, design and tell stories that enhance understanding (Scott-Simmons, Barker, & Cherry, 2003), incorporate real-world examples, and demonstrate that they really care about their students' learning (Sousa). Also of relevance to foreign language teaching is that learners typically ask themselves two questions when faced with new ideas or information, the answers to which will determine whether or not information is stored: "Does this make *sense?*" and "Does this have *meaning?*" (Sousa, p. 48). Brain scans have revealed that when learning is comprehensible or makes sense and is connected to past experiences, there is substantially greater cerebral activity and improved retention (Maquire, Frith, & Morris, 1999). According to Sousa, however, *meaning* is the criterion that has the greatest impact on the probability that information will be stored. Consequently, Kennedy (2006) has proposed content-based instruction (CBI) as an avenue through which language teachers might integrate more meaning in their teaching, thus addressing an important principle of brain-based learning. You will read more about this in a later section of this chapter.

Note that in brain-based research, an important principle is that practice does not make *perfect,* but rather *permanent,* allowing the learner to use a learned skill in a new situation (Sousa, 2006). Furthermore, practice alone doesn't make perfect unless the learner understands what needs to be done to improve and is motivated to do so; you will explore this issue further in Chapter 8. According to brain-based research, there are two variables that lead to permanent learning: *frequency* of practice (or use) and *saliency,* or the degree to which a language feature is noticed by the learner. That is, multiple exposures are required in order to make language permanent. However, a language feature that is made salient because of novelty, emotional investment, or a stimulating situation, as discussed above, may also lead to permanency (R. Donato, personal communication, June 22, 2008).

The implications of brain-based research presented in this section will undergird the approach to organizing content and planning for integrated language instruction to be explored in this chapter.

Bloom's Taxonomy of Thinking Processes

For over fifty years, Bloom's Taxonomy of Thinking has been used in educational circles as a model for promoting higher-order thinking (Bloom, Engelhart, Furst, Hill, & Krathwohl, 1956). First developed in the 1950s, Bloom's classification depicts six levels of complexity of human thought (see Figure 3.3), with *knowledge* as the lowest level of complexity and *evaluation* as the highest. This taxonomy served as the basis for early work on the design of instructional objectives and curricula. In the 1990s, the original taxonomy was revised by Anderson, one of Bloom's former students, in order to reflect more recent understandings of learning (Anderson & Krathwohl, 2001). Figure 3.3 illustrates the old and new versions. In the new version, nouns have been changed to verbs, *knowledge* has been changed to *remember*, and the top two levels exchanged places and were renamed.

In the new Bloom's Taxonomy (Anderson & Krathwohl, 2001), *remember* refers to the rote recall and recognition of learned material, *understand* is the ability to make sense of material, *apply* is the ability to use learned information and concepts in completing new tasks, *analyze* refers to the ability to break information into smaller segments so that it can be understood, *evaluate* is the ability to judge the value of material

FIGURE 3.3 Old and New Versions of Bloom's Taxonomy

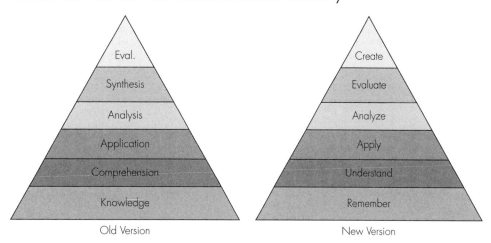

Old Version

New Version

Source: "Bloom's Taxonomy," developed by R. C. Overbaugh and L. Schultz, Old Dominion University. Retrieved from http://www.odu.edu/educ/roverbau/bloom/blooms_taxonomy.htm. Reprinted by permission of Richard Overbaugh.

by developing and applying specific criteria and/or standards, and *create* relates to putting information and ideas together to develop an original idea or engage in critical thinking. The lower three levels (remember, understand, apply) describe a *convergent* thinking process, since the focus is on information that the learner has learned. The higher three levels (analyze, evaluate, create) describe a *divergent* thinking process because the learner's processing leads to new insights, discoveries, and creations that were not part of the original information learned (Sousa, 2006). Although there are still six separate levels in the revised taxonomy, the hierarchy is not as rigid as in the original version, reflecting more recent brain research indicating that different brain areas are used to solve different types of problems and that the levels of thinking tend to overlap one another (Sousa).

Bloom's Taxonomy can be useful for language teachers in several ways. First of all, the taxonomy promotes active learning and provides teachers with common language about learning objectives (Clark, 2002). Secondly, it helps teachers to understand the level of thinking required by their classroom objectives and activities. The chart in Appendix 3.1, developed by Shrum and Glisan (2010) based on the revised taxonomy, illustrates (1) action verbs for each of the levels, depicting specific learning activities for each level of thinking and (2) sample activities that students in foreign language classes can perform at each level. This chart can be useful in writing unit and lesson plans, as you will see later in the chapter. Examples of activities that use *lower-level thinking* include naming objects in the foreign language, matching visuals to words, identifying objects in a Total Physical Response (TPR) activity, and interviewing a classmate using a given set of questions. *Higher-level thinking*, also called *higher-order thinking* or *critical thinking*, is exemplified in activities such as comparing L1 and L2 cultural perspectives, debating an issue, enacting a spontaneous role-play, and creating a travel brochure. Thirdly, the taxonomy can help teachers move students to higher levels of thinking. Thinking should not be limited to the *remember* and *understand* levels, and teachers might use Bloom's Taxonomy for ideas on how to move students toward higher-level thinking. To this end, the taxonomy can help them differentiate between *complexity* and *difficulty*. According to Sousa (2006), *complexity* refers to the thought process that the brain uses to process information, as shown in the taxonomy. *Difficulty,* on the other hand, refers to "the *amount of effort* that the learner must expend *within* a level of complexity to accomplish a learning objective" (Sousa, p. 256). Teachers may easily think they are making an activity more complex when in reality they are making it more difficult. For example, language teachers often ask students to identify the main idea of an audio segment they heard, which would be the *remember* level of thinking. If they ask students to identify details of the segment, this activity makes the task more difficult, but it is still at the *remember* level. The task could be made more complex by asking students to summarize the main idea of the segment in their own words, which moves the task up to the *understand* level. The notions of complexity and difficulty are important to *differentiated instruction*, a topic that will be explored in Chapters 5 and 10.

Bloom's Taxonomy helps teachers to understand the level of thinking required by their classroom objectives and activities.

Considerations in Providing Input and Selecting Content

Devising a lesson plan involves more than just completing a form or following a template. Planning for foreign language instruction in the current paradigm requires maximum use of the target language, meaningful teacher feedback, integration of oral and printed authentic texts, and identification of interesting and pertinent content. Attention to these elements enables the foreign language teacher to develop interesting topics and contexts in which to communicate, which leads to engagement of students and increased interest in language learning. Teachers make decisions as they plan that will influence student learning. This section of the chapter provides a discussion of the elements identified above in order to help you answer some questions you will probably ask yourself as you approach unit and lesson planning:

- What characteristics should my teacher talk or L2 input have?
- How should I respond to what students say?
- What should I keep in mind as I select oral and printed texts?
- How can I integrate language and content in my teaching?

L2 Input and Teacher Talk

In Chapter 1, you learned about the key role of comprehensible input in the acquisition process (Krashen, 1982). If students are to acquire a foreign language, they must have maximum opportunities to hear the target language at a level a little beyond their current range of competence, but understandable through strategies such as their use of background knowledge, context, and other extralinguistic cues. In order for language teachers to provide a classroom environment that is rich in TL input, their own level of proficiency must be high enough to allow them to speak in an unscripted, spontaneous manner and to tailor their speech so that it is comprehensible to students.

However, recent studies have shown that teacher talk must have other characteristics in addition to being in the TL. As part of her research on classroom interaction, Hall (1995) studied the discourse of a high school Spanish classroom (see Case Study One in Chapter 1). The term *discourse* refers to a back-and-forth communication of thought by means of a connected series of utterances shared through social interaction and collaboration. According to Wells (1999), "Discourse builds on understanding which has come to be over time and various situations with both the students and the teachers acting as speakers and listeners throughout communication" (p. 68, as cited in Mantero, 2002, p. 440). In examining classroom discourse, Hall found that although the teacher's talk contained features of comprehensible input, such as simple syntax and multiple rephrasings, it lacked topic development and provided no foundation upon which students could add to and extend the talk in a meaningful way. According to Hall, classroom discourse was limited to "lexical chaining," the "linking of utterances through the use of the same or similar words that had no connection to any larger topically related goal" (p. 34).

Similarly, in his study of a university Spanish classroom, Toth (1997) found that teacher talk negatively affected learners' ability to participate in the conversation activity because it did not contribute to a larger topic or goal-directed agenda. Toth (2004) suggests that during discussions that focus on the teacher's grammatical agenda, students need more time to respond because they have to focus simultaneously on what they want to say while satisfying the grammatical goals of the teacher. In these types of exchanges, students report being confused and frustrated in their attempts to understand the teacher's motivation for the questions asked. On the other hand, when exchanges are organized in terms of meaningful, natural conversations, students are able to process the content of an utterance without having to figure out the grammar-focused agenda of each question.

These studies illustrate that in order to facilitate students' communicative development, teacher talk must not only be in the TL, but it must also contribute to the development of a topic and a larger, activity-based communicative goal (Hall, 1999, 2004). In addition, for collaborative talk to occur, participants need to share conversational goals, recognize these goals as being legitimate, and understand how each participant's actions move the interaction forward (Donato, 2004).

Classroom Discourse: Teacher Feedback vs. Evaluation

Another aspect of teacher talk is the nature of the teacher's responses to learners' utterances. Planning meaningful and helpful responses is important in addressing the communicative goals of a standards-based curriculum. In Chapter 1, you explored the importance of developing learners' interactional competence so that they are able to manage discussions in relevant ways. As Hall (1995, 1999) points out, the rhetorical structure of most classroom talk is *IRE*:

- The teacher *initiates* an assertion or asks a question.
- The student *responds*.
- The teacher *evaluates*, by giving an evaluative statement such as "very good" or by asking the same or similar question of another student (Mehan, 1979).

The purpose of this type of questioning is for the teacher to find out whether the student has learned specific material (a grammatical structure or set of vocabulary). For example, in order to find out whether students can tell time in the foreign language, the teacher might use a cardboard clock with movable hands, ask students to tell what time is displayed on it, and then provide feedback to indicate whether the response was correct or not (e.g., "That's it," or "No, that's not right"). In this type of oral exchange, the teacher often asks *assessing* questions (i.e., questions that usually have one right answer or a predictable set of responses) and offers an evaluative response such as "very good," "right," "excellent" (Tharp & Gallimore, 1991). While IRE may be useful for the teacher in assessing achievement of material taught in a particular unit or lesson, it leads to mechanical, topically disjointed talk and limited student involvement (Hall, 1999). Moreover, it does not lead to use of the TL for interpersonal communication as defined in Standard 1.1.

Reread the scripted classroom discourse sample that appears in Case Study One in Chapter 1. What are some examples of IRE in this script? ▪

 IRE = teacher initiation → student response → teacher evaluation (assessing questions)

▪

As discussed earlier in this chapter, teacher talk must be more than "comprehensible" TL input and, from the perspective of "talk-as-discursive-practice," should be expanded to include the aspects of topic development and management (Hall, 1995). If learners are to acquire the skills necessary to be able to participate in conversations outside the classroom, then they must participate in more than just the typical IRE sequences that occur in most classrooms. Wells (1993) contrasts *IRE* with *IRF*, which he defines as the type of classroom communication that focuses on making meaning and extending discourse, not on evaluating responses:

- The teacher *initiates* an assertion or asks a question.
- The student *responds*.
- The teacher provides *feedback* in order to encourage students to think and to perform at higher levels (e.g., "Tell me more! Are you saying that . . . ?").

In this discourse model, teachers use *assisting* questions, which encourage learners to think, push learners to perform at higher levels, and integrate content and topics (Tharp & Gallimore, 1991). Examples of assisting questions are: "What do you mean by that?" and "That's incredible! Could you explain that a little more?"

Furthermore, students need experience in using turn taking, which Hall (1996) notes is a primary communicative resource in speech-based instructional practices and a crucial part of the development of sociality. In classrooms dominated by IRE, learners do not have real opportunities to engage in turn taking, as the teacher controls who will speak and when. The implications of Hall's research is that, when planning for instruction, the teacher should simulate real conversations in the classroom and thereby help learners develop interactional strategies, such as turn taking. This means that students would benefit from opportunities during which they assume the responsibility for taking a conversational turn rather than raise a hand and wait to be called upon by the teacher.

 IRF = teacher initiation → student response → teacher feedback (assisting questions)

▪

How Might Teachers Plan to Incorporate More IRF and Interpersonal Communication into Their Teaching?

- They can plan curriculum around interesting topics and contexts in which to anchor interpersonal communication.
- They can incorporate tasks that provide opportunities for engaging students in meaningful interaction and for asking assisting questions to move discussions forward.
- They can change the way in which the traditional warm-up is done at the beginning of class. Instead of asking each student a question that has little communicative value (e.g., "What's the weather like today?" or "What time is it?"), they can introduce an interesting and/or personalized topic (e.g., an upcoming dance or championship game) and engage only a few students in discussion so that they are able to take multiple turns. If time does not permit participation by the whole class,

those who don't speak on a particular day will benefit from observing a meaningful conversation and will have opportunities to participate on another day.

- They can plan opportunities for students to acquire new information and/or engage in activities in which there is an information gap with the teacher and/or peers on a topic important to them.
- They can seek students' input regarding the types of topics that they would be interested in discussing in an open discussion format where divergent answers, opinions, and IRF have a role and students are instructed in how to make feedback moves during an interpersonal exchange.

See Chapter 8 for additional ideas about developing oral interpersonal communication.

 How might teachers plan to incorporate more IRF and interpersonal communication into their teaching?

Now examine the following script of classroom discourse. What examples of IRF are there? How does this script differ from the one you analyzed in Chapter 1?

Note: This is a transcript and an English translation of a discussion that takes place in a French I high school class. The prelude for this discussion is a question posed by the teacher: "What plans do you have for Thanksgiving vacation?" A student responds that he is going hunting. The teacher, who is a native of France and unfamiliar with the concept of hunting, asks him for additional information.

> T: Tu vas chasser... pour... une personne?
>
> Ss: *[Rires...]*
>
> S1: Non... quelque... chose!
>
> T: Tu veux dire un animal?
>
> S1: Oui!
>
> T: Hum... chasser *[she writes the verb chasser on the board]*
>
> S1: Chasser. Euh... je... vais... euh... chasser... euh... dinde.
>
> T: Ah! Tu vas chasser la dinde?
>
> S1: Oui.
>
> S2: *[In English]* Shoot a turkey . . . that's not nice.
>
> Ss: *[Rires...]*
>
> T: Non, mais c'est bon la dinde! Et puis, c'est un sport la chasse, n'est-ce pas?
>
> S1: Oui, un sport.
>
> T: *[Looking at the class]* Vous ne chassez pas?
>
> Ss: NON!!!
>
> T: Oh! Vous êtes protecteurs des animaux?
>
> Ss: Non! *[Rires...]*
>
> T: Vous mangez les animaux, non? Oui, on mange les animaux! En plus, c'est stupide une dinde, non?
>
> S1: Hum... la dinde domestique... euh... *domesticated turkeys*... c'est stupide!
>
> T: Ah? Mais la dinde sauvage est intelligente?
>
> S1: ... oui... très intelligente. *[Rires...]*

T: You're going hunting . . . for . . . a person?

Ss: *[Laughter . . .]*

S1: No . . . some . . . thing!

T: You mean an animal!

S1: Yes!

T: Hum . . . to hunt *[she writes the verb chasser on the board]*

S1: To hunt. Eh . . . I'm . . . going . . . uh . . . to hunt . . . uh . . . turkey.

T: Ah! You're going to hunt turkey?

S1: Yes.

S2: *[In English]* Shoot a turkey . . . that's not nice.

Ss: *[Laughter . . .]*

T: No, but turkeys are nice! So . . . hunting is a sport, right?

S1: Yes, a sport.

T: *[Looking at the class]* The rest of you don't hunt?

Ss: NO!!!

T: Oh! You are animal protectors?

Ss: No! *[Laughter . . .]*

T: You eat animals, right? Yes, we eat animals! Besides, turkeys are dumb, aren't they?

S1: Hum . . . domesticated turkeys . . . uh . . . *domesticated turkeys* . . . are dumb!

T: Oh? But wild turkeys are intelligent?

S1: Yes, very intelligent. *[Laughter . . .]*

Source: R. Donato, personal communication, June 3, 1998.

Integration of Authentic Oral and Printed Texts[1]

As you have seen, the teacher's use of meaningful target language input and IRF can only occur in the presence of communicative contexts and interesting topics. In Chapter 2, you learned that a top-down approach uses an initial oral or printed text that provides the context, theme, or topic featured in the unit. Of critical importance is selecting texts that reflect natural language use and bring content and interest to learning tasks. As early as 1983, Oller maintained that certain kinds of texts are more easily internalized than others. According to Oller's Episode Hypothesis, "Text (i.e., discourse in any form) will be easier to reproduce, understand, and recall, to the extent that it is motivated and structured episodically" (Oller, 1983, p. 12). Although Oller's Episode Hypothesis is more than two decades old, we believe that it is still applicable today in facilitating the task of selecting texts. Episodic organization has two aspects: *motivation*, or affect, and *logical structure*. According to Oller, a text that has *motivation* has an apparent purpose, holds the attention and interest of the listener or reader, introduces a conflict of some sort, and is not dull and boring. A text that is logically organized has the characteristics of a good story and connects meaningfully to our experience in the world (Oller).

Carrell also found that text organization is an important factor in comprehension. Her research revealed that readers comprehend most effectively texts that feature the typical "problem-solution" type of organization (1984). In discussing the implications of the Episode Hypothesis for language teaching, Oller states that "perhaps second language teaching would be more successful if it incorporated principles of good story-writing along with the benefits of sound linguistic analysis" (1983, p. 12). Unfortunately, language textbooks often still contain boring texts and dialogues that do not reflect real-world language or situations, although they usually contain multiple examples of the grammar being presented.

 "Text (i.e., discourse in any form) will be easier to reproduce, understand, and recall, to the extent that it is motivated and structured episodically." ▪

In addition to episodic organization, another key characteristic of texts in bringing meaningful content to the classroom is the degree to which they are *authentic*. Remember from Chapter 2 that Galloway defined *authentic texts* as "those written and oral communications produced *by* members of a language and culture group *for* members of the same language and culture group" (Galloway, 1998, p. 133). According to Villegas Rogers and Medley, authentic materials reflect a "naturalness of form and an appropriateness of cultural and situational context" found in the language as used by native speakers (1988, p. 468). Authentic texts include realia, magazine and newspaper articles, literary excerpts, poems, audio recordings, videotapes, satellite broadcasts, radio programs, and so forth. Through exploring these materials, students have the opportunity to see and hear real language that serves a purpose. Another convincing reason to use authentic samples is for their richness in cultural content. Because these texts are prepared for native speakers, they reflect the details of everyday life in a culture as well as its societal values. Galloway suggests that "authentic texts, as total communicative events, invite observation of a culture talking to *itself*, not to outsiders; in its own context; through its own language; where forms are referenced to its own people, who *mean* through their own framework of associations; and whose voices show dynamic interplay of individuals and groupings of individuals within the loose general consensus that is the culture's reality" (p. 133). In Chapter 6, you will review a series of research findings that lend support for the use of authentic texts in foreign language classrooms.

 Authentic texts = "those written and oral communications produced *by* members of a language and culture group *for* members of the same language and culture group" ▪

The types of texts used for listening and viewing can be classified along a continuum as *unauthentic scripted, semiscripted*, and *authentic*. *Unauthentic scripted* texts are prepared, scripted out, and recorded by speakers of the TL onto an audiotape, CD, or video. Since these texts are not prepared by and for speakers of the target culture, but rather to accompany textbook chapters, they are considered unauthentic. They typically contain multiple examples of grammatical structures and vocabulary presented in the chapter, their context is often artificial, and since they are read aloud, they usually sound stilted and unnatural (i.e., pronunciation is deliberate and exaggerated, there are few or no natural pauses and/or repetition, and the rate of speech is abnormally slow). At the other end of the continuum are *authentic* segments, which are prepared by and for native speakers of the target culture, and NOT for language learning purposes. They may also be scripted (e.g., radio/television commercials, news/weather broadcasts, public service announcements) or unscripted (e.g., face-to-face or telephone conversations that are tape recorded, interviews, talk show segments) (Galloway, 1998; Villegas Rogers & Medley, 1988). In between unauthentic scripted and authentic texts are *semiscripted* segments, which are recorded by native speakers who speak spontaneously within a situation that they are given (similar to a role-play activity). Although semiscripted segments are not authentic, they have many features of authentic language, such as natural pauses, repetition, normal rate of speech and pronunciation, and negotiation of meaning (Geddes & White, 1978). Some newer textbook programs include semiscripted segments, which offer better examples of natural language use and contexts than do their unauthentic scripted counterparts.

www.cengagebrain.com

Visit the *Teacher's Handbook* Web site to listen to the following example of a dialogue from a beginning-level Spanish textbook program (Terrell, Andrade, Egasse, & Muñoz, 2006). Is it episodically organized? That is, does it reflect logical organization and motivation, according to Oller's definition? Does it captivate the interest of the reader? Does it have a real-world context? Is there an exchange of information that isn't already obvious to the speakers? Is it unauthentic scripted, semiscripted, or authentic?

Oral Text Sample A:

Nora y Esteban hablan de la ropa que llevan los estudiantes y la profesora.

Nora: Esteban, la blusa rosada de Lan es bonita, ¿no?

Esteban: Sí, es muy bonita, pero... ¿es rosada o roja?

Nora: ¡Es rosada, Esteban!

Esteban: ¿De qué color son los pantalones de Alberto?

Nora: Son grises. Y su camisa es anaranjada.

Esteban: *[Disgusted]* El color gris con el color anaranjado... ¡yuck!

Nora: Oye, ¿Es morada la chaqueta de Luis?

Esteban: *[Unsure]* Eh... hummm... es azul... ¿no?

Nora: Sí, Esteban. La chaqueta de Luis es azul.

Esteban: Pero el abrigo de la profesora Martínez es morado, right?

Nora: ¡Correcto! ¡Y es muy elegante!

Esteban: *[Unconvinced]* ¿Elegante? Bueno, un poquito...

[English translation]

Nora and Esteban talk about the clothing that the students and professor are wearing.

Nora: Esteban, Lan's pink blouse is pretty, isn't it?

Esteban: Yes, it's very pretty, but . . . is it pink or red?

Nora: It's red, Esteban!

Esteban: What color are Alberto's pants?

Nora: They are gray. And his shirt is orange.

Esteban: *[Disgusted]* The color gray with the color orange . . . yuck!

Nora: Hey, is Luis's jacket purple?

Esteban: *[Unsure]* Uh . . . hmmm . . . it's blue . . . right?

Nora: Yes, Esteban. Luis's jacket is blue.

Esteban: But Professor Martínez's coat is purple, right?

Nora: Right! And it's very elegant!

Esteban: *[Unconvinced]* Elegant? Well, a little . . .

www.cengagebrain.com

Visit the *Teacher's Handbook* Web site and listen to the following conversation (Chastain & Guntermann, 2004, p. 75); then compare it to the dialogue that you heard previously. How does this conversation reflect the typical organization of a conversation that is not intended to teach grammar and vocabulary? Is the conversation "motivated"? Does it leave the listener wondering about anything at the end of the conversation? How would you classify this segment along the authenticity continuum?

Oral Text Sample B:

Una joven le cuenta a su amiga sobre su cita con Roberto el viernes pasado.

Rosa: Elena, ¡qué casualidad! Justo la persona a quien quería ver.

Elena: Sí, Rosa, y ¿por qué?

Rosa: Porque te quería contar sobre mi cita del viernes pasado.

Elena: ¿Qué cita? No me digas.

Rosa: Pues tuve una cita con Roberto, un chico que conocí en clase.

Elena: Y, ¿qué tal es?

Rosa: Bueno, es encantador. Es alto, guapo, va a ser ingeniero...

Elena: Uy, pero, ¡qué bien!

Rosa: Y fíjate que la cita fue maravillosa.

Elena: ¿Qué hicieron?

Rosa: Pues me vino a buscar a la casa. Me llevó a cenar. Luego fuimos a bailar, y terminamos la noche en una fiesta.

Elena: ¿Y baila bien?

Rosa: Es encantador y baila divinamente bien.

Elena: Ay, pero Rosa, ¡qué maravilla! ¿Y lo vas a volver a ver?

Rosa: Sí, ¡vamos a salir otra vez este fin de semana!

Elena: ¡Qué bien!

[English translation]

A young girl tells her friend about her date with Roberto last night.

Rosa: What a coincidence! Just the person I wanted to see.

Elena: Yes, Rosa, and why?

Rosa: Because I wanted to tell you about my date last Friday.

Elena: What date? You're kidding!

Rosa: Well, I had a date with Roberto, a guy I met in class.

Elena: And so, what's he like?

Rosa: Well, he's so sweet! He's tall, handsome, he's going to be an engineer . . .

Elena: Wow, how great!

Rosa: And listen, the date was fantastic.

Elena: What did you do?

Rosa: Well, he came to my house to pick me up. He took me out to dinner. Then we went out dancing and we ended the evening at a party.

Elena: And does he dance well?

> Rosa: He's delightful and he dances really well.
>
> Elena: Wow, Rosa, how great! And are you going to see him again?
>
> Rosa: Yes, we're going out again this weekend!
>
> Elena: How great!

www.cengagebrain.com

See the *Teacher's Handbook* Web site for other sample taperecorded segments in English, French, German, and Spanish.

In recent years, particularly with the publication of *SFLL* and the availability of technology, there has been an increasing impetus for using authentic materials in language instruction. One of the challenges teachers often describe when using authentic texts is that these materials contain linguistic structures and vocabulary that students may not have already learned. Although a text may have varying levels of sophistication or complexity, its difficulty is determined by what learners are asked to do with it. Thus, the difficulty level lies within the tasks that learners are asked to complete based on that material, and not within the text itself (Terry, 1998). The suggestion "Edit the task, not the text" has become a well-known instructional guideline for teachers as they design activities around an authentic text. Because of the richness of these materials, the teacher might use a particular text for the first time and ask students simply to identify certain pieces of information; he or she might present the same text at a later time and ask students to explore it in more depth. In Chapters 5 and 6, you will learn more about how to integrate authentic materials as a strategy for addressing the Cultures and Communication goal areas and how to guide students through authentic texts.

Making Connections: Integrating Language and Content Learning[2]

You have seen that the absence of meaningful contexts and topics in the classroom often results in the use of IRE and a focus on grammatical accuracy in a void. The previous section identified key characteristics of authentic texts that make them effective in bringing context to language teaching. Language teachers can use oral and printed authentic texts as the theme for unit and lesson plans, as the context for activities, and as interesting content for students to explore. Another option for contextualizing language instruction is to merge language learning with content from other subject areas, disciplines, or cultures. This merging of language and content is at the heart of the Connections and Cultures *SFLL* goal areas and planning for standards-oriented instruction. In recent years, there has been increasing interest in *content-based, content-related, content-enriched,* and *theme-based* approaches, all of which propose interweaving content to varying degrees with language instruction. Curtain and Dahlberg (2010, in press) distinguish between *content-based* programs and *content-related* programs. *Content-based programs* take responsibility for teaching a specific portion of the regular school curriculum for that grade level in the target language (e.g., math or social studies classes). *Content-related programs* use some of the concepts or topics from the regular curriculum as the vehicle for integrating content (e.g., integrating geography and map skills while exploring target language regions). Any standards-based program that teaches language through theme-based or thematic units can be described as content-related.

CBI has historically received a great deal of attention, as it has been widely implemented in early language programs (traditionally called Foreign Language in the Elementary School [FLES]) and ESL (English as a Second Language) programs. CBI became the foundation of immersion and foreign language programs for K–12 students as early as the 1960s, and its success in immersion programs in Canada has been widely documented (Lambert, 1984). Research from foreign/second language immersion programs confirms that content-based approaches promote L2 proficiency and facilitate skill learning in relevant ways for second language learners (Genessee, 1998; Johnson & Swain, 1997; Pica, 2002; Stoller, 2002). According to Stoller, CBI views "language as a medium for learning content and content as a resource for learning and improving language" (as cited in Pessoa, Hendry, Donato, Tucker, & Lee, 2007, p. 103). CBI uses the content, learning objectives, and activities from the school curriculum as the vehicle for teaching language skills, and it has been shown to result in enhanced motivation, self-confidence, language proficiency, and cultural literacy (Leaver & Stryker, 1989; Met, 1991, 1999b; Snow & Brinton, 1997; Stoller, 2004).

The range of programs that integrate language and content learning are depicted in Curtain and Dahlberg's (2010, in press) continuum of programmatic possibilities, shown in Figure 3.4. One end of the continuum shows those programs that are primarily language-driven but use content as the vehicle for communicative language use, while the other end illustrates the most content-based or content-driven language programs, such as immersion. Although historically CBI has been implemented primarily at the elementary school level (see Chapter 4 for more information), its potential for blending language and content instruction at secondary and post-secondary levels has also been acknowledged (Dueñas, 2004a, 2004b; Glisan & Fall, 1991; Met, 1999a; Snow & Brinton, 1997). For example, on the right side of the continuum, subject courses taught in

FIGURE 3.4 Continuum of Intensity and Focus for Early Language Programs Leading to Proficiency

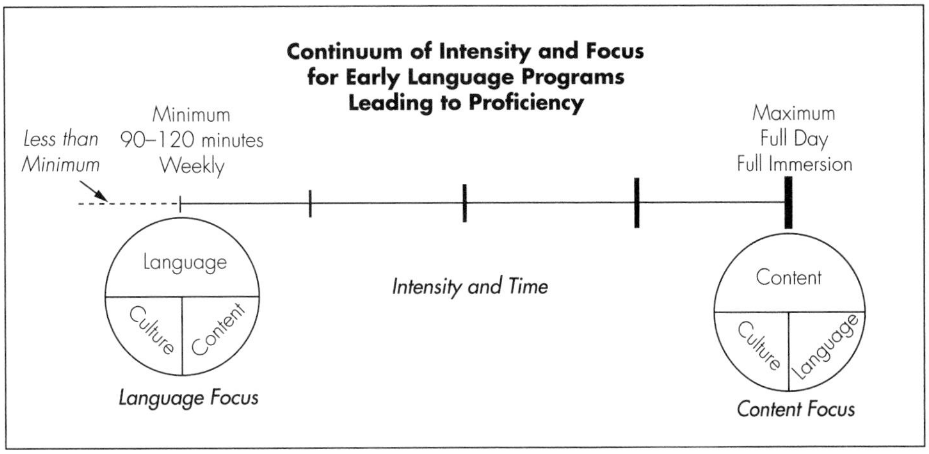

Language, Culture, and Curriculum content are essential elements in every program model. The *focus* changes as time on task and intensity increase across the continuum, from language focused programs on the left to content focused full immersion on the right. A number of variations are possible along the continuum.

PROGRAMS WITH LESS INTENSITY:

Early language programs that meet less than 30–40 minutes daily, and/or less than three times per week, may not be able to meet the performance goals anticipated by the *Standards for Foreign Language Learning* and the K–12 Performance Guidelines.

Source: From *Languages and Children – Making the Match,* 4th ed., by H. Curtain and C. A. Dahlberg, Boston: Allyn & Bacon. Copyright © 2010 Pearson Education. Reprinted by permission of the publisher.

L2 might include sheltered classes in which content is made accessible to learners who have less than native-like proficiency, such as those typically found in ESL progams (Brinton, Snow, & Wesche, 1989), and university courses that integrate foreign language immersion or L2 course readings, such as in a political science seminar taught in a foreign language (Met, 1999a). Further along the continuum, subject courses are supplemented with language instruction, such as in "adjunct courses," where content instructors and language instructors share the responsibility for student learning and in courses such as English for Academic Purposes and Business French at the secondary and post-secondary levels (Met, 1999a). Closer to the language-driven end of the continuum is theme-based instruction, in which the language instructor chooses a theme from which language outcomes are derived. Whereas traditional courses tend to focus more on language rules, theme-based language courses provide learners with interesting topics to explore in L2, such as those that relate to politics, culture, literature, and personal interests (Eskey, 1997). Theme-based instruction may also develop around thematic units (see a later section in this chapter). At the other end of the continuum is the use of content for practice of language, such as in the contextualized or content-based activities often found in content-related early language and secondary/post-secondary language classes.

We believe that CBI holds promise for integrating content and language across levels of instruction in at least two ways. First, it can offer ideas for designing instruction around meaningful themes, texts, topics, and tasks (Stoller & Grabe, 1997). To this end, units might be developed around topics such as the environment, immigration, and contemporary music, or themes may be selected because they are of interest to learners (Met, 1999a). Secondly, at the secondary level for upper levels of language instruction (e.g., levels 4, 5, Advanced Placement, and beyond) and at post-secondary levels, special-topics courses can be designed that integrate the exploration of interesting topics with continued development of language abilities (e.g., Contemporary Social Issues in Germany, French Women Writers). At the post-secondary level, CBI programs can be designed with the goal of advanced language acquisition (Byrnes, 2005). An excellent source of information regarding CBI is the project Web site for Content-Based Language Teaching With Technology (CoBaLLT), which provides professional development and online resources to assist foreign language and immersion teachers in developing content-based lessons/units using technology to enhance students' language proficiency and content or cultural knowledge; see the *Teacher's Handbook* Web site for link.

CBI uses the content, learning objectives, and activities from the school curriculum as the vehicle for teaching language skills.

Regardless of the degree to which language and content are integrated, several important factors to consider when planning connections with content are:

- the content-area skills and concepts that can interrelate most effectively with the language goals;
- the language competencies needed to work with the content selected;
- the cognitive skills necessary to perform the tasks in the lesson; and
- the potential for integration with cultural concepts and goals (Curtain & Dahlberg, 2010, in press).

The challenge in implementing CBI in whatever form described above is in developing students' content knowledge as well as L2 abilities, and several research studies have identified this as a key concern. Pica (2002) pointed out a concern in SLA research that classroom experiences with subject-matter content might not provide sufficient attention to the kinds of L2 input, feedback, and output that are critical to interlanguage development. In her study of two content-based ESL classes, Pica found that the strategy used most often by instructors was "discussion" involving subject-matter content, but that these discussions featured very limited use of negotiation of meaning and attention to form-focused intervention or instruction. In this scenario, learners may demonstrate achievement in content knowledge while making few gains in L2 development. A similar finding occurred in a study that examined the extent to which advanced undergraduate literature courses provide discourse opportunities for students to develop advanced-level language functions (Donato & Brooks, 2004); see Chapter 8 for a more detailed discussion.

This issue was further examined in a more recent investigation that examined the use of CBI in two sixth grade Spanish classrooms from a classroom discourse perspective. The researchers found that the way in which teachers monitor oral interactive practices shapes the language and content knowledge that are gained by students (Pessoa, Hendry, Donato, Tucker, & Lee, 2007). In this study, learners who had opportunities to engage in meaningful discussions of content, participate in IRF interactions with the teacher, and attend to and co-construct grammatical form when necessary performed significantly better on writing assessments (including vocabulary, comprehension, language control) than learners who received explicit grammar instruction and overt correction embedded in IRE sequences. Further, this investigation revealed that in classrooms in which the discourse balanced academic content and a focus on language, including implicit error correction and opportunities for attention to form, students engaged in interpersonal communication that had characteristics of real conversations. Their findings led these researchers to suggest that teachers should (1) include explicit language objectives in the CBI curriculum, (2) use the maximum amount of IRF in leading conversations on content-based topics, (3) encourage student language development and metalinguistic awareness by collaboratively negotiating form, and (4) limit their use of English and use translation only for specific purposes (Pessoa et al.). Lending support to these suggestions is a recent study by Rodgers (2006) carried out in a university-level Italian geography CBI course, which confirmed that students make gains in both subject matter content and linguistic form when they are given opportunities to focus on grammatical form when the need arises, produce more TL output, and are pushed to modify this output.

Pica (2002) also proposed that teachers use the "discussion" strategy as an initial activity to introduce or review subject-matter content and then implement interactive form-focusing tasks that elicit more targeted input, feedback, and student production of modified output. For example, students might reconstruct a scene from a film or story by taking notes on it and then using the notes to collaboratively reconstruct the scene; as students collaborate on reconstruction tasks, they provide each other with feedback that focuses on grammar and edits discourse, and they can then use this input as a basis for modifying their output (Pica). An additional related strategy is to engage students in writing journal entries as a way to enable them to explore subject-matter content and focus on their linguistic output.

This is an area ripe for future research, particularly to discover the most effective strategies for integrating focus on form within content-based teaching. In a recent study on integrating focus on form in content-enriched lessons, Grim (2008) found that a planned focus on form by college-level instructors in a content-enriched French class led students to perform better on tests of grammar, vocabulary, and content than their counterparts who either received an incidental focus on form (i.e., when students posed questions) or exclusive focus on meaning. Clearly, further research is needed to shed more light on how to integrate focus on form in both content-based and content-enriched lessons, and language teachers are encouraged to seek additional information regarding how to effectively blend language and content instruction; for example, see Byrnes (2005), Snow and Brinton (1997), and Stoller (2004). A discussion of CBI within the context of elementary school instruction can be found in Chapter 4. In Episode Two of the Teach and Reflect for this chapter and in Episode One of the Teach and Reflect for Chapter 4, you will have opportunities to develop specific strategies for integrating language and content.

In sum, in planning for meaningful, standards-based instruction, the teacher should consider:

1. ways to provide maximum opportunities for students to hear meaningful teacher talk in the TL;
2. ways in which optimal amounts of IRF can be incorporated to promote meaningful discourse in the classroom;
3. the nature of oral and printed texts to be integrated (according to episodic organization and degree of authenticity); and
4. strategies for bringing context into the learning experience by integrating language and subject-matter content using an approach that promotes development of both content knowledge and language proficiency.

Long-Term Planning for Instruction

"Backward Design" Planning

Recent approaches for planning have been called "backward design" or "top-down," since the process begins with a focus on the end results that are desired, whether they are for the entire program, a particular level of study, a unit of study, or daily lesson plans. Figure 3.5 depicts the three stages of backward design, a model that stands in sharp contrast to the traditional approach to planning that is centered on the textbook or lesson activities. In the first stage of the model, teachers identify the end results

FIGURE 3.5 Stages of Backward Design

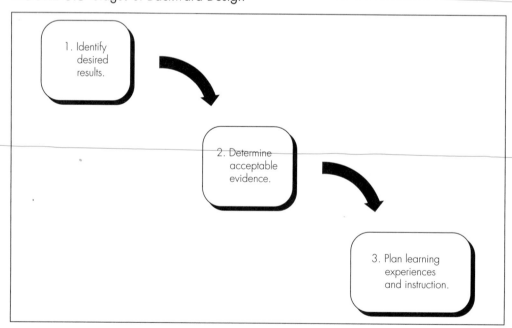

Source: From *Understanding by Design* (p. 18), by G. Wiggins and J. McTighe, 2005. Alexandria, VA: Association for Supervision and Curriculum Development. Copyright © 2005 by ASCD. Reprinted by permission. Learn more about ASCD at www.ascd.org.

of instruction in terms of what students should know, understand, and be able to do (Wiggins & McTighe, 2005). Wiggins and McTighe suggest that teachers identify the "understandings" that students will develop together with the "essential questions" that students will answer by the end of instruction. They advocate planning around "big ideas"—concepts, themes, or issues that give "meaning and connection to discrete facts and skills" and that have merit beyond the classroom (p. 5). This involves examining goals; content standards at the national, state, and district levels; and district foreign language curricula. In the second stage, teachers determine the evidence that will confirm that the end results have been met; this evidence is gathered through a variety of formal and informal assessments, not through a single end-of-teaching test or culminating task (Wiggins & McTighe). In the third stage, teachers plan learning experiences and instruction that students will need in order to achieve the desired results—i.e., teaching methods, sequencing of lessons, and resource materials. Appendix 3.2 at the back of this book is a planning template that provides an overall view of backward design by enabling teachers to check the extent to which assessments (Stage 2) and learning activities (Stage 3) align with desired end results or goals (Stage 1) (p. 22).

www.cengagebrain.com

Egan (1986) has suggested that teachers design curriculum and lessons using the characteristics of a good story. This does not imply that stories should be used in every lesson, but rather that the lesson should reflect the qualities of a story to be told rather than individual skills or objectives to be mastered. He maintains that every unit, lesson, and activity should have a clear beginning that motivates and engages the learner, a middle that elicits participation by the learner in working toward the lesson goal, and an ending in which there is an outcome, product, solution, resolution, or achievement of the goal by the learner (Curtain & Dahlberg, 2010, in press). An example of "story form in curriculum" is structuring the unit around tasks or projects that lead to some kind of culminating activity so that learners have a sense of completion and accomplishment (Curtain & Dahlberg, 2010, in press).

Beginning: Motivation; Engagement of Learner
Middle: Activity Toward a Goal, Participation by the Learner
End: Outcome, Product, Solution, Resolution, Achievement of Goal by the Learner
(Curtain & Dahlberg, 2010, in press)

In backward design planning, the desired end result drives the creation of unit and lesson plans and assessment. ▬

From State Framework to Year-Long Planning

Appendix 3.3 presents an excerpt from the state of Nebraska's framework that is based on the national standards (Nebraska Department of Education, 1996a). You will note that the framework describes what learners are able to do at three levels of ability: beginning, developing, and expanding. School districts use such state frameworks as the basis for program and course development.

At some point in your teaching career, you will be involved in writing a curriculum for a language program. As illustrated in Figure 3.6, curriculum planning might begin with the question: What should students know and be able to do . . .

- at the end of the entire language program?
- at the end of the individual language program (if each program is planned separately)?
- at the end of the course (course structures vary across districts: some are organized by courses, some by levels, others by semesters or years)?

FIGURE 3.6 Curriculum Planning

Curriculum Planning—Where Do You Begin?

Program
Are all languages offered in one program?
Examples: Exploratory + 1st–5th year; 1st–2nd year;
4th–6th grade + 1st–5th year

▼

Language-Specific Program
Is each language program planned separately?
Examples: Spanish: 1st–4th year;
German 1st–2nd year

▼

Course/Level/Semester/Year
Does your district go by courses? Levels? Is the time period in
semesters or years?
Examples: Spanish 1 (one year); French 7–8 (one year);
German 2 (one semester)

▼

Units
What units are offered within the course?
Examples: Shopping at the market;
Functioning at social gatherings

▼

Concept Lessons
What specific skills/knowledge are needed to achieve the
progress indicators, context/outcomes, and standards?
Examples: Food customs and vocabulary and phrases,
use of adjectives, expressing preferences

▼

Daily Lessons
What concepts (skills/knowledge) are interwoven each day to
achieve the standards and progress indicators?
Examples: Pairs practice expressing the food preferences;
video/group discussions of the customs of shopping
at market to buy food; review adjective use as
it applies to describing food; practice a situation
where students shop at a market

Source: From *Nebraska K–12 Foreign Language Frameworks,* 1996, p. 201. Used by permission of the Nebraska Department of Education.

- at the end of the unit (a series of units is offered within each course)?
- at the end of the concept lessons (these vary by district; lessons on essential skills and knowledge)?
- at the end of daily lessons? (Nebraska Department of Education, 1996b, pp. 199–200)

As teachers engage in curriculum planning, one of the factors is the type of class scheduling that the school district has adopted. Many districts still use the traditional 40-minute classes that meet every day. However, in recent years, an increasing number of districts have adopted "block scheduling," which typically features two different formats. In the "straight block," also known as the "4 × 4 model," students take four 90-minute classes a day, five days a week. Courses that were previously taught for a full year of 40- to 50-minute classes are scheduled for half a year of 90-minute classes. Students may now take eight courses each year for a total of 32 courses over four high school years, as compared with 24 in the traditional scheduling model. In the "rotating block model," students take four 90-minute classes Monday, Wednesday, and Friday, and four different 90-minute classes on Tuesday and Thursday. Each course runs for the entire school year, and so students on this schedule also may complete eight courses during a school year, or 32 courses during four high school years. In earlier editions of *Teacher's Handbook,* we discussed the advantages and disadvantages of block scheduling at a time when it was new. As of this writing, block scheduling is being used extensively, and several studies that compared block vs. traditional scheduling have found no significant differences between the two in terms of their effect on foreign language learning; see Wallinger, 2000; Lapkin, Harley, and Hart, 1997; American Council on the Teaching of Foreign Languages (ACTFL), 1996. Case Study Two on the *Teacher's Handbook* Web site illustrates the two block scheduling models and presents a discussion of strategies for teaching foreign language within a block scheduling format.

 What is the connection between the national standards and the state framework in Appendix 3.3?

Since long-term objectives must be valid regardless of which textbook is used, teachers should write a curriculum for any given level without reference to a particular textbook. The text should then be adapted to reflect the objectives rather than vice versa.

Appendix 3.4 is an example of an excerpt from a year planner for a Level 1 language class from the state of Nebraska (Nebraska Department of Education, 1996b).

 What is the relationship between the year planner in Appendix 3.4 and the state framework in Appendix 3.3?

Thematic Unit Planning

The next task in planning is to divide the long-term plan into teachable chunks, called *units of instruction.* In recent years, teachers have focused on creating *thematic units,* a series of related lessons around a topic (e.g., travel), a particular context (e.g., a story), or a particular subject-content theme (e.g., the effect of geography on daily living). While thematic units may correspond to unit divisions in the textbook, they often include objectives, activities, and materials that are not part of the textbook. The following are some steps that teachers might follow in designing a unit plan. Note the same type of backward design presented in the discussion of year-long curriculum planning.

1. **Standards as a Mind-Set:** Identify the goal areas (the Five Cs) and specific standards to be addressed.
2. **Unit Theme/Context:** Identify the theme or functional context of the unit.
3. **Objectives/Progress Indicators:** Describe what students will be able to do by the end of the unit. Progress indicators from national or state standards might be used or adapted when setting these objectives.
4. **Performance Assessments:** Design performance assessments through which students will demonstrate that they have achieved the unit objectives and attained the targeted standards. These assessments should integrate the three modes of communication and other goal areas addressed in the unit.
5. **Essential Skills/Knowledge:** Identify the key elements from the *ACTFL Performance Guidelines for K–12 Learners* (ACTFL, 1998) that learners should demonstrate in order to achieve unit objectives—e.g., language control: grammar/pronunciation, vocabulary use, communication strategies, cultural awareness.
6. **Instructional Strategies:** Select and/or design appropriate instructional strategies that will form the best approach to teach the lessons contained in the unit.
7. **Resources:** Select and/or design appropriate resources that will enhance student learning in the unit. Remember that the textbook is only one resource of many! (Adapted from the Nebraska K–12 Foreign Language Frameworks documents, 1996a, 1996b, and the Wisconsin Department of Public Instruction's Planning Curriculum for Learning World Languages, 2002.)

Figure 3.7 summarizes the steps described above in planning units of instruction. Note that the steps involving assessments, essential skills/knowledge, and instructional strategies (steps 4, 5, 6) are recursive and that each element informs and improves the other. Appendix 3.5 illustrates a sample unit plan for a unit on "Shopping at the Market," which

FIGURE 3.7 The Relationship of Curriculum-Planning Elements

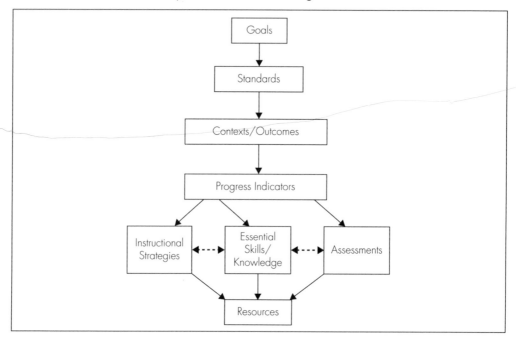

Source: From *Nebraska K–12 Foreign Language Frameworks,* 1996, p. 210. Used by permission of the Nebraska Department of Education.

integrates the five goal areas (Nebraska Department of Education, 1996b). Note that some units, depending on their themes and objectives, may integrate only three or four goal areas. The "progress indicators" listed in this sample refer back to the Nebraska K–12 Foreign Language Frameworks. As you use this template, you may find it more helpful to list the specific performance objectives that relate to your unit theme and which would also appear on daily lesson plans for the unit (e.g., Students will be able to . . . ask a sales clerk questions about prices, sizes, etc., . . . identify the key details regarding a department store sale advertised in the newspaper . . . express likes and dislikes about clothing on sale at a market/department store).

In designing thematic units, teachers benefit greatly from feedback from their students, peers, and supervisors concerning the effectiveness of their unit design. Wiggins and McTighe (2005) encourage teachers to solicit ongoing feedback, which is both helpful and necessary in making adjustments to plans. See the *Teacher's Handbook* Web site for a link to information on the concept of lesson study, a practice used by Japanese teachers to study the effectiveness of their lessons.

www.cengagebrain.com

A thematic unit is a series of related lessons around a topic, a particular context, or a particular subject-content theme.

Daily Lesson Planning[3]

Writing Objectives

Working from the broader thematic unit plans, language teachers organize the material to be presented in daily lessons. One of the most important aspects of planning a daily lesson is to identify the objective(s) that you want to achieve by the end of the class period. Effective objectives are measurable and describe what learners will be able to do in the target language in terms of meaningful language use, such as that which is described by the *SFLL*. For example, the objective may focus on learners' ability to accomplish some language function—to communicate real information. Examples of good objectives are: learners will be able to describe their daily routine; learners will be able to identify prices of clothing given in a radio commercial; learners will be able to compare the educational systems of the United States and target cultures; learners will be able to write an e-mail message to a key pal from a target country. Objectives use action verbs that represent desired student behavior. Verbs such as "learn" or "understand" are too vague for use in objectives.

Objectives should also contain an indication of the realistic context in which students will be able to use the TL that they learn. Objectives should not consist of a listing of textbook exercises or grammar points, although these may be a part of the instructional strategies. As discussed earlier, as you plan lessons and write objectives, you may find it helpful to refer to the Foreign Language Planning Model in Appendix 3.1 to ensure that you are designing learning experiences that span the levels of Bloom's Revised Taxonomy of Thinking. In addition, Wong and Wong (2005) provide helpful suggestions for beginning teachers in how to use the taxonomy to design daily lessons.

As you think about how to write lesson objectives, examine the list below.

Which of the following are appropriate functional lesson objectives and why? Which lead to critical or higher-level thinking skills?

1. The student will learn about typical dinner foods in the target culture.
2. The teacher will present ways to tell time.
3. The student will describe his or her family.

4. The student will understand how to form the future tense.
5. The student will compare and contrast daily teenage life in the native and target cultures.
6. The student will identify numbers given in a taped airline announcement.
7. The student will create a magazine feature article about a popular singer from the target culture.
8. The student will summarize the main ideas of an authentic news report.

 An objective describes what learners will be able to do in the target language in terms of meaningful language use.

The *ACTFL Proficiency Guidelines* and Design of Objectives

The teacher might use the *ACTFL Proficiency Guidelines—Speaking* (ACTFL, 1999) to design objectives in two ways. First, the guidelines can be used to establish a performance level to be attained by the end of a given program. For example, teachers might establish Intermediate-Mid as the minimal speaking performance level to be attained by the end of a four-year high school sequence of study. In this case, the ACTFL guidelines would be used to develop broader objectives or outcomes that describe Intermediate-Mid proficiency. For example, these proficiency-based objectives describe what the student should be able to do at this level:

- ask and answer questions related to personal needs and familiar topics;
- participate in short conversations and express basic courtesy; and
- successfully handle a number of uncomplicated situations necessary for survival in the target culture.

It is important to note that while the proficiency guidelines can be helpful in establishing performance expectations, they are not curriculum and cannot be used verbatim as objectives since they are written as assessment descriptors for testers. However, they can be helpful in setting expectations of learner performance. Second, teachers might use proficiency principles for both unit and daily planning. Expected learner outcomes can be defined in terms of the functions learners can perform (lesson objectives), the specific contexts in which they can use the language, and the accuracy of their language (Swender, 1999).

 How were the terms *function, context/content areas, accuracy*, and *oral text type* defined in Chapter 2?

Designing a Daily Lesson Plan

Freeman (1996) points out the results of research that examined how teachers actually plan lessons—that is, what they thought about ahead of time for the lesson and what they were thinking about as they taught (Nunan, 1992). Teachers do informal planning first by assessing what their students already know or bring to the learning task and then figuring out what they need to teach them to get them to the appropriate objective. They tend to visualize lessons as clusters or sequences of activity and to blend content with activity (Clark & Peterson, 1986; Freeman).

Next, teachers plan more formally by creating a written daily lesson plan, such as the one that appears on pages 99 and 100. This format reflects the three stages of the backward design model as well as a fourth stage for reflection on the lesson and its results. Teachers first identify desired results by describing the lesson theme or "big idea" and delineating what students will be able to do by the lesson's end. In this initial stage, they think about their learners in terms of their background knowledge to be brought to the experience as well as how instruction may be differentiated (see Chapter 10). In the second stage, teachers indicate the type of evidence that will confirm that students have produced the desired results. This might be a culminating performance task, quiz, or observation of student participation.

In the third stage, teachers outline the sequence of teaching and learning experiences that engage students. The lesson might begin with the *Anticipatory Set* to capture students' attention on the lesson context, to activate their background knowledge, and to prepare them for the learning process (Hunter, 2004). Ausubel, Novak, and Hanesian recommend the use of *advance organizers*, that is, "appropriately relevant and inclusive introductory materials that are maximally clear and stable . . . introduced in advance of the learning material itself, used to facilitate establishing a meaningful learning set" (1978, pp. 170–171). Advance organizers, such as visuals and pre-listening/pre-reading activities, can be used to activate students' existing knowledge and facilitate meaningful learning. This stage might include TL input by the teacher, comprehension checks, opportunities for learners to be actively involved with the teacher and peers, scaffolded assistance offered to the learner (novice) by the teacher and/or more capable peers (experts) in helping the learner to solve a problem or perform a task, and opportunities for pairs/groups of students to participate in culminating activities that integrate multiple skills and standards. Teachers might bring the lesson to a close by asking students to recall what they learned and/or by describing how the current lesson will be used as the basis for the next lesson.

Throughout the lesson teachers conduct *informal assessment* gauging how well students have achieved the objectives of the lesson. Informal assessment does not necessarily require an additional step in the lesson plan but rather can be done as students are performing activities throughout the lesson. Some of the informal assessments may guide the teacher to redesign activities or develop additional ones. More formal assessments, such as a short quiz, may also be recorded for a grade. See Chapter 11 for further explanation and examples of informal and formal assessments. The fourth phase of the lesson design is completed after the learning experience has occurred in order to determine the effectiveness of the lesson and impact on future learning.

It is important to keep in mind that planning a lesson does not always occur in a linear process; that is, teachers sometimes begin with a learning objective, begin to plan activities, and then realize that they need to alter the objective. Sometimes a classroom activity or authentic text provides an idea for a lesson objective and a way to address a particular student standard. Therefore, planning can be more appropriately viewed as an iterative process.

 Which principles of brain-based research and Bloom's Taxonomy will you keep in mind as you design daily lessons?

STAGE 1: IDENTIFY DESIRED RESULTS: What will learners know and be able to do by the end of the lesson?

A. Context/Theme/Topic/ "Big Idea":
B. Objectives: Learners will be able to. . .
C. Grammar/Vocabulary:
D. Goal Areas/Standards:
E. Learners: What do I need to know about the learners in order to plan instruction? What background knowledge do they need? What experiences, if any, have they had with this content? What special needs of my students must be addressed in instruction? What adaptations will I need to make to differentiate instruction in order to meet the diverse needs of my students?
F. Materials:

STAGE 2: DETERMINE ACCEPTABLE EVIDENCE: What evidence will show that learners have produced desired results?

STAGE 3: PLAN LEARNING EXPERIENCES: What activities are part of this lesson? What are the learners doing? What am I doing? (List instructional sequence.)

A. . . .
B. . . ., etc.

STAGE 4: REFLECT ON LESSON EFFECTIVENESS: How effective was this lesson?

A. Did I achieve my lesson objectives? How do I know?
B. What worked especially well and why?
C. What would I change if I were to teach this lesson again?

TEACH AND REFLECT ································

NC&TE_____

EPISODE ONE
Planning for Instruction

ACTFL/NCATE 4.a. Understanding and Integrating Standards in Planning

TESOL/NCATE 3.a. Planning for Standards-Based ESL and Content Instruction

Task A: Writing Daily Lesson Objectives

Use the Sample Unit Plan from Nebraska's Foreign Language Frameworks Sample Units in Appendix 3.5. Imagine that you are beginning the "Shopping at the Market" unit in your Level 1 language class. Design Part I (Content) of the lesson plan outline presented earlier for the first two days of this unit. Describe the context/theme, the objectives (what learners will be able to do), grammar/vocabulary addressed, and the goal areas/standards addressed.

Task B: Creating a Daily Lesson Plan

Now use Part I of the lesson plan that you designed for Day 1 of the unit and create Parts II, III, and IV for a typical 42-minute class period. Your instructor may ask you to present this lesson to your classmates.

Task C: Designing a Unit of Instruction

Using the Year Planner in Appendix 3.4 and the Sample Unit Plan in Appendix 3.5, design another unit of instruction for a Level 1 language class that reflects the goals of the Year Planner. Follow the steps provided earlier in this chapter for creating a unit plan. Be sure to structure your lesson around authentic materials, and use the textbook only as a secondary source.

NC&TE_____

EPISODE TWO
Developing a Content-Based Level 5 Foreign Language Class

ACTFL/NCATE 4.a. Understanding and Integrating Standards in Planning

TESOL/NCATE 3.a. Planning for Standards-Based ESL and Content Instruction

You are a high school foreign language teacher whose teaching assignment for next year includes a Level 5 class. This is the first time that your program has had enough students for Level 5, and you want to make the course a valuable experience that will motivate other students to take it in the future. You would like to design a content-based course instead of a skills-based one.

1. What are some possibilities for incorporating subject matter and cultural content at this level in the high school curriculum?
2. Identify four or five strategies that you might want to incorporate into your teaching in order to address current issues concerning integration of language and content.

Your instructor may ask you to work with one or two classmates on this assignment.

Note: If you are preparing to teach at the post-secondary level, you might design an advanced-level course that focuses on specific subject matter, culture, or literature.

EPISODE THREE
Comparing State Framework and Curriculum Documents

ACTFL/NCATE 4.a. Understanding and Integrating Standards in Planning

TESOL/NCATE 3.b. Managing and Implementing Standards-Based ESL and Content Instruction

States have different ways of designing their state frameworks and curricular plans. The purpose of this assignment is to engage you in comparing model standards documents from several states. Even though they are organized differently, each represents an effective approach for the design of standards and curriculum. Choose two of the tasks below, or your instructor might assign you specific tasks from the list. To access the frameworks listed, go to the *Teacher's Handbook* Web site, where you will find links to documents and/or the documents themselves, e.g., Appendix 3.6, which is a sample thematic unit on careers/work for grade 8.

www.cengagebrain.com

1. Compare the Connecticut Standards Frameworks with the Nebraska Standards Frameworks. Describe the similarities and differences. What are Connecticut's "Curriculum Trace Maps" and what purpose do they serve?
2. Compare the Wisconsin thematic unit sample (Appendix 3.6 on the *Teacher's Handbook* Web site) with the unit plan from Nebraska (Appendix 3.5 of text). How does the organization of these two units differ? What role do the three modes of communication play in the Wisconsin thematic unit plan format?
3. Relate New Jersey's "Horizontal Design" model to the development of oral proficiency (i.e., *ACTFL Proficiency Guidelines—Speaking*, ACTFL, 1999) and to the ideas presented in this chapter regarding integration of language and content.
4. Look at the American Sign Language (ASL) standards in the Texas Frameworks. What differences do you see between these standards and those of other foreign languages?

Your instructor may ask you to compare the frameworks for your state with those of Connecticut, Nebraska, New Jersey, Texas, and/or Wisconsin. See the *Teacher's Handbook* Web site for a link to state frameworks.

EPISODE FOUR
Exploring Options for CBI at the Post-Secondary Level

ACTFL/NCATE 2.c. Integrating Other Disciplines In Instruction and 4.a. Understanding and Integrating Standards In Planning.

TESOL/NCATE 3.b. Managing and Implementing Standards-Based ESL and Content Instruction.

If you are preparing to teach or are already teaching at the post-secondary level (beyond K–12), this task is designed to engage you in reflecting upon ways in which CBI can be implemented at the post-secondary level as a way to mend the traditional split between the teaching of linguistic form and the teaching of content (e.g., cultures, other disciplines, literature). First, read "Content-Based Foreign Language Instruction" by Byrnes (2005), and then access the following Web site to examine an innovative content-based curriculum in the German Department at Georgetown University, called *Developing Multiple Literacies*: http://data.georgetown.edu/departments/german/programs/curriculum/

1. Describe one of the initiatives in CBI in collegiate foreign language departments that was mentioned in the chapter. What are some of the challenges in implementing these programs?
2. What does Byrnes propose as a new conceptualization of CBI at the college level?
3. Describe the goals of the *Developing Multiple Literacies* Program at Georgetown University. What groups of student learning needs does the program address? Describe three key features of the program.

DISCUSS AND REFLECT ·····················

www.cengagebrain.com

See the *Teacher's Handbook* Web site for additional case studies:
    Case Study Two: The Effect of Class Scheduling on Planning for Instruction
    Case Study Three: Using Learners' Needs to Plan for Instruction

NCATE_____

CASE STUDY ONE
Analyzing the Use of Content and Context in a Japanese Lesson

ACTFL/NCATE 3.a. Understanding Language Acquisition and Creating a Supportive Classroom; 3.b. Developing Instructional Practices That Reflect Language Outcomes and Learner Diversity; 4.a. Understanding and Integrating Standards in Planning; 4.b. Integrating Standards in Instruction; and 4.c. Selecting and Designing Instructional Materials.

TESOL/NCATE 1.a. Language as a System and 1.b. Language Acquisition and Development.

Sensei Hiroshi has been teaching Japanese for ten years at Rifton City High School, where he is the only Japanese teacher and teaches Levels I, II, and III. He is a popular foreign language teacher who has built a strong Japanese program at this school. Although his initial preparation as a language teacher was traditional in nature, Mr. Hiroshi has regularly attended conferences and workshops and learned about current approaches to language instruction. Language teachers in Mr. Hiroshi's school district are observed at least once a year by the district foreign language supervisor, Dr. Bonnie Herbert, who is knowledgeable about the current state of the art in language teaching and always offers helpful guidance.

Today Dr. Herbert is observing Mr. Hiroshi's Japanese I class during the traditional 42-minute period. Mr. Hiroshi greets students in Japanese as they enter the classroom and begins today's class with several warm-up questions in Japanese dealing with today's date, weather, time of day, and the clothing and colors students are wearing. As students answer in Japanese, he provides IRE responses to offer praise and indicate whether the answers were accurate; this activity lasts for ten minutes. Next Mr. Hiroshi continues the lesson on food that he began the previous day by distributing plastic food items and having students, as a whole class, name them and answer questions about their colors and food group connections. Students seem to enjoy this activity, which takes 12 minutes. Then Mr. Hiroshi presents a new grammatical concept in English: use of the particle "o" after direct objects. He explains in English the new pattern, writes examples on the board, and asks students to analyze similar examples in the textbook; this lasts for ten minutes. For the last ten minutes, students complete mechanical workbook exercises on the new grammar point, in which they fill in blanks and answer questions using the particle. After the lesson, Dr. Herbert and Mr. Hiroshi meet for a post-observation conference.

Ask yourself these questions:

1. Based upon what you have learned about language acquisition and instruction in Chapters 1, 2, and 3, which instructional strategies in this lesson are effective and why? Which strategies could be improved and how?
2. How would you characterize the use of content and/or contexts in this lesson?
3. How would you characterize Mr. Hiroshi's use of Japanese in this lesson in terms of meaningful target language use, IRE, and IRF?
4. What might be some students' reactions to the different parts of the lesson?

To prepare for class discussion:

1. Imagine that you are Dr. Herbert, have observed Mr. Hiroshi's class, and must now have a conference with him. What specific suggestions would you make regarding the role of context in his teaching, his use of Japanese, and the responses he gives to students' utterances? Use the document *7 Best Practices for World Languages Instruction* (Pittsburgh Public Schools, 2003), which is also used in Mr. Hiroshi's school district, to support your suggestions. See the *Teacher's Handbook* Web site for Chapter 1.
2. Imagine that you are Mr. Hiroshi and have been given several suggestions by your supervisor regarding ways to integrate more content and contexts into your teaching. How might you obtain the knowledge and skills that you need in order to make these changes? You might refer back to the Preliminary Chapter for some ideas on how your professional organizations might be of assistance.

TECHNO FOCUS: Explore additional examples of content-based instruction by visiting the modules prepared by participants in the CoBaLLT project through the Center for Advanced Research on Language Acquisition (CARLA) at http://www.carla.umn.edu/technology/modules/examples-intro.html. Related to this particular case study, Mr. Hiroshi might download the module on Appreciation of Music: Japanese Traditional and Healing Music. Note the following:

 a. Which standards are addressed in this unit?
 b. How many days of instructional time are allocated?
 c. What are the topics of the four lessons and how do they engage student interest?
 d. How is the unit assessed?

REFERENCES

ACTFL Professional Issues Report. *ACTFL Newsletter, 6* (2): 11–15. Yonkers, NY: Author.

American Council on the Teaching of Foreign Languages (ACTFL). (1996). Block scheduling and second-language instruction.

American Council on the Teaching of Foreign Languages (ACTFL). (1998). *ACTFL performance guidelines for K–12 learners.* Yonkers, NY: Author.

American Council on the Teaching of Foreign Languages (ACTFL). (1999). *ACTFL proficiency guidelines—Speaking.* Yonkers, NY: Author.

Anderson, L. W., & Krathwohl, D. R. (Eds.). (2001). *A taxonomy for learning, teaching and assessing: A revision of Bloom's Taxonomy of educational objectives.* New York: Longman.

Armstrong, T. A., Kennedy, T. J., & Coggins, P. (2002). Summarizing concepts about teacher education, learning and neuroscience. Northwest Passage: *NWATE Journal of Education Practices, 2,* 9–13.

Ausubel, D. P., Novak, J. D., & Hanesian, H. (1978). *Educational psychology: A cognitive view.* New York: Holt, Rinehart and Winston.

Bloom, B. S. (Ed.), Engelhart, M. C., Furst, E. J., Hill, W. H., & Krathwohl, D. R., (1956). *Taxonomy of educational objectives: The classification of educational goals, by a committee of college and university examiners. Handbook 1: Cognitive domain.* New York: Longman.

Bragger, J. D., & Rice, D. B. (1998). Connections: The national standards and a new paradigm for content-oriented materials and instruction. In J. Harper,

M. Lively, & M. Williams (Eds.), *The coming of age of the profession* (pp. 191–217). Boston: Heinle & Heinle.

Brinton, D. M., Snow, M. A., & Wesche, M. B. (1989). *Content-based second language instruction.* Boston: Heinle & Heinle.

Byrnes, H. (2005). Content-based foreign language instruction. In C. Sanz (Ed.), *Mind and context in adult second language acquisition: Methods, theory and practice* (pp. 282–302). Washington, DC: Georgetown University Press.

Cahill, L., & McGaugh, J. (1998). Mechanisms of emotional arousal and lasting declarative memory. *Trends in Neuroscience, 21,* 294–299.

Carrell, P. L. (1984). The effects of rhetorical organization on ESL readers. *TESOL Quarterly, 18,* 441–469.

Chastain, K., & Guntermann, G. (2004). *¡Imagínate!: Managing Conversations in Spanish.* Boston: Thomson Heinle.

Clark, B. (2002). *Growing up gifted: Developing the potential of children at home and at school.* Upper Saddle River, NJ: Merrill Prentice Hall.

Clark, C., & Peterson, P. (1986). Teachers' thought processes. In M. Wittrock (Ed.), *Handbook of research on teaching* (3rd ed.) (pp. 255–296). New York: Macmillan.

Curtain, H., & Dahlberg, C. A. (2010, in press). *Languages and children—Making the match* (4th ed.). Boston: Pearson Allyn & Bacon.

Donato, R. (2004). Aspects of collaboration in pedagogical discourse. In M. McGroarty (Ed.), *Annual Review of Applied Linguistics (Vol. 24): Advances in language pedagogy* (pp. 284–302). West Nyack, NY: Cambridge University Press.

Donato, R., & Brooks, F. B. (2004). Literary discussions and advanced speaking functions: Researching the (dis)connection. *Foreign Language Annals, 37,* 183–199.

Dueñas, M. (2004a). A description of prototype models for content-based language instruction in higher education. *Barcelona English Language and Literature Studies, 14.* Retrieved June 1, 2008, from http://www.publications.ub.es/revistes/bells12/PDF/art04.pdf.

Dueñas, M. (2004b). The *whats, whys, hows,* and *whos* of content-based instruction in second/foreign language education. *International Journal of English Studies, 4,* 73–96.

Egan, K. (1986). Teaching as story telling. Chicago: University of Chicago Press.

Eskey, D. E. (1997). Syllabus design in content-based instruction. In M. A. Snow & D. M. Brinton (Eds.), *The Content-Based Classroom* (pp. 132–141). White Plains, NY: Longman.

Freeman, D. (1996). Redefining the relationship between research and what teachers know. In K. M. Bailey & D. Nunan (Eds.), *Voices from the language classroom* (pp. 88–115). Cambridge, UK: Cambridge University Press.

Galloway, V. (1998). Constructing cultural realities: "Facts" and frameworks of association. In J. Harper, M. Lively, & M. Williams (Eds.), *The coming of age of the profession* (pp. 129–140). Boston: Heinle & Heinle.

Geddes, M., & White, R. (1978). The use of semi-scripted simulated authentic speech in listening comprehension. *Audiovisual Language Journal, 16,* 137–145.

Genessee, F. (1998). Content-based language instruction. In M. Met (Ed.), *Critical issues in early second language learning* (pp. 103–105). Glenview, IL: Scott Foresman-Addison Wesley.

Glisan, E. W., & Fall, T. F. (1991). Adapting an elementary immersion approach to secondary and post-secondary language teaching: The methodological connection. In J. K. Phillips (Ed.), *Building bridges and making connections* (pp. 1–29). Burlington, VT: Northeast Conference on the Teaching of Foreign Languages.

Goals 2000: Educate America Act. (1994). Washington, DC: Department of Education.

Grim, F. (2008). Integrating focus on form in L2 content-enriched instruction lessons. *Foreign Language Annals, 41,* 321–346.

Hall, J. K. (1995). "'Aw, man, where we goin'?": Classroom interaction and the development of L2 interactional competence. *Issues in Applied Linguistics, 6,* 37–62.

Hall, J. K. (1996). The discursive formation of Spanish as a foreign language classroom community. Paper presented at AILA 1996, 11th World Congress of Applied Linguistics Symposium.

Hall, J. K. (1999). The communication standards. In J. K. Phillips & R. M. Terry (Eds.), *Foreign language standards: Linking research, theories, and practices* (pp. 15–56). Lincolnwood, IL: National Textbook Company.

Hall, J. K. (2004). Language learning as an interactional achievement. *The Modern Language Journal, 88,* 607–612.

Hunter, M. (2004). *Mastery teaching.* Thousand Oaks, CA: Corwin Press.

Jensen, E. (1998). *Teaching with the brain in mind.* Alexandria, VA: ASCD.

Johnson, R. K., & Swain, M. (1997). *Immersion education: International perspectives.* New York: Cambridge University Press.

Kennedy, T. J. (2006). Language learning and its impact on the brain: Connecting language learning through the mind through content-based instruction. *Foreign Language Annals, 39,* 471–486.

Krashen, S. (1982). *Principles and practice in second language acquisition.* Oxford, UK: Pergamon Press.

Lambert, W. E. (1984) (Ed.). An overview of issues in immersion education. In *Studies on immersion education: A collection for United States educators.* Sacramento, CA: California State Department of Education.

Lapkin, S., Harley, B., & Hart, D. (1997). Block scheduling for language study in the middle grades: A summary of the Carleton case study. *Learning Languages, 2* (3), 4–8.

Leaver, B. L., & Stryker, S. B. (1989). Content-based instruction for foreign language classrooms. *Foreign Language Annals, 22,* 269–275.

Lee, J. F., & VanPatten, B. (2003). *Making communicative language teaching happen.* (2nd ed.). New York: McGraw-Hill.

Liskin-Gasparro, J. E. (1982). *ETS oral proficiency testing manual.* Princeton, NJ: Educational Testing Service.

Mantero, M. (2002). Bridging the gap: Discourse in text-based foreign language classrooms. *Foreign Language Annals, 35,* 437–455.

Maquire, E. A., Frith, C. D., & Morris, R. G. M. (1999). The functional neuroanatomy of comprehension and memory: The importance of prior knowledge. *Brain, 122,* 1839–1850.

Mehan, H. (1979). What time is it, Denise? Asking known information questions in classroom discourse. *Theory Into Practice, 28* (4), 285–294.

Met, M. (1991). Learning language through content; learning content through language. *Foreign Language Annals, 24,* 281–295.

Met, M. (1999a). *Content-based instruction: Defining terms, making decisions.* NFLC Reports. Washington, DC: National Foreign Language Research Center.

Met, M. (1999b). Making connections. In J. K. Phillips & R. M. Terry (Eds.), *Foreign language standards: Linking research, theories, and practices* (pp. 137–164).

National Standards in Foreign Language Education Project (NSFLEP). (2006). *Standards for foreign language learning in the 21st century (SFLL).* Lawrence, KS: Allen Press.

Nebraska Department of Education. (1996a). *Nebraska K–12 foreign language frameworks.* Retrieved June 3, 2008, from http://www.nde.state.ne.us/FORLG/Frameworks/Frameworks.pdf.

Nebraska Department of Education. (1996b). *Nebraska K–12 foreign language frameworks.* Retrieved June 3, 2008, from http://www.nde.state.ne.us/FORLG/Frameworks/FLFCurric.pdf.

Nunan, D. (1992). The teacher as decision-maker. In J. Flowerdew, M. Brock, & S. Hsia (Eds.), *Perspectives on second language teacher education* (pp. 135–165). Hong Kong: City Polytechnic of Hong Kong.

Oller, J., Jr. (1983). Some working ideas for language teaching. In J. Oller, Jr. & P. A. Richard-Amato (Eds.), *Methods that work* (pp. 3–19). Rowley, MA: Newbury House.

Patrick, P. (2007). *The keys to the classroom.* Alexandria, VA: The American Council on the Teaching of Foreign Languages.

Pessoa, S., Hendry, H., Donato, R., Tucker, G. R., & Lee, H. (2007). Content-based instruction in the foreign language classroom: A discourse perspective. *Foreign Language Annals, 40,* 102–121.

Pica, T. (2002). Subject-matter content: How does it assist the interactional and linguistic needs of classroom language learners? *The Modern Language Journal, 86,* 1–19.

Pittsburgh Public Schools. (2003). *7 best practices for world languages instruction.* Pittsburgh, PA: Author.

Rodgers, D. M. (2006). Developing content and form: Encouraging evidence from Italian content-based instruction. *The Modern Language Journal, 90,* 373–386.

Scott-Simmons, D., Barker, J., & Cherry, N. (2003). Integrating research and story writing. *The Reading Teacher, 56,* 742–745.

Shrum, J. L. & Glisan, E. W. (2010). *Teacher's handbook: Contextualized language instruction* (4th ed.). Boston: Cengage.

Snow, M. A., & Brinton, D. M. (1997). *The content-based classroom: Perspectives on integrating language and content.* New York: Addison Wesley Longman.

Sousa, D. A. (2006). *How the brain learns.* Thousand Oaks, CA: Corwin Press.

Stoller, F. (2002). Promoting the acquisition of knowledge in a content based course. In J. Crandall & D. Kaufman (Eds.), *Content-based instruction in higher education settings* (pp. 109–123). Alexandria, VA: TESOL.

Stoller, F. (2004). Content-based instruction: perspectives on curriculum planning. *Annual Review of Applied Linguistics, 24,* 261–283.

Stoller, F. L., & Grabe, W. (1997). A six-T's approach to content-based instruction. In M. A. Snow & D. M. Brinton (Eds.), *The Content-Based Classroom* (pp. 78–94). White Plains, NY: Longman.

Swender, E. (1999). (Ed.) *The ACTFL oral proficiency interview tester training manual.* Yonkers, NY: ACTFL.

Terrell, T., Andrade, M., Egasse, J., & Muñoz, J. (2006). *Audio program to accompany Dos Mundos* (6th ed.). Columbus, OH: McGraw-Hill.

Terry, R. M. (1998). Authentic tasks and materials for testing in the foreign language classroom. In J. Harper, M. Lively, & M. Williams (Eds.), *The coming of age of the profession* (pp. 277–290). Boston: Heinle & Heinle.

Tharp, R. G., & Gallimore, R. (1991). *The instructional conversation: Teaching and learning in social activity.* Washington, DC: National Center for Research on Cultural Diversity and Second Language Learning.

Toth, P. (1997). The pragmatics of foreign language communities. Paper presented at the 1997 meeting of the American Association of Applied Linguistics, Orlando, FL.

Toth, P. (2004). When grammar instruction undermines cohesion in L2 Spanish classroom discourse. *The Modern Language Journal, 88,* 14–30.

Villegas Rogers, C., & Medley, F. W., Jr. (1988). Language with a purpose: Using authentic materials in the foreign language classroom. *Foreign Language Annals, 21,* 467–478.

Wallinger, L. M. (2000). The effect of block scheduling on foreign language learning. *Foreign Language Annals, 33,* 36–50.

Wells, G. (1993). Reevaluating the IRF sequence. *Linguistics and Education, 5,* 1–38.

Wells, G. (1999). *Dialogic inquiry: Toward a sociocultural practice and theory of education*. Cambridge, UK: Cambridge University Press.

Wiggins, G., & McTighe, J. (2005). *Understanding by design*. Alexandria, VA: Association for Supervision and Curriculum Development.

Wisconsin Department of Public Instruction. (2002). *Planning curriculum for learning world languages*. Milwaukee, WI: Author.

Wong, H. K., & Wong, R. T. (2005). *The first days of school*. Mountain View, CA: Harry K. Wong Publications, Inc.

NOTES

1. The focus of this section is to explore the nature of oral and printed texts used in language teaching in terms of their episodic organization and authenticity. Other characteristics of texts, as well as instructional strategies for guiding students through them, will be discussed in Chapter 6.

2. This chapter presents some options for merging language and content teaching and key issues as they relate to the development of language skills and learning of content.

In Chapter 4, you will explore content-based instruction as it relates to the Connections goal area of the standards and to specific strategies for subject-content teaching at the elementary school level.

3. See Patrick (2007) for suggestions to beginning teachers on a variety of issues ranging from surviving the first week of teaching to communicating with parents and handling unexpected classroom situations.

Connecting Language Learning to the Elementary School Curriculum

In this chapter, you will learn about:

- role of age and social/psychological factors in language acquisition
- benefits of early language learning
- characteristics of elementary school learners
- mythic stage of development
- program models: early language learning, immersion, sheltered instruction, dual language
- thematic planning webs
- content-based/content-related (content-enriched) FLES
- content-obligatory/content-compatible language

- graphic organizers
- semantic maps
- Venn diagrams
- Total Physical Response (TPR)
- storytelling
- Language Experience Approach
- story maps
- cooperative learning
- global units
- performance assessment strategies
- Connections Goal Area

Teach and Reflect: Designing a Content-Based Elementary School Lesson; Developing a Storytelling Lesson

Discuss and Reflect: Teaching Fourth-Grade Content in French

CONCEPTUAL ORIENTATION

In the last decade, increasing attention has been given to introducing language instruction to students in the elementary grades.[1] A steady stream of studies published over the past 30 years has confirmed that an early start provides increased time for learning and the opportunity to attain a functional level of language proficiency (see, for example,

Carroll, 1975; Domínguez & Pessoa, 2005). Much of the research in early language learning focused on the outcomes of early language learning as compared to those of later language learning. This continues to be a key area of investigation as we seek to provide language learning experiences at optimal times during learners' cognitive and social development. It is important to note that, until recently, the vast majority of studies in early language acquisition had been done in immersion settings or with immigrant children arriving in the U.S at a young age. As you will see later, only since the mid-1990s have we examined the performance of younger language learners in elementary school foreign language classrooms.[2]

Traditionally the term *FLES* (Foreign Language in the Elementary School) has been used to refer to all programs for languages other than English at the elementary school level. However, as Curtain and Dahlberg (2010) note, this term has more appropriately been used to describe a specific type of program taught three to five times per week for class times of 20 minutes to an hour or longer. The term is falling out of use as the profession is advocating for elementary programs that are part of the full K–12 sequence of language courses. Instead, the field has begun to use more general terms such as *early start programs, early language learning programs,* or *programs for young learners* (Curtain & Dahlberg).

Additional information about these program models will be provided later in this chapter.

 An early start provides increased time for learning and the opportunity to attain a functional level of language proficiency.

An Optimal Age for Language Acquisition?

The Factor of Age

Much of the research in early language acquisition has examined the question: Is there a *critical* (or *sensitive*) period for language acquisition, "a time in human development when the brain is predisposed for success in language learning"? (Lightbown & Spada, 2006, p. 68). Since the 1960s, this has been one of the most widely debated issues in second language acquisition (SLA) research (Hyltenstam & Abrahamsson, 2003). Early work in this area was done by Lenneberg (1967), who used results from studies of patients who recovered from aphasia to suggest that humans lose their biological predisposition for language acquisition due to the completion of hemispheric brain lateralization that occurs around the time of puberty. Lenneberg labeled the time span beween the age of two and puberty as a *critical period* for language acquisition (as cited in Hyltenstam & Abrahamsson, p. 539). According to one of the biological explanations supporting the Critical Period Hypothesis, neuropsychological functioning of the brain in the early childhood years may facilitate first- or second language acquisition up until the time of puberty or even earlier. Studies in neuropsychology (i.e., the study of how the functions of the brain relate to psychological processes and behavior) claim that the brain of a younger learner is malleable and is shaped by its own activity, while the brain of an older learner is stable and is not as equipped to reorganize itself. Therefore, "the old brain encountering a new task must make do with the brain structure that has already been set" (Hoff-Ginsberg, 1998, p. 35). In this view, as one matures, more of the brain is used for new functions, and there is less uncommitted capacity to access. Also important in this process is *associative memory,* that is, memory that relies on association of objects or concepts that are linked together in the mind; for example, a green traffic light means "go." It appears that the declines in associative memory and incremental learning elements of language learning begin in early childhood and continue throughout one's life span (Birdsong, 2006). The Critical Period Hypothesis postulates a sudden offset of language acquisition capabilities; another view is that these abilities fade away over a longer, *sensitive,* period of time, perhaps covering later childhood, puberty, and adolescence (Harley & Wang, 1997). Despite the difference in meaning between *critical* and *sensitive,* the two terms have typically been used interchangeably in SLA research.

Although there are other factors related to success in language acquisition, recent studies have confirmed that "age of acquisition is reliably the strongest prediction of ultimate attainment" of language (Birdsong, 2006, p. 12). One of the claims of the Critical Period Hypothesis that has been widely corroborated in research studies is the role of age in the acquisition of pronunciation and "accent." The work of Scovel (1999) and others (Long, 1990; Thompson, 1991) has confirmed that language learners who begin as children are able to achieve a more native-like accent than those who begin as adolescents or adults. An upper limit for the acquisition of phonology has been proposed as being the age of 6 "in many individuals" and at the age of 12 for the rest (Long, 1990, as cited in Hyltenstam & Abrahamsson, 2003, p. 559).

Beyond the issue of a critical period for the acquisition of pronunciation, the research supports the notion of multiple critical periods for other aspects of language, also referred to as the *Windows of Opportunity* Hypothesis (Schacter, 1996), which explains that biological properties become available to individuals at particular points in their linguistic development (p. 183):

- Competency in Syntax/Grammar: Evidence indicates that children tend to acquire a higher level of competence in syntax, morphology, and grammar than older learners (DeKeyser, 2000; Harley & Wang, 1997; Johnson & Newport, 1989). This finding was corroborated in a more recent study that documented greater gains in both speaking and writing for students who began Spanish in kindergarten as compared to their counterparts who began language in sixth grade (Domínguez & Pessoa, 2005). The critical age for syntactical/grammatical accuracy is likely to be later than for pronunciation—around age 15 (Patkowski, 1990). However, some studies have proposed the age of six or seven as the upper limit for morphosyntax and lexicon (Hyltenstam, 1992). It is interesting to note that Newport (1990) suggested that children may have a cognitive advantage in analyzing morphology because they can only hold shorter segments of what they hear in memory, which allows them to focus on and inspect more closely the grammatical features that might go unnoticed by adults, who try to attend to multiple chunks of input simultaneously and often unsuccessfully (Newport). According to Newport's Less Is More Hypothesis, children may be better equipped to analyze what they hear because they store less information than their adult counterparts, who must try to attend to multiple chunks of input simultaneously and often unsuccessfully. Consequently, it seems that younger learners of L2 are able to analyze word relationships quite easily—for example, between words in French such as *ami* (friend), *amitié* (friendship), *amical* (friendly)—as native speakers do. Adult L2 learners, however, find it more difficult to recognize these relationships, which may mean that older learners would benefit from meaningful tasks that enable them to attend to morphological features such as those associated with word families (R. Donato, personal communication, June 24, 2008).
- Language Proficiency: Evidence indicates that younger learners may reach higher levels of functional proficiency than those who begin language learning at a later age. Cummins (1981a) found that younger learners perform better

on communicative tasks measuring interpersonal skills such as oral fluency and phonology. Evidence indicates that younger learners may make more uniform gains as a group than older learners do (Tucker, Donato, & Antonek, 1996).

- Rate of Language Acquisition: Some earlier studies suggested that adult language learners may have a greater advantage than younger learners where the rate of acquisition of language is concerned (Krashen, Long, & Scarcella, 1979; Snow & Hoefnagel-Höhle, 1978). However, later evidence suggested that this rate advantage is short-lived and does not indicate that older children and adults are better learners in the long run (Long, 1990; Patkowski, 1990).

Social/Psychological Factors

While age has been cited as a key variable in language acquisition, other factors have been identified that interact with maturation in interesting ways. Up to the age of 6 or 7, all learners automatically attain a level of speaking that identifies them as native speakers, provided that they have sufficient input and that they do not experience deficient learning environments. After this age, however, social and psychological factors such as motivation and language aptitude can compensate for the negative effects of maturation (Hyltenstam & Abrahamsson, 2003). That is, older learners may require more motivation, effective L2 input and instruction, and language aptitude to reach the same levels that are automatically attained by younger learners (DeKeyser, 2000). In contrast, these social and psychological factors appear to play only a marginal role in early childhood when biological conditions are still optimal (DeKeyser, 2000; Hyltenstam & Abrahamsson).

 What theories or concepts from Chapter 1 relate to age and social/psychological factors affecting language acquisition?

Benefits of an Early Start: Cognition, Academic Achievement, Attitudes about L2

There may be other reasons to justify an early start to language learning that transcend the issue of age. Studies of bilingualism and cognition reveal that children who begin to study a second language in the early years reap cognitive, academic, and attitudinal benefits (Caccavale, 2007; Robinson, 1998). As supported by Vygotsky's (1962) theory of language as a mediator that guides thought and shapes social development (see Chapter 1), bilingual students demonstrate an enhanced ability to engage in problem solving (Bialystok, 2001), and they can also read earlier because they can more effectively recognize the symbolic relationship between letters or characters and sounds (Bialystok, 1997). It has also been found that children who have studied a foreign language score higher on standardized tests and tests of basic skills in English and math than those who have not experienced language study (Rafferty, 1986; Rosenbusch, 1995; Taylor-Ward, 2003). Caccavale reviewed the research findings from a number of studies that examined the relationship between early language learning and native language skill development. Her summary illustrated that, in studies of performance on standardized achievement tests, students who received early foreign language instruction did better than their non-FL counterparts, even when the latter received more instruction in the content being tested (i.e., in language arts and math) (Blanchard & Nelson, 2007; Rafferty; Saunders, 1998; Taylor-Ward). These results led Caccavale to surmise that "...if language learning is considered to be a *cognitive*, rather than a *linguistic* exercise, students' enhanced cognitive ability would translate into overall higher achievement test scores" (p. 31). Further support for this assertion can be seen in a recent study revealing that cognitive gains in an early language program positively impacted reading comprehension and vocabulary in a standardized test of elementary school basic skills (Taylor, Feyton, Meros, & Nutta, 2008).

Additionally, according to Lambert and Klineberg (1967), the age of 10 seems to be a crucial time in developing attitudes toward nations and groups perceived as "other." Children who are 10 years of age appear to be more open toward people who are different from themselves than are 14-year-olds. Since they are in the process of proceeding from egocentricity to reciprocity, they are open to new information introduced during this time (Lambert & Klineberg; as cited in Robinson, 1998). Children between the ages of 7 and 12 also demonstrate role-taking ability and seem to be the most open to learning about people from other cultures (Muuss, 1982). This research, most of which has been conducted with immersion students, confirms various benefits of language study for younger learners that include a heightened level of oral proficiency, more complex cognitive processing, higher performance on standardized tests and tests of basic skills, and a greater openness to other cultures.

Benefits of an Early Start: L2 Oral Proficiency and Literacy

Until recently, there have been few empirical studies that have investigated the specific L2 accomplishments of students in a traditional FLES setting that would serve to shed light on the possible benefits of an early start to language learning. Donato, Tucker, Wudthayagorn, and Igarashi (2000) reported on a longitudinal study of program ambiance and learner achievement in early language learning. The study tracked progress of North American students who studied Japanese for five or six consecutive years, since kindergarten, in a FLES program by means of 15-minute daily lessons, 5 days per week.[3] At the mid-point in this study (after the third year of Japanese study), results indicated that children in grades 3–5 performed better than those in K–2 in comprehension, fluency, vocabulary, and grammar, but not in pronunciation, which supports previous research findings dealing with the effect of age on development of pronunciation. Of importance is that there was less variability among scores in the K–2 group; that is, the older learners exhibited a wider range of abilities, while the younger children made more uniform progress overall. At the end of both the first and second years of instruction, children scored highest in pronunciation and lowest in grammar.

In the second phase of the study (after 5 or 6 years of Japanese study), findings revealed that students who had been in the program longer expressed more positive attitudes about learning Japanese, students with more positive attitudes were able to assess themselves more positively (i.e., they assessed themselves in terms of what they *could* do and their assessments were accurate), and students with positive self-assessments also performed better on the oral interview. Thus "time on task, attitude, and self-assessment relate closely to individual achievement" (Donato et al., 2000, p. 386). The study also showed that students' oral proficiency had progressed over the six-year period, and that learners require a good deal of time on task to progress through the various stages of proficiency.

This longitudinal study revealed that learners progressed in their language development in a differentiated manner; that is, some children made more progress in fluency, some more in vocabulary, and others more in pronunciation. Thus language acquisition did not develop in exactly the same way for all young learners (Donato, Antonek, & Tucker, 1996). This same finding was echoed in a study that charted the proficiency-based achievement of fourth graders enrolled in a Spanish FLES program (Montás, 2003). These studies provide further support to the claim that young language learners demonstrate differentiated achievement—that is, they progress in varied ways and at different rates.

Early language study also enables learners to begin literacy development in foreign language in the early grades. The fourth grade Spanish students in the study described by Montás (2003) made significant gains in their ability to interpret written Spanish. The Japanese study documented by Donato et al. (2000) revealed that middle school students of Japanese showed signs of emerging literacy skills through their sensitivity to the meanings and shapes of *kanji* characters (Chinen, Donato, Igarashi, & Tucker, 2003). Furthermore, this study found evidence that elementary school language learners are able to go beyond literal comprehension and interpret printed texts; they are able to anticipate what is coming next in a story, they are willing to hypothesize about what is happening or may happen, and they are often eager to share their opinions of what the story's message might be (R. Donato, personal communication, February 25, 2004).

The role of attitude and language learning in FLES programs was also examined in a study that compared attitudinal differences between K–5 FLES students and their peers who were not exposed to language learning (Kennedy, Nelson, Odell, & Austin, 2000). Results revealed that the FLES group had significantly more positive attitudes toward school, beliefs about being able to learn a foreign language, motivation for learning a second language, foreign people and cultures, and self-confidence. The researchers concluded that FLES programs motivate students to participate, persist, and succeed in second language study. This finding was also corroborated by results of two studies conducted over a 10-year period, in which the majority of students demonstrated positive attitudes over an extended period toward foreign language speakers, foreign cultures, and how FL study impacts their education (Heining-Boynton & Haitema, 2007).

The results obtained through all of these empirical studies reveal the following about the effects of early language learning experiences in traditional classroom settings: (1) elementary school language learners make significant gains in pronunciation; (2) children in grades K–6 are able to demonstrate notable progress in developing oral proficiency over a 6-year period of instruction; (3) since younger learners can generally keep up with older learners in the language learning process, being older may not be a distinct advantage for learning a language; (4) some evidence suggests that an early start in language learning may result in more uniform gains for the majority of learners, although this remains to be researched further by means of additional longitudinal studies; (5) young learners generally form a positive attitude toward language study, which may affect their ability to self-assess accurately and perform successfully in the target language; (6) literacy can be introduced from the beginning of language instruction and young learners demonstrate gains in this area; (7) young learners demonstrate progress in language acquisition in differentiated ways; and (8) young learners require significant time on task to show progress in moving up the proficiency scale (Donato et al., 2000; Donato, Antonek, & Tucker, 1994, 1996; Tucker, Donato, & Antonek, 1996). This last finding is especially significant in terms of understanding that language acquisition takes a great deal of time and that learners' language develops in varied ways. However, as we will see in a later section in this chapter, time alone is not sufficient to develop language proficiency in extended sequences of instruction; instructional approaches must also maintain the interest and motivation of students (Chinen et al., 2003).

The Elementary School Learner

Curtain and Dahlberg (2010) defined the following key characteristics of elementary and middle school learners:

- Preschool students (ages 2–4): absorb languages effortlessly and imitate speech sounds well; are self-centered and do not work well in groups; respond best to activities relating to their own interests; have a short attention span; respond best to concrete experiences and to large-motor involvement; benefit from activities that develop phonological awareness such as rhymes and tongue twisters.

- Primary students (ages 5–7; kindergarten, grades 1 and 2): learn best through concrete experiences and immediate goals; are imaginative and respond well to stories of fantasy and dramatic play; learn through oral language and can develop solid oral skills, pronunciation, and intonation when they have a good model; learn well through dramatic play, role play, and use of stories; have a short attention span and require large-muscle activity; need structured and specific directions and regular routines.

- Intermediate students (ages 8–10; grades 3–5): are at their peak for being open to people different from themselves; benefit from a global emphasis in language study; begin to understand cause and effect; work well in groups; continue to need concrete learning experiences; often dislike working with classmates of the opposite sex; learn well from imagination and stories that feature binary opposites (e.g., good vs. evil) and real-life heroes and heroines; are able to work with rubrics and enjoy peer editing and scoring activities.

- Early adolescent students (ages 11–14; grades 6–8): experience more dramatic developmental changes than at any other time in life; reach a cognitive plateau for a time; have multiplying and rapidly changing interests; feel a need to assert their independence, develop their own self-image, and become members of a peer group; benefit from the encouragement of positive relationships and a positive self-image; respond well to opportunities to learn about subjects of interest to them and to learning experiences with a strong affective component; respond well to content-based units with a culminating product (in press).

 What implications for instruction are suggested by the characteristics of elementary and middle school learners?

Egan (1979) describes the educational development of learners in terms of a process of accumulating and exercising "layers" of ability to engage with the world. In this view, as learners develop, they add new layers of sophistication onto the qualities of earlier layers, so that each layer contributes to their ability to make sense of the world by the time they are mature adults (as cited in Curtain & Dahlberg, 2010, in press). Egan (1979) described the "mythic" layer or stage of development in which children ages 4 or 5 to 9 or 10 make sense of the world by responding in terms of emotional categories, such as love, hate, fear, and joy, and morals, such as good or bad. They want to know how to *feel* about whatever they are learning, and they perceive the world as feeling and thinking like the child. Learners in the mythic stage are engaged in a topic or theme through exploration of polar opposites such as "a wicked witch vs. the perfect princess" (Curtain & Dahlberg). In order to plan effective learning experiences for children in the mythic stage, Egan suggests experiences that enable students (1) to interpret what they are learning in terms of their emotions and broad moral categories; (2) initially to build new information in terms of contrasting qualities, such as big/little and good/bad; and (3) to illustrate clear, unambiguous meaning, such as good or evil. Using a story form approach to instruction, as discussed in Chapter 3, is an ideal approach for teaching these learners. Instruction should incorporate story elements such as strong opposites, absolute meanings, and strong emotional and moral appeal (Curtain & Dahlberg).

 Children in the mythic stage (ages four/five to nine/ten) make sense of the world by responding in terms of emotional categories, such as love, hate, fear, and joy, and morals, such as good or bad.

In sum, it is important for language teachers to be familiar with the characteristics of young learners so that they are equipped to plan instruction that maximizes the learning potential of these learners and addresses their cognitive and social needs.

Program Models

From Language-Focused to Content-Focused Models

As school districts across the nation examine ways to expand language programs by introducing instruction at the elementary school level, they are faced with the need to choose from several different program models. As you learned in Chapter 3, early language learning program models range on a continuum from language-focused to content-focused programs (refer back to Figure 3.4). Figure 4.1 presents the types of elementary school foreign language programs together with a description of each and the amount of instructional time spent in the foreign language; remember that the label *FLES* has been used historically to refer to a program that is taught three to five times per week for class sessions of 20 minutes to an hour or longer.[4]

Attainment of specific goals in an early language program in grades K–6 depends upon the amount of instructional time that is allotted. Generally, developing a functional proficiency, understanding of other cultures, and acquiring subject content taught in the TL are key goals. An early language program should begin before middle school and continue in an articulated fashion throughout the entire program sequence (Curtain & Dahlberg, 2010). Classes should meet during the school day and throughout the school year. According to Swender and Duncan (1998), in order to meet the expectations described in the *ACTFL Performance Guidelines for K–12 Learners*, classes should meet no less than 30 to 40 minutes each day and no fewer than 3 to 5 days each week. Curtain and Dahlberg warn that early language programs with less frequent scheduling than three to five days per week are at risk of failure because students will be unable to meet language goals and programs may be eliminated when budgets are tight and program results are not met.

As you learned in Chapter 3, early language programs can be either *content-based*, in which the foreign language teacher teaches certain parts of the regular elementary school curriculum through the foreign language, or *content-related* (also called *content-enriched*), in which the foreign language teacher uses concepts from the regular elementary school curriculum to enrich the language program with academic content (Curtain & Dahlberg, 2010).

 Early language learning program models range on a continuum from language-focused to content-focused programs.

School districts have historically offered *exploratory* programs (traditionally called *FLEX*—Foreign Language Exploratory or Experience) in the middle school, designed to introduce learners to one or several languages and cultures. A minimal amount of instruction is provided, as little as once a week, for 6 to 9 weeks a year (Hoch, 1998). Because exploratory programs do not typically have language proficiency as an outcome and are not always part of an articulated sequence of courses, many districts have replaced them with the first full year of language instruction. You will learn more about exploratory programs in Chapter 5.

In immersion programs, the foreign language is the vehicle for teaching academic content in the regular elementary school curriculum (e.g., mathematics, science, art) rather than the subject of instruction itself. In total immersion, all instruction is conducted in the foreign language; students learn to read in the foreign language first, then in English. In partial immersion programs, students receive instruction in the foreign language for up to 50% of the school day; reading and language arts are taught in English (Hoch, 1998). Curtain and Dahlberg (2010) identified the following goals common to immersion programs:

- functional proficiency in the second language
- maintenance and development of English language arts comparable to or surpassing that of students in English-only programs
- mastery of subject content material of the school district curriculum
- cross-cultural understanding (in press).

www.cengagebrain.com

In immersion teaching, although language is simplified, it is not grammatically sequenced. Language reflects the themes and concepts of the elementary curriculum and the communicative and conceptual needs of the students. Reading instruction is based on previously mastered oral language. See Appendix 4.1 on the *Teacher's Handbook* Web site for a description of total or full immersion, partial immersion, early immersion, late immersion, continuing immersion, one-way immersion, two-way immersion, and indigenous immersion.

In immersion programs, the foreign language is the vehicle for teaching academic content in the regular elementary school curriculum rather than the subject of instruction itself. ▪

Sheltered Instruction and Dual Language Programs

Sheltered instruction (SI) refers to making academic content comprehensible to English language learners (ELLs) while simultaneously promoting their second language acquisition of English. Teachers of SI help learners understand the content knowledge specific to math, science, social studies, and language arts through the medium of their second language (Cloud, Genessee, & Hamayan, 2000). SI is also referred to as Specially Designed Academic Instruction in English (SDAIE). An observation tool called the Sheltered Instruction Observation Protocol (SIOP) was developed by Echevarria, Vogt, and Short (2000, 2004, 2008) to provide guidance for all teachers as they enable ELLs to understand the content of their math, science, social studies, or language arts classes. The SIOP model has evolved from the use of the protocol. The model consists of 30 instructional practices grouped into three main areas: preparation, instruction, and review/assessment. Teachers can use the model to guide their lesson planning, observe instructional practices in action, and review or reflect on their methods of instruction. SIOP is used primarily in schools where minority native language speakers learn a language spoken by the majority, e.g., Somali students learning English in the U.S. The importance of preserving the home culture and language led to two-way immersion programs that promote the goals of bilingualism, biliteracy, and cross-cultural competence, balanced across two languages. Often, the leadership of the ESL teachers is key to successful implementation of the SIOP model. SIOP has been modified by Howard, Sugarman, and Coburn (2006) and is now called the Two-Way Immersion Observation Protocol (TWIOP). See the *Teacher's Handbook* Web site for links to SIOP and TWIOP. See Chapter 10 for additional ways to teach diverse learners.

FIGURE 4.1 Elementary School Foreign Language Programs: Time Allocations and Descriptions

CONTENT-FOCUSED (CONTENT-DRIVEN) PROGRAMS

Goal: To become functionally proficient in the new language
Goal: To acquire an understanding of and appreciation for other cultures
Goal: To master subject content taught in the foreign language

Program Type	Time Allocations and Descriptions
	Note: Achievement of the goals will vary depending on how much time is allocated for the program.
Total Immersion (Full Immersion) Grades K–6	50–100% of the school day Focus is on learning subject matter taught in FL; language learning per se incorporated as necessary throughout curriculum Student population in the U.S and Canada is English speakers who are learning a new language **Description** The second language is used for the entire school day during the first 2 or 3 years. In early total immersion programs, reading is taught through the second language. In some programs instruction by means of English is introduced gradually, often in grade two, and the amount of English is increased until the fifth or sixth grade (the last grade in elementary school), where up to half the day is spent in English and half in the second language. In other programs, once English is introduced (usually at grade two or three) the percentage of time spent in English remains constant throughout the program, at approximately 20%. In some other programs the entire day is conducted in the second language for a much greater period of time and English is not introduced until grades four or five.
Two-Way Immersion Grades K–6 Also called Two-Way Bilingual, Dual Immersion and Developmental Bilingual Education	At least 50% of the school day Student population is both native speakers of English and of the target language. **Description** Two-way immersion programs are similar to one-way immersion programs except that the student group includes native speakers of the target language as well as native speakers of English. Thus, all students learn subject matter through their native language as well as through the second language, and both language groups have the benefit of interaction with peers who are native speakers of the language they are learning. The ideal goals of two-way immersion, in addition to subject content mastery, are that the English-speaking students become functionally proficient in the second language and that the second language speakers become functionally proficient in English. At the same time all students continue to develop skills and proficiency in their native language.
Partial Immersion Grades K–6	At least 50% (time is spent learning subject matter taught in FL; language learning per se incorporated as necessary throughout curriculum) **Description** All instruction is in the second language for part (at least half) of the school day. The amount of instruction in the foreign language usually remains constant throughout the elementary school program. In early partial immersion programs, students frequently learn to read in both languages at the same time; in some programs, notably Chinese and Japanese partial immersion, literacy skills are taught first in the native language.

The achievement of the goals will vary depending on how much time is allocated for the program.

(Continued)

FIGURE 4.1 *(Continued)*

LANGUAGE-FOCUSED (LANGUAGE-DRIVEN) PROGRAMS

Goal: To become functionally proficient in the new language
Goal: To acquire an understanding of and appreciation for other cultures
Goal: To master subject content taught in the foreign language
These goals are the same as for immersion programs

Program Type	Time Allocations and Descriptions
	Note: Achievement of the goals will vary depending on how much time is allocated for the program.
Early Language Learning Programs Grades K–6 Also Known As Early Start Programs And Programs For Young Learners Sometimes referred to as FLES	Minimum 30–40 minutes per class, at least 3–5 days per week This time allotment should be considered a minimum for an effective (non-immersion) early language program. **Description** The focus is on language learning with the integration of culture and content objectives. A program that begins before middle school and is articulated vertically throughout the entire program sequence. A student learns a single language throughout the program sequence. (This does not imply that only one language is offered throughout the school district.) Classes meet within the school day, throughout the entire school year. The amount of time allotted to a language-focused program in the elementary school is one of the most important variables in its potential for success. The vision of the Standards calls for an elementary school program that invests the time necessary for students to achieve significant outcomes. In order to achieve the performances described in the *ACTFL Performance Guidelines for K–12 Learners,* committee members advised that elementary school programs should meet no less than 30 to 40 minutes per day, and no fewer than 3 to 5 days per week (Swender & Duncan, 1998).

Underlying every program description is the fact that language proficiency outcomes are related to the amount of time spent by students in meaningful communication in the target language. Met and Rhodes (1990) suggest that the amount of time spent on language learning and the intensity of the learning experience may be among the most important factors determining the rate of language acquisition and the level of proficiency that can be attained in a language program. These results also assume the role of a well-qualified and dedicated teacher. Planners should seek to design a program that will result in the highest level of proficiency possible, given the resources they have available.

If the program design includes less time than the stated minimum, planners must be sure to give stakeholders adequate information about the types of student outcomes that may be expected due to the limited nature of the contact time in the program.

Source: From *Languages and Children – Making the Match,* 4th ed., by H. Curtain and C. A. Dahlberg, 2010, Boston: Allyn & Bacon. Copyright © 2010 Pearson Education. Reprinted by permission of the publisher.

In recent years, dual language programs have received increased attention in the U.S. *Dual language* refers to a form of bilingual education in which students are taught literacy and content in two languages; the *partner language* (the language other than English) is used for at least half of the school day in the elementary years. Programs typically begin in kindergarten or first grade and continue for at least 5 years, although many continue into middle and high school. According to the National Dual Language Consortium (NDLC) (2008),

FIGURE 4.2 Dual language Umbrella

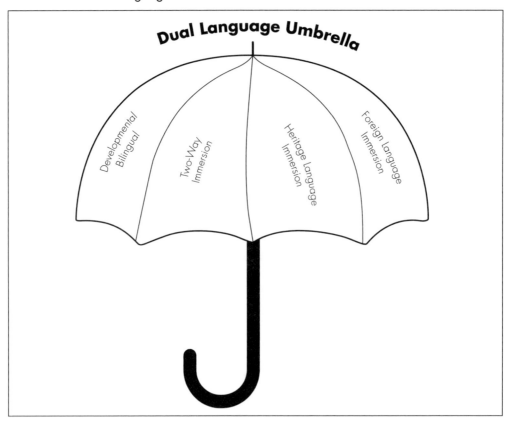

Source: From *The Dual Language Program Planner: A Guide for Designing and Implementing Dual Language Programs* (p. 3), by E. R. Howard, N. Olague, and D. Rogers, 2003. Center for Research on Education, Diversity & Excellence. Reprinted by permission.

the majority of dual language programs in the U.S. teach in English and Spanish, although growing numbers of programs use a partner language other than Spanish, such as Arabic, French, Hawaiian, Japanese, Korean, or Mandarin. Figure 4.2 depicts the four program models that are part of the dual language umbrella: *developmental,* or *maintenance, bilingual programs* enroll students who are primarily native speakers of the partner language; *two-way bilingual immersion programs* enroll a balance of native English speakers and native speakers of the partner language; *foreign language immersion, language immersion,* or *one-way immersion programs* enroll primarily native English speakers; and *heritage language programs* enroll students dominant in English but whose parents or grandparents spoke the TL.

All elementary school dual language programs use the partner language for 50% of the school day. The two models are:

- Total immersion (90/10 model): the partner language is used most or all of the day in the elementary grades (80–90%). Foreign language (one-way) immersion programs that implement full immersion use the partner language for 100% of subject matter instruction. In all cases, the partner language and English are used equally in the later grades.
- Partial immersion (50/50 model): the partner language and English are used equally throughout the program.

Although there are various types of dual language programs, according to Lindholm, they all have the following four characteristics:

1. Instruction through two languages where the target language is used for a significant portion of the students' instructional day.
2. Periods of instruction during which only one language is used.
3. Both native English speakers and native speakers of the target language are participants.
4. The students are integrated for most content instruction (2000, p. 13; as cited in Torres-Guzmán, 2002, p. 3).

The principles underlying dual language programs are that it takes most learners from 5 to 7 years to acquire L2 well enough to function academically, learners can transfer the knowledge and skills acquired in one language to the other, and learners' educational and cognitive development is enhanced by developing the two languages (Cummins, 1992; Torres-Guzmán, 2002). Dual language programs follow clear linguistic, sociocultural, and pedagogical policies. Linguistic policies include strict language separation of languages, avoidance of simultaneous translation, language taught through content, and heterogeneous language grouping. Sociocultural policies include appreciation of cultural diversity, culturally relevant teaching, development of self-esteem, cooperative group learning structure, and parental involvement. Among the pedagogical policies are academic achievement for all children, developmental-level team-teaching structures, thematic organization of units of study, teachers as monolingual models, and ongoing staff development (Torres-Guzmán). Dual language programs are unique in that they ensure equal status of the minority language with English, protect the minority language and culture and ensure its use among English-speaking students, and focus on quality education for all learners (Morrison, 1995). It is essential that teachers in these programs have appropriate teaching certification and knowledge of subject matter, curriculum and technology, instructional strategies, and classroom management; have appropriate academic background and experience; are fully credentialed bilingual or ESL teachers and have knowledge of bilingual education and second language acquisition; and have native or native-like ability in the language(s) of instruction (monolingual English speakers who provide English model MUST understand the partner language in early grades) (Howard, Sugarman, Christian, Lindolm-Leary, & Rogers, 2007, pp. 21–22).

Among the benefits of dual language programs, studies have revealed that language minority and language majority students outperform their peers in their first language and, by the upper elementary grades, in the second language; all students master skills in both languages; and most students in both groups show achievement in subject content at or above their grade level (see Torres-Guzmán for a review and discussion of these studies). See the *Teacher's Handbook* Web site for a link to the Spanish Language Arts Standards developed by the World-Class Instruction and Design Assessment (WIDA) Consortium, which can be used in planning curriculum for bilingual and two-way immersion programs and for the link to *Guiding Principles for Dual Language Education* available from the Center for Applied Linguistics.

Other Instructional Models

Other instructional models that have gained increasing attention are *media-based programs* and *distance learning*, which provide alternatives to the programs described above, particularly in the face of challenges such as budgetary considerations or difficulty in finding teachers. *Media-based programs* feature the use of a particular type of media, such as videotape, interactive television, CDs, audiotapes, or computers, with follow-up by the classroom teacher or traveling specialist. The key to the success of these programs is the quality of the follow-up, since in the past programs that have not been staffed by a qualified teacher have not produced effective results (Curtain & Dahlberg, 2010). Another instructional model uses interactive television as a vehicle for *distance learning*, where the language teacher is located at a base site with a group of students, and one or more groups of students are located at a remote site or sites. Communication occurs by means of interactive teleconferences via computer, audio, or video networks, offering opportunities for interaction between the learner and instructor (Moore & Thompson, 1997).

Although few empirical studies have been conducted in the area of distance learning, the existing research points to the possibility that students in distance learning programs may achieve as well as or even better than those taking traditional courses (Martin & Rainey, 1993). In one study examining the effectiveness of videoconferencing technology in a K–3 Spanish program, students at the remote site performed higher on achievement tests than students at the base site (Glisan, Dudt, & Howe, 1998). The researchers attribute this difference to the role of the facilitators at the remote site and the review sessions that they voluntarily conducted between class sessions. An additional interesting finding of this study was that 65% of the students who participated in this project reported having used Spanish outside the classroom, either with friends or to teach family members Spanish words (Glisan et al.). This illustrates the enthusiasm of elementary school learners toward language study and may lend further support for an early start to language learning. Although much more research is needed in this area, distance learning may hold promise for the future as one way for school districts to provide language learning opportunities to *all* students. Appendix 4.2 on the *Teacher's Handbook* Web site presents the guidelines for distance learning programs published by the National Council of State Supervisors for Languages (NCSSFL, 2008).

www.cengagebrain.com

Factors to Consider in Planning an Early Foreign Language Program

The following are key considerations in planning an early foreign language program (adapted from Curtain & Dahlberg, 2000; Hoch, 1998):

1. Desired level of proficiency: As Curtain and Dahlberg state, "The level of language fluency a student will gain in an elementary and middle school foreign language program is directly related to the amount of time students spend learning the language and on the intensity of that language experience" (2010, in press). A sequence of instruction that includes sufficient time on task is necessary in order to develop proficiency. Immersion programs enable students to attain the greatest amount of proficiency over time, traditional FLES programs lead to some functional proficiency depending on the amount of instructional time, and exploratory programs are not designed with functional proficiency goals in mind because of the minimal amount of instructional time. In view of the K–16 sequence set forth in the *Standards for Foreign Language Learning in the 21st Century [SFLL]* (National Standards in Foreign Language Education Project [NSFLEP], 2006), Swender and Duncan (1998) proposed that elementary school programs meet from 3 to 5 days per week for no less than 30–40 minutes per class; middle school programs meet daily for no less than 40–50 minutes; and that high school programs equal four units of credit.

2. Length of sequence: Immersion programs require a commitment by the school district to invest in an uninterrupted sequence of language courses. The vision of the *SFLL* is an articulated program of study that begins in the early grades and continues throughout the secondary years and into post-secondary programs. Successful early language programs are part of a sequential, well-articulated program that continues beyond the elementary

grades to enable students to build on and strengthen the skills they developed earlier. There is a caveat with long-term sequences of instruction, however: Instructional strategies and learning experiences must be varied from year to year, or else students may lose interest in the face of language experiences that become routinized and dull (Chinen, Donato, Igarashi, & Tucker, 2003). Curtain and Dahlberg (2000) suggest that implementation of a new program should not occur in all grades at the same time in order to allow sufficient time for teachers to develop materials and lessons; for them, a more effective approach would be to implement a new program in one or two grades during the first year and then add another grade each year until it is in place at all levels.

3. Nature of language(s) taught and integration within curriculum: An issue that often poses a challenge is deciding which language(s) to offer in an early language program. Factors that should be taken into consideration include community interest, which can be ascertained by means of a survey; availability of materials and staff; and potential for articulation and continuation of the language at higher levels of instruction (Curtain & Dahlberg, 2010). Presently it is desirable to introduce into the elementary school the less commonly taught languages, such as Arabic, Chinese, Japanese, and Russian, in view of their critical importance to our national agenda (Curtain & Dahlberg); the National Security Language Initiative (2006) labeled these languages as *critical needs languages* and they have been called *strategic languages* by the U.S. Department of Defense (2005). Whatever the language chosen, it should be recognized as a valid academic subject with the same status and importance as other subjects. Early language programs should also reinforce the goals of the general school curriculum by integrating other content areas and the basic mission of the school (Curtain & Dahlberg, 2000).

4. Teacher qualifications and workload: In order to be effective, all of the program models require qualified foreign language teachers. According to Curtain and Dahlberg, "Teachers at all levels need to be fully proficient in the language they teach" (2000, p. 3). Trained immersion teachers are usually not plentiful; districts may need to hire teachers from other countries and must be willing to provide ongoing in-service training. Early language learning programs require specialists with functional proficiency in the TL, an understanding of the nature of first- and second language acquisition for young learners, and the ability to create their own instructional materials. Further, teachers' schedules should be arranged so that they have time for the additional responsibilities of an early language teacher, such as developing curriculum and materials, interacting with fellow teachers, communicating with parents and community, and building public relations. The Georgia Department of Education has stipulated that foreign language elementary school teachers should teach no more than eight classes per day (Curtain & Dahlberg).

5. Funding and resources: An adequate budget is needed to support the start up costs of a language program to subsidize instructional materials, technology, teacher salaries, professional development, and staff development time for writing curriculum and developing materials since ready-made materials are not always readily available (Curtain & Dahlberg, 2010).

6. Community and parental support: For immersion programs to be successful, the parents and community must believe in the possibility that students can learn skills and subject content in a second language. In early language programs, it is important that the regular classroom teachers view language as an important component of the curriculum rather than as a frill. Faculty, parents, and administrators need to provide feedback about scheduling so that they are not concerned about time for language being "taken away" from the other subject areas. As indicated in the study by Donato, Tucker, Wudthayagorn, and Igarashi (2000), parental attitudes may not always be in consonance with the goals of an early language program. In their study, parents reported that their

top two goals for their children's study of Japanese were to enjoy language learning and acquire cultural knowledge, with the development of fluency not a high priority.

See the *Teacher's Handbook* Web site for a link to a description of four models of elementary school Latin programs.

www.cengagebrain.com

Traditional FLES Programs of the Past and Early Language Programs of the Present

While elementary school language programs are being developed at an increasing rate, the profession is trying to avoid the problems experienced by the traditional FLES programs of the 1960s. The heyday of audiolingualism brought with it a burst of enthusiasm, albeit short-lived, for elementary school language instruction. Unfortunately, despite government funding and public support, the new elementary school programs declined rapidly after 1964. Rosenbusch cites seven primary reasons for the demise of the FLES programs of the 1960s:

1. FLES teachers often lacked linguistic proficiency and skill in teaching young children. In 1961, a survey by Alkonis and Brophy indicated that in sixty-two elementary school language programs, the majority of teachers had no foreign language background.
2. FLES programs were begun quickly without sufficient coordination and planning.
3. Program goals were unrealistic or inappropriate and promised too much linguistic fluency in too short a time.
4. Few programs had a coordinator to provide supervision and articulation across levels.
5. FLES programs featured inappropriate methodologies as they relied on memorization and pattern drills, often with little real communication.
6. Programs lacked adequate instructional materials.
7. Many schools made no attempt to assess student progress (1995, pp. 2–3).

Caveats for Present and Future Early Language Learning Programs

The programs of today and tomorrow must be careful not to repeat the mistakes of the past. On the positive side, the revolution in language teaching over the last several decades has affirmed the importance of communicative language teaching. Early language learning programs are being planned and organized to match the age of the learners. New programs are emphasizing content-based learning that provides an integrated place for language in the elementary school curriculum. Culture and global connections are becoming integral components of the foreign language curriculum. New teacher training programs are enabling elementary school teachers to acquire proficiency in a foreign language and expertise in integrating language instruction into their curricula. (See Appendix 4.3 on the *Teacher's Handbook* Web site for an observation guide to assess the effectiveness of the elementary and middle school foreign language teacher, and Appendix 4.4 on the *Teacher's Handbook* Web site for a guide to assess the effectiveness of the immersion teacher.) More effective teaching materials that contextualize language instruction continue to appear on the market.

www.cengagebrain.com

Program developers must be careful to set realistic expectations of what students are able to achieve as a result of elementary school language study. Clearly much more research is needed in this area. The FLES study reported on by Montás (2003) illustrates the effectiveness of using a meaningful, context-centered curriculum in order to develop learners' language proficiency, especially when teaching with limited instructional time. However, the study of a Japanese FLES program by Donato et al. (2000) found that after 5 or 6 consecutive years of language study, students' proficiency was still rated in the novice level. Students rarely demonstrated the ability to engage in unplanned, interpersonal communication, they were unable to narrate stories orally, and they were unable to produce language beyond isolated words and sentences (Donato et al.).

These findings echo a concern that has arisen in other investigations, which is that early language learners, whether in early language learning or immersion programs, may not become independent language users (Igarashi, 1997). Current research seems to point to the possibility that (1) contextualization and culture do not necessarily lead to language creativity and (2) interaction between students and teachers does not automatically promote interpersonal communication skills and negotiation of meaning (Donato et al., 2000). These claims imply that teachers must carefully design opportunities for learners to create with the language and communicate with one another within the context of the lesson or thematic unit.

Such claims and implications are significant as we consider the development of early language learning programs in the future because:

1. They lend support for extended sequences of instruction given the fact that children advance slowly through novice performance and only reach intermediate levels after a significant period of time following the start of language study.
2. They illustrate the key role of instructional practices in influencing what children can and cannot do with the foreign language. If we want children to speak in sentences, engage in interpersonal communication, and narrate stories, then teachers must provide these types of opportunities in class and must assess students' progress in achieving these skills over time.
3. They stress the benefits of a literacy-rich classroom environment in which learners are engaged in exploring printed materials and in interpreting them.
4. They indicate an important need for additional research by means of longitudinal studies of learners' accomplishments in elementary school programs.

Strategies for Teaching Language to Elementary School Learners

Elementary school foreign language instruction involves careful planning and the use of a wide variety of approaches and techniques designed to involve students actively in language use. In the sections that follow, you will be introduced to several instructional strategies within the *SFLL* framework that are considered to be key in teaching languages to children. Since space permits the description of only a few of the most salient techniques, you may find it helpful to consult one or more of the references listed at the end of this chapter in order to explore other strategies in greater detail. Note that all of these techniques can be adapted and used effectively in secondary classrooms as well. Subsequent chapters will also address implications for teaching at the elementary school level as they relate to the topics presented in those chapters.

It is important to note the pivotal role of *context* and *attention to integration of meaning* in all activities that take place in the elementary school setting. As Curtain and Dahlberg (2004) point out, FLES programs have historically had (1) an emphasis on recitation (lists; labels; memorized patterns and dialogues, usually cued by a teacher question; songs, often not integrated into the rest of the language curriculum; games, used for a change of pace or for grammar practice; rhymes and poems chosen at random; and reading for recitation or reading aloud) and (2) pervasive use of English for discipline, giving directions, clarifying the target language, checking comprehension, and teaching culture. These types of strategies strip language of meaning, affect students' attitudes about language learning in a negative way, and contribute to the deterioration of early start programs.

Thematic Unit and Lesson Planning

The focus of planning for elementary school foreign language instruction is usually the *thematic unit*, to which you were introduced in Chapter 3. Curtain and Dahlberg (2010) emphasize that at the elementary school level, thematic planning (1) makes instruction more comprehensible, because the theme creates a meaningful context; (2) changes the instructional focus from the language itself to the use of language to achieve meaningful goals; (3) provides a rich context for standards-based instruction; (4) offers a natural setting for narrative structure and task-based organization of content; (5) involves students in real language use in a variety of situations, modes, and text types; (6) involves activities or tasks that engage learners in complex thinking and more sophisticated use of language; (7) avoids the use of isolated exercises with grammatical structures, practiced out of context, that tend to fragment language at the word or sentence level and neglect the discourse level; and (8) connects content, language, and culture goals to a "big idea." They stress that the thematic unit fits within a curriculum design that accounts for a K–12 sequence of instruction. At the center of this framework for curriculum development is the *thematic center*, which includes the theme, targeted standards, broad unit outcomes, enduring understanding and essential questions, and a culminating performance assessment, as illustrated in Figure 4.3 (Curtain & Dahlberg). This framework reflects the principles of backward curricular design described in Chapter 3.

FIGURE 4.3 A Curriculum Development Framework for Language Learning Programs

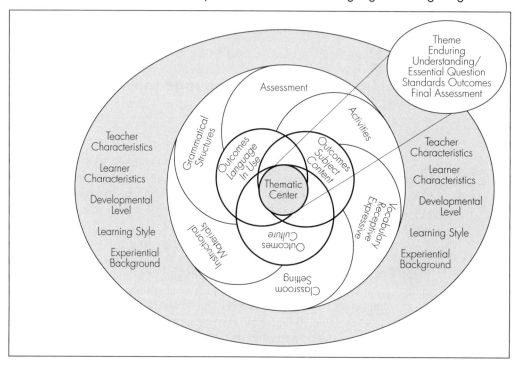

Source: From *Languages and Children – Making the Match,* 4th ed., by H. Curtain and C. A. Dahlberg, 2010, Boston: Allyn & Bacon. Copyright © 2010 Pearson Education. Reprinted by permission of the publisher.

Selection of a thematic center is based on the interests of the learners and teacher, relationship to curricular goals, potential for integration with culture, and potential for developing appropriate language functions and modes of communication. The focus of the thematic center could be a topic from the general school curriculum or one taken from the culture or literature of the target language; a "generative" theme around a question such as "What do we explore and what do we find?"; a story or book; a work of art, or an artist; or music, or a composer; however, it must reflect a "big idea"—that is, one that is at the heart of the discipline and has enduring value beyond the classroom (Curtain & Dahlberg, 2010). The topic might be a broad one (e.g., "the environment") that lasts for several weeks or might be developed into a more focused theme (e.g., a single story) that would last for a week. Once a topic or theme has been selected, the teacher might brainstorm in order to develop the theme more fully into meaningful subtopics. Useful in this brainstorming is a *thematic planning web*, a cognitive organizer that illustrates a visual representation of concepts and their relationships (see Appendix 4.5 for an example). It is important to note that not every element in the web may be included in the unit, and the information organized in the web may be included in future planning. The selected ideas from the planning web can then be used to design the unit plan and lessons plans according to the models presented in Chapter 3.

Content-Based Instruction

In Chapter 3, you learned about the general concept of content-based instruction (CBI). CBI is, of course, an integral component of immersion instruction. However, content-based lessons can also be designed in FLES or content-related (content-enriched) FLES programs. These lessons provide the means for contextualizing instruction and for integrating foreign language and elementary subject-content. Met (1999) emphasizes that the "content" in content-based programs "represents material that is cognitively engaging and demanding for the learner, and it is material that extends beyond the target language or target culture" (p. 150). Integrating CBI into language instruction requires planning and considerations about the nature of subject-content tasks that learners are asked to perform as well as the target language abilities that they will need to develop.

According to Cummins (1981b), communicative activities should be developed keeping in mind the *degree of contextual support* that is available as well as the *degree of cognitive involvement*, or the amount of information a learner must process simultaneously in order to complete a task. *Context-embedded language* is supported by a range of clues (e.g., illustrations, physical gestures, realia), while *context-reduced language* offers little extra support, which means that learners must rely on the language itself for meaning (e.g., telephone conversations, explanations without diagrams or examples). Figure 4.4 illustrates the way in which language/subject-content tasks can be classified into four categories according to the degree of contextual support provided and cognitive involvement required.

One implication of Cummins' classification is that language teachers might make new concepts less language dependent by incorporating more visuals and realia, meaningful contexts, hands-on learning, vivid examples and analogies, learners' background knowledge and past experiences, and rephrasing and natural repetition. Another implication is that language tasks can be made more cognitively engaging by integrating language and concepts in the general school curriculum; involving students in higher-order thinking skills such as classifying, categorizing, predicting, comparing, imagining, evaluating, debating, etc., even when the language itself might be simple; and providing opportunities for learners to practice new language in problem-solving situations, rather than relying on imitation and rote learning (Curtain & Dahlberg, 2010).

FIGURE 4.4 Range of Contextual Support and Degree of Cognitive Involvement in Communicative Activities

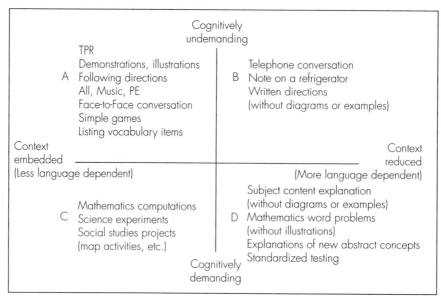

Source: From *Languages and Children – Making the Match,* 4th ed., by H. Curtain and C. A. Dahlberg, 2010, Boston: Allyn & Bacon. Copyright © 2010 Pearson Education. Reprinted by permission of the publisher.

 The "content" in content-based programs "represents material that is cognitively engaging and demanding for the learner, and it is material that extends beyond the target language or target culture."

The following are some steps that the teacher might follow in planning for CBI at the elementary school level and beyond, depending on the type of CBI program:

1. Identify possible concepts from the subject-content curriculum (i.e., in math, social studies, geography, science). Sources of these concepts include school district curriculum documents, state department of education standards for instruction, the *SFLL*, and the *PreK–12 English Language Proficiency Standards* (Teachers of English to Speakers of Other Languages [TESOL], 2006).
2. Select concepts that lend themselves to concrete, hands-on learning that is characteristic of the language classroom. A key issue to consider is whether or not the concepts can be taught using the language of learners at a particular level (e.g., novice, intermediate) or whether they require more abstract, sophisticated language.
3. Identify the language needed in terms of both content vocabulary for the subject area and new language necessary for students to understand the lesson. *Content-obligatory language* is the language (concept vocabulary, grammar, language functions) that must be taught in order to teach the subject-content concept. *Content-compatible language* is the language that may be integrated logically into the curriculum concept, although it is not required for comprehension or mastery of the subject-content concept (Lorenz & Met, 1989). See example below; also, in Appendix 4.6 on the *Teacher's Handbook* Web site, you will find a partial lesson plan for a grade 1 mathematics lesson with these two kinds of objectives illustrated.

www.cengagebrain.com

4. Locate, adapt, and/or create the instructional materials to be used in the lesson.
5. Create integrated, contextualized, hands-on instructional activities for teaching and practice of the new concept.

6. Provide for multiple opportunities for assessing student progress; both *Teacher's Handbook* and the CoBaLTT Web site suggest the use of the Integrated Performance Assessment (IPA) as a CBI assessment format, which will be presented in Chapter 11 (adapted from Curtain & Dahlberg, 2010, in press).

Content-obligatory language is the language (concept vocabulary, grammar, language functions) that must be taught in order to teach the subject-content concept.

Content-compatible language is the language that may be integrated logically into the curriculum concept, although it is not required for comprehension or mastery of the subject-content concept.

The following are sample content-obligatory and content-compatible objectives:

Language Objectives — Content Obligatory: Students will be able to...

- identify geographic features (e.g., *las montañas* [mountains], *el río* [river], *el desierto* [desert], *el bosque* [forest])
- identify locations using direction words (e.g., *norte* [north], *sur* [south], *este* [east], *oeste* [west])

Language Objectives — Content Compatible: Students will be able to...

- ask about geographic location (using question words such as *¿Dónde?,¿Qué?* [Where? What?])
- express likes/dislikes related to geographic preferences (using expressions such as *prefiero* [I prefer], *me gusta/n* [I like] and *no me gusta/n* [I don't like]).
- compare Spain and the U.S. with respect to geographical features (e.g., *El oeste de España (Extremadura) es como el estado de Nuevo México.* [The west of Spain is like the state of New Mexico.] (adapted from Fortune, 2008)

For a wealth of sample CBI units and lesson plans, consult the CoBaLTT Web site. The URL can be found on the *Teacher's Handbook* Web site.

As you learned in Chapter 3, implementing content-based instruction requires attention to both content and linguistic goals so that students learn subject-area content and make progress in L2 development. Chapter 3 described a recent study that examined CBI from a classroom discourse perspective and found that teachers envision and implement CBI in different ways, as manifested by their classroom discourse practices, classroom tasks, and students' performance on literacy assessments (Pessoa, Hendry, Donato, Tucker, & Lee, 2007). Simply inserting academic content into language lessons will not foster students' ability to engage in L2 discussions of content beyond formal language practice unless the teacher provides discursive opportunities (Pessoa et al.). As illustrated in the findings of this research, CBI teachers are reminded to:

1. include explicit language objectives in the curriculum, as illustrated in the framework for curriculum development depicted in Figure 4.3;
2. develop the ability to lead conversations with their students that reflect a cohesive academic topic and conversational features of interpersonal communication (IRF rather than IRE);
3. encourage students to elaborate on academic content using discursive features such as open-ended questions and topic development;

4. limit their use of English and use translation only for specific purposes;
5. integrate a focus on grammatical form when necessary and engage students in co-constructing the form so that they actively work to understand and internalize it;
6. avoid explicit error correction and unnecessary lecture on grammatical rules (Pessoa et al.).

In Chapter 7, you will learn more about how to lead students in co-constructing a grammatical form. For now, the following is an example of how a sixth-grade CBI Spanish teacher integrated a brief focus-on-form discussion with her class within the content-based discussion of fossil fuels:

Teacher: *¿Están de acuerdo? ¿Está bien? ¿Si tenemos los combustibles fósiles "es" o "son"?* [Do you agree? Is it good? If we have fossil fuels is it "is" or "are"?]

Student: *son* ["are"]

Teacher: *Daniela dice "son." ¿Por qué "son"? ¿Los combustibles fósiles es plural o singular?* [Daniela says "are." Why "are"? Fossil fuels is plural or singular?]

Student: *plural*

Teacher: *Los combustibles fósiles son. En este caso si estoy de acuerdo. ¿Cuál es el sustantivo de la oración? Aquí el sustantivo es porciento y cuál es el sustantivo de esta? ¿Natalia?* [Fossil fuels are. In this case yes I agree. What is the noun of the sentence? Here the noun is percentage and what is the noun of this? Natalia?]

Student: *Combustibles fósiles.* [Fossil fuels]

Teacher: *Sí, ¡muy bien! Los combustibles y es un sustantivo plural.* [Yes, very good! Fossil fuels, and it is a plural noun.] (Pessoa et al., 2007, p. 113)

As you can see, the teacher takes advantage of the opportunity to engage students in focusing on their L2 development within their content-based discussion. Note that the exchange is not lengthy, students are led in co-constructing form with the teacher's assistance, and the teacher does not use overt error correction nor provide a long grammatical explanation. Afterwards, the discussion returns to the content topic.

 What would be an example of an exchange in this sixth-grade class that focuses on the subject content and features an IRF sequence?

According to Pessoa and colleagues (2007), implementation of a fully integrated CBI program at the elementary school level may require that the teacher have a more thorough grounding in academic subject-matter teaching, perhaps even dual certification in both the foreign language and elementary school content. Another option is for language teachers to collaborate with their content-area counterparts in designing content-based language lessons. Further, teachers are encouraged to engage in ongoing professional development, including doing peer observations and providing feedback to one another.

In sum, CBI offers interesting possibilities for students to learn academic content, acquire new information and perspectives, and further develop their L2 within meaningful contexts. It offers a vehicle through which students stand to make significant gains in content knowledge and L2 language development.

Helping Students to Organize and Explore Content

Graphic organizers, such as semantic maps and Venn diagrams, are visuals that display words or concepts in categories to illustrate how they relate to one another (Curtain & Dahlberg, 2010). They can be an effective means of helping students organize subject-content topics and concepts. *Semantic maps* depict words or concepts in categories and show how they relate to each other. A key word or question is placed at the center or top of the map; students and teacher create the map together. In this way, students organize what they are learning and are able to see how it fits with the language and information previously learned (Curtain & Dahlberg). Appendices 4.7 and 4.8 illustrate two different types of semantic maps. *Venn diagrams* can be used for making comparisons and contrasts; they consist of two or more intersecting circles that depict relationships among concepts (see Appendix 4.9 on the *Teacher's Handbook* Web site).

www.cengagebrain.com

Graphic organizers are visuals that display words or concepts in categories to illustrate how they relate to one another.

Acquisition of Vocabulary

In Chapter 2, you learned that children acquire vocabulary as a result of attending to large quantities of meaningful input and by interacting with the concrete objects referred to in the input through a process referred to as *binding* (Terrell, 1986). You were also introduced to some ways in which binding can be facilitated in the classroom, such as presenting vocabulary in thematic groups, providing meaningful input, using visuals and objects, and using Total Physical Response (TPR) to actively engage students in connecting the vocabulary they hear to actions they perform or objects that they manipulate.

In TPR (Asher, 1986), the teacher gives a series of oral commands in the target language, and students demonstrate comprehension by responding physically. At first, students imitate the teacher performing the commands; later, they perform the commands without the teacher's assistance. The following is a typical series of commands that the teacher might give early in the language learning experience (these would be given in the target language):

Stand up. Sit down. Stand up. Sit down. Stand up. Walk to the door. Stop. Turn around. Walk to the blackboard. Stop. Turn around. Jump up and down. Stop. Turn around. Walk to the door. Stop. Turn around. Walk to your seats. Sit down.

At first, the teacher performs the commands along with students until they begin to bind the oral command forms to the physical activities; then the teacher gives the commands and students respond without seeing the teacher's physical responses first. Note that the series of commands is repetitive in nature because students need to hear the input multiple times in order for binding to occur. At some point after students have acquired the forms, the teacher may move beyond the comprehension stage by having students produce the commands themselves and asking their classmates to respond physically.

TPR can be used effectively to teach concrete vocabulary words, with the use of oral input and visuals or objects. In addition to physical responses, students can give yes-no answers, choose the correct word, or manipulate visuals while listening to input. For example, the teacher might teach vocabulary for food by showing plastic or real food items, presenting the items one at a time, and providing comprehensible input that also builds on students' background knowledge in the target language, as in the following example (substitute your target language for the English version that appears below):

Class, we're going to talk about some fruits and vegetables today in preparation for the recipe that we will be making later this week. *[Teacher holds up a shopping bag full of groceries.]* I went shopping early this morning and bought several things for our recipe. What do I have in the bag? Let's see. *[Teacher lifts an object out of the bag.]* Oh, I have here an apple, an apple. What color is the apple? [A student responds "red."] Yes, it's red, and delicious, too. Some apples are green but this one is red. Apples are good for our health. How many of you like apples? *[Teacher asks for a show of hands or takes individual responses.]* OK. I usually bring an apple in my lunch once or twice a week. *[Teacher lifts another item out of the bag.]* Class, is this an apple—yes or no? *[Class responds "no."]* No, it's not an apple, but it is a type of fruit. It's an orange. What color is it? *[A student responds "orange."]* Yes, it's orange and the apple is.... *[Class responds "red."]* Oranges are also good for you; they have a lot of vitamin C. *[Teacher holds the apple in one hand and the orange in the other.]* I like to snack on oranges at home. Point to the apple. Now point to the orange. *[The teacher goes up to several students and has them point to the fruit.]* Which is this? *[Students identify the name of the fruit.]*...

? What makes the input comprehensible in this TPR example?

This type of discussion continues with the remainder of the items in the bag until students have demonstrated some degree of acquisition and the ability to name the items in the target language. During a TPR lesson, it is important for the teacher to present the items one at a time and return to the previous items presented so that students can gradually acquire the words. If the teacher rushes through the presentation without proper "build-up," students will not be able to remember the words.

At the conclusion of the lesson, the teacher might show students the written names of the items so that they can associate the oral language they acquired with the written representations. They might copy the words from the board or overhead projector into their notebooks. It is important that the teacher not show students the written words before or during the TPR lesson so that acquisition of oral language may occur. If students see the words first, they will tend not to acquire the oral forms but rather just read the written forms. Students will pronounce new words more accurately if they acquire them orally first, since they will acquire what they hear—which will minimize the likelihood that they will project their L1 pronunciation onto L2 words that they read.

The teacher might also engage students in the following activities to further facilitate acquisition of the new words:

- numbering drawings of foods according to the order in which the teacher says them
- drawing and labeling their favorite foods
- matching labels of the words to visual representations of the foods
- coloring drawings of the foods according to the teacher's verbal instructions
- playing games that incorporate the food vocabulary
- singing songs that incorporate the food vocabulary
- identifying pictures of the foods in an authentic TL advertisement (with prices)
- making lists of food items that need to be purchased for a party, meal, etc.
- conducting surveys of which foods their classmates like/don't like, eat regularly, etc.
- making posters with labeled drawing of the food pyramid, authentic dishes from the target cultures, etc.

Note that many of these vocabulary activities involve interaction with peers. A recent study has revealed the positive impact that peer collaboration can have on the acquisition of L2 vocabulary. Kim (2008) found that students who had opportunities to work with peers on tasks performed significantly better on vocabulary tests and resolved their linguistic problems more effectively through peer assistance than they could by working alone. Chapter 8 will discuss more fully the role of collaboration in acquiring language and developing proficiency.

In sum, vocabulary acquisition can be facilitated if learners encounter new vocabulary in meaningful contexts and if they work collaboratively with peers to use the vocabulary for meaningful purposes.

Literacy: From Interpretive Listening to Reading and Writing

At the elementary school level, interpretive listening is used as the vehicle through which students first begin to acquire language. Many studies show the benefits of providing an initial period of instruction in which students listen to input without being forced to respond in the target language, through strategies such as TPR (Postovsky, 1974; Winitz & Reeds, 1973). Such a "comprehension before production" stage allows students to mentally associate input with meaning and instills the self-confidence necessary for producing language (Terrell, 1986). However, younger learners need to move quickly beyond this comprehension stage and begin to produce output within meaningful tasks and contexts.

In Chapter 2, you learned ways to contextualize language instruction by presenting an initial authentic oral or written segment. At the elementary school level, teachers use children's stories within age-appropriate contexts to provide an integrated-skills approach to L2 acquisition and development of literacy skills. Oral language provides the basis for reading in both the first and second language. Meaningful reading experiences in first- and second language classrooms depend on students' ability to comprehend what they hear and on their background knowledge and experiences (Curtain & Dahlberg, 2010). Students who have learned to read in their native language transfer these skills (e.g., decoding a word, identifying the main idea, discriminating between fact and opinion) to the new language (Cloud, Genessee, & Hamayan, 2000). See Curtain and Dahlberg (2010) for first steps to take in teaching young learners to read and write in the TL.

According to Curtain and Dahlberg (2010, in press), "narrative structure is emerging as one of the most valuable of all teaching tools." The human brain is "wired" for narratives and the emotional element of story form makes them memorable. Storytelling can develop interpretive abilities, even at very early stages of acquisition, especially when the story (1) is highly predictable or familiar to children from their native language, (2) is repetitive, (3) lends itself to dramatization and pantomime, and (4) lends itself to use of visuals and realia to illustrate meaning (Curtain & Dahlberg, 2004). The teacher tells the story a number of times over an extended period of time (without resorting to English), while also showing pictures and using gestures and mime to demonstrate meaning. After students hear the story numerous times, they are then involved through TPR and acting out story parts. Story mapping may be used to help students recall and visually organize the central theme and main components of a story setting, as well as the problem, characters, events, solution, and ending (Heimlich & Pittelman, 1986). See Appendix 4.10 on the *Teacher's*

www.cengagebrain.com

Handbook Web site for a sample story map. Students can begin to write at the word level by labeling visuals of story characters or scenes, completing graphs or charts, making a list of actions; at the sentence level by writing captions for story scenes, creating journal entries, describing story characters; and at the paragraph level by summarizing the story and describing story scenes. Teachers should realize that, for young learners, literacy in writing should involve more than labeling and copying. Writing should require children to make choices and have options concerning what they want to express. For example, they should learn to combine and recombine written familiar words in personal ways and keep personal vocabulary logs that they can refer to when completing writing tasks (R. Donato, personal communication, June 23, 2008).

Children's literature from the countries where the target language is spoken serves as an excellent source for story texts and provides another avenue for integrating culture into the program. In addition to helping students experience culture, authentic literature can serve as the foundation for a whole-language curriculum and appeals to children in Egan's (1979) mythic stage of learning, as described earlier. Pesola (1991) suggests the use of both folktales and contemporary children's literature in the elementary school classroom. Folktales, which present cultural information and describe solutions to human challenges, make effective stories since they come from a culture's oral tradition. Contemporary children's literature lets young students identify with the feelings and moral challenges faced by story characters (Pesola).[5]

One of the ways in which the transition to reading from hearing a story or attending to other oral input is made is through the use of the Language Experience Approach. This technique uses previously learned oral language as the basis for practicing reading and writing skills. The context is an experience that is shared by the class, such as a field trip, story, film, or cultural experience. This approach features the following steps: (1) the teacher provides target language input that describes the shared experience, in a top-down fashion as described in Chapter 2; (2) the teacher checks comprehension through TPR and questions requiring one-word and then longer responses; (3) students retell the story or experience with the teacher's help as the teacher writes their account on large "language experience chart" paper (lined paper on an easel); (4) students copy this version into their notebooks; and (5) this permanent record is used for a variety of reading and writing tasks (Allen, 1970; Hall, 1970; Hansen-Krening, 1982).

The Language Experience Approach exemplifies the ZPD since it is an activity in which the expert allows novices to set their own learning agendas, and it fosters reciprocal learning in which novices work toward their potential developmental level by interacting with the teacher and more capable peers. The technique has been used with success by both first- and second language learners (Dixon & Nessel, 1983). It is particularly helpful for poor readers, who benefit from the progression from listening and speaking (while experiencing) to reading and writing.

You will learn more about interpretive listening and reading in Chapter 6 and interpersonal and presentational writing in Chapter 9.

Interpersonal Communication: Cooperative Learning

It is important to recall that interpersonal communication is two-way communication while presentational communication is one-way communication to an audience of listeners or readers. The elementary school teacher uses a repertoire of techniques for actively involving children in communicating with one another. Through cooperative learning, in which students interact with one another in pairs and small groups in order to accomplish a task together, opportunities for using the target language are significantly increased. Research on cooperative learning by Johnson and Johnson (1987) suggests that the benefits of group and pair work include higher retention and achievement, development of interpersonal skills and responsibility, and heightened self-esteem and creativity. Cooperative learning is most successful when students depend on one another, participate in face-to-face interaction, take responsibility for the skills being learned by the group, use appropriate social skills (following directions, asking for help, taking turns), and analyze what is working and not working in the group activity. Curtain and Dahlberg (2004) suggest that students assume roles such as the following when participating in a cooperative learning activity:

- *Encourager/Praiser* ensures that group members perform well and stay on task.
- *Manager/Timekeeper/Supervisor/Checker* organizes the group, keeps the group on task, makes sure everyone contributes.
- *Recorder/Secretary* records group answers.
- *Spokesperson/Speaker/Reporter* reports back to the whole class (p. 100).

Through cooperative learning, students interact with one another in pairs and small groups in order to accomplish a task together.

Examples of cooperative learning activities that promote interpersonal communication are paired interviews, information-gap activities, jigsaw activities, and interviews or surveys (see Chapter 8 for explanations of these activities and examples). In planning for cooperative learning tasks, the teacher should consider the following: (1) the source of the message(s) to be exchanged (Is there an information gap or reason for students to want to know the information?); (2) the appropriate target language vocabulary and grammar required to complete the activity; (3) the product that results from the activity and how it will be shared or evaluated; (4) how the language will be guided, controlled, or scaffolded; (5) how partners or group members will take turns; (6) how students will find out whether they have been successful; (7) how the teacher will follow up on the activity in a communicative way; (8) how the activity can be extended for groups that finish early; and (9) the plan for a student who does not have a partner (Curtain & Dahlberg, 2010). See Chapter 8 for more information regarding group/pair activities as well as the role of collaboration in cooperative learning. See Curtain & Dahlberg and Lipton (1998) for numerous examples of cooperative learning activities as well as other strategies used to promote oral interpersonal communication and hands-on learning, such as the use of games, finger plays, puppets, and role play.

Presentational Speaking

Detailed information about presentational speaking and writing is featured in Chapters 8 and 9, together with specific strategies for integrating presentational communication into instruction. An effective avenue for encouraging presentational speaking at the elementary school level is through the performance of skits and dramatic songs. Presentations and performances are often used as culminating activities for a thematic unit. Examples include plays; performances of authentic songs, accompanied by culturally appropriate instruments; small-group presentations of scenes from an authentic story; puppet shows; PowerPoint presentations; short skits; and videotaped productions of "how-to" shows. Student interest in presentations is greatly heightened if students can perform for an audience. Students might perform for other classes, school assemblies, special classroom programs, and parent-teacher organization meetings (Curtain and Dahlberg, 2004).

Learning Through Culture

Culture is a key component in a content-based elementary school language program, since it is integrated with all subjects in the curriculum. The next chapter introduces the Cultures goal area of the *SFLL* and presents some strategies for engaging students, including those in elementary school, in exploring the products, practices, and perspectives of the target cultures. Pesola (1991) suggests that students explore cultural perspectives through the study of (1) cultural products such as traditional stories and legends, folk arts, visual arts and artists, musical arts and composers, and realia such as currency, coins, and stamps; and (2) cultural practices such as forms of greeting, use of gestures, recreational activities, home and school life, types of pets and attitudes toward pets, and how children and families move from place to place.

As described earlier in this chapter, the use of authentic literature can be an effective way to introduce many elements of cultural heritage in the classroom. The teaching of thematic units such as "Nutrition" or "Holidays" also provides the opportunity to present visual materials that show certain characteristics of the target culture—photographs, magazine pictures, and realia obtained from the target culture are rich in cultural information.

Pesola (1991) suggests the following activities for integrating culture within the elementary school content areas:

- Social Studies: For display create banners or other items that reflect symbols used for the target city; celebrate an important holiday in the target city, preferably one that is not celebrated locally, or at least not celebrated in the same way.
- Mathematics and Science: Apply the concepts of shapes and symmetry to the folk arts and other visual arts from the target culture; use catalogs from the target culture for problem-solving mathematics activities involving budgeting and shopping.
- Art and Music: Replicate authentic crafts from the target culture in classroom art activities; incorporate typical rhythms from the target culture in the development of chants and rhymes to reinforce new vocabulary and concepts (pp. 341–343).

See Pesola (1991) for other ideas on ways to integrate culture with these content areas.

Just as acquiring a language means more than knowing about its linguistic system, understanding another culture involves more than learning facts about it. Rosenbusch (1992b) suggests the development of *global units* to help elementary school students develop a global perspective and deeper awareness of key issues in the target culture. For example, she describes a global unit called "Housing," in which students compare housing in the native and target cultures through activities such as viewing and discussing slide presentations and making drawings, graphs, and housing models to illustrate similarities and differences.

Students can also gain a deeper awareness of the target culture by role playing authentic situations or participating in "fantasy experiences" (Curtain & Dahlberg, 2010, in press). For example, Curtain and Dahlberg describe an airplane fantasy experience in which children pretend that they are taking a trip, acting out each phase from checking baggage to finding their seats to landing. A truly integrated elementary school program carefully connects language and culture and provides many opportunities for students to learn about the culture through contextualized instruction and meaningful interaction.

 Global units help elementary school students develop a global perspective and deeper awareness of key issues in the target culture.

Contextualized Performance Assessment

Current approaches to assessment emphasize standards-based, contextualized, and performance-based assessment and the development of multiple forms of assessment administered in an ongoing manner (see Chapter 11 for further discussion). In performance-based assessments, learners use their repertoire of knowledge and skills to create a product or a response, either individually or collaboratively (Liskin-Gasparro, 1996). The focus on performance is one that relates well with the hands-on nature of the elementary school language program. Wiggins (1992) offers the following suggestions concerning the design of performance assessment tasks:

- Contextualize the task. Provide rich contextual detail.
- Aim to design "meaningful" tasks that are interesting to the learner and relevant/practical.
- Design performances, not drills. Performance is not about desired bits of knowledge, but about "putting it all together."
- Refine the tasks you design by building them backwards from the models and scoring criteria. Students should know the target and the standard in advance (as cited in Curtain & Dahlberg, 2010, in press).

In addition, when assessing students' achievement of material covered, it is a good idea to test what has been taught in the way it has been taught and to use the test primarily as a vehicle for discovering what children *know* and *can do*, as opposed to what they don't know and can't do (Curtain & Dahlberg, 2010).

The elementary school language curriculum uses both *formative assessments* (e.g., those that are administered throughout the year, are integrated into the teaching and learning process, and serve to inform and change instructional practices), and *summative assessments* (e.g., those that occur at the end of a course or at instructional benchmarks, such as after the first 3 years of instruction, in order to determine what the learner can do with language at a specific point in the language program). Both types of assessments should play a key role in the elementary program in order to verify achievement in an ongoing manner, provide feedback to students and parents, track long-term progress in terms of proficiency goals, provide information to teachers so that improvements in instruction can be made, and obtain data that can be used to evaluate the program.

Below are some examples of formative assessments, which may easily integrate culture and/or content in an effort to assess within meaningful contexts. It is important to select assessment tasks that:

1. suit the characteristics of young learners; see the characteristics of elementary and middle school learners presented earlier in this chapter;
2. assess the abilities that children need to be successful in their language learning;
3. give children the opportunity to show their best performance; and
4. engage children intellectually (McKay, 2006, pp. 109–111).

Interpretive Listening and Reading:

- Students respond to TPR commands.
- Students respond to "listen (read)-and-do" tasks, such as drawing or building things (McKay).
- Students select a visual or object to match an oral or written description.
- Students listen to or read a narrative and number pictures or put them in order.
- Students complete true-false, matching, fill-in-the-blank, or short response items to demonstrate comprehension of an oral or printed text.
- Students read (listen) and retell what they have read (heard) (McKay).
- Students create short oral or written summaries of stories heard or texts read.

Interpersonal Speaking:

- Students enact spontaneous role plays in pairs.
- Students converse with the teacher or respond to questions on familiar topics.
- Students discuss a familiar topic or a cultural/subject-content concept with the teacher and/or with one another.
- Students ask classmates questions about familiar topics and respond to their classmates' questions, taking multiple turns to do so in order for negotiation of meaning to be possible.

Presentational Speaking and Writing:

- Students create and present skits, plays, or puppet shows to an audience.
- Students describe a picture, objects, realia, etc., in oral or written form, or create a story about it.
- Students give an oral or written monologue or narration.
- Students tell a story with the use of visuals or a story book.
- Students fill in speech bubbles in a cartoon story (McKay).
- Students write short compositions, friendly letters, or notes on a familiar topic.

Note that rubrics may be used effectively to assess many of the tasks described above. They will be discussed in Chapter 11.

Appendix 4.11 on the *Teacher's Handbook* Web site illustrates an early language learning summative program assessment that might be administered to individual students at the end of the elementary school sequence, such as in grades 4 or 5.[6] The following are several examples of summative assessments, which use the criteria of the *ACTFL Performance Guidelines for K–12 Learners* (American Council on the Teaching of Foreign Languages [ACTFL], 1998) and the *ACTFL Proficiency Guidelines* (ACTFL, 1982, 1999, 2001) to assess students' performance holistically.

- Student Oral Proficiency Assessment (SOPA) and Early Language Listening and Oral Proficiency Assessment (ELLOPA): Developed by the Center for Applied Linguistics (CAL) (2008), these language proficiency assessment instruments elicit younger learners' highest level of performance in oral fluency, grammar, vocabulary, and listening comprehension. The SOPA is appropriate for learners in grades 2–8, and the ELLOPA is for learners in grades PreK–2. These interactive listening and speaking assessments feature hands-on activities and are conducted entirely in the foreign language. Students are assessed in pairs by two trained test administrators and, during the activities or tasks, are encouraged to interact with each other as well as with the interviewers.

- Center for Applied Linguistics Oral Proficiency Exam (COPE): Designed by CAL (2008) for learners enrolled in immersion programs in grades 5–8, this assessment consists of an oral interview/role play with two students at a time. The COPE measures a student's ability to understand, speak, and be understood by others in a second language. The test assesses cognitive-academic language skills (ability to discuss subject matter effectively, e.g., social studies, geography, and science) as well as social language (ability to discuss family, leisure-time activities, etc.).[7]

- Pittsburgh Public Schools Oral Ratings Assessment for Language Students (PPS ORALS): The PPS ORALS is a summative program assessment based on the OPI and the Center for Applied Linguistics Simulated Oral Proficiency Interview (SOPI) (Stansfield & Kenyon, 1992; 1996). It is an online testing program that makes large-scale oral testing feasible, as well as easy to create, administer, and rate (Fall, Adair-Hauck, & Glisan, 2007). See Chapter 11 for a full discussion of this assessment.

- Integrated Performance Assessment (IPA)[8]: The IPA (Adair-Hauck, Glisan, Koda, Swender, & Sandrock, 2006; Glisan, Adair-Hauck, Koda, Sandrock, & Swender, 2003) is designed to measure student progress in attaining the competencies described in *SFLL* and the *ACTFL Performance Guidelines for K–12 Learners*. The IPA provides opportunities for students to demonstrate the ability to communicate within a specific content area or context (e.g., "Famous Person" or "Your Health") across the three modes of communication. It is structured so that students first complete an interpretive task, then use the information learned to perform an oral interpersonal task, and finally use the information from both tasks to complete a presentational activity (either oral or written). Rubrics guide the students' task completion as well as how to score the performance. See Chapter 11 for a more detailed discussion of the IPA.

In this section, you have explored ways to use the theoretical concepts about early language learning in order to plan thematic units and lessons; integrate content-based instruction; help students to organize content; facilitate vocabulary acquisition; develop literacy skills, interpersonal communication, and presentational speaking; help students to learn through cultural exploration; and assess students' performance. In the next section, you will see how the Connections goal area and *SFLL* might serve as the impetus for enabling students to acquire new information from other disciplines in the target language.

STANDARDS HIGHLIGHT: Making CONNECTIONS Between Language and the Elementary School Curriculum

The Connections Goal Area

The benefits of linking language and content have been explored in Chapter 3 and earlier in this chapter. The Connections goal area of the standards states that students should be able to "connect with other disciplines and acquire information" (NSFLEP, 2006, p. 53). The two Connections standards are the following:

- Students reinforce and further their knowledge of other disciplines through the foreign language.
- Students acquire information and recognize the distinctive viewpoints that are only available through the foreign language and its cultures (NSFLEP, pp. 54, 56).

When combined with other disciplines, knowledge of another language and culture shifts the focus from language acquisition alone to broader learning experiences. Students deepen their understanding of other subjects while they enhance their communicative skills and cultural awareness. Furthermore, as students learn a foreign language, they gain greater access to sources of information and a "new window on the world" (NSFLEP, p. 56). The foreign language can be used as the vehicle for acquiring new knowledge.

Connections enable students to further their knowledge of other disciplines, acquire new information, and recognize the distinctive viewpoints that are available only through the foreign language and its cultures.

Implications of the Connections Standards on Instruction

Teachers who begin to experiment with making connections with other areas of the curriculum should start with a simple connection, such as addressing one small content piece of another subject (e.g., art, music, social studies, math). In lower levels of instruction, the foreign language teacher might continue the presentation of content introduced in science, mathematics, and social studies. For example, students in a science class might continue to explore weather, seasons, and temperatures in the foreign language class (NSFLEP, 2006). At various levels of instruction, students might read authentic documentation in the foreign language to support topics being explored (e.g., autobiographical accounts of historical figures, achievements of artists and musicians). These types of connections can be made by means of the thematic or interdisciplinary unit. In addition, the teacher might team teach a language course or a portion of it with a teacher from another subject area (e.g., history and foreign language). Also, individuals with language expertise who reside in the community might be invited to give presentations on certain content areas (e.g., art, music).

A recent endeavor that addresses the Connections standards is Global Learning and Observations to Benefit the Environment (GLOBE), a worldwide network of students and teachers representing over 18,000 schools in more than 100 countries. GLOBE students collect atmospheric, hydrologic, geologic, and biometric data from their schools' study site and report their scientific data to GLOBE and NASA/NOAA scientists via the Internet (Kennedy, 2006). This program provides an excellent foundation for interdisciplinary and content-based study and a vehicle for learning a foreign language while studying science, mathematics, social studies, and technology. Since GLOBE manuals and materials are available in various foreign languages, language teachers have access to content curriculum that can be easily incorporated in their classrooms.[9]

As students become more proficient in the target language, they can be expected to take more responsibility for acquisition of knowledge in areas of interest to them. They can find materials of interest, analyze the content, compare it to information available in their own language, and compare the linguistic and cultural characteristics (NSFLEP, 2006, p. 56). For example, students might research fashion, cars, music, art, and other topics of meaning and interest to them. In this way, teachers and students can be co-investigators, acquiring new information together. The teacher acts as a coach, helping students to select materials and to interpret language appropriately; students become the content experts.

As you have seen in this chapter, there are many reasons to begin foreign language study in the elementary grades. Younger learners bring a unique learning capacity and enthusiasm to the language classroom. Beginning language learning in the elementary grades ensures a long sequence of instruction, which is extremely important in developing language proficiency and cultural understanding. This chapter has presented a variety of strategies for addressing the standards in instruction in the elementary grades and for developing a hands-on approach in which younger learners are actively involved in and excited about learning another language.

TEACH AND REFLECT ·

EPISODE ONE
Designing a Content-Based Elementary School Lesson

ACTFL/NCATE 2.c. Integrating Other Disciplines in Instruction; 3.a. Understanding Language Acquisition and Creating a Supportive Classroom; 4.b. Integrating Standards in Instruction

TESOL/NCATE 3.a. Planning for Standards-Based ESL and Content Instruction; 3.b. Managing and Implementing Standards-Based ESL and Content Instruction

Design a content-based lesson that addresses a subject-content learning objective for grade 1. You may choose ONE of the following learning objectives or design your own:

- Grade 1 Mathematics: The student will identify halves, thirds, and fourths of a region or set.
- Grade 1 Science: The student will classify objects by size, shape, and color.
- Grade 1 Science: The student will make accurate observations using the senses.

(Adapted from Curtain & Dahlberg, 1994, pp. 407–419)

Assume that your lesson is 30 minutes in length and that this is the first day spent on this topic. Use the lesson plan format presented in Chapter 3, being sure to include both content-obligatory and content-compatible language objectives, as described earlier in this chapter and as exemplified in Appendix 4.6. Plan your presentation and two or three student activities. As you plan the lesson, keep in mind the following guidelines:

- Design a lesson that is appropriate, given the developmental characteristics of your students.
- Present oral language before written language.
- Involve students in hands-on activities from the start of the lesson.
- Do not lecture or overwhelm students with information they do not understand. They learn by being involved actively.
- Use the target language. Make yourself understood by using realia, gestures, and mime.
- Check comprehension often through TPR or short-response questions.

Your instructor may ask you to present part of this lesson to the class.

Next, write a paragraph explaining how you would adapt this grade 1 lesson for a grade four class. You might find it helpful to refer back to the description of intermediate students on page 113.

EPISODE TWO
Developing a Storytelling Lesson

ACTFL/NCATE 2.b. Demonstrating Understanding of Literary and Cultural Texts and Traditions; 3.a. Understanding Language Acquisition and Creating a Supportive Classroom

TESOL/NCATE 2.e. Understand and Apply Concepts about the Interrelationship between Language and Culture; 3.a. Planning for Standards-Based ESL and Content Instruction; 3.b. Managing and Implementing Standards-Based ESL and Content Instruction

www.cengagebrain.com

Design a 10-minute storytelling lesson in which you present a story that is familiar to the children from their native culture (such as "Goldilocks and the Three Bears") or a simple, authentic children's story or folktale (see http://teacher.scholastic.com/products/instructor/multicultural.htm for multicultural stories). Prepare visuals and realia as necessary for depicting meaning. Follow the suggestions given in this chapter for presenting the story orally and incorporating student involvement. Prepare a lesson plan, remembering that this is the first day using the story. Your instructor may ask you to present all or part of your story to the class. Be prepared to discuss how you would use the Language Experience Approach to progress to reading after spending sufficient time working with the oral version of the story.

DISCUSS AND REFLECT ·

www.cengagebrain.com

See the *Teacher's Handbook* Web site for an additional case study:
Case Study Two: Implementing an Elementary School Language Program

CASE STUDY ONE
Teaching Fourth-Grade Content in French

ACTFL/NCATE 2.c. Integrating Other Disciplines In Instruction; 3.a. Understanding Language Acquisition and Creating a Supportive Classroom; 4.b. Integrating Standards In Instruction

TESOL/NCATE 3.a. Planning for Standards-Based ESL and Content Instruction

Amy Guilderson and Georges Arnault have been teaching fourth grade at the elementary school in Milford City for 2 years, ever since they began their teaching careers. Georges is of French descent and grew up speaking French at home. Amy studied French in college and completed a semester-long study abroad experience in France before graduating. She also had a minor in History. Amy enjoys the opportunity to speak French with Georges.

While having lunch together one day, they began talking about integrating some French instruction into their teaching, although their school did not have a French program. Georges had been reading some recent journal articles that presented the idea of combining foreign language and subject-content instruction. They wondered if they could develop a social studies unit that incorporated French. Much to their surprise, when they consulted *SFLL*, they found the following learning scenario that integrates a social studies concept into a fourth-grade French lesson. Since this fit in perfectly with an upcoming social studies unit in their school district curriculum, they decide to try the unit and introduce the teaching of French.

Les Voyageurs: The French *Voyageurs* (elementary)

A study of the colorful and demanding life of the French *voyageurs* and their role in the fur trade provides an excellent complement to the elementary school social studies curriculum. The teacher can introduce the topic in French via videotape (for example, *Les Voyageurs* from the French Canadian Film Society), by reading the French coloring book about the *voyageurs* from the Minnesota Historical Society, or by playing the role of a voyageur himself/herself. Students then learn to describe the clothing worn by the *voyageurs*, discovering as they do which items are European in origin and which are adapted from Native American dress. They also make red *toques*, the woolen caps so readily identified with the *voyageurs*. The students dramatize each facet of the life of the *voyageurs*, including loading the canoe, paddling and singing, portaging, resting, eating pea soup, trading with Native Americans, and dancing at a *rendez-vous*. They also learn to identify and describe the animals hunted for their fur, and they make a map showing the itinerary of the *voyageurs'* travels. Students may also perform a reenactment of the life of the *voyageurs*, including songs and dances, in a presentation for students in other classes and/or for parents (NSFLEP, 2006, pp. 285–286).

Ask yourself these questions:

1. What are some dos and don'ts Amy and Georges should keep in mind as they teach their students this social studies unit?
2. What specific standards are addressed in the learning scenario?
3. How are the three modes of communication integrated into the activities described in the scenario?
4. What are the academic and social benefits of this type of interdisciplinary instruction for fourth graders?

To prepare for class discussion:

1. Imagine that you are Georges or Amy and are planning your first lesson in this social studies unit. What is the content-obligatory language students (language structures, functions, vocabulary) will need to know? What is the content-compatible language you have selected?
2. How might Georges and Amy expand this project so that students receive more content-based instruction in French? How would parents and school administrators be convinced that this plan is both beneficial academically and cost-effective?

www.cengagebrain.com

TECHNO FOCUS: Georges and Amy want to integrate some Native American legends into their social studies project, and they discovered that the media specialist in their school is planning a technology unit with their students. They found a lesson plan online at http://www.nclrc.org/eils/index.html (go to Chapter 5, Fourth Grade, Organize/Plan, Comic Strips). The plan was designed to help learners build strategies for organizing/planning, using French, and focusing on the content area of social studies. Students use technology to create comic strips about folk tales of the Native American cultures that they have already begun to study. Go to the Web site indicated and examine the plan. What elements of CBI do you see in this plan and how can Georges and Amy implement the plan? In what ways does this plan address the Cultures and the Connections standards?

REFERENCES

Adair-Hauck, B., Glisan, E. W., Koda, K., Swender, E., & Sandrock, P. (2006). The Integrated Performance Assessment (IPA): Connecting Assessment to Instruction and Learning. *Foreign Language Annals, 39,* 359–382.

Alkonis, N. V., & Brophy, M. A. (1961). A survey of FLES practice. *Reports and studies in the teaching of modern foreign languages,* 1959–1961 (pp. 213–217). New York: The Modern Language Association of America.

Allen, R. V. (1970). *Language experience in reading.* Chicago: Encyclopaedia Britannica Press.

American Council on the Teaching of Foreign Languages (ACTFL). (1998). *ACTFL performance guidelines for K–12 learners.* Yonkers, NY: Author.

American Council on the Teaching of Foreign Languages (ACTFL). (1982). *ACTFL provisional proficiency guidelines.* Hastings-on-Hudson, NY: Author.

American Council on the Teaching of Foreign Languages (ACTFL). (1999). *ACTFL proficiency guidelines—Speaking.* Yonkers, NY: Author.

American Council on the Teaching of Foreign Languages (ACTFL). (2001). *ACTFL proficiency guidelines—Writing.* Yonkers, NY: Author.

Asher, J. J. (1986). *Learning another language through actions: The complete teachers' guidebook.* Los Gatos, CA: Sky Oaks Publications.

Bialystok, E. (1997). Effects of bilingualism and biliteracy on children's emerging concepts of print. *Developmental Psychology, 33,* 429–440.

Bialystok, E. (2001). *Bilingualism in development: Language, literacy and cognition.* London: Cambridge University Press.

Birdsong, D. (2006). Age and second language acquisition and processing: A selective overview. *Language Learning, 56,* 9–49.

Blanchard, C., & Nelson, S. (2007). The correlation of foreign language instruction on tenth grade MCAS test scores. Franklin, MA: Paper presented at the Conference of the Massachusetts Secondary School Administrators Association.

Caccavale, T. (2007). The correlation between early language learning and native language skill development. *Learning Languages, 13,* pp. 30–32.

Campbell, R. N., Gray, T. C., Rhodes, N. C., & Snow, M. A. (1985). Foreign language learning in the elementary schools: A comparison of three language programs. *The Modern Language Journal, 69,* 44–54.

Carroll, J. B. (1975). *The teaching of French as a foreign language in eight countries.* New York: John Wiley.

Center for Applied Linguistics (2008). *Testing/Assessment: SOPA, ELLOPA, COPE.* Retrieved December 30, 2008, from http://www.cal.org/topics/ta/sopa_ellopa.html.

Chinen, K., Donato, R., Igarashi, K., & Tucker, G. R. (2003). Looking across time: Documenting middle school Japanese FLES students' attitudes, literacy and oral proficiency. *Learning Languages, 8,* 4–10.

Cloud, N., Genessee, F., & Hamayan, E. (2000). *Dual language instruction: A handbook for enriched education.* Boston: Heinle & Heinle.

Clyne, M. (Ed.). (1986). *An early start: Second language at primary school.* Melbourne, Australia: River Seine Publications.

Cummins, J. (1981a). Age on arrival and immigrant second language learning in Canada: A reassessment. *Applied Linguistics, 2,* 132–149.

Cummins, J. (1981b). The role of primary language development in promoting educational success for language minority students. In *Schooling and language minority students: A theoretical framework.* Los Angeles: Evaluation, Dissemination, and Assessment Center, California State University.

Cummins, J. (1992). Empowerment through biliteracy. In J. V. Tinajero & A. F. Ada (Eds.), *The power of two languages: Literacy and biliteracy for Spanish-speaking students* (pp. 9–25). New York, NY: Macmillan/McGraw-Hill.

Cummins, J. (2000). *Language, power and pedagogy: Bilingual children caught in the crossfire.* Clevedon, UK: Multilingual Matters.

Curtain, H., & Dahlberg, C. A. (2000). Planning for success: Common pitfalls in the planning of early foreign planners.

CAL Digests. EDO-FL-00-11. Retrieved June 13, 2008, from http://www.cal.org/resources/Digest/0011planning.html.

Curtain, H., & Dahlberg, C. A. (2004). *Languages and children—Making the match* (3rd ed.). Boston: Pearson Education.

Curtain, H., & Dahlberg, C. A. (2010). *Languages and children—Making the match* (4th ed.). Boston: Pearson Allyn & Bacon.

Curtain, H., & Pesola, C. A. (1994). *Languages and children—Making the match* (2nd ed.). White Plains, NY: Longman.

DeKeyser, R. M. (2000). The robustness of critical period effects in second language acquisition. *Studies in Second Language Acquisition, 22,* 499–533.

Dixon, C., & Nessel, D. (1983). *Language experience approach to reading (and writing): Language experience reading for second language learners.* Hayward, CA: Alemany Press.

Domínguez, R., & Pessoa, S. (2005). Early versus late start in foreign language education: Documenting achievements. *Foreign Language Annals, 38,* 473–483.

Donato, R., Antonek, J. L., & Tucker, G. R. (1994). A multiple perspectives analysis of a Japanese FLES program. *Foreign Language Annals, 27,* 365–378.

Donato, R., Antonek, J. L., & Tucker, G. R. (1996). Documenting a Japanese FLES program: Ambiance and achievement. *Language Learning, 46,* 497–528.

Donato, R., Tucker, G. R., Wudthayagorn, J., & Igarashi, K. (2000). Converging evidence: Attitudes, achievements, and instruction in the later years of FLES. *Foreign Language Annals, 33,* 377–393.

Echevarria, J., Vogt, M., & Short, D. J. (2000, 2004, 2008). *Making content comprehensible for English language learners: The SIOP model.* Boston: Allyn and Bacon.

Egan, K. (1979). *Educational development.* New York: Oxford University Press.

Egan, K. (1992). *Imagination in teaching and learning: The middle school years.* Chicago: University of Chicago Press.

Fall, T., Adair-Hauck, B., & Glisan, E. W. (2007). Assessing students' oral proficiency: A case for online testing. *Foreign Language Annals, 40,* 377–406.

Fortune, T. (2008) A scaffold for writing language objectives using the formula. Retrieved June 12, 2008, from http://www.carla.umn.edu/cobaltt/modules/index.html?curriculum/main.html.

Glisan, E. W., Adair-Hauck, B., Koda, K., Sandrock, S. P., & Swender, E. (2003). *ACTFL integrated performance assessment*. Yonkers, NY: ACTFL.

Glisan, E. W., Dudt, K. P., & Howe, M. S. (1998). Teaching Spanish through distance education: Implications of a pilot study. *Foreign Language Annals, 31,* 48–66.

Hall, M. A. (1970). *Teaching reading as a language experience*. Columbus, OH: Merrill.

Hansen-Krening, N. (1982). *Language experiences for all students*. Reading, MA: Addison-Wesley.

Harley, B., & Wang, W. (1997). The critical period hypothesis: Where are we now? In A. M. B. de Groot & J. F. Kross (Eds.), *Tutorials in bilingualism: Psycholinguistic perspectives* (pp. 19–51). Hillsdale, NJ: Lawrence Erlbaum.

Heimlich, J. E., & Pittelman, S. D. (1986). *Semantic mapping: Classroom applications*. Newark, DE: International Reading Association.

Heining-Boynton, A. L., & Haitema, T. (2007). A ten-year chronicle of student attitudes toward foreign language in the elementary school. *Foreign Language Annals, 91,* 149–168.

Hoch, F. S. (1998). A view from the state level. In M. Met (Ed.), *Critical issues in early second language learning: Building for our children's future* (pp. 5–10). Glenview, IL: Addison-Wesley.

Hoff-Ginsberg, E. (1998). Is there a critical period for language acquisition? In M. Met (Ed.), *Critical issues in early second language learning: Building for our children's future* (pp. 31–36). Glenview, IL: Addison-Wesley.

Howard, E. R., Olague, N., & Rogers, D. (2003). *The dual language program planner: A guide for designing and implementing dual language programs*. Washington, DC, and Santa Cruz, CA: Center for Research on Education, Diversity & Excellence.

Howard, E. R., Sugarman, J., & Coburn, C. (2006). Adapting the Sheltered Instruction Observation Protocol (SIOP) for two-way immersion eduation: An Introduction to the TWIOP. Center for Applied Linguistics. Retrieved June 16, 2008, from http://www.cal.org/twi/twiop.htm.

Howard, E. R., Sugarman, J., Christian, D., Lindholm-Leary, K. J., & Rogers, D. (2007). *Guiding principles for dual language education*. (2nd. ed.) Washington, DC: Center for Applied Linguistics. Retrieved June 2, 2009, from http://www.cal.org/twi/Guiding_Principles/pdf.

Hyltenstam, K. (1992). Non-native features of near-native speakers: On the ultimate attainment of childhood L2 learners. In R. J. Harris (Ed.), *Cognitive processing in bilinguals* (pp. 351–368). Amsterdam: Elsevier Science.

Hyltenstam, K, & Abrahamsson, N. (2003). Maturational constraints in SLA. In C. J. Doughty & M. H. Long (Eds.), *The handbook of second language acquisition* (pp. 539–588). Malden, MA: Blackwell Publishing Ltd.

Igarashi, K. (1997). *Early oral production of child second language learners in a Japanese immersion kindergarten*. Unpublished master's thesis, University of Oregon, Eugene.

Johnson, D., & Johnson, R. (1987). *Learning together and alone: Cooperation, competition, and individualization*. Englewood Cliffs, NJ: Prentice Hall.

Johnson, J., & Newport, E. (1989). Critical period effects in second language learning: The influence of maturational state on the acquisition of English as a second language. *Cognitive Psychology, 21,* 60–99.

Kennedy, T. J. (2006). Language learning and its impact on the brain: Connecting language learning through the mind through content-based instruction. *Foreign Language Annals, 39,* 471–486.

Kennedy, T. J., Nelson, J. K., Odell, M. R. L., & Austin, L. K. (2000). The FLES attitudinal inventory. *Foreign Language Annals, 33,* 278–287.

Kim, Y. (2008). The contribution of collaborative and individual tasks to the acquisition of L2 vocabulary. *The Modern Language Journal, 92,* 114–130.

Krashen, S. D., Long, M. A., & Scarcella, R. C. (1979). Age, rate and eventual attainment in second language acquisition. *TESOL Quarterly, 13,* 573–582.

Lambert, W. E., & Klineberg, O. (1967). *Children's views of foreign people*. New York: Appleton-Century-Crofts.

Lenneberg, E. (1967). *Biological foundations of language*. New York: John Wiley.

Lightbown, P. M., & Spada, N. (2006). *How languages are learned*. Oxford: Oxford University Press.

Lindholm, K. (2000). Biliteracy for a global society: An idea book on dual language instruction. Washington, DC: National Clearinghouse for Bilingual Education.

Lipton, G. C. (1998). *Practical handbook to elementary foreign language programs (FLES*)* (3rd ed.). Lincolnwood, IL: NTC/Contemporary Publishing Group.

Liskin-Gasparro, J. E. (1996). Assessment: From content standards to student performance. In R. C. Lafayette (Ed.), *National standards: A catalyst for reform*. The ACTFL Foreign Language Education Series (pp. 169–196). Lincolnwood, IL: NTC/Contemporary Publishing Group.

Long, M. (1990). *Input, interaction and second language acquisition*. Unpublished doctoral dissertation, University of California at Los Angeles.

Lorenz, E. B., & Met, M. (1989). *Planning for instruction in the immersion classroom*. Rockville, MD: Montgomery County Public Schools.

Martin, E., & Rainey, L. (1993). Student achievement and attitude in a satellite delivered high school science course. *The American Journal of Distance Education, 7,* 54–61.

McKay, P. (2006). *Assessing young language learners*. Cambridge: Cambridge University Press.

Met, M. (1999). Making connections. In J. K. Phillips & R. M. Terry (Eds.), *Foreign language standards: Linking research, theories, and practice* (pp. 137–164). Lincolnwood, IL: National Textbook Company.

Montás, M. (2003). Observing progress and achievement of beginning students in a fourth-grade Spanish FLES program. *Learning Languages, 9,* 8–20.

Moore, M., & Thompson, M. (1997). The effects of distance learning. American Center for the Study of Distance Education. *Research Monograph, 15.*

Morrison, S. H. (1995). A Spanish-English dual language program in New York City. *Annals of the American Academy of Political & Social Science, 508,* 160–169.

Muuss, R. (1982). Social cognition: Robert Selman's theory of role taking. *Adolescence, 17*(65), 499–525.

National Council of State Supervisors for Languages. (2008). *NCSSFL position statement on distance learning in foreign languages.* Retrieved June 11, 2008, from http://www.ncssfl.org/papers/index.php?distancelearning.

National Dual Language Consortium (NDLC). (2008). National Dual Language Consortium Web site. Retrieved June 13, 2008, from http://www.dual language.org/index.htm.

National Security Language Initiative. (2006). Fact sheet. Washington, DC: U.S. Department of State. Retrieved June 13, 2008, from http://www.state.gov/r/pa/prs/ps/2006/58733.htm.

National Standards in Foreign Language Education Project (NSFLEP). (2006). *Standards for foreign language learning in the 21st century (SFLL).* Lawrence, KS: Allen Press.

Newport, E. L. (1990). Maturational constraints on language learning. *Cognitive Science, 14,*11–28.

Patkowski, M. (1990). Age and accent in a second language: A reply to James Emir Flege. *Applied Linguistics, 11,* 73–89.

Pennsylvania State Modern Language Association (PSMLA). (2003). *PSMLA standards and guide to assessment: What to teach and how to test it!* PSMLA.

Pesola, C. A. (1991). Culture in the elementary school foreign language classroom. *Foreign Language Annals, 24,* 331–346.

Pesola, C. A. (1995). *Background, design, and evaluation of a conceptual framework for FLES curriculum.* Unpublished Ph.D. dissertation. University of Minnesota, Minneapolis, MN.

Pessoa, S., Hendry, H., Donato, R., Tucker, G. R., & Lee, H. (2007). Content-based instruction in the foreign language classroom: A discourse perspective. *Foreign Language Annals, 40,* 102–121.

Postovsky, V. (1974). Effects of delay in oral practice at the beginning of second language learning. *The Modern Language Journal, 58,* 5–6.

Rafferty, E. (1986). *Second language study and basic skills in Louisiana.* Baton Rouge, LA: Louisiana Department of Education.

Rhodes, N. (1985). *Elementary school foreign language program goals.* Washington, DC: Center for Applied Linguistics.

Robinson, D. W. (1998). The cognitive, academic, and attitudinal benefits of early language learning. In M. Met (Ed.), *Critical issues in early second language learning: Building for our children's future* (pp. 37–43). Glenview, IL: Addison-Wesley.

Rosenbusch, M. H. (1992a). *Colloquium on foreign languages in the elementary school curriculum. Proceedings 1991.* Munich: Goethe Institut.

Rosenbusch, M. H. (1992b). Is knowledge of cultural diversity enough? Global education in the elementary school foreign language program. *Foreign Language Annals, 25,* 129–136.

Rosenbusch, M. H. (1995). Language learners in the elementary school: Investing in the future. In R. Donato, & R. M. Terry (Eds.), *Foreign language learning: The journey of a lifetime.* The ACTFL Foreign Language Education Series (pp. 1–36). Lincolnwood, IL: NTC/Contemporary Publishing Group.

Saunders, C. M. (1998). *The effect of the study of a foreign language in the elementary school on the scores on the Iowa test of basic skills and an analysis of student-participant attitudes and abilities.* Athens, GA: University of Georgia.

Schacter, J. (1996). Maturation and the issue of universal grammar in second language acquisition. In W. C. Ritchie and T. K. Bhatia (Eds.), *Handbook of Second Language Acquisition* (pp. 159–193). San Diego, CA: Academic Press..

Scovel, T. (1999). 'The younger the better' myth an bilingual education. In R. D. Gonzalez & I. Melis (Eds.). *Language ideologies: Critical perspectives on the English only movement.* Urbana, IL: National Council of Teachers of English.

Snow, C., & Hoefnagel-Höhle, M. (1978). The critical age for language acquisition: Evidence from second language learning. *Child Development, 49,* 1114–1128.

Stansfield, C. W., & Kenyon, D. M. (1992). The development and validation of a simulated oral proficiency interview. *The Modern Language Journal, 76,* 129–41.

Stansfield, C. W., & Kenyon, D. M. (1996). Simulated oral proficiency interviews: An update. *ERIC Digest.* Washington, DC: Center for Applied Linguistics.

Swender, E., & Duncan, G. (1998). ACTFL performance guidelines for K–12 learners. *Foreign Language Annals, 31,* 479–491.

Taylor, G., Feyten, C., Meros, J., & Nutta, J. (2008). Effects of FLES on reading comprehension and vocabulary achievement: A multi-method longitudinal study. *Learning Languages, 13,* 30–37.

Taylor-Ward, C. (2003). *The relationship between elementary foreign language students in grades three through five and academic achievement on the Iowa test of basic skills (ITBS) and fourth grade Louisiana educational assessment program for the 21st century (LEAP21) test.* Baton Rouge, LA: Louisiana State University, Department of Curriculum and Instruction.

Teachers of English to Speakers of Other Languages (TESOL). (2006). *PreK–12 English language proficiency standards.* Alexandria, VA: Author.

Terrell, T. D. (1986). Recent trends in research and practice: Teaching Spanish. *Hispania, 68,* 193–202.

Thompson, E. (1991). Foreign accents revisited: The English pronunciation of Russian immigrants. *Language Learning, 41,* 177–204.

Torres-Guzmán, M. E. (2002). Dual language programs: Key features and results. *Directions in Language and Education, 14.* National Clearinghouse for Bilingual Education. Retrieved June 11, 2008, from http://www.ncela.gwu.edu/pubs/directions/14.pdf.

Tucker, G. R., Donato, R., & Antonek, J. L. (1996). Documenting growth in a Japanese FLES program. *Foreign Language Annals, 29,* 539–550.

U. S. Department of Defense. (2005). Defense Language Transformation Roadmap. Retrieved June 11, 2008, from http://www.globalsecurity.org/military/library/policy/dod/d20050330roadmap.pdf.

Vygotsky, L. (1962). *Thought and language.* Cambridge, MA: MIT Press.

Wiggins, G. (1992). Creating tests worth taking. *Educational Leadership, 49,* 26–33.

Winitz, H., & Reeds, J. (1973). Rapid acquisition of a foreign language by the avoidance of speaking. *International Review of Applied Linguistics, 11,* 295–317.

NOTES

1. See the *Teacher's Handbook* Web site for the link to the National Network for Early Language Learning (NNELL), an organization that provides leadership in support of successful early language learning and teaching. This organization offers a wealth of information, resources, and professional development opportunities to its members.

2. For two exceptions, see Campbell, Gray, Rhodes, and Snow (1985) and Clyne (1986).

3. See Donato, Antonek, and Tucker (1994, 1996) and Tucker, Donato, and Antonek (1996) for earlier reports on this study.

4. Lipton (1998) uses the term FLES* to refer in general to any type of foreign language instruction in elementary and middle schools.

5. See Chapter 5 for the use of children's literature in a middle school setting.

6. For examples of standards-based language assessments, see Pennsylvania State Modern Language Association (PSMLA), 2003.

7. Training for the SOPA, ELLOPA, and COPE is available through the Center for Applied Linguistics (http://www.cal.org). It is also offered at language conferences and available to school districts upon request.

8. IPA training and manual are available upon request from ACTFL.

9. See Kennedy (2006) for additional details of the GLOBE program.

Integrating Cultures and Comparisons into Middle School Language Instruction

In this chapter, you will learn about:

- the definition of middle school
- the middle level learner
- No Child Left Behind Act (NCLB)
- middle level programs
- sequential vs. exploratory language programs
- classroom management
- Cultures and Comparisons Standards

- the three Ps: practices, products, perspectives
- Kluckhohn Method
- Byram's Intercultural Communication
- sample thematic units
- assessment of middle school performance

Teach and Reflect: Developing Culture-Specific Examples of the Three Ps; Unit and Lesson Design Around a Story, Myth, or Folktale; Viewing and Analyzing Lessons on the Three Ps

Discuss and Reflect: It's McLicious! Staying in the Target Language

CONCEPTUAL ORIENTATION

Current emphasis on teaching language at the middle school level is due in part to two factors: (1) a growing change in approach to teaching 11- to 13.5-year-old learners, and (2) an attempt to begin language learning experiences as early as possible so that students benefit from a longer, uninterrupted period of language study. By 1993, a variety of configurations of schools between grades 5 and 9 had been defined by these perspectives:

- Purpose: Developmentally responsive to the needs of young adolescents;
- Uniqueness: A unique autonomous unit, separate from the elementary school and the high school;
- Organization: Includes the grade levels with the largest number of students who are becoming adolescents;
- Curriculum and instruction: Content is connected to everyday lives of students and instruction actively involves them in learning (adapted from Clark & Clark, 1994).

Currently, the most popular grade-level configuration includes grades 6–8, but other models do exist. Research shows that grade level configuration does not determine effectiveness (Johnston, 1984; National Middle School Association [NMSA], 2003). Recognizing that middle school learners are actively involved in maturing as well as in learning, the NMSA recommends a curriculum that is relevant, challenging, integrative, and exploratory to be delivered in a climate of high expectations. It should enable learners to "pursue answers to questions they have about themselves, content, and the world" (2005, p. 1). According to Nerenz, "Good middle level education allows students to experience old things in new ways and entirely new fields of learning in varied ways" (1990, p. 95).

A middle school concept generally presumes the presence of five components that have been empirically recognized as beneficial to middle level learners by educators, associations, foundations, state boards of education, and researchers:

1. interdisciplinary teaming, consisting of two to five team members in two, three, or four subject areas whose schedules allow them to plan and collaborate on interdisciplinary lessons;
2. advisory programs that consist of a small group of students (usually 20 or fewer) assigned to a teacher, administrator, or other staff member for a regularly scheduled meeting to discuss topics of concern to students;
3. varied instruction integrating learning experiences, addressing students' own questions, focusing upon real-life issues relevant to the student; actively engaging students in problem solving and accommodating individual differences; emphasizing collaboration, cooperation, and community; seeking to develop good people, caring for others, democratic values, and moral sensitivity;
4. programs that capitalize on the innate curiosity of young adolescents, exposing them to a range of academic, vocational, and recreational subjects for career options, community service, enrichment, and enjoyment;
5. transition programs that focus on creating a smooth change of schools for the young adolescent (adapted from the NMSA, 2003).

 "Good middle level education allows students to experience old things in new ways and entirely new fields of learning in varied ways."

The Middle Level Learner

Social Aspects

Eichhorn (1966) termed learners ages 11 to 13.5 as *transescents*. Middle school children are different from elementary and high school learners because of the many physical, cognitive, and emotional changes that happen to them within a short period of time.

Middle school learners are a diverse student group. As Mead maintains, they are "more unlike each other than they have ever been before or ever will be again in the course of their lives" (1965, p. 10). Rapidly occurring physical changes often accompany periods of restlessness and variable attention span (Nerenz, 1990). As Martin states, "Young adolescent students may have alternating periods of high energy and listlessness. They may need to squirm and move around, and may need to vent energy through physical exercise" (1993, pp. S-24). Middle level learners are aware of their physiological changes and become preoccupied with self-image. Nerenz suggests that these feelings often make students sensitive to typical classroom discussions concerning physical descriptions, daily routines with reflexive verbs, comparisons of clothing sizes, and other similar topics that refer to appearance.

Egan (1979) characterizes middle school students as being in the *"romantic"* stage of development, since they enjoy knowledge for its own sake, and bring a great deal of curiosity to the classroom. They have begun to develop a sense of their own identities within the bigger world; they seek out the limits of the real world, exploring its challenges that are beyond daily living, such as nobility, courage, genius, energy, or creativity (Curtain & Dahlberg, 2010). Though they are curious about this new world beyond themselves, it is nevertheless a potentially threatening and alien world. Emotional and physical safety of their students is a concern of all middle schools (NMSA, 2003).

The research of Andis (1981), Egan (1979, 1986), Johnston (1984), Lipsitz (1980), and Wiseman, Hunt, and Bedwell (1986) reveals that middle level learners view issues as either right or wrong, demonstrate a strong sense of justice and will work conscientiously for an important cause, are fascinated with the extremes of what exists and what is known, are able to memorize and retain massive amounts of detail, strive for individual definition of self, and gain identity by becoming part of a group. They are searching for and developing "a sense of romance, of wonder and awe" (Curtain & Dahlberg, 2010, in press)

Middle school learners need to see a connection between language learning and their real lives and interests in order to be motivated to learn. Since these learners place much importance on peer norms, they are less accepting of differences and are susceptible to developing negative stereotypes of individuals from other cultures (Met, 1994). However, they do tend to have more positive feelings toward people unlike themselves when they know more about them and when they understand more about the "way other people think and feel" (Robinson, 1981, p. 106). These young learners offer a rich opportunity to "grow the cross-cultural mind" (Galloway, 1985).

Cognitive Aspects

As you saw in Chapter 3, the emphasis on meaningfulness, as shown in recent brain research (Sousa, 2006), is important for all language learners. In addition, we now know more about the ways in which the brains of middle school learners function. Recent advances in brain research show that the brain changes its structure in response to external experiences (Diamond & Hopson, 1998; Wolfe & Brandt, 1998); that the search for meaning is innate (Caine & Caine, 1997, as cited in Curtain & Dahlberg, 2010); that the brain seeks meaning by looking for patterns in the information it receives (Curtain & Dahlberg); and that emotions drive attention to meaning and remembering (Caskey & Ruben, 2003; Jensen, 1998, 2000). Earlier research by Epstein and Toepfer (1978) indicates that brain growth in children between the ages of 11 and 13.5 slows down progressively, which may make them less able to acquire new cognitive skills and handle complex thinking processes than before. Thus, the difficulty many middle school learners experience in understanding abstract grammatical concepts, such as verb conjugation, may be a reflection of cognitive maturity (Met, 1994).

Cognitively, middle school learners demonstrate a wide diversity of skills and abilities. Sociocultural theory provides teachers with a way to tap the wide range of Zones of Proximal Development (ZPD) among this group of learners. Teachers should be aware that the range of abilities across learners in this group is wider than among other learners (Mead, 1965), and that the difference between the actual and the potential ZPD for each learner offers a rich environment for learning. In addition, story form, with emphasis on real-life heroes and heroines and realistic detail, continues to be a valuable tool for learners in the romantic stage (Curtain & Dahlberg, 2010).

You have now learned about two of the four stages of development of learners—mythic and romantic. Learners ages 14 to 15 through 19 to 20 are in the "philosophic" stage, as they understand the world to be a unit; they organize facts and details collected in the romantic layer to create their own systems for making sense of the world; they tend to think that since they found the system, they know everything. Individuals ages 19 to 20 through adulthood are in the "ironic" stage, where they recognize that systems are necessary to make sense of information although no one system is adequate to organize all knowledge (as cited in Curtain & Dahlberg, 2010, in press).

Language Instruction in the Middle School

The *Standards for Foreign Language Learning in the 21st Century (SFLL)* (National Standards in Foreign Language Education Project [NSFLEP], 2006) call for language instruction for all students in grades K–12. Attainment of the standards requires an early start and an extended, uninterrupted sequence of foreign language learning. In the 1990s, school districts with high school language programs responded to the emphasis on middle education and expanded instruction into the middle school in an effort to pique students' interest in other languages and cultures, provide them with more time to study a language, and enable them to reach specific levels of oral proficiency (Adair-Hauck, 1992). However, the effects of the federally mandated Elementary and Secondary Education Act (ESEA) of 2001 (U.S. Department of Education, 2002), known as the No Child Left Behind Act (NCLB) Act, has focused attention on math, science, reading, and support for English language learners, threatening instructional time and resources for foreign language programs in schools. NCLB is the reauthorization of the Elementary and Secondary Education Act, first approved in 1965 to provide better education for students in poverty groups through increased instructional services (Rosenbusch, 2005). The goal of NCLB is to raise academic achievement in the nation by requiring schools to assess all students on specific subject areas and report their progress. Although the *core academic subjects* have been identified as English, reading/language arts, mathematics, science, foreign languages, civics and government, economics, arts, history and geography (U.S. Department of Education, 2002), currently students are only being tested in the areas of reading/language arts, mathematics, and science.[1] A study conducted by the Council for Basic Education (2004) surveyed almost 1,000 principals in grades K–5 and 6–12 in Illinois, Maryland, New Mexico, and New York, and held focus groups with principals from across the U.S. Approximately three-quarters of the principals reported an increase in instructional time for the subject areas tested as a result of the NCLB Act (i.e., reading/language arts, mathematics), with a decrease in time for the arts, elementary social studies, and foreign languages (Rosenbusch, 2005). In high-minority schools, even more principals anticipated decreases in foreign language instructional time and professional development for teachers, and more than half of these principals expected the decreases to be large. Similar results were revealed in a 2003 survey conducted by the Northeast Conference on the Teaching of Foreign Languages, in which respondents reported cuts in their FL programs, including a scaling back often occurring in the upper elementary and middle school grades (Rosenbusch & Jensen, 2005). Although the Council for Basic Education report (2004) acknowledges that inclusion of a foreign language in the entire K–12 curriculum enhances student learning in other areas because it develops critical thinking, supports cognitive development, and improves native language reading and writing skills, financial limitations often restrict the extent to which fully articulated programs across grade levels can be implemented. This is a moment in time when foreign language teachers, learners and their families, and affiliated professional groups can use research to advocate for well-articulated programs of foreign language study.

Verkler (1994) examined the language competency and attitudes toward language study of middle school and high school students, all enrolled in Spanish I. Middle school students demonstrated higher competencies in all four language skills (listening, speaking, reading, and writing) than did their high school counterparts, and their attitude toward the foreign language learning experience was significantly more favorable. Verkler attributes these findings to the positive climate of middle school, which fosters students' social, emotional, and academic needs, and to the tenets of second language acquisition, which stress the key role of a positive and meaningful learning environment. Because of their unique openness and curiosity about challenges in the world around them, middle level learners can benefit from opportunities for language learning.

Lending further support for the importance of middle school language instruction is a recent study that examined the use of the Integrated Performance Assessment (IPA) at the post-secondary level. Glisan, Uribe, and Adair-Hauck (2007) found a positive correlation between years of FL study in middle school and college students' performance in the interpersonal mode of communication. That is, students who studied Spanish at the middle school level performed significantly better on oral interpersonal tasks than did their counterparts who began study at the high school level. The researchers attributed these results to the fact that "many middle school programs in the United States tend to be communicative and interactive, emphasizing novice-level language development through listening and speaking" (Glisan et al., p. 53).

Middle schools are often organized around interdisciplinary teams, which consist of four to five teachers who serve approximately 100 to 120 students (Met, 1995). These teams meet regularly and often to plan jointly and to deliver instruction that integrates content from various subject areas. Teams develop thematic units that integrate content and skills around a specific theme, establish interdisciplinary connections, and provide opportunities for students to use critical thinking skills. Although teams have usually been comprised of teachers of mathematics, science, social studies, and English/reading/language arts, more innovative middle schools now include foreign language teachers. Being part of a team enables foreign language teachers to integrate language instruction into the regular curriculum and helps teachers of other subject areas to understand the role of language study.

 How does middle school structure and organization match the characteristics of middle school learners?

Middle School Language Program Design[2]

Until recently, there has been little consistency in the type of language program developed for the middle school, due in part to the lack of consensus regarding the goal of language instruction at this level. Is the goal to offer exploration of languages and cultures or to begin to develop proficiency in a language? Accordingly, there is a divided opinion in the profession about whether middle school programs should be *exploratory* or *sequential*.[3] Many middle school programs have been exploratory, based on the middle school philosophy that students should have opportunities to explore a wide range of subjects.

The term *exploratory* has been interpreted in a variety of ways. Kennedy and DeLorenzo (1994) argue that exploratory programs offer middle school learners a "learner-friendly" way of beginning language study. In their view, effective exploratory courses include an introduction to linguistics, an option to explore several languages, development of survival language skills, fostering of strategies for language learning and readiness for language study, connections of other languages to English, exploration of cultures related to the languages being learned, and connections between languages and career paths (p. 70).[4]

In contrast, Knop and Sandrock (1994) maintain that many of the goals of exploratory programs can be achieved just as well, if not better, by sequential language programs, which are more likely to enable students to acquire functional language ability in a cultural context, rather than talking in English about language and culture. They identify the following limitations of traditional exploratory programs: students have a superficial exposure to many languages; students often do not advance beyond rote memorization of vocabulary and sentences; the same vocabulary is often taught in all of the languages, resulting in student boredom; courses are frequently taught in English, particularly when cultural knowledge is the primary goal; language potpourri courses are taught by teachers who may be less qualified in one language than another; and students' choice of which language to study in a sequential course is an uninformed one, often based on the exploratory teacher's popularity or personality (pp. 78–79).

In a position paper for the National Council of State Supervisors for Languages (NCSSFL), Sandrock and Webb (2003) point out that language programs in middle schools should be available for all learners, provide interdisciplinary connections, connect courses from one level to the next, and strive for the proficiency levels required for the workplace. Like all standards-based programs, effective programs for middle school learners incorporate the following goals into curriculum and instruction:

- develop students' ability to communicate effectively in real-life situations
- broaden students' educational background through language development and cross-cultural awareness
- foster healthy attitudes about people of other cultures through the interdisciplinary study of language and culture
- provide motivation for continued language study so that students can achieve higher levels of proficiency in the language (p. 6).

Additionally, Sandrock and Webb (2003) recommend that the longest possible sequence of language learning be provided, beginning in the elementary school, followed by middle school courses in a single language with multiple levels of instruction to allow for multiple entry points for new and transfer students (see Kentucky Department of Education, 2008b). They also advocate opportunities to add another language later in middle school, followed by continuing courses in two or three languages in high school (p. 9). Sandrock and Webb caution that some practices common to exploratory programs should be avoided in sequential programs, such as talking about languages in English; learning about cultures in English; learning only grammar rules until students are ready to speak; learning vocabulary in isolation; focusing on abstract data and facts unrelated to students' lives; and relying solely on the textbook as a teaching resource (p. 6). The College Board has reported higher Advanced Placement (AP) scores for students who have experienced long sequences of language study, beginning in elementary school and continuing through high school (Baum, Bischof & Rabiteau, 2002). One large school division has set the goal of having its graduates be able to communicate in English and at least one other language by 2015. Through planned expanded programming, their goal by 2025 is to have 90% of their students enrolled in foreign language since grade 1 (Fairfax County Public Schools, 2007).

The longest possible sequence of language learning should be provided, beginning in the elementary school, followed by middle school courses in a single language with multiple levels of instruction to allow for entry points for new and transfer students. Additionally, opportunities should be provided to add another language later in middle school, followed by continuing courses in two or three languages in high school. ▪

Principles for Middle School Language Instruction

According to Beane (1986), the ideal middle school environment is one in which the adults are "nice"; that is, they know students' names and are interested in them as individuals. The curriculum should be lively and contain activities that vitalize ideas through doing, creating, building, and dramatizing. Learners should have frequent opportunities to work together in pairs or in small groups. In their summary of the research on characteristics of effective middle school teachers, Johnston and Markle (1979) noted that, among other qualities, these teachers have a positive self-concept; demonstrate warmth; are optimistic, enthusiastic, flexible, and spontaneous; accept students; demonstrate awareness of developmental levels; use a variety of instructional activities and materials; use concrete materials and focused learning strategies; and incorporate indirectness and "success-building" behavior in teaching.

The middle school language curriculum should be lively and should contain activities that vitalize ideas through doing, creating, building, and dramatizing. ▪

It is the philosophy of *Teacher's Handbook* that the ideal characteristics of the middle school environment, curriculum, and teachers, as presented above, are applicable to all levels of instruction. Regardless of the instructional level, the curriculum should be learner-centered; organized around the social, cultural, and communicative use of language; and driven by what learners will know and be able to do with language rather than the grammatical concepts they can recite. A Vygotskyan approach, as explored in Chapter 1, engages learners so that they can derive meaning and use the language by means of guided participation, scaffolding, and assisted problem solving. Curriculum should encourage the negotiation of meaning for expression of ideas, engaging learners in tasks that are of interest to them and related to the real world. These principles are key to language instruction at all levels of instruction, including the middle school level.

Brain-based research has confirmed that activities related to the arts—such as music, dance, and drama—are fundamental to brain functioning: in music, certain structures in the auditory cortex respond only to musical tones; in dance, a part of the cerebrum and most of the cerebellum are dedicated to initiating and coordinating movement; and in drama, areas of the cerebrum focus on spoken language acquisition and rely on the limbic system to provide the emotional component (Sousa, 2006). Integration of the arts into the middle school curriculum addresses not only students' expressive and affective needs, but also their cognitive competencies, including developing their ability to perceive relationships, attend to nuance, understand that problems have multiple solutions, and see the world from an aesthetic perspective (Eisner, 2002). Further, studies have shown that in schools where the arts are integrated, where all subjects are experienced through the arts, students have a greater emotional investment in their classes, and they work more diligently and learn from each other better (Rabkin & Redmond, 2004). Language teachers are encouraged to integrate music, the visual arts, and movement into instruction, particularly at the middle school level, when students respond best to lessons that feature varied activities. Movement and other sensory experiences have been shown to help children with autism and attention deficit hyperactivity disorder (ADHD) to focus their attention to complete a task (Sousa). According to Sousa, "at some point in most lessons, students should be up and moving around, talking about the new learning" (p. 233). The following are some activities for middle school language programs that integrate the arts and movement:

- drawing, sketching, and painting according to instructions heard in the foreign language or to represent the main idea of an audio or video segment;
- creating a poem or play in the foreign language;
- acting out a play that peers wrote, using dance;
- learning dances from the target culture;
- sharing their reactions to songs from the target culture;
- learning the lyrics to a favorite song from the target culture;
- listening to music when entering and leaving class in order to foster a positive emotional mood;
- hearing soft music in the background while performing a task alone or in groups in order to facilitate the learning task;
- moving around the room to conduct a survey or interview in the foreign language.

Differentiated instruction is often suggested for instructional practices at the middle school level to address the diversity found among learners from ages 11 to 13.5. Differentiated instruction refers to a systematic approach to planning curriculum and instruction for academically diverse learners (Tomlinson & Eidson, 2003). The approach suggests that teachers design their instruction keeping in mind three student characteristics:

- *readiness*—what a student knows, understands and can do today in light of what the teacher is planning to teach today, much like considering the student's ZPD
- *interest*—what a student enjoys learning and doing
- *learning profile*—how a student prefers to learn, depending on learning style, intelligence, gender, and culture (adapted from p. 3).

In addition, Tomlinson and Eidson guide teachers to match these student characteristics to modifications in five classroom elements:

1. *content*—what we teach and how we give students access to information
2. *process*—how students come to understand knowledge and skills
3. *products*—how a student demonstrates what he or she has come to know, understand, and be able to do
4. *affect*—how students link thought and feelings
5. *learning environment*—the way the classroom feels and functions (adapted from p. 3).

As you saw in Chapter 3, students learn in differentiated ways and at varied paces, making it important for teachers to adjust the complexity and difficulty level of tasks. Strickland's (2003) standards-based differentiated unit for French I uses flexible grouping and pacing, learning centers, varied levels of questions, metacognitive thinking, multiple intelligences, and ongoing tiered assignments and assessments with rubrics to match learners' progress toward goals. In this unit, she presents authentic images to show young French people engaging in culturally accurate activities, then leads students from noticing the activities to using French to describe them in listening, reading, writing, and speaking. A key strategy she uses is *tiering*, in which she develops activities at different levels of difficulty but focused on the same key learning goals. She provides guided practice in tiers, using color coding to distinguish activities appropriate for students who are performing below, on, or above expectation level. For example, working *below* expectation level requires students to recognize and use only those verbs that have already been introduced and practiced in class. Students performing *at* expectation level recognize and use the same verbs but within verb phrases. Students performing *above* expectation level recognize and use familiar as well as unfamiliar verbs, and they complete a creative thinking task. Students are informed of the level at which they are working, sometimes through self-assessment and sometimes through consultation with the teacher. Guided practice worksheets and assessments are all keyed to the level at which the students are working, with the understanding that their performance may vary from level to level depending on their interest and progress. You will learn more about differentiated instruction in Chapter 10.

At the middle school level, the curriculum uses a spiral approach in which previously taught material is recycled and new expressions and more complex language are integrated within a familiar framework. As is the case with language teaching at all levels, a variety of classroom techniques and multimedia presentations should be used in the middle school language class. Since middle school learners are concerned with their self-image and the opinions of their peers, topics for thematic units and discussions should be selected with care (e.g., again, middle school learners may be uncomfortable describing the physical appearance of themselves and others). To appeal to students' curiosity and fascination with adventure and drama, a top-down approach as shown in Chapter 7 might be implemented, in which culturally appropriate myths, folktales, science fiction, and adventure stories are presented (Adair-Hauck, 1992).

How is second language instruction in middle school consistent with goals for middle school learning? What aspects of second language learning add uniqueness to the middle school program?

Managing a Middle School Classroom

Teaching middle level learners can be a thrilling experience. They are energetic, enthusiastic, and ready to explore. In the words of middle school teachers, they

- want to know about "stories from real life, real people";
- want to know the "weirdities" in their own culture as well as in others;
- love to compare and contrast;
- are more concerned with getting their point across (although accuracy is beginning to develop);
- want to explore beyond their "safe" world;
- need to feel grown up;
- still need structure (Curtain & Dahlberg, 2010, in press).

Thus, in order to explore the world of dissimilar others without allowing "weirdities" to create alienation, teachers might pose questions such as "What similarities and differences between the first and second culture can we see?", "What is particularly appealing or unappealing to us, and why?", "What is unexpected or difficult to understand?", and, especially, "What might others find strange about our ways of speaking or thinking?" (Knutson, 2006, p. 595). In this way learners explore their views of themselves as a way to explore others.

Managing a middle school classroom must involve thorough planning to engage the learners' interest and positive responses to behavior. When planning is inadequate, student attentiveness wanders and undesirable behaviors often erupt. Middle school learners are perhaps the most energetic of all learners due to their innate curiosity and the physical developmental changes they are experiencing. A number of factors beyond the teacher's control can affect how the students perform in class. For example, middle school learners are often sleepy early in the morning, while at midday they are hungry and watching the clock for lunch; in the afternoon they are eager to move around. Sometimes the language class is held in an auditorium, or in another teacher's classroom, which can be disruptive to the students.[5]

Consequently, teachers sometimes seek more skills in *classroom management*. Wong and Wong (2001) point out that the well-managed classroom is one that keeps learners engaged in meaningful tasks and that establishes procedures and routines for everything from turning in papers to asking to go to the restroom. When these student behaviors happen without prompting, they can provide opportunites for learners to use L2. Teachers who consider brain-based learning in their instruction and in their approaches to classroom events can effect more orderly classrooms, as shown in Chapter 3. Jensen (2000) shares six premises that reflect the fundamentals of establishing a brain-based approach to classroom management that supports learners:

1. Disruptions are a normal part of living and should be accepted in a positive and productive way.
2. The classroom is a learning environment requiring moderate stress to inspire motivation, enough novelty to inspire curiosity, and enough challenge to move students to achieve more.
3. Students are all basically good and are not plotting to make you miserable; show them how their need for control, expression, and love can become more appropriate for the classroom.
4. The best discipline is the kind nobody notices when you keep the focus on learning, not control.
5. Discipline problems are simply feedback to you that can be handled by redirecting the activity or its pace.
6. Prevention solves 95% of the problems by engaging learners in interesting topics, minimizing transitional times between activities, and working with students who need more attention behind the scenes (adapted from pp. 295–296).

Regardless of the circumstances in which they teach, however, the most successful middle school second language teachers find these tips useful:

- Plan your lesson thoroughly to engage learners every single moment—and beyond.
- Establish clear procedures that are observable, enforceable, in the target language, non-judgmental, and important to you so that you can teach effectively.
- Establish the connection between behavior and consequences.
- Establish routines for opening the class, ending the class, and other regularly occurring events.
- Involve parents and the community (adapted from Curtain & Dahlberg, 2010).

www.cengagebrain.com

Observing a talented middle school teacher will provide you with many strategies for keeping the focus on learning in a student-centered classroom. See Appendix 5.1 on the *Teacher's Handbook* Web site for suggestions to use when observing a middle school class.

STANDARDS HIGHLIGHT: Integrating CULTURES and COMPARISONS into Middle School Language Instruction

Earlier in the chapter we saw that middle school learners have begun to develop a sense of their own identities, are curious about the world beyond themselves, and tend to have more positive feelings toward people unlike themselves when they know more about them. In this chapter, we present the Cultures and Comparisons goal areas and standards because the middle school is an ideal level for exploring target cultures and comparing the target cultures with their own. Because language and culture are inextricably related (Schulz, 2007), these goal areas should also be an integral part of language instruction at other levels of instruction as well.

The Cultures Goal Area

Middle school language instruction should emphasize the acceptance of diversity, developing students' sensitivity to the differences they encounter in others, both within and beyond their classrooms, thus providing support for students' self-esteem (Met, 1995). The foreign language program is in a unique position to address the issue of diversity by exposing students to the cultures in which the foreign language is spoken. The Cultures goal area of the national standards states that students should be able to "gain knowledge and understanding of other cultures" (NSFLEP, 2006, p. 47). The two Cultures standards are:

- Students demonstrate an understanding of the relationship between the practices and perspectives of the cultures studied.
- Students demonstrate an understanding of the relationship between the products and perspectives of the cultures studied (pp. 50–51).

Practices are the patterns of behavior accepted by a society; they represent knowledge of "what to do when and where," e.g., how individuals address one another, the social strata, the use of space, gestures, mealtime etiquette. *Products* refer to what is created by members of the culture, both tangible and intangible, e.g., a house, an eating utensil, a painting, a piece of literature as well as a system of education, a ritual, an oral tale, a dance. Practices and products are derived from the *perspectives* of the culture, that is, traditional ideas, attitudes, meanings, and values (NSFLEP). For example, in some Asian cultures, social hierarchy (a perspective) is very important and is based on age, education, and social status. In those cultures, people often exchange business cards (a product) that facilitate social interaction, and are treated with respect such that one should not scribble another name or phone number on the business card. The information on the business card thereby affects the nonverbal behavior of those involved in communication (a practice). It is important to note that (1) not every product or practice has a perspective that is easily identifiable, and (2) sometimes the perspective has lost its historical significance and is no longer a perspective embraced by the contemporary culture.[6] Language teachers should be careful not to make up possible perspectives, but rather they should engage in cultural investigations with students to try to discover perspectives or confirm that perspectives have been lost or are unknown.

 Practices are the patterns of behavior accepted by a society; they represent knowledge of "what to do when and where."

 Products refer to things created by members of the culture, both tangible and intangible.

FIGURE 5.1 The Cultures Paradigm

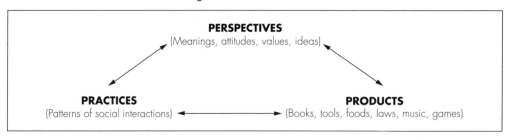

Source: From *Standards for Foreign Language Learning in the 21st Century*, 2006, p. 47. Used by permission of the American Council of the Teaching of Foreign Languages.

 Perspectives of the culture are the traditional ideas, attitudes, meanings, and values of members of that society.

Figure 5.1 illustrates how practices and products reflect the philosophical perspectives that form the world view of a cultural group, and it depicts the interrelatedness of these three cultural components. This model reflects the sociocultural framework posited by Fantini (1997), which consists of *sociofacts* (how people come together and for what purpose—practices), *artifacts* (things people make—products), and *mentifacts* (what people think or believe—perspectives). Since language is used to express cultural perspectives and to participate in social practices, language study offers students insights into a culture that are available in no other way. Although some cultural knowledge can be obtained from other kinds of courses, "only second language study empowers learners to engage successfully in meaningful, direct interaction, both orally and in writing, with members of other cultures" (NSFLEP, 2006, p. 49).

 Only language study empowers learners to engage in direct interaction with members of other cultures.

To help her students analyze cultural practices, products, and perspectives, a Japanese instructor asked them to brainstorm what they had learned about Japanese culture in a thematic unit they were studying (Curtain & Dahlberg, 2010). The teacher renamed the three Ps with more "child-friendly" terms and the students categorized the recalled information as shown in the cultures paradigm in Figure 5.2. Products are things the Japanese make, such as Pokemon and origami; practices are what they do, such as sumo wrestling or serving lunch; and perspectives are how they think, such as liking to keep indoors clean.

The cultures paradigm, with its anthropological approach to representing culture, lends itself to a *constructivist approach* to learning about culture, in which learners construct their views of culture through social interaction and interpersonal communication. Such an approach emphasizes the use of (1) a constructive process to understand the three Ps and their interrelatedness, and (2) connections, associations, and linkages between new and existing knowledge (Poplin & Stone, 1992). That is, learners construct their understandings of a culture by examining the relationships between products, practices, and perspectives, and by focusing initially on their own values and sense of self that evolve out of their respective native cultural perspectives (Wright, 2000). This approach contrasts with an *information-acquisition approach* through which students learn information and facts about the target culture as provided by the teacher.

Wright (2000) compared the effect of these two approaches on the development of cultural receptivity of beginning college-level German students, as identified on a measure of cross-culture adaptability. Over a 15-week period, the control group received

FIGURE 5.2 Products, Practices, and Perspectives in a Japanese Fifth Grade Class

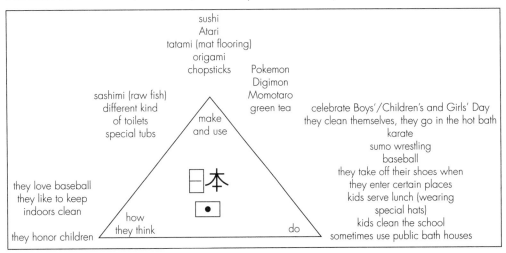

Source: From *Languages and Children – Making the Match,* 3rd ed. (p. 228), by H. Curtain and C. A. Dahlberg, 2004, Boston: Pearson Education. Reprinted by permission of Jessica Haxhi.

traditional instruction, in which cultural information was presented in terms of factual knowledge and discussions that referred to the information in or claims made by the textbook. In addition, they were given five lessons on language learning strategies and they designed a strategy portfolio. The experimental group, using a constructivist approach, received not only the same factual information, but they also participated in five lessons on cross-cultural awareness and designed a culture portfolio. The cross-cultural awareness lessons had five goals: (1) to pose authentic problems/topics that lead to a mild sense of confusion; (2) to encourage students to try to address the problems in their own way while the teacher acts only as mediator; (3) to help students put their own reasoning into words by sharing opinions, solutions, and strategies with the teacher and other students; (4) to use probing questions and allow enough wait time for students to think about answers; and (5) to give students an opportunity to reflect on the topic at hand in relationship to their own personal goals of second language and culture learning (Wright, p. 334). Findings of the study revealed that students who experienced the constructivist approach showed statistically significant gains in flexibility, openness, personal autonomy, and on an overall composite score of cultural awareness. Students who experienced a constructivist standards-based approach were able to separate facts from cultural assumptions and beliefs about those facts; they could shift their perspectives about culture, language, and people; they could differentiate between personal discomfort and intellectual disagreement; and they would be likely to function better in a culture unlike their own (pp. 335–336). The culture lessons and the culture portfolio had enhanced the constructivist students' sense of empowerment. See Appendix 5.2 on the *Teacher's Handbook* Web site for instructions on how to design the instructional culture portfolio.[7] Later in this chapter you will learn how to use a culture portfolio for assessment.

In a follow-up study, Abrams (2002) used the same culture portfolio as Wright to study how learners' use of the Internet shaped their views of culture, specifically with regard to stereotypes and use of the Internet to investigate them. In her study the students who used the culture portfolio (1) were better able to perceive culture from an *emic* or "insider's" perspective, (2) reflected a developing sensitivity to diversity within the cultures of the German-speaking countries, and (3) demonstrated an awareness of the idea that political boundaries are not adequate for determining memberships in cultural groups (p. 151).

These studies (Abrams, 2002; Wright, 2000) provide empirical evidence that an information-acquisition approach to culture "may lack essential dimensions that help students to comprehend, internalize, and feel comfortable with unfamiliar social demands" (Wright, p. 337). It lends support for a process-oriented constructivist approach to culture, which provides learners with the experiences they need to approach, appreciate, and bond with people from other cultures.

A process-oriented constructivist approach to culture provides learners with the experiences they need to approach, appreciate, and bond with people from other cultures.

The Comparisons Goal Area

The Comparisons goal area is presented here with the Cultures goal area because a deeper understanding of one's own culture comes about as a result of understanding another. The Comparisons goal area of the national standards states that students "develop insight into the nature of language and culture" (NSFLEP, 2006, p. 57). The two Comparisons standards are:

- Students demonstrate understanding of the nature of language through comparisons of the language studied and their own.
- Students demonstrate understanding of the concept of culture through comparisons of the cultures studied and their own (pp. 58, 60).

The second Comparisons standard can be addressed effectively with the Cultures standards as students analyze cultural products, practices, and perspectives between the target and native cultures. For example, as part of a thematic unit on family and celebrations, middle school students studying French explore how different cultures celebrate the birth of a baby. Students might imagine that their family receives two birth announcements, like those shown in Figure 5.3. Students compare the two birth announcements, and through analysis and discussion, they discover that in both announcements the parents introduce the baby; both have statistics about the baby's size and birthdate; both make comments about parts of the baby's body (fingers, toes, face, nose). The North American announcement mentions "welcomed with love" while the French announcement points out how long the wait has been since they learned of his coming in March until his arrival in November. Perhaps incidentally, the North American announcement mentions siblings, while the French one does not, nor does it mention parents' last names. Students might also note the differences in pounds/inches vs. kilograms/centimeters.

As you consider using the three Ps of the Cultures goal area coupled with the Comparisons standard, keep in mind that there can be multiple perspectives related to a single product or practice, that it is impossible to know all of the perspectives of your own culture and the target culture, and that your openness to learning new aspects of cultures will contribute greatly to your students' development of cultural perspectives.

One way to think about your own culture and to help your students understand it as well is to make cross-cultural comparisons using the Kluckhohn Values Orientation Method (Kluckhohn, 2004; Kluckhohn & Strodtbeck, 1961; Ortuño, 1991). The method categorizes five basic concerns common to all human beings: (1) What is a person's assessment of innate human nature (perception of self and others)?; (2) What is a person's relation to nature (world view)?; (3) What is the person's temporal focus of life (temporal orientation)?; (4) What is the principal model of activity (forms of activity) for a person, or the group to which he or she belongs?; (5) What is the modality of the person's or the group's relationships to others (social relations)? (adapted from Ortuño, p. 450).

FIGURE 5.3.A. Birth Announcement—North America

Ten tiny fingers and ten tiny toes
But this one came with ribbons and bows!
Introducing
Meredith Abigail Witry
June 19, 2013 2:42 a.m.
7 pounds, 6 ounces
18¾ inches

Welcomed with love by
Scott, Mary Beth, and
Big Brothers Jake and Ben

Image copyright Adam Borkowski, 2009. Used under license from Shutterstock.com.

FIGURE 5.3.B. Birth Announcement—France

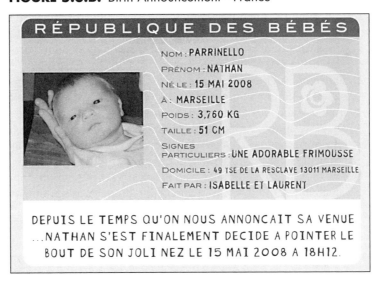

RÉPUBLIQUE DES BÉBÉS

NOM : PARRINELLO
PRÉNOM : NATHAN
NÉ LE : 15 MAI 2008
À : MARSEILLE
POIDS : 3,760 KG
TAILLE : 51 CM
SIGNES
PARTICULIERS : UNE ADORABLE FRIMOUSSE
DOMICILE : 49 TSE DE LA RESCLAVE 13011 MARSEILLE
FAIT PAR : ISABELLE ET LAURENT

DEPUIS LE TEMPS QU'ON NOUS ANNONCAIT SA VENUE
...NATHAN S'EST FINALEMENT DECIDE A POINTER LE
BOUT DE SON JOLI NEZ LE 15 MAI 2008 A 18H12.

Source: Dassier, 2008, modified.[8]

www.cengagebrain.com

Appendix 5.3 on the *Teacher's Handbook* Web site depicts the range of variations that exist across cultures within each of these value orientations. Students might use this framework for understanding their own culture and for comparing it to that of the target culture. For example, the dominant mode of activity in North American society is *doing*, as individuals are judged primarily by what they can accomplish. In the non-Western world, the emphasis is on who and what a person *is* rather than what he or she does. Ortuño (1991) cautions that a given culture cannot necessarily be classified on one side of the continuum in all five areas, although it might be plotted more on one than the other. Also, the Kluckhohn Method is not designed to make sweeping cultural generalizations, since much variation may also exist within a specific culture, but rather to account for dominant cultural patterns and perspectives.

A number of simulations have been devised to increase cross-cultural awareness among professionals, such as police officers, medical personnel, coaches, etc., who often face cross-cultural situations. Adaptation of simulations such as *Barnga* (Thiagarajan, 2007) and *Rafá Rafá* (Shirts, 2006b) for students in grades 5–8 and *Bafá Bafá* (Shirts, 2006a) for high school students can help learners understand their native culture and the target culture (Wright, 2003). Use of simulations coupled with reflection on standards of the Cultures and Comparisons goal areas can be especially useful for middle school learners forming a sense of *otherness*, as they explore a potentially threatening outside world, and as they seek the limits of the real world. See Appendix 5.4 on the *Teacher's Handbook* Web site for a description of the use of Barnga in a second language class. See Appendix 5.5 on the *Teacher's Handbook* Web site for a scenario in which an ESL teacher helps learners to perceive and compare the impact of the idioms in use around them.

www.cengagebrain.com

In addition to understanding their own willingness to adapt to other cultures, it is important that students learn how to use language to bridge the gaps between C1 (native culture) and C2 (target culture). Savignon and Sysoyev (2002) explored the use of sociocultural strategies to make the connection between language and cultural understanding, offering them as a taxonomy (Savignon & Sysoyev, 2005) that could be used in foreign language classrooms. They developed four strategies learners could use to initiate and sustain contact with people from other cultures (strategies 1–4 below) and four strategies learners could use to create accurate portraits of a C2 (strategies 5–8 below).

1. Initiate and maintain intercultural contact to learn about values, norms, spiritual heritage, etc., of the C2 and to represent the C1, e.g., U.S. students use English (L2 for Russian students learning EFL) to explain why certain activities are associated with a national holiday in the U.S. culture.
2. Anticipate sociocultural gaps that can result in misunderstandings or false stereotypes, e.g., examining a situation in which a member of C1 misinterprets a cultural norm from C2, such as arriving late to class.
3. Avoid misunderstandings, explaining C1 and asking for explanations of C2, e.g., apologizing in L2 for not removing shoes because in C1 there is not much mud and shoe removal is not necessary when entering a home.
4. Use diplomacy to redirect conversation to more neutral topics, or to dissimulate personal views and thus avoid conflict, e.g., see Alex's conversation on p. 161.
5. Compare the facts and realities of C1 and C2 using analogies, oppositions, and generalizations, e.g., after studying a reading selection on "Family Life in Britain," L2 learners prepared a similar report on family life in their own culture.
6. Identify and interpret unfamiliar features of C2, e.g., viewing authentic video multiple times to focus on cultural patterns of greeting, dress, and social interaction after meaning and story line have been understood.
7. Classify, compile, and generalize sociocultural information from mass media, the Internet and other sources of information, e.g., compiling a written report or oral presentation on environmental protection issues in the C2.
8. Review authentic cultural material, e.g., write a review of an authentic article or brochure published in the L2 for C2 users on a topic such as acid rain or other environmental issues (adapted from 2002, pp. 513–518; and 2005, pp. 362–364).

Savignon and Sysoyev (2005) then helped students in 11th-grade English-as-a-foreign (EFL) language classes in Russia as they collaborated in groups to develop sample interactive cultural conversations in which these strategies were used. For instance, for strategy 4, groups of students were given the following situation and asked to construct a dialogue, using diplomacy to avoid cross-cultural conflict by changing the topic of discussion.[9]

Situation: Pavel, Misha, and Tom are university students majoring in music. They play the piano, violin, and flute. They consider themselves to be musicians with a capital *M,* and they cannot stand modern popular music. Another student, Alex, becomes involved in a conversation that turns against pop music/musicians and has to find a way out of the situation.

Misha: I cannot stand that music. It drives me crazy.

Pavel: Right. You don't need to know anything about music to play like that.

Misha: And those people who come to their concerts. They are idiots. They can't understand that music like that is not art. It kills their minds and pollutes their souls.

Pavel: Yeah, those fans are so dumb. What do you think, Alex?

Alex: Well, I don't know.

Tom: You mean to say that you like that pop junk?

Alex: I would say that sometimes people do things that don't make any sense. And you guys, you sound like professionals. How long have you been playing musical instruments? (adapted from Savignon & Sysoyev, 2002, p. 517)

Notice how Alex uses diplomatic language to change the topic and redirect the focus of the conversation to the expertise of the musicians. Results of the research conducted by Savignon and Sysoyev showed that students were able to use the strategies in spontaneous communication beyond the classroom.

The following sections of this chapter will help you design instruction to enable your students to use language to communicate effectively in C2.

Implications of the Cultures and Comparisons Standards for Instruction

For decades, culture has been divided into two areas: "big C" (formal) culture—arts, literature, music, history; and "little c" (daily life) culture—anthropological and sociological aspects, such as social behavior, beliefs, housing, food, and transportation (Brooks, 1975). Culture has been treated traditionally in the classroom in terms of imparting facts and information, as teachers often lack sufficient cultural experiences themselves and have difficulty integrating culture into the linguistic component of the language program. Galloway (1985) characterized four common approaches to teaching culture:

- The Frankenstein Approach: a taco from here, a flamenco dancer from there, a gaucho from here, a bullfight from there
- The 4-F Approach: folk dances, festivals, fairs, and food
- The Tour Guide Approach: identification of monuments, rivers, and cities
- The "By-the-Way" Approach: sporadic lectures or bits of behavior selected indiscriminantly to emphasize sharp differences (as cited in Hadley, 2001, p. 348–349)

Making culture an integral part of language learning is a challenging task for teachers, and learners sometimes do not understand the relationship of culture to language. In a constructivist view, culture is something that people construct in the living of their daily lives, and language is the primary means by which they make their culture vibrant (Roberts, Byram, Barro, Jordan, & Street, 2001). In this sense, working through the ZPD, teachers can assist learners in shaping their views of their own culture and their understanding of the target culture. As shown earlier in this chapter (Wright, 2000), a constructivist approach to culture

FIGURE 5.4 Factors in Intercultural Communication

	Skills Interpret and relate (savoir comprendre)	
Knowledge Of self and other; of interaction: individual and societal (savoir être)	**Education** Political education Critical cultural awareness (savoir s'engager)	**Attitudes** Relativizing self Valuing others (savoir être)
	Skills Discover and/or interact (savoir apprendre/faire)	

Source: Byram, 1997, p. 34.

learning enables students to exhibit cross-cultural adaptability, while cultural understanding is likely to be inhibited if the teaching approach has an information-only, factual base.

Over the years researchers have argued for the integration of cultural knowledge and intercultural competence into the foreign language curriculum. See, for example, Byrnes (1996), Kramsch (1993), and Galloway (1999). Learning about how to use cultural knowledge is an aspect of communicative competence that Byram (1997) termed *intercultural communicative competence* (ICC). Figure 5.4 depicts his conceptualization of ICC, which includes four kinds of knowledge starting out with an initial understanding of self and others and moving to a new understanding: (1) knowing oneself and others (*savoir être*), (2) knowing how to interpret and relate (*savoir comprendre*), (3) knowing how to engage oneself (*savoir s'engager*), and (4) knowing how to discover/interact (*savoir apprendre/faire*).

Working in a European context, Byram described *intercultural speakers*, that is, speakers of L1 and L2 who know something about the native as well as the target cultures and often function as teachers or business personnel in the language and culture they are learning or teaching. He proposed 29 objectives for intercultural speakers that are related to his conceptualization of ICC.

According to Byram and Risager (1999), the role and responsibility of foreign language teachers is to help learners develop those aspects of intercultural communicative competence that put learners in contact with the cultural world of native speakers and that enable the learners to reflect on their own culture as they analyze it from an external perspective. In this sense, language teachers function as professional mediators "to help learners understand others and otherness as a basis for the acquisition of cultural and communicative competence" (p. 58). Learners acquire an *in-between* culture, that is, one that is partially understood on the basis of their own culture and partially on the basis of their exposure to the target culture. Much like a meta-language, or interlanguage, this in-between culture is an exciting and exhilarating place to be (Knutson, 2006). While a native speaker's familiarity with the language and the culture offers much to learners, nonnative teachers bring an additional perspective of the in-between culture, as Murti (2002) points out, teaching "people from other cultures how to use somebody else's linguistic code in somebody else's cultural context" (Murti, p. 29).

 Learning about how to use cultural knowledge is an aspect of communicative competence termed *intercultural communicative competence* (ICC) by Byram (1997).

Deardorff (2006) views intercultural competence as a cyclical *process orientation* that begins with attitudes, as suggested by Byram (1997), including respect, openness, curiosity, and discovery. Individuals' attitudes blend with their personal knowledge and comprehension of cultural self-awareness, deep cultural knowledge, and sociolinguistic awareness. Skills in listening, observing, and evaluating play a facilitative role in bringing about desired outcomes, such as effective and appropriate communication and behavior in an intercultural situation. The external outcome might then lead to changes in attitudes, completing the process-orientation cycle and, in turn, stimulating its reinitiation. Deardorff's model also allows for important internal outcomes, e.g., an informed frame-of-reference shift relative to adaptability, flexibility, empathy, which may be termed an *ethnorelative* view. In a study of 20 top intercultural experts, Deardorff reported consensus that intercultural competence is an important element of study abroad, and that measurement of it is best accomplished via multiple assessments, preferably case studies, interviews, and a mix of quantitative and qualitative measures. Deardorff points out that language study alone and international study abroad alone are inadequate conditions for development of intercultural competence. A process orientation of intercultural competence requires the dedication of time and conscious effort focused on development of intercultural skills throughout a student's educational experience, see Figure 5.5.

FIGURE 5.5 Process Model of Intercultural Competence

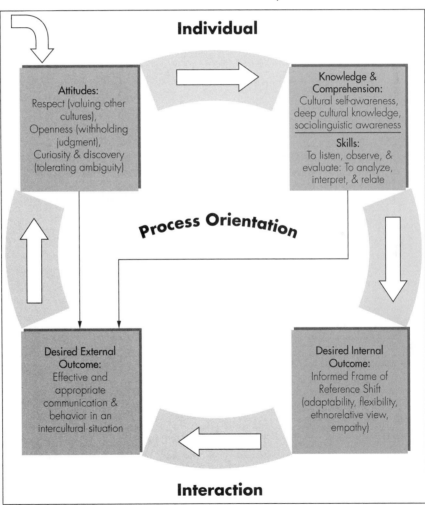

Source: From "A model of intercultural competence and its implications for the foreign language curriculum," by D. K. Deardorff, in S. Wilkinson (Ed.), *Insights from Study Abroad for Language Programs* (p. 90), American Association of University Supervisors, Coordinators, and Directors of Foreign Language Programs. Copyright © 2006 Heinle/Arts & Sciences, a part of Cengage Learning, Inc. Reproduced with permission. www.cengage.com/permissions.

Basing her work on the *SFLL* and the approaches of researchers such as Byram (1997) and Kramsch (1993), Schulz has proposed five fundamental objectives for culture learning and the development of cross-cultural awareness and understanding in a four-year high school or four-semester college foreign language learning sequence:

1. Students develop and demonstrate an awareness that geographic, historical, economic, social/religious, and political factors can have an impact on cultural perspectives, products, and practices, including language use and styles of communication.
2. Students develop and demonstrate awareness that situational variables (e.g., context and role expectations, including power differentials, and social variables such as age, gender, social class, religion, ethnicity, and place of residence) shape communicative interaction (verbal, nonverbal, and paralinguistic) and behavior in important ways.
3. Students recognize stereotypes or generalizations about the home and target cultures and evaluate them in terms of the amount of substantiating evidence.
4. Students develop and demonstrate an awareness that each language and culture has culture-conditioned images and culture-specific connotations of some words, phrases, proverbs, idiomatic formulations, gestures, etc.
5. Students develop and demonstrate an awareness of some types of causes (linguistic and nonlinguistic) for cultural misunderstanding between members of different cultures (2007, p. 17).

The Cultures Paradigm Across the Continuum of Learning. The Cultures paradigm can be effectively used to establish goals for culture learning across instructional levels, particularly when instruction is standards-based. Figure 5.6 shows how one state

FIGURE 5.6 A Cultures Standard Across the Grade Levels

ENTRY POINT: PRIMARY P1 OR P2 	WL-P-2.2.B1 Identify some common products (e.g., coins, costumes) of large culture(s). WL-P-2.2.B2 Identify some expressive forms (e.g., dance, artwork, songs) and contributions of target culture(s). WL-P-2.2.B3 Identify some objects, images and symbols of target culture(s) (e.g., Aztec calendar, lederhosen).	WL-PI-2.2.B4 Recognize and identify contributions and beliefs as reflected in products and contributions of target culture(s) (e.g., Ojo de Dios).	WL-PM-2.2.D1 Explain objects, images and symbols of target culture(s) (e.g., the Mexican flag). WL-PM-2.2.D2 Identify economic and social impact of products (e.g., music, soccer) on world markets. WL-PM-2.2.D3 Describe expressive forms of culture (e.g., art, literature, music, drama, dance).	WL-PH-2.2.E1 Discuss and explain external factors that impact products and contributions (e.g., effects of colonialization). WL-PH-2.2.E2 Identify and describe contributions of diverse groups within target culture(s) (e.g., Basque contribution to Spanish music). WL-PH-2.2.E3 Analyze relationships between cultural perspectives and products (as represented in expressive forms) [e.g., musical instruments, dances]. WL-PH-2.2.R1 Assess the significance of objects, images and symbols of other cultures. WL-PH-2.1.R2 Evaluate effects of cultures' contributions on other societies. WL-PH-2.1.R3 Assess economic and social impact of products on world market.

Source: From *Kentucky Multiple Entry Points Charts,* 2008. Used by permission of the Kentucky Department of Education, Frankfort, Kentucky 40601.

addressed the Cultures Standard 2.2 in World Languages (WL) across grade levels (Kentucky Department of Education, 2008b). If a student enters the school system at the primary school level (pre-K or K), note that the first column describes three ways in which the standard is addressed at the Beginning (B) level. The second column describes one way in which the standard is addressed as students study the beliefs of the culture as reflected in its products (e.g., *Ojo de Dios*). The third column describes how the standard is addressed at the Developing (D) level of competency in Primary through Middle school (PM), and the last column describes how the standard is addressed as student competency reaches the levels of Expanding (E) and Refining (R) in grade levels from primary through high school (PH). You can see how the expectation for students to demonstrate their understanding of the relationship between products and perspectives of the target culture is developed over the grade levels. For instance, if students begin language study at the primary level, an expectation is that they will develop an ability to identify some common products of the target culture, such as coins or costumes (WL-P-2.2.B1). In the intermediate grades, they begin to recognize and identify contributions and beliefs of the target culture. At the middle school level, they should be able to explain images and symbols of the target culture and identify the economic and social impact of products. Finally, at the high school level, it is expected that students would be able to demonstrate cultural competencies such as analyze relationships between cultural perspectives and products and evaluate the effects of cultures' contributions on other societies.

A Thematic Unit for Beginning and Intermediate Middle School Learners. You learned about ways to use children's literature and storytelling in Chapter 4. You also learned about the development of thematic units, thematic planning, and thematic planning webs to increase literacy among young language learners at the elementary level. In Chapter 3, you learned about backward planning design. All of these practices are also good educational practices recommended for use at the middle school and high school levels with age- and interest-appropriate adjustments. This knowledge will be helpful as you read about the following example that includes children's literature in a middle school foreign language program, designed by five French teachers (Coblin, Huss, Kirk, Lonneman, & Melville, 1998).

Crictor, written in French for French children by Tomi Ungerer (1980), is the tale of a boa constrictor named Crictor, who was sent from Africa to Madame Bodot, a teacher in a small village in France. The village experiences a crisis, and Crictor uses his unusual talents, saves the day, and is decorated as a hero for his bravery. Figure 5.7 shows a thematic web of the entire story and the lessons associated with it over several class lessons. You can see in the web how the teacher will integrate content of the book, culture, and language to enable students to explore mathematics, science, history, education, traditions, and literacy. The thematic planning web shows products and practices; as the teacher and students discover perspectives while working through the lesson, the web can be modified to place perspectives in the appropriate locations relative to products and practices. The story of Crictor is especially appealing to early middle level learners who are still somewhat tied to the fantasy and mythic worlds of their childhood but who are seeking heroes dealing with realistic problems (Egan, 1979).

www.cengagebrain.com

In Appendix 5.6 on the *Teacher's Handbook* Web site, notice how the teacher structures the language, content, and cultures to incorporate the products, practices, and perspectives of the Culture and Comparisons standards. Use of a Venn diagram provides a visual of the French village in the past that can then be compared to a French village of today, or to a small town in the students' country.[10]

Strategies for Integrating Language and Culture. At the heart of the cultural framework posited by the national standards is the importance of helping students to relate

FIGURE 5.7 Thematic Planning Web for "Crictor"

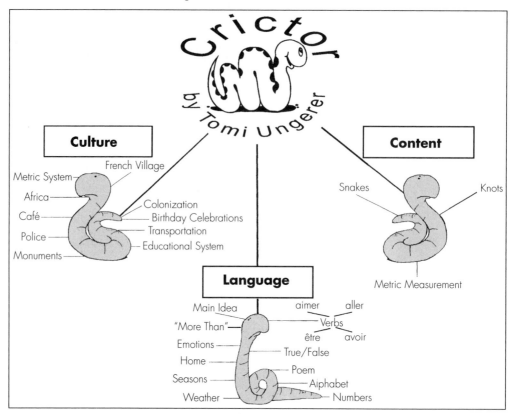

Source: From "A Standards-Based Thematic Unit: Crictor" (p. 2), by M. P. Coblin, D. Huss, B. Kirk, M. Lonneman, C. Melville, 1998, Ames, IA: Iowa State University, National K–12 Foreign Language Resource Center. Used by permission of Marcia Harmon Rosenbusch, Director, National K–12 Foreign Language Resource Center, Iowa State University.

cultural practices and products to each other and to their cultural perspectives. The following are a few examples of instructional strategies for integrating culture instruction at the middle and high school levels. Because *Teacher's Handbook* advocates integration of culture into the teaching of the other standards and skills, additional instructional strategies will be addressed within each of the subsequent chapters.

- Visual literacy: Students look at a scene from the target culture (e.g., a street scene with traffic lights) or an authentic magazine advertisement and discuss the possible practices and products depicted and the perspectives to which they relate.
- Integration of language and culture: As students learn vocabulary, they see and discuss culturally authentic visuals/realia[11] so that they acquire both language and cultural concepts. For example, in a lesson on housing, students look at photos of various types of housing from the target cultures, name features of each building type, and compare and contrast the housing types with each other and with housing from their own cultures.
- Semantic mapping: As presented in Chapter 4, semantic maps can be used to associate word clusters graphically around an idea, key word, or concept. Words can be grouped thematically according to cultural practices and products. See Appendix 4.7 for a sample semantic map based on the study of a river system.

- Use of authentic documents: Students discover information dealing with practices and products by analyzing authentic documents, such as movie listings, restaurant ads, bus/subway schedules, invitations, and so on. For example, students might read a restaurant ad from a Spanish-speaking country and discuss why the restaurant's hours are different from the hours of a North American restaurant (cultural perspectives and comparisons).

- Investigation of cultural truths: Students communicate with target language counterparts via e-mail; gather information about their daily routines, school, and interests; and compare these data to their own responses.

- Interviews with native speakers or recent immigrants: These interviews enable learners to understand the lives of the interviewees. Knutson (2006) suggests conducting insider interviews in an ethnographic style in which learners first explore their home culture practices, for example, health practices, eating habits, etc. Once generalizations have been formed, learners interview members of the target culture, asking about their views of the same cultural practices. Knutson also suggests interviews from an outsider's perspective, using travel guides from the home culture and from the target culture as the basis for exploration of how others see the home culture. Bateman (2002) reports that through interviews, his students became aware of their lack of knowledge about other cultures; that they are capable of carrying on a conversation with a native speaker; that they have stereotypes that need to change; and that, realistically, their language is very limited (p. 326). Rings (2006) cautions that oral interviews are successful when both speakers trust each other and value the other's perspective. Phrases that can be taught in the TL include back-channeling behavior, e.g., "mm-hmm" or "I see" or repeating what the person said; phrases that seek clarification, such as "When you say X, what do you mean?" or "Can you give me an example/ tell me more about...?" (p. 47).[12] You will learn more about these techniques in Chapter 8.

- Storytelling: Telling stories enables learners to use presentational communication, as you will learn in Chapters 6, 7, and 9. Langer de Ramirez (2005/2006) describes how she presented fairy tales from Mexico, Argentina, and Colombia to her middle school students and helped them analyze the stories for the setting, initiating event, internal response, attempt/outcome, and reaction. Then the students created their own original stories in Spanish using narration in the past and present as well as indirect discourse.

- Learning centers: This is a designated area of the classroom that contains materials and directions for a specific learning task, such as a game, an interpretive listening activity, or an interpretive reading task. It may be a desk or group of desks, bulletin board, or computer center, but it always attracts attention because of its bright colors or attractive use of shapes and pictures (Glisan & Fall, 1991). The learning center should be thematically arranged, contain instructions for self-pacing, and allow for a range of student ability and interest levels. Learning centers may be effectively used for both individual and small-group activities and for differentiating instruction; i.e., engaging learners in activities designed to meet their individual learning needs.

Cultures and Comparisons in L1 or L2? The importance of input as explained in Chapter 1, as well as the *SFLL,* indicate a primary role for L2 with only minimal use of L1. Committed to provide as much input in L2 as possible, teachers often find themselves reverting to L1 when they sense that learners do not understand, do not pay attention, or behave inappropriately. Levine (2003) surveyed 600 foreign language learners and

163 instructors of first- and second-year university-level classes to learn the perceptions teachers and learners have of the amount of time spent in L1 and L2. He found that learners and instructors reported that 40–60% of the classes were taught in L2 80–100% of the time. Overall, the perceptions were that L2 is used most by teachers speaking with learners, less by learners speaking with teachers, and least of all by learners speaking with other learners (p. 350). L2 is used for theme-based communication, less for communication about grammar, and still less for communication about tests, quizzes, and assignments (p. 351). Kraemer (2006) points out that teaching assistants in higher education also use L1 to describe culture, explain activities, show solidarity with learners, explain grammar, and manage the administrative aspects of the classroom. They also use L1 when they feel unsure of vocabulary. Describing factors that influence student teachers to revert to L1, Bateman (2008) adds lack of time, teacher fatigue, and learners unaccustomed to L2 use. Finding that teachers approach instruction of culture and grammar, discipline, and the mechanics of running a class in L1, Warford (2007) concludes that there will always be an element of L1 in foreign language classes (see also Cook, 2001; Donato, 1994; Macaro, 2001) and that teacher education programs should provide strategies to promote extended L2 use in the classroom. Further, Kraemer's findings affirm the value of a solid foundation in language teacher education in enabling teaching assistants to make more use of L2. In sum, discussions on Cultures and Comparisons should be carefully planned to prevent students from using English-only to engage in discussion. For example, teachers need to provide vocabulary resources, tasks that enable students to move from planning what they want to say to sharing their opinions with one another, and scaffolding of student output. See Chapter 8 for further guidance.

Assessment of Middle School Performance

In Chapter 4, you learned about contextualized performance assessment; in Chapter 11 you will see a more elaborated explanation of assessment in general. In middle level education as well as in all levels of instruction, successful assessment improves learning, instruction, and program effectiveness (McNamara, 2001; Stowell & McDaniel, 1997). Consistent with the middle learner's interest in the real world, authentic assessment that makes use of real-life tasks and real audiences is recommended. Examples of types of assessment are performance tasks, portfolios, student self-assessment surveys and probes, peer assessments, journals, logs, products, and projects. As pointed out in Chapter 4, assessment is an essential part of teaching, and what is measured should reflect what is taught (Shrum, 1991). In addition to these types of classroom assessments, some states have developed tests appropriate for learners at various stages in their language learning processs. An example is New York's Second Language Proficiency Exam (SLP), appropriate for learners who have had two years of a foreign language prior to grade 8.[13]

For middle level learners who want to know how things work in the real world, it is important that they participate in assessment and evaluation, help set individual and group goals, help identify ways to measure progress, and evaluate their own accomplishments. Student self-evaluation is an important means of developing a fair and realistic self-concept (NMSA, 2003). Since early adolescence is a crucial period for establishing a clear self-concept and positive self-esteem, all assessment and evaluation should emphasize individual progress instead of comparison with other students. The goal is to help students discover and understand their strengths, weaknesses, interests, values, and personalities.

As you saw earlier in this chapter with the cultural portfolio used by Wright (2000), portfolios are an excellent way for middle level learners to accumulate examples of their work that show their progress. Portfolios allow for self-selection of items to be included and provide for reflection on the learning process. Portfolios as a recommended form of authentic assessment will be examined more completely in Chapter 11. One example of a portfolio that is especially useful for elementary and middle school learners is *Lingua-Folio*. Using the model of a European language portfolio developed by the Council of Europe (2000), VanHouten and Fulkerson (2006) created *LinguaFolio Kentucky!,* which appears in Appendix 5.7 on the *Teacher's Handbook* Web site. This record of learners' language capabilities is built over the early years of language learning and has three parts: a biography, a passport, and a dossier. The biography describes the learners' language background, what they can do with the languages and cultures they study and have experienced, and shows that they are learning more and more. The passport section is a short document that shows what learners know and can do in the languages they study, and the dossier contains samples of their work the learners have selected, e.g., sample recordings, poems, or papers they have written. See the *Teacher's Handbook* Web site for links about LinguaFolio to the National Council of State Supervisors for Languages and to several other states that have adopted this approach to documenting a language learner's progress over time from grades K–16.

www.cengagebrain.com

Although the grade-level focus of this chapter is middle school, the Cultures and Comparisons standards should be addressed at all instructional levels. To illustrate, we highlight a culture portfolio developed by Schulz (2007) for use at the post-secondary level, available as Appendix 5.8 on the *Teacher's Handbook* Web site, but which can also be adapted for use at the secondary level. The portfolio asks students to engage in performance tasks that are based on the five fundamental objectives presented in the previous section and to compare the U.S. culture and the target culture, in this case, German-speaking cultures. For example, the four tasks required of learners in meeting Objective V are scaffolded so that the first task involves learners in exploring authentic materials such as "newspaper articles, advertisements, Web sites, or other data sources to compare how an event, product, or practice of the home culture is viewed in the target culture and attempt to explain the reasons for the views" (p. 25). Next, learners identify two examples of explicit or implicit values observed in texts or events. At this point, students might find that the values naturally lead to identifying perspectives held by members of the culture. The third task asks learners to describe and explain three critical incidents the instructor provides in which cross-cultural misunderstanding occurs; and finally learners use a scale of 1 to 5 to indicate how representative certain statements provided by the instructor are to the viewpoints that are likely to be held by U.S. teens and German middle-class nonimmigrant teens (Schulz, pp. 25–26).

To summarize, you have seen in this chapter that the concept of middle school education revolves around the special characteristics of learners ages 11 to 13.5. Language and cultural learning are especially suited to their needs and interests, matching up well with the *SFLL* Cultures and Comparisons goal areas. You explored constructivist models of how to help learners demonstrate their understanding of the relationships between the products, practices, and perspectives of another culture and acquire intercultural communicative competence. You saw some ways to manage a middle level classroom and some forms of assessment for learning accomplished at this level. As the profession strives to provide language instruction for all students at all levels, increasing attention will need to be given to the unique needs of the middle level learner. Furthermore, clear goals will need to be articulated for this level of language instruction so that there is a smooth transition from elementary to middle to high school language courses and so that one level builds effectively on the next.

TEACH AND REFLECT ·

NC&TE_____

www.cengagebrain.com

EPISODE ONE
Developing Culture-Specific Examples of the Three Ps

ACTFL/NCATE 2.a. Demonstrating Cultural Understandings; 4.a. Understanding and Integrating Standards in Planning; 4.b. Integrating Standards in Instruction

TESOL/NCATE 2.a. Understand and Apply Knowledge about Cultural Values and Beliefs in the Context of Teaching and Learning; 2.e. Understand and Apply Concepts about the Interrelationship between Language and Culture; and 3.a. Planning for Standards-Based ESL and Content Instruction

Create three age-appropriate examples of products, practices, and perspectives for the cultures of the foreign language you are preparing to teach. For the first example, begin with the product and match a practice and perspective to it. For the second example, begin with the practice and match a product and perspective to it. For the third example, begin with the perspective and match a product and practice to it. Into what types of middle school lessons might these examples be integrated? How do these examples relate to the Kluckhohn Values Orientation Method? Into Schulz's (2007) five fundamental objectives for culture learning and the development of cross-cultural awareness and understanding?

See Activity A in the View and Reflect section of the *Teacher's Handbook* Web site for an example lesson that integrates the three Ps around Cajun folktales and Zydeco music.

EPISODE TWO
Unit and Lesson Design Around a Story, Myth, or Folktale

ACTFL/NCATE 2.b. Demonstrating Understanding of Literary and Cultural Texts; 3.a. Understanding Language Acquisition and Creating a Supportive Classroom; 4.a. Understanding and Integrating Standards in Planning; 4.b. Integrating Standards in Instruction

TESOL/NCATE 3.a. Planning for Standards-Based ESL and Content Instruction; 3.b. Managing and Implementing Standards-Based ESL and Content Instruction; and 3.c. Using Resources Effectively in ESL and Content Instruction

In Chapter 4, you designed a storytelling lesson appropriate for elementary school students. Now select a culturally authentic story, myth, or folktale that you will present to a middle school class in your target language. First, design a unit plan built around the story you select (use the unit plan model presented in Chapter 3.) Second, design a lesson plan for the first day devoted to this story. Follow the lesson plan format presented in Chapter 3. Be sure to include your objectives for the lesson and connections with the Cultures and Comparisons standards. Prepare visuals and realia to help demonstrate meaning. You might also read Langer de Ramirez (2005/2006) for ideas on storytelling. Your instructor may ask you to present part of your lesson to the class.

EPISODE THREE
Viewing and Analyzing Lessons on the Three Ps

ACTFL/NCATE 2.a. Demonstrating Culture Understandings; 3.a. Understanding Language Acquisition and Creating a Supportive Classroom; 4.a. Understanding and Integrating Standards in Planning; 4.b. Integrating Standards in Instruction.

TESOL/NCATE 3.a. Planning for Standards-Based ESL and Content Instruction; 3.b. Managing and Implementing Standards-Based ESL and Content Instruction; and 3.c. Using Resources Effectively in ESL and Content Instruction.

1. Consult the sample lesson plan in Appendix 5.9 (on the *Teacher's Handbook* Web site), "Hotels in Spain" by Merle Wilder (Allen, 2000). Identify the products, practices, and perspectives you see in these sample lesson plans. Modify the plans, which were originally created for high school students, to make them suitable for middle school students. What aspects of the learner in the romantic stage of development (Egan, 1979) will you need to consider as you make these adjustments?

> **TECHNO FOCUS:** For a little help and some ideas, sometimes it's good just to talk with an experienced teacher. "Ask Yana" is one such source of electronic communication, developed by Sheila Cockey through the National Capital Language Resource Center. To see the queries and responses about teaching culture and using technology, go http://nclrc.org/teachers_corner/classroom_solutions_yana.html. Click on "About Yana" to see the breadth of experience this teacher brings to her comments; then click on "Teaching culture" to see what she recommends about teaching music, popular culture, and using video and film in the classroom. Write three of her recommendations you found useful.

DISCUSS AND REFLECT ·

See the *Teacher's Handbook* Web site for an additional case study:
Case Study Two: Exploratory vs. Sequential Middle School Programs

CASE STUDY ONE
It's McLicious! Staying in the Target Language

ACTFL/NCATE 1.c. Identifying Language Comparisons; 2.a. Demonstrating Culture Understandings; 2.c. Integrating Other Disciplines in Instruction; 3.b. Developing Instructional Practices that Reflect Language Outcomes and Diversity; 4.a. Understanding and Integrating Standards in Planning; 4.b. Integrating Standards in Instruction; 4.c. Selecting and Designing Instructional Materials; 5.a. Knowing Assessment Models and Using Them Appropriately

TESOL/NCATE 3.a. Planning for Standards-Based ESL and Content Instruction; 3.b. Managing and Implementing Standards-Based ESL and Content Instruction; and 3.c. Using Resources Effectively in ESL and Content Instruction

Having completed his degree in German with licensure to teach, Greg secured his first teaching job at a middle school in Kentucky. As he began to plan his lessons for the year, he was delighted to find this learning scenario for his state on the Web (see Figure 5.8). He read through the scenario, noting its interdisciplinary nature, the use of the Cultures and Comparisons goal areas, and the appropriateness of the activities of the scenario for middle school learners. However, Greg found himself unsure of how to implement the scenario in his lessons because the words "TAUGHT IN THE TARGET LANGUAGE" seemed to present an almost impossible task to him.

He called his mentor teacher, Mr. Poff, who teaches French, and asked him how he would carry out the scenario in the target language. Mr. Poff was very helpful and gave Greg some tips such as wearing a button that says "Speak French" and posting key vocabulary from the scenario around the room with colorful photos and pictures.

Greg also decided to ask Ms. Loria, the Spanish teacher, how she approached the goal of keeping the class in the target language. She pointed out that, in her experience, keeping the languages separate results in more proficiency achievement than mixing them or translating them. She said that she gives simple instructions in Spanish for classroom activities and does not translate them into English. If her students know that she will supply the English after the Spanish instructions, they stop listening to the Spanish. Ms. Loria also said that if she knows she is not going to use English, she puts more thought into making the input comprehensible.

In a workshop for foreign language teachers from his school division, Greg brainstormed the following list of simple techniques to maximize use of L2:

1. Post L2 instructions for routine management on the walls. These include teacher statements such as "Open books to page...," "Please read number 3...," and "Please write on the board/on your paper/in your notebooks...," as well as student statements and questions such as "What page?", "Please repeat...," "How do you say...?", and "May I go to the bathroom/my locker/the office?"

2. Make instructions to activities simple, and say them while illustrating with a picture, image, gestures, or an example. Explain only a couple of steps at a time.

3. Accustom students to use of L2 by noting the direction lines in their textbooks, which are often in the L2 after the first several opening chapters.

4. Support what you say with the use of gestures, visuals, and contextualized clues. For example, if students are having difficulty understanding, point to visuals or objects in your classroom to provide assistance.

5. Break complex topics into smaller manageable pieces—don't try to explain all in one presentation the importance of French bread in the form of oblong *baguettes*. Instead, use the strategies suggested by the three Ps to help students compare in simple language what bread is for them and what it is for French people, how their shopping practices are related, and why.

6. Hang a card with the name of the L1 on one side and the L2 on the other side. Teach students that when the L2 side is showing, they may not use L1.

7. Set aside a specific time for exclusive use of L2, such as warm-up at the start of class, interpersonal conversational activities, presentational projects, or games in which winning is contingent on staying in L2. See Discuss and Reflect in Chapter 8 for a description of a game that middle/high school teachers developed to motivate students to speak exclusively in L2.

8. DEMONSTRATE more than you EXPLAIN, and show students examples/models of what they are to do.

Read the learning scenario entitled "It's McLicious! (C'est McLicieux! Es McLicioso! Es ist McLecker!)" in Figure 5.8 (Kentucky Department of Education, 2008a) and the guiding questions that follow it. Add your own suggestions on how Greg can find ways to promote and maintain target language usage in his class.

Ask yourself these questions:

1. What aspects of the learning scenario will appeal to middle level learners?
2. Where do you see the Cultures standards targeted in the scenario? How are products, practices, and perspectives highlighted for teaching? What activities and teaching practices are used to engage learners with culture?
3. Where do you see the Comparisons standards targeted in the scenario? How do you see students making linguistic comparisons? How do they make cultural comparisons? What activities and teaching practices are used to engage learners in this goal area? What interdisciplinary aspects do you see in the scenario?

To prepare for class discussion:

1. Although this scenario is intended for middle level learners, the designers stated that it is easily adapted for high school learners. Create an adaptation of this scenario for high school or college learners.

FIGURE 5.8 Kentucky World Language Learning Scenario "It's McLicious!"

> ### *Kentucky World Language Learning Scenario*
> ### *It's McLicious! (C'est McLicieux!*
> ### *¡Es McLicioso! Es ist McLecker!)*
>
> **Intended Level:** Middle School, Developing
>
> **Guiding Question:** How do cultural differences affect the marketing of products?
>
> **Activity Summary:** McDonald's Restaurants can be found in countries around the world, but we are often surprised at the differences we find there. Students will compare/contrast McDonald's in their regions to at least one in the target culture and explore the effects of culture and resources on business practices and products.
>
> **Task:** Individually or in pairs, students will prepare an advertisement **in the target language** in the medium of their choice for the opening of a new McDonald's or other fast food restaurant in their target country/culture.
>
> **Kentucky World Language Content:**
>
> WL-PM-1.3.D4 Interpret and present information from authentic material to audience.
>
> **WL-PM-2.2.D2 Identify economic and social impact of products on world markets.**
>
> WL-PM-4.2.XX Analyze the differences between target culture(s) and students' own cultures.
>
> **Kentucky Core Content for Assessment:**
>
> SS-M-3.4.1 Basic economic issues addressed by producers are production, distribution, and consumption of goods and services.
>
> **SS-M-3.4.2 Productivity can be improved by specialization, new knowledge, and technology/tools.**
>
> SS-M-3.4.3 Personal, national, and international activities are interdependent.
>
> PL-M-3.1.4 There are positive and negative aspects of advertising strategies (e.g., providing accurate or misleading information, gimmicks).
>
> **PL-M-1.4.2 Using dietary guidelines, food guide pyramid, and other nutritional resources (e.g., food tables) helps make daily food choices.**
>
> **Steps for Planning and Implementing: TAUGHT IN THE TARGET LANGUAGE**
>
> 1. Teacher uses TPR, visuals, manipulatives, and other communicative approaches to present food vocabulary and appropriate grammatical structures (e.g., imperatives, courtesies).
> 2. Teacher highlights cultural considerations as they relate to food in the target culture(s) (e.g., dietary staples, food guide pyramid).
> 3. Students use websites to investigate McDonald's restaurants in target language culture(s) by:
>
>   - preparing and sharing Venn diagrams that compare/contrast local and target-culture McDonald's menus;
>   - completing a list of common phrases or expressions found throughout the websites;
>   - preparing and sharing charts that examine marketing techniques (e.g., use of technology, toys, slogans, other icons).
>
> 4. Students role play ordering at a McDonald's counter in the target culture(s).
> 5. [Performance Task] Individually or in pairs, students prepare an advertisement in the medium of their choice for the opening of a new McDonald's or other fast food restaurant in their target country/culture.
>
> *(continued)*

(Resource URLs: http://www.nal.usda.gov:8001/py/pmap.htm;
http://www.mcdonalds.com; http://www.mcdonalds.fr; http://www.mcdonalds.es;
http://www.mcdonalds.de; http://monarch.gsu.edu/nutrition/Spanish2.htm;
http://www.diffu-sciences.com/pages/info_1.htm;
http://www.aid.de/aid.htm?ernaehrung/ernaehrungsforum/ernaehrungsforum.html~Hauptframe)

[May be easily modified to address High School Practical Living Core Content PL-H-3.1.4 Methods and
techniques of advertising exert an influence on consumer choices for products and services.]

Source: *The Kentucky Framework for World Language Learning: It's McLicious!* Kentucky Department of
Education, 2008. Retrieved January 31, 2008 from http://www.education.ky.gov. Used by permission of the
Kentucky Department of Education, Frankfort, Kentucky 40601.

REFERENCES

Abrams, Z. I. (2002). Surfing to cross-cultural awareness. *Foreign Language Annals, 35,* 141–160.

Adair-Hauck, B. (1992). Foreign languages in the middle schools: A curricular challenge. *Pennsylvania Language Forum, 64,* 12–18.

Allen, L. Q. (2000). Designing curriculum for standards-based culture/language learning. *NECTFL Review, 47,* 14–21.

Andis, M. F. (1981). Early adolescence. Skills essential to learning television project. Working paper. Bloomington, IN: Agency for Instructional Television.

Bateman, B. E. (2002). Promoting openness toward culture learning: Ethnographic interviews for students of Spanish. *The Modern Language Journal, 86,* 318–331.

Bateman, B. E. (2008). Student teachers' attitudes and beliefs about using the target language in the classroom. *Foreign Language Annals, 41,* 11-28.

Baum, D., Bischof, D., & Rabiteau, K. (2002). Before and beyond the AP foreign language classroom. Retrieved June 8, 2008, from http://www.collegeboard.com/prod_downloads/apc/ap04_beforeand beyond.pdf.

Beane, J. A. (1986). A human school in the middle. *Clearing House, 60,* 14–17.

Brooks, N. (1975). The analysis of language and familiar cultures. In R. C. Lafayette (Ed.), The cultural revolution (pp. 19–31). *Reports of the Central States Conference on Foreign Language Education.* Lincolnwood, IL: NTC/Contemporary Publishing Group.

Byram, M. (1997). *Teaching and assessing intercultural communicative competence.* Clevedon, UK: Multilingual Matters, Ltd.

Byram, M., & Risager, K. (1999). *Language teachers, politics and cultures.* Clevedon, UK: Multilingual Matters, Ltd.

Byrnes, H. (1996). The future of German in American education: A summary report. *Die Unterrichtspraxis/Teaching German, 29*(2), 253–261.

Caine, R. N., & Caine, G. (1997). *Education on the edge of possibility.* Alexandria, VA: Association for Supervision and Curriculum Development.

Caskey, M. M., & Ruben, B. (2003). Research for awakening adolescent learning. *Education Digest, 69*(4), 36–38.

Clark, S., & Clark, D. (1994). *Restructuring the middle level school: Implications for school leaders.* Albany, NY: State University of New York Press.

Coblin, M. P., Huss, D., Kirk, B., Lonneman, M., & Melville, C. (1998). A standards-based thematic unit: "Crictor." M. H. Rosenbusch & E. Lorenz (Eds.), Ames, IA: Iowa State University, National K–12 Foreign Language Resource Center.

Cook, V. (2001). Using the first language in the classroom. *The Canadian Modern Language Review, 57,* 402–423.

Council for Basic Education. (2004). *Academic atrophy: The condition of the liberal arts in America's public schools.* Washington, DC: Author.

Council of Europe. (2000). European Language Portfolio. Retrieved June 15, 2008, from http://www.coe.int/t/dg4/portfolio/default.asp?l=e&m=/main_pages/welcome.html.

Curtain, H., & Dahlberg, C. A. (2004). *Languages and children—Making the match* (3rd ed.). Boston: Pearson Education.

Curtain, H., & Dahlberg, C. A. (2010). *Languages and children—Making the match* (4th ed.). Boston: Pearson Allyn & Bacon.

Deardorff, D. K. (2006). A model of intercultural competence and its implications for the foreign language curriculum. In S. Wilkinson (Ed.), *Insights from Study Abroad for Language Programs* (pp. 86–98). Boston: American Association of University Supervisors, Coordinators, and Directors of Foreign Language Programs, Thomson Heinle.

Diamond, M., & Hopson, J. (1998). *Magic trees of the mind: How to nurture your child's intelligence, creativity, and healthy emotions from birth through adolescence.* New York: Penguin Putnam.

Donato, R. (1994). Collective scaffolding. In J. Lantolf & G. Appel (Eds.). *Vygotskyan approaches to second language acquisition research* (pp. 33–56). Norwood, NJ: Ablex.

Egan, K. (1979). *Educational development*. New York: Oxford University Press.

Egan, K. (1986). *Teaching as story telling*. Chicago: The University of Chicago Press.

Eichhorn, D. H. (1966). *The middle school*. New York: Center for Applied Research.

Eisner, E. (2002). *The arts and the creation of mind*. New Haven, CT: Yale University Press.

Epstein, H. T., & Toepfer, C. F., Jr. (1978). A neuroscience basis for reorganizing middle school education. *Educational Leadership, 36*, 656–660.

Fairfax County Public Schools. (2007). *Languages Student Achievement Goal 1.2*. LanguagesSAGFactSheet11-20-07. Retrieved June 8, 2009, from http://www.boarddocs.com/vsba/fairfax/Board.nsf/d62d9cb847ef1cbd87257328006795e4/16b5bc90faecbd0485257329004d6a8c?OpenDocument.

Fantini, A. E. (Ed.). (1997). *New ways in teaching culture*. Arlington, VA: Teachers of English to Speakers of Other Languages.

Galloway, V. B. (1985). *A design for the improvement of the teaching of culture in foreign language classrooms*. ACTFL project proposal. Yonkers, NY: American Council on the Teaching of Foreign Languages.

Galloway, V. (1999). Bridges and boundaries: Growing the cross-cultural mind. In M. A. Kassen (Ed.) *Language learners of tomorrow: Process and promise* (pp. 151–187). Lincolnwood, IL: National Textbook.

Glisan, E. W., & Fall, T. F. (1991). Adapting an immersion approach to secondary and postsecondary language teaching: The methodological connection. In J. K. Phillips (Ed.), *Building bridges and making connections, Northeast Conference Reports* (pp. 1–29). Burlington, VT: Northeast Conference on the Teaching of Foreign Languages.

Glisan, E. W., Uribe, D., & Adair-Hauck, B. (2007). Research on integrated performance assessment at the post-secondary level: Student performance across the modes of communication. *The Canadian Modern Language Review, 64*, 39-67.

Hadley, A. O. (2001). *Teaching language in context* (3rd ed.). Boston: Heinle & Heinle.

Jensen, E. (1998). *Teaching with the brain in mind*. Alexandria, VA: Association for Supervision and Curriculum Development.

Jensen, E. (2000). *Brain-Based Learning*. San Diego, CA: The Brain Store.

Johnston, J. H. (1984). A synthesis of research findings on middle level education. In J. H. Lounsbury (Ed.), *Perspectives: Middle school education, 1964–1984* (pp. 134–156). Columbus, OH: Middle School Association.

Johnston, J. H., & Markle, G. (1979). *What research says to the middle level practitioner*. Columbus, OH: National Middle School Association.

Kennedy, D. F., & DeLorenzo, W. E. (1985). *Complete guide to exploratory foreign language programs*. Lincolnwood, IL: NTC/Contemporary Publishing Group.

Kennedy, D. F., & DeLorenzo, W. E. (1994). The case for exploratory programs in middle/junior high school. *Foreign Language Annals, 27*, 69–73.

Kentucky Department of Education. (2008a). *The Kentucky Framework for World Language Learning: It's McLicious!* Retrieved June 15, 2008, from http://www.education.ky.gov/KDE/Instructional+Resources/High+School/Language+Learning/Other+World+Languages/Kentucky+Framework+for+World+Language+Learning.htm.

Kentucky Department of Education. (2008b). *The Kentucky Framework for World Language Learning: Kentucky Multiple Entry Point Charts*. Retrieved June 15, 2008, from http://www.education.ky.gov/KDE/Instructional+Resources/High+School/Language+Learning/Other+World+Languages/Kentucky+Framework+for+World+Language+Learning.htm.

Kluckhohn, F. R. (2004). *The Values Orientation Method*. Retrieved June 15, 2008, from http://www.valuescenter.org/method.html.

Kluckhohn, F. R., & Strodtbeck, F. L. (1961). *Variations in value orientations*. Evanston, IL: Row, Peterson.

Knop, C. K., & Sandrock, P. (1994). The case for a sequential second language learning experience at the middle level. *Foreign Language Annals, 27*, 77–83.

Knutson, E. M. (2006). Cross-cultural awareness for second/foreign language learners. *The Canadian Modern Language Review, 62*, 591–610.

Kraemer, A. (2006) Teachers' use of English in communicative German language classrooms: A qualitative analysis. *Foreign Language Annals, 39*, 435–450.

Kramsch, C. (1993). *Context and culture in language teaching*. Oxford, UK: Oxford University Press.

Langer de Ramirez, L. (2005/2006) Eighth-grade *griots*: Turning middle school students into storytellers. *NECTFL Review, 57*, 30–43.

Levine, G. (2003). Student and instructor beliefs and attitudes about target language use, first language use, and anxiety: Reports of a questionnaire study. *The Modern Language Journal, 87*, 343–364.

Lipsitz, J. S. (1980). The age group. In M. Johnson (Ed.), Toward adolescence: The middle school years (pp. 7–31). *Seventy-ninth Yearbook of the National Society for the Study of Education*, Part. 1. Chicago: University of Chicago Press.

Macaro, E. (2001). Analysing student teachers' code switching in FL classrooms: Theories and decision-making. *The Modern Language Journal, 85*, 531–548.

Martin, T. (1993). Turning points revisited: How effective middle-grades schools address developmental needs of young adolescent students. *Journal of Health Education*, Supplement, S-24–S-27.

McNamara, T. (2001). Language assessment as social practice: Challenges for research. *Language Testing, 18*, 334–399.

Mead, M. (1965). Early adolescence in the United States. *Bulletin of the National Association of Secondary School Principals, 49*, 5–10.

Met, M. (1994). Current foreign language practices in middle schools. *Foreign Language Annals, 27*, 43–58.

Met, M. (1995). Foreign language instruction in the middle schools: A new view for the coming century. In R. Donato & R. M. Terry (Eds.), *Foreign language learning: The journey of a lifetime* (pp. 76–110). The ACTFL Foreign Language Education Series. Lincolnwood, IL: NTC/Contemporary Publishing Group.

Mori, J. (2002). Task design, plan, and development of talk-in-interaction: An analysis of a small group activity in a Japanese language classroom. *Applied Linguistics, 23*, 323–347.

Murti, K. (2002). Whose identity? The nonnative teacher as cultural mediator in the language classroom. *ADFL Bulletin, 34*(1), 26–29.

National Middle School Association (NMSA). (2003). *This we believe: Developmentally responsive middle level schools*. Columbus, OH: Author. Retrieved June 10, 2008, from http://www.nmsa.org.

National Middle School Association (NMSA). (2005). *This we believe: Interactive characteristics chart (relevant, challenging, integrative, exploratory curriculum)*. Retrieved June 18, 2007, from http://www.nmsa.org/AboutNMSA/ThisWeBelieve/The14Characteristics/tabid/1274/Default.aspx

National Standards in Foreign Language Education Project (NSFLEP). (2006). *Standards for foreign language learning in the 21st century*. Lawrence, KS: Allen Press.

Nerenz, A. G. (1990). The exploratory years: Foreign languages in the middle level curriculum. In S. Magnan (Ed.), *Shifting the instructional focus to the learner* (pp. 93–126). Northeast Conference Reports. Middlebury, VT: Northeast Conference on the Teaching of Foreign Languages.

Ortuño, M. M. (1991). Cross-cultural awareness in the foreign language class: The Kluckhohn Model. *The Modern Language Journal, 75*, 449–459.

Poplin, M. S., & Stone, S. (1992). Paradigm shifts in instructional strategies: From reductionism to holistic/constructivism. In W. Stainback & S. Stainback (Eds.), *Controversial issues confronting special education* (pp. 153–179). Boston: Allyn & Bacon.

Rabkin, N., & Redmond, R. (2004). *Putting the arts in the picture: Reforming education in the 21st century*. Chicago, IL: Columbia College.

Redmond, M. L., & Lorenz, E. (1999). *Teacher to teacher: Model lessons for K–8 foreign language*. Lincolnwood, IL: National Textbook Company.

Rings, L. (2006). The oral interview and cross-cultural understanding in the foreign language classroom. *Foreign Language Annals, 39*, 43–53.

Roberts, C., Byram, M., Barro, A., Jordan, S., & Street, B. (2001). *Language learners as ethnographers*. Clevedon, UK: Multilingual Matters, Ltd.

Robinson, G. (1981). *Issues in second language and cross-cultural education: The forest through the trees*. Boston: Heinle & Heinle.

Rosenbusch, M. H. (2005). The No Child Left Behind Act and teaching and learning languages in U.S. Schools. *The Modern Language Journal, 89*, 250-261.

Rosenbusch, M. H., & Jensen, J. (2005). Status of foreign language programs in the NECTFL states. *NECTFL Review, 56*, 26–37.

Sandrock, P., & Webb, E. (2003). *Learning Languages in Middle School: Position paper*. Retrieved February 26, 2004, from http://www.ncssfl.org.

Savignon, S. J., & Sysoyev, P. (2002). Sociocultural strategies for a dialogue of cultures. *The Modern Language Journal, 86*, 508–524.

Savignon, S. J., & Sysoyev, P. (2005). Cultures and comparisons Strategies for learners. *Foreign Language Annals, 38*, 357–365.

Schulz, R. (2007). The challenge of assessing cultural understanding in the context of foreign language instruction. *Foreign Language Annals, 40*, 9–26.

Shirts, G. R. (2006a). *Bafá Bafá*. Del Mar, CA: Simulation Training Systems. Retrieved June 15, 2008, from http://www.stsintl.com/schools-charities/bafa.html.

Shirts, G. R. (2006b). *Rafá Rafá*. Del Mar, CA: Simulation Training Systems. Retrieved June 15, 2008, from http://www.stsintl.com/schools-charities/rafa.html.

Shrum, J. L. (1991). Testing in context: A lesson from foreign language learning. *Vision, 1*(3), 7–8.

Sousa, D. A. (2006). *How the brain learns*. Thousand Oaks, CA: Corwin Press.

Stowell, L. P., & McDaniel, J. E. (1997). The changing face of assessment. In J. L. Irvin (Ed.), *What current research says to the middle level practitioner* (pp. 137–150). Columbus, OH: National Middle School Association.

Strickland, C., (2003). There's a pattern here folks! In C. A. Tomlinson & C. C. Eidson (Eds.). *Differentiation in practice* (pp. 182-232). Alexandria, VA: Association for Supervision and Curriculum Development.

Thiagarajan, S. (2007). *Barnga: A simulation game on culture clashes*. Yarmouth, ME: Intercultural Press. Retrieved June 15, 2008, from http://www. interculturalpress.com.

Tomlinson, C. A., & Eidson, C. C. (2003). *Differentiation in practice: A resource guide for differentiating curriculum, grades 5-9*. Alexandria, VA: Association for Supervision and Curriculum Development.

Trillium Paper Inc. (2008). Birth announcement. Retrieved January 6, 2009, from http://www.shopbirthannouncements.com/detail.aspx?ID=1455.

Ungerer, T. (1980). *Crictor*. Paris, France: L'École des Loisirs.

U.S. Department of Education. Elementary and Secondary Education. (2002). *Title IX. General Provisions. Part A, Section 9101. Definitions [11] core Academic Subjects*. Retrieved June 17, 2008, from http://www.ed.gov/policy/elsec/leg/esea02/index.html.

VanHouten, J. B., & Fulkerson, G. (2006). *LinguaFolio Kentucky!* Retrieved June 15, 2008, from http://www.kde.state.ky.us/KDE/Instructional+Resources/High+School/Language+Learning/Other+World+Languages/LinguaFolio+Kentucky.htm.

Verkler, K. W. (1994). Middle school philosophy and second language acquisition theory: Working together for enhanced proficiency. *Foreign Language Annals, 27*, 19–42.

Warford, M. (2007). L1 vs. L2 in the foreign language classroom: New findings. *NECTFL Review, 60*, 50–67.

Wing, B. H. (1996). Starting early: Foreign language in the elementary schools. In B. H. Wing (Ed.). *Foreign Language for All: Challenges and choices* (pp. 21–55). Northeast Conference Reports. Lincolnwood, IL: NTC/Contemporary Publishing Group.

Wiseman, D. G., Hunt, G. H., & Bedwell, L. E. (1986). Teaching for critical thinking. Paper presented at the Annual Meeting of the Association of Teacher Educators, Atlanta, GA.

Wolfe, P., & Brandt, R. (1998). What do we know from brain research? *Educational Leadership, 56*(3), 8–13.

Wong, H. K., & Wong, R. T. (2001). *The first days of school.* Mountain View, CA: Harry K. Wong Publications.

Wright, D. A. (2000). Culture as information and culture as affective process: A comparative study. *Foreign Language Annals, 33*, 330–341.

Wright, D. A. (2003). Fostering cross-cultural adaptability through foreign language study. *NECTFL Review, 52*, 36–39.

NOTES

1. For a complete description of NCLB and its effect on foreign language programs, see Rosenbusch (2005).

2. The National Middle School Association (NMSA) advocates the elimination of the following practices in middle schools: curriculum consisting of separate subjects and skills taught and tested in isolation from one another; content judged to be more important than the process by which it is learned; the excessive use of lecturing, rote learning, and drills; and the domination of textbooks and worksheets (Sandrock & Webb, 2003, p. 3).

3. See Wing (1996) for examples of middle school exploratory, sequential, and immersion programs. See Curtain & Dahlberg (2010) for a guide to program planning and articulation, detailing how to build a middle school program.

4. For a comprehensive discussion about exploratory language programs, see Kennedy and DeLorenzo (1985).

5. See Curtain & Dahlberg (2010, in press) for tips about what materials to have available in your middle school classroom and how to best teach from a mobile cart. See also Redmond and Lorenz (1999) for K-8 lesson plans.

6. For example, in early times, an expected practice at mealtime was for those seated at the table to keep their hands on the table where they could be seen. The perspective underlying this practice was one of guarding one's safety and making sure that dinner guests did not conceal weapons under the table. This perspective is no longer operational in most contemporary cultures.

7. Note that German I students in Wright's (2000) study were asked to complete the culture portfolio in English.

However, we encourage teachers to integrate the target language and culture and guide students in using the target language as much as possible.

8. Many thanks to Dr. Jean-Louis Dassier, of Indiana University of Pennsylvania, for finding and modifying the French birth announcement.

9. See Savignon & Sysoyev (2002, 2005) for discussion of additional conversations for each of the strategies outlined.

10. For another middle school lesson (grade 8) on French cities, see **View and Reflect**, Activity B on the *Teacher's Handbook* Web site.

11. *Realia* (cultural products) are real items or objects from the target culture, such as menus, train tickets, newspaper articles, party invitations, eating utensils, and toys.

12. See Mori (2002) for a research study using Conversational Analysis (CA), mentioned in Chapter 1 of *Teacher's Handbook,* to study interactions of students in a small group activity in a Japanese classroom. The study describes the teacher's instructions for the task, the learners' planning for the task, and the actual development of the talk as the learners interact with native speakers.

13. The Second Language Proficiency Exam, Comprehensive Regents Examinations are downloadable from the New York State Education Department Web site by language in French, German, Italian, Latin, and Spanish at http://www.nysedregents.org/testing/loteslp. Secured booklets of actual speaking tasks are not available but other materials are.

CHAPTER

6

Using an Interactive Approach to Develop Interpretive Communication

In this chapter, you will learn about:

- the three modes of communication
- the interpretive mode for teaching listening, reading, and viewing
- Schema Theory
- the processes involved in listening and reading
- L1 vs. L2 interpretive processes
- reader-/listener-based and text-based factors in comprehension and interpretation

- integration of authentic texts
- exploration of literary texts
- *workshop-style* classroom for exploring texts
- acquisition of new vocabulary through text exploration
- use of L1 vs. L2 in checking comprehension
- the Interactive Model for developing listening, reading, and viewing

Teach and Reflect: Using the Interactive Model to Explore an Authentic Printed Text; Using the Interactive Model to Explore an Authentic Audio/Video Segment; Teaching Literature at the Post-Secondary Level

Discuss and Reflect: Reading Aloud

CONCEPTUAL ORIENTATION

Historically, communicative ability in a foreign language has been described in terms of the four skills of listening, speaking, reading, and writing. As you learned in Chapter 2, instructional methods such as the Audiolingual Method (ALM) even fostered the teaching of the four skills separately and in a prescribed sequence (Chastain, 1988). Communication in the world, however, occurs as skills are used in concert, not in isolation, and it is shaped by specific cultural contexts. Listening and reading are often catalysts for speaking and/or writing; discussion often leads to written communication; and all of these aspects of communication occur within a specific set of cultural perspectives that govern patterns of interaction among individuals and interpretations of the message. Therefore, comprehension and interpretation involve both cognitive processes, for the integration of all skills, and social processes, such as discussing the possible meanings of texts with others. For example, you may have approached the task of reading this chapter by taking some notes about and/or discussing your background knowledge of the information you hope to learn. You might take notes as you read the chapter. After reading you will probably discuss the information with your classmates. You will have used all skills both cognitively and socioculturally as you explore the new information presented in the chapter.

In this chapter, we will explore the nature of interpretive communication and strategies for developing it in the classroom. Using Schema Theory (see later discussion) as the basis for understanding how learners engage in the processes of comprehension and interpretation of text, we present an *interactive* approach for developing interpretive communication in which learners *build* comprehension of a text by means of their perceptions, background knowledge, and prior experiences. Further, *Teacher's Handbook* advocates the integration of interpretive communication with the other two modes of communication—interpersonal and presentational—and offers ideas in this chapter for how to accomplish this.

 The three modes of communication are interpersonal, interpretive, and presentational.

Framework of Communicative Modes

The standards define communication by means of the three communicative modes that emphasize the context and purpose of the communication and thus depict the four skills as working in an integrated fashion. The framework is based on the model proposed by Brecht and Walton (1995), the purpose of which is to illustrate how one participates in "cultural discourses," or within culturally defined contexts. Figure 6.1 illustrates the framework.

The Interpersonal Mode

This mode features two-way oral or written communication and negotiation of meaning among individuals, regardless of skill modality. Since participants observe and monitor one another, they can make clarifications and adjustments in their communication. Communication can be realized through face-to-face conversation and written correspondence—all four skills of listening, speaking, reading, and writing can be involved in the interpersonal mode. This mode will be explored further in Chapters 7 and 8.

 The interpersonal mode features two-way oral or written communication and negotiation of meaning.

The Interpretive Mode

This mode focuses on the interpretation of meaning in oral and printed texts when there is no possibility of negotiation of meaning with the writer or speaker. This interpretation of meaning takes into account the cultural context in which the text is situated. Interpretation can occur in activities such as listening to an authentic news broadcast, reading

FIGURE 6.1 Framework for the Communicative Modes

	INTERPERSONAL	**INTERPRETIVE**	**PRESENTATIONAL**
Definitions	Direct oral communication (e.g., face-to-face or telephonic) between individuals who are in personal contact Direct written communication between individuals who come into personal contact	Receptive communication of oral or written messages Mediated communication via print and non-print materials Listener, viewer, reader works with visual or recorded materials whose creator is absent	Productive communication using oral or written language Spoken or written communication for people (an audience) with whom there is no immediate personal contact or which takes place in a one-to-many mode Author or creator of visual or recorded material not known personally to listener
Paths	Productive abilities: speaking, writing Receptive abilities: listening, reading	Primarily receptive abilities: listening, reading, viewing	Primarily productive abilities: speaking, writing, showing
Cultural knowledge	Knowledge of cultural perspectives governing interactions between individuals of different ages, statuses, backgrounds Ability to recognize that languages use different practices to communicate Ability to recognize that cultures use different patterns of interaction	Knowledge of how cultural perspectives are embedded in products (literary and artistic) Knowledge of how meaning is encoded in products Ability to analyze content, compare it to information available in own language and assess linguistic and cultural differences Ability to analyze and compare content in one culture to interpret U.S. culture	Knowledge of cultural perspectives governing interactions between a speaker and his/her audience and a writer and his/her reader Ability to present cross-cultural information based on background of the audience Ability to recognize that cultures use different patterns of interaction
KNOWLEDGE OF THE LINGUISTIC SYSTEM The use of grammatical, lexical, phonological, semantic, pragmatic, and discourse features necessary for participation in the Communicative Modes.			

Source: From *Standards for Foreign Language Learning in the 21st Century* (p. 27), 2006. Used by permission of the American Council of the Teaching of Foreign Languages.

a novel, or viewing a film. Clarification of meaning is not possible as the creator of the text is absent or not accessible. Since the interpretive mode does not provide for active negotiation between the reader and writer or the listener and speaker, it may also require a deeper knowledge of culture in order to gain a cultural interpretation of a text.

The interpretive mode encompasses listening, reading, and viewing skills. It involves not only literal comprehension of a text but also the interpretation of it, including cultural perspectives, personal opinions, and points of view. It is important to note that interpretation goes beyond the traditional idea of "comprehension," since interpretation includes the reader's/listener's ability to "read (or listen) between the lines" and bring his or her own background knowledge and ideas to the task (National Standards in Foreign Language Education Project [NSFLEP], 2006, pp. 36–37).

This ability to interpret is based largely on one's ability to engage in *inferencing*, "a thinking process that involves reasoning a step beyond the text, using generalization, synthesis, and/or explanation" (Hammadou, 2002, p. 219). For example, when reading "My brother fell off the ladder and has to stay in bed for three days," the reader typically reasons beyond the text and infers what might have happened to the brother when he fell and why he might have to stay in bed.

To draw inferences, the reader/listener uses generalizations of typical events and explanatory reasoning of how those events might pertain to the text being explored (Hammadou, 2002). While typical comprehension questions that follow a text assess understanding of factual information, they may not engage the listener or reader in interpreting the text and drawing inferences, i.e., going beyond the literal level to bring in personal points of view and cultural perspectives that pertain to the text. It is important to note, additionally, that comprehension and interpretation of a text are *not* the same as translation of the text, since assigning meaning to a text involves much more than matching surface-level equivalencies from one language to another or only understanding the factual information in the text.

In addition to inferencing, interpretation of a text also includes predicting, reaching conclusions, giving opinions and explanations, questioning textual assertions, and relating the text to other texts or life experiences. Interpretation is not reserved for advanced-level high school or college students, but rather should be fostered in language instruction in the early grades. In their native language, children routinely engage in interpreting texts when they read stories or see movies—they give their opinions and explain why they liked or didn't like the story or movie, describe the qualities of the characters, predict how the story will end, describe the moral of the story, and compare the story to others with which they are familiar. Foreign language teachers at the elementary and middle school levels can capitalize on students' L1 interpretation abilities and engage them in interpreting stories and fables in L2. High school and post-secondary language teachers can then build on these interpretive skills and focus on higher level interpretation that may involve aspects such as author's intent, tone of the text, and L2 cultural perspectives.

In foreign language learning and teaching, the interpretive mode refers to both (1) a component of daily communication that enables one to make sense of and interpret oral, printed, and video texts, and (2) a vehicle for language acquisition (i.e., interpreting input and texts facilitates language acquisition and development). As you read this chapter, you will notice that the interpretive mode is explored with both of these purposes in mind.

 The interpretive mode refers to both (1) a component of daily communication that enables one to make sense of and interpret oral, printed, and video texts, and (2) a vehicle for language acquisition.

 Comprehension and interpretation of a text are *not* the same as translation of the text.

The Presentational Mode

This mode features formal, one-way communication to an audience of listeners or readers. Speaking and/or writing skills are involved, but no direct opportunity exists for active negotiation of meaning between the presenter and audience. Examples include giving a speech or oral report, preparing a paper or story, and producing a newscast. Substantial knowledge of the language and culture is necessary on the part of the speaker and of the audience, to some extent, since the goal is to ensure that the audience will be able to interpret the message (NSFLEP, 2006). This mode will be explored further in Chapter 9.

The presentational mode features formal, one-way communication to an audience of listeners or readers.

As shown in Figure 6.1, successful communication in all three modes requires knowledge of cultural products, practices, and perspectives so that understanding of the appropriate patterns of social interaction and encoding of meaning can occur.

STANDARDS HIGHLIGHT: Exploring the Interpretive Mode Through Listening, Reading, Viewing

Few would dispute the claim that comprehension is necessary in order for language acquisition to occur. To communicate successfully in the target language, learners depend upon their ability to comprehend the spoken and written word. As explored in Chapters 1, 2, and 3, current research in second language acquisition (SLA) and approaches to foreign language teaching acknowledge the role of input in the acquisition process. Integration of authentic oral and printed texts into language teaching serves to merge culture and context with language, provide engaging topics for learners to explore, stimulate learners' interest in language study, and offer a means for engaging learners in more challenging, higher-order thinking tasks. Historically, however, interpretive skills have received less attention in language teaching than have interpersonal skills. Due in part to a lack of knowledge about interpretive processes, teachers often assumed that comprehension would occur on its own or that translation would lead to comprehension and interpretation. However, as you have already seen, merely exposing learners to oral or printed input is not sufficient, since they also must be equipped to make meaning of this input through avenues such as comprehension strategies and interaction with others.

Interpretive Communication: Listening and Reading Processes

How Comprehension Processing Occurs

Much of what we know about comprehension, particularly reading comprehension, is based upon *Schema Theory,* originally proposed by Bartlett (1932) and later developed as a theoretical framework (Minsky, 1975; Schank & Abelson, 1977). The origin of Schema Theory can be traced to studies of cognition, and it developed as computer scientists attempted to create programs that mimic human processing (Minsky). The term *schemata* (plural of *schema*) is used to refer to the mental "connections that allow new experiences and information to be aligned with previous knowledge" (McCarthy, 1991, p.168). A detailed theoretical discussion of Schema Theory is beyond the scope of this text. However, of importance to language teachers is that one of the major insights of the theory draws attention "to the constructive nature of the reading process and to the critical role of the reader and the interaction between the text and the reader's background knowledge"

(Nassaji, 2007, p. 80). Simply put, the reader (and by extension, the listener) must be able to link incoming (or new) spoken or written input to the knowledge and bank of experiences that already exist in his or her memory structures, or schemata. Schemata are understood by some researchers to be higher-level complex knowledge structures (van Dijk, 1981) that provide scaffolding (see Chapter 1) (Anderson, 1977) and by others to be organized background knowledge on a topic that leads learners to make predictions (Anderson, Spiro, & Montague, 1977). In addition to the role of schemata, listening and reading comprehension also involve both cognitive and social processes, which will each be addressed here. Listening and reading are active cognitive processes that require an interplay between various types of knowledge. Listeners and readers draw upon the following as they attempt to interpret a text:

- their knowledge of the target language, e.g., vocabulary, syntax;
- their background knowledge and experiences in the world;
- their knowledge of how various types of discourse, such as magazine articles, literary texts, radio broadcasts, and talk shows, are organized, i.e., use of cohesive devices such as pronouns, conjunctions, and transitional phrases to link meaning across sentences, as well as the use of coherence to maintain the unity of the message;
- their ability to hold information in short-term memory as they attend to the text; and
- their ability to use a variety of strategies to help them bring meaning to the comprehension task.

Listeners and readers rely upon the types of knowledge and abilities described above as they perform a variety of tasks in the comprehension process. Some tasks or subskills reflect *bottom-up processing* (see Chapter 2), in which meaning is understood through analysis of language parts. Simply put, the listener or reader processes language in a sequential manner, combining sounds or letters to form words, then combining words to form phrases, clauses, and sentences of the text (Goodman, 1967). Bottom-up subskills include discriminating between different sounds and letters, recognizing word-order patterns, recognizing intonation cues, analyzing sentence structure, translating individual words, and examining word endings. Bottom-up models that seek to explain reading comprehension are *text-driven* and portray the reader as someone who "approaches the text by concentrating exclusively on the combination of letters and words in a purely linear manner" (Martinez-Lage, 1995, p. 70).

Other comprehension tasks or subskills reflect *top-down processing* (see Chapter 2), in which meaning is derived through the use of contextual clues and activation of personal background knowledge about the content of the text. These subskills include identifying key ideas and guessing meaning through a process called a "psycholinguistic guessing game" (Goodman, 1967). In his description of a top-down approach to reading, Goodman states that "Efficient reading does not result from precise perception and identification of all elements, but from skill in selecting the fewest, most productive cues necessary to produce guesses which are right the first time" (as cited in Chastain, 1988, p. 223). Top-down models of comprehension are *reader-driven* and focus on what the reader/listener brings to the text in terms of knowledge of the world (Lally, 1998).

The current view of the interpretive skills is that the listener/reader arrives at meaning by using *both* bottom-up and top-down processing, in concert (Bernhardt, 1991; Swaffar, Arens, & Byrnes, 1991). According to Scarcella and Oxford (1992), "Listening can best be understood as a highly complex, interactive operation in which bottom-up processing is interspersed with top-down processing, the latter involving guessing" (p. 142). Similarly, in their discussion of the reading process, Swaffar, Arens, and Byrnes state that reading comprehension "results from interactive variables that operate simultaneously rather than sequentially" (p. 21). Furthermore, they maintain that the message of the text interacts with reader perceptions and that these interactions have the following components:

Top-down factors: reader
1. reader background (semantic knowledge)
2. reader perspective (reading strategies)

Top-down factors: text
3. text schema (topic)
4. text structure (organizational pattern of the information)
5. episodic sequence (scripts or story grammar)

Bottom-up factors: text and reader
6. illustrative detail
7. the surface language features of the text in letters, words, and individual sentences
8. reader language proficiency (p. 24)

There is evidence to suggest that learners perceive top-down strategies to be the more immediate strategies needed for comprehension and bottom-up strategies to be necessary in "repairing" comprehension in the face of difficulty (Vogely, 1995). This finding is supported by Eskey's (1986) interactive reading model, which proposes that readers use both (1) lower-level "identification" skills through which they recognize words and structures necessary for decoding; and (2) higher-level "interpretive" skills through which they reconstruct meaning of whole parts of the text. Both of these skill types are interactive in that they blend into one as the reader or listener interprets a text and makes it a part of what he or she knows (Eskey).

In addition to these cognitive processes, listening and reading comprehension also involve social processes. In her sociocognitive view of second language reading, Bernhardt (1991) proposes that readers interact with the features of a text, select the features that they feel are important for processing the information, and then use the selected features to reconstruct the text and interpret the message.[1] This process involves a different concept of "text," one that includes not only linguistic elements, but also the text's pragmatic nature, its intentionality, its content, and its topic (Bernhardt). Furthermore, a great deal of comprehension and interpretation is based on the experiences learners bring to the text. The learners gain new insights about the meaning of a text as a result of text-based discussions they have with others. This social view of comprehension reflects the sociocultural view of language learning and instruction posited in Chapter 1, in which learners and the teacher interact in the Zone of Proximal Development (ZPD) in order to co-construct meaning and interpretation of a text. This type of mediation mirrors the way in which comprehension is constructed socioculturally in the world outside the classroom.

 Top-down and bottom-up processes are used together in comprehension.

Despite what we know about the comprehension process and text interpretation, many FL classrooms still engage learners in practices that either foster exclusive use of linear bottom-up processing or reflect mechanical activities not associated with comprehension at all. For example, teachers often check comprehension of a reading by asking questions that are worded in such a way as to reveal the answer by making it easy for the student to look back to the passage and make a match. Consequently, students might identify a sentence from the text that correctly answers the question, but they may have no idea of what either the question or the answer means. This strategy reflects the "look-back-and-lift-off approach" (Lee & VanPatten, 1995) to reading and is problematic, since these readers rarely end up reading the entire passage and their comprehension consists of unconnected fragments of information (p. 189). A similar strategy is often used in listening through "listen-to-a-text-and-answer-questions" format (Berne, 2004, p. 522). This type of approach to interpretive communication does not account for ways in which comprehension and interpretation occur, and it does not assist learners in building comprehension of a text.

 In the "look-back-and-lift-off approach" to reading, students' comprehension consists of unconnected fragments of information.

The Relationship of L1 and L2 Interpretive Processes

Much of the research in L2 listening and reading cognition is based on studies conducted in L1 (Bernhardt, 1986; Brown, 1998; Fecteau, 1999; Joiner, 1986; Rubin, 1994).[2] Many studies have examined the relationship between L1 and L2 comprehension. Bernhardt and Kamil (1995) found that both L1 reading skills and L2 linguistic knowledge contribute to one's L2 reading comprehension, with L2 knowledge having a somewhat greater contribution. Moreover, they maintain that linguistic knowledge contributes more at lower proficiency levels, while L1 reading skills play a greater role in reading at higher levels. In other words, the reading ability of novice L2 learners might be predicted more on the basis of the level of their linguistic knowledge, while the reading ability of advanced L2 learners might be related more closely to their L1 reading skills. Fecteau's study of U.S. college students enrolled in an introductory French literature course also revealed that L1 and L2 reading skills are more interrelated among more proficient language learners, in which case L1 reading skills contribute more to L2 comprehension at higher levels than does L2 proficiency. This study also showed that organization of the text and level of background knowledge are important factors that impact comprehension in both L1 and L2 reading tasks; the "story-like" organization of the text and activated background knowledge of readers led to greater comprehension. Similar results have been revealed in listening: a study done by Vandergrift (2006) found that while both L2 proficiency and L1 listening ability contribute to L2 listening comprehension ability, L2 proficiency seems to be a much better predictor of L2 listener success. In Vandergrift's study, however, L1 inferencing ability appeared not to transfer to L2 inferencing in listening, which indicates that learners would benefit from strategy training that assists them in making this transfer.

According to Koda (2007b), second language reading differs considerably from L1 reading because it involves two languages in virtually all of its processes. In her summary of L2 reading research, Koda illustrates that a learner's L1 literacy experience has a lasting impact on L2 reading development, as do factors relating to age and L2 proficiency.[3] In comparing L1 and L2 reading, an important consideration is how L1 and L2 readers differ. Koda has identified three major distinctions between readers of L1 and readers of L2:

1. Unlike beginning L1 readers, L2 learners can use their prior literary experience, which can offer a great deal of assistance.
2. Beginning L1 readers, as a result of oral communication, have developed their linguistic systems by the time their formal literacy work begins. Conversely, L2 reading instruction often begins before a great deal of L2 linguistic knowledge has been acquired. Therefore the focus in L2 reading instruction differs. L1 instruction emphasizes decoding to help young readers link print with oral vocabulary, while L2 instruction focuses on building learners' linguistic foundations. Hence, L2 readers can often decode (i.e., connect print to oral vocabulary), but this decoding does not ensure comprehension since L2 learners do not have a fully developed linguistic system and may not know the meaning of the words they are able to decode. In sum, L2 readers can *read aloud* with little or no comprehension.
3. L1 focuses on processing in a single language, whereas L2 reading involves skills and experiences in both L1 and L2 (2004, p. 7).

Studies have also compared L1 and L2 listening comprehension, particularly around the issue of *discourse signaling cues*, metalinguistic devices that function as directional guides to signal how readers and listeners should interpret the incoming information (Tyler, 1994). Examples of signaling cues are previews (e.g., *There are four stages of this culture shock*), summarizers (*To sum up so far*), emphasis markers (e.g., *This is the key*), and logical connectives (e.g., *and, or, first,* and *second*) (Jung, 2003, p. 563). Many studies confirm that the beneficial effects of signaling cues found in L1 reading research can also be found in L1 listening comprehension. Listeners who attended to signaled texts in their native language recalled significantly more main ideas and performed better on open-ended questions when tested (Hron, Kurbjuhn, Mandl, & Schnotz, 1985; Richards, Fajen, Sullivan, & Gillespie, 1997).

Jung (2003) conducted a study to determine whether the positive effects of signaling cues in L1 listening could also be applied to L2 listening. Results of her study revealed that students who listened to lectures in the target language that contained signaling cues recalled significantly more information (i.e., both main ideas and supporting details) than did their nonsignaled counterparts. These results corroborated the findings of several previous studies that examined the effect of signaling cues on L2 listening (Chung, 2000; Flowerdew & Tauroza, 1995). In these and other studies, as in the case of the L2 reading research presented earlier, text type was found to be important since certain text types make use of particular signaling cues or use them more or less frequently. For example, in texts that feature a "comparison-and-contrast" organization, signaling cues might not play a critical role in making the text comprehensible since the text structure is already evident to the listener (Dunkel & Davis, 1994; Jung, 2003). Similarly, students might not rely as much on signaling cues in certain text types where the chronological order might be more familiar to students, such as narratives, as compared to expository text types, which often present a more complex set of relationships among ideas and whose meaning could be clarified through signaling cues (Barry & Lazarte, 1998; Horiba, 2000).

Differences Between Listening and Reading

In the previous sections, you have seen that listening and reading are similar—both draw upon knowledge of the language, background knowledge, contextual clues, cognitive processing skills, and the use of comprehension strategies. However, there are also important differences between the two. Written texts, particularly those that are presentational and intended for an audience, are typically organized in grammatical sentences arranged in coherent paragraphs (Richards, 1983). Spoken texts, on the other hand, can include ungrammatical or reduced forms; are often marked by pauses, hesitations, and fillers; and may feature topics that shift as the conversation is co-constructed. Another difference deals with the "accessibility" of the text (Stevick, 1984). In the reading comprehension task, the reader can reread what was read before and can look ahead to anticipate what is coming. In listening comprehension, the listener may be forced to comprehend with only one opportunity to hear the oral segment; any inattention to what is being said at the moment may cause him or her to lose part of the message (Hadley, 2001). Lund (1991) found that presenting a text twice, either in listening or reading, can be beneficial to students. If students do not have multiple opportunities to hear an oral segment, there is a risk of depending too heavily on short-term memory, thus confusing comprehension with memory recall. This finding is corroborated by a study done with learners studying Arabic as a foreign language, in which repeated exposure to a listening passage was identified as the "single most important factor in improving listening comprehension" (Elkhafaifi, 2005b, p. 510).

The Viewing Process

The interpretive mode relates not only to listening to an oral message and reading a written text, but also to viewing videos, films, plays, and television programs. The viewing medium provides a unique way of bringing the target culture into the classroom and making learning more meaningful and stimulating. Gruba (2006) has noted that no single definition of *video-mediated listening comprehension* has been posited in the research. Nonetheless, a number of studies have verified the effectiveness of video instruction in the classroom (Gruba; Price, 1990; Secules, Herron, & Tomasello, 1992; Weyers, 1999). Students who view videos demonstrate greater listening comprehension than do students who do not view them (Price; Secules, Herron, & Tomasello; Weyers). Videos have also been found to have a positive effect on learning grammar in the foreign language (Ramsay, 1991), the development of advanced level proficiency skills (Rifkin, 2000), and learning cultural information (Herron, Corrie, Cole, & Dubreil, 1999). In addition, studies have indicated that video clips can prepare students for listening (Wilberschied & Berman, 2004), that videos shown as advance organizers prior to the reading of a passage facilitate the retention of cultural information in the written text (Chung, 1999; Herron & Hanley, 1992), and that videos are more effective advance organizers than are pictures used with teacher narratives (Hanley, Herron, & Cole, 1995). Furthermore, one study indicated that, in addition to gains made in listening comprehension, students who viewed an authentic Spanish-language *telenovela* (soap opera) video showed greater confidence in generating output and greater scope and breadth of discourse (Weyers).

Videos that feature definite storylines and clearly drawn main characters are good texts for viewing (Joiner, 1990; Voller & Widdows, 1993). Swaffar and Vlatten (1997) propose that the viewing process should begin with silent viewing, during which students explore the possible messages and cultural perspectives implied by the visual images. Then, as students are exposed to sound, they verify whether their visual comprehension matches their understanding of what they hear. They engage in comprehension tasks and use the new information they learn through the viewing as the basis for discussion, role playing, and creative writing (Swaffar & Vlatten). Thus the viewing process involves predicting and anticipating the meaning of the visual images and then comparing these predictions to what is understood in the oral message.

Several studies have examined the use of *captioning*, "the use of on-screen text in conjunction with same language audio," (Taylor, 2005, p. 422) in L2 viewing and have revealed positive effects in various areas, including comprehension (Markham, 1999; Markham, Peter, & McCarthy, 2001) and vocabulary recognition and acquisition (Duquette & Painchaud, 1996; Stewart & Pertusa, 2004). In their study comparing the advantages of using L1 vs. L2 captions, Stewart and Pertusa found that listeners who watched films with L2 subtitles recalled more vocabulary than did their counterparts who saw L1 subtitles; they suggest the use of L2 captions since they maintain that students will not learn to listen if they read in L1 to interpret L2 texts. Taylor's study led him to conclude that L2 captioning might be more effective for enhancing the comprehension of more experienced language learners, since novices may have difficulty engaging in both listening and reading simultaneously. Clearly more research is needed to confirm the extent to which captioning might enable learners to have more success in L2 viewing.

Research on the Variables Involved in Comprehension and Interpretation

Research documents a number of variables that affect comprehension and interpretation of a text, be it oral or printed. These variables relate to (1) reader- and listener-based factors, such as familiarity with the topic, use of memory, use of strategies, purpose for listening/reading/viewing, and level of anxiety; and (2) text-based factors, such as text length, text organization, content and interest of the text, and vocabulary (Knutson, 1997).

Reader- and Listener-Based Factors

Topic Familiarity.   The first reader- and listener-based variable is the key role that *topic familiarity*, or background knowledge, plays in facilitating comprehension, regardless of the learner's proficiency level (Hammadou, 2000; Schmidt-Rinehart, 1994). This variable has already been explored in Chapter 2 in terms of the importance of context and background knowledge in understanding input. The degree to which the reader or listener is able to actually merge input with his or her schemata (see earlier discussion) determines how successful he or she will be in comprehending (Minsky, 1982). This linking of new and existing knowledge helps the listener or reader make sense of the text more quickly. The key role of topic/context and background knowledge has been verified by many studies on listening (Bransford & Johnson, 1972; Chiang & Dunkel, 1992;) and reading (Hammadou, 2000; Hanley, Herron, & Cole, 1995; Hauptman, 2000; Herron & Hanley, 1992; Lee, 1986a; Mueller, 1980; Nunan, 1985; Omaggio, 1979). These experiments have shown that language learners who are provided with prior contextual assistance, such as pictures, video segments, or pertinent cultural information, comprehend more accurately than they do in the absence of such support. The use of contextual and background information aids understanding by limiting the number of possible text interpretations. Furthermore, Hammadou (2000, 2002) found prior knowledge of the topic to be a key factor in enabling students to recall what they read and to make more logical inferences (e.g., those that have direct support from the text). Even beginning language learners can engage in inferencing if they have background knowledge of the topic (Hammadou, 1991).

Teachers are cautioned to not confuse learners' background knowledge with their level of interest in a text topic. For example, Carrell and Wise (1998) found in their research that background knowledge and interest in a text topic may be essentially uncorrelated. Though on the surface this finding may seem to be counterintuitive, according to Baldwin, Peleg-Bruckner, and McClintock (1985), "It should not be surprising then to find that a group of above average students could be fairly knowledgeable about space exploration and American Indians, for example, without having any real enthusiasm for those subjects" (p. 502). Conversely, it is possible to encounter a learner who is very interested in space exploration and American Indians but may be very weak in background knowledge of the topics (Baldwin et al.). Therefore, teachers should realize that even if students have prior knowledge of a text topic, they may or may not have interest in exploring the text. You will read more about interest level later in this section.

Short-Term or Working Memory.   A second reader- and listener-based variable is the ability of the reader or listener to hold information in his/her *short-term* or *working memory* during comprehension processing. According to Just and Carpenter (1992), the working memory stores words, phrases, meaning, and grammatical or thematic structures for later retrieval, in addition to performing language processing, such as accessing word meaning while syntactically processing a phrase. They suggest that listeners and readers with a small working memory span may have difficulty maintaining syntactic information (e.g., phrases and sentences from the text) while attending to nonsyntactic information (e.g., use of context and background knowledge). A larger working memory span may be necessary in order to allow for interaction between syntactic and nonsyntactic information, ". . . which is necessary for developing multiple interpretations, using context, making inferences, or integrating information over large distances in a text" (Brown,

1998, p. 195). Although much more research is needed in this area, the role of memory may be one factor that accounts for individual differences in comprehension. Elkhafaifi (2005b) found that teachers can compensate for the memory factor by providing prelistening preparation; in his study with students of Arabic as a foreign language, students who were provided with comprehension questions prior to a listening test achieved significantly better scores than did their counterparts who either had no prior preparation or who did a vocabulary preview activity.

In sum, teachers can limit the load on memory during a comprehension task by preparing students for the oral/printed segment, showing students the task or activity before they attend to the segment so that they know the purpose of what they are about to listen to/read/view, allowing students to have the printed text available to them during the reading comprehension process, and permitting students to listen to or view a segment multiple times.

Strategies in Comprehending and Interpreting.   A third variable is the degree to which the reader or listener uses *strategies* in comprehending and interpreting a text. In both listening and reading, prediction of forthcoming input, or the "activation of correct expectancies," is one characteristic of native listener and reader processing (Oller, 1983, p. 10). Many studies support the claim that learners who interact with the oral or printed text through strategies such as predicting, skimming (for main ideas), scanning (for details), and using background knowledge comprehend much better than learners who fail to use these strategies (Bacon, 1992a; Barnett, 1988a; Carrell, 1985; Elkhafaifi, 2005b; Palinscar & Brown, 1984; Vandergrift, 1997a). In listening, a number of studies have identified the various strategies that more- and less-proficient L2 listeners use (Cohen, Paige, Shively, Emert, & Hoff, 2005; Cubillos, Chieffo, & Fan, 2008; Goh, 2000; O'Malley, Chamot, & Küpper, 1989; Vandergrift, 1997b, 2003).[4] See Appendix 6.1 on the *Teacher's Handbook* Web site for a chart that summarizes the results of research on listening comprehension strategies; the chart highlights the differences among language learners in terms of their abilities to process oral language and depicts the effects of listening strategy instruction. Berne (2004) summarized the key results of these studies, as depicted in Figure 6.2. Overall, more-skilled listeners engage in active interaction with the text, use a wider variety of strategies, are more purposeful in their approach to listening, monitor their comprehension for overall meaning, infer meaning from context using a top-down approach, and effectively use prior knowledge while listening (Chamot & Küpper; Vandergrift, 2003). On the contrary, less-skillful listeners tend to use a bottom-up approach in segmenting what they hear on a word-by-word basis, make fewer connections between new information and their own background knowledge, and are easily frustrated when encountering unknown language (Chamot & Küpper; Vandergrift, 2003). Similar findings regarding strategy use by L2 readers have been documented (Carrell, 1989; Chamot & El-Dinary, 1999). With this information in mind, language teachers should be able to assess their L2 listeners and readers more effectively, diagnose their problems, and assist them in using more efficient strategies.

Research has also revealed that a study-abroad setting seems to promote or reinforce the use of top-down and social listening strategies for comprehension. Cubillos, Chieffo, and Fan (2008) found that intermediate-level college students who participated in a short-term study-abroad program used primarily top-down strategies and made significantly higher comprehension gains than did their home campus counterparts, who favored bottom-up listening strategies.

Evidence suggests that students benefit from direct strategy training in listening (Bacon, 1992b; Rost & Ross, 1991), reading (Barnett, 1988b; Carrell, 1989; Hosenfeld, 1984; Kitajima, 1997), viewing (Thompson & Rubin, 1996), and language learning in general (Oxford, 1990). Vandergrift (1997b) suggests that instruction should promote the use of

www.cengagebrain.com

FIGURE 6.2 Differences Between More- and Less-Proficient Listeners

More-Proficient Listeners	Less-Proficient Listeners
use strategies more often	process input word by word
use a wide range of strategies	rely heavily on translation/key words as strategie
use strategies interactively	are negatively affected by linguistic and attentional constraints
are concerned with the overall rhetorical organization of text	are concerned with definitions/pronunciation of words

are better able to:
    attend to larger chunks of input
    monitor/redirect attention
    grasp overall meaning of input
    relate what they hear to previous
        experiences
    guess meanings of words
	make fewer inferences/elaborations

use existing linguistic knowledge to aid comprehension	do not verify their assumptions
	do not relate what they hear to previous experiences

Source: From "Listening comprehension strategies: A review of the literature," by J. E. Berne, 2004, *Foreign Language Annals, 37,* 521–533. Reprinted by permission of John Wiley & Sons, Inc.

successful strategies as observed among more skillful listeners: planning for completion of the task, monitoring of comprehension, and evaluation of their approach to listening in terms of the outcomes of the task. Further, Vandergrift (2006) proposes that students should be taught strategies to transfer L1 inferencing skills to L2 inferencing tasks and to use their world knowledge in L2 listening to compensate for gaps in understanding; this might best be accomplished through listening comprehension practice without the threat of evaluation to help learners who are afraid to take risks.

Purpose for Listening/Reading/Viewing.   A fourth reader- and listener-based variable that affects comprehension and interpretation is the *purpose* for listening/reading/viewing—that is, the nature of the task. Reading (and also listening and viewing) with a purpose means "approaching texts with a specific perspective or goal" (Knutson, 1997, p. 51). Munby (1979) identifies two kinds of reading that involve different goals and skills. *Extensive reading*, usually for pleasure, requires the ability to understand main ideas, find specific information, and read quickly. *Intensive reading*, most often for information, requires the ability to read for details, understand implications, and follow relationships of thought throughout a text. Knutson suggests strategies such as the following for providing learners with specific purposes for reading: asking learners to read from a particular point of view (e.g., that of a detective, child, etc.); providing a reason for reading that reflects a real-world situation (e.g., looking through movie listings to find an appealing movie); giving groups of students a task to complete based on reading (e.g., students plan a trip after reading brochures, timetables, and maps, and listening to weather and traffic reports); guiding students in text analysis of rhetorical devices such as register and audience; developing language literacy by engaging students in reading and discussing literature; and providing opportunities for learners to learn new information and pursue their own interests and enjoyment through interpretive tasks (pp. 51–55).

Anxiety.   The fifth and final reader- and listener-based variable refers to the level of *anxiety* that the reader/listener brings to the comprehension task. In Chapter 1, you learned about how learners' anxiety can have negative effects on language learning. The issue of anxiety has been examined specifically in the contexts of reading and listening comprehension. In her study of university Spanish students, Sellers (2000) found that learners with higher levels of foreign language anxiety tended to have higher levels of foreign language reading anxiety and vice versa, recalled overall less passage content than students who claimed to experience only minimal anxiety, recalled fewer important ideas, and tended to experience more off-task, interfering thoughts. These results are similar to those obtained by Saito, Garza, and Horwitz (1999), whose work also showed that foreign language reading anxiety is distinguishable from general foreign language anxiety and that learners who perceive reading in their target language as relatively difficult have significantly higher levels of reading anxiety than learners who perceive it as somewhat difficult or as relatively easy. In addition, in this study, when reading, English-speaking learners of Japanese were the most anxious, followed by French learners, with Russian learners exhibiting the lowest anxiety; the researchers hypothesize that this difference may be due to the unfamiliar and non-Roman writing system and foreign cultural content in the texts. Other findings in this study reveal that students experience anxiety when (1) they encounter unfamiliar words and structures, because they feel a need to understand everything, and (2) they have to read about cultural topics with which they are unfamiliar. Although the curricula of the students in this study offered instruction on how to approach the reading task, many students reported using word-for-word translation when reading in their foreign language, and they reported a sense of anxiety when asked by their teachers to read aloud in class.

Similar studies have shown that anxiety impedes L2 listening comprehension (Bacon, 1989; Lund, 1991). According to Scarcella and Oxford (1992), students experience listening anxiety when they feel they must perform a task that is too difficult or unfamiliar to them. In Vogely's (1998) study examining L2 listening anxiety, beginning-level Spanish students reported four primary sources of anxiety: (1) oral input was too fast, poorly enunciated, and featured different accents; (2) listening comprehension exercises contained unfamiliar topics and vocabulary and complicated syntax; (3) there was a lack of visual support to help them with contextual guessing; and (4) they were only permitted to listen to oral segments once. Anxiety tends to decrease over time as learners become more proficient and gain more experience with listening tasks (Elkhafaifi, 2005a; MacIntyre & Gardner, 1991). These findings suggest that language teachers include more listening practice to familiarize students with tasks, teach specific listening strategies to help students listen more effectively and recall more of what they hear, help students to overcome unrealistic expectations about understanding every detail of what they hear, and encourage students to acknowledge and discuss their listening anxiety in class (Elkhafaifi). Further, teachers should resist the temptation to give students the printed script of a segment before they have attempted to interpret it aurally, as this may encourage "an inefficient on-line translation approach to listening" (Osada, 2001). L2 listeners will need to learn to rely on the text they hear, as in real-life listening, if they are to become successful listeners; thus, providing multiple opportunities to listen to a text should be a substitute for providing a script.

   Reader- and listener-based factors include topic familiarity, memory capacity, comprehension strategies, the purpose of the task, and anxiety level.

Text-Based Factors

Length of Text.   A sixth, text-based, variable relates to the *length of text* presented for comprehension and interpretation. In beginning-level classes, students are typically given shorter, edited texts to listen to or read. Learners who process shorter texts are more likely to use word-for-word processing strategies since the demands on memory permit greater attention to detail (Kintsch & van Dijk, 1978; Swaffar, Arens, & Byrnes, 1991). Recent studies suggest that longer texts may actually be easier for students to comprehend because they are more cohesive and provide more of a context from which meaning may be derived (Gascoigne, 2002a; Maxim, 2002; Swaffar & Arens, 2005). According to Swaffar and Arens, a longer text often contains redundancy and clues to content, such as "cognates, logical connectors, restatements, sentences of varying length, a fuller argument, and a broader scale of information" (p. 58) and are often easier to read. A longer text may provide students with the information necessary to compensate for their limited L2 proficiency (Hammadou, 1991; Maxim). Swaffar et al. have suggested that texts of more than 500 words are effective for activating the use of different reading strategies and recall. However, in her examination of beginning college French textbooks, Gascoigne (2002b) found that readings averaged 247 words in length, indicating a reluctance of textbook authors to give introductory students longer texts to read, despite support for this in the research.

Teachers are advised to select longer texts with great care and to develop strategies for guiding students through them, since longer texts may intimidate novice learners. Texts should be appropriate to the age and instructional level of students. Longer texts accompanied by visuals are much less daunting to students than multiple-page texts with dense prose. Also, the goal of reading longer texts should never be to comprehend every word; students may be expected to identify the main ideas and key details of a longer text on the first pass and perhaps later be asked to read more carefully for other details. Teachers should remember to *edit the task* to the level of students' interpretive abilities.

 Teachers should remember to *edit the task* to the level of students' interpretive abilities.

Organization of the Oral or Printed Text.   A seventh, text-based, variable in the comprehension/interpretation process pertains to the *organization of the oral or printed text presented*. Traditionally, the difficulty of texts has been judged on the basis of the simplicity of grammatical structures and the familiarity of the vocabulary. According to Lee (1987), this may be due to the fact that we have often tested comprehension itself on the basis of grammar and vocabulary recognition rather than on the reader's/listener's interaction with the text's message. Some research has shown that exposure to texts with unfamiliar grammar and vocabulary does not significantly affect comprehension (Lee). Further, there is evidence to show that the grammatical knowledge of the learner is not a significant predictor of L2 reading and listening comprehension ability; however, vocabulary knowledge may be a much more reliable predictor (Mecartty, 2000; Vandergrift, 2006). This finding stands in sharp contrast to the assumption that many teachers make concerning the impact of unknown grammatical structures on learners' ability to interpret a text. Indeed, other factors, such as the quality of the text itself in terms of factual consistency and coherence, and the background knowledge and motivation of learners, may be more important considerations for teachers when selecting texts (Swaffar, Arens, & Byrnes, 1991).

A great deal of research has revealed that text structure is an important factor in comprehension (Barry & Lazarte, 1998; Fecteau, 1999; Horiba, 2000; Riley, 1993; Roller, 1990). Several studies have found that texts that are organized according to a "story" format (those that have a beginning event, introduction of a conflict, development or attempt to resolve the conflict, outcome, and ending) have a positive effect on L2 readers' ability to recall the text (Fecteau; Riley).

Another aspect of text structure found to play a key role in comprehension is the use of signaling cues or features. Earlier in this chapter you read about the use of discourse signaling cues in the L2 listening process. Linguistic and nonlinguistic signaling features are also important in a printed text—they increase the redundancy for the reader and often provide helpful clues to content and structure of the text (Hauptman, 2000). Linguistic signaling in a printed text is similar to that of a spoken message and serves to indicate connections, transitions, and summaries of ideas, e.g., *in addition to, on the other hand, in summary.* Nonlinguistic signaling features in a printed text include graphic organizers, such as charts, graphs, pictures, diagrams, and maps, as well as structural organizers, such as titles, subtitles, numbering of sections, boldfacing, underlining, margin notes, indentation, and outline form. The presence of these types of signaling features may contribute to a text's "low linguistic load"; that is, these cues enable learners to rely less on the language of the text (e.g., vocabulary) in interpreting it (Hauptman, p. 626).[5]

How does the "story" format discussed here relate to Oller's Episode Hypothesis, presented in Chapter 3?

Content and Interest Level of the Text.   An eighth, text-based, variable relates to the *content and interest level of the text.* Is the content interesting, and relevant to students' interests and instructional objectives? Does the content provoke a topic to be discussed and ideas to be shared? Or does the content relate to the subject areas of the school curriculum (see Chapter 3 for discussion of content-based instruction)? The quality of the content will affect how successfully students will be engaged in exploring the text. In a study by Dristas and Grisenti (1995), students read one L2 text that reflected an area of interest for them but was judged to be more linguistically challenging and another L2 text that was not of interest to them but was judged to be less linguistically challenging. Students' ability to comprehend and interpret was greater with the L2 text that was more interesting to them, and they were able to say more about the information presented in the text, despite its linguistic challenge. This finding points to a possible relationship between interest level and content of a text and students' ability to interpret.

New Vocabulary.   A ninth, text-based, variable involves the treatment of *new vocabulary.* Koda (2004) maintains that vocabulary knowledge and reading comprehension may each enhance the development of the other; that is, acquiring more vocabulary helps one to become a better reader and reading ability expands one's vocabulary knowledge. Although the field has not reached universal consensus regarding how to help readers deal with unknown vocabulary, some studies have shed some light on this challenge. For example, the use of vocabulary lists with definitions does little to help the reader build vocabulary or comprehend more effectively while reading (Bensoussan, Sim, & Weiss, 1984; Johnson, 1982). Further, according to Swaffar and Arens, "a traditional gloss on a text tempts novice readers to translate rather than read, making the process of reading laborious (because it slows them down, while creating the impression that the linear sequence of words is the only way to understand a text's sentences)" (2005, p. 63). A more effective teacher strategy is to present new words in a pre-reading phase in terms of their thematic and discourse relationship to the text and link text information to the readers' background knowledge. According to Swaffar, Arens, and Byrnes, readers should be encouraged to build their own vocabulary banks, since not all students need to learn the same words (e.g., word banks organized thematically). In-class vocabulary practice can provide opportunities for students to "find additional words that relate to the same semantic category . . . ; identify how the same words are redefined by different contexts . . . ; increase awareness of pronounceability; and identify affixes, suffixes, or parts of speech" (1991, p. 68).

In a study that examined how learners use context to derive meaning, learners reported that, when faced with unknown words as they read, they (1) used the context to determine meaning, (2) identified cognates, and (3) used their previous knowledge of the meaning of the words (Frantzen, 2003). However, the context in which a word appears does not always lead a language learner to an accurate interpretation of its meaning. Many studies provide evidence that the use of contextual cues is often an insufficient way to narrow in on a word's meaning, and furthermore, that contextual guessing alone seldom allows the reader to arrive at the correct meaning (Frantzen; Kelly, 1990; Paribakht & Wesche, 1999; Stein, 1993). Accurate contextual guessing seems to depend in part on the type of context in which unknown words are found; vague and ambiguous contexts, contexts in which the text is too difficult and inaccessible to the learner, and contexts that are dense in unknown words yield little in terms of figuring out meaning. Similarly, context can dissuade learners from words they already know (i.e., cause them to change their minds from correct to incorrect meanings of words), and glossing of words can sometimes lead to misunderstanding of meaning (e.g., glosses for phrases instead of for individual words and supplying incorrect synonyms) (Frantzen).

Inaccurate guessing may also stem from four types of ineffective learner behaviors:

1. the inattentive use of contextual cues (not paying sufficient attention to the context);
2. "oblivious certainty," a term used by Frantzen (2003) to refer to learners' attitude that they already know certain words despite what the context may suggest;
3. overuse of the "just-get-the-gist" method of reading, which can lead to a contentment with a superficial understanding of the text, even when it isn't sufficient given the comprehension task at hand; and
4. the use of misplaced guesses based upon memory of the story in the text (Frantzen, pp. 175–184).

Nagy (1997) warns that "although deliberate use of context to infer meanings of new words is an essential reading strategy, any instruction in such a strategy should be based on recognition of the fact that natural context is relatively uninformative" (p. 83; as cited in Frantzen, 2003, p. 185). To assist learners in using contextual guessing more successfully, teachers might encourage them to re-evaluate their initial guesses by checking them against the context, since contexts can suggest a variety of meanings (Frantzen; Haynes, 1984; Nagy).

 Text-based factors include the length of text, organization of text, content/interest level of text, and treatment of new vocabulary.

Figure 6.3 sums up the key points regarding the text-based variables by illustrating the features of "more *readable* text" (Swaffar & Arens, 2005, p. 58).

According to the research presented throughout this section, we should take into consideration the following variables when we provide opportunities for students to comprehend and interpret oral, printed, and video texts: (1) topic familiarity and background knowledge of the learner, (2) the ability of the reader or listener to hold information in short-term memory during comprehension processing, (3) strategies the learner uses in the comprehension task, (4) the purpose for listening/reading/viewing, (5) the level of anxiety that the listener/reader brings to the comprehension task, (6) length of text, (7) organization of text, (8) content and interest level of text, and (9) treatment of new vocabulary. Above all, these factors should be kept in mind in light of the appropriateness of the text for the age and interests of the reader and the characteristics that make a text readable.

FIGURE 6.3 Features of a "More Readable Text"

Text Feature	Purpose for Reader
Is more redundant or longer with more than one point at which the reader can access it (including illustrations, titles, etc.)	To provide more context for the reader and multiple ways to approach the text
Is organized around concrete situations rather than abstract principles (unless abstract principles are L1 topics familiar to students)	To enable the reader to connect the text to real-world situations and contexts
Identifies the unfamiliar with respect to the familiar	To help the reader link new information to existing schemata
Deals with topics of interest or familiarity to intended audience	To capture the reader's attention and interest
Fits reader demographics of both L1 and FL cultures	To relate to topics and interests of age-appropriateness to the reader
Has a substantive, readily-discernible plot	To offer the reader an opportunity to think, learn, and enjoy reading
Has clear sequential development of events, well-marked episodes	To enable the reader to identify transitions in the story and follow the sequence of the various parts of the story
Has a recognizable agent or concrete subject	To help the reader relate the text to identifiable people
Has an unambiguous intent	To provide a straightforward point of view for the reader to explore

Source: Adapted from Swaffar & Arens (2005, p. 58), and Swaffar, Arens, & Byrnes (1991, pp. 137–139).

Integration of Authentic Texts

What was the definition of *authentic texts* given in Chapter 3?

Chapter 3 introduced the concept of using authentic materials in order to establish a meaningful context and reflect target-language cultures. Empirical studies have confirmed the positive results gained by listeners and readers who are given opportunities to interact with authentic oral or written texts. It has been well documented that students who listen to authentic oral segments, such as radio broadcasts, demonstrate significantly greater listening comprehension than do students who do not interact with authentic segments (Bacon, 1992b; Herron & Seay, 1991).

Several studies have examined the effect of introducing authentic readings early in language study. Maxim (2002) found that college students in their first semester of German were able to successfully read a full-length authentic novel in German while at the same time continuing to progress in their language development at the same level as their counterparts who were not exposed to such reading. The success of these readers can be attributed to several factors: (1) students experienced a guided approach as they explored the reading, progressing from identification to summarization, synthesis, and eventual analysis, while working collaboratively with classmates to construct meaning; (2) students experienced less anxiety because the cultural context of the romance novel was familiar to them and the length of the novel provided recurring situations, characters, and words, which seemed to facilitate comprehension; and 3) students received training in the use of effective reading strategies, such as identifying key information and focusing on major events in the story and their consequences (Maxim). The results of Maxim's investigation in German were corroborated by Gascoigne's (2002a) study of beginning French students who successfully read authentic French texts of several hundred words in length within the first 12 hours of class meetings.

The benefits of exploring authentic texts seem to go beyond that of improving comprehension, as students in several studies have also experienced improvement in oral and written language performance as a result (Vigil, 1987; Weyers, 1999). The reading success of these beginning students would seem to dispute claims often made by teachers that reading in language programs adversely affects the beginning language learner's second language development. In fact, Maxim (2002) suggests that allowing time for extensive reading on a regular basis may contribute to the development of grammatical and communicative competence, and Gascoigne (2002a) encourages teachers to incorporate authentic reading into the L2 classroom from the very first weeks of instruction. These and other studies confirm the advantage of presenting unedited, authentic texts to students as early as possible in language study.

Many teachers feel a need to "simplify" or "edit" authentic texts in order to make texts easier for students in early levels of language study to understand. However, the research has verified that the opposite is true; that is, learners demonstrate a significantly higher level of comprehension on texts that are read in their unedited, authentic forms as opposed to versions simplified through lexical changes (Vigil, 1987; Young, 1993, 1999). Two implications of these studies merit attention. First, teachers in Young's (1999) study who were asked to simplify authentic texts did so primarily by (1) changing words, i.e., they substituted words or phrases that were less common with those that students would be more apt to recognize, (2) changing passive voice to active voice, and (3) deleting verbiage that was thought to be redundant or superfluous (pp. 364–366). In a study of English-as-a-foreign-language textbooks approved in Japan, Oguro (2008) found that editing included changes in lexicon, simplification, and alteration of sentence, as well as changes in grammar and in the amount of elaboration contained in the original authentic text. The tasks required of students became literal rather than inferential, and the passages no longer reflected the target culture. These types of changes indicate that teachers, textbook authors, and governmental agencies believe that making lexical adjustments and shortening the text facilitate comprehension, and that they may also be convinced that students process texts by relying heavily on a word-for-word approach (Young, 1999). Evidence points to the possibility that language teachers may underestimate not only the abilities of their students to interact with authentic texts, but also the effect of a guided approach in greatly facilitating the comprehension process (Allen, Bernhardt, Berry, & Demel, 1988).

Simplifying an authentic text may actually be counterproductive, since the redundancy and richness of the context contributes to comprehension. This is important for language teachers to realize, since many textbooks still feature unauthentic oral and printed texts that carefully control for length and vocabulary, which may actually prove to be much more difficult for students to comprehend. The results of studies indicate that authentic texts should be used more extensively given their positive effects on comprehension and interpretation and on their overall second language development (see, for example, Bacon, 1989; Epstein, 2002; Lacorte & Thurston-Griswold, 2001; Weissenrieder, 1987). However, teachers should remember to choose authentic texts that are age- and level-appropriate, and to *edit the task, not the text.*

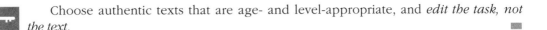 Choose authentic texts that are age- and level-appropriate, and *edit the task, not the text*.

Exploration of Literary Texts

While authentic materials are often primarily thought of as newspaper and magazine articles or news broadcasts, many other types of oral and written texts appropriate to specific age groups can be used effectively, including literary texts. Shook (1996) defines literature as "more than just informational in nature, but rather . . . compelling; that is, it makes the reader reflect inwardly, personally" (p. 202). Christensen (1990) suggests the use of authentic teenage adventure novels because of their potential for sustaining interest by means of suspense, intrigue, fast action, and cliff-hanging chapter endings.[6] Earlier chapters of this text have explored various possibilities for using folktales, stories, and legends. In their description of a holistic approach to post-secondary language teaching, Swaffar and Arens (2005) advocate integrating literature and culture into every level of the curriculum.[7] *Teacher's Handbook* advocates a prominent role for exploration of literary texts at all levels as a way to develop students' target culture and language competence, and to provide opportunities for students to use their cognitive skills and interact with one another through sharing of ideas.

 Teacher's Handbook advocates a prominent role for exploration of literary texts at all levels as a way to develop students' target culture and language competence, and to provide opportunities for students to use their cognitive skills and interact with one another through sharing of ideas.

In Chapter 5, you learned about a constructivist approach to engaging students in learning about culture and acquiring cultural perspectives (Wright, 2000), and the role of affective learning in helping students to become sensitive to cultural differences (Lange, 1999). Inspired by the approaches of Wright and Lange, Scott and Huntington (2002) conducted a study to explore the relationship between the study of a foreign language literary text and the development of competence in a second culture. Their study compared the attitudes and reactions of introductory-level university French students who read a fact sheet about the Ivory Coast with the attitudes and reactions of students who read a poem written by a poet from the Ivory Coast. Students who read the poem were able to generalize more personalized reactions to cultural themes, such as language and ethnicity, than were their counterparts who read the fact sheet. The authors conclude that exploration of literary texts can play a pivotal role in developing students' (1) affective awareness, i.e., awareness of feelings and attitudes, sensitivity to dimensions of emotion, empathy for others, and (2) cognitive flexibility, i.e., acknowledgment of multiple views, tolerance of ambiguity, nonjudgmental evaluation of others (Scott & Huntington, pp. 623–624). Further, their findings lend support for the claim that literary texts should be used, even at the earliest stages of language learning, as a basis for developing C2 competence and addressing the culture standards of the *Standards for Foreign Language Learning in the 21st Century (SFLL)* (National Standards in Foreign Language Education Project [NSFLEP], 2006).[8]

In addition to serving as a useful context for developing cross-cultural perspectives, literature can also be used to provide opportunities for lengthy turns at talk and for developing language proficiency (Donato & Brooks, 2004). Students' language use should be monitored for its targeted level of proficiency, discourse features, and sociolinguistic appropriateness (Bernhardt, 2001). Recent findings, however, indicate that language teachers may not always take advantage of the opportunity to develop their students' language proficiency while exploring literary texts. Studies done by Donato and Brooks, Musumeci (1996), and Zyzik and Polio (2008) described college literature classes in which teacher talk dominated lessons, negotiation of meaning rarely occurred, student participation was limited, and pressure was felt by the instructor to cover required content in a limited span of time. See Chapter 8 for a full discussion of the discourse of literature classes.

Foreign language teachers often express a concern that literary texts are too challenging for typical language students and restrict their use, if they use them at all, to the advanced level, particularly Advanced Placement classes. Many leading scholars who conduct L2 reading research warn that this perceived difficulty is a faulty one (Allen, Bernhardt, Berry, & Demel, 1988; Fecteau, 1999). Frantzen (2003) notes that one factor that contributes to the perceived difficulty of literature selections is that authors of works of literature do not write for L2 learners, but rather their fellow citizens, who most likely share the cultural and historical knowledge necessary to understand their work. Therefore, one of the principal reasons that students at all levels may find the literature difficult is because they often do not have this type of background knowledge (Bernhardt, 2001). To compound the problem, in the absence of effective strategies for helping guide students through literary texts, language teachers often expect learners to understand the entirety of a text, which means that students either use word-for-word translation to attempt to comprehend the text and/or teachers resort to an explanation and discussion of the text in English.

In selecting texts for beginning foreign language learner-readers, Shook (1996) suggests that teachers choose literary texts that express the basic, shared cultural beliefs of the target culture. The texts do not have to be direct descriptions of values but can indirectly reflect or hint at values. The teacher should select subsequent literary texts that build upon the knowledge of the native and target cultures already explored by the readers' interaction with previous texts (Shook). Building on students' background knowledge also facilitates their ability to formulate inferences about what they read, as suggested earlier (Hammadou, 1991, 2000). Galloway (1992) suggests that as students explore literary texts, they need frequent comprehension checks, and guidance in sorting information, assigning meaning, formulating and testing hypotheses, and integrating new ideas.

With respect to teaching literature at the advanced secondary level and at the post-secondary level, Hoecherl-Alden (2006) suggests that a learning community be created by means of a *workshop-style* literature classroom where learners are encouraged to provide a variety of responses to the text, rather than being given a ready-made interpretation by the teacher; this is similar to the approach proposed by reader-response theories (Rosenblatt, 1995).

The *workshop-style* literature classroom instruction, which could be applied to exploration of texts at any level of instruction, values student-initiated analysis, through which "students begin to take control of their interactions with a literary text and become comfortable making judgments" (Hoecherl-Alden, 2006, p. 248). Activities such as literature circles, journal keeping, peer writing groups, and role-plays facilitate the building of a community of learners. A *reader's theater* activity at the intermediate level engages students in literature-based, read-aloud sessions, which foster oral interpretation by individual learners and further modification by the class (Ratcliff, 1999). This socioculturally constructed type of classroom environment supports the suggestions offered by Mantero (2006) in his discussion of a model of instruction called *Applied Literacy in Second Language Education (ALL2E)*, through which literature instructors extend text-centered talk so that it addresses cognitive development and improves language proficiency. This approach focuses on interpretive and evaluative inquiry, rather than linguistically driven, discrete-point questions.

Similarly, Wolfe (2004) conducted a study that investigated ways in which adolescent ESL readers developed the ability to read literary texts in a more "adult-like" manner and learned to identify and understand abstract literary concepts. Wolfe tape-recorded study sessions in which 15 ESL students discussed a novel with their teacher. Through an analytic tool called "chains of signification," the researcher studied how the meanings of words changed, and ultimately how abstract ideas evolved, through the study sessions; for example, in the story, the word *owl* initially was used to discuss the animal, then to signify a messenger, then a symbol, and finally to refer to a more complex idea of a dichotomy in the novel. Wolfe attributes students' abilities to interpret the novel at an abstract level to the strategies used by the teacher who, as a facilitator, guided students to more abstract interpretations of the text as a result of rechaining of words and concepts— i.e., redefining lexical items with a new accepted definition, such as redefining *owl* from *animal* to *symbol*. Rechaining was accomplished by four key teacher strategies:

1. validating the value of student contributions and not judging any contributions as "off task";
2. restating student comments in more adult-like ways while giving the student credit as the contributor of the idea, thus legitimizing the student's interpretation and sometimes repairing the utterance;
3. tying complex ideas of symbolism and theme to more concrete examples from students' lives and other texts; and
4. taking advantage of opportunities to offer his own literary interpretations of the text, thereby enabling students to rechain lexical items constantly (p. 411).

Wolfe's study suggests that teachers must have a metacognitive awareness of how to "lift the level" of the literary discussion, which is best accomplished through small, consistent shifts toward more complex interpretations (Edelsky, Draper, & Smith, 1983).

 How do these teacher strategies relate to the concept of the ZPD as an interactive activity, discussed in Chapter 1?

Implications for Teaching Listening, Reading, Viewing

If we adopt the definition of reading as proposed by Swaffar, Arens, and Byrnes (1991) and extend it to listening and viewing, then reading, listening, and viewing comprehension in L2 are functions of "cognitive development, the ability to think within the framework of the second language" (p. 63). According to their framework and the results of the studies described earlier, research points to the following implications for teaching the interpretive skills:

1. Students need pre-reading, pre-listening, and pre-viewing activities that prepare them for the comprehension/interpretation task.
2. Students should be taught to interact with the text through the use of both bottom-up and top-down processes.
3. The information gained through interpreting a text can be used as the basis for interpersonal and presentational communication.
4. Students' comprehension will increase if they are trained to use strategies such as activation of background knowledge, contextual guessing, and use of nonverbal cues, which will also serve to lessen their anxiety.
5. In practicing contextual guessing, students should be encouraged to check their initial guesses against the context and revise them as necessary.
6. Students will have greater success if the texts selected deal with topics with which they are familiar and if they are encouraged to establish a purpose for exploring these texts.

7. Students, even in beginning levels of language study, can be engaged in drawing inferences from a text being explored if they have sufficient familiarity with the topic of the text and are provided with prompts and/or tasks that encourage them to do so.

8. Teachers should be aware of the load on memory that students may experience during the comprehension task, and they should plan to control for this by allowing students to have the printed text available while completing a reading comprehension task and allowing students to listen to an oral text or view a video text multiple times.

9. Factors to consider when selecting texts include the degree of contextual support, i.e., longer may be better; the organization of the text, i.e., story-like features and signaling features are helpful; and level of interest to students.

10. Effective strategies for helping students to deal with new vocabulary found in a text include helping them to explore new words in terms of their thematic and discourse relationship to the text; linking new words to their background knowledge; identifying words in similar semantic categories; identifying affixes, parts of speech, or word families; and building their individual vocabulary banks.

11. Teachers should encourage students to self-report periodically while listening, reading, and viewing so that teachers will be informed about the comprehension strategies their students are using.

12. Authentic texts provide an effective means for presenting real language, integrating culture, heightening comprehension, and stimulating interest in language learning.

13. Literary texts should be used from beginning levels of language instruction to develop affective awareness and cognitive flexibility, both of which will facilitate C2 competence.

14. Teachers should remember to *edit the task, not the text.*

15. An interactive, or workshop-style classroom format, can facilitate the interpretation task by enabling learners to collaborate on tasks, construct meaning together, use teacher and peer feedback in refining hypotheses, and assume more of an active role in developing interpretive abilities.

The Role of the Interpretive Mode Across Instructional Levels

In Chapters 4 and 5, you learned about the key role that interpretive listening plays in teaching foreign language to elementary and middle school students. Listening is used as the vehicle for language acquisition and serves as a springboard for integrating the other modes and content. Elementary and middle school teachers use many techniques for improving interpretive listening, such as gestures, Total Physical Response (TPR), exploration of visuals and realia, and hands-on student participation.

For elementary school children, the transition from interpretive listening and interpersonal speaking to interpretive reading is made through the use of the Language Experience Approach, as described in Chapter 4. At both the elementary and middle school levels, culturally appropriate stories, myths, folktales, science fiction, and adventure stories can be presented to combine cultural understanding and the teaching of interpretive reading. Chapter 5 presented an approach for using an oral or a printed text as the context for a thematic unit while integrating the practice of all three modes of Communication and Cultures.

At the middle/junior high school and high school levels and beyond, listening should also play a prominent role if students are to acquire language. Learners need to attend to large amounts of comprehensible input in the target language, and they benefit from training in strategy development. Authentic input provides the context and meaning stage for the story-based approach to grammar instruction that is presented in Chapter 7. The various types of authentic oral or printed texts, as described in earlier chapters, can be presented to students at all levels of instruction. Beginning language learners benefit from experience in top-down processing or listening/reading/viewing for the main idea, since this activity discourages the word-for-word decoding that often occurs in early language learning.

The research discussed earlier in this chapter refutes the notion of consistently matching text length and text type to particular levels of instruction or to students' proficiency levels. For example, beginning-level students should not just be given short texts dealing with concrete information, such as menus and advertisements. Instead, students should be given the opportunity to use the information in the text, grammar, vocabulary, and discourse markers that connect ideas and help with comprehension. In addition, by listening/reading/viewing from various perspectives, students can also gain additional insights about the text and the author's intent. Thus this type of interactive listening, reading, and viewing not only develops interpretive abilities but can also enable students to learn new ideas and improve global language competence.

Acquisition of New Vocabulary Through Reading/Listening/Viewing

A related issue concerning new vocabulary in a text concerns the difference between recognizing or correctly identifying the meaning of new words and learning their meaning. Many studies have pointed out that words that are correctly guessed or inferred in a text are not necessarily learned and/or remembered, perhaps because once the immediate comprehension need is met, further processing may not be seen as needed (Pressley, Levin, & McDaniel, 1987; Wesche & Paribakht, 2000). Research suggests that learning vocabulary through incidental exposure, i.e., reading and listening, is most effective when students know how to attend to new language—by being aware of word families and affixes for analyzing words into parts, by knowing how to use contextual cues, and by knowing when and how to use a dictionary effectively (Fraser, 1999).

Several researchers have suggested that for learning of new vocabulary, the degree of processing that occurs as meaning is figured out determines whether and to what degree a word will be learned (Mondria & Wit-DeBoer, 1991; Paribakht & Wesche, 1999). On the one hand, if the word appears in a rich context that makes the meaning of a word obvious, the word will likely not be acquired (Mondria & Wit-DeBoer; Nation & Coady, 1988). On the other hand, if the context is too difficult and reveals little about the word's meaning, then the word will not be inferred or learned, because the struggle in processing is too great (Paribakht & Wesche). It seems, then, that a "moderate" amount of struggling might lead to correct inference of a word's meaning and a greater likelihood that the word will be acquired (Frantzen, 2003).

The research has revealed the merit of exercises that engage readers in tasks such as locating selected words in the text, matching definitions to the new words, producing derivatives of words to create other parts of speech in word families, replacing underlined words in new sentences with similar words from the text, and arranging words into sentences (Paribakht & Wesche, 1996, 1997; Wesche & Paribakht, 2000). The use of these exercises along with a reading seems to make more L2 words more salient, or noticeable, to readers; guide readers' attention to different aspects of L2 word knowledge; and encourage them to explore some words on their own (Wesche & Paribakht). Thus, while reading, listening, and viewing provide effective contexts and activities for acquiring new knowledge and language, learners require opportunities to do focused work on the use of new vocabulary within a text if they are to acquire and retain new vocabulary and use it productively.

An Interactive Model for Integrating the Three Modes of Communication

Here we present a model for developing students' communicative skills, using integration of the three modes of communication as the framework. The modes and skills are integrated as students are engaged in interaction with oral, printed, and video texts and with one another. This model is called *interactive* because it accounts for ways in which the message of the text interacts with reader/listener perceptions in both top-down and bottom-up ways, as described by Swaffar, Arens, and Byrnes (1991) earlier in this chapter. Further, the model responds to the implications of current research in the interpretive mode inasmuch as it (1) reflects the phases through which learners should be guided, according to Swaffar and Arens (2005): pre-reading, initial reading for global ideas, rereading to identify and reproduce textual messages, rereading to express messages, and rereading to create discourses that express an independent viewpoint (p. 71); and (2) answers Berne's call for a listening model that expands beyond the traditional "listen-to-a-text-and-answer-questions" format, as discussed earlier in this chapter (2004, p. 522).

In other words, an interactive approach involves actively constructing meaning between the text and personal experience and/or background knowledge. Figure 6.4 illustrates the integrative aspects of the three modes in this model: (1) through the interpretive mode, students comprehend and interpret a text, acquiring new information and cultural perspectives; (2) through the interpersonal mode, students share information, inferences, and reactions with one another; and (3) through the presentational mode, students use their new knowledge and perspectives as they create a summary and/or an oral or written product. As depicted in Figure 6.4, real-world communication can begin with any of the three modes; for example, a story might be the springboard for discussion and for an oral presentation on a particular topic; a two-way discussion might prompt the viewing of a video text and lead to further sharing of ideas; a letter to the editor of a newspaper might serve as the basis for discussion and for listening to a news broadcast. The Interactive Model begins with the interpretive mode and continues with the interpersonal and presentational modes; however, the model could be adapted to begin with any of the three modes.

Figure 6.5 presents the Interactive Model for Integrating the Three Modes of Communication, which has been adapted since its 2005 version in the third edition of *Teacher's Handbook* to parallel more closely the Revised Bloom's Taxonomy presented in Chapter 3

FIGURE 6.4 Integrating the Three Modes of Communication

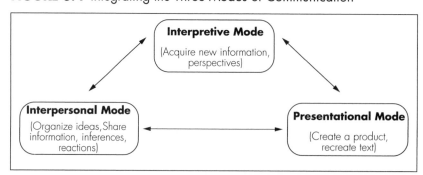

Source: Adapted from *Standards for Foreign Language Learning in the 21st Century,* 2006. Used by permission of the American Council of the Teaching of Foreign Languages.

FIGURE 6.5 An Interactive Model for Integrating the Three Modes of Communication

MODE	PHASE AND CLASS ACTIVITIES	PURPOSE	FORMAT OF ACTIVITIES
Interpretive	PREPARATION PHASE: Students preview the text, establish a purpose, predict meaning, activate background knowledge, preview unfamiliar content, anticipate new vocabulary and text language.	Prepare students for the task Pique student interest	Whole-class discussion; small-group collaboration
	COMPREHENSION PHASE: Students SKIM for the gist, SCAN for specific information. Students create a list of main ideas and match them to sections of text. Students match main ideas to key details.	Identify main ideas and details Connect main ideas and details Identify key discourse markers (word order, transitional words, parts of speech) and/or specific linguistic features Acquire new information	Pair- or small-group collaboration followed by whole-class discussion Activity formats: Multiple choice, T/F, matching, check-off list, short answer
Interpretive + Interpersonal	INTERPRETATION/DISCUSSION PHASE: Students read/listen/view "between the lines" and discuss content of text. Students guess meanings of new vocabulary in context. Students collaborate to identify the cultural products, practices, and perspectives found in the text (depending on nature of text). Students ask each other questions about the content, inferences, and author intent/perspectives of the text. Students share their opinions of and reactions to the text and create alternative interpretations.	Read and interpret the text Use the context to construct meaning Discuss cultural products, practices, perspectives Interpret inferences and share reactions Personalize and evaluate information and ideas in text	Students read text for homework or in class Pair- or small-group collaboration; whole class discussion Activity formats: Completion, fill-in-blank, question-answer, tasks, debates
Interpersonal + Presentational	CREATIVITY PHASE: Students participate in open-ended role-plays, create a written summary of text, and/or design an oral/video presentation for a specific audience. Students create a follow-up product such as a letter, advertisement, brochure, new beginning or ending for text.	Use new information acquired in text to participate in role-plays, create a summary of text, design a presentation or product	Hypothetical situations, role-plays, mini-dramas done in class Presentations and products done partially in class and partially outside of class
Interpretive (revisited)	EXTENSION PHASE (Optional): Students analyze features of two texts (intertextuality) and compare content and organization.	Compare text to another text (content, organization, perspective)	Authentic text—printed, video, audio, live broadcast

Source: Shrum & Glisan, original material, 2010; adapted from Shrum & Glisan, 2005.

and to include more suggestions regarding the formats of class activities possible for each phase. This model engages students in interaction with the text, helps them build strategies for comprehending and interpreting a text, and provides ways for them to use their newly acquired knowledge and skills in meaningful tasks. The model is interactive and procedural in nature, guiding the learner as he or she interacts with the text by using both bottom-up and top-down processes. It is also integrative, since it provides opportunities for students to combine skills from the three modes and cultural perspectives as they derive meaning from the text, recreate the text, and react to the text in a personal way. Note that students are guided through the text by means of a Preparation Phase, Comprehension Phase, Interpretation/Discussion Phase, Creativity Phase, and an optional Extension Phase.

Teachers should spend sufficient time in the Preparation Phase so that students have the necessary skills, background knowledge, and motivation for the comprehension and interpretation tasks. This phase should include activation of prior knowledge about the content of the text, setting a purpose for exploring the text, opportunities for learners to predict and anticipate events in the text, and opportunities for learners to explore and predict new vocabulary; see the earlier section in this chapter dealing with the treatment of new vocabulary. In the Comprehension Phase, learners demonstrate that they have understood the main ideas through skimming and important details through scanning and that they can link these aspects to the text. In this phase, students can also identify linguistic features of the text such as discourse markers and vocabulary grouped by parts of speech or word families. It is recommended that learners complete the Preparation and Comprehension Phases in class before they read the entire text outside of class so that they have a better chance of having success in their interpretation when reading alone. In the Interpretation/Discussion Phase, students read the text and interpret inferences and the author's intent as they exchange ideas and opinions with one another orally. It is important to note that students may draw inferences on their own as they assign meaning to the text, even before being asked to do so. The Creativity Phase provides the opportunity for learners to use knowledge and reactions gained in exploring the text to create a product. The optional Extension Phase brings the model full circle as learners explore *intertextuality*—that is, they compare two texts in terms of content and organization (Kristeva, 1980). For example, after the class has used the Interactive Model to interpret a printed text, the teacher could present an audio segment that deals with the same topic and ask students to compare the two in terms of content, organization, intended audience, and other features. Another option is to ask students to bring a new text to class and explain to their classmates why they think the two texts are similar or different or why they chose to compare the two texts (R. Donato, personal communication, July 18, 2008).

Teachers might also include some discussion of grammatical form, if helpful in exploring the text, sharing opinions, and creating presentations and products; this attention to form should occur in the Interpretation/Discussion Phase after students have read the text.

The Interactive Model can be implemented with any type of oral or printed text including literary texts, for it addresses potential comprehension difficulties noted in the research. For example, Bernhardt (1990) notes that an initial misunderstanding of how the main idea of a story relates to its details can distort a reader's entire comprehension and interpretation of it. Students work best with literary texts by gleaning information collaboratively in stages and by applying a heavy dose of top-down reading strategies. During the initial stages of reading, students focus on what the text says as they identify the "who, what, where," clarifying the difference between what the text says and what they think it says. Only after students have an accurate understanding of the main ideas and details of the text does the teacher lead them in making inferences and exploring the "how and why" of the story. Using this model to explore a text may take several classes, depending on the nature of the text as well as on the instructional objectives. See Chapter 12 for a Web-based module using the Interactive Model. Appendix 6.2 presents an example of how an authentic reading in Spanish can be used as the impetus for communication in all three modes, and Appendix 6.3 (see the *Teacher's Handbook* Web site) provides an example of how the model can be used with a semiscripted audio segment in English.

www.cengagebrain.com

What role can the ZPD play as the teacher guides students through a text, using the Interactive Model?

L1 or L2? One issue that teachers confront when teaching listening and reading is how much of the native language to use when checking students' comprehension of texts. Several studies have shown that learners receive higher comprehension scores when they are tested in their native language (Davis, Glass, & Coady, 1998; Godev, Martínez-Gibson, & Toris, 2002; Wolf, 1993). In a study by Davis, Glass, and Coady, undergraduate and graduate students of Spanish demonstrated significantly higher recall of a written text when tested in their native language. The results of their investigation led these researchers to conclude that the language of recall affects FL readers' performance in terms of (1) the amount of textual information recalled accurately, and (2) the number of inferences, elaborations, and metacognitive statements produced. These findings support Lee's earlier conclusion that "assessing comprehension with a target language task may limit learners' ability to demonstrate what they [have] comprehended" (1986a, p. 353). Another factor in using L2 for checking comprehension is that it sometimes promotes the use of the "look-back-and-lift-off approach" to reading, described earlier in this chapter as a strategy whereby students use the wording of the comprehension questions to look back to the passage and make a match without necessarily understanding either the question or the text. When the native language is used to check for comprehension and recall, comprehension skill is not confused with productive use of the target language (Lee, 1986b; Swaffar, Arens, & Byrnes, 1991).

It might be beneficial to conduct pre-listening, pre-reading, and pre-viewing activities in the native language, particularly if students require new background information prior to the listening or reading task. Clearly, the decision to use either the native or target language for each phase of the interactive model presented here must be made by the teacher after considering the level of students' proficiency and the task to be accomplished. Godev, Martínez-Gibson, and Toris (2002) suggest that if teachers decide to use an all-L2 comprehension format, especially for testing purposes, this format should have "(1) questions that circumvent the potential problem of not being understood, (2) questions that preclude the possibility of answering correctly without understanding, and (3) a device that would prevent the mistaking of limited writing skills for limited reading comprehension" (p. 213). While some use of L1 in the comprehension phase may be advantageous for the reasons mentioned above, teachers should make every effort to use L2 in the Interpretation/Discussion, Creativity, and Extension Phases of the Interactive Model. Since we have already established that the three modes of communication are used in concert in real-world communication, an important goal of interpreting audio, printed, and video texts is to enable learners to use the target language to engage in oral and written tasks using the information and ideas acquired from these texts. Teachers should remember, however, that learners should not be expected to discuss a text at the same linguistic level at which the text itself was created. Therefore, tasks should be designed so that learners use the L2 at an appropriate level—i.e., *edit the task, not the text.* Further, while it might be easier or intuitively appealing to use L1 to engage novice-level learners in higher-level tasks when working with a text,[9] teachers are cautioned that (1) even novice-level learners can be assisted in engaging in critical thinking in L2 through tasks such as creating a new ending to a story or evaluating an action of a story character, and (2) if novices do not have at least some opportunities to engage in L2 tasks in their exploration of texts, they may find it increasingly difficult to do so at higher levels of language study. Undoubtedly, this is an area that needs further investigation in the field. See Chapters 2, 5, 8, and 9 for further discussion of L1 vs. L2 use in the classroom.

This chapter presented the overall framework of the communicative modes together with a model for developing communication by integrating the modes. The focus here was on the interpretive mode as the processes underlying reading, listening, and viewing were discussed and implications for instruction were explored. Each of the next three chapters will examine a particular aspect of the other two modes—interpersonal and presentational—in an effort to explore specific issues relating to grammar, speaking, and writing. These modes and skills are analyzed somewhat separately in order to help the reader focus on particular issues one at a time. However, keep in mind that the approach advocated by *Teacher's Handbook* is to teach the modes and skills in an integrative manner, using the model presented in this chapter as well as other strategies.

TEACH AND REFLECT •

Note: You may want to review the characteristics of authentic texts, presented in Chapter 3, before completing the following tasks.

NC&TE_____

EPISODE ONE
Using the Interactive Model to Explore an Authentic Printed Text

ACTFL/NCATE 2.b. Demonstrating Understanding of Literary and Cultural Texts and Traditions; 4.a. Understanding and Integrating Standards into Planning; 4.b. Integrating Standards in Instruction, 4.c. Selecting and Designing Instructional Materials

TESOL/NCATE 3.a. Planning for Standards-Based ESL and Content Instruction; 3.b. Managing and Implementing Standards-Based ESL and Content Instruction; and 3.c. Using Resources Effectively in ESL and Content Instruction

For this activity, you will need to select a targeted level of instruction: elementary school, middle/junior high school, high school, or post-secondary.

Option 1:   Select an authentic magazine or newspaper article of at least 750 words.

Option 2:   Select an authentic literary text (folktale, story, novel excerpt, poem, etc.).

Check the text for the characteristics of good episodic organization (see Chapter 3) and *readability*, as described in this chapter. First, decide how this text might be used in a particular thematic unit in order to address short- and long-range objectives. Second, design a plan for teaching the text by using the Interactive Model presented in this chapter. Begin with the interpretive mode and then integrate interpersonal and presentational communication. Remember that you may need to devote a portion of several class periods to this activity in order to complete your work on the text. For each day you plan to spend on the reading, describe what students will do in all stages of the procedure. Your instructor may ask you to present an element of your plan to the class.

TECHNO FOCUS: One source of authentic texts is a *blog,* which is an electronic journal that allows people to write comments on the World Wide Web. A blogger is a person who sets up or writes comments on such a Web site. Usually a blog is maintained by one person who sets the topic and monitors comments from other users/readers/writers, forming a community. Communication on a blog is asynchronous but highly personalized, which heightens interest in reading or writing on the blog. Blogs are low-cost and can easily be set up by a teacher (http://www.blogger.com, or http://www.blog-city. com) for use within a class. Teachers can also encourage their language learners to look at blogs among native-speaking students and to make cultural inferences. For example, read Ducate and Lomicka (2005) to see how German language learners were responsible for researching and writing on a blog about products, practices, and perspectives (see Chapter 5) in German culture on these topics: computers and the German computer company Medion; opening and closing times of German stores; and the German voting system (p. 417). After you read the article, comment on the following:

a. How did French learners from the U.S. and native French speakers get to know each other on a blog before, during, and after a study abroad trip for both groups?

b. How can you find a blog site in L2 for your learners to read or write comments? What caveats should you recognize before engaging your students with an assignment on a L2 blog?

EPISODE TWO
Using the Interactive Model to Explore an Authentic Audio/Video Segment

ACTFL/NCATE 4.a. Understanding and Integrating Standards into Planning; 4.b. Integrating Standards in Instruction; 4.c. Selecting and Designing Instructional Materials

TESOL/NCATE 3.a. Planning for Standards-Based ESL and Content Instruction; 3.b. Managing and Implementing Standards-Based ESL and Content Instruction; and 3.c. Using Resources Effectively in ESL and Content Instruction

For this activity, you will again need to select a targeted level of instruction: elementary school, middle/junior high school, high school, or beyond.

Option 1: Select an authentic segment on audiotape/CD or videotape, an authentic live broadcast, or an authentic audio segment from the Internet (e.g., conversation, commercial, news report, talk show, song).

Option 2: Semiscript your own recorded conversation: Give two native speakers a particular situation or subject to discuss (for example, ask them to pretend that they are two students who meet for the first time while standing in the registration line); ask the speakers to talk spontaneously for 2 to 3 minutes. Do not prepare a written script, since the conversation should be as natural as possible.

Decide how this segment might be used in a particular thematic unit in order to address short- and long-range objectives. Then design a plan for teaching the segment by using the interactive approach presented in this chapter. Begin with the interpretive mode and then integrate interpersonal and presentational communication. Describe what students will do in each stage of the procedure. Your instructor may ask you to present your taped segment and an element of your lesson to the class.

EPISODE THREE
Teaching Literature at the Post-Secondary Level

ACTFL/NCATE 2.b. Demonstrating Understanding of Literary and Cultural Texts and Traditions; 3.a. Understanding Language Acquisition and Creating a Supportive Classroom; 3.b. Developing Instructional Practices That Reflect Language Outcomes and Learner Diversity; 4.b. Integrating Standards in Instruction, 4.c. Selecting and Designing Instructional Materials

TESOL/NCATE 3.a. Planning for Standards-Based ESL and Content Instruction; 3.b. Managing and Implementing Standards-Based ESL and Content Instruction; and 3.c. Using Resources Effectively in ESL and Content Instruction

If you are preparing to or are already teaching at the post-secondary level, this task is designed to engage you in reflecting upon the teaching of literature in undergraduate language and literature classes.

Read Chapter 10 in *SLA and the Literature Classroom: Fostering Dialogue* (Bernhardt, 2001): "Research into the teaching of literature in a second language: What it says and how to communicate it to graduate students." Then complete the following tasks:

1. Describe the impact of the student's knowledge base when reading L2 literary texts.
2. Explain the significance of the "lang-lit split" that Bernhardt describes as it pertains to the nature of the teaching of literature.
3. Name three misconceptions that graduate students have about teaching literature to undergraduates.
4. Explain the principles of literature learning that deal with:

- time on task
- appropriate feedback
- situated learning
- release of control

5. Explain two ways in which a literature instructor could tap a student's conceptualization of a literary text.

Your instructor might also ask you to read Chapter 3 in Swaffar and Arens (2005): "The Holistic Curriculum: Anchoring Acquisition in Reading." You might consider the following questions as you read and use them to discuss this chapter with your classmates:

1. What is a holistic FL curriculum?
2. How might texts be sequenced within a curriculum in terms of their readability?
3. What types of assignments might be created to address specific goals within a holistic approach to FL learning?

www.cengagebrain.com

See Appendix 6.4 on the *Teacher's Handbook* Web site for a description of a framework for teaching literature to the undergraduate foreign language major (Barnes-Karol, 2003).

DISCUSS AND REFLECT . . . .

www.cengagebrain.com

See the *Teacher's Handbook* Web site for an additional case study:
Case Study Two: Developing Interpretive Listening: Scripts or No Scripts?

NCATE_____

CASE STUDY ONE
Reading Aloud

ACTFL/NCATE 3.a. Understanding Language Acquisition and Creating a Supportive Classroom; 3.b. Developing Instructional Practices That Reflect Language Outcomes and Learner Diversity, 4.b. Integrating Standards in Instruction

TESOL/NCATE 3.a. Planning for Standards-Based ESL and Content Instruction; 3.b. Managing and Implementing Standards-Based ESL and Content Instruction; and 3.c. Using Resources Effectively in ESL and Content Instruction

For 12 years, Ms. Dayton has been teaching French at Big Sky High School in a rural midwestern town. One of the first things she noticed about her students when she began teaching was the transference of students' regional English accent to their French pronunciation. She began to ask her students to read aloud in French to help them practice their pronunciation. Generally, her procedure is to introduce the activity by telling students that it's time to practice pronunciation. Sometimes she puts them through some practice exercises, repeating words that have a particularly troublesome sound. She then models for the students a short sentence that embodies the sound and asks for whole-class repetition. Finally, she asks individuals to read aloud subsequent sentences that also contain the troublesome sound.

Ms. Lilly teaches Spanish in the same school as Ms. Dayton and has roughly the same amount of teaching experience. Ms. Lilly also uses reading aloud in her Spanish classes, but for a different reason. She believes that reading aloud focuses students' attention on the text so that they can comprehend the language and then discuss what it means; the students listening to the oral reader also use the oral reading to figure out meaning. Earlier this week, for example, students in Ms. Lilly's Spanish III class read aloud a passage from Mosén Millán, after which they discussed what they had understood from it.

Today is a teachers' in-service day, and Ms. Dayton and Ms. Lilly's foreign language department is fortunate to have a workshop that focuses on a current topic in their subject area. Dr. Janet Farwell, a well-known specialist in second language reading comprehension, is scheduled to talk about "Strategies for Developing Interpretive Communication in the Foreign Language Classroom." Dr. Farwell begins the workshop by presenting teachers with an interactive hands-on activity, in which they are asked to give their opinions on a series of statements concerning the development of reading and listening comprehension. One of the statements prompts a lively discussion and some debate among the teachers: "Reading aloud isn't really reading."

Ask yourself these questions:

1. Why do you think that the teachers in this workshop engaged in a "lively discussion and some debate" concerning the statement, given by the workshop presenter, about reading aloud?
2. What are some possible metacognitive strategies that Ms. Dayton's students use during oral reading? How about Ms. Lilly's students?
3. What issues or factors related to the reading process presented in this chapter can you relate to the two approaches to reading aloud used by these teachers?
4. Do you agree with Ms. Lilly's belief that her students' comprehension is enhanced by listening to their classmates read aloud? Explain.

To prepare for class discussion:

1. Conduct your own mini-experiment. Ask a student to read a paragraph aloud; ask two other students to listen and then to answer the following questions. Summarize your findings.

   - What was the first thing you did to make sense of this paragraph?
   - Did you do anything else to help yourself understand the text at any point during the listening?
   - Did you change your mind regarding what this passage was about or what to listen for at any point during the listening?
   - What can you remember hearing?
   - Can you remember anything else that you heard? Any new information?

- Did you learn anything new?
- Do you remember anything else?
- Do you remember any new words?
- On a scale of one to ten, how confident are you that you understood this passage?
- On a scale of one to ten, how much did you already know about this topic? (adapted from Bacon, 1992a)

2. Write a description of the effectiveness or ineffectiveness of using reading aloud as a strategy in your foreign language classroom.

REFERENCES

Allen, E., Bernhardt, E. B., Berry, M. T., & Demel, M. (1988). Comprehension and text genre: An analysis of secondary foreign language readers. *The Modern Language Journal, 72,* 63–72.

Anderson, R. C. (1977). The notion of schemata and the educational enterprise. In R. C. Anderson, R. J. Spiro & W. E. Montague (Eds.), *Schooling and the acquisition of knowledge* (pp. 415-431). Hillsdale, NJ: Lawrence Erlbaum Associates.

Anderson, R. C., Spiro, R. J., & Montague, W. E. (1977). *Schooling and the acquisition of knowledge.* Hillsdale, NJ: Lawrence Erlbaum Associates.

Bacon, S. M. (1989). Listening for real in the foreign-language classroom. *Foreign Language Annals, 22,* 543–551.

Bacon, S. M. (1992a). Phases of listening to authentic input in Spanish: A descriptive study. *Foreign Language Annals, 25,* 317–334.

Bacon, S. M. (1992b). The relationship between gender, comprehension, processing strategies, and cognitive and affective response in foreign language listening. *The Modern Language Journal, 76,* 160–178.

Baldwin, R. S., Peleg-Bruckner, Z., & McClintock, A. H. (1985). Effects of topic interest and prior knowledge on reading comprehension. *Reading Research Quarterly, 20,* 497–504.

Barnes-Karol, G. (2000). Revising a Spanish novel class in the light of Standards for Foreign Language Learning. *ADFL Bulletin, 31,* 44–48.

Barnes-Karol, G. (2003). Teaching literature to the undergraduate foreign language major: A framework for a methods course. *ADFL Bulletin, 34,* 20–27.

Barnett, M. (1988a). Reading through context. *The Modern Language Journal, 72,* 150–159.

Barnett, M. (1988b). Teaching reading strategies: How methodology affects language course articulation. *Foreign Language Annals, 21,* 109–119.

Barry, S., & Lazarte, A. (1998). Evidence for mental models: How do prior knowledge, syntactic complexity, and reading topic affect inference generation in a recall task for nonnative readers of Spanish? *The Modern Language Journal, 82,* 176–193.

Bartlett, F. C. (1932). *Remembering.* Cambridge: Cambridge University Press.

Bensoussan, M., Sim, D., & Weiss, R. (1984). The effect of dictionary usage on EFL test performance compared with student and teacher attitudes and expectations. *Reading in a Foreign Language, 2,* 262–276.

Berne, J. E. (2004) Listening comprehension strategies: A review of the literature. *Foreign Language Annals, 37,* 521–533.

Bernhardt, E. B. (1986). Reading in the foreign language. In B. H. Wing (Ed.), *Listening, reading, writing: Analysis and application* (pp. 93–115). Northeast Conference Reports. Middlebury, VT: Northeast Conference on the Teaching of Foreign Languages.

Bernhardt, E. B. (1990). A model of L2 text reconstruction: The recall of literary text by learners of German. In A. Labarca & L. M. Bailey (Eds.), *Issues in L2: Theory as practice/practice as theory* (pp. 21–43). Norwood, NJ: Ablex.

Bernhardt, E. B. (1991). A psycholinguistic perspective on second language literacy. Association Internationale de la *Linguistique Apliquée Review, 8,* 31–44.

Bernhardt, E. B. (2001). Research into the teaching of literature in a second language: What it says and how to communicate it to graduate students. In V. Scott & H. Tucker (Eds.), *SLA and the literature classroom: fostering dialogues* (pp. 195–210). Boston: Heinle & Heinle.

Bernhardt, E. B. (2005). Progress and procrastination in second language reading. *Annual Review of Applied Linguistics, 25,* 133–150.

Bernhardt, E. B., & Kamil, M. L. (1995). Interpreting relationships between L1 and L2 reading: Consolidating the linguistic threshold and the linguistic interdependence hypotheses. *Applied Linguistics, 16,* 15–34.

Bransford, J. D., & Johnson, M. K. (1972). Contextual prerequisites for understanding: Some investigations of comprehension and recall. *Journal of Verbal Learning and Verbal Behavior, 11,* 717–726.

Brecht, R. D., & Walton, A. R. (1995). The future shape of language learning in the new world of global communication: Consequences for higher education and beyond. In R. Donato & R. M. Terry (Eds.), *Foreign language learning: The journey of a lifetime* (pp. 110–152). The ACTFL Foreign Language Education Series. Lincolnwood, IL: NTC/Contemporary Publishing Group.

Brown, C. (1998). L2 reading: An update on relevant L1 research. *Foreign Language Annals, 31,* 191–202.

Carrell, P. (1985). Facilitating ESL reading by teaching text structure. *TESOL Quarterly, 19,* 727–752.

Carrell, P. (1989). Metacognitive awareness and second language reading. *The Modern Language Journal, 73,* 121–134.

Carrell, P. L., & Wise, T. E. (1998). The relationship between prior knowledge and topic interest in second language reading. *Studies in Second Language Acquisition, 20,* 285–309.

Chamot, A. U. (1995). Learning strategies and listening comprehension. In D. J. Mendelsohn & J. Rubin (Eds.), *A guide for the teaching of second language listening* (pp. 13–30). San Diego: Dominie Press.

Chamot, A. U. & El-Dinary, P. B. (1999). Children's learning strategies in language immersion classrooms. *The Modern Language Journal, 83,* 319–338.

Chamot, A. U., & Küpper, L. (1989). Learning strategies in foreign language instruction. *Foreign Language Annals, 22,* 13–24.

Chastain, K. (1988). *Developing second language skills: Theory and practice.* San Diego, CA: Harcourt Brace Jovanovich.

Chiang, C. S., & Dunkel, P. (1992). The effect of speech modification, prior knowledge, and listening proficiency on EFL lecture learning. *TESOL Quarterly, 26,* 345–374.

Christensen, B. (1990). Teenage novels of adventure as a source of authentic material. *Foreign Language Annals, 23,* 531–537.

Chung, J.-M. (1999). The effects of using video texts supported with advance organizers and captions on Chinese college students' listening comprehension: An empirical study. *Foreign Language Annals, 32,* 295–308.

Chung, J. S. (2000). Signals and reading comprehension: Theory and practice. *System, 28,* 247–259.

Cohen, A. D., Paige, R. M., Shively, R. L., Emert, H., & Hoff, J. (2005). *Maximizing study abroad through language and culture strategies: Research on students, study abroad program professionals, and language instructors.* Final Report to the International Research and Studies Program, Office of International Education, DOE. Minneapolis: Center for Advanced Research on Language Acquisition, University of Minnesota.

Cubillos, J. H., Chieffo, L., & Fan, C. (2008). The impact of short-term study abroad programs on L2 listening comprehension skills. *Foreign Language Annals, 41,* 157–185.

Davis, J. N., Glass, W. R., & Coady, J. (1998). Use of the target language versus the native language to assess foreign/second language reading comprehension: Still an issue? Unpublished manuscript.

Donato, R., & Brooks, F. B. (2004). Literary discussions and advanced speaking functions: Researching the (dis)connection. *Foreign Language Annals, 37,* 183–199.

Dristas, V. M., & Grisenti, G. (1995). Motivation: Does interest influence reading and speaking proficiency in second language acquisition? Unpublished manuscript.

Ducate, L. C., & Lomicka, L. L. (2005). Exploring the blogosphere: Use of web logs in the foreign language classroom. *Foreign Language Annals, 38,* 410–421.

Dunkel, P.A., & Davis, J. N. (1994). The effects of rhetorical signaling cues on the recall of English lecture information by speakers of English as a native and second language. In J. Flowerdew (Ed.), *Academic listening: Research perspectives* (pp. 55–74). New York: Cambridge University Press.

Duquette, L., & Painchaud, G. (1996). A comparison of vocabulary acquisition in audio and video contexts. *The Canadian Modern Language Review, 24,* 239–255.

Edelsky, C., Draper, K., & Smith, K. (1983). Hookin' 'em in at the start of school in a "whole language" classroom. *Anthropology and Education Quarterly, 14,* 257–281.

Elkhafaifi, H. (2005a). Listening comprehension and anxiety in the Arabic language classroom. *The Modern Language Journal, 89,* 206–220.

Elkhafaifi, H. (2005b). The effects of prelistening activities on listening comprehension in Arabic learners. *Foreign Language Annals, 38,* 505–513.

Epstein, S. (2002). The news as a textbook in the Spanish classroom: A language/social studies approach to teaching. *NECTFL Review, 51,* 27–31.

Eskey, D. E. (1986). Theoretical foundations. In F. Dubin, D. E. Eskey, & W. Grabe (Eds.), *Teaching second language reading for academic purposes* (pp. 3–23). Reading, MA: Addison-Wesley.

Fecteau, M. L. (1999). First- and second-language reading comprehension of literary texts. *The Modern Language Journal, 83,* 475–493.

Flowerdew, J., & Tauroza, S. (1995). The effect of discourse markers on second language lecture comprehension. *Studies in Second Language Acquisition, 17,* 435–458.

Frantzen, D. (2003). Factors affecting how second language Spanish students derive meaning from context. *The Modern Language Journal, 87,* 168–199.

Fraser, C. (1999). Lexical processing strategy use and vocabulary learning through reading. *Studies in Second Language Acquisition, 21,* 225–241.

Galloway, V. (1992). Toward a cultural reading of authentic texts. In H. Byrnes (Ed.), *Languages for a multicultural world in transition* (pp. 87–121). Northeast Conference Reports. Lincolnwood, IL: NTC/Contemporary Publishing Group.

Gascoigne, C. (2002a). Documenting the initial second language reading experience: The readers speak. *Foreign Language Annals, 35,* 554–560.

Gascoigne, C. (2002b). Reviewing reading: Recommendations versus reality. *Foreign Language Annals, 35,* 343–348.

Godev, C. B., Martínez-Gibson, E. A., & Toris, C. C. M. (2002). Foreign language reading comprehension test: L1 versus L2 in open-ended questions. *Foreign Language Annals, 35,* 202–221.

Goh, C. C. M. (2000). A cognitive perspective on language learners' listening comprehension problems. *System, 28,* 55–75.

Goodman, K. S. (1967). Reading: A psycholinguistic guessing game. *Journal of the Reading Specialist, 6,* 126–135.

Gruba, P. (2004). Understanding digitized second language videotext. *Computer Assisted Language Learning, 17,* 51–82.

Gruba, P. (2006). Playing the videotext: A media literacy perspective on video-mediated L2 listening. *Language Learning & Technology, 10,* 77–92.

Hadley, A. O. (2001). *Teaching language in context* (3rd ed.). Boston: Heinle & Heinle.

Hammadou, J. A. (1991). Interrelationships among prior knowledge, inference, and language proficiency in foreign language reading. *The Modern Language Journal, 75,* 27–38.

Hammadou, J. A. (2000). The impact of analogy and content knowledge on reading comprehension: What helps, what hurts. *The Modern Language Journal, 75,* 27–38.

Hammadou, J. A. (2002). Advanced foreign language readers' inferencing. In J. A. Hammadou Sullivan (Ed.), *Literacy and the second language learner* (pp. 217–238). Greenwich, CT: Information Age Publishing.

Hanley, J. E. B., Herron, C. A., & Cole, S. P. (1995). Using video as an advance organizer to a written passage in the FLES classroom. *The Modern Language Journal, 79,* 57–66.

Hauptman, P. C. (2000). Some hypotheses on the nature of difficulty and ease in second language reading: An application of schema theory. *Foreign Language Annals, 33,* 622–631.

Haynes, M. (1984). Patterns and perils of guessing in second language reading. In J. Handscombe, R. A. Orem, & B. P. Taylor (Eds.), *On TESOL '83: The question of control* (pp. 163–176). Washington, DC: Teachers of English to Speakers of Other Languages.

Herron, C., Corrie, C., Cole, S. P., & Dubreil, S. (1999). The effectiveness of a video-based curriculum in teaching culture. *The Modern Language Journal, 83,* 518–533.

Herron, C., & Hanley, J. (1992). Using video to introduce children to a foreign culture. *Foreign Language Annals, 25,* 419–426.

Herron, C. A., & Seay, I. (1991). The effect of authentic oral texts on student listening comprehension in the foreign language classroom. *Foreign Language Annals, 24,* 487–495.

Hoecherl-Alden, G. (2006). Connecting language to content: Second language literature instruction at the intermediate level. *Foreign Language Annals, 39,* 244–254.

Horiba, Y. (2000). Reader control in reading: Effects of language competence, text type, and task. *Discourse Processes, 29,* 223–267.

Hosenfeld, C. (1984). Case studies of ninth grade readers. In J. C. Alderson & A. H. Urquhart (Eds.), *Reading in a foreign language* (pp. 231–249). London, UK: Longman.

Hron, A., Kurbjuhn, I., Mandl, H., & Schnotz, W. L. (1985). Structural inferences in reading and listening. In G. Richheit & H. Strohner (Eds.), *Inferences in text processing* (pp. 221–245). Amsterdam, The Netherlands: North-Holland.

Johnson, P. (1982). Effects on comprehension of building background knowledge. *TESOL Quarterly, 16,* 503–516.

Joiner, E. G. (1986). Listening in the foreign language. In H. S. Lepke (Ed.), *Listening, reading, writing: Analysis and application* (pp. 43–70). Northeast Conference Reports. Middlebury, VT: Northeast Conference on the Teaching of Foreign Languages.

Joiner, E. G. (1990). Choosing and using videotexts. *Foreign Language Annals, 23,* 53–64.

Jung, E. H. (2003). The role of discourse signaling cues in second language listening comprehension. *The Modern Language Journal, 87,* 562–577.

Just, M., & Carpenter, P. A. (1992). A capacity theory of comprehension: Individual differences in working memory. *Psychological Review, 99,* 122–149.

Kelly, P. (1990). Guessing: No substitute for systematic learning of lexis. *System, 18,* 199–207.

Kintsch, W., & van Dijk, T. A. (1978). Towards a model of discourse comprehension and production. *Psychological Review, 85,* 363–394.

Kitajima, R. (1997). Referential strategy training for second language reading comprehension of Japanese texts. *Foreign Language Annals, 30,* 84–97.

Knutson, E. M. (1997). Reading with a purpose: Communicative reading tasks for the foreign language classroom. *Foreign Language Annals, 30,* 49–57.

Koda, K. (2004). *Insights into second language reading: A cross-linguistic approach*. Cambridge: Cambridge University Press.

Koda, K. (Ed.). (2007a). *Reading and language learning*. Malden, MA: Blackwell Publishing.

Koda, K. (2007b). Reading and language learning: Crosslinguistic constraints on second language reading development. *Language Learning,* 1–44.

Kristeva, J. (1980). *Desire in language: A semiotic approach to literature and art*. New York: Columbia University Press.

Lacorte, M., & Thurston-Griswold, H. (2001). Music in the foreign language classroom: Developing linguistic and cultural proficiency. *NECTFL Review, 49,* 40, 49–53.

Lally, C. (1998). The application of first language reading models to second language study: A recent historical perspective. *Reading Horizons, 38,* 267–277.

Lange, D. L. (1999). Planning for and using the new national culture standards. In J. K. Phillips & R. M. Terry

(Eds.), *Foreign language standards: Linking research, theories, and practices* (pp. 57–135). Lincolnwood, IL: National Textbook Company.

Lee, J. F. (1986a). Background knowledge and L2 reading. *The Modern Language Journal, 70,* 350–354.

Lee, J. F. (1986b). On the use of the recall task to measure L2 reading comprehension. *Studies in Second Language Acquisition, 8,* 83–93.

Lee, J. F. (1987). Comprehending the Spanish subjunctive: An information processing perspective. *The Modern Language Journal, 71,* 51–57.

Lee, J. F., & VanPatten, B. (1995). *Making communicative language teaching happen* (2nd ed.). New York: McGraw-Hill.

Lund, R. J. (1991). A comparison of second language listening and reading comprehension. *The Modern Language Journal, 75,* 196–204.

MacIntyre, P. D., & Gardner, R. C. (1991). Methods and results in the study of anxiety and language learning: A review of the literature. *Language Learning, 41,* 85–117.

Mantero, M. (2006). Applied literacy in second language education: (Re)Framing discourse in literature-based classrooms. *Foreign Language Annals, 39,* 99–114.

Markham, P. (1999). Captioned videotapes and second-language listening word recognition. *Foreign Language Annals, 32,* 321–328.

Markham, P., Peter, L. A., & McCarthy, T. J. (2001). The effects of native language versus target language captions on foreign language students' DVD video comprehension. *Foreign Language Annals, 34,* 439–445.

Martinez-Lage, A. (1995). Benefits of keeping a reading journal in the development of second language reading ability. In R. M. Terry (Ed.). *Dimension '95* (pp. 65–79). Roswell, GA: Southern Conference on Language Teaching. (ERIC Document Reproduction Service No. ED384235) *Dimension,* 65–79.

Maxim, H. H., II. (2002). A study into the feasibility and effects of reading extended authentic discourse in the beginning German language classroom. *The Modern Language Journal, 86,* 20–35.

McCarthy, M. (1991). *Discourse analysis for language teachers.* Cambridge: Cambridge University Press.

Mecartty, F. (2000). Lexical and grammatical knowledge in reading and listening comprehension by foreign language learners of Spanish. *Applied Language Learning, 11,* 323–348.

Minsky, M. (1975). A framework for representing knowledge. In P. H. Winston (Ed.), *The psychology of computer vision* (pp. 211–277). New York: McGraw-Hill.

Minsky, M. (1982). A framework for representing knowledge. In J. Haugeland (Ed.), *Mind design* (pp. 95–128). Cambridge, MA: MIT Press.

Mondria, J., & Wit-DeBoer, M. (1991). The effects of contextual richness on the guessability and the retention of words in a foreign language. *Applied Linguistics, 12,* 249–267.

Mueller, G. A. (1980). Visual contextual cues and listening comprehension: An experiment. *The Modern Language Journal, 64,* 335–340.

Munby, J. (1979). Teaching intensive reading skills. In R. Mackay, B. Barkenson, & R. Jordan (Eds.), *Reading in a second language* (pp. 142–158). Rowley, MA: Newbury House.

Musumeci, D. (1996). Teacher-learner negotiation in content-based instruction: Communication at cross-purposes? *Applied Linguistics, 17,* 286–325.

Nagy, W. (1997). On the role of context in first- and second-language vocabulary learning. In N. Schmitt & M. McCarthy (Eds.), *Vocabulary: Description, acquisition, and pedagogy* (pp. 64–83). Cambridge, UK: Cambridge University Press.

Nassaji, H. (2007). Schema theory and knowledge-based processes in second language reading comprehension: A need for alternative perspectives. *Language Learning, 57,* 79–113.

Nation, P., & Coady, J. (1988). Vocabulary and reading. In R. Carter & M. McCarthy (Eds.), *Vocabulary and language teaching* (pp. 97–110). New York: Longman.

National Standards in Foreign Language Education Project (NSFLEP). (2006). *Standards for foreign language learning in the 21st century (SFLL).* Lawrence, KS: Allen Press.

Nunan, D. (1985). Content familiarity and the perception of textual relationships in second language reading. *RELC Journal, 16,* 43–51.

Oguro, Y. (2008). *Presentation of culture in English-as-a-foreign-language reading textbooks in Japan.* Unpublished doctoral dissertation, Virginia Tech, Blacksburg, VA.

Oller, J. W. (1983). Some working ideas for language teaching. In J. W. Oller & P. A. Richard-Amato (Eds.), *Methods that work* (pp. 3–19). Rowley, MA: Newbury House.

Omaggio, A. C. (1979). Pictures and second language comprehension: Do they help? *Foreign Language Annals, 12,* 107–116.

O'Malley, J. M., Chamot, A. U., & Küpper, L. (1989). Listening comprehension strategies in second language acquisition. *Applied Linguistics, 10,* 418–437.

Osada, N. (2001). What strategy do less proficient learners employ in listening comprehension? A reappraisal of bottom-up and top-down processing. *Journal of the Pan-Pacific Association of Applied Linguistics, 5,* 73–90.

Oxford, R. (1990). *Language learning strategies: What every teacher should know.* Boston: Heinle & Heinle.

Palinscar, A., & Brown, A. (1984). Reciprocal teaching of comprehension-fostering and comprehension-monitoring activities. *Cognition and Instruction, 1,* 117–175.

Paribakht, T. S., & Wesche, M. (1996). Enhancing vocabulary acquisition through reading: A hierarchy of text-related exercise types. *The Canadian Modern Language Review, 52,* 250–273.

Paribakht, T. S., & Wesche, M. (1997). Vocabulary enhancement activities and reading for meaning in second language vocabulary development. In J. Coady & T. Huckin (Eds.), *Second language vocabulary acquisition: A rationale for pedagogy* (pp. 174–200). New York: Cambridge University Press.

Paribakht, T. S., & Wesche, M. (1999). Reading and "incidental" L2 vocabulary acquisition. *Studies in Second Language Acquisition, 21,* 195–224.

Pressley, M., Levin, J. R., & McDaniel, M. A. (1987). Remembering versus inferring what a word means: Mnemonic and contextual approaches. In M. G. McKeown & M. E. Curtis (Eds.), *The nature of vocabulary acquisition* (pp. 107–127). Hillsdale, NJ: Lawrence Erlbaum Associates.

Price, J. (1990). Improving foreign language listening comprehension. In J. A. Alatis (Ed.), *Georgetown University Roundtable on Languages and Linguistics 1990: Linguistics, language teaching, and language acquisition: The interdependence of theory, practice, and research* (pp. 309–316). Washington, DC: Georgetown University.

Ramsay, R. (1991). French in action and the grammar question. *French Review, 65,* 255–266.

Ratcliff, G. L. (1999). *Introduction to readers theatre. A guide to classroom performance.* Colorado Springs: Meriwether Publishing.

Richards, J. C. (1983). Listening comprehension: Approach, design, procedure. *TESOL Quarterly, 17,* 219–240.

Richards, J. P., Fajen, B. R., Sullivan, J. F., & Gillespie, G. (1997). Signaling, notetaking, and field independence-dependence in text comprehension and recall. *Journal of Educational Psychology, 89,* 508–517.

Rifkin, B. (2000). Video in the proficiency-based advanced conversation class: An example from the Russian-language curriculum. *Foreign Language Annals, 33,* 63–70.

Riley, G. L. (1993). A story structure approach to narrative text comprehension. *The Modern Language Journal, 77,* 417–432.

Roller, C. M. (1990). The interaction between knowledge and structure variables in the processing of expository prose. *Reading Research Quarterly, 25,* 79–89.

Rosenblatt, L. M. (1995). *Literature as exploration* (5th ed.). New York: Modern Language Association.

Rost, M., & Ross, S. (1991). Learner use of strategies in interaction: Typology and teachability. *Language Learning, 41,* 235–273.

Rubin, J. (1994). A review of second language listening comprehension research. *The Modern Language Journal, 78,* 199–221.

Saito, Y., Garza, T. J., & Horwitz, E. K. (1999). Foreign language reading anxiety. *The Modern Language Journal, 83,* 202–218.

Scarcella, R. C., & Oxford, R. L. (1992). *The tapestry of language learning.* Boston: Heinle & Heinle.

Schank, R., & Abelson, R. (1977). *Scripts, plans, goals and understanding: An inquiry into human knowledge structures.* New Jersey: LEA Publishers.

Schmidt-Rinehart, B. C. (1994). The effects of topic familiarity on second language listening comprehension. *The Modern Language Journal, 78,* 179–189.

Scott, V. M., & Huntington, J. A. (2002). Reading culture: Using literature to develop C2 competence. *Foreign Language Annals, 35,* 622–631.

Scott, V. M., & Huntington, J. A. (2007). Literature, the interpretive mode, and novice learners. *The Modern Language Journal, 91,* 3–14.

Secules, T., Herron, C., & Tomasello, M. (1992). The effect of video context on foreign language learning. *The Modern Language Journal, 76,* 480–490.

Sellers, V. D. (2000). Anxiety and reading comprehension in Spanish as a foreign language. *Foreign Language Annals, 33,* 512–521.

Shook, D. J. (1996). Foreign language literature and the beginning learner-reader. *Foreign Language Annals, 29,* 201–216.

Stein, M. (1993). The healthy inadequacy of contextual definition. In T. Huckin, M. Haynes, & J. Coady (Eds.), *Second language reading and vocabulary learning* (pp. 203–212). Norwood, NJ: Ablex.

Stevick, E. (1984). Similarities and differences between oral and written comprehension: An imagist view. *Foreign Language Annals, 17,* 281–283.

Stewart, M. A., & Pertusa, I. (2004). Gains to language learners from viewing target-language closed-captioned films. *Foreign Language Annals, 37,* 438–447.

Swaffar, J., & Arens, K. (2005). *Remapping the foreign language curriculum: An approach through multiple literacies.* New York: The Modern Language Association.

Swaffar, J., Arens, K., & Byrnes, H. (1991). *Reading for meaning.* Englewood Cliffs, NJ: Prentice Hall.

Swaffar, J., & Vlatten, A. (1997). A sequential model for video viewing in the foreign language curriculum. *The Modern Language Journal, 81,* 175–188.

Taylor, G. (2005). Perceived processing strategies of students watching captioned video. *Foreign Language Annals, 38,* 422–427.

Thompson, L., & Rubin, J. (1996). Can strategy instruction improve listening comprehension? *Foreign Language Annals, 29,* 331–342.

Tyler, A. (1994). The role of syntactic structure in discourse structure: Signaling logical and prominence relations. *Applied Linguistics, 15,* 243–262.

van Dijk, T. A. (1981). Review of R. O. Freedle (Ed.) [Review of the book *New directions in discourse processing*]. *Journal of Linguistics, 17,* 140–148.

Vandergrift, L. (1997a). The Cinderella of communication strategies: Reception strategies in interactive listening. *The Modern Language Journal, 81,* 494–505.

Vandergrift, L. (1997b). The comprehension strategies of second language (French) listeners: A descriptive study. *Foreign Language Annals, 30,* 387–409.

Vandergrift, L. (2003). Orchestrating strategy use: Toward a model of the skilled second language listener. *Language Learning, 53,* 463–496.

Vandergrift, L. (2006). Second language listening: Listening ability or language proficiency? *The Modern Language Journal, 90*, 6–18.

Vandergrift, L. (2007). Recent developments in second and foreign language listening comprehension research. *Language Teaching, 40*, 191-210.

Vigil, V. D. (1987). Authentic text in the college-level Spanish I class as the primary vehicle of instruction. Unpublished doctoral dissertation. University of Texas, Austin.

Vogely, A. J. (1995). Perceived strategy use during performance on three authentic listening comprehension tasks. *The Modern Language Journal, 79*, 41–56.

Vogely, A. J. (1998). Listening comprehension anxiety: Students' reported scores and solutions. *Foreign Language Annals, 31*, 67–80.

Voller, P., & Widdows, S. (1993). Feature films as text: A framework for classroom use. *ELT Journal, 47*, 342–349.

Weissenrieder, M. (1987). Listening to the news in Spanish. *Foreign Language Annals, 71*, 18–27.

Wesche, M. B., & Paribakht, T. S. (2000). Reading-based exercises in second language vocabulary learning: An introspective study. *The Modern Language Journal, 84*, 196–213.

Weyers, J. R. (1999). The effect of authentic video on communicative competence. *The Modern Language Journal, 83*, 339–340.

Wilberschied, L, & Berman, P. M. (2004). Effect of using photos from authentic video as advance organizers on listening comprehension in an FLES Chinese class. *Foreign Language Annals, 37*, 534–543.

Wolf, D. F. (1993). A comparison of assessment tasks used to measure FL reading comprehension. *The Modern Language Journal, 77*, 473–489.

Wolfe, P. (2004). "The owl cried": Reading abstract literary concepts with adolescent ESL students. *Journal of Adolescent and Adult Literacy, 47*, 402–413.

Wright, D. A. (2000). Culture as information and culture as affective process: A comparative study. *Foreign Language Annals, 33*, 330–341.

Young, D. J. (1993). Processing strategies of foreign language readers: Authentic and edited input. *Foreign Language Annals, 26*, 451–468.

Young, D. J. (1999). Linguistic simplification of SL reading material: Effective instructional practice? *The Modern Language Journal, 83*, 350–366.

Zyzik, E., & Polio, C. (2008). Incidental focus on form in university Spanish literature courses. *The Modern Language Journal, 92*, 53–70.

NOTES

1. See Bernhardt (2005) for detailed information regarding the process of second language reading.

2. For a review of L2 reading research based on L1 reading research, see Brown (1998); for a review of L2 listening, see Berne (2004) and Vandergrift (2007).

3. See Koda (2007a) for a series of articles that represent new approaches to exploring critical issues in L2 reading.

4. Researchers such as Berne (2004), Chamot (1995), and Rubin (1994) have reviewed the studies on listening strategies.

5. For a detailed discussion of text structure and comprehension, see Chapter 8 in Koda (2004).

6. For excellent series of authentic French and Spanish magazines for children and adolescents, contact Bayard Presse, 9709 Sotweed Drive, Potomac, MD 20854; (301)/299–5920.

7. See Swaffar and Arens (2005) for a thought-provoking guide to post-secondary foreign language programs in how to rethink the "teaching of literature, culture, and language as the teaching of *multiple literacies*: the ability to engage with culture, with its forms of knowledge and communication, and with its various publics" (p. xii). In addition to its insightful discussion, the text contains a number of helpful templates and matrices to help design interpretive tasks at the beginning, intermediate, and advanced level as well as to redesign curricula.

8. For an interesting description of how a college-level instructor revised a Spanish novel class in order to address the *SFLL*, see Barnes-Karol (2000).

9. See Scott and Huntington (2007) for a discussion of using L1 to engage novice-level readers in discussion of literary texts.

Using a Story-Based Approach to Teach Grammar

By Bonnie Adair-Hauck, Ph.D. (University of Pittsburgh). and Richard Donato, Ph.D. (University of Pittsburgh).[1]

In this chapter, you will learn about:

- deductive and inductive approaches to grammar instruction
- focus on form
- re-conceptualizing grammar instruction
- story-based language learning

- co-constructing grammar explanations
- dialogic grammar explanations
- the PACE Model: Presentation, Attention, Co-Construction, Extension

Teach and Reflect: Examining Grammar Presentations in Textbooks; Designing a Story-Based PACE Lesson; Developing a PACE Lesson for the Post-Secondary Level

Discuss and Reflect: Contrasting Explanations of Form

CONCEPTUAL ORIENTATION

In this chapter, you will explore a dialogic approach to the teaching of grammar using cultural stories as the centerpiece of a lesson in standards-based foreign language instruction. The model that will be presented in this chapter is based on the concept that as learners are guided to reflect on meaningful language form, they develop grammatical concepts in the target language. Additionally, the model of grammatical instruction, referred to as PACE, includes conscious attention to the target language and the need for learners to discuss form from the perspective of meaning and use. Although this shares some similarities with other approaches, it differs in three important ways. First, learners are neither left alone to reflect on form in the input nor are they the passive recipients of "ready-made" grammatical rules. Second, reflecting on form is raised as a topic of conversation in its own right rather than as a mini-lesson during communicative tasks and activities. Finally, through dialog with the teacher and each other, learners develop grammatical concepts through problem-solving activity where they are asked to reflect upon form and the relationship of forms to meanings that have been established in the context of cultural stories.

Throughout *Teacher's Handbook* so far you have explored how the *Standards for Foreign Language Learning in the 21st Century (SFLL)* (National Standards in Foreign Language Education Project [NSFLEP], 2006) emphasize communication as being at the core of second language learning. You have also learned that communication involves personal expression, interpretation, and negotiation of meaning where information, feelings, and ideas are exchanged in various forms of human interaction (Lee & Van Patten, 2003). Traditional foreign language instruction emphasized the mastery of grammatical rules as the goal of instruction. Unfortunately, as a result, many learners who spent years learning the formal properties of the language (the sound system, verb conjugations, rules of syntax, vocabulary, etc.) were not able to exchange information, participate in target language cultures, or develop and nurture a social relationship in a second language (Adair-Hauck & Cumo-Johanssen, 1997; Barnes, 1992; Hall, 1995, 1999).

Traditional approaches to grammar instruction often involve planning lessons based on the "grammar point of the day" and teaching grammar largely through teacher explanation of grammatical rules. In contrast, the model we propose in this chapter views grammar teaching as a focus on a well-chosen form of language after the meaning of this form has been established in interesting and compelling contexts, such as stories, folktales, and legends. In this model, learners are not required to master all aspects of a grammatical topic (e.g., past tense formation, the French partitive, *ser* vs. *estar*, aspect markers in Chinese) but rather focus solely on the part of the language that is relevant to understand the story and to express opinions, ideas, and feelings about the text. In this way, the language is examined in smaller installments rather than in lists of decontextualized rules and exceptions to these rules characteristic of many textbook grammar presentations.

Teachers who are committed to teaching language for communication often find it difficult to include "grammar instruction" into their curriculum and lessons. The *SFLL* stress that knowledge of the language system, including grammar, vocabulary, phonology, and pragmatic and discourse features, contributes to the accuracy of communication. Researchers agree that reflecting on aspects of the language that are relevant to the communication task, or what is referred to as "focus on form," is beneficial to learners and is critical to making progress as language users (Adair-Hauck & Donato, 1994; Anton, 1999; Ellis, 1988, 2004; Gass & Selinker, 2001; Herron & Tomasello, 1992; Hinkel & Fotos, 2002; Larsen-Freeman, 2003; Lightbown & Spada, 1990; Long, 1991; Salaberry, 1997). In contrast to traditional grammar teaching, focus on form largely depends on what learners need for communicative purposes rather than on a predetermined grammatical syllabus. J. Liskin-Gasparro (personal communication, September 15, 1999) illustrates what teachers attempt to do when they focus students' attention on form for purposes of communication. She states that teachers are "supplying information about how the language works when one or more students experience what we might call communicative urgency, a need to say something and, thus, a desire for grammatical information."

From this perspective, focus on form can emerge spontaneously as learners need to understand language to express themselves and deepen their comprehension of texts. In addition to spontaneous focus on form, teachers can also draw students' attention to form when the form is particularly relevant to the context of the lesson. The model presented in this chapter allows for both types of focus on form to occur. In summary, in this chapter the term *grammar instruction* will be used to refer to a focus on a particular form of language that is relevant to the context, such as a cultural story, and essential to developing the ability to make meaning in the foreign language.

"Focus on form" largely depends on what learners need for communication purposes rather than on a predetermined grammatical syllabus.

Ellis (2008) points out that there is now widespread acceptance that acquisition requires learners to attend to form. However, learning grammatical structures apart from their use and function is pointless unless one wants to be a linguist or describe a language systematically without becoming a communicatively competent user of that language (Larsen-Freeman, 2003). Like road signs, grammatical structures take on meaning only if they are situated within a context, within people, and within connected discourse. They become internalized only if the learners are placed in a situation in which they need to use the structures for communication and participation in communicative events (Adair-Hauck & Donato, 2002; DeKeyser & Sokalski, 1996; Fotos & Ellis, 1991; Salaberry, 1997; Shaffer, 1989; VanPatten & Cadierno, 1993). Thus, an important role of the language teacher is to create learning situations in which students perceive how grammar can be used to comprehend and interpret the target language and how to use grammar in meaningful exchanges. In other words, learners need to understand how grammar will enable them to become better meaning makers.

The Deductive and Inductive Dichotomy

Although many researchers agree on the benefits of some grammar instruction, the term "teaching grammar" has a variety of meanings (Ellis, 2008). Most applied linguists agree that *deductive* and *inductive* approaches are the two predominant types of grammar instruction in classrooms today. Other language teaching specialists include the use of tasks where learners are directed to pay attention to preselected forms or preplanned forms to complete tasks successfully. Despite this ostensibly neatly organized view of grammar teaching, deductive and inductive approaches to learning represent two dichotomous perspectives on how grammar is taught and learned. On the *deductive* side of the dichotomy is explicit grammar instruction that involves teacher explanations of rules followed by related manipulative exercises intended to practice the new structure. The expected outcome of a deductive approach is that students learn the designated forms of the language, so that later they will be able to perform selected communicative or meaning-making activities. In this paradigm, structures and grammar are viewed as *a priori* knowledge that will enable the learner to eventually communicate (Hopper & Thompson, 1993; Mantero, 2002; Van Patten, 1998).

Many language learners have experienced the deductive approach of grammar instruction. Most textbooks still present grammar explanations in this fashion, followed by manipulative drills that are cast in shallow and artificial contexts unrelated to the real communicative intentions of learners (Aski, 2003; Walz, 1989). Thus, these practice opportunities are often meaningless to learners and are not capable of engaging their language problem-solving skills and their desire to communicate using the forms they are learning (Adair-Hauck & Donato, 1994; Brooks & Donato, 1994). It is common for teachers to observe that these artificial opportunities for practice after the teacher's grammatical explanation is delivered often result in unmotivated and lethargic responses in learners, no matter how much context is given in the directions or how much personalization is provided.

A possible explanation for these disappointing results from a deductive approach to grammar instruction is that it invests the teacher with the responsibility for understanding and constructing grammatical knowledge and, consequently, assigns a passive role to the learners. Learner interaction takes place, if it occurs at all, only after the teacher's grammatical explanations and practice exercises consisting of disconnected sentences unrelated to an overall theme. Additionally, a deductive approach to grammar teaching has the disadvantage of requiring learners to focus on grammatical forms before experiencing their meaning and function in a communicative encounter (Larsen-Freeman, 2003). This linear model of teaching a form before using a form has distinct disadvantages and does not support learning grammatical knowledge. When learners are presented with ready-made explanations of grammar by the teacher, they are denied the opportunity to explore and construct for themselves an understanding of the form; predictably, they do not perceive a valid reason for learning the particular grammar point no matter how skilled at explanation the teacher is or how succinctly a grammatical feature is presented in a rule-based formula. Moreover, when learners are presented with ready-made explanations of grammar by the teacher, they are denied the opportunity to explore, problem-solve and construct for themselves an understanding of the form, and they do not perceive a valid reason for learning the particular grammar point. As we learned in Chapter 1, sociocultural theory (Rogoff, 1990; Vygotsky, 1978; Wertsch, 1991) reminds us that it is dialogic, joint problem solving that leads to cognitive development.

What is deductive grammar instruction? Why does it appeal to some educators? What are its disadvantages?

On the other side of the instructional dichotomy is the *inductive* grammar approach. The inductive approach, as presented by Krashen (1985), Terrell (1977), and Dulay and Burt (1973), rejects the need for any explicit focus on form. Proponents of inductive teaching argue that learners can acquire language naturally if they are provided with sufficient comprehensible input from the teacher. Furthermore, the approach maintains that grammatical development follows its own natural internal syllabus; thus, any explicit teaching of form is pointless and not worth the instructional time and effort of the teacher and the students. If learners are exposed to a sufficient amount of language that interests them and is globally understandable to them, they will eventually be able to induce how the structures of the language work. As the theory goes, learners should be able to perform hypothesizing and language analysis on their own as comprehensible input becomes intake.

However, research has shown that some learners do not attend to or "induce" the teacher's preselected grammatical point on the basis of input alone. One reason for this may be that the implicit approach clearly places little importance on mediating the students' understanding of the grammatical feature in question, reducing the teacher to a provider of input rather than of responsive instructional assistance. Herron and Tomasello (1992) also state that the inductive approach cannot guarantee that the learner will discover the underlying concepts or that the induced grammatical concepts will actually be correct. In the research of Adair-Hauck (1993), it was found that when learners were asked about their emerging understandings and self-generated "discoveries" about form, they often had inaccurate or partial understandings of the grammatical concept. Additionally, some students failed to perceive the grammatical pattern that the teacher presented even when the structure was embedded in a meaningful context and made salient through repetitions in the input. Even in the studies of input enhancement, where the target form is highlighted or manipulated in some way to draw the individual learner's attention to the target form, findings of successful outcomes are inconsistent. Furthermore, the inductive approach can frustrate adolescent or adult learners, many of whom have already become analytical with regard to the rules that govern their native languages. These learners often want to hasten the learning process by consciously comparing and contrasting their own native language rules to the rules that govern the new target language.

What is the inductive grammar instructional approach? What are its advantages? What are some disadvantages?

Reconceptualizing Grammar Instruction

Although deductive and inductive grammar instruction are clearly opposite approaches to teaching and learning grammar, they share some notable deficiencies. Neither approach acknowledges the critical role of the teacher in mediating understandings of how the new language works, and neither acknowledges the contributions and backgrounds that the learners bring to the instructional setting for collaborating with the teacher on constructing a grammatical explanation (Donato & Adair-Hauck, 1992). Moreover, neither approach recognizes the social aspects of learning that take place routinely among people in the world, outside of the classroom. In deductive and inductive approaches, learning is seen as exclusively located in the individual rather than situated in the dialogic interactions between them. A sociocultural approach to instruction (see Chapter 1) indicates that learning is an emerging, social, and interactive process situated in cultural contexts, such as schools and classrooms, and assisted through tools, the most notable being language. Therefore, theory and research have provided two dichotomous approaches to learning and processing grammatical information, both of which fail to take into account the collaborative, dialogic, and social aspects of learning (Adair-Hauck, 1993, 2007; Adair-Hauck & Donato, 1994, 2002; Donato, 2004). Neither approach recognizes the dialogic interactions that are fundamental to learning as it occurs naturally between humans in everyday life (Adair-Hauck, 1993; Adair-Hauck & Donato, 1994; Donato, 2004; Forman, Minnick, & Stone, 1993; John-Steiner, 2000; Lave & Wenger, 1991; Rogoff, 1990; Stone, 1993; Wenger, 1998).

In this chapter, we advocate a story-based and dialogic approach (Adair-Hauck, 1993; Donato & Adair-Hauck, 1992) that contrasts with both the traditional deductive approach and the inductive approach to learning. This dialogic approach allows teachers and students to build understandings of form as they are encountered in meaningful contexts. It must be pointed out, however, that a dialogic co-constructed approach to grammar instruction does not assume that students must reinvent or discover the generalizations about grammar that we already know (Karpov, 2003; Negueruela & Lantolf, 2005). Conversely, this approach also recognizes, as Vygotsky (1986) has pointed out in his theories of concept formation, that concepts—and we include here grammatical concepts—cannot be given to learners ready-made and that they are subject to continual revision and development. A dialogic approach can reconcile the polarized views of grammar teaching, as shown in Figure 7.1. For a number of reasons that will be discussed later in this chapter, we believe that a dialogic approach embedded in the use of meaningful contexts found in compelling and interesting stories might hold the key to dramatic improvements in the acquisition of grammar.

FIGURE 7.1 A Dialogic Story-Based Approach to Grammar Instruction

INDUCTIVE APPROACH	DIALOGIC APPROACH	DEDUCTIVE APPROACH
Learners analyze the grammar explanation for themselves.	*Teacher and learners* collaborate on and co-construct the grammar explanation.	Teachers provide explanation for learners

Source: Adapted from *A Descriptive Analysis of a Whole Language/Guided Participatory versus Explicit Teaching Strategies in Foreign Language Instruction* (p. 6), by B. Adair-Hauck, 1993. Used by permission of the author.

Basic Principles of Dialogic Story-Based Language Teaching

Before discussing some practical applications of this approach, we present the rationale for a story-based and dialogic approach to focus on form. It is said that the whole is always viewed as being greater than the sum of its parts, and it is the whole that gives meaning to the parts (Vygotsky, 1978). Words, phrases, or sentences are not linguistic islands unto themselves. On the contrary, these linguistic elements gain meaning and function— for example, giving advice on good eating habits to a friend using the subjunctive in French, Spanish, or Italian—only when they are placed in context and in a whole text. In this example, the use of the subjunctive takes on meaning and is used for a function in the whole context of giving advice. Compare this to simply giving students a deductive explanation of the subjunctive, which does not situate its use and fails to illustrate how the form is used to make meaning in the language, resulting in a decontextualized academic exercise in language analysis rather than language use.

If words only take on their meaning and function when used in connection to each other, learners need to encounter grammar in action in contextualized language and connected discourse (e.g., stories, legends, poems, listening selections, cartoons, songs, recipes). Emphasis needs to be placed on meaning-making and sense-making before a focus on form can be a productive instructional activity. In this way, a story-based language approach stresses connected discourse and encourages learners to comprehend meaningful texts from the very beginning of the lesson. As learners comprehend meaningful texts (e.g., stories), the forms of the language take on meaning and their uses become transparent. Once learners understand the meaning of the whole text, they will be better able to focus on and understand the contribution of the parts of the text to the meaning of the whole (Adair-Hauck & Cumo-Johanssen, 1997; Adair-Hauck & Donato, 1994; Fountas & Hannigan, 1989; Freeman & Freeman, 1992; Hughes & McCarthy, 1998).

 A story-based language approach stresses connected discourse and encourages learners to comprehend meaningful texts from the very beginning of the lesson. ▪

By introducing a lesson with a whole text, the teacher uses the grammatical feature in a meaningful way by making obvious the meaning and function of the grammar structure to be taught. In this way, the teacher foreshadows the conversation about grammar that will occur after comprehension of the meaning of the feature has been achieved. Galloway and Labarca (1990) explain how foreshadowing of new language elements is beneficial: It provides "learners with a 'feel' for what is to come and can help learners cast forward a familiarity net by which aspects of language prompt initial recognition and later, gradually, are pulled into the learner's productive repertoire" (p. 136). The story or text highlights the functional significance of the grammatical structure before learners' attention is focused on the systematic grammatical features of the specific form. This approach is also in agreement with Ausubel, Novak, and Hanesian's (1968) idea of using advance organizers to assist learners, providing an "anchoring framework" for the new concepts to be learned; in this approach, the story "anchors" the new structure.

Unlike many classroom textbooks, which may offer a group of disconnected sentences or a "contextualized" drill (Walz, 1989), a story-based approach invites the learner to comprehend and experience the meaning and function of grammar through integrated discourse in the form of a story. The process of understanding a story in a foreign language also creates a Zone of Proximal Development (ZPD) (see Chapter 1) where responsive assistance is provided and target language development occurs. As a result, from the very beginning of the lesson, the teacher and learners are engaged in authentic use of language through joint problem-solving activities and interactions to render the story comprehensible. By using simplified language, pictures, and gestures, the teacher scaffolds (see Chapter 1) and guides learners to comprehend the story. Once comprehension is achieved, the teacher can then productively turn the learners' attention to various linguistic elements previously encountered and anchored in the narrative.

 Foreshadowing of new language elements provides learners with a "feel" for what is to come.

Why Use Stories?

Many specialists in first language literacy development have explored the implications of story-based teaching and narrative ways of knowing for quite some time. The rationale for storytelling is multifaceted. Storytelling is an ancient human pastime, often used to entertain, to explain the human condition, and to share an aesthetic experience through expressive language (Pellowski, 1984). Furthermore, storytelling is a natural activity that is socially mediated on a daily basis outside the walls of the classroom. Cross-culturally, there is a deep need for human beings to exchange and tell stories (Morgan & Rinvolucri, 1983). Likewise, research in sociocultural theory has turned attention to the importance of collaborative interaction in several academic disciplines. In an effort to situate grammar instruction in sociocultural theory, we will discuss the principles of a story-based approach to grammar instruction, and then present how to use collaborative dialogic problem solving in a story-based lesson to enhance the learning and use of grammar.

Storytelling is particularly adaptable to second language instruction, since it is natural to tell stories orally, interpret their contents, and extend the story in various ways (e.g., talk about favorite parts, speculate on why an event occurred, express personal opinions about a character). Oller (1983) states that the episodic organization represented in stories aids comprehension and retention. Since individuals have prior knowledge concerning how stories are structured and expectancies about what should take place in stories, their comprehension is facilitated and meaning is established. Furthermore, using "multiple passes" and recycling the storyline through picture displays, Total Physical Response (TPR) activities, and role-playing scenarios deepen comprehension. The framework of the story provides a flow of mental images that help the learners to assign meaning and functions to the forms they hear. After these initial activities and interactions have helped learners to understand the meaning of the discourse, the teacher turns learners' attention to specific language forms or structures. This approach is in agreement with Celce-Murcia's suggestion concerning grammar instruction for ESL learners, that "one of the best times for them [the learners] to attend to form is after comprehension has been achieved and in conjunction with their production of meaningful discourse" (1985, p. 301).

 "One of the best times for them [the learners] to attend to form is after comprehension has been achieved and in conjunction with their production of meaningful discourse." ■

 Which elements of the story-based approach make it appealing? ■

A Model for Dialoguing about Form in a Story-Based Language Approach

Language teaching should never be driven by grammar instruction alone, nor should grammar instruction be literally interpreted to mean instruction on morphology (e.g., adjective or subject-verb agreement, rules for pluralization, etc.) or meaningless, decontextualized manipulation of forms. When the teacher or students focus on form, attention is drawn to the formal properties of the language, which include its sound system, word formation, syntax, discourse markers, and devices for relating one sentence to another, to name a few. Additionally, focus on form needs to include how grammatical forms function in texts. That is, to know only how to form a grammatical structure will never enable learners to use the structure for meaning-making. Therefore, the issue is not whether a teacher should focus on form; instead, the issue is how, when, and where to focus on form in a lesson that will ultimately clarify this important design feature of foreign language instruction. The PACE model for grammar instruction presented below is a way for learners to develop concepts about target language structures that includes form and focus. This approach also challenges teachers to reflect upon their own grammatical understandings and learn new ways of viewing grammar functionally beyond rules of word formation. For example, although language teachers are well aware of how comparative and superlative forms of adjectives are formed (e.g., place *plus* before the adjective in French followed by *que*), explaining how and why comparatives and superlatives are used and how their meanings differ is often rather difficult for teachers to articulate. Why a particular grammatical choice is made rather than selecting another form from a large set of possibilities is at the crux of what it means to know grammar.

The PACE Approach

The following four sections present PACE, a model for contextualizing lessons with learners about language form in the context of interesting cultural texts. *PACE* (Donato & Adair-Hauck, 1994) is an acronym for the four steps we have developed for integrating focus on form in the context of a story-based unit of study. The PACE model should be viewed as the framework for a unit of study that is carried out in multiple lessons over several days. In addition to the opportunities for developing cultural understandings, rich vocabulary, and modes of communication, the PACE model also allows for learners to construct understandings of relevant and meaningful form in collaboration with the teacher and each other. This approach, as will be illustrated below, contrasts sharply with deductive teacher explanation of grammar and inductive approaches that assume that all structures can be analyzed by students on their own, solely on the basis of the input they hear.

P: PRESENTATION of Meaningful Language

This first step of PACE represents the "whole" language being presented in a thematic way. It can be an interesting story (folktales and legends work well), a TPR lesson, an authentic listening segment, an authentic document, or a demonstration of a real-life, authentic task, such as playing a sport, making a sandwich, or conducting a science experiment. Even materials from a textbook chapter (narratives, dialogues, stories) may be used if they are found to be interesting and episodically organized. Episodically organized stories include stageable actions and events that are well-suited for presentation, since the meanings of these texts can be made transparent and comprehensible through dramatization, actions, or TPR storytelling. Given that this text will be foreshadowing a future grammar conversation, the grammatical feature should be well-represented in the text and used meaningfully throughout the story.

In the Presentation phase, the teacher presents the story orally, which facilitates aural comprehension and the acquisition of meaning and form; students do not see the written script of the story in this phase. The Presentation does not consist of isolated, disconnected sentences illustrating the target form in question; rather, it is presented in a narrative intended to capture learner interest and provide opportunities for the teacher to create comprehension through various meaning-making and negotiation strategies (see Chapter 1). Care should also be taken to ensure that the presentation adequately illustrates the structure in question and that the story and target structure are appropriate to the learners' actual and potential levels of development, as instruction in the ZPD suggests. The structure should appear often enough during the Presentation to be salient to learners, without making the language sound unnatural or stilted (see suggestions on creating a storytelling lesson below). Many stories contain *naturally occurring repetitions*; for example, think of the fairytale Goldilocks and the Three Bears and the natural repetitions of certain grammatical features that occur in the story.

The Presentation should also be interactive. By creating student participation in the storytelling event, teachers can guide learners through the new element of the language to be learned. Student participation during the presentation of the text may take the form of learner repetitions of key phrases cued by the teacher during a storytelling session, the use of student actors to portray the events of the story as it is told, cloze exercises based on listening segments, K-W-L activities,[2] or questions that ask students to anticipate what will happen next. The goal here is to enable learners to stretch their language abilities by comprehending new elements of the target language in meaningful texts, through the mediation of the teacher during storytelling.

The Presentation phase may last for part of a class, an entire class session, or even across several class sessions, depending on the story selected and the sequencing of its presentation. For example, a storytelling lesson should be planned using a three-part design involving pre-storytelling, while-storytelling, and post-storytelling activities. These three design features may include focusing on prior knowledge, content, cultural references, key vocabulary, dramatization, pair-work comprehension checks, or story-retelling exercises. The length of time required ultimately depends on the nature of the story, its length, and the amount of negotiation work required to establish meaning. See below for more suggestions on designing and delivering the presentation phase of PACE.

In the Presentation phase, the teacher presents the story orally, which facilitates aural comprehension and the acquisition of meaning and form; students do not see the written script of the story in this phase.

A: ATTENTION

This second PACE step focuses learners' attention on some aspect of the language used during the Presentation. In the Presentation phase, language is transparent and students may not notice important aspects of the language that will help them progress in proficiency. The Attention phase takes place after the class has understood the story and is ready to move to a conversation about an important grammatical feature of the story. Thus, in this phase, the teacher highlights the grammatical feature of the language to be discussed. Highlighting can be achieved in several ways. Teachers can ask questions about patterns found in the text or about words and phrases repeated in a story. Overhead transparencies or PowerPoint presentations of example sentences from the Presentation story can be prepared, with important words and phrases circled or underlined. The point of this step is to help learners to focus attention on the target form without needless elaboration or wasted time.

The important purpose of this step is to ensure that learners are focused on the grammatical element chosen for discussion, which is, after all, the original purpose of following the PACE model. Recall that research has shown that learners do not always process or attend to input in ways that we expect (Herron & Tomasello, 1992). Adair-Hauck

(1993) found that when learners were presented with contextualized sentences (examples taken from the "Le lion et la souris" story with sentences both in the present and in the past using the new past-tense verb form) and were asked by the teacher what they noticed about these sentences, the learners were unable to answer. Instead, they responded with puzzled looks. However, when the teacher provided responsive and graduated assistance and included the words *aujourd'hui* (today) and *hier* (yesterday), which are semantic, not syntactic, clues, learners were able to articulate the differences in the meanings of the sentences. After paying attention to the *semantic clues* (focus on meaning), the learners were able to attend to the *syntactic clues* (focus on form). This classroom-based observation highlights the role of the teacher in guiding and assisting the learners in attending to the lesson objective and the importance of focusing on meaning before form.

It should also be pointed out that learners might show curiosity about certain aspects of the language. That is, if teachers are truly in the ZPD of the learners, they will be attentive to where their students' development is headed and not just the lesson objective as determined by the teacher. In addition to having clear goals and outcomes for the lesson, teachers should allow for the possibility that the grammatical agenda may be set by students when their curiosity about the language emerges. By assessing whether attention was drawn to a particular structure and what structures students express interest in understanding more about, the teacher can determine aspects of the language that were not transparent and need clarification. In summary, the Attention phase recognizes that joint attention between teacher and student needs to be established in order for learning to occur. Joint attention to specific grammatical features of the language can be established explicitly and directly through various mediational means, such as printed text with enhancements or questions that direct attention.

If teachers are truly in the ZPD of the learners, they will be attentive to where their students' development is headed and not just the lesson objective as determined by the teacher.

C: CO-CONSTRUCT—Explanation as Conversation

Learners and teachers should be co-constructors of grammatical explanations. Co-construction involves collaborative talk between the teacher and the students to reflect on, hypothesize about, and create understandings about the form, meaning, and function of the new structure in question. This phase occurs after joint focus of attention on the target form is achieved. At this step, the teacher assists learners in developing a concept of the target structure and enables them to contrast the structure with what they already know. This phase directly addresses the Comparisons goal area, at a time when language comparisons are appropriate and can be discussed in a meaningful context. During this conversation about form and meaning, learners are guided to hypothesize, make predictions, and come to generalizations about the target form, all higher-order thinking skills requiring observation, evaluation, analysis, and synthesis.

One way to begin a conversation where grammatical knowledge is co-constructed is to ask questions. Co-constructing an explanation requires teacher questions that are well-chosen, clear, and direct. Questions are powerful tools in the hands of teachers who can adjust their questioning "in flight" to meet the emergent understandings of their learners. For example, asking learners questions such as, "What words do you hear or see repeated in the text, and what could they mean?", "What pattern do you see in this group of words?", and "How do certain words change as their meanings change?" is a way to help learners draw insights from the language. These assisting questions (see Chapter 1) help learners discover regular grammatical patterns, sound systems, word order, unique cultural meanings of words, and grammatical functions. Additionally, questions cannot be predicted in advance and need to be contingent upon learner contributions. Learners should also be encouraged to ask the teacher and each other questions, if the explanation is to be truly co-constructed. As learners hypothesize and generalize about the target form, teachers build upon and extend learners' knowledge without overwhelming them with superfluous grammatical detail. Hypothesis testing can also be conducted, with teachers leading learners in trying out their new knowledge by applying their generalizations to new situations. Teachers need to be aware that the help they provide is graduated and may range from brief hints about the target form to explicit instruction if needed (Aljaafreh, 1992; Aljaafreh & Lantolf, 1994).

It is important to note that, unlike guided induction techniques, which rely primarily on teacher questioning, a co-constructed explanation is not an inquisition; instead, co-constructed explanations recognize that learners may not be able to perceive the formal properties of language on the basis of the teacher's questions alone. Just as in conversation in everyday life, one individual does not interrogate another in a barrage of questions. What is obvious to the teacher is often a mystery to the novice. A co-constructed explanation is as participatory for the teacher as it is for the learners; that is, teachers need to assess the abilities of their learners and assist them by providing and eliciting information when necessary. Teachers can be conversation partners and offer their own observations, thereby modeling for the students the process of reflecting on language forms. As Tharp and Gallimore (1988) point out, teaching is responsive assistance and cannot be reduced to a series of actions (such as questions) to be performed in the same order in every instructional circumstance. By listening closely to learner contributions during this step, teachers can assess how much help is needed to attain the concept. Over time, learners will develop the ability to reflect on language on their own and some learners may be able to work in small groups on grammar problems and report back to the class about their observations and hypotheses (Fotos & Ellis, 1991).

The use of English for co-construction of grammatical knowledge may be necessary, depending on the level of the class and the structure under investigation. Indeed, it is hard to imagine that beginning language students can analyze language and arrive at generalizations in the target language. It is common to observe, however, that when students reflect on language form, they do so in their native language (Brooks & Donato, 1994; Brooks, Donato, & McGlone, 1997; Swain & Lapkin, 2002). However, if the grammatical conversation can be simplified—and this simplification would be largely determined on the basis of the structure being discussed and the level of the class—then the use of the target language may be possible and useful. As students progress, the teacher should be attentive to changes in students' language and observational abilities and determine if the co-construction can take place in the target language.

In summary, a conversation about grammar involves both teacher and students in discussion about the grammatical form focused upon in the Attention step of the PACE lesson. The purpose of the conversation is neither to engage in a didactic presentation of the form by the teacher (deductive approach) nor require the students to discover the grammatical concept on their own (inductive approach). Rather, teachers elicit students' observations, understandings, and misunderstandings and respond with their own observations or assisting questions. Finally, teachers need to understand grammar in a new manner to help students observe the meaning-making potential of the forms they are learning. This means that simply thinking that the students' ability to explicitly recite a textbook grammar rule is equal to knowing how to use this rule is misguided. Rather, teachers need to move students to understand how grammar functions in spoken and written texts, such as stories, so that they understand why certain grammatical choices were made over others and how they might use grammar for their own communicative purposes.

To conclude this section, the following example of a grammar conversation between a teacher and her first-year French class illustrates how the teacher skillfully manages the conversation about comparative forms of adjectives in French. In this dialogic encounter, the teacher moves students from a superficial observation about word placement to a conceptual understanding that links the formation of adjectives with their functional significance.

 Co-constructing an explanation requires teacher questions that are well-chosen, clear, and direct.

Dialoguing About Grammar: A Co-constructed Grammar Lesson

The teacher has just presented the authentic French folktale of a curious boy who asks what parts of nature are stronger than other parts (e.g., Is the mountain stronger than the wind?). The following day the teacher reviews the contents of the story, provides a printed text of the story, and distributes the text to the class. The teacher's goal for one part of this class is to call attention to the form of the French comparative (*plus + adj + que*), its meaning (superiority of one item over another), and its use (describe and compare two things where one is greater than the other). Then the teacher assists students to engage in *self-explanation* of this form through a conversation about the comparative as it is used in the story. Note the *instructional moves* and the critical thinking that takes place about language form, meaning, and use.

ATTENTION PHASE OF LESSON: FOCUS ON FORM

T: Look at the text of the story. Do you see any phrase that is repeated?

S: Yes, there's *PLUS FORT.*

T: Is this all? Look again, I see another word.

S: *QUE.*

T: So what is the phrase that is repeated?

S: *PLUS FORT QUE.*

Co-construction of Grammatical Concept Phase: Form-Meaning Connections

T: *OK, look at these sentences. [Teacher writes on board* LE CHAT EST PLUS FORT QUE LE RAT. LE ROCHER EST PLUS FORT QUE LE BATEAU. LE BATEAU EST PLUS FORT QUE LA MER.*]*

T: And what's before *PLUS* and after *QUE* in the first sentence?

S: *LE CHAT* before *QUE* and *LE RAT* after *QUE.*

T: So what is the relationship between the cat and the rat?

S: (Confused . . . no response)

T: Well, what do we know about the cat and the rat in this sentence?
How are they described? I see the word *FORT,* which means the cat and the rat are strong. But are they the same?

S: No, the cat is stronger than the rat.

T: The cat is stronger than the rat. OK, but how do you know this? What is in the sentence that tells you the cat is stronger than the rat is?

S: *PLUS*

T: Just *PLUS*?

S: *PLUS FORT QUE*

T: Yes, all the words tell you this, not just one word. Can we say the same about the rock and the boat?

S: Yes, they also have *PLUS FORT QUE* . . .

T: So when you see *PLUS* and a word that describes (an adjective) and a *QUE*, what does the sentence mean?

S: Means one thing is more than the other, like stronger.

T: And when would you use a sentence like the sentences on the board?

S: When you tell a story?

T: Well, yes, to tell a story, but what kind of story? Why are you using *PLUS + ADJECTIVE + QUE*? Why not just use the adjective *FORT* and not use *PLUS . . . QUE*?

S: Because you're comparing two things.

T: OK, yes. We use this kind of sentence to describe and compare two things. Anyone want to try to explain the meaning of the comparison? Are the two things equal? (teacher writes = on the board)

S: No, one is more than the other. Not equal.

T: So if you want to *describe* two things and *compare* these two things and one is superior to the other, how do you make a sentence like this in French?

S: You say the first thing, then say it is *PLUS* + description (adjective), then use *QUE* and say the second thing.

T: Do you all agree with this explanation? (Everyone says yes.) We can try it with some other descriptions and comparisons. Let's see if our generalization works. Let's compare these two things.

Eiffel Tower and our school building

Porsche and Ford

Pennsylvania and California (etc.)

T: OK, take 3 minutes and write your explanation for describing and comparing two things in your notebooks. Tonight, read your textbook explanation about this and see if the textbook gives the same explanation as you. [Teacher then assigns homework using the comparative structure, which moves the PACE lesson into Extension phase.]

Homework: Write a paragraph describing two people or things of your choice and compare them in five different ways. Tomorrow we will see if the class can guess how you compared your two people or objects. You will then present your comparison to the class.

E: EXTENSION Activities

Focus on form is only useful if it can be pressed into service by the learners in a new way at a later time. In story-based language teaching, the teacher never loses sight of the "whole." Therefore, the Extension activity phase of PACE provides learners with the opportunity to use their new grammar skill in creative and interesting ways while at the same time integrating it into existing knowledge. Extension activities should be interesting, be related to the theme of the lesson in some way, and, most importantly, allow for creative self-expression. Extension activities are not worksheets on which learners use the target form to fill in blanks of disconnected sentences; instead, they can be information-gap activities, role-play situations, dramatizations, games, authentic writing projects, paired interviews, class surveys, out-of-class projects, or simulations of real-life situations (see Chapter 8). The possibilities are endless, as long as the learners have the chance to try to use the target form in ways that they see as useful, meaningful, and connected to the overarching theme of the lesson. Moreover, the Extension phase of the lesson allows the teacher to address other goal areas of the standards, such as Cultures, Communities, and Connections: The Extension activities can address cultural perspectives embodied in the story (Adair-Hauck & Donato, 2002; West & Donato, 1995), bring learners into contact with target language members of the community for further investigations of the story's country of origin, or link the story's theme to an academic subject area.

The Extension activity phase closes the circle of the PACE lesson and puts the "whole" back into story-based language teaching (see Figure 7.2). As is the case in the Presentation phase, the Extension phase can take several days as students are engaged in multiple communicative and interpersonal activities.

 The Extension activity phase closes the circle of the PACE lesson and puts the "whole" back into story-based language teaching.

FIGURE 7.2 A Story-Based Approach to Language Instruction and Focus on Form

1

Presentation
Teacher foreshadows
the grammar explanation
through the use of
integrated discourse
(stories, poems, taped
selections, songs, etc.).
Emphasis is on literal comprehension
and meaning.

Extension
Through integrative extension
activities, the learners need to
use the grammatical structure(s)
in order to carry out a particular
function or task.

4

Attention
Teacher assists the learners in
focusing their attention on a
particular language form or
grammatical structure.

2

Co-Construction
Using guiding questions, teacher
and learners co-construct the
grammar explanation by
discovering the underlying patterns
or consistent forms.

3

Source: From "PACE: A model to focus on form," by R. Donato and B. Adair-Hauck, 1994. Paper presented at the annual meeting of the American Council on the Teaching of Foreign Languages. Used by permission of Bonnie Adair-Hauck.

Elements of Story-Based Language Learning

Figure 7.3 summarizes the differences between a story-based language approach and the traditional deductive approach to teaching grammar. The earlier discussion should have led you to the conclusion that language learning is a thinking process. Teachers need to manage cognitively demanding conversations about grammar and extension activities that will encourage learners to hypothesize, predict, take risks, make errors, and self-correct (Adair-Hauck & Donato, 2002; Fountas & Hannigan, 1989). By doing so, learners become active participants in the learning process. All the story-based activities described later in this chapter have a common denominator—they all encourage learners to be active thinkers and hypothesizers as they collaborate in conversations about language and language learning activities with the teacher or with their peers.

Whether listening to a storytelling activity, co-constructing a grammar explanation, or collaborating with peers during an extension activity, learners are actively discovering and hypothesizing about the target language. This approach reflects the framework of the Communication goal area of *SFLL*, which advocates that learners be engaged in cognitively challenging activities that encourage them to use communication strategies, such as guessing intelligently, deriving meaning from context, asking for and providing clarification, making and checking hypotheses, and making inferences, predictions, and generalizations. Moreover, all of the classroom activities described encourage functional and interactional use of language by giving learners opportunities to share information, ask questions, and solve problems collaboratively.

FIGURE 7.3 Teaching of Grammar: A Story-Based PACE Approach vs. Traditional Approach

STORY-BASED PACE APPROACH	TRADITIONAL APPROACH
1. Use of higher-level thinking skills and language before moving to procedural skills	1. Sequencing of tasks from simple to complex
2. Instructional interaction between Teacher ("expert") and Learners ("novices")	2. Little teacher/learner interaction; teacher-directed explanation
3. Dialogic co-constructed explanation	3. Explicit explanation of grammar
4. Encourages performance before competence (approximations encouraged).	4. Learner must master each step before going to next step (competence before performance).
5. Learners participate in problem-solving process and higher-order thinking skills (opportunity for learners' actions to be made meaningful).	5. Learners are passive and rarely participate in constructing the explanation.
6. Language and especially questions must be suitably turned to a level at which performance requires assistance.	6. Few questions—mainly rhetorical
7. Lesson operationalizes functional significance of grammatical structure before mechanical procedures take place.	7. The functional significance of a grammatical point often does not emerge until end of lesson.

Source: From "PACE: A model to focus on form," by R. Donato and B. Adair-Hauck, 1994, p. 20. Paper presented at the annual meeting of the American Council on the Teaching of Foreign Languages. Used by permission of Bonnie Adair-Hauck.

Finally, a distinguishing theme of a dialogic story-based approach to grammar instruction is that learning needs to be integrated, contextualized, and meaning-centered (Pearson, 1989). In Appendices 7.1.0 to 7.1.14 on the *Teacher's Handbook* Web site, we have included a sample story-based language lesson to teach the past definite in French with *avoir* (story suggested and edited by Terry [1986] and based on a well-known Aesop's fable). The lesson begins with a story, "The Lion and the Mouse" ("Le lion et la souris"), which foreshadows the functional significance of the grammar point. All of the subsequent classroom activities—for example, role-playing, paired activities to retell the story, and team activities using graphic organizers—are contextualized and relate to the theme of "The Lion and the Mouse." In this way, the unit is contextualized and integrated, which enables the instructional events to flow naturally. As noted earlier, integrated and meaning-centered activities facilitate comprehension and retention on the part of learners. Furthermore, the extension activities encourage learners to integrate meaning, form, and function while experiencing language in context.

It should be mentioned that creating integrated and meaning-centered activities is probably one of the most difficult aspects of story-based language teaching, since many textbooks still stress context-reduced practice and fragmented materials. The following activities will provide you with suggestions on how to incorporate integrated and story-based language activities into your classroom. See the View and Reflect section of the *Teacher's Handbook* Web site for a video of a lesson that has features of the PACE approach.

 How does a dialogic story-based approach lead to language learning?

Suggestions for Selecting, Preparing, Designing, and Delivering a Story-Based Language Lesson

Actualizing a PACE lesson will enable the teacher to transform the classroom into a socially mediated environment where the teacher and learners co-construct meaning of "texts" (stories, poems, songs, etc.) from the beginning of the lesson. In particular, we suggest embedding stories (fables, legends, fairytales, etc.) into your lesson plans. Integrating story-based activities enables the teacher to create a meaning-making classroom that parallels the home or out-of-school environment. This explains why first language reading and language arts programs value story-based language learning. Golden (2000) explains: "Like homes, libraries, book clubs, workplaces and many other social contexts, classrooms are special places where human beings interact with stories, story-based tasks, and with each other to make meaning" (p. 4).

Selecting an Appropriate Text. One of the first steps in designing a story-based lesson is selecting an appropriate text for learners and for your instructional purposes. Text selection is not an easy task, given the many texts that exist, their contents, and their complexity. Interactive storytelling, rather than "story-reading," is an excellent way to make use of the myriad stories that exist in target language cultures. Through storytelling, natural simplifications can occur, and teachers can shape the story to be within learners' ZPDs. The following are guiding principles for selecting a good text for a PACE lesson:

1. Do you like the text and find it appealing?
2. Will the learners enjoy the story you selected? Is it an age-appropriate story dealing with issues, experiences, and themes that reflect the lives of your learners? Does the story incite imagination or reflection?
3. Does the story lend itself to "stageable actions"?

4. Does the story suggest connections to academic content?
5. Does the story represent some aspect of the target culture that you will address?
6. Does the story present stereotypes or reasonable and fair depictions of the target language culture?
7. Is the language accessible or can it be made accessible through storytelling simplifications to the learners' current stage of linguistic development?
8. Is the theme of the story one that can be expanded upon and extended into various activities?
9. Does the story adequately represent a grammatical structure on which you will later focus?
10. Does the story lend itself to addressing some of the goal areas of the *SFLL*?

One of the best places to find stories is in the children's section of a large public library. Many libraries have well-illustrated children's books (folktales, fairytales, fables, myths, legends, humorous tales, tall tales) in different languages. Folktales seem to work particularly well, since they were originally created to be delivered orally in a cultural context, and they have withstood the test of time (Seeley, 1993). The Internet is also a rich source of authentic stories in your target language. However, when using the Internet, or when searching materials marketed by publishers of second language materials, remember that an authentic story is one written by a member of the target language community for purposes other than language instruction. Usually, the writer's motivation is to tell an interesting tale, entertain, explain the human condition, or illustrate a moral or theme (Pellowski, 1984). Some Web sites and second language material developers offer texts that do not follow the above criteria. For example, some stories are translations containing illustrations and cultural references that have not been modified to match the cultures of the language into which the story has been translated. Many of these stories would never be read by members of the target culture. Unfortunately, the major goal of some material developers and Web sites is to sell products, not to share a well-written story representing various cultures.

An authentic story worthy of being integrated into the curriculum should have the following characteristics:

- a compelling theme
- characters with personality
- a problem
- plot or stageable events
- quick resolution to the problem.

Fairytales are appropriate for PACE lessons. They are internationally known (e.g., Pinnochio, Red Riding Hood, Peter Pan, etc.) and find their origins in many different cultures. For example, Adair-Hauck and Cumo-Johanssen (1997) designed a PACE lesson that embedded the story of *Red Riding Hood* to teach the past tense (*passé composé* with *être*) to French II high school students. Although the students were familiar with this well-known story, follow-up questionnaires demonstrated that it was a challenge for them to listen and comprehend the story told orally in French and to participate in the story-based language learning activities. However, the students found the challenge well worth the effort, and much more interesting than a traditional approach to grammar (Adair-Hauck, 1993). Furthermore, the students were intrigued to learn how the French version of this universal fairytale differs from the American version. As they learned, the French version of *Red Riding Hood* has a different ending from the story they heard as children.

Preparing and Delivering Stories. Storytelling needs to be a social event. When students listen to stories, the quality of their listening is dramatically different when compared to listening to an audio selection or viewing a videotape in the foreign language. For the latter, the students are "eavesdropping" on exchanges and social interactions occurring between *other* individuals (Morgan & Rinvolucri, 1983). In other words, they are involved in secondhand listening rather than participatory listening. Storytelling, however, is a co-constructive listening experience, which Morgan and Rinvolucri succinctly elucidate: "To be told a story by a live storyteller involves the learners in "I-Thou" listening where the listeners can directly influence the telling" (1983, p.2). Stated differently, through storytelling, both the teacher and learners influence the meaning-making event.

What are some participation strategies used by professional storytellers that keep their listeners engaged? First, the story you want to tell needs to become a familiar friend (Livo & Rietz, 1986). You may not need to memorize every word verbatim, but you do need to know exceptionally well the introduction, characters, main events, transition words that keep the story flowing, the resolution to the conflict, and the ending. Practicing storytelling in front of a mirror can be quite useful. A dress rehearsal for a friend or family member can inform you about which techniques are particularly valuable for helping students comprehend the story. For this dress rehearsal, it doesn't matter if your audience doesn't know your second language. If your illustrations, visuals, props, and facial expressions support the meaning of the story, even those who do not know the language should be able to comprehend some of the major events of the story and learn from your dress rehearsal.

The types of strategies you select to engage the listeners into the storytelling event will depend on the age, proficiency level, backgrounds of the learners, and the nature of the story. Some techniques, however, are essential for participatory storytelling. It is difficult to engage an audience if you are far away, so seating should be arranged so that everyone can see you clearly (a semicircle works well). Concentration, especially for elementary language learners, can be a difficult challenge; therefore, make sure that the story is not too long (many effective stories can be told in 5–10 minutes). If you have a favorite story that is longer but appropriate, divide the presentation step of the PACE lesson into two parts and introduce the second part of the story on day two.

Successful storytellers know how to engage the audience by using audience participatory techniques, such as hand motions (thumbs-up/thumbs-down for comprehension checks), character signs that learners hold up when the character is mentioned, cued repetitions of lines from the story, or silent dramatizations of parts of the story as it is being told (McWilliams, 2008). Visual aids will also hold learners' attention and assist in building comprehension. Most stories require at least 10–12 illustrations that depict the main characters and events. Oftentimes, artistic students are willing to create the illustrations and take pride in contributing to the class enterprise. Arranging the illustrations on the chalk runner or hanging them on a story "clothesline" will keep the story alive for the learners. A flannelgraph story can be useful to demonstrate connections between characters and events (McWilliams). Some teachers prefer to use puppets, prompts (such as costumes for different characters), and concrete objects to help learners understand the story. These visuals aids are particularly important for elementary and intermediate-level classes. To be sure, students are not going to understand every word of the story, so using these storytelling comprehension-building strategies and participatory techniques will help to hold their attention and increase their level of understanding.

Finally, successful storytellers are skilled at incorporating kinesthetic cues that encourage the audience to concentrate and follow the events of the story. These cues may include eye contact, facial gestures, hand motions, and pantomime and/or body movements (e.g., standing one way for one character and another way for the narrator). Voice techniques, such as changing the tone of one's voice (high or low pitch), rhythm (fast or slow paced), and sound effects and silent pauses when appropriate will also help to hold learners' attention (Livo & Rietz, 1986).

To deepen learners' comprehension, the teacher may need to tell the story two or three times. For the second telling of the story, the teacher may want to use a story-cubing activity to focus learners' attention on the why-questions, or the who-what-where-when elements of the story (Cassidy & Hossler, 1992). If a third pass of the story is necessary, the teacher and learners together can retell the story by using the illustrations. Alternatively, the teacher may want to make smaller versions of the visuals and have students work in pairs or groups to recreate the storyline and retell the story. As stories are retold, the teacher should increase the level of student verbal or nonverbal participation in each telling of the story.

As a comprehension check, the teacher might play the "I Have: Who Has" game with students (Polette, 1991). This is an attentive listening comprehension game that can be constructed from any story and can be played as a whole-class activity or in groups as a final meaning-making activity. The teacher constructs a number of questions concerning the setting, character, major events, and final outcome of the story. Each student receives a card with one question and one answer to a different question written on it. The learner who has the starred card reads the first question. For "Le lion et la souris," the first question is "Where does the story take place?" The learner holding the card with the answer reads it and then provides the next question. By listening carefully, the learners should be able to respond correctly and thereby retell the story.

Creating Extension Activities. Creative extension activities are critical because they allow learners to use the new grammatical feature from the story in interpersonal communication, where they create their own thoughts in the foreign language. Extension activities also encourage learners to collaborate and cooperate in meaningful, interpersonal contexts. Although these activities may be challenging for learners, students will be able to express their own thoughts with more confidence, and their interpretive, interpersonal, and oral and written presentational communication will improve (Adair-Hauck, 1993).

 Creative extension activities are critical because they allow learners to use the new grammatical feature from the story in interpersonal communication.

Extension activities often incorporate graphic organizers (such as story mapping, character mapping, or discussion webbing) to serve as anchoring devices to help learners organize their thoughts and ideas concerning the story. Vygotsky (1978) would argue that these graphic organizers may be viewed as mediational tools to organize learners' thinking, such as perception, attention, and memory. Story mapping and character mapping can be accomplished in pairs or in groups. During story mapping activities, learners work together to construct the principal elements of the story. The story map encourages learners to focus on the principal characters, problems, major events, and solutions to the problem. In character mapping activities, learners focus on a number of elements, such as the character's physical and intrinsic traits, and the character's good and bad actions. For

www.cengagebrain.com

sample PACE lessons and accompanying story-based activities in French, German, Japanese, and Spanish, see Appendices 7.2 to 7.6 on the *Teacher's Handbook* Web site.

At some point, the teacher will want to move the lesson from mere comprehension activities to activities that stimulate the learners' critical thinking skills. These activities encourage learners to analyze the events of the story and then to draw conclusions about the story. Alvermann (1991) suggests that critical thinking activities should be carried out collaboratively and cooperatively since "some of the best thinking results in a group's collaborative efforts" (p. 92).

Discussion webbing (Alvermann, 1991) is a critical thinking activity that can be developed for any story. Discussion webbing moves learners from what happened in the story to why it happened. For example, using "Le lion et la souris," the teacher can develop a discussion webbing activity around the question "Should the mouse help the lion?" Discussion webbing encourages groups of learners to think about an even number of yes/no answers. Learners try to form a consensus on the best reason WHY the mouse should or should not help the lion. This encourages learners to look at both sides of an issue. Later, the groups can share their results from the discussion webbing activity in a class discussion. For sample discussion-webbing activities, see Appendix 7.1.13 on the *Teacher's Handbook* Web site.

www.cengagebrain.com

www.cengagebrain.com

Discussion webbing moves learners from what happened in the story to why it happened.

Finally, the teacher may want to integrate an *intertextual* activity as a way to encourage learners to move beyond the mere recalling of events to higher critical thinking skills. During intertextual activities, learners working in pairs or groups analyze the components of stories by juxtapositioning two different texts or stories. Intertextual links can be made at various levels, by juxtaposing characters, content, plot development, style, and so on (Bloome & Egan-Robertson, 1993). A Venn diagram is often used as a graphic organizer (Christenbury & Kelly, 1983; Edwards, 1989; Redmond, 1994) to help learners analyze their thoughts (see Chapter 4). Note again that learners are encouraged to work in participatory groups during these intertextual activities, since a story-based approach emphasizes meaning-making and the *interpersonal* nature of language and literacy. For a sample intertextual activity, see Appendix 7.1.12 on the *Teacher's Handbook* Web site.

Many teachers might wonder how learners with limited L2 resources will be able to participate in some of the more challenging story-based activities. Discussion webbing and intertextual activities tap into learners' higher critical thinking skills; therefore, during these activities learners use their cognitive processes to concentrate on comparing and contrasting, analyzing, and synthesizing new information gleaned from the story with their prior background knowledge. In order to participate in these immersion-type activities, learners exploit a variety of compensation strategies to communicate their ideas in L2. As a result, their productive use of L2 varies. For example, some learners feel comfortable mixing L1 and L2, other learners seek assistance from the teacher or a more capable peer, and other learners feel more comfortable consulting a resource such as a dictionary (Adair-Hauck, 1996). The teacher creates a community that assists and supports learners in activities that they would be unable to do alone or unassisted. According to Vygotsky (1986), instruction (assisted performance) leads to development (unassisted performance): "Therefore the only good kind of instruction marches ahead of development and leads it. It must be aimed not so much at the ripe, but at the ripening functions" (p. 188).

To illustrate this point, one foreign language teacher who uses a story-based approach encourages her learners to negotiate meaning in L2 using discourse strategies such as comprehension checks and clarification requests. To do so, she decorates her room with large, colored, laminated signs highlighting discourse facilitators, such as: "*Répétez, s'il vous plaît*"; "*Comment?*"; "*Je n'ai pas saisi ça*"; "*Comment dit-on ___ en français?*"; "*Comment dirai-je ____?*", and so on. She explained that in this way she provides assistance to her learners and, at the same time, decorates her classroom with the "curriculum." ACT-FL's standards-based assessment research project (Glisan, Adair-Hauck, & Gadbois, 2000) has revealed that many learners are not aware of and cannot use discourse compensation strategies, which, in turn, deters their performance on standards-based interpersonal tasks. Therefore, we need to integrate these discourse facilitators and compensation strategies into a standards-based curriculum early in the language learning sequence.

PACE and the Accuracy Issue. Elementary/intermediate level learners certainly will make grammatical errors while participating in extension activities, even with the new grammatical feature of the lesson. As learners work in groups, the teacher needs to observe the various groups and provide assistance (e.g., requisite vocabulary, verb tense, etc.) when necessary. But in many instances, learners will be capable of expressing their opinions regarding the events/outcomes of the story, even if those opinions are at times not grammatically perfect. Frustration on the part of the teacher and/or learners will be reduced if the teacher places an emphasis on *meaning-making* or *sense-making* as learners try to create and construct meaning during these interpersonal and socially mediated activities.

As a debriefing activity after the extension activities, the teacher may want to focus attention on some common or frequently made errors or remind the students of what they had discussed in the co-construction phase of the lesson. It is important to note that during interactions between native and nonnative speakers in the world outside of the classroom, error correction tends to be limited to errors regarding meaning, including vocabulary choice, rather than on pronunciation and grammar. Errors that do not interfere with meaning tend to be overlooked by native speakers (Lightbown & Spada, 2003). Unfortunately, in many formal second language classroom settings, accuracy has precedence over meaningful communication, and, therefore, errors are frequently corrected. Too much error correction can stifle learner motivation (Hadley, 2001).

A collaborative approach to error correction is advantageous, since it includes the learners in the learning process. For example, during the debriefing session, the teacher can remind learners that errors are a natural part of language development (Lightbown & Spada, 2003). In the natural second language setting, errors regarding meaning would prompt a native speaker to correct or to ask for clarification.

Learners enjoy collaborating with the teacher and investigating which of their mistakes cause misunderstanding of the message (Adair-Hauck, 1995; Vavra, 1996). Using an overhead or LCD projector, the teacher can show learners examples of contextualized mistakes and errors in meaningful exchanges with longer stretches of discourse.

Another strategy that encourages learners to pay attention to accuracy is to show elementary or intermediate level students a sample oral interview in which students from previous years participated. This interview could be one that had been done at the end of the year as a summative assessment. Before playing the interview, the teacher could briefly discuss the *ACTFL Proficiency Guidelines—Speaking* (1999) for novice, intermediate, and advanced level speakers. This explanation may have to be conducted in L1, depending on the level of the learners. Students could then identify the functions that they see and they could identify the structures that the interviewee needs to work on in order to improve. Another idea is to show an actual OPI (to the extent that one may be available) and have learners discuss with their teacher why the interviewee is at a particular proficiency level and which accuracy structures the interviewee needs to work on in order to receive a higher rating. Furthermore, the class can discuss what language functions or tasks the interviewee was able to carry out during the interview. In this way, the teacher crystallizes the importance of the functions and grammatical structures embedded in the curriculum. As Christenbury (1996) succinctly explains, "Grammar and usage cannot be taught effectively if students see no real need for it and if teachers cannot persuade them to see the need" (p. 12).

Moving to Independent Practice

At some point, the teacher will want learners to practice the target language independently. Ideally, group activities or working together on an interpersonal level will have prepared learners to function independently (Vygotsky, 1978). As an independent extension activity, the teacher may ask learners to create a different ending to the story.

Learners may also use the story mapping technique to create their own stories. A number of foreign language teachers have reported that learners enjoy creating humorous stories or "spoofs" related to the story in class. As a final presentational activity, learners can share their stories either with their class or with other members of the community (e.g., younger learners in the district, target culture student exchange groups).

Voices of the Learners

Before concluding, one should acknowledge the thoughts and opinions of learners regarding story-based language learning activities for foreign language learners. Adair-Hauck (1993) conducted a three-month, classroom-based research project using a story-based approach to teach intermediate level French to a class of 20 learners ranging from 15 to 16 years of age. At the end of the project, learners' responses were overwhelmingly positive. For example, when asked, "Was it easier to learn French by listening to stories?" 90% of the learners answered "yes," one learner answered "no," and one learner answered "yes" and "no." Learners' qualitative responses to the question "What did you like most about the storytelling activities?" were particularly enlightening. One perceptive learner commented, "I liked learning with pictures and props. That way, if there was something I didn't understand, then I knew what it was." Another learner responded, "I liked the storytelling activities because they had a good effect. You seem to remember things better if you have something to do with the words you are learning." Finally, one learner made this comment regarding a positive, affective climate: "I liked the fact that it gets the class into the story and it makes it more fun. I think I learn better when I enjoy the class."

TEACH AND REFLECT ·

NCATE_____

EPISODE ONE
Examining Grammar Presentations in Textbooks

ACTFL/NCATE 3.a. Understanding Language Acquisition and Creating a Supportive Classroom; 3.b. Developing Instructional Practices that Reflect Language Outcomes and Learner Diversity; 4.c. Selecting and Designing Instructional Materials.

TESOL/NCATE: 1.b. Candidates Understand and Apply Theories and Research of Language Acquisition and Development to Support Their ESOL Students' Learning; 3.a. Planning for Standards-Based ESL and Content Instruction; 3.b. Managing and Implementing Standards-Based ESL and Content Instruction; and 3.c. Using Resources Effectively in ESL and Content Instruction.

Examine at least two textbooks in the target language. Decide whether the textbooks use a deductive or inductive approach to grammar explanation. To do so, answer the following questions for each textbook:

1. Does the textbook offer some form of grammatical analysis? If so, does the textbook advocate a deductive or inductive approach to grammar explanation?
2. When is the teacher supposed to focus the learners' attention on form or on grammatical structures—at the beginning of the chapter, the middle, the end, or not at all?
3. Analyze the role assigned to the learner regarding grammar explanations. Is the learner a passive listener during the explanation? Is the learner supposed to be an active hypothesizer? Is the learner supposed to hypothesize alone or in collaboration with others?

4. Now identify a particular language function, such as asking and giving directions, making purchases, or describing people or things. (Turn to the chapter that focuses on your selected language function.) How does the chapter relate language function to form? Hint: Are students asked to do mechanical practice before communicative practice?

5. Examine the chapter to see if the learners are exposed to meaningful, integrated discourse. If so, how—through stories, poems, songs, videotapes, or drama? And when—at the beginning, the middle, or the end of the chapter?

6. In your opinion, how well does the chapter integrate (1) meaning—the thoughts and ideas of the message being conveyed; (2) form—the various linguistic and grammatical elements; and (3) function—the way to carry out a particular task by exploiting the appropriate grammatical structures?

7. In your estimation, is one particular dimension—meaning, form, or function—emphasized more than the others? If so, which one? Can you offer an explanation of why one dimension might be emphasized at the expense of the others?

TECHNO FOCUS: In this Teach and Reflect, you have analyzed how textbooks present grammar. Now you will see how college faculty members supplemented their textbooks using technology and lessons built around the PACE model. This project, called *Taller Hispano* (Hispanic Workshop), uses authentic materials on the Web in multimedia activities for basic Spanish language instruction. The activities lend themselves to teaching listening using video and audio. There are 10 modules that cover the topics of *La familia, Los colegios y las universidades, Las mascotas y otros animales, El gobierno, El ocio, La gastronomía, El vestuario, El turismo,* and *El cajón de sastre – Potpourri.* To view the *Taller Hispano,* go to http://www.merlot.org/merlot/viewMaterial.htm?id=88097

Answer the questions listed below:

1. How do you think learners might work in their ZPDs using the song presented on the Web page ?
2. In what ways do you think students might develop interlanguage by viewing and listening to the materials presented on the Web page?
3. What role do you think authentic materials like these will play in learner motivation?
4. Go to the Multimedia Educational Resource for Learning and Online Teaching (MERLOT) main page at http://www.merlot.org/merlot/index.htm, click on "world languages," and explore other items in the collection.

NCATE

EPISODE TWO
Designing a Story-Based PACE Lesson

ACTFL/NCATE 2.b. Demonstrating Understanding of Literary and Cultural Texts and Traditions; 3.a. Understanding Language Acquisition and Creating a Supportive Classroom; 3.b. Developing Instructional Practices that Reflect Language Outcomes and Learner Diversity; 4.b. Integrating Standards in Instruction; 4.c. Selecting and Designing Instructional Materials.

TESOL/NCATE: 1.b. Candidates Understand and Apply Theories and Research of Language Acquisition and Development to Support Their ESOL Students' Learning; 3.a. Planning for Standards-Based ESL and Content Instruction; 3.b. Managing and Implementing Standards-Based ESL and Content Instruction; and 3.c. Using Resources Effectively in ESL and Content Instruction.

You are now going to design a lesson that emphasizes a story-based language approach to grammar instruction. First, you need to identify a particular linguistic function—for example, asking questions, making purchases, or describing people or things. Think of an appropriate context in which you would need to use this function. Then decide which structures should be incorporated into the lesson so that learners are capable of carrying out the function. Using the following steps as guidelines, decide how you are going to PACE the story-based language lesson.

1. Identify an integrated discourse sample that foreshadows the selected linguistic function, context, and accuracy structures. Remember that the "text" can be in the form of a story, poem, taped listening selection, advertisement, videotaped interview, and so on. Consult the section on selecting a text in this chapter before beginning this step.

2. Decide what you need to do to help learners comprehend the meaning of the text. For example, will it help learners' comprehension if you use visuals, mime, gestures, and props? Gather all necessary supplemental materials. This phase is critical to the success of the lesson. Be creative!

3. Demonstrate for your fellow classmates how you plan to introduce the story-based text. Even if your classmates do not know your target language, see if you can convey the general meaning or significance of the text. (Make use of those props!)

4. Discuss how you will use "multiple passes" to recycle the storyline. What kinds of TPR activities, role-playing scenarios, or other activities would be appropriate to deepen the learners' comprehension? Remember that at this stage the learners will become more participatory.

5. Write a short description of how you will focus the learners' attention on form. What hints or helping questions are you going to ask? How do you plan to co-construct the explanation?

6. Now design at least three extension activities that relate to the selected context. (Note: Use the extension activities in Appendix 7.1, including Appendices 7.1.12 to 7.1.15 on the *Teacher's Handbook* Web site as guidelines.) These activities should create a need for the learners to use the identified structures. In doing so, the learners will develop a fuller understanding of the function of the grammatical structures.

www.cengagebrain.com

NCATE

EPISODE THREE
Developing a PACE Lesson for the Post-Secondary Level[3]

ACTFL/NCATE 2.b. Demonstrating Understanding of Literary and Cultural Texts and Traditions; 3.a. Understanding Language Acquisition and Creating a Supportive Classroom; 3.b. Developing Instructional Practices that Reflect Language Outcomes and Learner Diversity; 4.b. Integrating Standards in Instruction; 4.c. Selecting and Designing Instructional Materials.

TESOL/NCATE: 1.b. Language Acquisition and Development; 3.a. Planning for Standards-Based ESL and Content Instruction; 3.b. Managing and Implementing Standards-Based ESL and Content Instruction; and 3.c. Using Resources Effectively in ESL and Content Instruction.

If you are preparing to teach or are already teaching at the post-secondary level, this task is designed to engage you in developing a PACE lesson for a college or university level class that is working toward advanced level speaking functions. You might find it helpful to read about advanced-level discourse on pages 278–279 in Chapter 8 before you begin this task. Design your lesson according to the following steps:

1. Select a new grammatical form that you would like to target for a PACE lesson, but be sure that it is one that is useful in developing advanced-level discourse, such as the use of the imperfect subjunctive and conditional for hypothesizing in Spanish or the use of cohesive devices such as conjunctions and connector words (e.g., *therefore, on the other hand, however*). Decide how the grammatical form will be used in a specific advanced-level function.

2. Select an authentic text, preferably one that is in story form.

3. Design a lesson using the four stages of the PACE model (see the steps in Episode Two). Remember to incorporate visuals and props to clarify meaning. In your Extension Phase, be sure to engage your students in interpersonal communication, using the new structure in context. Your instructor may ask you to present your lesson to your classmates.

DISCUSS AND REFLECT ·

www.cengagebrain.com

See the *Teacher's Handbook* Web site for an additional case study:
Case Study Two: Using a Story-Based Language Approach to Teach Reflexive Verbs

NCATE_____

CASE STUDY ONE
Contrasting Explanations of Form

ACTFL/NCATE 3.a. Understanding Language Acquisition and Creating a Supportive Class-room; 3.b. Developing Instructional Practices that Reflect Language Outcomes and Learner Diversity; 4.b. Integrating Standards in Instruction.

TESOL/NCATE: 1.b. Candidates Understand and Apply Theories and Research of Language Acquisition and Development to Support Their ESOL Students' Learning; 3.a. Planning for Standards-Based ESL and Content Instruction; 3.b. Managing and Implementing Standards-Based ESL and Content Instruction; and 3.c. Using Resources Effectively in ESL and Content Instruction.

Review the co-constructed conversation between a teacher and student that appeared earlier in this chapter on pp.227–228; we will refer to this conversation as Scenario I. Then compare it to the conversation in Scenario II below (Antón, 1999). Study both wconversations—perhaps even act them out—and use the questions at the end of each to guide your discussion about them.

Scenario II: In this scenario, an Italian instructor has presented some new vocabulary and read several times a dialogue that students have repeated chorally.

1. T: In this lesson, you are doing two important things. We are learning possessive adjectives and another past tense. You've already had the *Passato Prossimo*. They are both past tenses but they have different uses in Italian. Intricate for the speaker of English, not so intricate for speakers of other Romance languages. Let's talk about possessives first. What's the word for *book*?

2. Ss: *Libro*.

3. T: What's the word for *house*?

4. Ss: *Casa*.

5. T: OK. Let's get a masculine and singular. *The book*?

6. Ss: *Il libro*.

7. T: *The house*?

8. Ss: *La casa*.

9. T: That's correct. Now we have masculine and feminine. Masculine article *il*, feminine *la*. We've also learnt that adjectives agree with nouns they modify [louder]. An adjective agrees with the noun it modifies. That was important until now, but it becomes more im-portant now in this lesson, so, the . . . *beautiful book, il bel libro, the beautiful house, la bella casa*. Now we are going to adjectives, possessive adjectives. Adjectives are words which describe other words, other nouns, pronouns, or other adjectives. *The beautiful book, beautiful* is an adjective, the *red* book, *red* is an adjective modifying *book*. Posses-sives in English and Italian are also adjectives, possessive adjectives. *My house, my* is a possessive in Italian, it's next to the noun, it is also an adjective. Now, what did we just

say? Adjectives agree with the thing modified. *My book, il mio libro. This book is red, il mio libro è rosso. My house is white, la mia casa,* adjectives agree with the noun they modify [louder]. So, when you are saying *my book* and *my house,* adjectives agree with the noun they modify. Okay, that goes for all of them: *my things, your things, his or her things, our things, your things, and their things.* [writing the paradigm on the board] *Il mio libro, il tuo libro, il suo libro, la mia casa, la tua casa, la sua casa.* (My book, your book, *i miei, i miei libri, i tuoi libri, i suoi libri, le mie case, le tue case* (pp. 308–309).)

Guide your discussion of the preceding scenarios with the following questions:

1. Identify the "expert" and the "novice" players in each scenario.
2. How does the expert draw novices' attention to the forms in each scenario?
3. Does the teacher draw the learners' attention to form, meaning, and use in each scenario? If yes, how?
4. How does the role of the teacher in Scenario I differ from that of the teacher in Scenario II?
5. Which scenario illustrates guided assistance, scaffolding, and development through the ZPD? Cite specific examples of each from the scenario.
6. Describe the role of interaction and collaboration in each of these scenarios.
7. What do you think would be the result of student learning in each of these scenarios?
8. How might students react as learners engaged in each of these scenarios?

To prepare for class discussion:

1. Imagine that you are a student participating in the French conversation presented earlier in this chapter on pp. 227–228. Write an entry in your journal reflecting on what you learned in Scenario I.
2. Imagine that you are a student in the Italian class in Scenario II. Write a journal entry reflecting on what you learned in that scenario.
3. Using these two scenarios as examples, write a brief description comparing a traditional deductive approach to teaching grammar and an approach that is based upon dialogic explanation and collaboration of teacher and learners.

REFERENCES

Adair-Hauck, B. (1993). *A descriptive analysis of whole language/guided participatory versus explicit teaching strategies in foreign language instruction.* Unpublished doctoral dissertation, University of Pittsburgh, Pittsburgh, PA.

Adair-Hauck, B. (1995). Are all grammar errors created equal? Seminar presented at Millersville University Summer Graduate Program in French. Millersville, PA.

Adair-Hauck, B. (1996). Practical whole language strategies for secondary and university level FL learners. *Foreign Language Annals, 29,* 253–270.

Adair-Hauck, B. (2007). The PACE Model: A dialogic and co-constructive approach to grammar explanation. Paper presented at the New Jersey State Foreign Language Teachers Consortium, Princeton, NJ.

Adair-Hauck, B., & Cumo-Johanssen, P. (1997). Communication goal: Meaning making through a whole language approach. In J. K. Phillips (Ed.), *Collaborations: Meeting new goals, new realities* (pp. 35–96). Northeast Conference Reports. Lincolnwood, IL: NTC/Contemporary Publishing Group.

Adair-Hauck, B., & Donato, R. (1994). Foreign language explanations within the zone of proximal development. *The Canadian Modern Language Review, 50,* 532–557.

Adair-Hauck, B., & Donato, R. (2002). The PACE Model: A story-based approach to meaning and form for standards-based language learning. *The French Review, 76,* 265–296.

Aljaafreh, A. (1992). *The role of implicit/explicit error correction and the learner's zone of proximal development.* Unpublished doctoral dissertation, University of Delaware, Newark, DE.

Aljaafreh, A., & Lantolf, J. (1994). Negative feedback as regulation and second language learning in the zone of proximal development. *The Modern Language Journal, 78,* 465–483.

Alvermann, D. (1991). The discussion web: A graphic aid for learning across the curriculum. *The Reading Teacher, 45,* 92–98.

American Council on the Teaching of Foreign Languages (ACTFL). (1999). *ACTFL Proficiency Guidelines—Speaking.* Yonkers, NY: Author.

Antón, M. (1999). The discourse of a learner-centered classroom: Sociocultural perspectives on teacher-learner interactions in the second language classroom. *The Modern Language Journal, 83,* 303–318.

Aski, J. M. (2003). Foreign language textbook activities: Keeping pace with second language acquisition research. *Foreign Language Annals, 36,* 57–65.

Ausubel, D., Novak, J., & Hanesian, H. (1968). *Educational psychology: A cognitive view.* New York: Holt, Rinehart & Winston.

Barnes, D. (1992). *From communication to curriculum.* Portsmouth, NH: Boynton/Cook.

Bloome, D., & Egan-Robertson, A. (1993). The social construction of intertextuality in classroom reading and writing lessons. *Reading Research Quarterly, 28,* 305–334.

Brooks, F., & Donato, R. (1994). Vygotskyan approaches to understanding foreign language learner discourse during communicative tasks. *Hispania, 77,* 262–274.

Brooks, F., Donato, R., & McGlone, J. (1997). When are they going to say it right? Understanding learner talk during pair-work activity. *Foreign Language Annals, 30,* 524–541.

Cassidy, J., & Hossler, A. (1992). Help your students get the main idea with graphic organizers. *Learning, 21*(2), 75–77, 82.

Celce-Murcia, M. (1985). Making informed decisions about the role of grammar in language teaching. *Foreign Language Annals, 18,* 297–301.

Christenbury, L. (1996). The great debate (again): Teaching grammar and usage. *English Journal, 85,* 11–12.

Christenbury, L., & Kelly, P. (1983). Questioning: A path to critical thinking. In *TRIP: Theory and research in practice.* Urbana, IL: National Council of Teaching of English. (Eric Document Reproduction Service No. ED226 372).

DeKeyser, R., & Sokalski, K. (1996). The differential role of comprehension and production practice. *Language Learning, 46,* 613–642.

Donato, R. (1994). Collective scaffolding in second language learning. In J. P. Lantolf & G. Appel (Eds.), *Vygotskian approaches to second language research* (pp. 33–56). Norwood, NJ: Ablex.

Donato, R. (2004). Aspects of collaboration in pedagogical discourse. In M. McGroarty (Ed.), *Annual Review of Applied Linguistics (Vol. 24), Advances in language pedagogy* (pp. 284–302). West Nyack, NY: Cambridge University Press.

Donato, R., & Adair-Hauck, B. (1992). Discourse perspectives on formal instruction. *Language Awareness, 2,* 73–89.

Donato, R., & Adair-Hauck, B. (1994). *PACE: A model to focus on form.* Paper presented at the annual meeting of the American Council on the Teaching of Foreign Languages, San Antonio, TX.

Dulay, H., & Burt, M. (1973). Should we teach children syntax? *Language Learning, 23,* 245–258.

Edwards, A. (1989). Venn diagrams for many sets. *New Scientist, 121,* 51–56.

Ellis, R. (1988). *Classroom second language development.* Englewood Cliffs, NJ: Prentice Hall.

Ellis, R. (1998). Teaching and research: Options in grammar teaching. *TESOL Quarterly, 32,* 39–60.

Ellis, R. (2004). *The study of second language acquisition.* Oxford: Oxford University Press.

Ellis, R. (2008). *Principles of instructed second language acquisition.* CAL Digest. Washington, DC: Center for Applied Linguistics.

Forman, E., Minnick, N., & Stone, A. (1993). *Contexts for learning.* New York: Oxford University Press.

Fotos, S., & Ellis, R. (1991). Communicating about grammar: A task-based approach. *TESOL Quarterly, 25,* 605–628.

Fountas, I., & Hannigan, I. (1989). Making sense of whole language: The pursuit of informed teaching. *Childhood Education, 65,* 133–137.

Freeman, Y., & Freeman, D. (1992). *Whole language for second language learners.* Portsmouth, NH: Heineman Educational Books.

Galloway, V., & Labarca, A. (1990). From student to student: Style, process and strategy. In D. Birckbichler (Ed.), *New perspectives and new directions in foreign language education* (pp. 111–158). Lincolnwood, IL: NTC/Contemporary Publishing Group.

Gass, S. M., & Selinker, L. (2001). *Second language acquisition: An introductory course.* London: Lawrence Erlbaum Associates.

Glisan, E. W., Adair-Hauck, B., & Gadbois, N. (2000). *Designing standards-based assessment tasks: A pilot study.* Paper presented at the annual meeting of the American Council on the Teaching of Foreign Languages. Boston.

Golden, J. (2000). *Storymaking in elementary and middle school classrooms: Constructing and interpreting narrative texts.* Mahwah, NJ: Erlbaum.

Hadley, A. O. (2001). *Teaching language in context* (3rd ed.). Boston: Heinle & Heinle.

Hall, J. K. (1995). "Aw, man, where we goin'?" Classroom interaction and the development of L2 interactional competence. *Issues in Applied Linguistics, 6,* 37–62.

Hall, J. K. (1999). The communication standard. In J. Phillips (Ed.), *Foreign language standards: Linking research, theories, and practices* (pp. 15–56). Lincolnwood, IL: NTC/Contemporary Publishing Group.

Herron, C., & Tomasello, M. (1992). Acquiring grammatical structures by guided induction. *The French Review, 65,* 708–718.

Hinkel, E., & Fotos, S. (Eds.) (2002). *New perspectives on grammar teaching in second language classrooms.* Mahwah, NJ: Lawrence Erlbaum Associates.

Hopper, P., & Thompson, S. (1993). Language universals, discourse pragmatics, and semantics. *Language Sciences, 15*(4), 357–376 .

Hughes, R., & McCarthy, M. (1998). From sentence to discourse: Discourse grammar and English language teaching. *TESOL Quarterly, 32,* 263–287.

John-Steiner, V. (2000). *Creative collaboration.* New York: Oxford University Press.

Karpov, Y. V. (2003). Vygotsky's doctrine of scientific concepts: Its role for contemporary education. In A. Kozulin, B. Gindis, V. S. Ageyev, & S. M. Miller (Eds.), *Vygotsky's educational theory in cultural context* (pp. 65–82). Cambridge, UK: Cambridge University Press.

Krashen, S. (1985). *The input hypothesis.* New York: Longman.

Larsen-Freeman, D. (2003). *Teaching language: From grammar to grammaring.* Boston: Thomson Heinle.

Lave, J., & Wenger, E. (1991). *Situated learning: Legitimate peripheral participation.* Cambridge, MA: Cambridge University Press.

Lee, J., & VanPatten, B. (2003). *Making communicative language teaching happen* (2nd ed.). New York: McGraw-Hill.

Lightbown, P., & Spada, N. (1990). Focus on form and corrective feedback in communicative language teaching. *Studies in Second language Acquisition, 12,* 429–448.

Lightbown, P., & Spada, N. (2003). *How languages are learned* (2nd ed.). New York: Oxford University Press.

Livo, N., & Rietz, S. (1986). *Storytelling process and practice.* Littleton, CO: Libraries Unlimited, Inc.

Long, M. (1991). The least a second language acquisition theory needs to explain. *TESOL Quarterly, 24,* 649–666.

Mantero, M. (2002). Evaluating classroom communication: In support of emergent and authentic frameworks in second language assessment. *Practical Assessment, Research & Evaluation, 8*(8). Retrieved June 1, 2008, from http://PAREonline.net/getvn.asp?v=8&n=8.

McWilliams, B. (2008). *Eldrbarry: The art of telling stories.* Retrieved June 12, 2008, from http://www.eldrbarry.net.

Morgan, J., & Rinvolucri, M. (1983). *Once upon a time: Using stories in the language classroom.* Cambridge, MA: Cambridge University Press.

National Standards in Foreign Language Education Project (NSFLEP). (2006). *Standards for foreign language learning in the 21st century (SFLL).* Lawrence, KS: Allen Press.

Negueruela, E., & Lantolf, J. P. (2005). *Concept-based instruction: Teaching Spanish in an intermediate advanced Spanish L2 classroom.* CALPER Working Papers (3), Penn State University, University Park, PA.

Oller, J., Jr. (1983). Some working ideas for language teaching. In J. Oller, Jr. and P. Richard Amato (Eds.), *Methods that work* (pp. 3–19). Rowley, MA: Newbury House.

Pearson, D. (1989). Reading the whole-language movement. *Elementary School Journal, 90,* 231–241.

Pellowski, A. (1984). *Story Vine: A source book of unusual and easy-to-tell stories from around the world.* Fort Worth, TX: Alladin Paperbacks.

Polette, N. (1991). *Literature-based reading.* O'Fallon, MO: Book Lures.

Redmond, M. L. (1994). The whole language approach in the FLES classroom: Adapting strategies to teach reading and writing. *Foreign Language Annals, 27,* 428–444.

Rogoff, B. (1990). *Apprenticeship in learning.* Oxford, UK: Oxford University Press.

Salaberry, R. (1997). The role of input and output practice in second language acquisition. *The Canadian Modern Language Review, 53,* 422–453.

Seelye, H. N. (1993). *Teaching culture: Strategies for intercultural communication.* Lincolnwood, IL: National Textbook Company.

Shaffer, C. (1989). A comparison of inductive and deductive approaches to teaching foreign languages. *The Modern Language Journal, 73,* 395–403.

Stone, A. C. (1993). What is missing in the metaphor of scaffolding? In E. A. Forman, N. Minnick, C. Addison Stone (Eds.), *Contexts for learning, sociocultural dynamics in children's development* (pp. 169–183). New York: Oxford University Press.

Swain, M., & Lapkin, S. (2002). Talking it through: Two French immersion learners' response to reformulation. *International Journal of Educational Research, 37,* 285–304.

Terrell, T. (1977). A natural approach to second language acquisition and learning. *The Modern Language Journal, 61,* 325–337.

Terry, R. M. (1986). *Let Cinderella and Luke Skywalker help you teach the passé composé and the imparfait.* Hastings-on-Hudson, NY: ACTFL Materials Center.

Tharp, R., & Gallimore, R. (1988). *Rousing minds to life: Teaching, learning and schooling in social context.* New York: Cambridge University Press.

VanPatten, B., (1998). Perceptions of and perspectives on the term "communicative." *Hispania, 81,* 925–932.

VanPatten, B., & Cadierno, T. (1993). Explicit instruction and input processing. *Studies in Second Language Acquisition, 15,* 225–241.

Vavra, E. (1996.) On not teaching grammar. *English Journal, 85,* 32–37.

Vygotsky, L. S. (1978). *Mind in society: The development of higher psychological processes.* Cambridge, MA: Harvard University Press.

Vygotsky, L. S. (1986). *Thought and language.* Cambridge, MA: MIT Press.

Walz, J. (1989). Context and contextualized language practice in foreign language teaching. *The Modern Language Journal, 73,* 161–168.

Wenger, E. (1998). *Communities of practice.* New York: Cambridge University Press.

Wertsch, J. (1991). *Voices of the mind.* Cambridge, MA: Harvard University Press.

West, M., & Donato, R. (1995). Stories and stances: Cross-cultural encounters with African folktales. *Foreign Language Annals, 28,* 392–406.

NOTES

1. These individuals were asked to co-author this chapter since their research in the teaching of grammar supports the premise of contextualized language instruction espoused in *Teacher's Handbook*.

2. K-W-L activities are a way to organize classroom tasks around learners' background knowledge and their goals for learning. From the learners' perspective, K stands for what I know already; W stands for what I want to know; and L stands for what I have learned. For instance, if the topic is grasshoppers, the K activities might include making a list on the board of everything learners know about grasshoppers; the W activities might include the creation of a list of questions students have about grasshoppers, (e.g., "How long do grasshoppers live?"); and the L activities might include a videotaped presentation of a skit students wrote about the life of a grasshopper.

3. Thanks to Dr. Bonnie Adair-Hauck for the inspiration for this activity.

Developing Oral and Written Interpersonal Communication

In this chapter, you will learn about:

- the ACTFL oral proficiency scale and speaking from a proficiency perspective
- implications of proficiency for instruction
- nature of interpersonal communication
- willingness to communicate (WTC)
- instructional conversations (ICs)
- strategies for helping students interact orally
- turns-at-talk, routines and gambits, gestures
- student discourse in pair/group activities
- collaborative dialogue
- conversational repair

- strategy training
- cooperative learning: task-based instruction
- developing advanced-level discourse through the study of literature and culture
- developing interpersonal writing
- dialogue journals
- key pal and pen pal letter exchanges and synchronous electronic interaction
- providing feedback in oral interpersonal contexts
- types of teacher feedback (trouble, repair, noticing, uptake)

Teach and Reflect: Creating Information-Gap Activities for Various Levels of Instruction; Integrating Speaking Tasks with Oral or Printed Texts; Integrating Advanced-Level Discourse at the Post-Secondary Level

Discuss and Reflect: "Survivor" Game: Keeping Students in the Target Language

CONCEPTUAL ORIENTATION

For over three decades, the foreign language teaching profession has made astounding progress in enabling students in foreign language classrooms across the country to use the target language (TL) orally and in writing to communicate with one another, thanks to an ever-increasing body of research in second language acquisition (SLA) and experience in assessing oral proficiency. Since the early 1980s, the concept of proficiency has had a major impact on how we view communication in a foreign language and how we articulate the goals of language study. The publication of *Standards for Foreign Language Learning in the 21st Century (SFLL)* (National Standards in Foreign Language Education Project [NSFLEP], 1996, 1999, 2006) expanded our notion of oral and written interpersonal communication and emphasized the key role that it plays in learning content, acquiring new information, gaining cultural understanding, and engaging in activities and inquiry within communities beyond the classroom.

This chapter will explore the pivotal role that interpersonal communication plays in a classroom that reflects a sociocultural framework to language learning, in which learners have frequent opportunities to interact meaningfully with others. Historically, interpersonal communication has been treated primarily within the context of speaking, and the literature on interpersonal writing is still scant. In an attempt to treat the interpersonal mode in an inclusive manner, however, this chapter will explore interpersonal communication as it occurs in oral, visual, and written forms. The theme of oral interpersonal communication dominates the chapter, due to the complexity of speaking in interpersonal contexts and the vast number of issues that are pertinent to the discussion. At times throughout the chapter, oral and written interpersonal communication are treated as one topic in light of similarities of speaking and writing in this mode. At other times, speaking and writing in the interpersonal mode are explored separately in order to focus on their unique aspects and implications for instruction.

The *ACTFL Proficiency Guidelines—Speaking* (American Council on the Teaching of Foreign Languages [ACTFL], 1999) and the *ACTFL Proficiency Guidelines—Writing* (ACTFL, 2001) are applicable to both the interpersonal and presentational modes of communication. However, since the *ACTFL Proficiency Guidelines—Speaking* have the most applicability to and impact on the interpersonal mode, we present them in this chapter for review and implications for teaching. The *ACTFL Proficiency Guidelines—Writing* are presented in Chapter 9 as they are more applicable to presentational writing.

Interpersonal Speaking from a Proficiency Perspective

The concept of proficiency, as developed and explored for almost three decades, has generated more discussion concerning the role of speaking in the curriculum than perhaps any other topic in the history of foreign language teaching. In her analysis of the survival of the *ACTFL Proficiency Guidelines* and the Oral Proficiency Interview (OPI), Liskin-Gasparro (2003) discusses three areas in which both have had a major impact on the field:

1. They served as a catalyst for major changes in foreign language teaching at all levels of instruction as the profession moved from a focus on grammar to a focus on communication. Accordingly, they sparked a new generation of pedagogical materials that contained novel features, such as multiple presentations of key grammatical structures in the same textbook, student-to-student interviews, set-ups for role-plays and skits, and strategy instruction. They promoted attention to performance-based outcomes that would bridge communicative language teaching and language assessment. Furthermore, the two decades of emphasis on proficiency placed the profession in an ideal position to develop the *SFLL*.

2. The wealth of speech samples from OPIs continue to provide rich data regarding the nature of the language that is produced in face-to-face oral tests, the nature of

language acquisition during study abroad experiences, and discourse analyses. These data are a valuable resource to researchers as they investigate issues pertaining to the development of language acquisition and speaking proficiency.

3. The guidelines and OPI have also had an impact on classroom testing, both formative and summative, in significant ways; see Chapter 11 (pp. 486–488).

What can we expect students at each level of language study to be able to communicate orally in the foreign language? What classroom strategies might enable students to develop speaking proficiency? In the early years of proficiency, Liskin-Gasparro's (1987) statement, "If you can't use a language, you don't know a language," reflected the basic idea underlying proficiency, one that is still applicable today (p. 26). Therefore, the current concept of proficiency describes the competencies that enable us to define in more specific terms what it means to know a language. As explained in Chapter 2, proficiency is the ability to use language to perform global tasks or language functions within a variety of contexts/content areas, with a given degree of accuracy, and by means of specific text types. In Chapter 2, you learned about how the proficiency concept evolved; you may find it helpful to review the summary chart in Appendix 2.2 on the *Teacher's Handbook* Web site in order to understand more fully the development of the proficiency concept.

www.cengagebrain.com

Proficiency is the ability to use language to perform global tasks or language functions within a variety of contexts/content areas, with a given degree of accuracy, and by means of specific text types.

What are the characteristics of speech at each of the major borders of the ACTFL proficiency scale?

The *ACTFL Proficiency Guidelines* (Appendix 2.3 on the *Teacher's Handbook* Web site) provide detailed information about the performance characterized for listening, speaking, reading, and writing at each major level (or border)—novice, intermediate, advanced, superior—and sublevel—low, mid, high. These criterion-referenced descriptions are experientially based, describing how speakers typically function at various levels of ability. Figure 8.1 illustrates the four major levels of the rating scale in the form of an inverted pyramid, demonstrating that language facility increases exponentially, rather than arithmetically; in other words, it takes progressively more language ability to climb from one level to the next. Figure 8.2 illustrates the assessment criteria for speaking at each major level in terms of global tasks and functions, context/content, accuracy, and text type.

At this point, you will find it beneficial to familiarize yourself with the major levels of the rating scale.

It is important to note the following with respect to the sublevels:

- Speakers at the "low" sublevel use their linguistic energy to sustain the requirements of the level. They show less fluency and accuracy, more lapses in vocabulary, and more self-correction than the "mid" speaker. The "low" speaker functions primarily within the level with little or no demonstrated ability at the next higher level.
- Speakers at the "mid" sublevel represent a number of speech profiles, based on their mix of quantity (how much they say) and/or quality (efficiency and effectiveness with which message is communicated) at level, and/or the degree to which they control language features from the next level.
- Speakers at the "high" sublevel communicate with confidence when performing the functions of their respective level. They are capable of functioning for at least half of the time at the next higher level but are unable to sustain their performance

FIGURE 8.1 Inverted Pyramid Showing Major Levels of the ACTFL Rating Scale

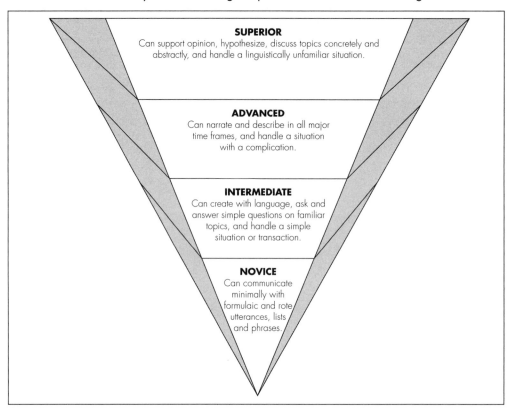

Source: From *ACTFL Oral Proficiency Interview Tester Training Manual* (p. 9), by E. Swender, 1999. Used by permission of the American Council of the Teaching of Foreign Languages.

at that next higher level without difficulty or intermittent lapses. Therefore, the dynamic of the "high" level is best understood in a top-down representation of proficiency: the "high" represents a fall from the next higher level rather than a strong ability demonstrated at the general level (Swender, 1999, pp. 18–19).

Teachers who experience training in using the OPI to elicit speech samples and rate proficiency and those who work in proficiency-oriented programs are able to develop reasonably accurate intuitions and predictions about their students' levels of proficiency (Glisan & Foltz, 1998). ACTFL conducts a rigorous training and practice program for those who wish to qualify as official oral proficiency testers and be certified to conduct interviews and accurately rate speaking skill (Swender, 1999). Chapter 11 discusses the interview procedure itself and its significance to classroom testing.

Figure 8.3 illustrates the relationship of the ACTFL rating scale to that of the original Interagency Language Roundtable (ILR) scale used by the government (see Chapter 2 for history). The ACTFL scale represents four of the six major levels of the ILR scale. The ACTFL Superior level rating corresponds to performance that comprises ILR levels 3–5 (Swender, 1999).

Classroom Instruction and Oral Proficiency Levels

The emphasis on the development of proficiency over the past several decades continues to spark an interest in examining the extent to which classroom instruction and the language curriculum may influence students' abilities to reach specific levels of proficiency. The research in this area began with an analysis of how much time (i.e., years of

FIGURE 8.2 Assessment Criteria—Speaking

PROFICIENCY LEVEL*	GLOBAL TASKS AND FUNCTIONS	CONTEXT/ CONTENT	ACCURACY	TEXT TYPE
Superior	Discuss topics extensively, support opinions, and hypothesize. Deal with a linguistically unfamiliar situation.	Most formal and informal settings/ *Wide range of general interest topics and some special fields of interest and expertise.*	No pattern of errors in basic structures. Errors virtually never interfere with communication or distract the native speaker from the message.	Extended discourse
Advanced	Narrate and describe in major time frames and deal effectively with an unanticipated complication.	Most informal and some formal settings/*Topics of personal and general interest.*	Understood without difficulty by speakers unaccustomed to dealing with nonnative speakers.	Paragraphs
Intermediate	Create with language; initiate, maintain, and bring to a close simple conversations by asking and responding to simple questions.	Some informal settings and a limited number of transactional situations/ *Predictable, familiar topics related to daily activities.*	Understood, with some repetition, by speakers accustomed to dealing with nonnative speakers.	Discrete sentences
Novice	Communicate minimally with formulaic and rote utterances, lists, and phrases.	Most common informal settings/*Most common aspects of daily life.*	May be difficult to understand, even for speakers accustomed to dealing with nonnative speakers.	Individual words and phrases

*A rating at any major level is arrived at by the sustained performance of the functions of the level, within the contexts and content areas for that level, with the degree of accuracy described for the level, and in the text type for the level. The performance must be sustained across ALL of the criteria for the level in order to be rated at that level.

Source: From *ACTFL Oral Proficiency Interview Tester Training Manual* (p. 31), by E. Swender, 1999. Used by permission of the American Council of the Teaching of Foreign Languages.

classroom instruction) students spend in language study compared to what levels of oral proficiency they attain. In recent years, however, the focus has turned to an examination of what happens in classrooms—i.e., the degree to which learners are engaged in meaningful communication—and how instructional practice may have an effect on levels of oral proficiency that learners attain.

Several studies have used OPI results to examine the relationship between oral proficiency and length of language instruction, only a few of which have focused on the secondary level. Two studies (Glisan & Foltz, 1998; Huebner & Jensen, 1992) showed that, after two years of Spanish study, students' mean proficiency rating was Novice-High. After four years of study, however, results were mixed, with the mean rating for Level 4 students in the Glisan and Foltz study approaching Intermediate-Low, while in the Huebner and Jensen study the mean rating was Intermediate-Mid. An earlier study by Steinmeyer (1984) reported similar findings in German: After two years of secondary school German

FIGURE 8.3 Illustration Showing Relationship of ACTFL Scale to ILR Scale

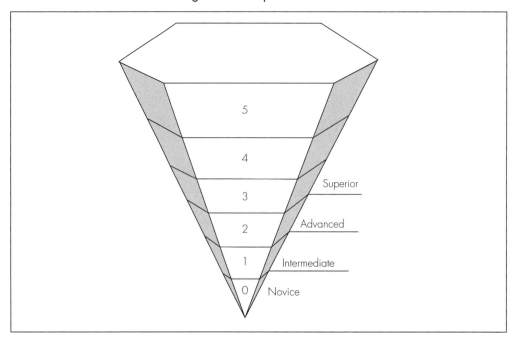

Source: From *ACTFL Oral Proficiency Interview Tester Training Manual* (p. 20), by E. Swender, 1999. Used by permission of the American Council of the Teaching of Foreign Languages.

instruction, the oral proficiency of students ranged from Novice-Mid to Novice-High, while after four years the mean rating was Intermediate-Mid. The Huebner and Jensen findings in French and German also revealed proficiency in the Novice range after two years of study, and proficiency in the Intermediate range after four years of study.[1] Figure 8.4 is adapted from Tschirner and Heilenman (1998) and depicts the results of the studies that have examined length of secondary school instruction in French, German, and Spanish with the oral proficiency levels attained.

A few studies have reported oral proficiency levels using assessment instruments that were based on the oral proficiency construct, but that were not face-to-face OPIs conducted with certified OPI testers. Using the Simulated Oral Proficiency Interview (SOPI), Adair-Hauck and Pierce (1998) investigated the results of SOPI testing with 40 French and 34 Spanish high school students in levels 3 through 5 across four school sites. Their findings were similar to those revealed in the OPI studies inasmuch as: (1) the mean rating for Spanish 3, 4, and 5 was Intermediate-Low, with 41% of the Spanish 4/5 students being rated Intermediate-Mid/High, and (2) the mean rating for French 3 and 4 was Intermediate-Mid. See Chapter 11 for a full description of the SOPI assessment format. A recent study reports the results of large-scale oral proficiency testing using an assessment format based on the OPI and SOPI (Fall, Adair-Hauck, & Glisan, 2007). Between 2003 and 2006, over 6,000 students between grades 5 and 12 were tested in French, German, Japanese, and Spanish; Italian was added in 2006. Among the results, between 2004 and 2006, the majority of students in levels 4 through 6 attained a proficiency level of Intermediate-Mid to Intermediate-High, and in 2006, 41% of Level 3 students met the Intermediate-Low goal in place in the school district (Fall et al.). These results are similar to those described in the OPI studies above, which found that students with four years of language study demonstrated Intermediate-Low to Intermediate-Mid oral proficiency. See Chapter 11 for a description of the Pittsburgh Public Schools Oral Rating Assessment for Language Students (ORALS) model.

FIGURE 8.4 Range of OPI Scores After 1, 2, 3, 4, and 5 Years of Secondary School Instruction in French, German, and Spanish

STUDY	1 YEAR	2 YEARS	3 YEARS	4 YEARS	5 YEARS
Steinmeyer (1984) German (N=25)		NM – NH (NM)	NM – NH (NH)	NH – IH (IM)	IM – A (IH)
Moeller & Reschke (1993) (N=84)	NL – IM (NH)	NM – IM (NH)			
Huebner & Jensen (1992) German (N=65)		NM – IM (NH)	NL – IH (IL)	NL – IH (IL)	
Huebner & Jensen (1992) French (N=241)		NL – IH (NM)	NM – IH (IM)	IL – AH (IH)	IH – A (A)
Huebner & Jensen (1992) Spanish (N=550)		NL – AH (NH)	NM – A (IL)	NH – AH (IM)	IH – A (A)
Glisan & Foltz (1998) Spanish (N=59)		NL – IL (NH)		NM – IH (IL)	

Note: Median scores provided in parentheses. Median scores in Huebner & Jensen (1992) calculated from tabled data in original.

Source: From "Reasonable expectations: Oral proficiency goals for intermediate-level students of German," by E. Tschirner and L. K. Heilenman, 1998, *The Modern Language Journal, 82*, 147–158, p. 149. Used by permission of Blackwell Publishing.

Figure 8.5 illustrates the results of key studies that compared length of college-level instruction in French, German, and Russian, and OPI ratings attained. Results of these studies generally revealed a mean rating of Intermediate-Mid range for students who completed two years of instruction, Intermediate-High after three years, and Advanced-Low after four years. Rifkin (2003) reported on the results of testing students entering the Middlebury Russian School, who had formally studied Russian for various numbers of hours. His data revealed that "students entering at the Intermediate-Mid level alone represented a range of 180–600 hours of prior classroom instruction (with an average of 350 hours of classroom instruction)" (p. 583). This finding illustrates that perhaps time alone is not as critical a factor as was once thought in terms of its effect on growth in oral proficiency (more on this below).

Swender (2003) reported the proficiency levels of undergraduate foreign language majors using data collected from 501 official OPIs conducted through the ACTFL Testing Office between 1998 and 2002. The interviews were conducted face-to-face or telephonically and were double-rated and certified through the ACTFL Testing Office. The students assessed were foreign language majors in their junior or senior years, although

FIGURE 8.5 Range of OPI Scores After 1, 2, 3, and 4 Years of College Instruction in French, German, and Russian

STUDY	1 YEAR	2 YEARS	3 YEARS	4 YEARS
Magnan (1986) French (N=40)	NM–IM/IH (IL/IM)	IL–A (IM)	IM/IH–A/AH (IH/A)	IM–AH (A)
Tschirner (1993) German (N=40)	NH–IM (IL)	IL–IM (IM)		
Thompson (1996) Russian (N=56)	NL/NM–IL/IM (NM)	NH/IL–IH/A (NH/IL)	IL/IM–AH/S (IM/IH)	IM–AH (IH/A)
Dugan (1988) French (N=?)	? (NH)	? (IL)		
Kaplan (1984) French (N=25)			NH–AH (IH/A)	? (A)
Freed (1987) French (N=206)		IL–A (IM)		
Tschirner (1992) German (N=549)	NH–IM (IM)	NM–A (IM)		

Note: OE = Other Evidence; T = Performance Task

Source: From "Reasonable expectations: Oral proficiency goals for intermediate-level students of German," by E. Tschirner and L. K. Heilenman, 1998, *The Modern Language Journal, 82,* 147–158, p. 149. Used by permission of Blackwell Publishing.

the report did not correlate proficiency ratings to the specific number of semesters or years of study completed. Swender reports that the greatest concentration of ratings (55.8%) was in the Intermediate-High/Advanced-Low range (p. 523). According to the data analysis, slightly less than half (47%) of the foreign language majors tested were rated above the Advanced-level border, and slightly more than half (53%) received ratings below Advanced. These statistics seem to lend support to the findings described above.

Perhaps the most significant finding revealed by these research studies is the range of oral proficiency levels attained by students *in* a given level of study. This is corroborated by Magnan's (1986) study, which found that proficiency levels form "bands" at each level of study and that the bands overlap from one level or year of study to the next. Magnan concludes that "this banding and overlapping reminds us that the process of language learning is a continuum on which learners progress at different rates, regardless of course boundaries" (p. 432). You may recall that in Chapter 4, you read about several studies that revealed a similar finding with elementary school students in a FLES program (Donato, Antonek, & Tucker, 1996; Montás, 2003). These studies are important because they indicate the extended sequence of instruction that most learners need to progress from one level of proficiency to the next and the variation of levels attained by learners who experience the same number of years of instruction. However, what this also indicates is that time is not the only factor in advancing in oral proficiency, given (1) the wide variance in proficiency levels among students who experience the same amount of instructional time (refer to the Magnan study), and (2) the similar range of proficiency levels among students who experience significantly different lengths of instruction (refer to the Rifkin [2003] study). Glisan and Donato (2004) suggest that what may be more critical than time itself is the type of classroom instruction that learners experience and the degree to which they are engaged in meaningful, goal-directed interaction with others in the TL. Study abroad and immersion programs that provide this type of experience and supportive assistance to students have a role to play in fostering growth in proficiency (Brecht, Davidson, & Ginsberg, 1993; DeKeyser, 1991; Wilkinson, 2002). However, in order to ensure maximum impact, these programs should be integrated with and be a natural extension of what occurs in secondary and post-secondary language classrooms.

 "Language learning is a continuum on which learners progress at different rates, regardless of course boundaries."

Implications of the OPI for Language Instruction

Research on the OPI and analysis of speech samples continue to shed light on features of spoken communication at each major proficiency border and what students need to be able to do in speaking in order to climb the scale. At the same time, an understanding of student performance at each level may help us to re-envision the types of instructional practices that lead to the development of learners' oral proficiency, keeping in mind that the *ACTFL Proficiency Guidelines* themselves do not represent a curricular outline, syllabus, sequence of instruction, or method of teaching (Hadley, 2001). Therefore, what implications for teaching does the proficiency concept offer teachers? First of all, teachers should become familiar with the *ACTFL Proficiency Guidelines* and the ILR rating scale. As discussed earlier, these rich descriptions of oral performance provide a clear picture regarding what students must be able to do at each level in terms of global tasks or functions, contexts/content areas, text types, and accuracy.

 What are some key factors in advancing oral proficiency in addition to time spent in foreign language study?

What types of practice do students need as they work toward proficiency at each of the major levels?:

- *Novice:* acquiring concrete vocabulary in context through activities such as Total Physical Response (TPR) to acquire and retain it well; using contextualized vocabulary in short conversations and oral presentations; developing a personalized vocabulary
- *Intermediate:* engaging in spontaneous conversations on familiar topics related to self and personal environment, as well as work and/or school; asking questions; speaking in complex sentences (with dependent clauses); participating in simple survival situations (e.g., making invitations, asking for directions, ordering a meal); negotiating meaning in conversations; interpreting what a conversational partner says
- *Advanced:* conversing in a participatory manner; speaking in paragraphs (or extended utterances) using connector words such as adverbial expressions, subordinating conjunctions, and ordinal numbers (e.g., *therefore, although, before/after, first/second,* etc.); narrating and describing in present, past, future; participating in situations with unanticipated complications (e.g., losing one's luggage, reporting a car accident)

- *Superior:* discussing topics concretely and abstractly; supporting and defending an opinion through development of a logical argument, hypotheses, and extended discourse; circumlocuting in the absence of specific words/expressions (i.e., getting around unknown vocabulary by saying something in a different way); conversing in linguistically unfamiliar situations (Swender, 1999)

www.cengagebrain.com

Appendix 8.1 on the *Teacher's Handbook* Web site presents a detailed description of performance at each of the major borders according to the levels on the OPI/ILR scale, together with language learning activities that relate to each level of the scale (Herzog, 2003).

A second implication of the proficiency concept is that students must go beyond their traditional role as responder to the teacher's questions, and their interactions must take on the characteristics of typical conversations that occur between native and nonnative speakers outside of the classroom (Pica & Long, 1986; Rubio, 2003). In Chapter 3, you learned that discourse refers to a back-and-forth communication of thought by means of a connected series of utterances shared through social interaction and collaboration. Ellis (1994) distinguishes between traditional instructional discourse and *natural discourse,* which fosters the development of oral proficiency:

> Instructional discourse arises when the teacher and the students act out institutional roles, the tasks are concerned with the transmission and reception of information and are controlled by the teacher, and there is a focus on knowledge as a product and on accuracy. Natural discourse is characterized by more fluid roles established through interaction, tasks that encourage equal participation in the negotiation of meaning, and a focus on the interactional process itself and on meaning (p. 580, as cited in Rubio, p. 547).

Research on advanced-level speech indicates that learners who had extensive exposure to natural native discourse have an advantage in terms of their fluency (Lennon, 1990; Rubio, 2003). Fostering more natural conversations means that teachers must modify their traditional ways of interacting with students through strategies such as listening and responding to the content of students' messages, rather than listening exclusively for accuracy, and not interrupting while students are speaking in order to correct errors (Bragger, 1985).

Current research points to the third implication: the need to provide opportunities for students to hear a great deal of comprehensible and authentic language, to use the language in meaningful interaction with others, to negotiate meaning in cooperation with others, and to participate in an environment that encourages and motivates self-expression in a nonthreatening way (Gass & Selinker, 1994; Krashen, 1982; Lightbown & Spada, 2006; Long, 1983; Vygotsky, 1978); see Chapter 1.

STANDARDS HIGHLIGHT: Exploring the Interpersonal Mode Through Speaking and Writing

The Nature of Oral Interpersonal Communication

As you learned in Chapter 2, the interpersonal mode of communication refers to two-way interactive communication (NSFLEP, 2006). It is important to understand the characteristics of oral communication that make it interpersonal:

- Two or more speakers are engaged in conversation and exchange of information, either a face-to-face discussion or a phone conversation. Interpersonal communication is spontaneous; it is not scripted and read or performed as a memorized skit.

- Interpersonal communication is meaningful and has as its objective a communicative task or reason for communicating. Consequently, working in pairs to do mechanical grammar exercises out of the textbook does not constitute interpersonal communication.
- There is usually an "information gap"; that is, one speaker seeks to acquire information that the other speaker has, or at the very least, one speaker doesn't know what the other is going to say or how he or she will respond. Therefore, pair activities in which Student A and Student B know in advance how the other will respond do not reflect true interpersonal communication.
- Since interpersonal communication is spontaneous, conversational partners must listen to and interpret what the other speaker says.
- Conversational partners often find it necessary to negotiate meaning with one another in order to interpret meaning. Thus, the interpretive mode of communication is implied in interpersonal communication. Negotiating meaning involves asking for repetition, clarification, or confirmation, or indicating a lack of understanding. Natural conversations have pauses as speakers think of what they want to say and repetitions as they repeat, restate, or even correct their utterances.
- Conversational partners often find it necessary to use gestures to make their message clear and to circumlocute, or express a thought in an alternative way when specific words or expressions are unknown.

Interpersonal communication can also be written whenever a printed message, in the form of a letter, note, or e-mail exchange, is intended to prompt a response on the part of the recipient and/or engage two individuals in communication with each other. In this case, speaking and writing share similarities in the interpersonal mode. In written interpersonal communication, the reader must interpret the printed message and create a response.

Interpersonal communication stands in sharp contrast to the *presentational* mode of communication, which refers to one-way communication—one person produces language in oral or written form for an audience of listeners/viewers/readers. Although you will explore presentational communication fully in Chapter 9, it bears mentioning here that teachers have a tendency to include many opportunities for presentational communication and label them as interpersonal communication. It is important to distinguish between these two modes of communication in planning for instruction and to include a balance of both in language classrooms.

Learners' Willingness to Communicate in L2

A challenge in fostering a classroom rich in interpersonal communication lies in engaging learners' participation in speaking, referred to in the research as *Willingness to Communicate (WTC),* and defined as "the probability of speaking when free to do so" (MacIntyre, 2007, p. 564). According to MacIntyre, issues regarding motivation and anxiety (see Chapter 1) interact and are played out in the decision that a learner makes at a specific moment in time regarding whether or not to communicate in L2. WTC has been conceptualized in L2 communication as a *situation-based variable,* one that is influenced by a particular situation that offers the possibility for speaking to occur. In this view, WTC brings together motivational processes with communicative competencies and perceived self-confidence (MacIntyre). Figure 8.6 illustrates The Pyramid Model of Willingness to Communicate, originally developed by MacIntyre, Clément, Dörnyei, and Noels (1998). The pyramid depicts a range of potential influences on WTC in the L2 in terms of both *situational influences,* or those that are transient and unique to the immediate situation, and *enduring influences,* or those that represent long-term characteristics of the environment or person that apply to almost any situation.

FIGURE 8.6 The Pyramid Model of Willingness to Communicate

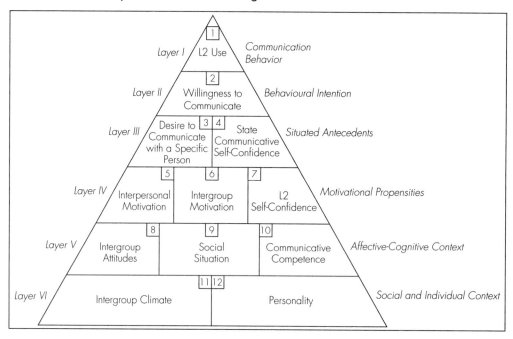

Source: From "Conceptualizing willingness to communication in a L2: A situational model of L2 confidence and affiliation," by P. D. MacIntyre, R. Clement, Z. Dornyei, and K. Noels, 1998, *The Modern Language Journal, 82,* p. 547. Reprinted with permission.

Situational influences (Layers I–III) include the desire to communicate with a specific person and knowledge of the topic, while enduring influences (Layers IV–VI) pertain to intergroup relations, learner personality, and communicative competence (MacIntyre et al.). As shown in Figure 8.6, reaching the point at which a learner is faced with the decision to communicate, the top of the pyramid is affected by both situational and more enduring influences. The pyramid shape of the model shows the immediate effect of some factors and the more distant effect of others; the broadest factors such as personality and intergroup climate are considered to be the basis on which the rest of the influences operate.

What implications does the WTC have for L2 instruction? MacIntyre (2007) summarized the results of a number of studies that examined WTC and found that:

1. Extroverts showed higher WTC than introverts when studying new L2 vocabulary words in a moderately unfamiliar situation; however, in a familiar situation, the introverts showed higher WTC than the extroverts (MacIntyre, Clément, & Noels, 2007). The researchers attribute this to the fact that introverts learn better in familiar situations because they prefer routine, while extroverts thrive on change and novel situations.
2. An event that leads to low WTC is when a learner whose native language is English initiates L2 communication with an L2 speaker and the L2 speaker switches to English (Baker & MacIntyre, 2000). The rejection of the speaker's volition to communicate in L2 apparently reduces the WTC.
3. Situations resulting in low WTC include those in which speakers feel a lack of self-confidence when communicating with strangers and when they feel they are being criticized by the listener, especially for accent and grammatical errors (MacDonald, Clément, & MacIntyre, 2003).

For classroom teachers, helping learners to develop a WTC "appears to be a crucial component of modern L2 pedagogy" (MacIntyre et al. 1998, p. 558). Although more research is needed to shed light on clear implications for L2 teaching, the WTC model can enable teachers to become more aware of the factors involved in prompting a learner to communicate. Teachers should become familiar with the personality types of their students, their levels of anxiety about speaking the L2 with others, and how they interact with peers and other L2 speakers. This information can then be used to structure experiences for learners within a classroom designed to be a community of learners, whereby hopefully learners have the support that they need to make the decision to communicate.[2]

 How does what you learned about motivation in Chapter 1 relate to WTC?

Strategies for Teaching Interpersonal Speaking

Below are sample techniques for interpersonal speaking that are based on the research findings presented in Chapter 1, as well as on the implications of proficiency introduced in this chapter. These activities may be adapted for use with elementary school, middle school, high school, and post-secondary classes. Note that, while these activities relate primarily to the interpersonal mode, speaking activities often address both the interpersonal and presentational modes of communication. Students interact with one another to perform a task in the interpersonal mode and then present this information to an audience in the presentational mode. Furthermore, they are often based on or can lead to an interpretive task.

The reader is encouraged to review the information from Chapter 1 dealing with negotiation of meaning, which is a vital concept in developing interpersonal speaking. In the spirit of sociocultural theory, *Teacher's Handbook* advocates an approach to teaching interpersonal communication that actively engages learners in constructing and negotiating meaning.

Teacher Interaction with Students

The extent to which oral interpersonal communication is fostered in the classroom depends to a great extent on the types of interactions that the teacher has with learners. In Chapter 3, you learned about the importance of the following features of teacher talk and classroom interaction:

- The teacher provides maximum use of the TL that is both comprehensible and contributes to a larger topic or goal-directed agenda.
- The teacher uses a maximum amount of Initiation-Response-Feedback (IRF) activities to stimulate meaningful conversations and push learners to perform at higher levels.
- The teacher integrates authentic oral and printed texts that reflect natural language use and bring context and interest to the classroom.
- The teacher incorporates subject-matter content into the language learning experience in order to provide interesting context to explore and discuss.

Hall (1999) suggests the use of "instructional conversations" (ICs) as a way to facilitate a conversation with students on a topic or theme that is interesting to them and intellectually challenging, while providing them with assisted performance. Instructional conversations are defined as "discussion-based lessons geared toward creating opportunities for

FIGURE 8.7 Features of an Instructional Conversation

INSTRUCTIONAL FEATURES	CONVERSATIONAL FEATURES
• Thematic focus • Activation of background knowledge and schema • Direct teaching when necessary • Promotion of more complex language and expression • Promotion of bases for statements or positions	• Few "known-answer" questions • Responsiveness to student contributions • Connected discourse • A challenging, but non-threatening atmosphere • General participation, including self-selected turns

Source: Summarized from Tharp & Gallimore (1988) & Goldenberg (1991).

students' conceptual and linguistic development. They focus on an idea or a concept that has educational value and that has meaning and relevance for students" (Goldenberg, 1991, p. 1). According to Tharp and Gallimore (1988), the concept underlying ICs is also referred to as *responsive teaching*, i.e., the way that mothers teach their children language and letters, chat that accompanies action, and the natural conversational method of language instruction; ICs can also "wear the mask of a third-grade reading lesson or a graduate seminar" (p. 111). Text-based discussions are good opportunities for using ICs while addressing the interpretive mode of communication, since interpretation often occurs in the context of these types of conversations.

Figure 8.7 illustrates the features of an IC. Appendix 8.2 presents a description of the key features of the IC.

Teachers use "instructional conversations" (ICs) as a way to facilitate a conversation with students on a topic or theme that is interesting to them and intellectually challenging, while providing them with assisted performance.

Tharp and Gallimore (1988) and their colleagues (Goldenberg, 1991; Patthey-Chavez, Clare, & Gallimore, 1995; Rueda, Goldenberg, & Gallimore, 1992) proposed ICs in order to foster assisted performance in ways reflected in Vygotsky's (1978) Zone of Proximal Development (ZPD) concept. In ICs, the teacher "acts as a discussion leader and facilitator, allowing students to initiate turns while making sure that all student voices are included in the discussion and, when necessary, drawing out and helping students to draw out their ideas" (Hall, 1999, p. 30). The teacher also assists students in connecting their background experiences to the discussion by making certain that responses are interconnected and build upon one another through extending previous turns. With guidance from the teacher, "learners' assisted performance extends beyond their current individual level of performance" (Todhunter, 2007, p. 606).

ICs may include the following teacher actions:

- modeling of how students might approach a given topic or task;
- brief focus on form in the face of difficulty in expression using a particular structure;
- linking a comment to what was said previously (this will also serve as an example of what students should learn to do in order to develop a coherent conversation);
- assisting questions to elicit clarification and/or further information;
- explanation or direct teaching, primarily when requested by students when they need additional information about a topic, text, concept, etc.; and
- expressive reactions to what students say.

Although ICs were initially created for use in bilingual academic lessons, where they serve a key role in the curriculum (Tharp & Gallimore, 1988), they often emerge in foreign language classrooms in unplanned discourse that occurs "in the cracks of the lesson" (Todhunter, 2007). For example, several studies have identified ways in which ICs appear in spontaneous communication in the classroom. Donato (2000) found that ICs occurred "spontaneously between activities; as digressions from homework checking, vocabulary review, or grammar practice; and during management activities such as distributing papers" (as cited in Todhunter, p. 606). Todhunter's study revealed the use of ICs during classroom management tasks, the warm-up at the beginning of the lesson and other spontaneous exchanges, and planned discussion of curriculum topics; the longest ICs were based on students' experiences (e.g., weekend) and cultural topics. Todhunter found that the ICs provided evidence that students were developing interactional competence (see Chapter 1) because they initiated topics, guided the topic development so that it was coherent, negotiated meaning and form, and assumed a share in the control of the discourse. For an example of an IC that emerged in a warm-up to a French lesson, see Chapter 3, pp. 83–84. For another example of an IC, see Appendix 8.3.

The type of discourse fostered by ICs differs from other types of classroom discourse because utterances are dependent on one another, familiar knowledge is connected to new knowledge, and the conversation unfolds in an unpredictable manner (van Lier, 1996). ICs help to foster interpersonal communication in ways that focus on the IRF pattern of teacher-to-learner interaction. Chapter 3 presented ideas on how to incorporate more interpersonal communication and IRF into classroom instruction. You may find it helpful to review this discussion. ICs can be used effectively as the teacher:

- engages students in "warm-up" discussions of a personalized topic of interest to them or a timely topic concerning the school community (e.g., a championship game, the prom);
- leads a discussion as learners interpret an authentic oral, printed, or video text;
- sparks a discussion or the creation of a story based on a visual or cultural artifact;
- elicits opinions about a topic of high interest to learners, e.g., mandatory drug testing for athletes;
- acquires new information with learners on a content-based or cultural theme;
- explores with learners the relationship among specific products, practices, and perspectives in C2 and makes comparisons with C1; and
- guides learners through the process of designing a presentation or creating a product for an audience.

While these specific types of strategies and activities are effective in promoting interpersonal communication, it is essential that the language classroom environment be one in which sharing opinions, offering a variety of possible responses, asking questions, negotiating meaning, and initiating unexpected conversations are welcomed. In her 2007 study, Todhunter attributed much of the success of the ICs to the teacher's genuine interest in the students' lives and her identification of community building as a pivotal course goal. Consequently, the teacher should set up ICs so that:

1. the unexpected discourse events in the classroom are exploited, including management tasks and students' questions and comments—i.e., the *teachable moments of interpersonal talk* (Todhunter, 2007, p. 617);
2. students have opportunities to take multiple turns in a given conversational exchange;
3. students practice taking the floor in conversations;
4. students have sufficient time to respond as participants in conversations;
5. a variety of responses are accepted;

6. short answers are permitted where they would naturally occur (e.g., answers to yes-no questions);

7. students are encouraged and taught how to respond to statements made by their classmates in order to develop conversations that are connected and coherent; and

8. the teacher assumes the role of facilitator and guide, providing assistance and scaffolding as needed.

Todhunter suggests that the teacher might ask hesitant speakers forced choice questions (e.g., Do you think X or Y?) and offer more wait time to ease them into conversation. Further, in her opinion, smaller teacher-led groups might encourage better participation in an IC.

Teaching Strategies for Group Interaction

Turns-at-Talk

In conducting interactive tasks, the teacher must often teach the interaction skills that are lacking or in need of improvement, such as taking turns at talking. Kramsch (1987) suggests that teachers use the following strategies for encouraging students to take control of turn-taking as they would in natural discourse:

- Tolerate silences; refrain from filling the gaps between turns. This will put pressure on students to initiate turns.
- Direct your gaze to any potential addressee of a student's utterance; do not assume that you are the next speaker and the student's exclusive addressee.
- Teach the students floor-taking gambits; do not grant the floor.
- Encourage students to sustain their speech beyond one or two sentences and to take longer turns; do not use a student's short utterance as a springboard for your own lengthy turn.
- Extend your exchanges with individual students to include clarification of the speaker's intentions and your understanding of them; do not cut off an exchange too soon to pass on the floor to another student (p. 22).

 The teacher must often teach the interaction skills that are lacking or in need of improvement.

Routines and Gambits

In order to interact spontaneously with others, students need to incorporate the use of what Yorio (1980) calls *routines*: words, phrases, or sentences that are predictable in a typical communicative situation by members of a speech community. The following are four types of routine formulae:

1. situation formulae, which are very culturally specific; for example, "You had to be there" when relating a humorous story;

2. stylistic formulae, which are normally used in written interpersonal communication; for example, "To whom it may concern";

3. ceremonial formulae for ritualistic interaction; for example, "Dearly beloved"; and

4. gambits, as described below (Yorio, 1980; as cited in Taylor, 2002, p. 172).

The fourth category of routine formulae, *gambits,* are "devices that help the speaker maintain the smooth flow of conversation" (Taylor, 2002, p. 172). They function as (1) discourse organizers that introduce or frame what the speaker is about to say; (2) strategies to maintain the flow of conversations by signaling such actions as the desire to take a turn, offer an opinion, or express interest in the topic; and (3) pause fillers that buy time while the speaker thinks of a word or tries to hold a turn (Keller, 1981; as cited in Taylor, p. 172). Sample gambits are expressions used to interrupt to get the floor, such as *excuse me* and *wait a minute*; expressions used to buy time, such as *well, let's see,* and as *I was saying*; and expressions used to redirect the topic such as *by the way* and *on another topic.*

www.cengagebrain.com

Taylor (2002) conducted a study of university-level students in a beginning Spanish conversation course to examine the effect of direct instruction on their use of gambits during discussions and role-play situations. Students were divided into two groups (a discussion group and a role-enactment group) to assess their use of gambits before and after gambit training. See Appendix 8.4 on the *Teacher's Handbook* Web site for a list of the Spanish gambits used in this study. Both groups were given the list of gambits, identified and discussed gambits heard in authentic video segments, and reacted to their instructor's statements using gambits. After this training, the discussion group engaged in a discussion with a native Spanish speaker about cultural differences between the United States and Latin America. The native speaker played the role of a Latin American exchange student, having difficulty with cultural differences. The role-enactment group performed role-plays with a native Spanish speaker in a customer-clerk situation in which students played the role of the customer (Taylor).

Results of Taylor's (2002) study indicated that gambit training resulted in gambit use by both groups in the follow-up tasks. These results confirmed earlier findings that illustrated the effect of direct gambit instruction on subsequent gambit use (Dörnyei, 1995; Wildner-Bassett, 1984). Gambit categories that showed the largest increase in use within the discussion group were those related to opinions, counterarguments, refining points, and buying time. Gambit categories with the largest increases within the role-enactment group were those related to politeness formulae, such as thanking, requesting, greeting, leave taking, and expressing assent. Additionally, however, Taylor's study also revealed that the overall quality and variety of gambits increased significantly for the discussion group but not for the role-enactment group. This finding indicates that, while explicit instruction combined with practice can increase gambit use significantly, this may not occur in all contexts. The research on gambit use points to two implications for foreign language teachers:

1. Students incorporate gambits into their speech if they receive direct training and practice in gambit use.
2. Natural conversations (as exemplified earlier in ICs, for example) are an effective context for eliciting gambit use.

Gambits are "devices that help the speaker maintain the smooth flow of conversation."

Gestures

Not all interpersonal communication is verbal. According to McCafferty (2002), gestures have a mediational function, not only in play and drama, but also in verbal interaction, and thus are a symbolic tool, i.e., they assist verbal performance.[3] According to FL learners, the use of gestures by their instructor conveys meaning in certain contexts and facilitates the process of classroom interaction (Sime, 2008); further it contributes to the encouraging ambiance of the classroom (Allen, 2000). There is evidence to indicate that FL learners use gestures to elicit assistance with vocabulary and to show that they are moving on with communication without resolving a linguistic problem (Gullberg, 1998). Proficiency has also been found to have an effect on the use of gestures inasmuch as the lower the proficiency level, the more gestures produced (Gullberg). In his study of ESL students and an ESL instructor, McCafferty found that while students and the instructor used gestures to refer to lexical items (*iconic gestures*), not all gestures carried lexical meaning and some reflected cultural meaning. Students and teacher used gestures to illustrate concepts (*metaphoric gestures*), such as illustrating someone "thinking outside the box" by drawing a square in the air with one's fingers. They also used gestures to indicate images (*illustrators*), such as illustrating water being splashed by cupping both palms and "splashing" oneself by pumping one's arms up from a horizontal position on the lap inward toward oneself (p. 196). Finally, gestures were used to point out objects in the immediate environment and virtual or far-off contexts and thus indicate space and time (*deictic gestures*). Of interest is the fact that the students and the teacher imitated the gestures used by one another, scaffolded each other in their efforts to co-construct meaning, and created a shared history of signs, exemplifying the transformation of learner and instructor within the ZPD.

The implication of the research on the use of gestures for foreign language teachers is that L2 students exposed to natural contexts will benefit from becoming aware of the use of gestures as part of the process of making meaning. Thus, the use of gestures should be encouraged. McCafferty (2002) suggests that, in order to do this, students first need the opportunity to examine the use of gestures in L2 by watching videotaped interactions and by explicitly discussing gestures when performing role-plays and classroom scenarios. Awareness of gestures might help students both to comprehend the language and to express themselves more effectively.

 In what specific ways can gestures help language learners mediate between themselves and the world? See also Chapter 1.

Student Discourse in Pair/Group Activities

Several studies have revealed important findings regarding strategies and discourse that learners use when faced with interactive tasks and activities with their peers. A series of studies illuminates the ways students mediate their work on tasks in pairs and small groups over time (Alley, 2005; Brooks, Donato, & McGlone, 1997; Donato & Brooks, 1994; Liskin-Gasparro, 1996; Platt & Brooks, 1994). Brooks et al. (1997) identified four mediational strategies students use during pair-work activity: talk about talk, talk about task, the use of English, and whispering to self. The following excerpt from a jigsaw activity illustrates these four strategies used by students when they participate in a problem-solving task of this kind for the first time:

249 J: uh well, now I'm even more confused

250 K: ha! ha!

251 J: see, I have um

okay let me try to do this in Spanish.

I'll at least put up the effort

253 *En mi papel yo tengo muchos espacios algunos tienen películas otros están blancos* [On my paper, I have many spaces, some have movies, others are blank.]

254 K: uh huh

255 J: *y uh yo pienso que tú tienes un blancos donde yo tengo películas* [And, uh, I think you have blanks where I have movies.]

256 K: uh huh

257 J: *¿entiendes?* [Do you understand?]

258 K: uh *sí*

259 J: *Y* but that's not happening

. . .

264 J: I think um you're supposed to draw in what I have and I'm supposed to draw um um

(italics added)

(Brooks et al., pp. 524–525)

Typical student language in pairs includes: talk about talk, talk about task, the use of English, and whispering to self.

When participants talk about their own talk, sometimes called *metatalk*, they use statements such as *"¿Cómo se dice* 'through'?" ("How do you say 'through'?"), or "That's a good word for that" (Brooks, Donato, & McGlone, 1997, p. 528). This talk about talk is also accompanied by talk about task when students say things like "I don't know if I'm right," or *"¿Tú quieres mi hablar mi hablo en español y tú oye oír?"* ("You want me to speak and you listen?") (Brooks et al., p. 529). According to Swain (2000), learners often use metatalk (or talk about talk) to co-construct linguistic knowledge while engaging in a task by means of *collaborative dialogue*, which enables them to test hypotheses about the correct forms to use, discuss them, and decide which forms are best to express their meaning. Collaborative dialogues provide the context in which "language use and language learning can co-occur. It is language use mediating language learning. It is cognitive activity and it is social activity" (Swain, p. 97). Learners demonstrate that they *notice* a particular linguistic form as they discuss and attempt to resolve the problem; *noticing* is a cognitive process that exists within these dialogues (Swain). The following is an example of a collaborative dialogue between two eighth-grade French immersion students:

Rick: *Elle se… et elle se…* how do you say follow? (She [reflexive pronoun] . . . and she [reflexive pronoun] … how do you say follow?)

Kim: Hmmm?

Rick: How do you say follow?

Kim: *Suit.* (Follows.)

Rick: *Suit. Elle se suit* or *elle suit?* (Follows. She follows [reflexive form] or she follows? [nonreflexive form])

Kim: *Elle se… elle LE suive.* (She [reflexive pronoun] . . . she follows HIM.)

Rick: *Elle le?* (She [follows] him?)

Kim: *Elle LE suive.* (She follows HIM.)

Rick: *Jusqu'à l'école.* (To school.)

(Swain & Lapkin, 1998, p. 330)

Students use *metacognitive talk* in discussing how to do a particular task. As students think, act, and speak through a task, they mediate their work with the language that is available to them, most likely the native language. In the second language classroom this use of English is often distressing to teachers. Szostek (1994) points out that in her study insufficient time had been spent on preparing students for managing group dynamics, and they therefore resorted to English for exchanges. Brooks, Donato, & McGlone (1997) explain that use of English is normal and does not necessarily mean that TL use will not be achieved. They explain that students are learning to use the TL for such tasks, but they often start with the native language and move toward use of the TL as they resolve the problem of the task. Across time, English use diminishes dramatically as learners are provided with opportunities to complete similar tasks.

A final strategy identified by these researchers is *whispering to the self*. This mediation behavior appears early in L1 language acquisition, mostly when communication is difficult and thinking is verbal, and it is suppressed in adults except when under communicative duress. The subjects in these studies (Brooks, Donato, & McGlone, 1997; Donato & Brooks, 1994; Platt & Brooks, 1994) used this mediational tool in the native and the TL, and its use diminished over time as the tasks and how to resolve them became more familiar.

A study examining the interaction of Spanish II high school students during group tasks confirmed the findings of the earlier studies described above. Alley (2005) found that the majority of on-task talk was metatalk, through which students pooled their linguistic resources to complete tasks, as demonstrated by negotiation of meaning, turn taking, and frequent use of confirmation checks, while the next largest category of student discourse was metacognitive talk. Twenty-one percent of the discourse was categorized as off-task talk, with 94% of this talk occurring in English. Alley noted that off-task talk emerged when students first began the task, when a student attempted to distract another student, and when the group's work was interrupted by the teacher or another student. In summarizing the results of his study, Alley maintains that, although students tend to use English as the predominant language during group work, it serves to clarify procedures for completing tasks, and that off-task behavior promoted an effective group environment in which students assisted one another.

In sum, these studies indicate that if the purpose and function of learner language during problem-solving tasks is not clearly understood, learners might not be given the strategic opportunities that can lead to their successful performance of tasks using the TL; that is, they might have difficulty ever "saying it right" during such tasks (Brooks, Donato, & McGlone, 1997).

 How does whispering to the self relate to the concepts of private speech and mental rehearsal discussed in Chapter 1?

A feature of student discourse characteristic of communication in pairs or groups is the use of *repair*, which is "a mechanism used to deal with trouble in speaking, hearing, or understanding" (Schegloff, Jefferson, & Sacks, 1977; as cited in Liebscher & Dailey-O'Cain, 2003, p. 376). Repair has been discussed widely in SLA research (Seedhouse, 2004a; van Lier, 1988). It refers to more than just the replacement of an error with a correct utterance, since the presence of an identified error is not required for a repair process to be initiated. Repair has been found to consist of three components: the *trouble source* or "anything which participants judge to be impeding their communication" (Seedhouse, p. 143); the *repair initiation*, or the indication that there is trouble to be repaired; and the *outcome*, which is either the success or the failure of the repair attempt (Liebscher & Dailey-O'Cain; Seedhouse). In the earlier example of a collaborative dialogue, you saw an example of how students experienced *trouble* in a communicative exchange, *noticed* the linguistic problem, worked to *repair* the problem, and the *outcome*

resulted in communication of the message. A repair operation might begin as words are being retrieved or turn-taking is being negotiated. It is "both a forward and a backward mechanism, acting on both vocalized and nonvocalized language" (Buckwalter, 2001, p. 381). According to Seedhouse, in activities that focus on meaning and fluency, repair is conducted in a way that is similar to what happens in a typical conversation, i.e., for purposes of clarifying the message.

Repair can also be described in terms of who initiates the repair and who performs the repair. Buckwalter (2001) examined the use of repair by university-level Spanish students as they participated in communicative pair activities in their Spanish classes. She specifically examined the frequency of use of four repair strategies: self-initiated, self-repair; self-initiated, other-repair; other-initiated, self-repair; and other-initiated, other-repair. Findings indicated that learners overwhelmingly used self-initiated, self-repair, particularly as they attempted to deal with lexical and morphological difficulties. Self-initiated, other-repair, although used infrequently, was the second most-used strategy that occurred when learners recognized that their knowledge base was insufficient to carry out a repair action and sought help. Other-initiated repair strategies were rare in this study and were found primarily to signal non-understanding on the part of the listener.

The preference for self-repair mirrors L1 interaction and may be the result of attempts to maintain one's "public self-image" by not calling attention to or correcting problems in a partner's L2 production (Brown & Levinson, 1987). Another finding in this study is that the majority of repair work was "local"; that is, it focused on moving an utterance closer to the TL form as opposed to focusing on global features, such as message clarity. This finding supports earlier research indicating that, in the talk of language learners, repairs are mostly local, and as proficiency improves, repairs become increasingly more global and discourse related (Shonerd, 1994).

These studies on repair in pair/group interaction have the following important implications for language teachers:

1. Repair is possible only when students have opportunities for meaningful interaction in the classroom.
2. Repair is evidence of students becoming self-regulated in the language (i.e., they are able to function without assistance from others).
3. Long turns at talk provide many opportunities for use of self-initiated, self-repair strategies (Buckwalter, 2001).

See the last section in this chapter for further discussion of providing feedback in oral interpersonal contexts.

 Long turns at talk provide many opportunities for use of self-initiated, self-repair strategies.

Enhancing Small Group Communication Through Strategy Training

There is evidence to suggest that learners can be taught to engage with each other and with a task so that they reap benefits from group interaction. Naughton (2006) used the Cooperative Organization of Strategies for Oral Interaction (COSOI) to provide training for 45 Spanish students of English as a foreign language. Training featured the teaching of four strategies: (1) use of follow-up questions, (2) requesting and giving clarification, (3) correction or repair (see prior discussion in this chapter) of their peers' utterances, and (4) requesting and giving help. The results of the study illustrated that, in comparison to their counterparts who received no strategy training, students who were given strategy training increased their number of turns-at-talk, asked more follow-up questions, almost tripled their use of requesting and giving clarification, increased their use of repair, and showed the most progress overall in their ability to request and give help. This investigation yielded several insights of importance to language teachers:

1. Prior to the strategy training, students rarely engaged in the types of interaction included in the program.
2. Asking follow-up questions (Strategy 1) was the most frequently used strategy on both pre-test and post-test measures.
3. Requesting and giving information improved significantly but did not last beyond the experimental period.
4. The increase in the use of correction or repair (Strategy 3) was considerably less than for the other strategies, most likely because engaging in repair is often considered socially taboo or a hindrance to the flow of conversation.
5. The most successful outcome of the training was in students' use of requesting and giving help (Strategy 4), perhaps because it is not a complex strategy to learn.

Student Interaction

In Chapter 2, you explored the role of context in approaches to language teaching and in various types of activities and exercises used by instructors and characteristic of textbook programs. As you learned, mechanical types of drills and exercises have limited value in contributing to language acquisition and in developing communicative abilities (Brooks, 1990; Kinginger, 1990; Wong & VanPatten, 2003). Indeed, activities classified as "communicative" often consist of questions asked by the teacher and answers supplied by students (Lee, 1995). Studies dealing with the nature of classroom tasks confirm that when pair/group work entails discussion and negotiation of meaning, students perform a greater number of content clarifications, confirmation checks, and comprehension checks (Doughty & Pica, 1986; Porter, 1986) and use a greater number of conversational gambits (Taylor, 2002). In this section, you will learn how to engage learners in interactive tasks, including how to group students, prepare them for interaction with peers, conduct follow-up activities, and integrate attention to linguistic form.

Cooperative Learning: Task-Based Instruction

Foreign language teachers engage students in cooperative learning through a variety of classroom activities and tasks. Teachers often use the terms *activities* and *tasks* as synonyms. However, we will use Skehan's (1998) definition of *task* as an activity in which: "(1) meaning is primary, (2) listeners are not given other people's meanings to regurgitate, (3) there is some sort of relationship to comparable real-world activities, (4) task completion has some sort of priority, and (5) the assessment of the task is in terms of outcome" (as cited in Willis & Willis, 2007, p. 12). A strategy for restructuring the traditional question-answer type of class discussion is *task-based instruction*, which enables students to interact with others by using the TL as a means to an end (Lee, 1995). A task-based approach to language teaching, which has received increasing attention in recent years, is based on two concepts that we have explored in previous chapters of *Teacher's Handbook* in great detail: communication and negotiation of meaning (Wilson-Duffy, 2003a). It emphasizes that communication (1) is the expression, interpretation, and negotiation of meaning; (2) requires two or more autonomous participants; and (3) should focus on the learners' use of the language, not the instructor's (Lee, 1995, p. 440).

In *cooperative learning,* students work in pairs or in small groups of four or five to help one another complete a given task, attain a goal, converse, or learn subject matter. Each person in the group has a responsibility, and students depend on one another as they work to complete their task. Students learn to work together and respect their classmates. They are also encouraged to develop their own abilities and identities. The teacher may give points or some form of credit to the entire group for achieving the objectives and may also give individual students credit for their contributions.

Extensive research on cooperative learning by Johnson and Johnson (1987) suggests that this technique often produces higher achievement, increases retention, and develops interpersonal skills. Cooperative learning also has been shown to promote higher self-esteem and acceptance of differences, as well as to foster responsibility. Furthermore, it encourages creativity by giving students opportunities to observe the problem-solving approaches and cognitive processing strategies of others (Kohn, 1987). According to Johnson, Johnson, and Holubec (1988), cooperative of learning provides the vehicle for teaching students to process skills that are needed to work effectively within a group. By using process observers and peer feedback on group processing skills, students begin to analyze and improve the group interaction. Of particular benefit to foreign language study, cooperative learning activities teach students how to ask questions, negotiate meaning, and interact in groups. Figure 8.8 is an example of a questionnaire designed to encourage students to think about the group process and their own participation (Scarcella & Oxford, 1992).

As discussed in earlier chapters, foreign language teachers should remember the importance of designing cooperative learning activities that are meaningful, contextualized, and engage students in offering diverse responses and opinions. You may find it helpful

FIGURE 8.8 Questionnaire: Conversational Skills

IN TODAY'S ACTIVITY	OFTEN	SOMETIMES	NEVER
1. I checked to make sure that everyone understood what I said.			
2. I gave explanations whenever I could.			
3. I asked specific questions about what I didn't understand.			
4. I paraphrased what others said to make sure that I understood.			
5. I encouraged others to speak by making such remarks as "I'd like to know what _____ thinks about that" and "I haven't heard from _____ yet" and "What do you think, _____?"			

Source: From *The Tapestry of Language Learning* (p. 158), by R. C. Scarcella and R. L. Oxford. Copyright © 1992 Heinle/Arts & Sciences, a part of Cengage Learning, Inc. Reproduced with permission. www.cengage.com/permissions.

to consult Chapter 4 to review the considerations that elementary school teachers should make in planning for cooperative learning activities, as these considerations may also apply to the secondary and post-secondary levels of instruction.

 In cooperative learning tasks, each person in the group has a responsibility, and students depend on one another as they work to complete their task.

 Task-based instruction enables students to interact with others by using the TL as a means to an end.

Teachers may implement individual *tasks* or a *task sequence* (i.e., *task-based lesson*), which involves a sequence of tasks that relate to one another. The sequence typically begins with a teacher-led introduction that prepares or *primes* learners by engaging them in thinking about the topic of the task, activating their background knowledge, reviewing/generating key vocabulary and expressions to be used, and demonstrating what will be expected of them in the task(s) (Willis & Willis, 2007). Students then conduct the target task or tasks and share their products or information with the teacher and/or the class. Wilson-Duffy (2003a) suggests that *pedagogical tasks* might be used as a technique for preparation and scaffolding prior to engaging students in the culminating *real-world task*. For example, in preparation for the real-world task of reporting items stolen in a hotel burglary, students might complete the pedagogical task of comparing two pictures of hotel rooms and describing differences between where objects are located (Wilson-Duffy, 2003a, p. 3). Wilson-Duffy (2003b) describes an online task-based sequence in which students explore which movie they might like to see and convince their classmates to attend the movie they like. The sequence consists of the following interrelated tasks, described below in terms of directions to the student:

1. Ask and answer questions regarding your schedule in order to decide on a day and time to see a movie, using audio or video chats to communicate.
2. Using a movie theater Web site in the TL, find a movie that you would like to see that fits into your schedule.
3. Convince your classmates to attend the movie you have chosen, using a written or oral chat room (pp. 3, 6).

www.cengagebrain.com

In order to complete these tasks, students use computer-mediated communication, i.e., chat rooms and the Internet. See the *Teacher's Handbook* Web site for the link to a complete description of this lesson.

Tasks may be based on a printed or oral text (see Chapters 6 and 7), on subject-matter content (see Chapter 3), on cultures (see Chapter 5), on sharing of information, or on discussion. Figure 8.9 depicts a taxonomy of task types, as suggested by Willis and Willis (2007) in helping teachers to think of different kinds of tasks on a specific topic. Note that the task types are not mutually exclusive—for example, problem-solving tasks could involve tasks such as matching, ordering, and listing. Willis and Willis also suggest that not all topics lend themselves well to all types of tasks and that teachers should select the best three or four that link well together. The following are several examples of tasks, which can each be a part of a task sequence.

- *Think-pair-share* (Kagan, 1989): Students use the following response cycle in answering questions: (1) they listen while the teacher poses a question; (2) they are given time to think of a response; (3) they are told to pair with a classmate and discuss their responses; and (4) they share their responses with the whole group.
- *Jigsaw Sequence* (Kagan, 1989): Each member of the group assumes responsibility for a given portion of the lesson. These members work with the members from

FIGURE 8.9 The Task Generator: A Taxonomy of Task Types

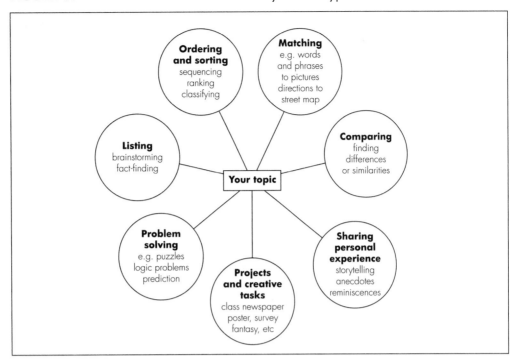

Source: From *Doing Task-Based Teaching* (p. 108), by D. Willis and J. Willis. Oxford, UK: Oxford University Press. Copyright © 2007. Reprinted by permission.

the other groups who have the same assignment, thus forming "expert groups." Eventually, each member must learn the entire lesson by listening to and sharing information with others in the group. Figures 8.10A, 8.10B, and 8.10C depict a sample jigsaw activity, together with suggestions for how to form teams and expert groups. Notice that the expert groups refer to the first series of groups in which students become "experts" by learning their assigned content; each member of the group must have the knowledge for their group—learning is not divided into separate assignments. The "home groups" refer to the second set of groupings of students, each of which is comprised of an expert from each of the expert groups; each group has the collective knowledge of all of the expert groups. Once in home groups, students use their collective knowledge in order to complete a task, such as the one shown in Figure 8.10C. See also the videotape entitled "Happy New Year!" for an example of a jigsaw activity in action (Annenberg/CPB, & ACTFL, 2003).

- *Information-gap activities (IGAs)* (Johnson, 1979; Walz, 1996): One student has information that another student does not have but needs. For example, pairs of students might be given the task of finding an hour that they both have free this week to play a game of tennis. Each student might have a copy of his/her schedule of activities for the week, and each has to ask questions in order to find out when the other person is free. As they share the information, the students eventually find a time slot that works for both of them. See Figure 8.11 "Where are my glasses?" for an example in English. On the *Teacher's Handbook* Web site, Appendices 8.5A and 8.5B (Dreke & Lind, 2000), 8.6A and 8.6B (Freed & Bauer, 1989), and 8.7A and 8.7B (Jansma & Kassen, 2004) are sample information-gap activities in German, Spanish, and French, respectively. Note that Appendices 8.5A and 8.5B illustrate an IGA in German that is somewhat different from the other examples that follow in that it deals with storytelling.[4] Student B has a series of drawings arranged and numbered

FIGURE 8.10A A Sample Jigsaw Activity

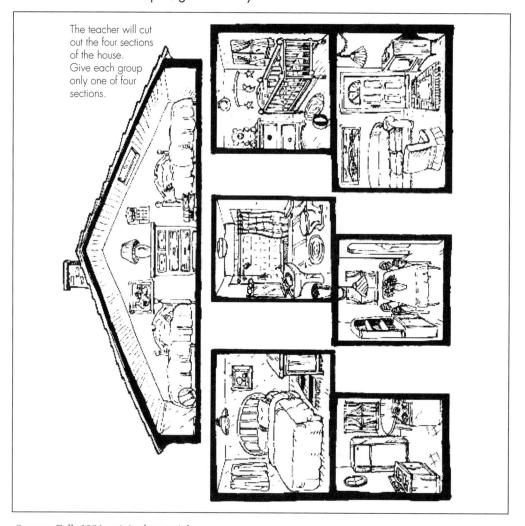

The teacher will cut out the four sections of the house. Give each group only one of four sections.

Source: Fall, 1991, original material.

in the correct order to represent a story; he or she tells the story to Student A by describing the drawings. Student A asks questions as needed and numbers the drawings accordingly. This activity is repeated for a second story, but this time Student A tells the story as Student B numbers the drawings. At the end, students are asked to create a title for the stories and relate them to the class.

Teachers should recognize that, in order for jigsaw activities and IGAs to be most effective, students need preparation before they begin to do them. Teachers should guide students in activating background knowledge and in recalling/reviewing key vocabulary and expressions that they will need in order to complete the task. If the activity includes visuals, students should have an opportunity to look at them to be sure that they understand what they are depicting and to brainstorm possible vocabulary. Furthermore, it is critical that students see a model of these activities before they engage in one themselves. The teacher might videotape students completing an information-gap activity and then show this video to students as an example of how this type of activity works. It is important to do several similar activities so that students can become comfortable managing intrapersonal communication—that is, figuring out in their own minds how they

FIGURE 8.10B Jigsaw Activity for Four Groups of Students

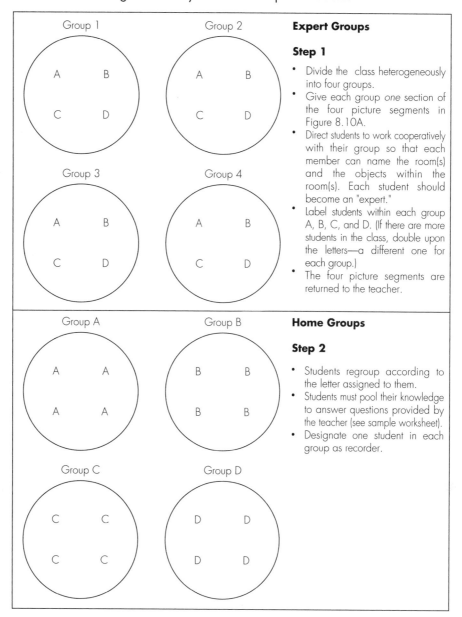

Source: Fall, 1991, original material.

will sustain their involvement in the task (Brooks, Donato, & McGlone, 1997). Finally, students must be held accountable for these activities by being expected to perform a follow-up task, such as reporting back to the class. See a later section in this chapter on how to structure group tasks.

Brooks (1992) describes another type of information-gap activity: "There are two parts to a whole diagram or picture, Part A and Part B. When both parts are superimposed, they form a complete diagram. One student receives Part A, the other Part B. The teacher then asks the students to talk to one another in the foreign language to find out how their part of the diagram is both different from and similar to that of the partner and to draw in or add the missing information

FIGURE 8.10C Jigsaw Activity Worksheet

Group _____

Names _____   _____

_____   _____

Each member of your group has seen one part of a house. You will need to work together to answer the following questions:

1. How many rooms are in the house?   _____
2. How many bathrooms are there?   _____
3. How many bedrooms are there?   _____
4. How many of the following did you see?

beds	_____	pictures	_____
tables	_____	sinks	_____
clocks	_____	doors	_____
chairs	_____	toys	_____
dressers	_____	pillows	_____
lamps	_____	bookshelves	_____
rugs	_____	waste baskets	_____
windows	_____		

5. How many children might live in this house?   _____
6. Do you think the children are older or younger?   _____

Variations: Selected readings may be given, or research assignments may be made, including biographies (each group studies one facet of the person's life) of cultural studies (each group studies one facet of a particular country or culture).

Target Language Use: To encourage use of the TL, give each student 5–10 bingo chips. Each time a student uses English, he or she must place a chip in a pile. Students receive bonus points depending on the number of chips they still have at the end of the activity.

Process Objectives: Students will work cooperatively.
Students will engage in peer teaching.

Content Objectives: Students will communicate in the TL.
Students will recall and/or name vocabulary items or basic facts and information.

Source: Fall, 1991, original material.

www.cengagebrain.com

so that, by the end of their conversation, they both have replicas of the same master diagram" (p. 67). Appendices 8.8A and 8.8B (on the *Teacher's Handbook* Web site) provide examples of this type of IGA in which students draw the missing information from each drawing of the house so that, at the end of the activity, both students have the same drawing of the complete house. Appendix 8.8 also illustrates how the same jigsaw activity used in Figure 8.10A can be adapted for use as an information-gap activity of the kind described above.

Information-gap activities provide a good opportunity for students to learn how to ask for clarification, how to request information, and how to negotiate

FIGURE 8.11 Where Are My Glasses? Student A

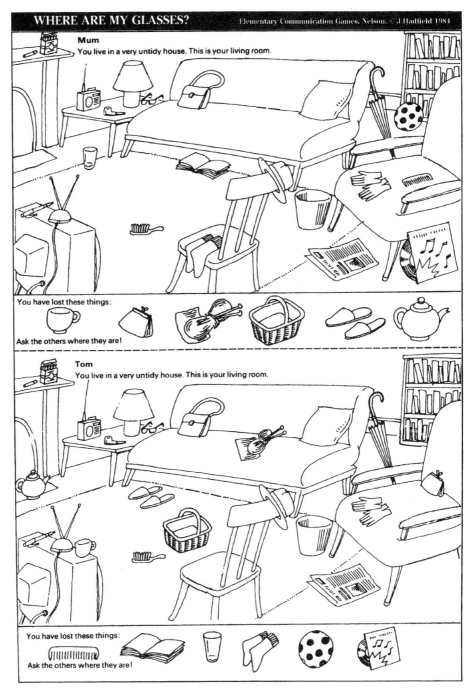

Source: From "The classroom dynamics of information-gap activities," by J. Walz, 1996, *Foreign Language Annals, 29,* 481–494. Used by permission of the American Council of the Teaching of Foreign Languages.

when faced with misunderstandings. Teachers should realize, however, that not all IGAs are created equal. Some provide formulaic practice of language utterances and vocabulary, e.g., those that require students to give prices of items, while others, such as the ones included in this chapter, promote creativity and meaning-making.

In information-gap activities, one student has information that another student does not have but needs.

- *Problem solving* (Willis & Willis, 2007): Group members offer advice and recommendations on problems ranging from general issues such as global warming to more specific problems such as what to do if your neighbor's cat is causing trouble in your garden. These tasks stimulate discussion and serve as the basis for writing activities including note-taking, drafting, and finalizing proposals for solutions (Willis & Willis, p. 93).

- *Sharing personal experiences: Storytelling, anecdotes, reminiscences* (Willis & Willis): Students work together to recreate a familiar story, add more details, and change the ending; they create a story with visuals. Students engage in social interactions by recounting their own experiences, making them entertaining and dramatic.

- *Cooperative projects* (Kagan, 1989): Group members work together to complete a group project such as a presentation, composition, or art project. Oxford (1992) describes the "Heritage Project," a successful cooperative model for teaching culture in language classes, in which students design a culture-related project and have a large degree of freedom in topic choice, grouping, implementation, and time management.

- *Movement activities* (Bassano & Christison, 1987): Students get up from their seats and walk around the room in order to obtain information from classmates. For example, students might have a list of 10 activities in the present tense and ask classmates whether or not they do each activity (wake up at 6:00 A.M., eat breakfast every morning, etc.); students share the information with the class afterward.

- *Paired interviews*: Students interview each other for specific information and share their findings with the class.

- *Role-plays*: Students act out situations, such as a restaurant scene or a visit to a doctor. Beginning students can be given role-play cards with vocabulary/grammar hints, intermediate-level students can practice role-plays around survival situations, and advanced-level learners can present role-plays around a problematic situation in which someone must solve a conflict or persuade someone else to do something within a culturally specific context (DiPietro, 1987; Hadley, 2001).

  It is advantageous to present the situation card describing the role-play in the native language so that students completely understand the task. However, when preparing role-plays, students also benefit from well-organized instructions and guidance, such as a model situation and hints concerning vocabulary and grammar use. The extent to which the teacher offers specific suggestions will depend on the cognitive and linguistic levels of the students. Younger learners, for example, require more structured role-play directions in order to help them focus their ideas.

  While the advantage of the role-play is that it mirrors real life, it can prove challenging to learners because it asks them to solve a problem, and to act out a role simultaneously (Willis & Willis, 2007). A solution to this problem is to take learners through a sequence in which they first collaborate on how the problem might be solved, then learn to play a role, and, finally, learn to solve problems while playing a role (Willis & Willis).

- *Discussion tasks*: Students share opinions, debate, narrate, describe, and explain. For example, students might discuss and share their opinions of a text or controversial topic. An opinion survey might be used to assist learners in formulating an opinion (Willis & Willis, 2007). It is important to note that the complexity of task-based discussions depends on the linguistic level of students. That is, the discussions that novices have are typically short and based on information collected in a task, whereas students at higher levels are able to exchange opinions and have more of an interactive discussion. Discussion tasks are particularly useful as students move into the advanced level of study, since they provide the impetus for self-expression, use of paragraph-length and extended discourse, and manipulation of more sophisticated vocabulary and grammatical structures.

- *Imaginative activities*: Sadow (1987) developed a number of *imaginative activities* for the language classroom in which students are asked to "solve a problem they would not normally have to face, concoct a plan they would never have dreamt of on their own, reconstruct the missing parts of stories, and act in outlandish ways" (p. 33). When students first begin to do imaginative work, Sadow suggests that they work with structured paired activities, such as rewriting conversations or dialogues to change the characters, perhaps by switching male and female roles or altering age and status. Beginning-level students might be engaged in activities such as designing a mask with unusual facial features, designing half-built houses, or inventing a job interviewer they would like to encounter. At the intermediate and advanced levels, challenging problem-solving activities can be presented that promote interaction and critical thinking through what Sadow (1994) terms "concoctions." Students are presented with an unusual problem to solve creatively; for example, students might create a new animal, plan model cities, invent a heroine for a country that lacks one, and write plays with happy endings (Sadow, 1994, p. 242).[5]

As illustrated above, there are various types of tasks and task sequences that can be planned so that students are engaged in meaningful interaction.[6] However, there is a caveat of which language teachers should beware. The nature of certain tasks may lead learners to use minimal TL and take short turns at talk with simple syntax (Seedhouse, 2004b). Since the completion of the task is the goal, there may be a tendency on the teacher's part to pay little attention to the language that is being used. Given that Seedhouse suggests that task-based instruction not be used as the basis for an entire methodology, teachers might (1) use tasks as one of several strategies for engaging students in interaction, (2) take care to integrate as much TL use as possible in the task sequence—a follow-up or reporting back phase might an effective avenue for eliciting more language from learners, and (3) integrate some focus on form after the task sequence has been completed.

Conducting Cooperative Learning Activities

Grouping Students.   Research in cooperative learning shows that the most effective way to configure small groups is to put together four students who represent a cross-section of the class in terms of level of past performance in the subject area, race or ethnicity, and sex (Slavin, 1986). Slavin suggests that "a four-person team in a class that is one-half male, one-half female, and three-quarters white, one-quarter minority might have two boys and two girls and three white students and one minority student. The team would also have a high performer, a low performer, and two average performers" (p. 16). Students should be assigned to groups or teams by the teacher, since they tend to choose partners who are like themselves. Periodically, teachers should consider grouping students more homogenously, particularly so that more advanced learners can challenge each other and be pushed to exceed their current abilities.

When a class does not evenly divide up into groups, the extra students can be assigned the role of "floater." Floaters can have several functions, such as collecting information from each group (during paired interviews, for example), eavesdropping and reporting back to the class what he or she discovered, and serving as an observer of group processing. In this way, the extra students can contribute to the class at the end of the activity or during group reporting (R. Donato, personal communication, June 14, 1992).

Structuring Group Tasks.   The following are helpful guidelines for structuring cooperative learning and interactive activities:

1. Ensure that students do, in fact, need to cooperate in order to complete the task. They should not be able to complete it without interaction.
2. Keep the group size small; start with pair activities. Groups are most effective when they are no larger than five.
3. Set the stage; motivate the activity with drama, actions, or visuals.
4. Set clear goals; describe outcomes clearly for the students.
5. Make sure the students have the TL they need to accomplish the activity, that they know how to say what they will need to say.
6. Give exact directions for every step of the task. Model the sequence of the activity in precise steps.
7. Set a time limit to help students feel accountable and to make the best use of the time available. Use a kitchen timer with a loud bell or buzzer to provide a neutral timekeeper and a clear signal for the end of the activity.
8. Circulate among the students throughout the activity. This will enable you to monitor use of the TL, offer assistance, and check progress.
9. Establish a system for directing the attention of the students back to you, e.g., a hand signal such as a raised right hand, dimming the lights.
10. Elicit responses at random from each group after the activity, which will hold students accountable for staying on task (adapted from Curtain & Dahlberg, 2010, in press).

 Elicit responses at random from each group after the activity, which will hold students accountable for staying on task.

Detailed attention must be given to providing clear directions and examples before the task is begun (Johnson, Johnson, & Holubec, 1988). Modeling the task with students in front of the class and talking about the task while it is performed is another good way to provide support for the activity. While students are engaged in group activities, the teacher acts as both a process observer and a resource person. At the conclusion of the group activity, the groups report back to the whole class on their progress and on the process, thus helping the teacher to plan for future activities. Circulating around the room to monitor progress and making students responsible for reporting back to the class after the activity will encourage students to use the TL and may prevent them from reverting to the use of the native language. See Appendix 8.9 for a description of Donato's (2004) "Talk Scores," a technique for monitoring and evaluating group speaking activities.

Developing Interpersonal Speaking Through Study of Literature and Culture

In Chapters 6 and 7, you explored strategies for guiding students through oral and printed texts and using these texts as springboards for discussion and creative extension activities, including following the Interactive Model for Integrating the Three Modes of Communication. One of the advantages of this model, presented in Chapter 6, is that it helps students understand a text and feel comfortable with it before being asked to engage in creative speaking. The difficulty students often experience when trying to discuss readings, particularly literary texts, is that they cannot communicate orally in the same style or at the same level as the text. The Interactive Model compensates for this difference in skill level by encouraging students to express their thoughts in their own words and at their own speaking level, while using parts of the text prose for additional support. Breiner-Sanders (1991) suggests that, when beginning to use reading as a basis for conversation, teachers select reading materials that are targeted more closely to students' speaking level, in order to help them gain confidence in discussing texts.

Sadow (1987) suggests the use of simulations or reenactment of scenes from a literary passage or historical event as a strategy for integrating interpersonal speaking with the study of literature and history. According to Cazden (1992), reenactments or performance activities stimulate discussion as groups plan and decide upon an interpretation of the text, and again later, in the post-performance discussion when the small groups' interpretive decisions are explained and compared. These activities provide opportunities for students to use the TL in preparing their reenactments while interacting with the text and assimilating text language into their linguistic repertoire.

Undoubtedly, students cannot be taught to engage in effective interpersonal communication without cultural understanding. *Teacher's Handbook* advocates the integration of culture and communication across the three modes. In Chapter 5, you learned about a constructivist approach to learning about culture, in which learners construct their views of culture through social interaction and interpersonal communication. In Chapters 6 and 7, you explored ways in which culture can be integrated in an oral, printed, or video text and used as the basis for communication.

In her reading process for using authentic texts to guide learners' cross-cultural discovery, Galloway suggests that students use speaking as they transfer and reflect on cultural information and insights acquired through exploration of a text. In oral interpersonal tasks, students might:

- role play a scenario using appropriate cultural and linguistic protocols, given the context;
- verbally support or refute a position from the point of view of a native from the target culture, using citations from an authentic text;
- debate an issue from the viewpoints of both the native and target cultures;
- analyze a possible TL utterance by determining the likelihood that it would have been said at all and identifying the type of speaker from whom it might have come; and
- respond to open-ended questions relating to cultural information they discovered in an authentic text (1992, pp. 120–121).

www.cengagebrain.com

You may find it helpful to refer back to Viewing Activity B in Chapter 6 on the *Teacher's Handbook* Web site—"Hearing Authentic Voices"—to see how this teacher engages students in viewing a video of Spanish-speaking youths who discuss their leisure activities as a prelude for the students' own discussions.

Another example of integrating interpersonal speaking and culture is the series of cross-level collaborative projects undertaken by the 1997 Northeast Conference on the Teaching of Foreign Languages to address the standards in classroom practice (Phillips, 1997). Two of the projects exemplify how interpersonal speaking and writing can be effectively integrated into exploration of cultures, comparisons of language and cultures, communication with native speakers, connections to other disciplines, and interaction with TL communities.

First, Haas and Reardon (1997) designed and taught an interdisciplinary unit on Chile to a seventh-grade Spanish class. Interpersonal speaking was integrated in various ways as students (1) discussed, in Spanish, slides and literary texts (including poetry) dealing with Chile; (2) interviewed a guest informant from Chile; and (3) as a culminating activity, visited a Chilean bakery in their local community and interacted with the store owners in Spanish, making purchases, asking questions about a food preparation

www.cengagebrain.com

demonstration, etc. A key component of this project was that students also engaged in interpersonal writing by corresponding by e-mail with Chilean key pals (more on this in the next section). See the Chapter 10 video segment on the *Teacher's Handbook* Web site for the bakery visit.

Second, Schwartz and Kavanaugh (1997) taught a unit on immigration to a ninth-grade Spanish class through the study of conditions in Guatemala and the viewing of various video materials. Interpersonal speaking was incorporated by means of (1) discussion of video segments from the movie on video "El norte"; (2) role-plays from video scenes; (3) interviewing a Guatemalan informant; and (4) debate on immigration to the United States.[7]

Using Literary Exploration to Develop Advanced-Level Discourse

One of the challenges of teaching interpersonal speaking is moving students' proficiency from the intermediate-low and -mid levels to the intermediate-high and advanced levels. This is difficult for several reasons, because at the advanced level:

- Students must move from sentences to connected paragraphs.
- Students must narrate and describe in present, past, and future time frames.
- Students must expand their discourse beyond their immediate worlds to topics of public interest.
- Students must deal with unanticipated complications.
- Students must be understood without difficulty by speakers unaccustomed to dealing with nonnative speakers (Swender, 1999).

Advanced-level discourse competence requires attention to the use of cohesive devices, such as pronouns and conjunctions, which serve to illustrate a relation between one element or idea and another; for example, conjunctions such as *therefore* and *however* connect the idea in one sentence with an idea in a subsequent sentence. Advanced-level discourse also has *coherence*, which refers to the organization of ideas within a text; that is, the orderly presentation of ideas, consistency of facts and opinions, and completeness of the discussion (Canale, 1982). See Chapter 9 for a fuller discussion of cohesion and coherence as they deal with presentational writing.

Advanced-level discourse requires interesting content to talk and learn about, beyond the scope of self, daily life, and weekend activities. In Chapters 5, 6, and 7, you explored ways in which *Teacher's Handbook* advocates pivotal roles for literature and culture in language instruction because they provide the means for more stimulating content, acquisition of interesting content, and extension of linguistic skills. Also, upper-level classes at the secondary level and literature classes at the post-secondary level should offer the ideal environment for developing discourse into the advanced range of oral proficiency.

However, several studies have called into question the degree to which the discourse conditions of typical literature classes foster interactions that reflect advanced levels of language functioning. As mentioned in Chapter 6, research examining the discourse of college foreign language literature classes revealed the lack of student participation and negotiation of meaning and the predominance of teacher-centered presentation of texts and teacher talk (Donato & Brooks, 2004; Musumeci, 1996; Zyzik & Polio, 2008). According to Mantero, difficulties in interpreting literary texts "may be caused by a lack of opportunity to comprehend the text through classroom dialogue" (2006, p. 105). In their study of teacher-directed TL discussions of literary texts in a senior-level undergraduate Spanish literature course, Donato and Brooks found that (1) the discourse pattern established by the instructor inhibited students' elaboration of responses and prevented them from moving beyond word- and sentence-level utterances; (2) most of the teacher's questions were display questions, to which the instructor already knew the answer, and which provided an invitation for her to take the floor; (3) the range of time frames used in discussions was limited and the present tense was the predominant tense; and (4) students generally did not "uptake" speech modeled by the teacher (i.e., they did not show evidence of altering or correcting their language after instructor modeling or recasting, primarily due to the fact that the instructor accepted utterances that were incorrect and/or inappropriate in the context of the discussion).

Findings of the Donato and Brooks (2004) study echo those of an earlier study that also examined the discourse of an undergraduate Spanish literature class. Mantero (2002) found that most text-centered classroom talk occurred at the level of dialogue and featured extensive use of IRE patterns, and that students' cognitive behavior focused on knowledge of specific pieces of information. As mentioned in Chapter 6, Mantero (2006) suggests extending text-centered talk so that it addresses cognitive development as well as improving language proficiency. In this approach, the literature instructor would rely more on interpretive and evaluative inquiry, rather than linguistically driven, discrete-point questions. Consequently, the instructor would assist learners in creating background information for putting tasks into the appropriate context, activating prior knowledge by focusing on word meaning rather than vocabulary memorization, questioning and posing problems through open-ended questions, learning to have an inner dialogue with themselves about their understanding of the text before sharing their interpretation, and using metacognitive strategies to think aloud or write and thus monitor their own understanding and language use (Mantero, 2006). This type of text-centered talk, which reflects the features of the instructional conversations explored earlier in this chapter, could lead to richer discussions of literary texts in which students have extended turns at talk, engage in negotiation of meaning with the teacher and peers, and have opportunities to practice advanced-level functions.

In sum, Donato and Brooks cite five implications of current research regarding the role of interpersonal speaking and advanced-level functions in literary discussions:

1. Discussions that take place in literature courses have the potential to incorporate advanced proficiency goals.
2. Literature classes need to include a variety of interaction patterns to provide for elaborated responses, one feature of an advanced speaker.
3. The potential of literary discussion to move students into advanced speaking tasks needs to be raised in the minds of instructors and students.
4. Literature instructors need to know the *ACTFL Proficiency Guidelines—Speaking*, the range of functions at each level of proficiency, and the modes of communication as described in the *SFLL*.
5. There is a critical need for more research into the literary discussion and its relationship to developing functional language abilities at the advanced level (2004, pp. 195–196).

Teaching Interpersonal Writing

Two-way interpersonal communication can also be accomplished through written means, such as dialogue journals, letters, and e-mail projects.

Dialogue Journals

A *dialogue journal* is a written conversation in which students communicate individually with the teacher (Peyton, 1993; Peyton & Reed, 1990). It can also be used to engage students in interaction with one another or in small groups. Various studies have shown the effectiveness of using journal writing to help students create personal meaning and increase their motivation to write (Peyton, 1987, 1990; West & Donato, 1995). According to Hall and Robinson (1994), interactive journal writing can facilitate children's writing skills, aid in the transition from oral to written communication, and give students the chance to be an "author." Learning to write occurs when children are given a reason to write and a real audience to address (Jensen, 1993). Shohamy (1998) advocates the use of dialogue journals because they involve young learners in the learning process and provide the teacher with information about their perspectives on the language learning process.

The interactive dialogue journal is effective for learners of all ages and at all levels of language development. Curtain and Dahlberg (2010) suggest that, at very beginning stages of language learning in elementary school, students can write or copy the words they have learned and combine them with pictures, and then share this with the teacher for response. At more advanced stages, they suggest using the journal to engage in discussions of cultural issues or other content, as well as more personal feelings and opinions. It is important that the teacher respond to the content of each journal entry rather than using it as an opportunity to correct grammar, vocabulary, and spelling errors.

The dialogue journal can also be used as a tool to help students make sense of new content that they are learning in the language classroom. They might, for example, keep lists of new vocabulary, respond to questions posed by the teacher, or organize content through charts or outlines. Students might share their journal entries with the teacher or use them to engage in a private conversation with themselves in order to mediate learning. When the dialogue journal is shared with the teacher in this way, it also functions as a tool for alternative formative assessment since students continually provide feedback about what they understand in class as they progress with their language development, and this can enable the teacher to improve instruction (Peyton & Reed, 1990). Figure 8.12 shows the types of journal writing that might be used to foster student learning of content areas. A table such as this one helps the teacher monitor learning in the various subject areas by means of interpersonal written tasks. Although this table was developed to monitor learning in bilingual or immersion second language settings, it can also be used in foreign language classrooms that incorporate content-based instruction.

Borich (2001) reported on the use of the dialogue journal with a second-grade FLES class to assess learning related to the Cultures and Connections goal areas in a thematic unit on the Yucatan. Data obtained from the students' journal entries revealed their ability to identify cultural similarities and differences, identify cultural products and practices, and acquire new information related to other disciplines. Borich concluded that the journal enabled students to show what they had learned in a variety of ways, to use higher-order thinking skills, and to provide their own perspectives on what had been taught. One disadvantage of the journal for teachers is the amount of time that it takes to read and respond. In a similar vein, some teachers in Borich's study expressed dissatisfaction with the amount of time taken out of the school day for students to write in their journals. However, as you will see in Chapter 11, taking time to integrate valuable assessment is justified, particularly since effective assessment informs and improves instruction and should be closely integrated with it.

At secondary and post-secondary levels, the interactive dialogue journal may be used through e-mail. Wang (1998) observed that using e-mail to conduct dialogue journals in an intermediate ESL class had advantages over the paper-and-pencil journals: Students who used e-mail wrote more per writing session, asked more questions, used more language functions, and adopted a more conversational tone in their language than did their traditional counterparts. These findings were also reflected in a study of university Spanish students, whose electronic dialogue journals were found to have more language, a greater variety of topics and language functions, more student-initiated interactions, and more personal and expressive language use (González-Bueno, 1998).

FIGURE 8.12 Types of Journal Writing Used to Foster Learning of Content Areas

JOURNAL TYPE AND PURPOSE	SCIENCE	LANGUAGE ARTS	MATHEMATICS	SOCIAL SCIENCE
Dialogue/Buddy: to share with another	Explain to teacher or to friend what is happening in class and what is understood	Share with another about a story or poem being read; share other aspects of class	Let teacher or friend know how class or assignments are going	"Discuss" information pertaining to topics in class
Notebook: to take notes to assist memory	Write down information pertaining to an experiment in class	Take down conversations overheard for use in a story to be written	Keep notes about math concepts	Write down key information discussed in class
Learning logs: to discuss and process information from class	Write down notes about what one understands in the class and about what might seem unclear	Write down key concepts from class such as definitions of concepts: setting, theme, characterization	Try to explain math concepts for oneself or perhaps for another; clarify or try to apply a new concept	Take notes on causes of Civil War or other key ideas; ask self to identify and clarify ideas
Response journals: to respond openly and freely to any topic	Respond to feelings about scientific experimentation or use of animals as subjects of biogenetics	Make any comments on characters or conflicts presented in a story being read	Respond to math in an interesting way, such as ask questions about why people who would never admit to being illiterate will seemingly brag about their math ignorance	Respond to politicians' handling of peace after World War I or about attitudes of pilgrims toward Native Americans

Source: From *Reading, Writing and Learning in ESL: A Resource Book for K–12 Teachers,* 3rd ed. (p. 354), by S. F. Peregoy and O. F. Boyle, 2005, Upper Saddle River, NJ: Pearson Education. Used by permission of Pearson Education, Upper Saddle River, NJ.

Use of the electronic medium for interpersonal exchanges seems to facilitate participation by students who are reluctant to engage in face-to-face conversations, it allows time to process input and output, and it increases language production. Evidence suggests that the electronic dialogue journal improves students' attitudes toward language learning, promotes communicative and personalized interaction, increases the amount of language produced by students, and enables students and instructor to develop a positive rapport (González-Bueno, 1998; González-Bueno & Pérez, 2000; Warschauer, 1995; Warschauer & Healey, 1998). However, research results are mixed concerning whether or not the electronic format poses any significant advantage over the paper-and-pencil version in terms of improving lexical and grammatical accuracy (Florez-Estrada, 1995; González-Bueno & Pérez; Ittzes, 1997; Reichelt, 2001).

Key Pal and Pen Pal Letter Exchanges

Written interpersonal communication with members of the target culture not only provides a way to practice communication skills but is also an effective means of acquiring new information and cultural perspectives. A number of studies describe e-mail exchanges as an interpersonal communication activity that enhances student autonomy (Bernhardt & Kamil, 1998; Fischer, 1998; Van Handle & Corl, 1998). Fischer suggests that small talk in letter writing helps to form personal relationships and a sense of community. Van Handle and Corl suggest that students should be informed that their primary focus is on communication rather than linguistic accuracy and that they should write as much and as freely as they can. According to Kern (1998), e-mail correspondence stresses speed and conciseness of expression, while paper-and-pen writing is an intensive, recursive process that fosters development and elaboration of ideas (p. 75; as cited in Yamada & Moeller, 2001, p. 32).

In an interdisciplinary unit on Chile that Haas and Reardon (1997) designed and taught to a seventh-grade Spanish class in New York, an integral component was the correspondence by e-mail with Chilean key pals. Over the course of the school year, three rounds of e-mail messages were sent back and forth to the students' peers in Chile. Students shared cultural differences and similarities, exchanged photos of themselves and their schools, and formed friendships. The U.S. teacher assisted students' writing of the letters by helping them to brainstorm information they could use in their replies and questions they could ask their Chilean key pals. The key pal exchange proved to be a pivotal part of the unit, bringing the Chilean world into the Spanish classroom.

At the post-secondary level, Jogan, Heredia, and Aguilera (2001) report similar findings in their study of dialogue journals and key pals in a U.S. class of advanced Spanish conversation and composition and a Chilean class of advanced ESL. In addition to their asynchronous e-mail exchanges, U.S. students wrote reflections about the cultural knowledge they had gained, pointing out a lessening of stereotypes and an increase in understanding.

Yamada and Moeller (2001) report on a pen pal letter exchange conducted between students enrolled in a second-year Japanese class at a liberal arts college in the Midwest and a group of college students in Japan. Handwritten letters were electronically scanned and posted to a Web site, which enabled immediate access to the letters. Letters were exchanged three times during the semester; the entire process for one round of letter writing took three to four weeks and included the following steps: writing the draft, peer editing, writing the second draft, feedback from the instructor, writing the final draft, submission of the letter for grading and correcting, completion of the final letter and posting on the Web, reading the response letter from the pen pal, and bringing the letter to class when help was needed in interpreting it. Results of the study indicated that students felt a sense of accomplishment by being able to engage in interpersonal communication with native Japanese speakers, they were motivated to write better as a result of peer editing, they became curious about the people of Japan and were prompted to make comparisons and contrasts, they improved their interpretive skills by reading pen pal letters, and they learned about age-appropriate cultural practices and perspectives. Similar results were reported by Hertel (2003), whose students reported greater understanding of the cultural practices of their Mexican key pals.

Synchronous Electronic Interaction

Modern technology has made it possible for learners to share ideas and receive responses immediately through real-life chats, or text-based instantaneous communication. Like face-to-face conversation, computer-mediated communication (CMC) takes place in real-time interaction in which language users negotiate meaning in written forms. A message is typed on a computer keyboard and is displayed immediately on the screen. During online negotiation, learners attend to input, feedback, and output similarly to the way they experience face-to-face spoken interaction (Lee, 2002). Research studies have revealed the positive effects of synchronous online discussion on teaching and learning as well as on fostering student interest and motivation for language learning (Beauvois, 1998; Lee, 1997, 1999; Pelletieri, 2000). The research indicates three benefits of CMC: (1) it offers opportunities for more equal participation than face-to-face interaction, (2) it allows the learner sufficient time to process input and monitor and edit output through a self-paced process, and (3) it increases language production and complexity (Lee, 2002, p. 17). There is also evidence to suggest that online chat leads students to scaffold each other's performance collaboratively and to pool each other's resources in the face of uncertainty concerning language choice (Shekary & Tahririan, 2006). Additionally, students who engage in online chat have been found to *notice* TL forms and subsequently make changes to their interlanguage (Shekary & Tahririan). Lee (2002) describes the use of an online chat room and task-based instruction to create a learning environment in which third-year college Spanish students used the TL to discuss, exchange, and debate issues related to real life. Students accessed online communication tools through *Blackboard* (an e-learning environment) and then completed task-based online activities, wrote online essays, and participated in online discussions on real-world topics of interest.[8] Lee proposes that "the combined use of online interaction and task-based instruction empowers students' communication skills by creating a lively environment in which they respond to real-time conversation about topics relevant to their interests" (2002, p. 21). Lee (1999) also found that students who participate in online communication acknowledge the necessity of being prepared for the chats and the value of working collaboratively with their peers. In Chapter 12, you will explore further the use of technology such as this to promote language acquisition.

In sum, strategies such as dialogue journals, pen pal/key pal letter exchanges, and synchronous electronic interaction are effective ways to engage students in written interpersonal communication while simultaneously addressing other goal areas.

Providing Feedback in Oral Interpersonal Contexts[9]

Language teachers have traditionally given students feedback in response to the correctness of language use. A "very good" awarded by the teacher undoubtedly means that the student used accurate grammar, vocabulary, and/or pronunciation, or used the designated linguistic pattern being practiced. See discussions of IRE in Chapter 3 and earlier in this chapter. Oral feedback given by the teacher in the classroom can generally be of two types: (1) error correction, and (2) response to the content of the student's message, much as in natural conversation. In classrooms that focus on negotiation of meaning (as defined in Chapter 1), the teacher provides feedback that helps learners figure out meaning, make themselves understood, and develop strategies for interacting effectively in groups (Platt & Brooks, 1994).

 In Chapter 3, what did the discussion of IRE/IRF reveal about the nature of teacher feedback?

Types of Teacher Feedback. In the earlier section of this chapter dealing with student discourse in pair/group activities, you learned about conversational repair in interactive activities. As you learned, learners often experience *trouble* in an exchange, *notice* the problem, work to *repair* the problem, and have either a positive or negative *outcome* in terms of communicating the message. Another concept that is often a part of the discussion on repair is *uptake*, which refers to how the learner incorporates feedback (i.e., from the teacher) into subsequent utterances (Lyster & Ranta, 1997). There are two types of student uptake: (1) uptake that results in repair of the error, and (2) uptake that results in an utterance that is still in need of repair (Lyster & Ranta). Students might demonstrate uptake by repeating the teacher's feedback that includes the correct form (provided by the teacher), incorporating the correct form into a longer utterance, self-correcting, or using peer correction.

In their hallmark (1997) study with French immersion students in grades four and five, Lyster and Ranta examined the effect of teacher correction strategies on student uptake. Their study identified six types of teacher feedback:

1. *Explicit correction:* The teacher corrects the student, indicating clearly that what the student said was incorrect: "You should say . . . ."
2. *Recast:* The teacher reformulates all or part of a student's utterance minus the error. Recasts are implicit and are not introduced by "You should say . . . ." They may focus on one word, grammatical modification, or translation of the student's use of the native language: S: "I go not to the movies last night." T: "Oh, you didn't go to the movies last night."
3. *Clarification request:* The teacher identifies a problem in either comprehensibility or accuracy or both: "Pardon me" or "What do you mean by X?"
4. *Metalinguistic feedback:* The teacher makes comments or asks questions about the form of the student's utterance without providing the correct form. These comments indicate that there is an error somewhere: "Can you find your error?" or "It isn't said in that way." This feedback includes some grammatical metalanguage that refers to the nature of the error: "It's masculine."
5. *Elicitation:* The teacher repeats part of the student's utterance and pauses to allow the student to complete the utterance at the place where the error occurred: S: "I had already went to the library." T: "I had already. . . ." The teacher can also use questions to elicit correct forms (e.g., "How do we say 'X' in French?"), or the teacher asks students to reformulate their utterance: "Try again, using the conditional."
6. *Repetition:* The teacher repeats the student's erroneous utterance, usually changing the intonation to highlight the error: S: ". . . many money." T: ". . . many money?" (1997, pp. 46–48).

The teachers in Lyster and Ranta's (1997) study used recasts more than any other strategy for correcting errors (55% of the time), with the other strategies occurring in the following order of decreasing frequency: elicitation (14%), clarification request (11%), metalinguistic feedback (8%), explicit correction (7%), and repetition (5%). Interestingly, recast was the strategy that proved *least likely* to lead to uptake: Recast strategies led students to make attempts at repairing their utterances only 31% of the time. Explicit correction led to uptake only 50% of the time. Clarification requests, metalinguistic feedback, and repetition were effective strategies for eliciting uptake from students (88%, 86%, and 78%, respectively). The most effective strategy with respect to uptake was elicitation. In all cases, elicitation led to uptake. Lyster and Ranta's study illustrated that elicitation may be a more effective strategy because it is a way for the teacher to signal to the student that there is a problem with form and consequently with meaning.

Recasts. The Lyster and Ranta (1997) study sparked a number of subsequent investigations into teacher feedback, particularly in the area of recasts, since this strategy appears to be favored by most language teachers, including those who teach content such as literature (Zyzik & Polio, 2008). In fact, according to Ellis and Sheen (2006), there have been more published articles in SLA journals on the topic of recasts than on any other single topic since 2001. At the writing of this fourth edition of *Teacher's Handbook*, there continues to be debate and lack of consensus in the field regarding the effectiveness of using recasts in order to lead to effective learner uptake. This is due in part to the fact that the studies up to this point have been conducted with different learner populations, in different settings (classrooms vs. one-on-one experimental settings), have been defined in a variety of ways, and have been implemented by teachers for various instructional purposes. Since learners in these studies were of various ages and at various levels of L2 development, it is difficult to generalize the findings and what implications they have for foreign language classrooms. Additionally, some of the studies were not conducted in classrooms but rather were conducted in a tutorial setting. Since a comprehensive review of the research on recasts is beyond the scope of *Teacher's Handbook,* the reader is encouraged to consult Ellis and Sheen for a detailed discussion of the studies on recasts completed in recent years. However, what should foreign language teachers know about the use of recasts in their classrooms? The chart in Figure 8.13 illustrates six key findings of current recast research together with the implications for using recasts in foreign language classrooms. Undoubtedly these findings and suggestions are subject to change as our understanding of recasts is refined through further research.

Other Feedback for Focusing on Content of the Message.   In addition to recasts, other feedback strategies have a role to play in the classroom. Some strategies, such as clarification requests, focus on the message while signaling to the student that there is a problem, most likely due to a grammatical or vocabulary error. The following is an example of an exchange between a Spanish teacher and a student where a clarification request is made by the teacher:

Estoy cansada hoy, clase. Trabajé hasta muy tarde anoche. ¿Qué hicieron Uds. anoche? Sí, Susana, ¿qué hiciste tú? [I'm very tired today, class. I worked until very late last night. What did all of you do last night? Yes, Susana, what did you do?]

Pues, tú no hiciste nada. [Well, you didn't do anything.]

¿Quién? ¿Yo? Sí, yo hice mucho anoche. [Who? Me? Yes, I did a lot last night.]

¡Oh! Yo no hice nada. [Oh! I didn't do anything.]

In this exchange, the focus on form happened in a meaningful context, as it resulted from a misunderstanding. It was not arbitrary or dependent on the teacher's hidden grammatical agenda. When errors are treated in this way, students must think about what went wrong in communication while they are developing strategies for negotiating meaning.

Another type of teacher feedback strategy that has been found to be effective in student uptake is *corrective confirmation checks,* in which the teacher provides learners with an appropriate L2 alternative in the form of a question, such as *"Did you mean, 'he goes?'"* (O'Relly, Flaitz, & Kromrey, 2001). These types of confirmation checks call attention to a linguistic problem in an unambiguous way. There are data to suggest that the use of feedback strategies such as clarification requests and corrective confirmation checks are most effective in reinforcing linguistic features that have already been introduced to and internalized by learners (O'Relly, Flaitz, & Kromrey), particularly since they have the knowledge necessary to make repairs.

Liebscher and Dailey-O'Cain (2003) compared conversational repair strategies in exchanges between teacher and advanced learners of German to repair strategies used in discourse outside the classroom. Their data revealed that repair initiation in classroom interaction differs from repair initiation in discourse outside the classroom. In the face of trouble in speaking, hearing, or understanding in a conversation, native speakers in naturally occurring discourse tend to use other-initiated strategies that are "less specific" at first (e.g., *Pardon?, Huh?, Hmm?*) (Schegloff, Jefferson, & Sacks, 1977). If these strategies are unsuccessful, they move on to "more specific" strategies as necessary, such as individual question words (e.g., *Who?, Where?, When?*), then to partial repeats of the trouble source, to partial repeats plus question words, to the most specific devices consisting of

FIGURE 8.13 Research on Recasts: Implications for FL Teaching

FINDINGS OF STUDIES ON RECASTS	IMPLICATIONS FOR USING RECASTS IN FL TEACHING
Given the various functions that recasts can serve, learners are likely to have difficulty deciding how to respond to them (Lyster, 1998). For example, since instructors often repeat even learners' *correct* utterances, learners are not sure whether teachers are echoing what they have said in order to be supportive or whether they are providing them with correction (Han, 2002).	Teachers can make recasts less ambiguous—i.e., more *salient* or noticeable—by focusing them on a single linguistic feature and signaling correction by the use of emphatic stress on the targeted form (Ellis & Sheen, 2006). Lightbown and Spada suggest a method of signaling to the student, through a tone of voice, gesture, or facial expression, which says to the student, "I think I understand what you are saying and I'm telling you how you can say it better" (2006, p. 193).
Learners in content-based classes (e.g., immersion) are likely to perceive recasts as a focus on message content rather than a focus on language (Sheen, 2004). In these settings, teachers often do not allow time for students to uptake their recasts but rather they continue with topic development.	Teachers in content-based classes should allow more time for learners to demonstrate uptake of recasts and should integrate focus on form into the curriculum or course.
Learners with well-developed metalinguistic knowledge (such as adults who have had form-focused instruction) are more likely to perceive recasts as explicit correction than are learners with less-developed metalinguistic knowledge (such as elementary school immersion students) (Sheen, 2004). Recasts may allow students with higher proficiency to notice the corrected linguistic forms better than students with lower proficiency, for whom recasts tend to go unnoticed (Lin & Hedgcock, 1996; Mackey & Philp, 1998).	Teachers might reserve the use of recasts for older students who have more metalinguistic knowledge and a higher proficiency level.
If the recasts target linguistic features that a learner is developmentally ready to acquire, those recasts may be effective in leading to uptake. If the recasts target features that are far beyond the learners' current stage of development, they are likely to be unsuccessful (Mackey & Philp, 1998). In addition, the timing of the recast may contribute to its salience—i.e., ability to be noticed; if recasts occur at *teachable moments*, when the learner is temporarily switching to a hypothesis-testing mode when speaking, they will have the best chance of being noticed and processed (Han & Kim, 2008).	Teachers should take care to provide recasts for linguistic forms that learners have the ability to notice and correct. They should also time the use of recasts so that they occur at teachable moments when the learner is entering a hypothesis-testing mode.
Recasts have been found to lead to uptake with repair if they are short (requiring one or two changes), declarative (as opposed to interrogative with rising intonation), focused on pronunciation and vocabulary rather than on grammar, and involve substitution of an item in the learner utterance (Philp, 2003; Sheen, 2006).	When using recasts, teachers should remember to keep them short, declarative, focused primarily on pronunciation or vocabulary, and involving substitution of an item in the learner utterance.
Recasts do not work as well as feedback that elicits output from learners or that offers metalinguistic information (Lyster, 2004; Lyster & Ranta, 1997).	Elicitation and clarification requests may be more effective overall because they elicit pushed output from learners, which provides evidence of uptake. Another option is to provide recasts along with negotiation of meaning (Han & Kim, 2008).

Source: Shrum & Glisan, 2010, original material.

"you mean" plus a possible understanding of the prior turn (Liebscher & Dailey-O'Cain, pp. 376–377). The most specific devices to which they refer are the corrective confirmation checks described in the previous paragraph.

In the Liebscher and Dailey-O'Cain (2003) study, the teacher often used "less specific" repair initiations with students (i.e., those found in naturally occurring discourse). These repair initiations enabled students to effectively modify their output and thus make successful conversational repairs. This finding corroborates that of the Lyster and Ranta (1997) study that identified clarification requests to be an effective strategy for eliciting uptake from students. On the other hand, students in this study showed a marked preference for using more specific repair initiation techniques, i.e., those not found as prevalent in natural discourse, when they didn't understand what the teacher was saying, in an effort to avoid behaving in what might seem to be a confrontational manner, outside of the norms for student-to-teacher interaction. In initiating repairs themselves, students usually asked for specific vocabulary items, showing the teacher that they were trying to understand the vocabulary used and that they were following classroom discourse—thus enacting their designated roles as typical learners.

Liebscher and Dailey-O'Cain (2003) interpret the findings of their study to mean that (1) what keeps students from using certain types of repairs is an understanding of their roles in the classroom rather than an insufficient knowledge of L2; (2) the teaching of naturally occurring repair strategies must occur in classroom environments in which students are free to use such strategies and thus step out of their traditional learner roles; (3) students should be encouraged to use less-specific repair initiations, especially in interactions with the teacher, because these are most effective in leading to modified output by the teacher and modified input for students; and (4) teachers should use repair strategies such as less-specific repairs in order to facilitate modified output by students.

In highly communicative or group activities, the teacher might do best to make mental notes of patterns of errors and use them as the focus for subsequent language activities. Kramsch (1987) suggests extensive use of natural feedback (i.e., IRF) rather than overpraising everything students say. Statements such as "Yes, that's interesting," "I can certainly understand that!" "That's incredible!" and "Hmm, that's right" show students that teachers are listening to what they're saying, and this strategy encourages students to focus more on meaning. When conversing with the class as a follow-up to group interaction, Kramsch also proposes that teachers give students explicit credit for their contributions by quoting them ("As X just said, . . ."). In this way, teachers are not taking credit for what students have said by using it to suggest their own ideas.

At more advanced levels of study, where one of the goals is to refine language use, students can be given increasingly greater responsibility for their accuracy. The following are a few ideas that merit further research:

- *Peer editing of oral language samples*: The teacher records role-plays or situations that students enact in the classroom, after which pairs of students listen to the tapes in order to correct linguistic errors and identify ways to improve the content.
- *Teacher feedback*: At certain designated times throughout the year or semester, perhaps following speaking exams, the teacher gives helpful feedback to each student concerning progress made in speaking. This feedback can include patterns of errors that merit attention, with specific suggestions on how to improve accuracy.
- *Error tracking system*: As a class, students listen to tapes of themselves and, with the teacher's help, compile a listing of the kinds of errors they hear. They focus on eliminating certain errors over a specified period of time and agree on a system to check and reward their efforts.

Clearly, a great deal of research is still needed in order to understand more fully the role of feedback in interpersonal communication contexts. The research presented here points to the following implications regarding error correction and feedback in the classroom:

1. Students benefit most when the feedback they receive focuses on comprehensibility of the message itself, not just on accuracy of form.
2. The feedback strategies that lead to negotiation of form most effectively appear to be elicitation, clarification requests, metalinguistic feedback, and repetition.
3. Learners may not recognize teacher response as corrective in nature unless the teacher has a strategy for signaling this to the learner.
4. Recasts may have a place in the classroom but only if the teacher uses them in a salient manner and if learners are cognitively and linguistically ready to notice their corrective value.
5. Student-generated repairs may help learners to access TL forms and revise hypotheses about the TL.
6. The classroom environment should be one in which learners are encouraged to step out of their traditional learner roles when engaging in conversational repair.
7. Teachers should use less-specific repair initiations with students and provide opportunities for students to use them as a strategy for facilitating uptake or modified input.
8. In order to focus on fluency and comprehensibility of speech, it is best to avoid trying to coerce correction of errors in speaking and to allow the interaction to develop as it would in natural discourse.
9. Teacher feedback should include comments that help the student to focus on negotiation of meaning.
10. Students should be made increasingly more responsible for their language accuracy so that their oral proficiency can improve.

This chapter presented many ideas for developing oral and written interpersonal communication. Continue to keep in mind that the approach of *Teacher's Handbook* is that all three modes of communication should be integrated closely, as described in the Model presented in Chapter 6.

TEACH AND REFLECT ·

NCATE____

EPISODE ONE
Creating Information-Gap Activities for Various Levels of Instruction

ACTFL/NCATE 3.a. Understanding Language Acquisition and Creating a Supportive Classroom; 3.b. Developing Instructional Practices That Reflect Language Outcomes and Learner Diversity; 4.b. Integrating Standards in Instruction; 4.c. Selecting and Designing Instructional Materials

TESOL/NCATE 3.a. Planning for Standards-Based ESL and Content Instruction; and 3.b. Managing and Implementing Standards-Based ESL and Content Instruction

Create the following information-gap activities in the language you teach, according to the following instructions:

1. Elementary-school level: Design an information-gap activity that would be appropriate for elementary school children. You might create this for the content-based lesson you

designed in the Teach and Reflect section of Chapter 4, or you could create it for practice within another context. Decide what the purpose of the activity is and how it relates to your unit objectives. Include specific directions for students and your procedure for grouping students, i.e., what you will do if you don't have an even number. Your instructor may ask you to present your activity to the class.

2. Secondary or post-secondary level: Create an information-gap activity to promote interpersonal speaking among your students. Decide what the purpose of the activity is and how it relates to your thematic unit objectives. What functions/contexts will students practice? What grammar and vocabulary are integrated? Include specific directions for students and your procedure for grouping students. Your instructor may ask you to present your activity to the class.

EPISODE TWO
Integrating Speaking Tasks with Oral or Printed Texts

ACTFL/NCATE 3.a. Understanding Language Acquisition and Creating a Supportive Classroom; 3.b. Developing Instructional Practices That Reflect Language Outcomes and Learner Diversity; 4.b. Integrating Standards in Instruction; 4.c. Selecting and Designing Instructional Materials

TESOL/NCATE 3.a. Planning for Standards-Based ESL and Content Instruction; and 3.b. Managing and Implementing Standards-Based ESL and Content Instruction

For this activity, work from the authentic reading or taped segment that you prepared in the Teach and Reflect section of Chapter 6, or work with a literary reading, such as a short story. Design a task sequence in which you engage students in interpersonal speaking as a follow-up to exploration of the oral or written text. You might choose from one of the following options:

1. an interactive task sequence, such as a jigsaw activity, paired interview, or role-play
2. an imaginative task sequence, such as changing the text or reenacting a part of the text
3. an instructional conversation that deals with some idea or issue from the text

Identify the objective of the task sequence. Include instructions to the students and your procedure for grouping students, if applicable. Your instructor may ask you to present a part or all of your task sequence to the class.

EPISODE THREE
Integrating Advanced-Level Discourse at the Post-Secondary Level

ACTFL/NCATE 3.a. Understanding Language Acquisition and Creating a Supportive Classroom; 3.b. Developing Instructional Practices That Reflect Language Outcomes and Learner Diversity; 4.a. Understanding and Integrating Standards in Planning; 4.b. Integrating Standards in Instruction; 4.c. Selecting and Designing Instructional Materials

TESOL/NCATE 3.a. Planning for Standards-Based ESL and Content Instruction; and 3.b. Managing and Implementing Standards-Based ESL and Content Instruction

If you are preparing to teach or are already teaching at the post-secondary level, this task is designed to engage you in incorporating advanced-level discourse into your teaching. Select an authentic oral, printed, or video text for a course that you are teaching on culture, literature, conversation, or a content-based topic, in which students are working on using advanced-level functions. Develop three ideas for how you will build advanced-level discourse into your exploration of the content of the text. Your instructor may ask you to use the Interactive Model for Integrating the Three Modes of Communication that you learned about in Chapter 6 to develop a lesson plan for guiding students through the text.

DISCUSS AND REFLECT ·

See the *Teacher's Handbook* Web site for additional case studies:
Case Study Two: Friday is Culture Day
www.cengagebrain.com Case Study Three: Interpersonal Speaking? I Already Do That!

NCATE_____

CASE STUDY ONE
"Survivor" Game: Keeping Students in the Target Language[10]

ACTFL/NCATE 3.a. Understanding Language Acquisition and Creating a Supportive Class-room; 3.b. Developing Instructional Practices That Reflect Language Outcomes and Learner Diversity; 4.a. Understanding and Integrating Standards in Planning; 4.b. Integrating Standards in Instruction

TESOL/NCATE 2.a. Understand and Apply Knowledge about Cultural Values and Beliefs in the Context of Teaching and Learning; 3.a. Planning for Standards-Based ESL and Content Instruction; and 3.b. Managing and Implementing Standards-Based ESL and Content Instruction

Tim and Karen Richardson are both Spanish teachers in a suburban high school where Karen is also chairperson of the World Languages Department. Karen has been teaching Spanish for some 15 years, while Tim has just completed his sixth year of teaching in the district. They are known for their enthusiasm and up-to-date approach to the teaching of Spanish, and they enjoy a positive rapport with their students. The Richardsons travel abroad regularly and usually take students on yearly summer trips to Spanish-speaking countries. They keep abreast of current SLA research, work with student teachers from a local university on a regular basis, and have begun to do presentations at professional conferences to share their ideas for FL teaching.

Over the years, the Richardsons have developed an approach to teaching in which they use Spanish close to 100% of the time in the classroom, and, in recent years, they designed an effective strategy for encouraging their students to speak only the TL—the "Survivor" game. Visitors to their classrooms, including teachers from other districts, student teachers, and university supervisors, are extremely impressed when they witness that their students indeed speak only in Spanish, even when engaging in "chit-chat" with one another before class begins. The Richardsons seem to have simulated an immersion atmosphere in their classes, and students appear to be motivated to speak in Spanish.

Students leaving the program have often demonstrated oral proficiency at the Intermediate-High/Advanced-Low levels. Further, the number of students enrolling in upper-level courses has increased significantly, and 75% of students taking the Advanced Placement Exam now score a 4 or 5 compared to a score of 2 or 3 prior to participating in Survivor. Finally, new classes and language events have been added. These impressive results have prompted their colleagues in other languages to initiate the Survivor game, and although first created for upper levels of Spanish, the game has been introduced in beginning levels as well. Their colleagues from the district and the local university have encouraged them to share their game with other teachers since the results have been so impressive. Below is a description of the Survivor game as explained by the Richardsons; a complete explanation of rules and procedures is available on the *Teacher's Handbook* Web site in Appendix 8.10.

www.cengagebrain.com

> The game "Survivor" has been developed for use in all levels of language to get students and teachers to exclusively use L2 every day for the entire class. The game is **always** being played while lessons are presented and normal class activities are completed. The "game" is better explained as a classroom procedure based on total simulated

immersion. The goal is to get students to use L2 exclusively as soon as possible and help students to think in L2 and use L2 exclusively to learn new material. The game is designed to simulate the immersion situation a student would encounter if he/she were suddenly introduced into an L2 culture with no one around who spoke L1.

The procedure is presented to the students as a "game," with prizes to be won or lost. If students can "survive" by not being eliminated from the game, they will have success in receiving prizes and in learning L2. During the first day of class, students are given the rules and procedures for Survivor. What follows is a brief summary of the rules (which are the only classroom rules).

Students may not speak English under any circumstance without first asking permission in L2 from the teacher. If given permission, they may ask for only one word at a time. Students must participate every day in individual, pair, small group, and whole class activities. If they speak English, they are first given a warning or a series of warnings and then they are eliminated or "thrown off the island." While they are still in the game, they may eliminate two questions from exams, participate in tribal games, be eligible to receive tribal points, and redeem the points for prizes. They may also be considered for an upgrade at the end of nine weeks. Students who are eliminated receive none of the above perks. If they speak English again after being eliminated, they will receive a percentage point off their grade for each instance. They may also be required to complete extra assignments. Once students are eliminated, they remain eliminated until the end of the game (nine weeks, the entire course or at the teacher's discretion). After level I, since students are more comfortable with not using English, fewer and fewer students are eliminated as the levels progress. (On rare occasions, the teacher may permit a discussion in English and then indicate when L2 is again obligatory.)

Students are asked to sign a contract stating that the game and the consequences of not playing have been explained. An explanation letter is sent home to parents that answers frequently asked questions. After level I, most students and parents are aware of the simulated immersion classroom methodology, and there are fewer questions and concerns.

The teacher's responsibility is to communicate entirely in the TL and negotiate meaning with the students to ensure comprehension. To do this, teachers use visuals, symbols, pictures, gestures, facial expressions, PowerPoint presentations, photographs, maps, flashcards, chalkboard drawings, and acting out words. The game "Survivor" ensures that all students are always trying to negotiate meaning in the TL. Translation is avoided and not considered helpful in retaining vocabulary in the long term.

The teachers begin in level I with a period of time for students to prepare to play the game. Students are given "tools" they are encouraged to use while playing the game to support their negotiation of meaning. The tools consist of an ongoing reference list of common and useful expressions, notes, flashcards, visual dictionaries, and textbooks. The expressions are enlarged to poster size and placed on the walls throughout the classroom. The expressions are modified and added to as necessary. Eventually, teachers begin to eliminate some of the more basic tools as students become more confident and no longer need them. Students practice pronouncing and manipulating the common expressions and practice playing the game "Survivor" for several classes until they become comfortable with not using English. Students who would have been eliminated are identified, and the class then discusses different things the student could have said to avoid elimination.

By participating in this game and underlying approach to L2 acquisition, students become very comfortable using only L2 and have great success in their language experience.

Ask yourself these questions:

1. How would you describe the approach of the Richardsons to teaching interpersonal speaking?
2. What role do you think the following elements play in their classrooms?:

   - turns-at-talk
   - routines and gambits
   - gestures

3. In the description of the Survivor game, the Richardsons indicate that their students experience a period of time in which they prepare to begin the game. What type of strategy training might the Richardsons offer students as part of this preparation? See earlier discussion in this chapter.
4. How might the Survivor game help learners to develop a high willingness to communicate? Refer to Figure 8.6.
5. Why do you think the Survivor game has led to such an improvement in student performance in Spanish?

To prepare for class discussion:

1. In order to implement Survivor, what does a teacher need to know about SLA and motivation of students? You might want to review some of the SLA theories from Chapter 1 and the information about interpersonal speaking presented earlier in this chapter.
2. As a teacher preparing to implement the Survivor game for the first time, what challenges might you face ,.e.g., from students, parents, fellow teachers?

TECHNO FOCUS: Making a Case for the Pedagogical Use of Cell Phones: Go to the following link for the Spring 2008 issue of the CLEAR Newsletter and read the article, "The Case for Banned Technology in the Language Classroom," paying particular attention to the discussion of using cell phones as a teaching tool (pp. 3, 6): http://clear.msu.edu/clear/newsletter/files/spring2008.pdf. Using the ideas presented in this article, describe three ways that the Richardsons might incorporate cell phone usage into their Spanish classes, provided that the school administration permits the use of cell phones in the school and that students are willing to share their phone numbers with their classmates. What pedagogical advantages does the use of cell phones offer the FL classroom? How might this strategy be used to address the issues discussed earlier in the chapter related to willingness to communicate (WTC)?

REFERENCES

Adair-Hauck, B., & Pierce, M. (1998). Investigating the simulated oral proficiency interview (SOPI) as an assessment tool for second language oral proficiency. *Pennsylvania Language Forum, LXX,* 6–25.

Allen, L. (2000). Nonverbal accommodations in foreign language teacher talk. *Applied Language Learning, 11,* 155–176.

Alley, D. C. (2005). A study of Spanish II high school students' discourse during group work. *Foreign Language Annals, 38,* 250–258.

American Council on the Teaching of Foreign Languages (ACTFL). (1999). *ACTFL Proficiency Guidelines—Speaking.* Yonkers, NY: Author.

American Council on the Teaching of Foreign Languages (ACTFL). (2001). *ACTFL Proficiency Guidelines—Writing.* Yonkers, NY: Author.

Annenberg/CPB, & American Council on the Teaching of Foreign Languages (ACTFL). (2003). *Teaching Foreign Languages K–12: A library of classroom practices.* Boston: WGBH Boston and ACTFL.

Baker, S. C., & MacIntyre, P. D. (2000). The role of gender and immersion in communication and second language orientation. *Language Learning, 50,* 311–341.

Bassano, S., & Christison, M. A. (1987). Developing successful conversation groups. In M. H. Long & J. C. Richards (Eds.), *Methodology in TESOL: A book of readings* (pp. 201–207). New York: Newbury House/Harper.

Beauvois, M. H. (1998). Write to speak: The effects of electronic communication on the oral achievement of fourth-semester French students. In J. A. Muyskens (Ed.), *New ways of learning and teaching: Focus on technology and foreign language education* (pp. 93–116). Boston: Heinle & Heinle.

Bernhardt, E., & Kamil, M. (1998). Enhancing foreign culture learning through electronic discussion. In J. A. Muyskens (Ed.), *New ways of learning and teaching: Focus on technology and foreign language education* (pp. 39–55). Boston: Heinle & Heinle.

Borich, J. M. B. (2001). Learning through dialogue journal writing: A cultural thematic unit. *Learning Languages, 6,* 4–19.

Bragger, J. (1985). The development of oral proficiency. In A. Omaggio (Ed.), *Proficiency, curriculum, articulation: The ties that bind* (pp. 41–75). Northeast Conference Reports. Middlebury, VT: Northeast Conference on the Teaching of Foreign Languages.

Brecht, R. D., Davidson, D., & Ginsberg, R. B. (1993). *Predictors of foreign language gain during study abroad.* Washington, DC: National Foreign Language Center.

Breiner-Sanders, K. E. (1991). Higher-level language abilities: The skills connection. In J. K. Phillips (Ed.), *Building bridges and making connections* (pp. 57–88). Northeast Conference Reports. Middlebury, VT: Northeast Conference on the Teaching of Foreign Languages.

Brooks, F. B. (1990). Foreign language learning: A social interaction perspective. In B. VanPatten & J. F. Lee (Eds.), *Second language acquisition—Foreign language learning* (pp. 153–169). Clevedon, UK: Multilingual Matters.

Brooks, F. B. (1992). Can we talk? *Foreign Language Annals, 25,* 59–71.

Brooks, F. B., Donato, R., & McGlone, V. (1997). When are they going to say "it" right? Understanding learner talk during pair-work activity. *Foreign Language Annals, 30,* 524–541.

Brown, P., & Levinson, S. C. (1987). *Politeness: Universals in language usage.* Cambridge, UK: Cambridge University Press.

Buckwalter, P. (2001). Repair sequences in Spanish L2 dyadic discourse: A descriptive study. *The Modern Language Journal, 85,* 380–397.

Canale, M. (1982). *Evaluating the coherence of student writing in L1 and L2.* Paper presented at annual Teachers of English to Speakers of Other Languages (TESOL) convention. Honolulu, HI.

Cazden, C. B. (1992). Performing expository texts in the foreign language classroom. In C. Kramsch & S. McConnell-Ginet (Eds.), *Text and context: Cross disciplinary perspectives on language study* (pp. 67–78). Lexington, MA: Heath.

Curtain, H., & Dahlberg, C. A. (2010). *Languages and children—Making the match* (4th ed.). Boston: Pearson Allyn & Bacon.

DeKeyser, R. M. (1991). Foreign language development during a semester abroad. In B. F. Freed (Ed.), *Foreign language acquisition research and the classroom* (pp. 104–119). Lexington, MA: D.C. Heath.

DiPietro, R. J. (1987). *Strategic interaction: Learning languages through scenarios.* New York: Cambridge University Press.

Donato, R. (2000). Sociocultural contributions to understanding the foreign and second language classrooms. In J. Lantolf (Ed.), *Sociocultural theory and second language learning* (pp. 29–52). Oxford, UK: Oxford University Press.

Donato, R., Antonek, J. L., & Tucker, G. R. (1996). Documenting a Japanese FLES program: Ambiance and achievement. *Language Learning, 46,* 497–528.

Donato, R., & Brooks, F. B. (1994). *Looking across collaborative tasks: Capturing L2 discourse development.* Paper presented at annual meeting of the American Association for Applied Linguistics. Baltimore, MD.

Donato, R., & Brooks, F. B. (2004). Literary discussions and advanced speaking functions: Researching the (dis) connection. *Foreign Language Annals, 37,* 183–199.

Dörnyei, Z. (1995). On the teachability of communication strategies. *TESOL Quarterly, 29,* 55–85.

Dörnyei, Z. (2005). *The psychology of the language learner: Individual differences in second language acquisition*. London: Erlbaum.

Doughty, C., & Pica, T. (1986). Information gap tasks: Do they facilitate acquisition? *TESOL Quarterly, 20,* 315–326.

Dreke, M., & Lind, W. (2000). *Wechselspiel*. New York: Langenscheidt.

Ellis, R. (1994). *The study of second language acquisition*. Oxford, UK: Oxford University Press.

Ellis, R., & Sheen, Y. (2006). Reexamining the role of recasts in second language acquisition. *Studies in Second Language Acquisition, 28,* 575–600.

Fall, T., Adair-Hauck, B., & Glisan, E. W. (2007). Assessing students' oral proficiency: A case for online testing. *Foreign Language Annals, 40,* 377–406.

Fischer, G. (1998). Toward the creation of virtual classrooms: Electronic mail and cross-cultural understanding. In A. Moeller (Ed.), *Celebrating diversity in the language classroom*. Lincolnwood, IL: National Textbook Company.

Florez-Estrada, N. (1995). *Some effects of native-nonnative communication via computer e-mail interaction on the development of foreign language proficiency*. Unpublished doctoral dissertation, University of Pittsburgh, PA.

Freed, B., & Bauer, B. W. (1989*). Contextos: Spanish for communication*. New York: Newbury House.

Galloway, V. (1992). Toward a cultural reading of authentic texts. In H. Byrnes (Ed.), *Languages for a multicultural world in transition, Northeast Conference Reports* (pp. 87–121). Lincolnwood, IL: NTC/Contemporary Publishing Group.

Gass, S., & Selinker, L. (1994). *Second language acquisition*. Hillsdale, NJ: Lawrence Erlbaum.

Glisan, E. W., & Donato, R. (2004). It's not just a matter of "time:" A response to Rifkin. *Foreign Language Annals, 37,* 465–471.

Glisan, E. W., & Foltz, D. A. (1998). Assessing students' oral proficiency in an outcome-based curriculum: Student performance and teacher intuitions. *The Modern Language Journal, 82,* 1–18.

Goldenberg, C. (1991). *Instructional conversations and their classroom implication*. Washington, DC: The National Center for Research on Cultural Diversity and Second Language Learning. (ERIC Document Reproduction Service No. 341–253).

González-Bueno, M. (1998). The effect of electronic mail on Spanish L2 discourse. *Language Learning and Technology, 1*(2), 55–70. Retrieved March 17, 2004, from http://www.polyglot.cal.msu/llt/num1vol2/article3.

González-Bueno, M., & Pérez, L. C. (2000). Electronic mail in foreign language writing: A study of grammatical and lexical accuracy, and quantity of language. *Foreign Language Annals, 33,* 189–198.

Gullberg, M. (1998). *Gesture as a communication strategy in second language discourse*. Lund: Lund University Press.

Haas, M., & Reardon, M. (1997). Communities of learners: From New York to Chile. In J. K. Phillips (Ed.), *Collaborations: Meeting new goals, new realities, Northeast Conference Reports* (pp. 213–241). Lincolnwood, IL: NTC/Contemporary Publishing Group.

Hadley, A. O. (2001). *Teaching language in context* (3rd ed.). Boston: Heinle & Heinle.

Hall, J. K. (1999). The communication standards. In J. K. Phillips & R. M. Terry (Eds.), *Foreign language standards: Linking research, theories, and practices* (pp. 15–56). ACTFL Foreign Language Education Series. Lincolnwood, IL: NTC/Contemporary Publishing Group.

Hall, N., & Robinson, A. (Eds.). (1994). *Keeping in touch: Using interactive writing with young children*. ERIC Database: ERIC Document Reproduction Service No. ED 367–996.

Han, Z. (2002). A study of the impact of recasts on tense consistency in L2 output. *TESOL Quarterly, 36,* 543–572.

Han, Z.-H., & Kim, J. H. (2008). Corrective recasts: What teachers might want to know. *Language Learning Journal, 36,* 35–44.

Hertel, T. J. (2003). Using an e-mail exchange to promote cultural learning. *Foreign Language Annals, 36,* 386–396.

Herzog, M. (2003). Impact of the proficiency scale and the oral proficiency interview on the foreign language program at the Defense Language Institute Foreign Language Center. *Foreign Language Annals, 36,* 566–571.

Huebner, T., & Jensen, A. (1992). A study of foreign language proficiency-based testing in secondary schools. *Foreign Language Annals, 25,* 105–115.

Ittzes, Z. (1997). *Written conversation: Investigating communicative foreign language use in written form in computer conference writing and group journals*. Unpublished doctoral dissertation, University of Arizona, Tucson, AZ.

Jansma, K., & Kassen, M. A. (2004). *Motifs*. Boston: Heinle.

Jensen, J. M. (1993). What do we know about the writing of elementary school children? *Language Arts, 70,* 290–294.

Jogan, M. K., Heredia, A. H., & Aguilera, G. M. (2001). Cross-cultural e-mail: Providing cultural input for the advanced foreign language student. *Foreign Language Annals, 34,* 341–346.

Johnson, D. D., & Johnson, R. T. (1987). *Learning together and alone: Cooperation, competition, and individualization*. Englewood Cliffs, NJ: Prentice Hall.

Johnson, D. D., Johnson, R. T., & Holubec, E. J. (1988). *Cooperation in the classroom*. Edina, MN: Interaction Book Company.

Johnson, K. (1979). Communicative approaches and communicative processes. In C. J. Brumfit & K. Johnson (Eds.), *The communicative approach to language teaching* (pp. 192–205). Oxford, UK: Oxford University Press.

Kagan, S. (1989). *Cooperative learning: Resources for teachers*. San Juan Capistrano, CA: Resources for Teachers.

Keller, E. (1981). Gambits: Conversational strategy signals. In F. Coulmas (Ed), *Conversational routine*. The Hague: Mouton.

Kern, R. (1998). Technology, social interaction, and foreign language literacy. In J. A. Muyskens (Ed.), *New ways of learning and teaching: Focus on technology and foreign language education* (pp. 57–92). Boston: Heinle & Heinle.

Kinginger, C. (1990). *Task variation and classroom learner discourse*. Unpublished doctoral dissertation, University of Illinois, Urbana-Champaign, IL.

Kohn, A. (1987, October). It's hard to get left out of a pair: Profile: David & Roger Johnson. *Psychology Today*, 53–57.

Kramsch, C. (1987). Interactive discourse in small and large groups. In W. Rivers (Ed.), *Interactive language teaching* (pp. 17–30). Cambridge, UK: Cambridge University Press.

Krashen, S. (1982). *Principles and practice in second language acquisition*. New York: Pergamon Press.

Lee, J. (1995). Using task-based instruction to restructure class discussions. *Foreign Language Annals, 28,* 437–446.

Lee, L. (1997). Using Internet tools as an enhancement of L2 cultural teaching and learning. *Foreign Language Annals, 30,* 410–427.

Lee, L. (1999). Student perspectives on the internet: The promise and process of online newspapers and chats. In M. A. Kassen (Ed.), *Language learners of tomorrow: Process and promise* (pp. 124–149). Lincolnwood, IL: National Textbook Company.

Lee, L. (2002). Enhancing learners' communication skills through synchronous electronic interaction and task-based instruction. *Foreign Language Annals, 35,* 16–24.

Lennon, P. (1990). Investigating fluency in EFL: A quantitative approach. *Language Learning, 40,* 387–417.

Liebscher, G., & Dailey-O'Cain, J. (2003). Conversational repair as a role-defining mechanism in classroom interaction. *The Modern Language Journal, 87,* 375–390.

Lightbown, P. M., & Spada, N. (2006). *How languages are learned*. Oxford, UK: Oxford University Press.

Lin, Y.-H., & Hedgcock, J. (1996). Negative feedback incorporation among high-proficiency and low-proficiency Chinese-speaking learners of Spanish. *Language Learning, 46,* 567–611.

Liskin-Gasparro, J. E. (1987). If you can't use a language, you don't know a language. *Middlebury Magazine,* (Winter): 26–27.

Liskin-Gasparro, J. E. (1996). Circumlocution, communication strategies, and the ACTFL proficiency guidelines: An analysis of student discourse. *Foreign Language Annals, 29,* 317–330.

Liskin-Gasparro, J. E. (2003). The ACTFL Proficiency Guidelines and the Oral Proficiency Interview: A brief history and analysis of their survival. *Foreign Language Annals, 36,* 483–490.

Long, M. H. (1983). Native speaker/non-native speaker conversation in the second language classroom. In M. A. Clarke & J. Handscomb (Eds.), *On TESOL '82: Pacific perspectives on language learning and teaching* (pp. 207–205). Washington, DC: TESOL.

Lyster, R. (1998). Recasts, repetition, and ambiguity in L2 classroom discourse. *Studies in Second Language Acquisition, 20,* 51–81.

Lyster, R. (2004). Differential effects of prompts and recasts in form-focused instruction. *Studies in Second Language Acquisition, 26,* 399–432.

Lyster, R., & Ranta, L. (1997). Corrective feedback and learner uptake. *Studies in Second Language Acquisition, 19,* 37–61.

MacDonald, J. R., Clément, R., & MacIntyre, P. D. (2003). *Willingness to communicate in a L2 in a bilingual context: A qualitative investigation of Anglophone and Francophone students*. Unpublished manuscript, Cape Breton University, Sydney, Nova Scotia, Canada.

MacIntyre, P. D. (2007). Willingness to communicate in the second language: Understanding the decision to speak as a volitional process. *The Modern Language Journal, 91,* 564–576.

MacIntyre, P. D., Clément, R., Dörnyei, Z., & Noels, K. A. (1998). Conceptualizing willingness to communicate in a L2: A situational model of L2 confidence and affiliation. *The Modern Language Journal, 82,* 545–562.

MacIntyre, P. D., Clément, R., & Noels, K. A. (2007). Affective variables, attitude and personality in context. In D. Ayoun (Ed.), *Handbook of French applied linguistics* (pp. 270–298). Philadelphia: John Benjamins.

Mackey, A., & Philp, J. (1998). Conversational interaction and second language development. Recasts, responses, and red herrings? *The Modern Language Journal, 82,* 338–356.

Magnan, S. S. (1986). Assessing speaking proficiency in the undergraduate curriculum: Data from French. *Foreign Language Annals, 19,* 429–438.

Mantero, M. (2002). Bridging the gap: Discourse in text-based foreign language classrooms. *Foreign Language Annals, 35,* 437–455.

Mantero, M. (2006). Applied literacy in second language education: (Re)Framing discourse in literature-based classrooms. *Foreign Language Annals, 39,* 99–114.

McCafferty, S. G. (2002). Gestures and creating zones of proximal development for second language learning. *The Modern Language Journal, 86,* 192–203.

McCafferty, S. G., & Stam, G. (Eds.). (2008). *Gesture: Second language acquisition and classroom research*. New York: Routledge.

Montás, M. (2003). Observing progress and achievement of beginning students in a fourth-grade Spanish FLES program. *Learning Languages, 9,* 8–20.

Musumeci, D. (1996). Teacher-learner negotiation in content-based instruction: Communication at cross-purposes? *Applied Linguistics, 17,* 286–325.

National Standards in Foreign Language Education Project (NSFLEP). (1996). *Standards for foreign language learning: Preparing for the 21st century.* Lawrence, KS: Allen Press.

National Standards in Foreign Language Education Project (NSFLEP). (1999). *Standards for foreign language learning in the 21st century.* Lawrence, KS: Allen Press.

National Standards in Foreign Language Education Project (NSFLEP). (2006). *Standards for foreign language learning in the 21st century.* Lawrence, KS: Allen Press.

Naughton, D. (2006). Cooperative strategy training and oral interaction: Enhancing small group communication in the language classroom. *The Modern Language Journal, 90,* 169–184.

O'Relly, L. V., Flaitz, J., & Kromrey, J. (2001). Two modes of correcting communicative tasks: Recent findings. *Foreign Language Annals, 34,* 246–257.

Oxford, R. L. (1992). Encouraging initiative and interest through the cooperative "Heritage Project." *Northeast Conference on the Teaching of Foreign Languages Newsletter, 32,* 13–16.

Patthey-Chavez, G. G., Clare, L., & Gallimore, R. (1995). *Creating a community of scholarship with instructional conversations in a transitional bilingual classroom.* Washington, DC: The National Center for Research on Cultural Diversity and Second Language Learning.

Pelletieri, J. (2000). Negotiation in cyberspace: The role of chatting in the development of grammatical competence. In M. Warschauer & R. Kern (Eds.), *Network-based language teaching: Concepts and practice* (pp. 59–86). Cambridge, UK: Cambridge University Press.

Peregoy, S. F., & Boyle, O. F. (2005). *Reading, writing and learning in ESL: A resource book for K–12 teachers* (4th ed.). New York: Addison-Wesley Longman.

Peyton, J. K. (1987). *Dialogue journal writing with limited English proficient students.* Washington, DC: Center for Applied Linguistics.

Peyton, J. K. (1990). *Students and teachers writing together: Perspectives on journal writing.* Alexandria, VA: TESOL.

Peyton, J. K. (1993). Dialogue journals: Interactive writing to develop language and literacy. *ERIC Digest.* Retrieved February 28, 2004, from http://www.cal.org/ericcll/digest/peyton01.html.

Peyton, J. K., & Reed, L. (1990). *Dialogue journal writing with non-native English speakers: A handbook for teachers.* Alexandria, VA: TESOL.

Phillips, J. K. (Ed.). (1997). *Collaborations: Meeting new goals, new realities.* Northeast Conference Reports. Lincolnwood, IL: NTC/Contemporary Publishing Group.

Philp, J. (2003). Constraints on "noticing the gap": Non-native speakers' noticing of recasts in NS-NNS interaction. *Studies in Second Language Acquisition, 25,* 99–126.

Pica, T., & Long, M. H. (1986). The linguistic and conversational performance of experienced and inexperienced teachers. In R. R. Day (Ed.), *Talking to learn: Conversation in second language acquisition* (pp. 85–98). Rowley, MA: Newbury House.

Platt, E., & Brooks, F. B. (1994). The acquisition-rich environment revisited. *The Modern Language Journal, 78,* 497–511.

Porter, P. A. (1986). How learners talk to each other: Input and interaction in task-centered discussions. In R. R. Day (Ed.), *Talking to learn: Conversation in second language acquisition* (pp. 200–224). Rowley, MA: Newbury House.

Reichelt, M. (2001). A critical review of foreign language writing research on pedagogical approaches. *The Modern Language Journal, 85,* 578–598.

Rifkin, B. (2003). Oral proficiency learning outcomes and curricular design. *Foreign Language Annals, 36,* 582–588.

Rubio, F. (2003). Structure and complexity of oral narratives in advanced-level Spanish: A comparison of three learning backgrounds. *Foreign Language Annals, 36,* 546–554.

Rueda, R., Goldenberg, C., & Gallimore, R. (1992). *Rating instructional conversations: A guide.* Washington, DC: The National Center for Research on Cultural Diversity and Language Learning.

Sadow, S. A. (1982). *Idea bank: Creative activities for the language class.* Rowley, MA: Newbury House.

Sadow, S. A. (1987). Speaking and listening: Imaginative activities for the language class. In W. M. Rivers (Ed.), *Interactive language teaching* (pp. 33–43). Cambridge, UK: Cambridge University Press.

Sadow, S. A. (1994). "Concoctions": Intrinsic motivation, creative thinking, frame theory, and structured interactions in the language class. *Foreign Language Annals, 27,* 241–251.

Scarcella, R. C., & Oxford, R. L. (1992). *The tapestry of language learning.* Boston: Heinle & Heinle.

Schegloff, E. A., Jefferson, G., & Sacks, H. (1977). The preference for self-correction in the organization of repair in conversation. *Language, 53,* 361–382.

Schwartz, A. M., & Kavanaugh, M. S. (1997). Addressing the culture goal with authentic video. In J. K. Phillips (Ed.), *Collaborations: Meeting new goals, new realities* (pp. 97–139). Northeast Conference Reports. Lincolnwood, IL: NTC/Contemporary Publishing Group.

Seedhouse, P. (2004a). The organization of repair in language classrooms. *Language Learning, 54,* S-1, 141–180.

Seedhouse, P. (2004b). The organization of turn taking and sequence in language classrooms. *Language Learning, 54,* S-1, 101–140.

Sheen, Y. (2004). Corrective feedback and learner uptake in communicative classrooms across instructional settings. *Language Teaching Research, 8,* 263–300.

Sheen, Y. (2006). Exploring the relationship between characteristics of recasts and learner uptake. *Language Teaching Research, 10,* 361–392.

Shekary, M., & Tahririan, M. H. (2006). Negotiation of meaning and noticing in text-based online chat. *The Modern Language Journal, 90,* 557–573.

Shohamy, E. (1998). Assessing foreign language abilities of early language learners: A reaction. In M. Met (Ed.), *Critical issues in early second language learning: Building for our children's future* (pp. 185–191). Glenview, IL: Scott Foresman-Addison Wesley.

Shonerd, H. (1994). Repair in spontaneous speech: A window on second language development. In V. John-Stiner, C. P. Panofsky, & L. W. Smith (Eds.), *Sociocultural approaches to language and literacy* (pp. 82–108). Cambridge, UK: Cambridge University Press.

Sime, D. (2008). "Because of her gesture, it's very easy to understand"—Learners' perceptions of teachers' gestures in the foreign language class. In S. G. McCafferty & G. Stam (Eds.), *Gesture: Second language acquisition and classroom research* (pp. 259–279). New York: Routledge.

Skehan, P. (1998) *A cognitive approach to language learning.* Oxford, UK: Oxford University Press.

Slavin, R. E. (1986). *Using student team learning.* Baltimore, MD: Johns Hopkins University Press.

Steinmeyer, G. (1984). Oral proficiency interviews at Amherst Regional High School: Report of a pilot project. *Unterrichtspraxis, 17,* 330–334.

Swain, M. (2000). The output hypothesis and beyond: Mediating acquisition through collaborative dialogue. In J. P. Lantolf (Ed.), *Sociocultural theory and second language learning.* Oxford, UK: Oxford University Press.

Swain, M., & Lapkin, S. (1998). Interaction and second language learning: Two adolescent French immersion students working together. *The Modern Language Journal, 82,* 320–337.

Swender, E. (1999). *ACTFL oral proficiency interview tester training manual.* Yonkers, NY: ACTFL.

Swender, E. (2003). Oral proficiency testing in the real world: Answers to frequently asked questions. *Foreign Language Annals, 36,* 520–526.

Szostek, C. (1994). Assessing the effects of cooperative learning in an honors foreign language classroom. *Foreign Language Annals, 27,* 252–261.

Taylor, G. (2002). Teaching gambits: The effect of instruction and task variation on the use of conversation strategies by intermediate Spanish students. *Foreign Language Annals, 35,* 171–189.

Tharp, R. G., & Gallimore, R. (1988). *Rousing minds to life: Teaching, learning, and schooling in social context.* New York: Cambridge University Press.

Todhunter, S. (2007). Instructional conversations in a high school Spanish class. *Foreign Language Annals, 40,* 604–621.

Tschirner, E., & Heilenman, L. K. (1998). Reasonable expectations: Oral proficiency goals for intermediate-level students of German. *The Modern Language Journal, 82,* 147–158.

Van Handle, D. C., & Corl, K. A. (1998). Extending the dialogue: Using electronic mail and the Internet to promote conversation and writing in intermediate level German language courses. *CALICO Journal, 15,* 129–143.

van Lier, L. (1988). *The classroom and the language learner.* London: Longman.

van Lier, L. (1996). *Interaction in the language classroom: Awareness, autonomy and authenticity.* New York: Longman.

Vygotsky, L. (1978). *Mind in society: The development of higher psychological processes.* Cambridge, MA: Harvard University Press.

Walz, J. (1996). The classroom dynamics of information-gap activities. *Foreign Language Annals, 29,* 481–494.

Wang, Y. (1998). Email dialogue journaling in an English as a Second Language (ESL) Reading and Writing Classroom. *International Journal of Educational Telecommunications 4*(2), 263–287. Charlottesville, VA: Association for the Advancement of Computing in Education.

Warschauer, M. (1995). *E-mail for English teaching.* Alexandria, VA: TESOL.

Warschauer, M., & Healey, D. (1998). Computers and language learning. *Foreign Language Annals, 31,* 51–72.

West, M. J., & Donato, R. (1995). Stories and stances: Cross-cultural encounters with African folktales. *Foreign Language Annals, 28,* 392–406.

Wildner-Bassett, M. (1984). *Improving pragmatic aspects of learner's interlanguage.* Tubingen: Narr.

Wilkinson, S. (2002). The omnipresent classroom during summer study abroad: American students in conversation with their French hosts. *The Modern Language Journal, 86,* 157–173.

Willis, D., & Willis, J. (2007). *Doing task-based teaching.* Oxford, UK: Oxford University Press.

Wilson-Duffy, C. (2003a). Creating online language activities: Putting task-based language teaching to use (Part 1). *CLEAR News, 7*(1), 1, 3–4.

Wilson-Duffy, C. (2003b). Creating online language activities: Putting task-based language teaching to use (Part 2). *CLEAR News, 7*(2), 1, 3, 6–7.

Wong, W., & VanPatten, B. (2003). The evidence is IN: Drills are OUT. *Foreign Language Annals, 36,* 403–423.

Yamada, Y., & Moeller, A. J. (2001). Weaving curricular standards into the language classroom: An action research study. *Foreign Language Annals, 34,* 26–33.

Yorio, C. (1980). Conventionalized language forms and the development of communicative competence. *TESOL Quarterly, 14,* 433–442.

Zyzik, E., & Polio, C. (2008). Incidental focus on form in university Spanish literature courses. *The Modern Language Journal, 92,* 53–70.

NOTES

1. It should be noted that uncertified testers were used in the Huebner and Jensen (1992) and Steinmeyer (1984) studies.

2. Dörnyei (2005) refers to the point at which the language learner commits to taking action in terms of speaking as *crossing the Rubicon*. See MacIntyre (2007) for an explanation of this metaphor.

3. For a full discussion of the research on gesture within the field of SLA and classroom research, see McCafferty and Stam (2008).

4. Many thanks to Dr. Thekla Fall for her translation of the German in this IGA.

5. For a wealth of activities designed to promote divergent thinking and language production, consult Sadow (1982).

6. For other types of tasks and additional suggestions on how to implement task-based instruction, see Willis and Willis (2007).

7. In both the Schwartz and Kavanaugh (1997) and the Haas and Reardon (1997) projects, students also designed and presented oral presentations on related cultural topics that they had researched.

8. For more information, consult http://www.blackboard.com and Lee (2002).

9. Providing feedback for written work is discussed in Chapter 9.

10. Many thanks to Tammy and Kevin Lyons, Spanish teachers in the Greensburg-Salem School District, Greensburg, PA, for sharing their Survivor game with us.

Developing Oral and Written Presentational Communication

In this chapter, you will learn about:

- presentational communication in speaking and writing
- the nature and purposes of oral and written presentational communication
- a problem-solving model of the L1 writing process
- teaching presentational writing and speaking as a process
- the importance of audience
- formats for presentational communication at the elementary, middle, and high school levels

- reading-to-write
- writing as product: *ACTFL Proficiency Guidelines—Writing*
- technologically enhanced presentations
- providing feedback on writing
- peer revision
- ways to evaluate writing
- evaluating oral and multimedia writing presentations
- pronunciation: feedback and instruction

Teach and Reflect: Designing a Presentational Process-Oriented Writing Activity for Secondary Levels or Beyond; Finding the Oral and Written Presentational Elements in Prepared Project Units

Discuss and Reflect: Integrating Peer Revision into the Presentational Writing Process

CONCEPTUAL ORIENTATION

In this chapter we will explore presentational communication as it occurs in speaking and writing. The spontaneity you saw in interpersonal commuication in Chapter 8 disappears in the presentational mode because speakers and writers need time to think, draft, obtain feedback, and revise as they construct appropriate ways to communicate ideas to an audience that has expectations for the form and context of the presentation (Phillips, 2008). Historically, presentational communication has been explored by means of the development and evaluation of writing skills. However, a growing body of literature has offered ideas for guiding students in the creation of oral or multimedia presentations in the foreign language (FL), which are also important components of the presentational mode. In this chapter, we treat presentational communication by discussing writing as well as presentational communication that is accomplished by speaking and projects such as those supported by multimedia. However, a great deal of our attention will still be devoted to writing, since it is the vehicle for much of the presentational communication that is currently the focus in language classes and because the bulk of the research deals with important issues involved in teaching and acquiring writing abilities. Throughout the chapter, where appropriate, we will explore oral and written presentational communication as one topic, while at other times we will focus on them separately in order to discuss their unique aspects and pedagogical implications for each. Finally, on several occasions, in the absence of research on oral presentational communication, we will glean implications from writing research and explore their applicability to speaking.

 ## STANDARDS HIGHLIGHT: Exploring the Presentational Mode Through Speaking and Writing

The Nature of Oral and Written Presentational Communication

In the *presentational mode* of communication, one person produces a message in oral or written form for an audience of listeners, viewers, or readers. Communication is one-way; unlike interpersonal communication, no opportunity exists for the negotiation of meaning to occur between the presenter and those who read, listen to, or view what is presented (National Standards in Foreign Language Education Project [NSFLEP], 2006). The presentation is in the form of one-to-many; that is, one person speaks or writes to an audience of many people. The creator of the message may be present, but he or she is not personally known or accessible to the audience. In learning how to communicate in this mode, students primarily use the productive skills of speaking and writing. In order to successfully communicate with an audience, speakers and writers need to know the cultural perspectives, backgrounds, and expectations of their listeners/readers.

Characteristics of presentational communication are:

- A presenter gives an oral or multimedia presentation to an audience of listeners/viewers, or prepares a written message, text, or product for an audience of readers.
- Oral, multimedia, and written presentations are prepared in advance and may require research on a given topic.
- Presenters may conduct an oral/multimedia presentation while reading from a script, they may use notes periodically during the presentation, or they may deliver a pre-planned talk spontaneously.

Presentational communication, oral and written, requires knowledge of how to communicate with audiences and an ability to present cross-cultural information based on the background of the audience. The purposes of oral and written presentational communication can be categorized into five major types: descriptive, narrative, demonstrative, explanatory, and transformative (O'Hair, Friedrich, Wienmann, & Wienmann, 1995). In *descriptive* presentations, we describe something or someone, e.g., our experiences, our feelings, physical objects, places, people, or events. In *narratives*, we tell a story or describe an event. *Demonstrations* allow us to show our understanding of how something works or offer instructions on how to do something. In *explanatory* presentations, we seek to create an understanding of a concept by providing evidence or justifying why something is so. We use *transformative* presentations to persuade an audience to adopt our point of view or rethink an idea (O'Hair et al., 1995, as cited in Hall, 1999, p. 42).

In writing in the presentational mode, often called *writing for publication*, learners produce written language for an audience of readers. This involves the creation of texts through which writers display what they know and explore what they do not know.

 Presentational communication, oral and written, requires knowledge of how to communicate with audiences and an ability to present cross-cultural information based on the background of the audience.

Presentational Writing and Speaking: Product vs. Process

Traditionally, presentational communication focused on the skill of writing and had a rather narrow focus: (1) writing to practice grammar and vocabulary, and (2) writing to produce a written product, such as compositions in the form of a five-paragraph essay. Development of a product that illustrated grammatical and syntactic accuracy was the teacher's primary goal when asking students to write. Research in the 1980s and 1990s, however, began to focus on writing in order to communicate meaningful messages and on the writing *process*[1]—the steps involved in producing a written text—as well as the writing *product*—the written text created by the writer (Barnett, 1989; Kern & Schultz, 1992; Scott, 1996).

In this chapter, you will explore in greater detail the thought processes involved in creating presentational communication; later, you will learn how to implement a process-oriented approach to help learners communicate in the presentational mode in various tasks that provide students with opportunities to observe and create a variety of written genre and genre-based formats. First, however, we turn our attention to how learners go about engaging in presentational communication in L1 and how we can use this information to better understand how to help learners develop presentational writing and speaking in L2.

Presentational Communication: L1 vs L2

Much of what we know about presentational communication stems from research in L1, particularly as it occurs in writing. In 1981, Flower and Hayes proposed a comprehensive problem-solving model of the L1 writing process, which has since become the most frequently cited model in connection with L2 writing instruction. Their model, depicted in Figure 9.1, attempts to explain the diverse set of thought processes in which writers engage while writing, and it is organized around three components: (1) the task environment, (2) the writer's long-term memory, and (3) writing processes (Flower & Hayes). The *task environment* refers to the rhetorical problem and the written text that is developing and providing direction for what comes next. The *rhetorical problem* is the writing situation, topic, audience, and writer's goals. The term *exigency*, listed in the model as an element in the rhetorical problem, refers to the situation that sparks a need to write. The second element in the model, the writer's long-term memory, contains stored knowledge, not only of the topic, but also of the audience and of various writing plans. The third element contains the writing processes described below, which are under the control of a *Monitor* that functions as a metacognitive editor or writing strategist and determines when the writer moves from one process to the next:

- *Planning:* Writers form an internal, abstract representation of the knowledge that will be used in writing. This involves subprocesses such as generating ideas, organizing thoughts, and setting goals for writing. Generating ideas includes retrieving information from long-term memory, grouping ideas, and forming new concepts. Organization of thoughts is often guided by setting goals that may involve *content* (e.g., "I have to get a definition of _____ worked into this essay") as well as *procedures* (e.g., "Should I start with a definition and then give an example, or provide an example and then logically extract a definition?") (Lee & VanPatten, 2003, p. 248). The nature of the goal is very important and affects the quality of the written product. If a writer's goal is to write a certain number of words rather than to appeal to the interest of the reader, for instance, the quality of the product might be different. Goal setting may account for some of the differences between more successful and less successful writers (Lee & VanPatten).

- *Translating:* Writers put ideas into language. It is important to note that, in this context, the term *translation* does not mean translation of L1 utterances to L2. Instead, it describes the process that L1 writers go through as they convert ideas into written language. Teachers of second languages need to be aware that there is an important difference in L1 and L2 process writing. In L1, writers begin by organizing their ideas and putting them into suitable language. They decide which aspects they will consciously attend to—for example, grammar, spelling, and organization. This process differs from the process typically used by L2 writers, which is to collect and organize words and phrases they will need to express ideas; for L2 writers, more time is spent in creating a word inventory and putting phrases and sentences together in the L2 with the help of some thinking in L1. In addition, research shows that students often use L1 during the L2 planning process to facilitate organization and coherence (Cohen & Brooks-Carson, 2001; Friedlander, 1990) and that use of L1 during prewriting activities does not alter the quality of compositions (Lally, 2000; Qi & Lapkin, 2001). Learners often use L1 in the L2 writing process to compensate for difficulties they have in using the second language, such as searching for vocabulary (Jones & Tetroe, 1987) and figuring out what to say and how to say it (Roca de Larios, Manchón, & Murphy, 2006); to shape ideas and assess their use of linguistic form (Cumming, 1990; Qi, 1998); and to check on their restructuring processes once they realize that their plan needs to be revised (Roca de Larios, Murphy, & Manchón, 1999).

- *Reviewing:* Writers revise and evaluate their writing by reading, examining, changing, and correcting the text. They make surface changes that do not alter the meaning of the text, such as spelling, punctuation, verb tenses; and they make meaning or content changes that alter the meaning, such as additions, deletions, substitutions. Inexperienced writers tend to make more surface changes and fewer global meaning changes than do more expert writers (Scott, 1996). Revising and evaluating may occur at any time during the writing process and are usually repeated

FIGURE 9.1 Cognitive Processes of Writing (L1)

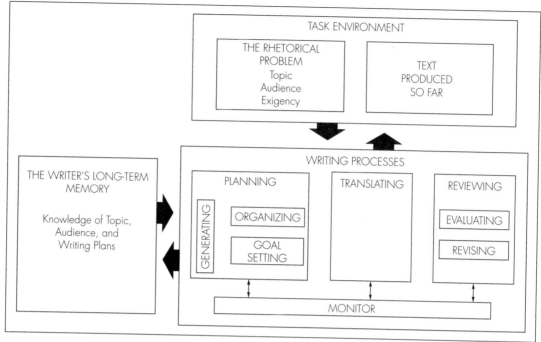

Source: Flower & Hayes, 1981, p. 370.

many times. Furthermore, Kobayashi and Rinnert (2007) showed that instruction in L1 writing carries across languages to influence writing in L2, and vice versa. For teachers and students the implications of this research are that successful writers in L1 can be expected to be successful in L2, and that learning to write in L2 can influence first-language writing.

As depicted in Figure 9.1 and in subsequent L2 writing research, the overall writing process is not viewed as a linear sequence of stages, e.g., organizing followed by drafting followed by revising, but rather a set of thought processes that do not occur in a specific order and that influence each other:

> Writing processes may be viewed as the writer's tool kit. In using the tools, the writer is not constrained to use them in a fixed order or in stages. And using any tool may create the need to use another. Generating ideas may require evaluation, as may writing sentences. And evaluation may force the writer to think up new ideas (Flower & Hayes, 1981, p. 376).

In Figure 9.1, note how the arrows indicate that information flows from one box or process to another *in either direction*; knowledge about the writing task or knowledge from memory can be transferred or used in the planning process, and information from planning can flow back the other way. One of the key concepts of this cognitive process theory, therefore, is that writers are constantly orchestrating a set of cognitive processes as they integrate planning, remembering, writing, and rereading.

Although Flower and Hayes' (1981) model deals with the process of writing, the same process may be used in planning an oral presentation. Speakers often prepare their presentations in written form before they convert them to an oral format. Note that, in the case of oral presentations, the process may include planning for using visuals and/or multimedia support and reviewing by rehearsing the presentation.

To summarize, the processes in which writers and speakers engage can be described as:

- generating ideas, a key phase to ensure that students have the lexicon for their work;
- drafting, the first step toward combining ideas into connected discourse;
- obtaining feedback from the instructor or peers, allows for improved communication of ideas and of more accurate language;
- revising, to promote the clarity of ideas needed when one cannot negotiate meaning, i.e., the product must stand on its own; and
- publishing, to keep the focus on real-world performance for an audience (Phillips, 2008, p. 99).

 The overall writing process is not viewed as a linear sequence of stages, but rather a set of thought processes that do not occur in a specific order and that influence each other.

Successful vs. Unsuccessful Writers and Speakers

In order to understand how to help learners communicate in the presentational mode, it is useful to know about the ways in which they typically engage in presentational communication. Successful writers are reader-centered because they keep the audience and the meaning of the message in focus. Current research focuses on how written presentational communication occurs. Process-oriented writing research in ESL has shown that writing competence is not language-specific. The assumptions that students have about writing in their native language provide the foundation for making new hypotheses about writing in the FL (Edelsky, 1982; Kobayashi & Rinnert, 2007). Similarly, both successful and unsuccessful writing strategies transfer from L1 to L2 (Friedlander, 1990; Zamel, 1983). Successful writers, regardless of the language, spend time planning for writing, and they use a recursive, nonlinear approach; that is, they review and revise their written work as they compose. There is evidence that writers devote twice as much time to dealing with problems of formulating meaning in L2 than in L1 (Roca de Larios, Manchón, & Murphy, 2006), regardless of their proficiency level. Successful writers spend more time improving the expression of meaning or discovering a better match between what they want to write and how they write it (Roca de Larios, Marín, & Murphy, 2001; Roca de Larios et al., 2006). Proficiency level has a role to play in writers' planning. Sasaki (2004, 2007) reports that as writers increase in proficiency over a 3.5 year period, their planning changes from a local focus to a more global form of planning, i.e., from stopping to think what to write next to overall organizational planning of the writing product. In a recent study, Roca de Larios, Manchón, Murphy, and Marín (2008) report that more proficient writers self-regulate, balancing time between formulation and revision processes in writing, engaging "in a kind of inner dialogue: writer and reader/evaluator" (p. 43). Skilled writers view the writing process in a multidimensional way; they select from a range of resources at their disposal internally and externally to meet the demands of the task of creating a written text. Presentational communication develops over time, since it involves planning, recursive revision, and attention to purpose and audience.

Unsuccessful writers, by contrast, are more likely to devote little time to planning and to use a linear approach to composing, writing in a step-by-step fashion without going back to review what was written. Roca de Larios et al. (2008) explain that unsuccessful writers have a monodimensional view of themselves as writers and of the writing process, which leads them to view composition as a grammatically driven juxtaposition of sentences rather than the creation of a whole discourse with the ultimate purpose of simply completing the essay. Unsuccessful writers focus more on their own goals for completing the task rather than on the audience, and they use revisions primarily to correct form errors and mechanics (Magnan, 1985; Richards, 1990; Zamel, 1982). Khaldieh (2000) studied the learning strategies (Oxford, 1990) used by more- and less-proficient writers of upper intermediate/advanced Arabic as a FL. Both groups of writers used a variety of learning strategies, especially in the cognitive strategies, but the proficient writers used them more actively and with more control. For instance, the proficient writers had more control over the language structure and vocabulary, knew how to generate well-formed sentences, and connected structure and meaning. They addressed the writing task directly and used feedback from peers and the teacher. The writers' comments as they used learning strategies appear in Appendix 9.1 on the *Teacher's Handbook* Web site. As pointed out by Rinnert and Kobayashi (2001), successful versus unsuccessful writing can also be a matter of experience versus inexperience, with more experienced writers attending to clarity, logical connections, and organization, while inexperienced writers are more concerned with content, balance, and redundancy.

www.cengagebrain.com

Although currently there are no research studies that examine the nature of oral presentational communication, there are implications of presentational writing that we can glean and apply to presentational speaking. Using the research presented above, one could predict that successful speakers also use a process that allows for generation of ideas, revision of multiple drafts, and attention to impact of the message on the audience. In addition, successful speakers, whether in L1 or L2, have the following characteristics:

- They know the content of what they are presenting and have done the necessary background reading, writing, and other preparations necessary to produce the presentational product.
- They know when they should speak spontaneously and only refer to notes periodically so as to be more engaged with the audience, and when it would be appropriate to read from a script. For example, in an oral demonstration of how to prepare a typical dish from the target culture, presenters would find it more effective to speak spontaneously so that they are free to work with the food, whereas in a television news skit it would be more authentic to read news stories from a script.
- They maintain eye contact with the audience, whether they are speaking spontaneously or from a script.
- They use multimedia, including visuals, pictures, and props to facilitate understanding of the presentation and to enhance the impact of the message.
- As part of the process, they practice their presentations prior to presenting before the targeted audience.
- They know how to alter the presentation as needed, given the reaction of the audience. For example, if it appears that members of the audience do not understand the message, the presenter knows how to expand extemporaneously on certain points, talk more slowly, repeat, etc.
- When possible and appropriate, they offer the audience an opportunity to ask questions.

Research on Teaching Presentational Writing

You have learned about how writers and speakers communicate in the presentational mode. In this section, we explore the research on teaching writing for presentational communication. We focus on writing here because there are so many related factors that are important when presentational communication is taught. There is a lack of research on speaking specifically in the presentational mode, and research on interpersonal speaking was previously presented in Chapter 8.

Research on second language presentational writing has its roots in applied linguistics, L1 composition studies, and ESL/EFL studies. The connections with L1 composition studies have shown that learners transfer writing skills from one language to another, as discussed in the previous section (Kobayashi & Rinnert, 2007; Rinnert & Kobayashi, 2001; Silva & Leki, 2004). The connection with ESL/EFL research has been useful because learners share many commonalities of processing in planning, organizing, drafting, and revising written texts. However, ESL/EFL learners often have opportunities to use English with real purposes and with real audiences, while the L2 learners must consciously work to find real purposes and audiences apart from those in the classroom.

Since research in FL writing is a relatively young field, researchers have designed studies that examine many different aspects of writing, making it difficult to construct comparisons across studies or even draw many conclusions about the FL writing process. Reichelt (2001) conducted a thorough review of 32 research articles on FL writing, and Silva and Brice (2004) examined over 300 articles on research on writing from an ESL and FL perspective. This research focuses on the need to identify a purpose for writing and to include real-world writing tasks and genres in addition to traditional formal composition formats. The following are some key findings from the research on teaching presentational writing:

1. Explicit grammar instruction seems to have little to no effect on the grammatical accuracy of the written product (Frantzen, 1995; Manley & Calk, 1997; Wong & VanPatten 2003). In light of these findings, Reichelt (2001) suggests that FL teachers consider decreasing the emphasis on form in the instructions for tests of FL writing.

2. The use of computer technology for FL writing is an emerging field with the potential to facilitate L2 learning. Reichelt's (2001) review of the literature confirmed the fact that writing for interpersonal purposes is different from writing for presentational communication, and that the goal of writing in FL classrooms must be clarified: If the goal is to prepare students to write traditional compositions, then interactive computer writing may not be appropriate to achieve that goal (Reichelt). However, the use of the computer for word processing *has* been shown to result in greater fluency in writing based on word count when compared to the use of handwriting—for some students, using a computer to create written products will prompt them to write more (Nirenberg, 1989). Computer software continues to evolve and is now capable of identifying and correcting typical misspellings and morphological errors in multiple languages, and researchers are using keystroke-tracking software to study the composing processes of learners (Silva & Brice, 2004).

3. Different writing tasks lead students to produce texts with differing characteristics. For example, dialogue journals (see Chapter 8) and other writing tasks that are free from focus on form or free from a final grade tend to result in greater quantity of writing; furthermore, they are syntactically as complex and grammatically more accurate than writing in which form is emphasized (Chastain, 1990; Martinez-Lage, 1992). When students engage in sentence-combining activities (e.g., combining two sentences to form a single compound or complex sentence), their later essays contain more syntactic complexity than if they practice writing in typical workbook exercises (Cooper, 1981; Cooper & Morain, 1980). Kuiken and Vedder (2008), in a study of Dutch students learning French and Italian, found that more complex writing tasks resulted in greater accuracy. McKee (1980) found that when students write in their own voices, their

writing is more syntactically complex than in writing where they take on the role of another person.

4. The type of writing prompt also has an effect on the quality of students' writing. Way, Joiner, and Seaman (2000) compared the use of three kinds of writing prompts on writing samples produced by high school French students: a bare prompt, a vocabulary prompt, and a prose model prompt. Each prompt was presented in the context of a reply to Marie, a teenage pen pal from France. The *bare prompt* was a simple explanation of the task, presented in English only. The *vocabulary prompt* contained the same explanation along with a list of words and expressions in French with English definitions. The *prose model prompt*, advocated by researchers such as Terry (1989) and Dvorak (1986), contained the wording from the bare prompt plus a sample of a pen pal letter; i.e., a letter from a potential pen pal, with all the necessary kinds of content and grammatical structures used in context. Students were told to "write a letter back to Marie describing yourself, your family, your pets, your classes, your pastimes, and your likes and dislikes" (Way, et al., p. 183). Of the three types of prompts, the prose model prompt produced writing samples with the best overall quality, the greatest fluency, the greatest syntactic complexity, and the highest accuracy, while the vocabulary prompt produced better results than did the bare prompt. This research indicates that students benefit from reading target language (TL) examples of written products that they are expected to create.

5. Aziz (1995) found that training in strategy use can have an effect on writing. In Aziz's study, grammatical agreement and overall writing improved when students were trained in cognitive strategies as well as metacognitive strategies. Among the cognitive strategies were note-taking during dictation, reconstruction of the dictated passage, and error analysis. Training in the metacognitive strategies included self-monitoring and self-evaluating while writing. In Arabic writing of persuasive tasks, Khaldieh (2000) found that more-proficient as well as less-proficient writers used cognitive and metacognitive strategies in monitoring and reviewing their writing. These findings illustrate the importance of helping students to self-monitor and reflect on their writing while they write.

6. Process approaches to writing instruction have been shown to prompt students to write more and generate better-organized written products (Gallego de Blibeche, 1993). Kern and Schultz (1992) reported on the positive results of teaching writing as a process in upper-level French classes, targeting especially the text-based argumentative essay. They found that unsuccessful writers benefited most from instruction that focused on thesis statement development, planning, and development of paragraphs; successful writers benefited most from instruction that focused on refining interpretive analyses and developing a personal voice in their writing. An important implication of this study is that teachers should have realistic expectations concerning the level of sophistication with which students can write, given their L2 abilities.

 How can the type of writing task and type of writing prompt affect the written product that students create?

All of the studies reviewed above were carried out at secondary and post-secondary levels. As you learned in Chapter 4, there are few studies of FL literacy at the elementary school level. Since students benefit from the discovery that occurs as they read and compose using the TL, future research is needed to clarify findings and assist teachers in effectively integrating writing and literacy into language instruction right from the beginning (Blanton, 1998; Matsuda, 2001; Scott, 1995).

Research-Based Implications for Instructional Practices

The research summarized above points to the following suggestions for teachers as they incorporate presentational writing into the FL classroom (adapted from Scott, 1996, and Williams, 2005). Where appropriate, suggestions are also applied to the teaching of oral and multimedia presentations.

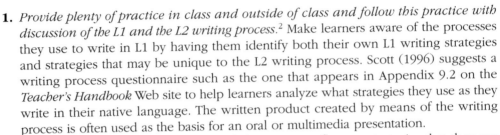

www.cengagebrain.com

1. *Provide plenty of practice in class and outside of class and follow this practice with discussion of the L1 and the L2 writing process.*[2] Make learners aware of the processes they use to write in L1 by having them identify both their own L1 writing strategies and strategies that may be unique to the L2 writing process. Scott (1996) suggests a writing process questionnaire such as the one that appears in Appendix 9.2 on the *Teacher's Handbook* Web site to help learners analyze what strategies they use as they write in their native language. The written product created by means of the writing process is often used as the basis for an oral or multimedia presentation.

2. *Teach about the FL writing process.* Ask learners to reflect on strategies that they use when they write in L2. A writing process should include *pre-writing*, usually led by the teacher in whole-class groups; *drafting*, done alone or in small groups; *sharing and responding* to writing with partners or in small groups; *revision*, done alone or in small groups; *editing*, with partners or in small groups; and *publishing* a final version (Curtain & Dahlberg, 2010, in press). Appendix 9.3 on the *Teacher's Handbook* Web site illustrates a FL writing process questionnaire that might be used to direct learners' attention to effective and ineffective strategies for writing in the TL (Scott, 1996) and Appendix 9.4 on the *Teacher's Handbook* Web site illustrates a teacher's checklist for preparing the writing task.

   According to Scott (1992), generating ideas is the most challenging feature of the FL writing process because learners tend to use L1 idea generation strategies and then try to transfer or translate their ideas from the native language to the TL. Thinking and planning in the native language is useful, but since L2 students may possess a limited amount of vocabulary and grammatical knowledge, their translated ideas often lack comprehensibility. Teachers can help students generate ideas by (1) providing topics that are familiar and personal to them, (2) encouraging them to recall words and expressions in the TL associated with the topic, and (3) providing enough direction to help them focus on the TL while generating ideas (Scott & Terry, 1992). Figure 9.2 illustrates a sample worksheet for helping learners to generate ideas at the word level in the TL (Scott, 1996). This type of worksheet might include or be a springboard for vocabulary exercises that provide linguistic "scaffolding" for a given writing task (Koda, 1993). In this way, the writing process can be approached as an activity that stimulates new ideas and discovery instead of the tedious task of translating (Scott, 1996).

 Help learners to generate ideas on a topic, recall words and expressions in the TL, and focus on the TL while generating ideas.

3. *Teach students to self-monitor and self-reflect.* Since another challenging aspect of the FL writing process is reviewing, learners must be taught to reread frequently while writing. Raimes (1987) suggests that students read their texts aloud, either to themselves or to a classmate, as this will help them edit what is on the page and generate new ideas. Similarly, students need to be taught to revise throughout the writing process and to make content changes as well as surface changes. Students should reread their written text for content and organization as a separate activity from rereading for linguistic accuracy (Scott, 1996). Changes in content often require direct suggestions from the teacher and can be incorporated in later drafts (Scott, 1995, p. 119). When

FIGURE 9.2 Sample Worksheet for Generating Ideas

SAMPLE WORKSHEET FOR GENERATING IDEAS
(Designed for use in the target language)

Topic: Describe your personality.

Underline the adjectives that describe you best:

intellectual	realistic	athletic	quiet
naïve	pessimistic	boring	loud
lazy	enthusiastic	anxious	active
serious	intelligent	calm	adventuresome
crazy	dull	depressed	loving
optimistic	hopeful	diligent	perfectionistic

Use the dictionary to find five more adjectives that describe you.

Use some of the following expressions as you describe yourself:

intellectual	realistic	athletic	quiet
always	rarely	often	when I'm tired
occasionally	never	regularly	when it's rainy
in the morning	during the day	at night	when it's sunny
with my friends	with my parents	on a date	at a party
on a trip	when I meet someone		

Source: From *Rethinking Foreign Language Writing* (p. 53), by V. M. Scott. Copyright © 1996 Heinle/Arts & Sciences, a part of Cengage Learning, Inc. Reproduced with permission. www. cengage.com/permissions.

it is time to reread for linguistic accuracy, students need explicit instructions on what types of errors to look for, e.g., subject-verb agreement, tense usage, noun-adjective agreement. Teachers can also model self-monitoring by sharing with students a draft of their own writing, for example, and thinking aloud as they contemplate revisions; they can also write a paragraph of self-reflection on the draft and share it with students. For oral presentations, students can tape record their talks and engage in self-monitoring and self-reflecting while they listen to them. These steps provide guidance and scaffolding for all tasks and activities (Williams, 2005).

4. *Design writing tasks to reflect authentic purposes and genres.* Whether the task reflects a real-world communication, such as a letter of application for a job or a research composition for a class, the real uses of the writing task should be made apparent to learners (Williams, 2005), as well as cultural differences in specific genres.

5. *Provide focused practice on syntax.* We have seen earlier that practice in sentence combining improves the syntactic complexity of student writing (Cooper, 1981; Cooper & Morain, 1980). Similarly, since syntactic complexity is an important aspect of good writing, Schultz (1994) suggests that learners be engaged in reformulation activities, through which they (1) analyze a poorly written text consisting of only three or four sentences, (2) work individually or in groups to rewrite the text, and (3) compare their rewritten version to one rewritten by a native speaker. This technique enables learners to integrate their knowledge of grammar, vocabulary, and syntax and make interpretive choices about the content of the text (p. 176).

When students' writing is difficult to understand, teachers should be careful not to interpret what students are trying to say and reformulate their writing without discussing with students what their intended message was supposed to be (Krueger, 2001). Individual writing conferences can be helpful in this regard, as they provide an opportunity for discussion between teacher and student about specific areas of difficulty, progress being made, and strategies for improvement of writing. See related discussion later in this section.

6. *Distinguish between writing for communication and writing as an academic exercise.* Learners need to know the difference between using writing as a tool for communicating messages to others (e.g., notes, letters, e-mail messages) and using writing as an academic exercise in order to learn content (e.g., writing an essay about cultural comparisons). Writing tasks should enable learners to learn how to write for both academic and communication purposes (Williams, 2005).

7. *Combine reading and writing.* There are at least two ways to combine reading and writing that result in the creation of presentational products. One way is to give learners authentic examples of written discourse as models to follow as they write. The use of writing prompts in the Way, Joiner, and Seaman (2000) research study was an interpersonal example of this method. A presentational example would be to provide students with a biographical poster and a photo of one of the athletes in their school's sports program. Students would then be asked to: "Create your own poster for another athlete in your school. Be sure to describe the athlete's birthplace and date, his or her likes and dislikes about playing this sport, how he or she got started in it, whom he or she admires in the sport, and what he or she hopes to accomplish in this season or in his/her career." A second strategy is to combine the interpretive and presentational modes of communication in a *reading-to-write* approach (Ruiz-Funes, 2001). The Interactive Model presented in Chapter 6 illustrates this approach—students first interpret a text and then use the information learned as a basis for the completion of a task or the creation of an oral or written product.

8. *Design writing tasks carefully.* Assign some writing tasks that are ungraded in order to prompt students to write more. Have realistic expectations for how well students will be able to write, given their levels of language proficiency. Williams (2005) suggests that expectations for student performance must be made clear. For example, if students struggle to write paragraphs, they can't be expected to demonstrate much of a personal voice in their writing. Recognize that certain types of writing may be more challenging for students, e.g., expository writing, and provide guidance and examples that will facilitate these types of writing. The same suggestion is applicable to oral presentational tasks: Remember that students need guidance and time to transform to an oral product what they may have prepared first in written form.

9. *Redefine "creative" writing.* Teach learners that one goal of FL writing is to create personal meaning with the TL. According to Scott (1996), students sometimes have the mistaken idea that in order to write creatively, they must possess the inspiration of a poet or novelist. When they don't feel inspired in this way, they often experience frustration with writing. Learners will be more likely to succeed if teachers can "remove the burden of creativity and teach the art of discovery" (Scott, p. 49). Various studies have shown the effectiveness of using journal writing in helping students create personal meaning and in increasing their motivation to write (Peyton, 1987, 1990; West & Donato, 1995). For example, in an interactive dialogue journal, which is effective at all age levels, the teacher and the student carry on a written conversation. Learners write about topics of interest to them, and the teacher participates in the dialogue by writing back with responses, comments, and observations. Since the learner and the teacher are focused on meaning, errors in language form are not corrected except by the teacher's use of correct modeling.

10. *Integrate a writing conference into your instructional approach.* The writing conference can occur at some point within the course or year, after students have done some writing and would benefit from discussion about their progress and ways in which they might improve. Effective conferences are those that engage students in talking about their writing process and in analyzing their written work. Teachers should avoid

using the conference as an opportunity for a one-way lecture. Teachers may also conduct conferences with students in order to discuss their progress in creating and conducting oral and multimedia presentations.

You will find many of these instructional implications embedded in the instructional applications that follow.

Teaching Presentational Writing and Speaking as a Process

Teacher's Handbook recommends the use of a process-oriented approach in teaching presentational writing and speaking—here, the problem-solving model of the L1 writing process posited by Flower and Hayes (1981), explored earlier in the chapter, which can also easily be applied to presentational speaking.

In both native and FL writing instruction, the shift away from a focus on writing as *product* toward a focus on writing as *process* has resulted in an emphasis on the steps that learners complete in order to create a written product (Barnett, 1989; Dvorak, 1986; Silva, 1990). A process-oriented approach calls for a "positive, encouraging, and collaborative workshop environment within which students, with ample time and minimal interference, can work through their composing processes" (Silva, p. 15). The teacher's role, according to Silva, is to assist students in developing strategies for (1) beginning to write, e.g., finding topics, generating ideas, focusing, planning, etc.; (2) drafting, e.g., revising by adding, deleting, modifying; and (3) editing, e.g., attending to grammar, vocabulary, sentence structure, mechanics.

In the Flower and Hayes (1981) model, two key elements of the writing process that are important for teachers to consider are (1) the *rhetorical problem*, which refers to the writing situation, audience, topic, and the writer's goals; and (2) knowledge of the topic. A third issue for language teachers is the vocabulary, grammar, and syntax that students must use in order to write effectively. We will now turn our attention to a discussion of each of these three elements.

Addressing the Rhetorical Problem: Goals and Audience

The rhetorical problem involves the writer's goals or purposes for completing a presentational task, as well as the targeted audience. According to Lee and VanPatten (2003), the nature of writing assignments in FL classrooms often, and unfortunately, leads students to have only one purpose for doing them: "getting the assignment done" (p. 247). Since their writing goal in this case becomes meeting what they think is the teacher's desired outcome, students' writing processes of planning and reviewing are minimized. Lee and VanPatten suggest an approach to engaging learners in writing that involves a series of "thoughtful processes," based on the Flower and Hayes (1981) model. You may find it helpful to refer to Figure 9.1 presented earlier. Figure 9.3 is an example of this approach applied to a typical presentational writing task given to a beginning FL class. Note that this writing task could easily be adapted for a presentational speaking task by having students present a talk instead of a composition. In oral and multimedia presentations, the process should include opportunities for students to conduct research if applicable, practice the oral presentations, conduct the presentations, and participate in critiquing and assessing the presentations.

 Which elements of the Flower and Hayes' cognitive process model can you identify in the task in Figure 9.3?

FIGURE 9.3 Writing Process Applied to a Task

A. Generating Content

Step 1. To each group of three or four students, the instructor will assign one of the following topics:
  a. Family life at the turn of the century
  b. Family life today

Each group will have __10__ minutes to make a list of as many ideas as possible relating its topic to each of the following:
  1. Family size
  2. Economic opportunities
  3. Educational opportunities
  4. Male and female roles
  5. Society

Step 2. Report to the rest of the class the ideas your group has generated. Create a master list on the board of the ideas generated on each topic. Are there any other ideas you can think of to add to the lists?

Step 3. Each member of the class should copy the lists from the board to use later in writing.

B. Selecting An Audience and Purpose

Step 1. Keeping in mind the ideas the class generated in the Activity A, think about an audience for your writing. Select an audience from the following list or propose one yourself:
  a. High school students you are addressing as part of a college recruitment program
  b. Readers of the school newspaper
  c. Members of a businesswomen's organization
  d. Members of a church council
  e. Panhellenic council that governs fraternities and sororities on campus
  f. Other suggestions _____

Step 2. Select one of the two topics. Then form groups of three with others working on the same topic and list your audience's characteristics. Report your list to the rest of the class. Try to help other groups by proposing characteristics they may not have considered. Take down any suggestions your classmates offer you.

C. Planning and Organizing

Step 1. Now that you have an audience, what will you say to them? Working in the same groups as in Activity B, examine the lists of ideas you prepared for Activity A, and indicate what information you might include in your composition.

Step 2. Working individually, prepare an outline of the composition. Once each of you has an outline, present it to each other. Have your partners thought of some things you didn't?

Step 3. (*Option*) Present your outline to someone who selected a different audience, and listen to his/her presentation. Can you offer any ideas or suggestions?

D. Composing

Step 1. Take your outline and list of ideas and keep them handy as you write a composition directed at the audience you selected. *Suggestion:* Write a draft of the work and let it sit for two days. Do not think about it or read it. At the end of the two days, pick it up and read it. As you do, answer the following questions:
  a. Content: Are these still the ideas you want to include?
  b. Organization: Does the order in which the ideas are presented help you get your message across to the audience?

If you answer "no" to either question, rewrite some of your composition.

Step 2. Once you think your composition is good enough to hand in, review the language you used:
  a. Verbs: Are the forms, spelling, and accents correct?
  b. Adjectives: What noun do they go with? Do the adjectives agree?
  c. [*Other elements of the language on which you want learners to focus*]

Source: Adapted from *Making Communicative Language Teaching Happen,* 3rd ed. (pp. 252–253), by J. F. Lee and B. VanPatten. Used by permission of the McGraw-Hill Companies.

What specific parts of this activity would need to be adapted if this task reflected presentational speaking?

It is the consideration of *audience* that makes presentational writing and speaking communicative *acts* rather than *activities* to practice language forms. Historically, the audience for such presentations has been the teacher. Experimental studies (Roca de Larios, Murphy, & Manchón, 1999; Storch & Wigglesworth, 2008; Zimmerman, 1996) focusing on how writers actually write for an audience of readers have elaborated on the processes of formulating text, generating ideas, and restructuring and reformulating text. Unlike their counterparts in ESL classes, students in FL classes are rarely required to write or speak in the L2 outside of class. Greenia (1992) calls for instructional practices and textbook materials for L2 classes that do not overlook the importance of the purpose of L2 writing, audiences that can be realistically accessed, and assignments that allow students to take ownership over their writing. Teachers should make every effort to find other audiences apart from their classroom so that students learn how to design presentations with various audiences in mind. Audiences can include students in other classes, students in specific clubs or organizations, parents, other faculty and administrators, and members of the local community, including native speakers of the TL.

Another approach to presentational writing for audiences is *genre* instruction in writing (K. Hyland, 2007). Here the term *genre* does not apply exclusively to a literary genre such as poetry, novel, fiction or non-fiction, short story, drama, or essay but rather to the kinds of texts that are easily recognized and shared by members of a speech community. Given that speech communities exist in all cultural groups, genre is culture-specific. A genre shares characteristics that all members of the cultural community recognize and expect as they engage in socially and culturally constructed acts of living day-to-day, reflecting the social turn in the writing products they produce daily (Trimbur, 1994). Swales (1991) points out that it is the communicative purpose of the genre that shapes its structure, style, and choice of content (p. 10). For example, planning a Chinese New Year Party might engage students of Chinese in researching how the New Year is celebrated in various provinces of China, then they might produce culturally appropriate written genres of invitations, e-mail reminders, and descriptive flyers of what to bring and how to get to the party site. They might also prepare written recipes for traditional moon cakes and newspaper ads for stores that sell traditional costumes and gifts. Genres share related purposes, similar presentations and language features, although how a culture enacts purpose, presentation, and function in writing will vary. For this reason, modeling representative samples of various cultural genres, e.g., ads, recipes, short messages, formal letters, for their key features is critical to a genre-based approach.

Acquiring Knowledge for Presentational Communication

Students need content knowledge about the topics on which they are to present, whether it be an oral or written product. A process-oriented approach involves learners in developing their own experiences and interests as possible sources of knowledge for writing. Reading other texts on the topic of their interests, conducting library and Internet research, and interviewing experts are other ways in which learners can acquire knowledge about a topic.

Reading-to-write. Some research proposes that reading may facilitate writing and that a well-read person has more knowledge about the conventions and features of writing (Scott, 1996). Reading can help learners to gain an understanding of patterns of discourse and connections between language and culture. Kern and Schultz (1992) found that composition instruction that is integrated with the reading of texts and that focuses on the writing process as well as on the final product helps learners improve their writing performance. In their study, undergraduate French students enrolled in an intermediate-level composition course read and discussed a series of texts, analyzed the texts as models of successful writing, received sequenced lessons on how to write based on the readings, and created in-class essays based on various topics. Over the course of a year, students made significant progress in terms of the syntactic complexity and overall quality of their writing.

A well-read person has more knowledge about the conventions and features of writing than a person who reads little.

Particularly in an academic setting, writing or speaking on a topic using knowledge from a source text such as a literary text, an online newspaper article, or a scholarly article involves the processes of planning, writing, revising, and editing, as one might expect. In a study of the presentational writings of skilled Spanish-as-a-second-language learners writing about a source text drama, Ruiz-Funes (1994, 1999) found that four processes were involved in reading-to-write text production in addition to planning, translating, and reviewing: (1) synthesizing served to design a framework or plan; (2) monitoring served to check for accuracy of information and to collect relevant information from the literary text; (3) structuring served to select relevant information from the literary text and structure it according to the writer's intent; and (4) elaborating served to generate new ideas and evaluate and judge existing ideas (p. 520). In writing to learn, students must use critical thinking skills such as analyzing, synthesizing, and decision making (Scott, 1996). In addition to acquiring knowledge about a topic by reading-to-write, learners also acquire vocabulary. Laufer and Hulstijn (2001) found that students retain more vocabulary if they acquire it through reading-to write than if they simply read glosses of new words.

Writing about literature can be employed at all levels of language learning, as pointed out in Chapters 4 and 5. Employing reading-to-write strategies with students at the secondary and post-secondary level, Debevec Henning (1992) outlined a proficiency-oriented scale of students' ability to analyze literature in the TL. Believing that literature is suitable input for novice learners as well as advanced learners, she suggests that a teacher might ask a novice student to write a composition that recognizes main themes in a literary work and separates them from minor subthemes. Students might produce program notes for the production of the literary work if it's a play, or jacket notes for the cover of the work if it's a novel. For advanced students, a teacher might ask for a description of the historical, sociopolitical, and sociocultural significance of the author's work. This description could be read at a local ceremony for international week, as a way to pay homage to the author.

The Web can be a valuable resource for information that students can use for their writing tasks. Reading-to-write using the Web, however, is not fully comparable to reading-to-write using printed texts. Web-page reading is more difficult than print reading (Thurstun, 2004) and requires that learners also figure out how to navigate the Web in the TL. Most importantly, they must construct knowledge from the nonlinear arrangement of information on a Web page, discriminate which information they need, verify the validity of the information, and convert it into oral or written presentational communication. Stapleton (2005) reported that his Japanese students using the Web for research produced academic compositions on topics of global interest, but learners were unable to judge the appropriateness of Web sites. For presentational assignments that require reading to acquire new information, FL teachers need to assist students in finding appropriate sources to read and in using effective interpretive strategies as they engage with these texts (see Chapter 6). These types of presentational tasks also provide an opportunity for the teacher to learn content along with students.

Using Vocabulary, Grammar, and Syntax in Presentational Communication

In a process approach to writing in L1, students elaborate ideas as a beginning step. L1 learners already have the vocabulary they need to explore ideas; L2 learners often need to create a word inventory. Researchers have found that the size of a learner's vocabulary and the number of associations with similar word families can distinguish proficiency differences between intermediate and advanced L2 learners (Zareva, Schwanenflugel, & Nikolova, 2005). Use of appropriate vocabulary enhances the effectiveness of the learner's presentational writing and speaking. Morin and Goebel's (2001) research study revealed the effectiveness of *semantic mapping* and *semantic clustering* as strategies that help learners recall and organize L2 vocabulary. Although their study dealt with vocabulary acquisition, their findings have applicability to use of vocabulary in presentational writing and speaking. *Semantic mapping* or *thematic clustering* refers to grouping words of any number of parts of speech around a thematic topic, e.g., *frog, green, pond, hopping, swim, slippery. Semantic clustering*, on the other hand, refers to words of a similar syntactical or semantic nature being grouped together, e.g., *apricot, peach, plum, nectarine, pear*. As students generate content for a presentational task, teachers might engage them in brainstorming vocabulary by using mapping or clustering strategies. See Chapters 4 through 6 for information about semantic mapping and acquisition of vocabulary in content-based instruction and the importance of vocabulary in the interpretive mode.

Another consideration pertaining to vocabulary is the use of varied vocabulary. The degree to which students need to use diverse vocabulary depends on the type of task; for example, descriptive tasks may require more varied vocabulary in order to produce greater imagery. For other types of tasks, such as narrative writing, the diversity of vocabulary may not be as critical as features such as topical progression, which will help the reader follow the linear progression of the text.

Although knowledge of grammatical rules correlates more with written skills than oral skills (Dykstra-Pruim, 2003), knowledge of grammar does not guarantee writing competence (Schultz, 1991). Writers' skill in using language structures to communicate successfully seems to develop independently of their knowledge and use of grammatical rules (Coombs, 1986). The degree to which writing contains the use of particular grammatical structures or is grammatically complex depends on the nature of the writing task. For example, writing a postcard may not require grammatically complex sentences; on the contrary, the norm might be to write short sentences and phrases. In comparison, narrative writing does require the appropriate use of tense and aspect. As teachers design tasks, they should determine ahead of time whether students have the grammatical structures necessary to complete the tasks. Furthermore, rather than designing tasks around a specific grammatical structure—which often results in disguised grammatical practice—teachers should design tasks that address their thematic unit or lesson objectives and then identify grammatical structures that might be necessary to engage in the tasks.

You have seen earlier the suggestion to engage students in sentence combining as a way to improve their skill in writing by using more complex sentences. Nonetheless, it is important to note that presentational communication is more than a list of isolated sentences. Communicating in the presentational mode requires that students write cohesively and coherently. Cohesive devices indicate "a semantic relation between an element in a text and some other element that is crucial to the interpretation of it" (Halliday & Hasan, 1976, p. 8). Halliday and Hasan cite five categories of cohesive devices: (1) reference, e.g., use of pronouns such as *he* or *it* to refer back to previously mentioned nouns; (2) substitution, e.g., use of pronouns such as *ones* that substitute for a noun referent when it is known, as in "There are big cookies and little cookies; I prefer the little ones"; (3) ellipsis or deletion of repeated words when the referent is known (e.g., "Yes, I will . . ."

for "Yes, I will come with you"); (4) conjunction, e.g., use of words that connect ideas across sentences such as *therefore, however*; and (5) lexical cohesion/repetition of the same word or use of a synonym to clarify the referent, e.g., "Jim finally got a job. It was the perfect job" (p. 119).

Appropriate use of cohesive devices contributes to the overall coherence of a text (Scarcella & Oxford, 1992). *Coherence* refers to the organization of ideas within a text. According to Canale (1982), the conditions of coherence are

- Development: Presentation of ideas must be orderly and convey a sense of direction.
- Continuity: There must be consistency of facts, opinions, and writer/speaker perspective, as well as reference to previously mentioned ideas; newly introduced ideas must be relevant.
- Balance: A relative emphasis (main or supportive) must be accorded each idea.
- Completeness: The ideas presented must provide a sufficiently thorough discussion (as cited in Scarcella & Oxford, 1992, p. 120).

In a recent qualitative study, Lei (2008) found that her participants mediated their writing by using four types of strategies, including cohesion and coherence:

1. artifacts, e.g., Internet, literary works, L1 and L2
2. rules, e.g., rhetoric devices such as the recommended form of an argumentative essay, and cohesion or coherence, or parallelism
3. community, e.g., evaluation and time allocation expectations, consultation with members of campus community and local society
4. role, e.g., authority and responsibility as author, language learner roles in preparation for career goals.

Lei suggested that teachers of second language writing might raise consciousness among their learners about how to use resources around them to mediate the writing process. Teachers should be aware that they need to address cohesion and coherence as they help students communicate in the presentational mode. For example, teachers can engage students in analyzing printed texts to identify the use of cohesion and coherence, developing presentational topics with cohesion and coherence in mind, analyzing their writing and revising based on specific features of cohesion and coherence, and conferencing with the teacher on these features of their writing.

In sum, you have now seen how a process-oriented approach might be used to engage students in written and oral presentational communication, and in using the cognitive processes presented in the Flower and Hayes (1981) model introduced earlier in the chapter. You have also seen some examples of strategies learners might use as they engage in presentational communication.

Presentational Writing as Product: *ACTFL Proficiency Guidelines—Writing*

Thus far we have examined presentational writing and speaking from the standpoint of process. Of course, another aspect of presentational communication is the type of *product* that is created. This section examines the nature of presentational written *products* as reflected through the lens of the *ACTFL Proficiency Guidelines—Writing* (ACTFL, 2001).

The *ACTFL Proficiency Guidelines—Writing* (ACTFL) were revised in 2001 to present the levels in a top-down fashion, from Superior to Novice, and were written to stress what students *can do* rather than what they cannot do. The 2001 revision addresses the reflective nature of advanced tasks, the increased awareness of audience, and the difference between written products that have been created in a *spontaneous* manner versus writing that has been created in a *reflective* way. Spontaneous writing does not allow the writer time for revision, rewriting, clarification, or elaboration. In contrast, reflective writing provides the writer with time to plan and be involved in the writing process by rereading, revising, and rewriting; this method results in a written presentation that accounts for audience and reception of the written product (Breiner-Sanders, Swender, & Terry, 2001). The guidelines serve to evaluate both types of writing since it is not the type of writing but the product that is being evaluated. In spontaneous as well as reflective writing, learners may not always begin FL writing at the novice level since they may transfer their writing competence from L1 to L2 (Henry, 1996; Valdés, Haro, & Echevarriarza, 1992).

The revised guidelines also indicate that as tasks shift upward on the scale, writing becomes more reflective in order to satisfy the demands of the higher levels. Writers become more aware of audience and the purposes of their writing. At higher proficiency levels, writers use a variety of tools for monitoring and revising their work—for example, proofreading, editing, dictionary, and spell checks. Upper-level writers edit their own work in order to enhance the content, style, and impact of their text. See the *Teacher's Handbook* Web site for a link to the revised ACTFL writing guidelines.

www.cengagebrain.com

The *ACTFL Proficiency Guidelines—Writing* (ACTFL, 2001) provide a framework for assessing writing proficiency. Appendix 9.5 on the *Teacher's Handbook* Web site summarizes the performance of writers across proficiency levels as stated by the guidelines. In terms of classroom instruction, teachers may find it useful to refer to the guidelines as they design presentational writing activities that address specific functions, contexts/content areas, text types, and levels of accuracy. For example, novices might produce posters that are labeled with words and phrases in L2 and that deal with familiar topics such as self, school, and activities; intermediate-level learners might write descriptions of famous people from the target culture; advanced-level learners might create narratives or stories in the past time frame. The guidelines can provide information that can be used to set long-term proficiency goals and to develop summative assessments.

Formats for Presentational Communication in the Classroom

In this section, you will find ideas for formats that can be used to teach oral and written presentational communication. The formats suggested also address sample progress indicators of the *Standards for Foreign Language Learning in the 21st Century (SFLL)* (NSFLEP, 2006) across grade levels. You will find examples that include all of the categories mentioned by Hall (1995), described on page 301:

- descriptive activities
- narratives
- demonstrations
- explanatory presentations
- transformative presentations

It is important to note that teachers should present these tasks within a process-oriented approach, as explored earlier in the chapter.

Formats for Presentational Communication in the Elementary and Middle School

In Chapters 4 and 5, you learned about some ideas for presentational communication appropriate for FL classes at the elementary and middle school levels. *Descriptive* presentational writing activities for elementary and middle school learners include materials that can be published for a public audience beyond their classroom and/or school. Presentational writing for young learners should offer scaffolding and provide for freedom and creativity of expression within guided frameworks. Beginning at the word level, elementary and middle school learners can create "concrete poetry" to connect meaning with visual representation, as shown in Figure 9.4. Writing is based on a clear pattern, and students contribute their own content to the pre-existing pattern, as in this poem frame taken from a second-grade classroom (Curtain & Dahlberg, 2010, in press):

Snow
Snow is as _____ as _____
Snow is as _____ as _____
Snow is as _____ as _____
Snow is as _____ as _____
by _____

Creative presentational writing activities for beginning learners include simple forms of poetry, such as fixed-form poetry and diamantes, through which learners can begin to play with language. Laidlaw (1989) suggests the use of fixed-form poetry to tap the creative processes of young learners while enabling them to synthesize information. A sample integrative activity, perhaps from a social studies lesson and resulting writing assignment, is the following fixed-form poem:

Monument Poem

Line 1: Name of the monument

Line 2: Four adjectives describing the monument

Line 3: Constructed in (date, century)

Line 4: Constructed by _____

Line 5: Which is (on the right bank, left bank, in Paris, . . .)

Line 6: Which is near (another monument or landmark)

Line 7: Don't miss (the monument name) because _____

(as cited in Nerenz, 1990, pp. 120–121.)

The following are sample directions for a diamante, a poem in the shape of a diamond, accompanied by an example in English (LaBonty & Borth, 2006, p. 32):

Line 1 noun for subject	Immaturity
Line 2 two adjectives describing subject	Young, Bothersome
Line 3 three participles describing subject	Making fun, Having fun, Laughing
Line 4 four nouns, two about subject, two about its antonym	Jokes, Games, Responsibilities, Jobs
Line 5 three participles describing the	Speaking, Working, Achieving antonym
Line 6 two adjectives describing the antonym	Respectful, Diligent, Hard-working
Line 7 the antonym	Maturity

FIGURE 9.4 Concrete Poetry

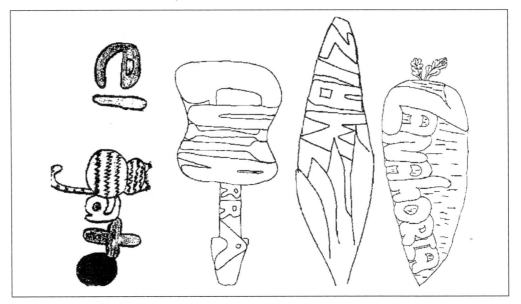

Source: From *Languages and Children – Making the Match,* 4th ed., by H. Curtain and C. A. Dahlberg, Boston: Allyn & Bacon. Copyright © 2010 Pearson Education. Adapted by permission of the publisher.

LaBonty and Borth (2006) also suggest "I used to be . . . but now . . ." poems to practice uses of past tenses in the following pattern, illustrating the past and present circumstances and giving brief presentations on them:[3]

I used to be _____, but now I'm _____.

Yo era _____, pero ahora soy _____.

Descriptive presentational activities for speaking at this level include:

- short speeches advertising the attractions of a city or a famous landmark in one of the countries in which the TL is spoken;
- PowerPoint or other types of media presentations to share the information gained through research into a topic drawn from a thematic unit;
- production of a video essay or podcast about the students' school and school life to send to a partner class or partner school in a country where the TL is spoken (Curtain & Dahlberg, 2010, in press).

Now reconsider the Language Experience Approach you learned about in Chapter 4 as you examine *narrative* and *demonstration* types of oral and written presentational activities. The *SFLL* suggest that *narrating* and retelling stories creates a connection between the interpretive mode and the presentational mode that helps young learners make sense of what they read and experience. In the following scenario from the *SFLL*, the teacher of a fourth-grade class presented La Fountaine's fable "Le cigale et la fourmi" ("The Grasshopper and the Ant") to her students. She used pictures, gestures, and Total Physical Response (TPR) activities to be sure that the students had interpreted the story well. Then the students began the presentational phase by dividing up into pairs. The teacher again narrated the story while the students spoke and acted the roles, each student playing the role of the ant or the grasshopper and then switching roles. The class then developed a short play that they videotaped and shared with parents and other French classes (NSFLEP, 2006). Aspects of presentational speaking included their narrative of the tale by demonstration of the actions of the grasshopper and the ant, and their depiction of French culture to others in their school and community through dramatization of the fable.

Additional narrative presentational activities for speaking include:

- plays in which every student takes a role
- small group presentations of scenes from an authentic story that accompanies a thematic unit
- student-created skits that tie together the language and information from a thematic unit
- puppet plays, written by students and presented before an audience (Curtain & Dahlberg, 2010, in press)

For oral *demonstrations*, students might produce a videotape production of "how-to" shows, such as how to prepare a recipe or the steps in a craft project, taken from the target culture (Curtain & Dahlberg, 2010, in press).

González-Bueno and Quintana-Lara (2007) identified several presentational activities, all related to using periodicals in the classroom. For example, they suggest the following for grade 4 students who see a photo of David Beckham and can read the words *Real Madrid* and *Manchester United* in the brief article and photo in Figure 9.5.

> Identify the subject(s) and setting(s) of photographs accompanying the articles in the newspaper/magazine.
>
> What are the overt and subtle meanings of the photos? Do they complement the article? Evaluate the captions. Propose alternative photos and captions to illustrate the article (p. 11).

Elementary school students might then demonstrate for their peers in their school how to play soccer, or another sport or game.

FIGURE 9.5 Presentational Writing for Grade 4 (Beckham)

From *El País* (Spain)
Beckham: "El Madrid ha sido mi familia"
El jugador británico del Real Madrid
David Beckham ha anunciado que abandonará el equipo blanco a final de temporada. El destino del capitán inglés será Los Ángeles Galaxy, equipo integrado en la MSL norteamericana y con el que ha firmado un contrato de cinco años de duración. Beckham, de 31 años, llegó al Real Madrid en junio del 2003 procedente del Manchester United y se convierte en el futbolista más importante que firma por la competición estadounidense desde que arrancase en 1996.

[Beckham: "The Madrid has been my family"
The British soccer player of Real Madrid, David Beckham announced that he will leave the white team at the end of the season. The English caption's new team will be Los Angeles Galaxy, which belongs to the American MSL, and with which he signed a five-year contract. Beckham, who is 31, arrived to the Real Madrid in June 2003 from the Manchester United, becoming the most important soccer player signing for the USA league since its beginnings in 1996.]

David R. Anchuelo/Real Madrid via Getty Images.

Source: From "The use of periodicals in the foreign language classroom," by M. González-Bueno and M. Quintana-Lara, 2007, *NECTFL Review, 60*, 7–19, p. 15. Reprinted by permission of Northeast Conference on the Teaching of Foreign Languages.

To explore interdisciplinary concepts, middle school students might select a bar graph, pie graph, or histogram in a TL newspaper or magazine. They might then answer the following questions in the form of a demonstration for their peers: What information must be understood in order to read it, e.g., values on the X and Y axes? Percentages? Summarize the information presented in the graph (González-Bueno & Quintana-Lara, 2007, p. 10).

For *explanatory* and *transformative* oral and written communication, consider the example of a thematic unit on trees. In one NSFLEP (2006) activity, the goal for a selected group of FL students in the Pacific Northwest is to publish a brochure in French and English that explains the importance of maintaining hardwood and redwood forests. The students perform oral presentations on local radio and television stations on the value of forests. The unit is interdisciplinary in nature, involving subject-area activities (biology, geography, ecology, art, music, math) and oral and written activities in the presentational mode. Students might begin by using the FL as a support tool for filling out visitor identification forms (Hadley, 2001) like those found at national forest centers; they might also create partial sentences that could later become key logos for the brochure and make posters of the logos. Additionally, they might explain in French and English to a bilingual immersion class the importance of maintaining proper soil pH for the preservation and long life of trees. A thematic planning web such as the one shown in Figure 4.5 in Chapter 4 might be used to generate ideas for these types of presentational activities.

Formats for Presentational Communication at the Secondary and Post-Secondary Levels

In a standards-based approach, presentational communication can develop naturally as a result of work in the interpretive mode. In Chapter 6, you learned how the interpretive mode serves as the basis for speaking or writing in the presentational mode. For example, the *SFLL* sample progress indicators for grade 12 in the interpretive mode state, "Students analyze the main plot, subplot, and characters, and their descriptions, roles, and significance in authentic literary texts" (NSFLEP, 2006, p. 44). For the presentational mode, the sample progress indicator says, "Students select and analyze expressive products of the culture, from literary genres or the fine arts" (p. 46). These analyses can be mapped (see semantic maps in Chapters 4 and 5) and used as a pre-writing stage for an assignment in which learners summarize a text or create their own similar type of text. Working in small groups, learners might construct written texts for an audience using the presentational mode, working toward the following sample progress indicator for grade 12: "Students create stories and poems, short plays, or skits based on personal experiences and exposure to themes, ideas, and perspectives from the target culture" (p. 46).

The NSFLEP (2006) *Il Barbiere di Siviglia (The Barber of Seville)* project is one in which all of the types of oral and written presentational texts can be incorporated to meet the above sample progress indicator. Advanced college-level students of Italian read, listen to, and view Web-based, print, and video material on the components of opera, how the libretto of the work results in the actual performance, the theatrical traditions of comedy in Italian opera, the visual representation of scenery and sets in opera, and the history of the period when *Il Barbiere di Siviglia* was written. As a *descriptive* oral or written presentation, students might write summaries of the historical period in which the opera was written, and deliver PowerPoint presentations to members of the music class. Presenting in Italian could be understood by the music class members if the PowerPoint presentation is sufficiently graphic to convey meaning. As *narratives*, the Italian students might then read the libretto and write presentational posters summarizing the main points of the plot. As *demonstrations*, the students might enact the roles of each of the characters of the *Commedia dell'arte*, wearing their traditional masks, in front of parents, other students, and school board members. An *explanation* of the history, plot, and characters of the play could be a part of the program handed out when parents visit the presentation of the opera put on by the students. Finally, related *transformational* oral or written presentations might be created to convince the school board to provide additional funds for the school's language programs (adapted from NSFLEP, 2006).

Task-Oriented Presentational Writing

In Chapter 8, you learned about task-based instruction as a strategy for engaging students in interpersonal communication. Task-based activities can also be used for developing oral and written presentational communication skills. Scott and Terry (1992) have suggested a task-oriented approach to teaching writing, which is based on the principle that learners need explicit guidelines in order to complete a writing assignment. They propose that the assignment include (1) a general situation; and (2) a series of tasks that specify the language functions, vocabulary, and grammar structures necessary for completing the activity. Figure 9.6 illustrates a task-oriented writing activity, while Figure 9.7 shows a task-oriented writing activity modified for three different levels of language study.

Using this task-based approach, Scott (1992) proposes a developmental writing program designed to initiate writing practice at the earliest levels of language instruction. In each writing assignment, the situation might remain the same while the tasks are changed to progress from simple to more complex language structures and functions. Figure 9.8 exemplifies one situation with tasks for first, second, and third years of study. Note that this particular activity also integrates the Communication, Cultures, and Comparisons goal areas of *SFLL*. It could also combine the three modes of communication if students were to read and interpret a text that pertains to the situation featured in the task, discuss their findings and opinions with classmates in the interpersonal mode, and complete the written task in a format suitable for presentation. Variations on the tasks suggested above that could apply to different audiences and perspectives include those suggested by Krueger (2001). For instance, at the post-secondary level, instead of asking students to describe themselves for the new student files, they could be given this prompt: Describe yourself from the point of view of someone who does not know you, but sees you reading in the library, the student union, or a café (p. 22).

FIGURE 9.6 Task-Oriented Writing Activity–Self Description

> **Situation: You have been asked to write a complete description of yourself for the new student files.**
>
> **Tasks:**
> 1. Describe yourself physically.
>   Function: Describing people
>   Grammar: Adjective position and agreement
>   Vocabulary: Hair color, body, face
> 2. Describe your personality, indicating positive as well as negative traits.
>   Grammar: Negation
>   Vocabulary: Personality
> 3. Conclude with a statement about how you feel about your school.
>   Function: Expressing an opinion

Source: Modified from Scott & Terry, 1992, p. 25.

FIGURE 9.7 Task-Oriented Writing Activity–Multi-Year

Situation: You have heard that American and French students are different. In order to promote cultural understanding, you are writing an article for a French magazine about American students.

First-year tasks:
1. Begin with a general remark about American students.
2. Describe the way a female student might look.
3. Describe the way a male student might look.
4. Indicate three things that some American students like to do.
5. Conclude with a personal opinion about American students.

Second-year tasks:
1. Begin with a general remark about American students.
2. Describe the way students, both male and female, might look.
3. Indicate at least five things that some American students like to do, and three things that they don't like to do.
4. Conclude with several personal opinions about the individuality or conformity of American students.

Third-year tasks:
1. You will argue either for or against the idea that all American students are alike. Begin with a thesis statement.
2. Describe American students.
3. Define the term "stereotype" as it relates to American students.
4. Conclude by showing how the argument supports the thesis statement.

Source: Modified from Scott, 1992, pp. 7–8.

Technologically Enhanced Presentations

In Chapter 8, you also explored the use of synchronous computer-mediated interaction, e.g., e-mail, online tasks, communication with key pals, etc., and its effectiveness in increasing the quantity of interpersonal communication and in improving students' attitudes toward language learning. As learners make use of more recent iterations of word processors in general, as well as TL word processors, the recursive and interactive aspects of the writing process model described by Flower and Hayes (1981) have become even more evident. Planning, writing, and revising can now occur simultaneously and in an ongoing fashion. Learners can access resources and reference materials without leaving the screen that contains their essay. Use of word processors can also help learners in the creation of a more polished, revised presentational product (K. Hyland, 2003). Pennington (1996) identifies five principal benefits of computer-assisted writing:

1. quality of written work, shown by higher holistic and analytic ratings;
2. quantity of writing, shown by longer compositions or more time spent on writing;
3. writing processes, shown by writers' use of more experimentation with language, and more flexible use of writing process;
4. revision behavior, shown by more revisions and more meaning-based revisions; and
5. affective/social outcomes, e.g., less apprehension and better attitude toward writing (as cited in Chikamatsu, 2003, p. 122).

Although there is currently insufficient evidence to point to clear conclusions, in general the research supports the use of the computer in producing more accurate written products because word processing can help students to think about and focus on form. The majority of studies done in this area have pointed out positive effects of using the computer by L2 learners of English and European languages (Pennington, 1996; Scott & New, 1994; Warschauer, 1995). Chikamatsu (2003) analyzed the effects of using the computer on writing efficiency and quality among intermediate undergraduate learners of Japanese. Results of this study revealed that (1) learners took more time to write using the computer, probably due in part to the time required to convert segments to *kanji* characters; (2) computer use improved word-level accuracy, but not the quality of sentence-level grammar or syntactic complexity; and (3) students whose ability in Japanese was low gained less advantage from computer writing; i.e., if a Japanese learner does not have sufficient knowledge of *kanji*, using a computer does not significantly increase *kanji* usage. Al-Jarf (2003) found that Web-based tools were effective for struggling EFL students; their writing became more complex, and sentences were longer and more accurate. In sum, studies indicate that use of word processing may produce different results depending on the FL being studied, the level of students' language abilities, and the goals of writing. Descriptions of writing assistant tools, *Système-D, Atajo,* PowerPoint, and Keynote, appear on the *Teacher's Handbook* Web site.

www.cengagebrain.com

The Web has been found to be widely useful in developing presentational products. When students prepare Web pages of their own or post an entry on a blog, they engage in presentational writing, since the audience is not present and the communication is one-way, at least initially. Similarly, in a wiki, which consists of several interlinked web pages, learners also engage in presentational writing often organized thematically by the wiki owner. In writing for the Web, learners have an authentic audience, a real purpose, and an opportunity to express their personal voice. In constructing a Web page, learners should attend to color, font size, scrolling, use of terms referred to as nominalization, graphics, and white space (Murray, 2005). The Internet offers new tools for researchers and teachers alike as writing shifts to real audiences outside the classroom. The challenge for teachers will be to bring real-world writing *into* the classroom and enable learners to produce presentational products for use *outside* the classroom. Below are some examples of how teachers helped their students produce presentational communication.

Goulah (2007) incorporates a technologically enhanced project into his study-abroad program with adolescent intermediate-high learners of Japanese by asking them to produce digital video related to topic units: "Japanese politics in a geopolitic context, and the environment, featuring a one-day poetry lesson selected because poem topics linked the politics and environment units" (p. 60). Students use their textbook, selected Web-based articles, teacher-led "why" questions, and vocabulary and grammar instruction, all in Japanese. During eight days of their study-abroad experience in three locations in Japan, students work collaboratively to construct one-minute personal films, called *un-commercials*, that represent their viewpoints derived from their readings and exploration of unit-based materials. They prepare storyboards with sketches and descriptions in Japanese, and present, defend, and discuss their storyboard ideas with each other, mediated by their teacher. They negotiate the roles of director, script writers, movie and music editors, camera person, staging, actors, etc., all in Japanese. Students produce two digital videos. The first asks the essential question: "What should ideal countries do?," as related to economics and the environment. Student actors represent weak/poor countries and strong/wealthy countries as clients in a store or on a street. The student/country actors try to buy or ask for food, drink, and medicine, but they have no money. The wealthy student/country provides something to drink for the poor student/country, who then provides medicine for the wealthy student/country, and both stop to pick up a student/country who has fallen on the street. The answer to the essential question rains down across the screen: "Ideal countries should help poor countries" (p. 68). Goulah reported that students learn new literacies as they use iTunes, iMovie, and learn how to create scenarios that educate. In addition to the scaffolding provided by the teacher, learners engage in *triadic scaffolding* as the music editor from the first project helps the new music editor in the second one, and as they interact with the computer screen. Further, students work in their Zones of Proximal Development (ZPDs) as they develop new literacy in FL computer terminology, mediate their learning through the search tools, and acquire new language by means of the teacher's scaffolded assistance. Sildus (2006) also reports improved vocabulary learning among students of German who produced video projects. Thus, technologically mediated projects can provide learners with opportunities to work in their own individual ZPDs, assisting and being assisted by others. Additional information about using technology in the FL classroom can be found in Chapter 12, and in the techno focus sections of each chapter in this edition.

You have now seen various formats that are possible for developing written and oral presentational communication. All of the suggested formats may be adapted for use at different levels of instruction and with students of different age groups. In the next two sections, we will turn our attention to ways in which we might respond to and provide feedback on students' presentational writing and speaking.

Responding to Presentational Writing

Traditionally, responding to presentational writing simply meant that the teacher corrected students' errors in grammar, vocabulary, and mechanics. However, in a process-oriented approach, feedback becomes part of the writing process as learners use feedback from peers and the teacher as they revise their work. The research indicates that learners want feedback on their writing (Leki, 1991, 2006; Schulz, 1996, 2001; Zhang, 1995), but they do not often find their teachers' comments useful because they are too short, uninformative, vague, authoritarian, and attempt to take over the student's writing (K. Hyland & F. Hyland, 2006). In a study of comments, reactions, and markings that university-level ESL instructors made on their students' compositions, Zamel (1985) found that instructors make comments about abstract rules and principles that are difficult for learners to interpret; they tend to give conflicting signals about what to improve; when providing suggestions, they respond to some problems but not others; and they tend not to revisit their own initial feedback when reviewing a revised composition (as cited in Lee & VanPatten, 2003).

Students typically handle teacher feedback by making a mental note or wanting additional teacher explanation (Cohen & Cavalcanti, 1990). In an extensive study of over 200 college students learning foreign and second languages, Cohen (1987) found that successful language learners paid greater attention to comments dealing with vocabulary, grammar, and mechanics than did unsuccessful language learners. Effective error correction—that which is selective, prioritized, and clear—can and does help at least some student writers (Ferris, 1999; Ferris & Hedgcock, 1998; Reid, 1998). Research on corrective feedback shows conflictive results. In a summary of meta-analysis of the research, Truscott (2007) makes the case that corrective feedback has a small and negative effect on learners' ability to write accurately. He suggests that the time students spend dealing with corrective feedback would be better spent in additional writing practice. Nevertheless, teachers feel that feedback on student work is an important part of their relationship with students and one of the ways in which they facilitate learning. Furthermore, students are disappointed when they do not receive feedback since they view it as an important contribution to their goal of producing an error-free document (K. Hyland & F. Hyland, 2006).

In this section, we will explain what kinds of feedback teachers and peers offer on student writing, how students respond to feedback, and some formats for teacher/student writing conferences, as well as ways to evaluate final written products. Keep in mind that students often first create a written draft of an oral or multimedia presentation and can benefit from feedback on the draft as they then adapt it for a live presentation. A discussion of feedback for oral and multimedia presentations follows in a subsequent section of this chapter. We will attempt to answer these questions:

- When should feedback focus on form, e.g., grammar, vocabulary, and mechanics, and when should it focus on content, e.g., organization and amount of detail?
- What types of teacher feedback do learners report being most helpful to them in improving their writing?
- How can teachers best help learners to edit and revise their own writing and that of their peers?
- What are effective methods of assessing and scoring final written products?

You will see in Chapter 11 that an effective practice in instruction and assessment is to provide students with criteria for how they will be assessed on a particular task prior to having them begin the task. You will also learn how to accomplish this through the use of rubrics and work samples so that students have a clear idea of what the task expectations are, what they must consider to create their final product, and on what criteria their work will be evaluated. Although a full treatment of rubrics is given in Chapter 11, we will provide a definition of this term here since the use of rubrics is suggested at this point: "a criterion-based scoring guide consisting of a fixed measurement scale . . . and descriptions of the characteristics for each score point. Rubrics describe degrees of quality, proficiency, or understanding along a continuum" (Wiggins & McTighe, 2005, p. 173). As you read this section, you may find it helpful to consult the part of Chapter 11 that deals with rubrics and/or examine the sample set of rubrics for presentational communication found in appendices on the *Teacher's Handbook* Web site for this chapter and Chapter 11.

www.cengagebrain.com

Learners want feedback on their writing, but they do not often find their teachers' comments useful because they are too short and uninformative.

Types of Feedback Based on Goals for Writing

As pointed out previously in this chapter, the goal for writing often determines how students and their teachers carry out the process of writing. At the early stages of the writing process, the goal may be for students to produce large amounts of writing as they generate ideas, and the research indicates that at this phase feedback should comment encouragingly on content rather than form. If the goal is to produce written or spoken language that is accurate in terms of syntax, semantics and grammar, then feedback should focus on the details of the language forms as well as the format of the presentation. The following sections describe how various approaches to feedback, which appear to be contradictory, can be reconciled by keeping the above two goals in mind.

No Feedback.   Before discussing the benefits of certain kinds of feedback, let us first consider the condition of no feedback. Sometimes no feedback means that a teacher simply looks at student work to verify its completion, but does not comment on it or offer suggestions. Sometimes it means that the learner puts early drafts of work into a portfolio, planning to revise it with feedback later and develop a final version. Not every product of student work requires feedback. Graham (1983) found that students made no fewer errors when they got feedback on every third assignment than when they got feedback on every assignment. Fathman and Whalley (1990) reported that students significantly improved the content and length of their compositions when they did revisions in the absence of teacher feedback, which suggests that the mere act of rewriting is valuable and that teacher feedback may not always be necessary (see also Truscott, 1996,

2007). Chastain (1990) found that there may be some relationship between the quality of learner compositions and whether or not a grade is being given by the teacher. His study showed that (1) intermittent grades on compositions may motivate learners to work harder to increase the length of the written text and complexity of its sentences, and (2) including ungraded written work in language classes enables learners to work on developing their writing skills without constant preoccupation with grades.

The portfolio approach has been suggested as an alternative to grading every individual writing assignment. In this approach, learners set goals for what they hope to accomplish in their writing, compare drafts of how they revised and reformulated their writing, and write reflections on how their work has improved. The portfolio provides a record over time of how their writing has changed. From this record, the entire portfolio can be evaluated for a grade (Leki, 1990; Moore, 1994; Tierney, Carter, & Desai, 1991). Portfolios have been successfully used at all grade levels, including college-level advanced grammar and stylistics courses. Paesani (2006) used literary texts to initiate study of grammatical points in context, asked students to write a text following the literary model, and included peer review, self-evaluation, and instructor feedback, all presented within a portfolio.

A portfolio may contain presentational forms of writing since it is often shown in the format of one-to-many, with little opportunity for negotiation of meaning. Learners select items for inclusion, which may include stories, letters, surveys, poetry, learning logs, reading records, posters, artwork, and response and writing-conference logs (Peregoy & Boyle, 2005). Learners could prepare a news broadcast or a videotape of a skit that they have created, accompanied by reactions of a preliminary audience, followed by a final revised version of the skit. The portfolio might also include multiple ungraded drafts of these samples of writing in order to show progress over time. See Chapter 11 for additional information about portfolio assessment.

Focus on Content.   Much of the literature on correcting written errors supports the claim that learners' writing skills may improve with teacher responses that focus on content rather than on form (Donovan & McClelland, 1980; Kepner, 1991; Semke, 1984; Zamel, 1983). Semke's (1984) study researched the effects of four types of feedback on students' freewriting journal assignments: (1) comments only, (2) corrections only, (3) corrections with comments, and (4) errors signaled with a correction code for students to self-correct. The results indicated that there was no significant difference among the groups in terms of effect on writing accuracy, but that the group receiving comments wrote significantly more than the other groups and made more progress in general language ability. Similarly, Kepner (1991) compared the effects of sentence-level error correction and message-related comments. She found that sentence-level correction did not help students avoid surface errors and that responding to a message was more effective in helping learners improve the quality of their written ideas and grammatical accuracy.

Providing content-focused feedback is sometimes difficult for teachers whose attention is often drawn to grammatical or syntactical errors because of the expectations of the environment in which they teach. Despite teachers' wishes to provide content-focused feedback, F. Hyland (2003) reports that grammatical accuracy and focus on form accounted for 58–75% of the feedback given by teachers of ESL in her study in Hong Kong. Ashwell (2000) found that content feedback had only a moderate effect on the revisions that students made, indicating that perhaps providing useful content-focused feedback is more difficult than it seems. K. Hyland (2003) suggests that teachers who provide feedback that focuses on content should draw from statements of praise, criticism, and suggestions, as shown in these examples:

- Praise: You have dealt with this topic well. There is a good flow of ideas and a very clear plan.

- Criticism: There is no statement of intention in the essay—what is the purpose of your essay and how are you going to deal with it? You are not giving me [as reader] any direction.
- Suggestion: This conclusion is all a bit vague. I think it would be better to clearly state your conclusions with the brief reasons for them (pp. 187–189).

Focus on Form. Much of the research examining the effect of correction of form errors provides little support for overt correction, i.e., giving the correct forms (Ashwell, 2000; Hendrickson, 1978; Lee, 1997; Truscott, 1996, 1999, 2007), since students tend to simply copy the correct forms into the next draft. Focus-on-form feedback seems to produce only surface-level improvements. Furthermore, Robb, Ross, and Shortreed (1986) point out that even the most systematic and exhaustive attention to grammar correction produces insignificant improvement in subsequent writing tasks. Conversely, when teachers are selective about corrections, place feedback in the margins, and clearly indicate which errors are being addressed, writing accuracy increases (Fathman & Whalley, 1990; Goldstein, 2004.)

Grammar and content feedback, whether given alone or simultaneously, positively affect rewriting. In a study by F. Hyland (2003), students successfully revised 88–100% of the focus-on-form suggestions, perhaps because teachers usually expect form errors to be corrected. Some evidence also points to the likelihood that those learners who appreciate grammatical information may also be those who are able to identify gaps in their own grammatical knowledge (Manley & Calk, 1997). Also, students may benefit more from teacher feedback when the feedback is focused on two or three patterns of error rather than all errors at once (Ferris, 2002).

Ferris (1999) points out that students can learn to identify their own errors, describe their own work, and self-edit and revise their own texts if they are "focused on the importance of editing, trained to identify and correct patterns of frequent and serious errors, and given explicit teaching as needed about the rules governing those patterns of errors" (p. 5). Qi and Lapkin (2001) confirm students' ability to analyze their own work but point out that it is the more proficient learner who is better able to explain why a reformulated version of his composition is better. Although the use of error codes is somewhat productive, not all learners are sophisticated enough to understand and apply them, and some students may need explicit instructions about the underlying rules of the error codes.

An example of a focus-on-form error correction feedback system is Lalande's (1982) Essay Correction Code (ECCO), used for marking errors, and his Error Awareness Sheet (EASE), used for tracking errors. In his studies, the number of errors was reduced when teachers marked the errors with ECCO, used EASE to track errors, and required students to interpret the codes, correct their own mistakes, and rewrite their essays. See Appendix 9.6 on the *Teacher's Handbook* Web site for an adapted version of ECCO and Appendix 9.7, also on the *Teacher's Handbook* Web site for an adapted version of EASE.

www.cengagebrain.com

If the goal is that students produce large amounts of writing, the research indicates that feedback should comment encouragingly on content rather than form. If the goal is to produce written or spoken language that is accurate in terms of syntax, semantics and grammar, then feedback should focus on the details of the language forms as well as the format of the presentation.

Writing Workshop Conferences. Writing conferences, whether one-on-one or in small groups, are often touted as the preferred mode of giving feedback to learners. In a writing conference, the learner can ask the experts, the teacher or another content-area experts, for information about where writing might be weak. Teachers and expert can provide input that is focused on what the learner was trying to say. Negotiation of meaning is a two-way process during the conference, and provides scaffolding in an environment that is low-anxiety and generally perceived as helpful and productive. Among ESL learners, researchers found differences in individual learners' responses to the conferences, but more importantly, they found that even the weaker students attempted to incorporate the changes suggested during the conferences into their subsequent drafts (Goldstein & Conrad, 1990; Patthey-Chavez & Ferris, 1997).

To prepare for writing conferences, teachers should be certain that students know the purpose of the activity, perhaps by explicitly instructing learners on what to do and say during the session, modeling, role-playing, and explicitly teaching language to be used to facilitate interaction during the session. Figure 9.8 shows a sample worksheet that can be used to prepare for a writer's conference. Williams (2005) suggests that teachers allow students to begin the conference by asking questions and sharing concerns. Teachers should use general leading questions such as, "What was the hardest thing about writing this paper?," "What is the point of your paper/this paragraph?," "What do you mean here?" (p. 115).

 How can a ZPD be created during a writing conference?

There are various ways in which teachers may respond to student writing, and each has a specific purpose given the goal of the writing activity. Teachers will undoubtedly

FIGURE 9.8 Writing Conference Preparation Worksheet

Initial Conference (about a topic)

1. Topic for my essay ....
2. Intended purpose of my essay ....
3. Intended audience for my essay ....
4. Prewriting about my topic ....

Essay Draft Conference

Statements 1–3 above plus
1. In group work my peers asked the following questions about my topic ....
2. In group work my peers made the following suggestions ....
3. The problem(s) I'm having with this draft are ....

Revision Planning Conference

1. I thought the best part of my essay was ....
2. I thought the weakest part of my essay was ....
3. According to the teacher's comments, the strengths and problems in the draft are:

    Strengths   Problems

    (a) ....   (a) ....
    (b) ....   (b) ....
    (c) ....   (c) ....

4. Based on the feedback, here is my plan for revising the essay (list specific steps you intend to take and specific paragraphs you intend to revise):

    (a) ....
    (b) ....
    (c) ....

Three questions I want to ask you (the instructor) are:

    (a) ....
    (b) ....
    (c) ....

Source: From *Second Language Writing* (p. 196), by K. Hyland, 2003, Cambridge, UK: Cambridge University Press. Reprinted with permission of Cambridge University Press.

use a variety of strategies to provide feedback to students, but they should be sure to match the feedback type to the goal of the writing task.

 Why is it necessary to match feedback to the goals of writing?

Student Responses to Feedback

Another way to consider the usefulness of feedback is to explore the kinds of changes students make following teacher or peer feedback. Providing feedback is a time-consuming activity for teachers, who are often unconvinced that students make use of it in subsequent drafts (Guénette, 2007; Lee, 1997; Truscott, 2007). Lee and Schallert (2008) found that if the teacher and students have a trusting relationship, students incorporate teacher suggestions more readily in subsequent drafts. Chandler's (2003) study offers support for a way to provide feedback while requiring students to make corrections themselves. She studied four kinds of teacher feedback/error correction over 10 weeks in ESL classes: (1) direct correction, (2) underline and describe, (3) describe, and (4) underline. She found that direct correction produced the most accurate revisions because students simply copied the changes that the teacher indicated, and not surprisingly, students thought it was the fastest and easiest way to make revisions. However, this approach did not encourage students to take responsibility for learning how to improve their writing, and they admitted that they learned more from self-correction when teachers used simple underlining on first drafts. Nevertheless, this underlining technique should not be used in isolation as the only form of feedback because studies show that students tend to make surface-level changes when working on their own, but they make mostly meaning-level changes when working with peer or teacher feedback (Paulus, 1999). Bitchener (2008) reported that EFL students produced more accurate revisions if they received a combination of (1) direct corrective feedback written above their errors, and (2) written as well as oral explanations of the correct form. A teacher might deliver the explanation of form in a whole class setting, drawing attention to forms that may require additional practice by the group rather than individual errors.

Hedgcock and Lefkowitz (1996) interviewed FL and ESL writers about the types of responses they would like to have in order to improve their writing. They gave the following suggestions for teachers:

- more practice in writing and more systematic opportunities to revise, e.g., through the use of quickwriting, other short activities, and multiple drafts;
- more personalized and explicit written feedback from expert readers, e.g., experts in the topic content or the language, other than the teacher, e.g., writing conferences;
- grammatical and rhetorical feedback geared more specifically to writer's level of proficiency and degree of readiness, e.g., too much feedback or too much detail is overwhelming; students should be guided to work on selected aspects of their writing;
- individualized writing conferences with instructors, other expert readers, or both (Beach, 1989); see below for an example;
- more peer interaction and response, e.g., see the description of peer revision below;
- more student control over the nature and extent of instructor/expert feedback; e.g., students need to be able to ask for targeted help from experts in the areas they feel they are weak; and
- more extensive reading of L2 texts, particularly models that students are asked to imitate, e.g., reading more expository texts as models before being asked to write one (adapted from Hedgcock & Lefkowitz, 1996, p. 299).

Feedback from the teacher is one avenue for helping students to improve their writing. Another avenue for providing feedback comes from peers. The following section describes the process and benefits of peer review.

Peer Revision

Having students engage in peer revision can promote their autonomy as authors, provide them with an audience other than the teacher, and encourage them to work with others during the writing process (Scott, 1996). Research indicates that peer revision is successful because it allows students opportunities to take active roles in their own learning; reconceptualize their ideas, gain confidence, and reduce anxiety by seeing peers' strengths and weaknesses in writing; gain feedback from multiple sources; and build the critical skills needed for revision by responding to peers (Ferris, 2003; K. Hyland & F. Hyland, 2006). However, peers sometimes have difficulty identifying errors, and learners tend to trust teacher feedback more readily, and peers from different cultures have varying expectations for correction.

Initially, students may be reluctant to participate in peer review processes. Mangelsdorf and Schlumberger (1992) found that peer reviewers adopted one of three perspectives: (1) prescriptive, i.e., focused on form and on a predetermined notion of what the text should be; (2) interpretive, i.e., imposed their own ideas about the topic onto the text; and (3) collaborative, i.e., viewed the text from the author's perspective, made suggestions, and did not focus exclusively on form. Nearly half of the peer reviewers adopted a prescriptive approach, which the researchers attribute to the fact that they received the same kind of feedback from teachers in the past. In later research, Villamil and de Guerrero (1996) studied the audio recordings of 40 pairs of students during peer interactions. The peer review process was found to be a "total communicative experience in which students not only wrote and read but also spoke and listened" (p. 66). They found that the students engaged in sociocognitive behaviors such as reading, assessing, dealing with trouble sources, composing, writing comments, copying, and discussing task procedures. The students mediated their writing by using L1, symbols, and external resources; by providing scaffolding to each other; by resorting to interlanguage knowledge; and by vocalizing private speech. Significant aspects of social behavior found were management of control as an author (i.e., giving it up, taking it over, respecting/not respecting it, struggling for and maintaining it), collaboration, affectivity, and adopting reader/writer roles. These same researchers also highlighted the complexity of student relationships during peer review sessions, and showed how students are first controlled by their written drafts and do not wish to respond to directions from a peer. Then, as they become more accustomed to the process, students accept peer guidance. Finally, when the process has been helpful, students anticipate peer guidance and respond quickly and efficiently to suggestions from a peer. Recently, building on the de Guerrero and Villamil studies, Levi Altstaedter (2009) found that students who engaged in peer editing processes with guidance paid attention to the macro aspects of organization and clarity of communication as well as to the micro aspects of form as it relates to meaning. She also found that learners began to internalize the supportive role and guidance of the tutor. That is, students became more self-directed in questioning and editing their own writing and more self-reliant in making revisions.

One way to initiate a peer review process might be to involve students in a *collaborative* writing process in pairs, not just in the peer editing process after a completed composition has been written by one student in isolation. Students are paired (see Chapter 8 for formation of groups) and might be given a graphic prompt. Students write one to two paragraphs of text, collaborating with each other and recording their talk on a teacher-provided tape recorder. They make decisions about what the graphic means, how to shape their paragraphs, what to include or exclude, and comment on correct form. Their paragraphs are collected but not graded, and returned to them with teacher commentary and feedback. Storch (2005) noted that collaborative writing "affords students the opportunity to give and receive immediate feedback on language, an opportunity missing when students write individually. This may explain why pairs tend to produce texts with greater grammatical accuracy and complexity than individual writers" (Storch, p. 168). Storch and Wigglesworth (2008) summarize that collaborative writing leads to more accurate texts, and it supports learning in a scaffolded manner as students assist each other in the planning, writing, and reviewing processes, working through the ZPD (Donato, 1994, 2004; Storch, 2002; Swain, 2000). See Appendix 9.8 on the *Teacher's Handbook* Web site for a whole-class collaborative writing activity that might be used to launch in-pairs collaborative writing. As students progress through the stages of peer editing and collaborative writing, they will benefit from guidance on how to plan, what to look for, and how to revise their own and their peers' work in ways consistent with sociocultural theory, advocated in Chapters 1 and 7 of this book.

www.cengagebrain.com

According to the research, peer revision can be a positive experience if peer reviewers are given clear guidelines so that they know what to look for and what kinds of feedback will be most helpful (Amores, 1997; Hedgcock & Lefkowitz, 1996; Jacobs, Curtis, Braine, & Huang, 1998; Stanley, 1992). In fact, peer assistance might be just as useful as feedback provided by the teacher (Hedgcock & Lefkowitz). To conduct peer review, teachers typically assign students to groups of two, three, or four in order to exchange completed drafts and give comments on each others' work. Peer review works best if the teacher involves the students in the purposes and procedures for the activity, as shown in Figure 9.9. The actual review may happen during class, or online or in another informal setting. Students may bring a copy of their drafts to share with the others during class or may share their drafts via discussion board. Students typically work from a set of guidelines such as those in Figure 9.10. Roebuck (2001) provides a worksheet that appears in Appendix 9.9 on the *Teacher's Handbook* Web site for peer and self-analysis based on the sociocultural approach advocated in *Teacher's Handbook*. On the *Teacher's Handbook* Web site, see Appendix 9.10 for a sample Peer Response Sheet and Appendix 9.11 for a revision plan, or "what to do when the draft comes back" (Williams, 2005, p. 110).

The first step in conducting a peer review session is to introduce the concept of peer editing. K. Hyland (2003) suggests the following description to introduce students to the session:

FIGURE 9.9 What is Peer Editing?

What is Peer Editing?

Peer editing means responding with appreciation and positive criticism to your classmates' writing. It is an important part of this course because it can:
- Help you become more aware of your reader when writing and revising
- Help you become more sensitive to problems in your writing and more confident in correcting them

Rules for Peer responding:
- Be respectful of your classmate's work
- Be conscientious—read carefully and think about what the writer is trying to say
- Be tidy and legible in your comments
- Be encouraging and make suggestions
- Be specific with comments

Remember: You do not need to be an expert at grammar. Your best help is as a reader and that you know when you have been interested, entertained, persuaded, or confused.

Source: From *Second Language Writing* (p. 202), by K. Hyland, 2003, Cambridge, UK: Cambridge University Press. Reprinted with permission of Cambridge University Press.

K. Hyland (2003) also suggests that learners think about how they want peer reviewers to respond to their writing. Figure 9.10 is suggested as a sample:

FIGURE 9.10 Peer Response Sheet

Peer Response Sheet: Argument

Author's Name ....   Title of Draft ....
Write three questions you would like your responder to answer.
1.
2.
3.
Responder's Name ....
Read the questions above. Listen to the author read his/her draft aloud. Read the paper again if you want to. Then write a response for the author.

Author's Reflection

Read the response you have received carefully. Reflect on it and write what you have learned and what you intend to do next below.

Source: From *Second Language Writing* (p. 206), by K. Hyland, 2003. Cambridge, UK: Cambirdge University Press. Reprinted with permission of Cambridge University Press.

 Peer revision can be successful if peer reviewers are given clear guidelines so that they know what to look for and what kinds of feedback will be most helpful.

 What are the benefits of peer revision?

Summary of Research on and Implications of Responses to Writing

In this section, you have learned about the important research that deals with the effects of various types of responses to student writing. In addition, implications were drawn from this research, and suggestions were made to guide the FL teacher in responding to writing. The following are the key points to remember from the review of the research and implications:

- The goal for writing determines the type of feedback that is most effective.
- Feedback on content encourages students to produce more language and to use it creatively. Learners' writing improves most when students receive feedback dealing with the content of the message.
- Feedback that focuses on form will lead to greater accuracy in terms of syntax, semantics, and grammar, if it focuses on only a few patterns of error at once and allows students to self-correct.
- Feedback should be given by teachers and by peers.
- Students should be given the responsibility for revisions and correction of errors.
- Intermittent evaluation and simple underlining of errors are effective and provide some relief to the teacher overburdened with grading papers.
- Peer revision can be successful if learners are given explicit guidelines for how to review others' writing.

Ferris (2003) also suggests that teachers should recognize that, at the lower levels of proficiency, feedback should be targeted and brief, focusing on a couple of points, whether related to content or form, at a time. Teachers should examine their feedback to be certain that it is clear and helpful, and model the kinds of helpful feedback in peer editing settings (p. 134).

Scoring Methods for Evaluating Writing

The following are four methods for scoring and assigning a grade to compositions. Teachers will find it beneficial to use these types of scoring systems throughout the year with different writing assignments, depending on the nature and purpose of each task:

www.cengagebrain.com

- Holistic (also called integrative or global): The rater gives one grade as an overall impression of the entire text, based on a combination of aspects such as clarity, effectiveness of message, control of language, and so forth. According to Terry (R. Terry, personal communication, July 16, 2008), the holistic scoring instrument used by the Educational Testing Service for evaluating the Advanced Placement Evaluation in foreign languages, as shown in Appendix 9.12 on the *Teacher's Handbook* Web site, can be adapted to fit the level of students and the focus of instruction. The holistic method of scoring is most reliable when raters are trained to establish common standards based on practice rating the types of writing samples they will be evaluating (Cooper, 1977).
- Analytic: The rater scores various components of the composition separately and gives specific responses to the learner; scored components may include content, organization, vocabulary, language use, and mechanics. See Appendix 9.13 on the *Teacher's Handbook* Web site for the ESL Composition Profile Scale, an example of an analytic scoring tool. See Amores (1999, p. 457) for another scoring profile. The advantage of an analytic scoring method is that it offers feedback to show the quality of students' work in each of the criteria specified, thereby informing students of the specific areas in which they need to improve. See Chapter 11 on the *Teacher's Handbook* Web site for a sample set of presentational rubrics that are analytic in nature.
- Primary trait: The rater assigns a holistic score to one particular feature of writing that has been identified in the writing assignment, such as grammatical accuracy or vocabulary usage. Lloyd-Jones (1977) suggests using primary trait scoring to evaluate the quality of a particular mode of discourse such as explanatory, persuasive, or expressive, as shown in Appendix 9.14 on the *Teacher's Handbook* Web site.
- Multiple trait: The rater assigns a score on several qualities of writing that are important in a particular context or task, and allows the rater to score these qualities relative to each other. Hamp-Lyons (2003) points out that this scoring approach allows the rater to score some qualities higher than others, particularly within a specified context. See Appendix 9.15 on the *Teacher's Handbook* Web site.

In this section, you have explored ways to provide feedback to learners on their writing, incorporate peer revision, and assess final written products. We will now ponder additional considerations when providing feedback on oral and multimedia presentations.

Responding to Oral and Multimedia Presentations

Given that our current framework for describing communication within the three modes is still a relatively new concept, little research exists on ways to provide feedback on presentational communication, particularly that which occurs orally or with multimedia. Many of the suggestions offered in the previous section for giving feedback on presentational writing, together with implications regarding feedback in interpersonal communication (refer back to Chapter 8), can also be appropriately applied to presentational speaking.

Criteria Specific to Oral Presentations

As with presentational writing, responding to oral presentations includes giving feedback on accuracy of language, e.g., grammar and vocabulary. In presentational speaking, accuracy of grammar usually includes the criterion of formal language use appropriate for a presentation to an audience, e.g., use of the formal "you" when addressing the audience and avoidance of slang. However, there are other characteristics unique to oral presentations to be considered as well, which are illustrated in the sample oral presentation evaluation form that appears in Figure 9.11. In this evaluation instrument, note that the term *delivery* refers to the manner in which the student presents the message to the audience and includes features such as maintaining eye contact, projecting one's voice and

FIGURE 9.11 Sample Oral Presentational Evaluation Form

Sample Language Related Activities:

Giving Effective Presentations: Learners should consider the following evaluation rubric when preparing and delivering their presentations. The instructor and classmates can use this rubric to evaluate the presentations.

Sample Presentation Evaluation Form

Speaker:

Delivery

_____ Maintained eye contact with listeners in all parts of the room
_____ Spoke loudly and clearly
_____ Spoke in a natural, conversational manner
_____ Used effective posture, movement, and gestures
_____ Used notes effectively (if applicable)

Communicative Ability

_____ Pronunciation was clear
_____ Spoke fluently, without too much hesitation or repetition
_____ Grammar and vocabulary choices were reasonably accurate

Content

_____ Met time limit
_____ Developed topic with sufficient reasons, examples, and detail
_____ Chose a topic that was appropriate for the audience
_____ Organization
_____ Effective introduction
_____ Logical development of ideas
_____ Clear transitions
_____ Effective conclusion

Additional Comments:

Source: From "Evocando y paso a paso avanzando: A creative writing project for Spanish," by M. Espinosa-Dulanto, 2003, *CALPER Pedagogical Materials: Project Work*, No. 3, p. 7. Copyright © 2003 Center for Advanced Proficiency Education and Research (CALPER), The Pennsylvania State University, http://calper.la.psu.edu. Reprinted by permission.

articulating clearly, and using effective body language and gestures. In Chapter 11, you will learn about a standards-based performance assessment in which the term *impact* is used as a criterion referring to an aspect of delivery: the degree to which the message maintains the attention of the audience.

Also key to effective delivery is the use of notes, if any are used. Traditionally, students gave oral presentations by standing up and reading their written scripts word for word while the rest of the class often paid little attention to what was being said. Presentations that have *impact* are not read from a script, but rather are presented in a more extemporaneous form where the presenter uses notes periodically as a guide in remembering the order of ideas to be discussed. This frees the presenter to interact more with the audience, show visuals, or operate the computer in cases of multimedia presentations. Presentations that are totally memorized and read like the evening news scripts on television are lacking in impact and are often difficult for students in the class to comprehend because they lack natural pauses and other features of more extemporaneous speech that facilitate comprehension. Students need ample practice in doing presentations and receiving informal feedback before they are assessed on more formal presentations.

As depicted in Figure 9.11, the criterion of *communicative ability* includes pronunciation that makes the message comprehensible, fluency (not having too much hesitation or repetition), and grammar and vocabulary that have the expected level of accuracy given students' levels of language development. Finally, the criterion of *content* deals with the meaning of the message itself and completion of the assignment according to the instructions provided at the beginning. This criterion addresses specifically the depth with which the topic was developed, how the information was organized, the quality of the introduction and conclusion, the logical development of ideas, and the use of transitions. If the presentation required research on the part of the student, the quality of the research could be another element that is included here. Appendix 9.16 on the *Teacher's Handbook* Web site contains an example of a rubric that can be used to assess oral presentations. See Appendix 9.17, also on the *Teacher's Handbook* Web site, for a description of rubrics and a presentational communication project on children's literature delivered to elementary school students by high school Spanish students.[4] See also Chapter 10 for a presentational "real audience" community project conducted by recently immigrated ESL students.

www.cengagebrain.com

Criteria Specific to Multimedia Presentations

When students use multimedia to enhance their oral presentations, teachers should assess their use of media in addition to the other criteria discussed above that deal with language and content. Media might include visuals, paintings, cultural artifacts and other realia, video, audio, and music CDs, as well as Web-based connections and presentational software such as PowerPoint. Appendix 9.18 illustrates a rubric that might be used in assessing a multimedia presentation. Note the specific criteria that pertain to the use of media:

- selection of media type as an avenue for presenting the content;
- degree to which media elements accent the information being presented; and
- way in which media are manipulated during the presentation.

For presentations that use a presentational software program such as PowerPoint, the following are some questions that might be used to assess this aspect of the presentation:

- Does the visual component support and/or enhance the content of the presentation?

- Is the number of slides appropriate given the length of the presentation, e.g., between five to six slides in a 15-minute presentation?
- Is the layout of the slides visually appealing (e.g., color, design scheme, amount of text on each slide, font)?
- Are the backgrounds and design appropriate, i.e., colors don't clash, design not too "busy"?
- Is animation appropriate, e.g., movement and timing of figures, graphics, and text?
- Are the appearance and sound of transition effects appealing, e.g., not too loud?

When Web-based connections are used as part of the presentation, the teacher might also assess the appropriateness of these connections to the content of the presentation.

Although it is important to assess the multimedia aspects of presentations, teachers are cautioned to keep in mind that the most important characteristics of presentations are those that deal with language use and content of the presentation.

Pronunciation: Feedback and Instruction.   An important component of presentational speaking is using a pronunciation of the TL that is comprehensible to the audience. In the days of the audiolingual method (see Chapter 2), there was an emphasis on the use of *correct* pronunciation, which was thought to develop through rote repetition. However, teachers should realize that a learner's interlanguage includes pronunciation that is in development, just as grammatical knowledge is in a constant state of evolving. Hence, it is acceptable for learners to have an *accent*—i.e., pronunciation is always under construction during language learning (in development). Thus, the goal of feedback and instruction should be *comprehensible* pronunciation (i.e., developing) rather than native-like pronunciation. It is clear that longer periods of exposure to L2 can lead to improved pronunciation (Piske, MacKay, & Flege, 2001), and that experience hearing authentic L2 is pivotal for students to acquire a pronunciation that approaches the quality of the L2. With exposure to authentic L2, learners' pronunciation improves over time.

You might recall Case Study 2 in Chapter 6, which illustrated how one teacher used reading aloud for pronunciation practice. A few studies have shown that direct pronunciation instruction can help learners to improve, particularly if attention is given to suprasegmental features of L2, e.g., intonation patterns (Hahn, 2004; Jenkins, 2004). As an example, in Spanish, the teacher might include attention to intonation when engaging students in tasks that require the use of information questions, which require a falling intonation instead of a rising intonation as in English. Pronunciation instruction should involve more than teaching the discrete sounds of the language but it is not the same as teaching a phonology course for college students. Explicit pronunciation awareness instruction could address recurring pronunciation difficulties, L1–L2 pronunciation comparisons, and the relationship of pronunciation to formal or informal speech, always keeping in mind the age and cognitive development of the learner. This type of instruction stands in sharp contrast to the view that pronunciation instruction is only repetition after the teacher.

Pronunciation awareness instruction should always be taught in the service of meaning and in meaningful contexts. For example, pronunciation practice might best occur in oral presentational contexts such as jazz chants, poetry readings, readers' theater, or any activity in which attending to the sounds of language is important to understanding the language (R. Donato, personal communication, July 14, 2008). Furthermore, attention to pronunciation, just as in the case of grammar and vocabulary, can be handled within a learner-based approach in which focus on form occurs by engaging learners in the process of identifying specific sounds or intonation patterns, working to acquire them, and helping one another to improve. Thus, teachers "need not cast L2 pronunciation learning as a rote, meaningless, and largely teacher-driven process" (Trofimovich & Gatbonton, 2006, p. 532).

In sum, according to Lightbown and Spada (2006), it is clear that "decontextualized pronunciation instruction is not enough and that a combination of instruction, exposure, experience, and motivation is required" (p. 107).[5]

Feedback from Audiences

With oral and multimedia presentations, feedback may come from not only the teacher, but also from "real" audiences, including peers, other teachers and administrators, parents, and other invited guests, such as native speakers of the TL who live in the local community. It is a good idea for students to provide feedback to their peers because (1) this feedback is usually meaningful to students, and (2) this activity engages the rest of the class in listening and learning content from the presentations. Figure 9.12 illustrates a sample peer evaluation form for a group oral presentation. You will notice that in addition to providing evaluative comments, students are also held accountable for what they have learned as a result of having been the audience by describing what they learned, liked, and disliked about the presentation. Another format for holding students accountable as the audience is to have them write a brief summary of what they learned in the FL and then have them write one or two questions that they would like to ask the presenter.

Other types of audiences, such as parents and other teachers, might be invited to provide comments about the content of the presentation rather than an assessment of it. They could be given 3 × 5 note cards on which to place their comments; if they speak the TL, comments could be given in that language. Or they might write their comments on the bulletin board or other space dedicated to audience feedback.

Teachers will find it helpful to provide feedback throughout the process of creating the presentation as well as at the end. For group presentations or projects, teachers are encouraged to provide both individual grades and group grades so that students' individual and collaborative efforts are recognized and rewarded.

FIGURE 9.12 Sample Peer Evaluation Form for Oral Presentations

Project:	*"13 Jahre Deutsche Vereinigung"*					
Group:	Sub-Topic of the group					
Speaker:	_____					

SPEAKER:	−				++
The speaker is comprehensible	1	2	3	4	5
The presentation was well-organized (beginning, middle, end)	1	2	3	4	5
The speaker provided enough vocabulary to help me understand	1	2	3	4	5
The speaker used aids (OHP etc.) to help me understand	1	2	3	4	5
The speaker presented interesting and valuable information	1	2	3	4	5
GROUP:					
The group presentation reflected team effort	1	2	3	4	5

I:
What I learned from the presentation?
What I liked in this presentation?
What I disliked in this presentation?

Source: From "13 Jahre Deutsche Vereinigung: A sample project for advanced learners of German," by G. Appel, 2003, *CALPER Pedagogical Materials: Project Work,* No. 2, p. 4. Copyright © 2003 Center for Advanced Proficiency Education and Research (CALPER), The Pennsylvania State University, http://calper.la.psu.edu. Reprinted by permission.

In conclusion, in this chapter you have learned about a process-oriented approach to oral and written presentational communication, as well as formats for presentational tasks across levels of instruction and strategies for assessing presentational speaking and writing. It is important to note that, in the spirit of integrating the three modes of communication, presentational communication can be the culmination of work done in the other two modes. It can also be used as the catalyst for interpersonal discussion or acquisition of content through interpretive listening, reading, and/or viewing.

TEACH AND REFLECT ·

NCATE_____

www.cengagebrain.com

EPISODE ONE
Designing a Presentational Process-Oriented Writing Activity for Secondary Levels or Beyond

ACTFL/NCATE 4.b. Integrating Standards in Instruction; 4.c. Selecting and Designing Instructional Materials; 5.b. Reflecting on Assessment

TESOL/NCATE 3.a. Planning for Standards-Based ESL and Content Instruction; 3.b. Managing and Implementing Standards-Based ESL and Content Instruction; and 3.c. Using Resources Effectively in ESL and Content Instruction

For this activity, use a thematic unit for the target language you teach, as approved by your instructor. Develop a presentational process-oriented writing activity that you might assign as part of your work on this unit. Use the criteria provided in the teacher checklist in Appendix 9.4 on the *Teacher's Handbook* Web site as you prepare the task. Develop the assignment by using the process-oriented model applied to a task that is presented in Figure 9.3. Describe what students will do in each phase of their writing, how many days the activity might take, and how you will provide feedback and include peer review as well. Choose a scoring method from among those described in this chapter, and explain how you will assign a grade to the final product.

NCATE_____

www.cengagebrain.com

EPISODE TWO
Finding the Oral and Written Presentational Elements in Prepared Project Units

ACTFL/NCATE 3.a. Understanding Language Acquisition and Creating a Supportive Classroom; 4.b. Integrating Standards in Instruction; 4.c. Selecting and Designing Instructional Materials; 5.b. Reflecting on Assessment; 5.c. Reporting Assessment Results

TESOL/NCATE 3.a. Planning for Standards-Based ESL and Content Instruction; 3.b. Managing and Implementing Standards-Based ESL and Content Instruction; 3.c. Using Resources Effectively in ESL and Content Instruction; and 4.c. Classroom-Based Assessment for ESL

On the *Teacher's Handbook* Web site, Appendices 9.19, 9.20, and 9.21 are a set of "project units" from The Pennsylvania State University Center for Advanced Language Proficiency Education and Research (CALPER). These units are the result of Project Work, through which students engage in substantial inquiry over a period of time on a particular topic as the basis for designing an oral or written presentation; they analyze and evaluate their own learning, work collaboratively with others, and receive guidance and direction from the teacher. Project Work offers a constructivist perspective on language learning and enables students to develop the ability to become more self-directed while creating a product that is realistic and meaningful. The project units are designed for high intermediate or advanced students, grades 7–12, or undergraduate students.

Go to the *Teacher's Handbook* Web site and select one of the German, Spanish, or ESL projects:

- "Let's Make a Deal" (Johnson, 2003)
- "13 Jahre Deutsch Vereinigung" (Appel, 2003)
- "Evocando y paso a paso avanzando" (Espinosa-Dulanto, 2003)

Now complete the tasks below.

1. Analyze the project you selected for the following elements:
   a. real audiences
   b. opportunities to use a valid voice
   c. reading-to-write from source materials
   d. process approach to presenting (formulating/generating ideas, planning, writing, revising, restructuring, presenting)
   e. use of reference tools and source materials
   f. evaluation and critique possibilities

2. Describe how the final presentation for the particular project you read about is assessed. How does the assessment relate to the information presented in this chapter?

TECHNO FOCUS: With regard to a post-secondary use of oral presentational communication, Bueno (2006) incorporates the study of two films into a third-year composition and conversation course. Students view the films outside of class, engage in online asynchronous chats, and create a video journal. While the asynchronous chats are a form of interpretive and interpersonal communication, the video journals exemplify oral presentational communication. For example, in the video journal for the film *Yerma*, students relate what happened in the first act from the perspective of one of the main characters, either Yerma or Juan. The account must include a comparison of the different viewpoints of Juan and Yerma, and must elicit understanding and sympathy (p. 454). In preparing for their oral video journals, students report *stepping out of the comfort zone* of their usual present-tense narration and thinking of ways to use the past tense; they listen to each other and then form their own narrative; they record, edit, and re-record their journals two to six times, finally achieving a "really good flow and naturalness to it." (p. 463).

a. Re-read Chapter 6 and Bueno (2006) to see what characteristics of the film version of the play *Yerma* led Bueno to select it. Find another film that also meets these same characteristics that you can use with your students.

b. Create a video journal assignment based on a reading selection from your textbook, or based on a literary selection. In this journal assignment, ask your students to take the perspective of one of the characters in the film, or to narrate or act out a different ending of the film.

DISCUSS AND REFLECT ·

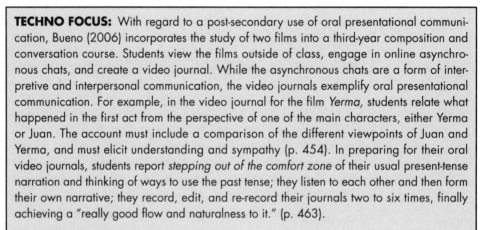

www.cengagebrain.com

See the *Teacher's Handbook* Web site for an additional case study:
Case Study Two: A Play for My Buddies (adapted from Blanton, 1998)

NCATE _____   **CASE STUDY ONE**
Integrating Peer Revision into the Presentational Writing Process

ACTFL/NCATE 5.a. Knowing Assessment Models and Using Them Appropriately; 5.b. Reflecting on Assessment

TESOL/NCATE 3.a. Planning for Standards-Based ESL and Content Instruction; 3.b. Managing and Implementing Standards-Based ESL and Content Instruction; and 3.c. Using Resources Effectively in ESL and Content Instruction; and 4.c. Classroom-Based Assessment for ESL

Ms. Reynolds has been teaching Spanish and German at Yuristown High School for three years. She has a heavy teaching schedule of seven classes, and one of her Spanish classes includes both Level 3 and Level 4 learners. Ms. Reynolds believes in teaching language for proficiency, and she provides many opportunities for her learners to use the language in meaningful contexts. Because of time constraints and her own training and teaching experience, she tends to focus more on interpersonal speaking and writing in her classroom.

Recently she spoke to Ms. Savage, who has been teaching English at Yuristown for seven years, about the issue of doing more presentational activities in her language classes. Ms. Reynolds assigns periodic written presentational tasks and even uses a process-oriented approach to some degree as she guides learners' writing. However, she is frustrated that learners do not seem to care much about correcting their errors, and she ends up practically rewriting their compositions for them. Ms. Savage suggests that Ms. Reynolds try peer revision, a technique that English teachers have been using for some time. She explains that learners work in pairs (usually with one weaker learner and one stronger) to help each other correct their mistakes. Ms. Savage also suggests the use of some type of correction code and the use of the Error Awareness Sheet to help learners keep track of their errors.

Ask yourself these questions:

1. At what stage of the presentational communication process would the peer revision be done?

2. What difficulties can Ms. Reynolds anticipate when introducing the peer revision technique to her classes?

3. What type of guidance will Ms. Reynolds need to give her learners so that they can use peer revision successfully?

4. How might peer revision be used effectively in oral or multimedia presentational activities?

To prepare for class discussion:

1. Imagine that you are Ms. Reynolds. Develop your own instruction sheet similar to those found in Figures 9.9 and 9.10 in this chapter and Appendices 9.9, 9.10, and 9.11 on the *Teacher's Handbook* Web site, to help learners use peer editing.

2. As Ms. Reynolds, remember that you have one class with both Level 3 and Level 4 Spanish learners. Describe how you might use this situation to your advantage for the purposes of peer editing.

3. Describe how you can incorporate underlining of errors into the peer editing process.

www.cengagebrain.com

REFERENCES

Al-Jarf, R. S. (2003). The effects of web-based learning on struggling EFL college writers. *Foreign Language Annals, 37*, 49–57.

American Council on the Teaching of Foreign Languages (ACTFL). (2001). *ACTFL proficiency guidelines— Writing.* Yonkers, NY: Author.

Amores, M. J. (1997). A new perspective on peer-editing. *Foreign Language Annals, 30*, 513–522.

Amores, M. J. (1999). Preparing graduate teaching assistants: An investment in excellence. *Foreign Language Annals, 32*, 441–468.

Appel, G. (2003). *13 Jahre Deutsche Vereinigung: A sample project for advanced learners of German.* CALPER Pedagogical Materials: Project Work, No. 2. The Pennsylvania State University: Center for Advanced Language Proficiency Education and Research.

Ashwell, T. (2000). Patterns of teacher response to student writing in a multiple-draft composition classroom: Is content feedback followed by form feedback the best method? *Journal of Second Language Writing, 9,* 227–257.

Aziz, L. (1995). *A model of paired cognitive and metacognitive strategies: Its effect on second language grammar and writing performance.* Unpublished doctoral dissertation, University of San Francisco, CA.

Barnett, M. A. (1989). Writing as a process. *The French Review, 63,* 39–41.

Beach, R. (1989). Showing students how to assess: Demonstrating techniques for response in the writing conference. In C. Anson (Ed.), *Writing and Response* (pp. 127–148). Urbana, IL: National Council of Teachers of English.

Bitchener, J. (2008). Evidence in support of written corrective feedback. *Journal of Second Language Writing, 17,* 102–118.

Blanton, L. L. (1998). *Varied voices: On language and literacy learning.* Boston: Heinle & Heinle.

Breiner-Sanders, K. E., Swender, E., & Terry, R. M. (2001). *Introduction to the ACTFL Proficiency Guidelines—Writing.* Yonkers, NY: ACTFL.

Bueno, K. (2006). Stepping out of the comfort zone: Profiles of third-year Spanish students' attempts to develop their speaking skills. *Foreign Language Annals, 39,* 451–470.

Canale, M. (1982). *Evaluating the coherence of student writing in L1 and L2.* Paper presented at the annual TESOL convention. Honolulu, HI.

Chandler, J. (2003). The efficacy of various kinds of error feedback for improvement in the accuracy and fluency of L2 student writing. *Journal of Second Language Writing, 12,* 267–296.

Chastain, K. B. (1990). Characteristics of graded and ungraded compositions. *The Modern Language Journal, 74,* 10–14.

Chikamatsu, N. (2003). The effects of computer use on L2 Japanese writing. *Foreign Language Annals, 36,* 114–127.

Cohen, A. D. (1987). Student processing of feedback on their compositions. In A. Wenden & J. Rubin (Eds.), *Learner strategies in language learning* (pp. 57–68). Englewood Cliffs, NJ: Prentice Hall.

Cohen, A. D., & Brooks-Carson, A. (2001). Research on direct versus translated writing: Students' strategies and their results. *The Modern Language Journal, 85,* 169–188.

Cohen, A. D., & Cavalcanti, M. C. (1990). Feedback on compositions: Teacher and student verbal reports. In B. Kroll (Ed.), *Second language writing: Research insights for the classroom* (pp. 155–177). Cambridge, UK: Cambridge University Press.

Coombs, V. M. (1986). Syntax and communicative strategies in intermediate German composition. *The Modern Language Journal, 70,* 114–124.

Cooper, C. R. (1977). Holistic evaluation of writing. In C. R. Cooper & L. Odell (Eds.), *Evaluating writing* (pp. 3–31). Urbana, IL: National Council of Teachers of English.

Cooper, T. (1981). Sentence combining: An experiment in teaching writing. *The Modern Language Journal, 65,* 158–165.

Cooper, T., & Morain, G. (1980). A study of sentence-combining techniques for developing written and oral fluency in French. *The French Review, 53,* 411–423.

Cumming, A. (1990). Expertise in evaluating second language compositions. *Language Testing, 7,* 31–51.

Curtain, H., & Dahlberg, C. (2010). *Languages and children—Making the match* (4th ed.). Boston: Pearson, Allyn & Bacon.

Debevec Henning, S. (1992). Assessing literary interpretation skills. *Foreign Language Annals, 25,* 339–355.

de Guerrero, M. C. M., & Villamil, O. S. (1994). Social-cognitive dimensions of interaction in L2 peer revision. *The Modern Language Journal, 78,* 484–496.

Donato, R. (1994). Collective scaffolding in second language learning. In J. P. Lantolf & G. Appel (Eds.), *Vygotskian approaches to second language research* (pp. 35–56). Norwood, NJ: Ablex.

Donato, R. (2004). Aspects of collaboration in pedagogical discourse. *Annual Review of Applied Linguistics, 24,* 284–302.

Donovan, T. R., & McClelland, B. W. (1980). *Eight approaches to teaching composition.* Urbana, IL: National Council of Teachers of English.

Dvorak, T. (1986). Writing in the foreign language. In B. H. Wing (Ed.), *Listening, reading, writing: Analysis and application* (pp. 145–167). Northeast Conference Reports. Middlebury, VT: Northeast Conference on the Teaching of Foreign Languages.

Dykstra-Pruim, P. (2003). Speaking, writing, and explicit-rule knowledge: Toward an understanding of how they interrelate. *Foreign Language Annals, 35,* 66–76.

Edelsky, C. (1982). Writing in a bilingual program: The relation of L1 and L2 texts. *TESOL Quarterly, 16,* 211–228.

Espinosa-Dulanto, M. (2003). *Evocando y paso a paso avanzando: A creative writing project for Spanish.* CALPER Pedagogical Materials: Project Work, No. 3. The Pennsylvania State University: Center for Advanced Language Proficiency Education and Research.

Fathman, A. K., & Whalley, E. (1990). Teacher response to student writing. In B. Kroll (Ed.), *Second language writing: Research insights for the classroom* (pp. 178–190). Cambridge, UK: Cambridge University Press.

Ferris, D. (1999). The case for grammar correction in L2 writing classes: A response to Truscott (1996). *Journal of Second Language Writing, 8,* 1–11.

Ferris, D. R. (2002). *Treatment of error in second language student writing.* Ann Arbor, MI: University of Michigan Press.

Ferris, D. R. (2003). Responding to writing. In B. Kroll (Ed.), *Exploring the dynamics of second language writing* (pp. 119–140). Cambridge, UK: Cambridge University Press.

Ferris, D. R., & Hedgcock, J. (1998). *Teaching ESL composition: Purpose, process, and practice.* Mahwah, NJ: Erlbaum Associates.

Flower, L., & Hayes, J. R. (1981). A cognitive process theory of writing. *College Composition and Communication, 32,* 365–387.

Frantzen, D. (1995). The effects of grammar supplementation on written accuracy in an intermediate Spanish course. *The Modern Language Journal, 79,* 324–344.

Friedlander, A. (1990). Composing in English: Effects of a first language on writing in English as a second language. In B. Kroll (Ed.), *Second language writing: Research insights for the classroom* (pp. 109–125). Cambridge, UK: Cambridge University Press.

Gallego de Blibeche, O. (1993). *A comparative study of the process versus product approach to the instruction of writing in Spanish as a foreign language.* Unpublished doctoral dissertation, The Pennsylvania State University, University Park, PA.

Goldstein, L. M. (2004). Questions and answers about teacher written commentary and student revision: Teachers and students working together. *Journal of Second Language Writing, 13,* 63–80.

Goldstein, L. M., & Conrad, S. (1990). Student input and negotiation of meaning in ESL writing conferences. *TESOL Quarterly, 24,* 443–460.

González-Bueno, M., & Quintana-Lara, M. (2007). The use of periodicals in the foreign language classroom. *NECTFL Review, 60,* 7–19.

Goulah, J. (2007). Village voices, global visions: Digital video as a transformative foreign language tool. *Foreign Language Annals, 40,* 62–78.

Graham, M. F. (1983). *The effect of teacher feedback on the reduction of usage errors in junior college freshmen's writing.* Unpublished doctoral dissertation, University of Southern Mississippi, Hattiesburg.

Greenia, G. (1992). Why Johnny can't escribir: Composition and the foreign language curriculum. *ADFL Bulletin, 24,* 30–37.

Guénette, D. (2007). Is feedback pedagogically correct? Research design issues in studies of feedback on writing. *Journal of Second Language Writing, 16,* 40–53.

Hadley, A. O. (2001). *Teaching language in context* (3rd ed.). Boston: Heinle & Heinle.

Hahn, L. D. (2004). Primary stress and intelligibility: Research to motivate the teaching of suprasegmentals. *TESOL Quarterly, 38,* 201–223.

Hall, J. K. (1995). "'Aw, man, where we goin'?": Classroom interaction and the development of L2 interactional competence. *Issues in Applied Linguistics, 6*(2), 37–62.

Hall, J. K. (1999). The communication standard. In J. K. Phillips (Ed.), *Foreign language standards: Linking research, theories, and practices* (pp. 15–56). Lincolnwood, IL: NTC/Contemporary Publishing Group.

Halliday, M. A. K., & Hasan, R. (1976). *Cohesion in English.* London: Longman.

Hamp-Lyons, L. (2003). Writing teachers as assessors of writing. In B. Kroll (Ed.), *Exploring the dynamics of second language writing* (pp. 162–189). Cambridge, UK: Cambridge University Press.

Hedgcock, J., & Lefkowitz, N. (1996). Some input on input: Two analyses of student response to expert feedback in L2 writing. *The Modern Language Journal, 80,* 287–308.

Hendrickson, J. M. (1978). Error correction in foreign language teaching: Recent theory, research, and practice. *The Modern Language Journal, 62,* 387–398.

Henry, K. (1996). Early L2 writing development: A study of autobiographical essays by university-level students of Russian. *The Modern Language Journal, 80,* 309–326.

Hyland, F. (2003). Focusing on form: Student engagement with teacher feedback. *System, 31,* 217–230.

Hyland, K. (2003). *Second language writing.* Cambridge, UK: Cambridge University Press.

Hyland, K. (2007). Genre pedagogy: Language literacy, and L2 writing instruction. *Journal of Second Language Writing, 16,* 148–164.

Hyland, K., & Hyland, F. (2006). Feedback on second language students' writing. *Language Teaching, 39,* 83–101.

Jacobs, G. M., Curtis, A., Braine, G., & Huang, S-Y. (1998). Feedback on student writing: Taking the middle path. *Journal of Second Language Writing, 7,* 307–317.

Jenkins, J. (2004). Research in teaching pronunciation and intonation. *Annual Review of Applied Linguistics, 24,* 109–125.

Johnson, K. E. (2003). *Let's make a deal: A sample project for advanced ESL learners.* CALPER Pedagogical Materials: Project Work, No.1. The Pennsylvania State University: Center for Advanced Language Proficiency Education and Research.

Jones, S., & Tetroe J. (1987). Composing in a second language. In A. Matsuhashi (Ed.), *Writing in real time: Modeling production processes* (pp. 34–57). Toronto: Ablex.

Kepner, C. G. (1991). An experiment in the relationship of types of written feedback to the development of second-language writing skills. *The Modern Language Journal, 75,* 305–313.

Kern, R., Ware, P., & Warschauer, M. (2004). New directions in online pedagogy and research. *Annual Review of Applied Linguistics, 24,* 243–260.

Kern, R. G., & Schultz, J. M. (1992). The effects of composition instruction on intermediate level French students' writing performance: Some preliminary findings. *The Modern Language Journal, 76,* 1–13.

Khaldieh, S. A. (2000). Learning strategies and writing processes of proficient vs less-proficient learners of Arabic. *Foreign Language Annals, 33,* 522–534.

Kobayashi, H., & Rinnert, C. (2007). Task response and text construction across L1 and L2 writing. *Journal of Second Language Writing, 17,* 7–29.

Koda, K. (1993). Task-induced variability in foreign language composition: Language-specific perspectives. *Foreign Language Annals, 26,* 332–346.

Krueger, C. (2001). Form, content, and critical distance: The role of "creative personalization" in language content courses. *Foreign Language Annals, 34,* 18–25.

Kuiken, F., & Vedder, I. (2008). Cognitive task complexity and written output in Italian and French as a foreign language. *Journal of Second Language Writing, 17,* 48–60.

LaBonty, J., & Borth, L. (2006). El elefante y la hormiga: Writing poetry in foreign language classes. *NECTFL Review, 58,* 25–36.

Laidlaw, A. (1989). Formula poetry fun. A presentation to the Washtenaw/Livingston Academic Alliance of Foreign Language Teachers. Ypsilanti, MI.

Lalande, J. F., II. (1982). Reducing composition errors: An experiment. *The Modern Language Journal, 66,* 140–149.

Lally, C. G. (2000). First language influences in second language composition: The effect of pre-writing. *Foreign Language Annals, 33,* 428–431.

Laufer, B., & Hulstijn, J. (2001). Incidental vocabulary acquisition in a second language: The construct of task-induced involvement. *Applied Linguistics, 22,* 1–26.

Lee, G., & Schallert, D. L. (2008). Meeting in the margins: Effects of teacher-student relationship on revision processes of EFL college students taking a composition course. *Journal of Second Language Writing, 17,* doi:10.1016/j.jslw.2007.11.002.

Lee, I. (1997). ESL learners' performance in error correction in writing. *System, 25,* 465–477.

Lee, J. F., & VanPatten, B. (2003). *Making communicative language teaching happen* (3rd ed.). New York: McGraw-Hill.

Lei, X. (2008). Exploring a sociocultural approach to writing strategy research: Mediated actions in writing activities. *Journal of Second Language Writing, 18,* doi:10.1016/j.jslw.2008.04.001.

Leki, I. (1990). Coaching from the margins: Issues in written response. In B. Kroll (Ed.). *Second language writing: Research insights for the classroom* (pp. 57–68). Cambridge, UK: Cambridge University Press.

Leki, I. (1991). The preferences of ESL students for error correction in college-level writing classes. *Foreign Language Annals, 24,* 203–318.

Leki, I. (2006). 'You cannot ignore': Graduate L2 students' experience of and responses to written feedback practices within their disciplines. In K. Hyland & F. Hyland (Eds.), *Feedback in second language writing: Contexts and issues* (pp. 266–285). New York: Cambridge University Press.

Lightbown, P., & Spada, N. (2006). *How languages are learned* (3rd ed.). New York: Oxford University Press.

Levi Altstaedter, L. (2009). *Writing instruction in foreign language courses: The impact of peer feedback on students' revision types and writing.* Unpublished doctoral dissertation, Virginia Polytechnic Institute and State University, Blacksburg, VA.

Lloyd-Jones, R. (1977). Primary trait scoring. In C. R. Cooper & L. Odell (Eds.), *Evaluating writing* (pp. 33–66). Urbana, IL: National Council of Teachers of English.

Magnan, S. (1985). Teaching and testing proficiency in writing: Skills to transcend the second-language classroom. In A. Omaggio (Ed.), *Proficiency, curriculum, articulation: The ties that bind* (pp. 109–136). Northeast Conference Reports. Middlebury, VT: Northeast Conference on the Teaching of Foreign Languages.

Mangelsdorf, K., & Schlumberger, A. (1992). ESL student response stances in a peer-review task. *Journal of Second Language Writing, 1,* 235–254.

Manley, J. H., & Calk, L. (1997). Grammar instruction for writing skills: Do students perceive grammar as useful? *Foreign Language Annals, 30,* 73–83.

Martinez-Lage, A. (September, 1992). Effect of grammar instruction on the development of accuracy and syntactic complexity of Spanish L2 written compositions. Paper presented at biennial meeting of the Northeast Regional American Association of Teachers of Spanish, Manchester, NH.

Matsuda, P. (2001). Voice in Japanese written discourse: Implications for second language writing. *Journal of Second Language Writing, 10,* 35–53.

Matsuda, P. (2003). Process and post-process: A discursive history. *Journal of Second Language Writing, 12,* 65–83.

McKee, E. (1980). *The effects of two types of simulations on measures of written performance in beginning college French.* Unpublished doctoral dissertation, The Ohio State University, Columbus, OH.

Moore, Z. (1994). The portfolio and testing culture. In C. Hancock (Ed.), *Teaching, testing, and assessment: Making the connection* (pp. 163–182). Northeast Conference Reports. Lincolnwood, IL: NTC/Contemporary Publishing Group.

Morin, R., & Goebel, J. (2001). Teaching strategies or teaching words. *Foreign Language Annals, 34,* 8–17.

Murray, D. E. (2005). Technologies for second language literacy. *Annual Review of Applied Linguistics, 25,* 188–201.

National Standards in Foreign Language Education Project (NSFLEP). (2006). *Standards for foreign language learning in the 21st century (SFLL).* Lawrence, KS: Allen Press.

Nerenz, A. G. (1990). The exploratory years: Foreign languages in the middle-level curriculum. In S. Magnan (Ed.), *Shifting the instructional focus to the learner* (pp. 93–126). Northeast Conference Reports. Middlebury, VT: Northeast Conference on the Teaching of Foreign Languages.

Nirenberg, E. (1989). *The effects of interactive writing assignments on the written language proficiency of first year students of Russian.* Unpublished doctoral dissertation, The University of California, Los Angeles, CA.

O'Donnell, M. (2007). Policies and practices in foreign language writing at the college level: Survey results and Implications. *Foreign Language Annals, 40,* 650–669.

O'Hair, D., Friedrich, G., Wienmann, J., & Wienmann, M. (1995). *Competent communication.* New York: St. Martin's Press.

Oxford, R. (1990). *Language learning strategies: What every teacher should know.* New York: Newbury House/ Harper & Row.

Paesani, K. (2006). Exercises de style: Developing multiple competencies through a writing portfolio. *Foreign Language Annals, 39,* 618–639.

Patthey-Chavez, G., & Ferris, D. (1997). Writing conferences and the weaving of multi-voiced texts in college composition. *Research in the Teaching of English, 31,* 51–90.

Paulus, T. (1999). The effect of peer and teacher feedback on student writing. *Journal of Second Language Writing, 8,* 265–289.

Pennington, M. (1996). *The computer and the non-native writer: A natural partnership.* Cresskill, NJ: Hampton Press.

Peregoy, S. F., & Boyle, O. F. (2005). *Reading, writing and learning in ESL: A resource book for K–12 teachers* (4th ed.). New York: Addison Wesley Longman.

Peyton, J. K. (1987). *Dialogue journal writing with limited English proficient students.* Washington, DC: Center for Applied Linguistics.

Peyton, J. K. (1990). *Students and teachers writing together: Perspectives on journal writing.* Alexandria, VA: Teachers of English to Speakers of Other Languages.

Phillips, J. (2008). Foreign language standards and the contexts of communication. *Language Teaching, 41,* 93–102.

Piske, T., MacKay, I. R. A., & Flege, J. E. (2001). Factors affecting degree of foreign accent in an L2: A review. *Journal of Phonetics, 29,* 191–215.

Qi, D. S. (1998). An inquiry into language-switching in second language composing. *The Canadian Modern Language Review, 54,* 413–435.

Qi, D. S., & Lapkin, S. (2001). Exploring the role of noticing in a three-stage second language writing task. *Journal of Second Language Writing, 10,* 277–303.

Raimes, A. (1987). Language proficiency, writing ability, and composing strategies: A study of ESL college student writers. *Language Learning, 37,* 439–467.

Reichelt, M. (2001). A critical review of foreign language writing research in pedagogical practices. *The Modern Language Journal, 85,* 578–598.

Reid, J. (1993). *Teaching ESL writing.* Englewood Cliffs, NJ: Prentice Hall.

Reid, J. M. (1998). "Eye" learners and "ear" learners: Identifying the language needs of international students and U.S. resident writers. In P. Byrd & J. M. Reid (Eds.), *Grammar in the composition classroom: Essays on teaching ESL for college-bound students* (pp. 3–17). Boston: Heinle & Heinle.

Richards, J. (1990). *The language teaching matrix.* Cambridge, UK: Cambridge University Press.

Rinnert, C., & Kobayashi, H. (2001). Differing perceptions of EFL writing among readers in Japan. *The Modern Language Journal, 85,* 189–209.

Robb, T., Ross, S., & Shortreed, I. (1986). Salience of feedback on error and its effect on EFL writing quality. *TESOL Quarterly, 20,* 83–93.

Roca de Larios, J., Manchón, R., & Murphy, L. (2006). Generating text in native and foreign language writing: A temporal analysis of problem-solving formulation processes. *The Modern Language Journal, 90,* 100–114.

Roca de Larios, J., Manchón, R., Murphy, L., & Marín, J. (2008). The foreign language writer's strategic behavior in the allocation of time to writing processes. *Journal of Second Language Writing, 17,* 30–47.

Roca de Larios, J., Marín, J., & Murphy, L. (2001). A temporal analysis of formulation processes in L1 and L2 writing. *Language Learning, 51,* 497–538.

Roca de Larios, J., Murphy, L., & Manchón, R. (1999). The use of restructuring strategies in EFL writing: A study of Spanish learners of English as a Foreign Language. *Journal of Second Language Writing, 8,* 13–44.

Roebuck, R. (2001). Teaching composition in the college level foreign language class: Insights and activities from sociocultural theory. *Foreign Language Annals, 34,* 206–215.

Ruiz-Funes, M. (1994). *An exploration of the process of reading-to-write used by skilled Spanish-as-a-foreign-language students.* Unpublished doctoral dissertation. Virginia Polytechnic Institute and State University, Blacksburg, VA.

Ruiz-Funes, M. (1999). Writing, reading, and reading-to-write in a foreign language: A critical review. *Foreign Language Annals, 32,* 514–526.

Ruiz-Funes, M. (2001). Task representation in foreign language reading-to-write. *Foreign Language Annals, 34,* 226–234.

Sasaki, M. (2004). A multiple-data analysis of the 3.5-year development of EFL student writers. *Language Learning, 54,* 525–582.

Sasaki, M. (2007). Effects of study-abroad experiences on EFL writers: A multiple data analysis. *The Modern Language Journal, 91,* 602–620.

Scarcella, R., & Oxford, R. (1992). *The tapestry of language learning.* Boston: Heinle & Heinle.

Schultz, J. M. (1991). Writing mode in the articulation of language and literature classes: Theory and practice. *The Modern Language Journal, 75,* 411–417.

Schultz, J. M. (1994). Stylistic reformulation: Theoretical premises and practical applications. *The Modern Language Journal, 78,* 169–178.

Schulz, R. A. (1996). Focus on form in the foreign language classroom: Students' and teachers' views on error correction and the role of grammar. *Foreign Language Annals, 29,* 343–364.

Schulz, R. A. (2001). Cultural differences in student and teacher perceptions concerning the role of grammar instruction and corrective feedback: U.S.A. Colombia. *The Modern Language Journal, 85,* 244–258.

Scott, V. M. (1992). Writing from the start: A task-oriented developmental writing program for foreign language students. In R. Terry (Ed.), *Dimension: Language '91* (pp. 1–15). Southern Conference on Language Teaching. Valdosta, GA: Valdosta State University.

Scott, V. M. (1995). Writing. In V. Galloway & C. Herron (Eds.), *Research within reach II* (pp. 115–127). Southern Conference on Language Teaching. Valdosta, GA: Valdosta State University.

Scott, V. M. (1996). *Rethinking foreign language writing.* Boston: Heinle & Heinle.

Scott, V. M., & New, E. (1994). Computer aided analysis of foreign language writing process. *Calico Journal, 11,* 5–18.

Scott, V. M., & Terry, R. M. (1992). *Système-D Teacher's Guide.* Boston: Heinle & Heinle.

Semke, H. D. (1984). Effects of the red pen. *Foreign Language Annals, 17,* 195–202.

Sildus, T. I. (2006). The effect of a student video project on vocabulary retention of first-year secondary school German students. *Foreign Language Annals, 39,* 54–70.

Silva, T. (1990). Second language composition instruction: Developments, issues, and directions in ESL. In B. Kroll (Ed.), *Second language writing: Research insights for the classroom* (pp. 11–23). Cambridge, UK: Cambridge University Press.

Silva, T., & Brice, C. (2004). Research in teaching writing. *Annual Review of Applied Linguistics, 24,* 70–106.

Silva, T., & Leki, I. (2004). Family matters: The influence of applied linguistics and composition studies on second language writing studies—past, present, and future. *The Modern Language Journal, 88,* 1–13.

Stanley, J. (1992). Coaching student writers to be more effective peer evaluators. *Journal of Second Language Writing, 1,* 217–233.

Stapleton, P. (2005). Using the Web as a research source: Implications for L2 academic writing. *The Modern Language Journal, 89,* 177–189.

Storch, N. (2002). Patterns of interaction in ESL pair work. *Language Learning, 52,* 119–158.

Storch, N. (2005). Collaborative writing: Product, process and students' reflection. *Journal of Second Language Writing, 14,* 153–173.

Storch, N., & Wigglesworth, G. (2008). Writing tasks: The effects of collaboration. In M. del P. García Mayo (Ed.), *Investigating tasks in formal language learning* (pp. 157–177). Clevedon, UK: Multilingual Matters Ltd.

Swain, M. (2000). The output hypothesis and beyond: Mediating acquisition through collaborative dialogue. In J. Lantolf (Ed.), *Sociocultural theory and second language learning* (pp. 97–114). Oxford: Oxford University Press.

Swales, J. (1991). *Genre analysis: English in academic and research settings.* Cambridge, NY: Cambridge University Press.

Terry, R. M. (1989). Teaching and evaluating writing as a communicative skill. *Foreign Language Annals, 22,* 43–54.

Thurstun, J. (2004). Teaching and learning the reading of homepages. *Prospect, 19* (2), 56–71.

Tierney, R. J., Carter, M. A., & Desai, L. E. (1991). *Portfolio assessment in the reading-writing classroom.* Norwood, MA: Christopher-Gordon.

Trimbur, J. (1994). Taking the social turn: Teaching writing post-process. *College Composition and Communication, 45,* 108–118.

Trofimovich, P., & Gatbonton, E. (2006). Repetition and focus on form in processing L2 Spanish words: Implications for pronunciation instruction. *The Modern Language Journal, 90,* 519–535.

Truscott, J. (1996). The case against grammar correction in L2 writing classes. *Language Learning, 46,* 327–369.

Truscott, J. (1999). The case for "The case against grammar correction in L2 writing classes": A response to Ferris. *Journal of Second Language Writing, 8,* 111–122.

Truscott, J. (2007). The effect of error correction on learners' ability to write accurately. *Journal of Second Language Writing, 16,* 255–272.

Valdés, G., Haro, P., & Echevarriarza, M. P. (1992). The development of writing abilities in a foreign language: Contributions toward a general theory of L2 writing. *The Modern Language Journal, 76,* 333–352.

Villamil, O., & de Guerrero, M. (1996). Peer revision in the L2 classroom: Social-cognitive activities, mediating strategies, and aspects of social behavior. *Journal of Second Language Writing, 5,* 51–75.

Warschauer, M. (1995). *E-mail for English teaching.* Alexandria, VA: TESOL.

Way, D. P., Joiner, E. G., & Seaman, M. A. (2000). Writing in the secondary foreign language classroom: The effects of prompts and tasks on novice learners of French. *The Modern Language Journal, 84,* 171–184.

West, M. J., & Donato, R. D. (1995). Stories and stances: Cross-cultural encounters with African folktales. *Foreign Language Annals, 28,* 392–406.

Wiggins, G., & McTighe, J. (2005). *Understanding by design.* Alexandria, VA: Association for Supervision and Curriculum Development.

Williams, J. (2005). *Teaching writing in second and foreign language classrooms.* Boston: McGraw-Hill.

Wong, W., & VanPatten, B. (2003). The evidence is IN: Drills are OUT. *Foreign Language Annals, 36,* 403–424.

Zamel, V. (1982). Writing: The process of discovering meaning. *TESOL Quarterly, 16,* 195–209.

Zamel, V. (1983). The composing processes of advanced ESL students: Six case studies. *TESOL Quarterly, 17,* 165–187.

Zamel, V. (1985). Responding to student writing. *TESOL Quarterly, 19,* 79–101.

Zareva, A., Schwanenflugel, P., & Nikolova, Y. (2005). Relationship between lexical competence and language proficiency. *Studies in Second Language Acquisition, 27,* 567–595.

Zhang, S. (1995). Reexamining the affective advantage of peer feedback in the ESL writing class. *Journal of Second Language Writing, 4,* 209–222.

Ziegler, R., & Ziegler, W. (2000). *Multimedia rubric.* Waco, NE: Learning for the Future.

Zimmerman, R. (1996). Formulating in L2 writing: Towards an empirical model. In A. Archibald and G. C. Jeffrey (Eds.), *Second language acquisition and writing: A multidisciplinary approach* (pp. 53–68). Southampton, UK: University of Southampton Press.

NOTES

1. According to Scott (1996), writing as a "process" means that "writing is a succession of actions undertaken to bring about some desired result" (p. 31). She also notes that the term process has never been clearly defined in the literature. Matsuda (2003) clarifies this notion and explains that process writing is a reaction to teacher-centered, product-oriented approaches to writing. The advocates of process pedagogy have changed the focus to a student-centered, process-oriented approach, with an emphasis on "the process of helping students discover their own voice, of recognizing that students have something important to say, of allowing students to choose their own topics, of providing teacher and peer feedback, of encouraging revision, and of using student writing as the primary text of the course" (p. 1).

2. The amount of writing practice varies, but in a survey of 66 college-level foreign language programs, O'Donnell (2007) found that 38% of the 66 programs required four to six graded compositions, and that 40% of the compositions were less than two pages in length. Just over half of the programs required graded drafts, counting them as 1–91% of the grade.

3. See LaBonty & Borth (2006) for additional examples of student work and patterned poetry, name and alphabet poems, terquians, cinquians, diamantes, "I like" poems, and definition poems.

4. Many thanks to Jill Surprenant for her contributions to Appendices 9.8 and 9.17 on the *Teacher's Handbook* Web site.

5. Many thanks to Dr. Rick Donato, University of Pittsburgh, for his assistance in this section.

Addressing Diverse Needs of Learners in the Language Classroom

In this chapter, you will learn about:

- diverse ways students learn language
- multiple intelligences
- learning styles
- teacher personality and teaching style
- language learning strategies
- addressing diverse learners' needs
- the inclusive classroom: accommodating learners with disabilities
- physical needs

- special learning needs
- at-risk learners
- gifted learners
- heritage learners
- differentiated instruction
- Communities Goal Area
- community-based and service learning

Teach and Reflect: Designing a Language Lesson Appropriate for Diverse Learning Styles; Working Within Communities

Discuss and Reflect: Differentiating Instruction: Three Classrooms

CONCEPTUAL ORIENTATION

As a language teacher, your commitment to addressing the needs of diverse learners is supported by professional organizations and the standards for foreign language and ESL learning. The American Council on the Teaching of Foreign Languages has issued a position statement on diversity and language programs (ACTFL, 2007), as follows:

ACTFL and its members are committed to developing and maintaining a teaching and learning environment that reflects the broad diversity of American society. We welcome teachers and students from diverse cultural, linguistic, and socio-economic backgrounds to language programs. We believe that all children should have the opportunity to learn other languages and support full access for all students to language programs. In this effort, ACTFL and its member organizations . . .

- support a teaching and learning environment where diversity is appreciated and respected;
- advocate diverse language learning opportunities for all socio-economic levels in urban, suburban, and rural communities;
- work to develop, support, promote and enhance the language skills of Native American and heritage language learners;
- initiate and support efforts to recruit and retain a diverse teaching force in the language profession;
- work to ensure that the organization's structure, services, professional development, and policies address the needs of our diverse profession;
- promote awareness and differentiation of language instruction to accommodate students' diverse learning styles; exceptional learning needs; cultural, ethnic, and linguistic backgrounds; and personal interests and goals;
- encourage the selection and use of instructional materials that integrate multicultural and diverse perspectives throughout the curriculum (ACTFL, 2007).

In addition, Teachers of English as a Second Language (TESOL) cites diversity in its statement of values:

- professionalism in language education
- individual language rights
- accessible, high-quality education
- collaboration in a global community
- interaction of research and reflective practice for educational improvement
- respect for diversity and multiculturalism (2008)

The *Standards for Foreign Language Learning in the 21st Century* (SFLL) (National Standards in Foreign Language Education Project [NSFLEP], 2006) affirm the importance of language education for *all* students:

"The United States must educate students who are equipped linguistically and culturally to communicate successfully in a pluralistic American society and abroad. This imperative envisions a future in which ALL students will develop and maintain proficiency in English and at least one other language, modern or classical. Children who come to school from non-English-speaking backgrounds should also have opportunities to develop further proficiencies in their first language" (p. 7).

The inclusive orientation of the *SFLL* implies that in any given language classroom there may be students who differ from each other in various ways, including motivation, goals for learning, aptitude, needs for instructional assistance, ethnic or national origin, gender, socioeconomic status, and linguistic or cultural heritage. Even in classes in which students appear to be relatively homogeneous in background and goals, they may differ along some other dimension. The challenge for the language teacher is to recognize and help learners appreciate these differences and similarities in the language classroom, and to design differentiated instruction so that each learner has opportunities to enhance thinking skills and learn how members of other cultures express themselves.

As the student population continues to grow in diversity, teachers will need to gain an understanding of the various needs that these learners bring to the foreign language classroom. The National Center for Education Statistics (NCES) reports that in 2005, 33% of the school-age population were members of minority groups.[1] The largest minorities among students were Black and Hispanic, each representing 12% and 14% respectively;

other groups included Asian/Pacific Islanders (4%) and American Indians/Alaskan Natives (1%). Interestingly, NCES projects that, by the year 2020, minority learners will constitute 39% of the public school population (NCES, 2007a). Only 16% of public school teachers are members of minority groups (NCES, 2007b, p. 65). The fact that many teachers may not belong to the minority groups represented by their students underscores the challenge the teachers may face in the classroom.

We often think of diverse populations of students in terms of gender, age, race, national origin, and ethnicity. However, diversity also includes the range of academic, linguistic, physical, and emotional characteristics that students bring to the classroom. Of particular interest to language teachers is linguistic diversity, one aspect of the changing complexity of U.S. schools. *Language minority* students are those who come from homes where a language other than English is actively used, who therefore have had an opportunity to develop some level of proficiency in a language other than English. A language minority student may be of limited English proficiency, bilingual, or essentially monolingual in English (August & Hakuta, 1997, p. 15). The presence of many language minority children in U.S. schools enriches the cultural and linguistic diversity of the classroom, and demands resources for those who speak English with difficulty. In the 2003–2004 school year, 3.8 million students, or 11% of the school-age population, received services for English Language Learners (ELLs) due to their limited literacy in English. These students were enrolled in 63% of the nation's public schools (NCES, 2008a). From 2000 to 2006 the percentage of the school-age population that spoke a language other than English at home increased from 18% to 20%. Students who spoke languages other than English or who spoke English with difficulty were three times more likely to be poor (NCES, 2008a). Relationships among language, economic condition, and education place tremendous importance on your role as a language teacher who understands the background, interests, and goals of students. The way you teach can be critical to the success of learners in your classroom.

Haley and Hancock (2007/2008) affirm the reality of changing demographics described above and call for training for teachers to enable them to work effectively with culturally, linguistically, and cognitively diverse (CLCD) learners. Thus, in addition to understanding the *ethnic, racial, linguistic*, and *cultural* diversity of learners, teachers should also understand that *all* learners are unique in the ways in which they approach language learning. The focus of this chapter is to explore the diverse needs of learners in language classrooms and to offer ideas to language teachers about how to address these needs so that language learning is facilitated for all learners. In this chapter, you will recognize that:

1. Learners approach language learning in a variety of ways.
2. Teachers can help learners to develop strategies that best use the teachers' teaching style and the learners' learning style.
3. In a standards-based approach, languages are for all learners but some may require special accommodations as illustrated by a parallel curriculum model.
4. Knowing about the special needs of disabled, gifted, and heritage learners will assist you in implementing a standards-based approach that benefits all learners.

The Diverse Ways in Which Learners Approach Language Learning

This section will examine the ways in which multiple intelligences, learning strategies, and language learning strategies have an impact on language learning.

Multiple Intelligences

Gardner's explanation of multiple intelligences captured the attention of researchers and practitioners alike (Díaz & Heining-Boynton, 1995). Through several refinements of his theory, he recently defined *intelligence* as "a capacity to process a certain kind of information" (Gardner, 2006, p. 6). In his view, an *intelligence* can be expressed in symbol systems such as numbers, language, or art; it can be developed and expanded and consists of skills for (1) resolving genuine problems or difficulties, and (2) finding or creating problems. Gardner's theory suggests eight intelligences with a ninth one—existential—identified and still being explored. Figure 10.1 categorizes the nine intelligences, and includes the characteristics of and sample foreign language classroom activities for each intelligence.

Díaz and Heining-Boynton (1995) point out four key elements to Gardner's theory:

1. Everyone possesses all intelligences, and others may exist, but this is a manageable list for educators.
2. Most of us have some of the intelligences highly developed; the other intelligences are either moderately developed or underdeveloped, but we can develop any of them to a moderate level.
3. The intelligences usually work in concert and not alone.
4. There are many ways to demonstrate intelligence within each category (adapted, p. 5).

www.cengagebrain.com

These multiple intelligences can enable us to understand how certain learners might more easily grasp a linguistic concept if it is presented in the form of a mathematical formula that allows them to access their logical/mathematical intelligence; how singing songs and doing Total Physical Response (TPR) activities help learners who have trouble focusing attention on printed pages by accessing their musical/rhythmic and bodily/kinesthetic intelligence; how interacting in pairs helps learners acquire a new linguistic or cultural concept by using interpersonal intelligence. It may be helpful to review Appendix 10.1 on the *Teacher's Handbook* Web site before continuing with your reading because it provides an extensive list of multiple intelligences activities, classroom environments, and assessments.

Haley and Hancock (2007/2008) and Haley (2001, 2004) reported results from a study involving primary and secondary language teachers and students in classrooms where a multiple-intelligence approach was incorporated that showed greater progress in learning the target language (TL) than those in teacher-centered classrooms. Feedback affirmed that learner-centered instruction from the perspective of multiple intelligences can have an impact on student achievement. See Appendix 10.2 on the *Teacher's Handbook* Web site for a survey that can be used to raise student and teacher awareness of students' dominant ways of processing information via multiple intelligences.

 An intelligence is a "capacity to process information in certain ways. Each intelligence can be activated in an appropriate cultural setting."

Language Learning Styles

A *learning style* is a general approach a learner uses to learn (Scarcella & Oxford, 1992, p. 61). In the previous section you saw how multiple intelligences allow us to understand how learners access and use information from a biopsychological perspective. The intelligence itself drives behaviors and actions. Learning styles are similar in that they represent another way learners perceive and process information. Proponents of learning styles attempt to describe an individual in terms of one learning style used across all content

FIGURE 10.1 Multiple Intelligences

CATEGORY OF INTELLIGENCE	CHARACTERISTICS	FL CLASSROOM ACTIVITIES
PERSONAL: Intrapersonal/Introspective	Self Smart: understanding oneself and taking responsibility for thinking on one's own	Goal setting; journals and personal reflection; problem-solving activities; independent assignments such as auto-biographies and family heritage study; open-ended expression
Interpersonal/Social	People Smart: understanding others, getting along with others, interpreting individuals' moods, motivations, inhibitions	Cooperative tasks such as think-pair-share and jigsaws; creative group tasks such as collages and story books; interactive technology such as e-mail, CD-ROM, and Internet
ACADEMIC: Logical/Mathematical	Logic Smart: logical reasoning, categorizing facts, sequential thought	Graphic organizers that show patterns and relationships; problem-solving manipulatives; puzzles and games; challenge tasks
Verbal/Linguistic	Word Smart: communicating by listening, speaking, reading, and writing; using language to link new knowledge to prior experiences	Graphic organizers to promote brainstorming and generating ideas; list making; mnemonics; verbal games; speakers; interviews; peer teaching; personal expression (opinions, reactions); logs or journals
EXPRESSIVE: Bodily/Kinesthetic	Body Smart: skillfully controlling body motions; showing a keen sense of direction and timing in movement	TPR; creative dramatics and mime; creating things; role-playing and interviews; projects, field trips, active learning
Visual/Spatial	Picture Smart: accurately comprehending the visual word; transforming mental images; seeing things in terms of pictures	Learning experiences using drawings, charts, props, posters, photographs; illustrations; demonstrations; use of overhead projector, chalkboard, video
Musical/Rhythmic	Music Smart: using pitch, rhythm, and so on, in enjoying and creating musical experiences; being attuned to rhythms, responding with actions	Songs, music, dance of the target culture; music mnemonics; jingles, raps, cheers; using movement or dance to illustrate ideas or concepts
EMERGING: Naturalist	Nature Smart: seeing deeply into the nature of living things; identifying and classifying things; problem solving	Data collection; demonstrations; research projects; logs; reports
Existential	Life Smart: Capturing and pondering the fundamental questions of existence; capacity to raise big questions about one's place in the cosmos	Reading literature or storytelling about life and living, e.g., as an immigrant or a member of a minority group

Source: Compiled from Von Károlyi, Ramos-Ford, & Gardner, 2003, p. 102; Lange, 1999, pp. 106–109; and Gahala & Lange, 1997, pp. 30–32; adapted from Gardner, 2006.

areas, whereas a learner may still select one of several multiple intelligences depending on the context. Research evidence continues to show the importance of recognizing and providing explicit instruction about their preferred and other available learning strategies to learners of foreign languages (Castro & Peck, 2005), as well as to learners of English as a Foreign Language (Khalil, 2005; Nisbet, Tindall, & Arroyo, 2005; Woodrow, 2005).

Learning styles research has had particular influence on helping teachers identify ways in which learners differ in their approaches to language learning. Oxford (1990a) and Scarcella and Oxford (1992) identify five key dimensions of language learning styles:

1. *Analytic-global:* This dimension illustrates the difference between a detail-oriented individual and a holistic one. Analytic learners concentrate on grammatical details and often do not participate well in communicative activities. They would rather find the meanings of words in a dictionary than guess in context. Global learners like interactive tasks in which they use main ideas. They have difficulty dealing with grammatical details and are content to use guessing strategies.

2. *Sensory preferences:* This dimension highlights the physical, perceptual avenues for learning, such as visual, auditory, and hands-on (kinesthetic or movement-oriented and tactile or touch-oriented). Visual learners prefer to read and visualize information; they usually dislike having to process oral input in the absence of visual support. Auditory learners enjoy conversations and other types of verbal interaction and often have difficulty with written work. Hands-on learners do well with movement around the classroom and work easily with objects and realia.

3. *Intuitive/random and sensory/sequential Learning:* This dimension deals with the type of organization learners prefer in the presentation of material. Intuitive/random learners think in an abstract, nonsequential, or random manner, making sense of the global picture. Sensory/sequential learners prefer to encounter new information by means of a step-by-step, ordered presentation. They perform tasks in a linear order and often have difficulty seeing the bigger picture. In the PACE model, presented in Chapter 7, for instance, intuitive/random learners are often quite comfortable with language used in context during the Presentation phase and find the Co-Construction phase an interesting puzzle.

4. *Orientation to closure:* This dimension refers to the degree to which learners need to reach conclusions and can tolerate ambiguity. Learners oriented toward closure want all rules spelled out for them and use metacognitive skills such as planning, organizing, and self-evaluating. However, they often tend to analyze prematurely and experience difficulty dealing with abstract or subtle issues. Ehrman and Oxford (1989) show that the desire for closure might have a negative effect on a learner's ability to participate in open-ended communication. Open learners, or those who have less need for closure, learn by osmosis rather than by conscientious effort and appear to use more effective language learning strategies than learners who require quick closure (Scarcella & Oxford, 1992, p. 62). As an example, also drawn from the PACE model, learners who have little tolerance for ambiguity ask for the grammatical rule early in the process, and find co-constructing the rule a time-consuming and risky activity.

5. *Competition-cooperation:* This dimension illustrates the degree to which learners benefit from competing against or cooperating with others. Competitive learners are motivated by competition in which winning is of utmost importance. Cooperative individuals prefer working with others in a helpful, supportive situation. Studies show that the high degree of competitiveness in education may account for the fact that learners seldom report using cooperative, social strategies (Reid, 1987). According to Bailey (1983), competition in language learning may result in feelings of anxiety, inadequacy,

hostility, fear of failure, guilt, and too strong a desire for approval. As you learned in Chapter 8, cooperative learning provides an avenue for student interaction while increasing self-esteem, achievement, motivation, and the use of cognitive strategies.

A *learning style* is a general approach a learner uses to learn.

What is your preferred learning style and why? Which intelligences do you use most often and in what contexts?

Teachers' Personality Types and Teaching Styles

www.cengagebrain.com

Often teachers prefer certain instructional practices because they comfortably match their personalities. Research on personality types using the Myers-Briggs Type Indicator (Myers & McCaulley, 1985) has shown a high percentage of *feeling* types among foreign language teachers (Heining-Boynton & Heining-Boynton, 1994; Hunt, 1986; Lawrence, 1996, 1997; Myers, McCaulley, Quenk, & Hammer, 1998). Cooper (2001) adapted Lawrence's work on matching personality types with instructional preferences and compared these instructional preferences with those of the beginning teachers in his methods class. He found a high percentage of feeling type personalities among the preservice teachers. As you can see in Appendix 10.3 on the *Teacher's Handbook* Web site, teachers who are characterized as *feeling* types place importance on personal rapport with students, incorporate small-group work whenever possible, think people are more important than things or ideas, give personal meaning to an assignment, seek ways to give learners benefits from learning, and seek harmony when working with others (Cooper). Sparks (2006) cautions, however, that matching teaching style to the learner's preferred learning style has not been shown to affect academic achievement, partly because of the limitations of learning styles inventories and language learning testing instruments. Castro (2006) nevertheless points out that teacher awareness of learners' preferred strategies and understanding of their own preferred teaching styles may be a mark of a good teacher, echoing Lawrence (1996), who wrote that "A sign of a good teacher is the ability to flex one's teaching style to better fit the needs of those being taught" (p. 74).

"A sign of a good teacher is the ability to flex one's teaching style to better fit the needs of those being taught."

If teachers' preferences for certain instructional practices reflect their personalities and their own learning styles, how do the various learners' preferences match? Oxford and Lavine (1992) examined the mismatch between instructors' teaching styles and their students' learning styles. They claim that "Students whose learning processes resemble the teacher's are more likely to achieve good grades (and want to continue studying the language) than are students with opposing styles, who may drop the course or even discontinue studying the language" (p. 38). The researchers further assert that style wars between teachers and students are often disguised as poor language aptitudes, personality clashes, and bad learner attitudes (p. 42). They suggest six ways in which teachers can realistically deal with these teacher–student style conflicts:

1. Assess your style and students' styles and use this information to understand classroom dynamics. As teachers and students become aware of their major learning style preferences, they may be able to help one another understand diverse views and

make an effort to compensate for any style mismatches. Instruments for assessing learning styles can be used, such as Oxford's (1990a) Strategy Inventory for Language Learning (SILL), which lists 80 items or the Language Learning Strategies (LLS) developed by Schmidt and Watanabe (2001) listing 24 items.

2. **Change your teaching behavior.** Teachers can orient their teaching styles to meet their students' needs by providing a variety of multisensory, abstract, and concrete learning activities that appeal to different learning styles. A standards-based teaching approach that provides for a variety of activities, individual guidance, and an emphasis on meaning can enable students to experience many ways of learning. Learners who are analytic, sequential, or closure-oriented usually like questions and exercises requiring unambiguous information such as completions, definitions, true-false, slash sentences, cloze passages, and guided writing. Learners who are global, intuitive, or open often prefer open-ended activities, personalized questions, simulations and games, interviews, reading for the gist, and social conversation. Visual learners need visual stimuli such as transparencies, slides, video, charts, maps, magnetic or felt boards, posters, board games, and puppets. They benefit from written directions and from being shown, not told, what to do. Auditory learners prefer auditory input from radio, television, video, songs, interviews, oral reports, discussions, telephone conversations, and recordings. They need oral instructions and must be told, not shown, what to do. Hands-on learners require hands-on experiences, such as creating things, manipulating real cultural items, taking notes, doing TPR activities, and following directions. If these learners "do not receive enough sensory stimuli, they might create their own movement activities unrelated to the learning task (such as tapping pencils, drawing, doodling, wiggling, or bouncing)" (Oxford & Lavine, 1992, p. 43).

3. **Change learners' behavior.** Language learners use their style preferences to their own advantage. Learners can benefit when teachers realize this and provide opportunities for students to move beyond their stylistic comfort zone through the use of strategies with which they might not initially feel comfortable (Scarcella & Oxford, 1992). For example, an analytic learner can benefit from an activity that involves understanding global meaning, while a global student similarly can benefit from specific linguistic analysis.

4. **Change the way students work in groups in your classroom.** Teachers can use the principles of cooperative learning when grouping students for interactive work. In certain tasks, students with similar learning styles might be grouped together, while in other activities, students might be grouped in a heterogeneous fashion so that members might practice stretching beyond their comfort zones.

5. **Change the curriculum.** Teachers can organize lessons as a series of activities or episodes, each with a different objective and style. New materials might be developed in learning-style modules. Multimedia materials can be integrated into the curriculum for classroom and individual use in order to guarantee the tapping of different sensory styles.

6. **Change the way style conflicts are viewed.** Teachers who encourage students to become aware of learning style preferences help promote flexibility and openness to the use of many styles.

 A standards-based teaching approach that provides for a variety of activities, individual guidance, and an emphasis on meaning can enable students to experience many ways of learning.

Language Learning Strategies

Scarcella and Oxford (1992) define language learning strategies as "specific actions, behaviors, steps, or techniques—such as seeking out conversation partners, or giving oneself encouragement to tackle a difficult language task—used by students to enhance their own learning" (p. 63). According to MacIntyre and Noels (1996), almost any tactic or plan that the student believes will help in learning some part of the language or in managing the language learning process can be considered a strategy. Studies have not been systematically replicated and results are conflictive, leading Woodrow (2005) to suggest that Likert-type assessments such as the SILLS and the LLS should be heavily supplemented by qualitative studies that more clearly reflect the environment of the classroom and the motivation and affective factors that influence students.

Nevertheless, two broad conclusions can be drawn from the research: (1) language learning strategies can be taught, and (2) these strategies are effective when students use them, although not all strategies are useful for all people in all situations. Figure 10.2 depicts a list of language learning strategies categorized in terms of four stages in the learning process: (1) planning for learning, (2) regulating or facilitating one's learning, (3) problem solving, and (4) evaluating one's progress in learning (Alatis & Barnhardt, 1998).

 Language learning strategies are specific actions, behaviors, steps, or techniques used by students to enhance their own learning.

Oxford (1990b) suggests that instructors teach students how to use strategies in order to help them in the language learning process. Earlier chapters of *Teacher's Handbook* presented ways to teach students effective strategies for using the three modes of communication. Strategy training can be integrated with language learning and communication activities and conducted through simulations, games, and other interactive tasks. Furthermore, MacIntyre and Noels (1996) add that strategy training can encourage the actual use of the strategy by building assurance in learners that they know the strategies well, that the strategies will work, and that they are not difficult to use. Oxford (1990a) developed the following eight-step model for integrating strategy training into classroom activities:

1. Identify students' needs to determine what strategies they are currently using, how effective the strategies are, and how they can be improved.
2. Choose relevant strategies to be taught.
3. Determine how best to integrate strategy training into regular classroom activities.
4. Consider students' motivations and attitudes about themselves as learners and about learning new ways to learn.
5. Prepare materials and activities.
6. Conduct *completely informed* training, in which students learn and practice new strategies, learn why the strategies are important, learn to evaluate their use of the strategies, and learn how to apply the strategies in new situations (refer to Figure 10.2 for an example of this training model in action).
7. Evaluate the strategy training.
8. Revise the strategy training procedure for the next set of strategies to be taught (pp. 48–49).

An alternative to direct strategy instruction is suggested in a study in which Donato and McCormick (1994) helped students in a French conversation class identify and create their own learning strategies by means of a portfolio assessment project. In this study,

FIGURE 10.2 Learning Strategies Model

PLAN		
Strategy name	**Question student asks self**	**Definition**
Goal setting	What is my personal objective? What strategies can help me?	Develop personal objectives, identify purpose of task, choose appropriate strategies
Directed attention	What distractions can I ignore? How can I focus my attention?	Decide in advance to focus on particular tasks and ignore distractions
Activate background knowledge	What do I already know about this topic/task?	Think about and use what you already know to help do the task
Predict/ Brainstorm	What kinds of information can I predict for this task? What might I need to do?	Anticipate information to prepare and give yourself direction for the task
REGULATE		
Self-Monitor	Do I understand this? Am I making sense?	Check your understanding to keep track of how you're doing and to identify problems
Selective attention	What should I pay most attention to? Is the information important?	Focus on specific aspects of language or situational details
Deduction	Which rules can I apply to help complete the task?	Apply known rules
Visualize	Can I imagine a picture or situation that will help me understand?	Create an image to represent information to help you remember and check your understanding
Contextualize/ Personalize	How does this fit into the real world?	Think about how to use material in real life, relate information to background knowledge
Cooperate	How can I work with others to do this?	Work with others to help build confidence and to give and receive feedback
Self-talk	I can do this! What strategies can I use to help me?	Reduce anxiety by reminding self of progress, resources available, and goals
PROBLEM-SOLVE		
Inference/ Substitute	Can I guess what this means? Is there another way to say/do this?	Make guesses based on previous knowledge
Question for clarification	What help do I need? Who/Where can I ask?	Ask for explanation and examples
Resource	What information do I need? Where can I find more information about this?	Use reference materials
EVALUATE		
Verify	Were my predictions and guesses right? Why or why not?	Check whether your predictions/guesses were right
Summarize	What is the gist/main idea of this?	Create a mental, oral, written summary

Source: From J. Alatis and S. Barnhardt, eds., *Portfolio Assessment in the Modern Language Classroom,* 1998, National Capital Language Resource Center, Washington, DC. Used by permission.

students were instructed to provide, in their portfolios, *evidence* of their learning. As they selected the evidence, they engaged in four cyclical steps: self-assessing, setting goals, using specific plans of action (strategies), and connecting to and reflecting upon past performance or evidence. For instance, a self-assessment statement such as "I can't speak quickly enough" could be turned into a goal such as "I'll speak more in class" (p. 459). This goal then became the strategy of talking with a friend in French twice a week on the telephone. Students demonstrated that they were connecting with their work and reflecting on past performance, saying, for example, "I listened to the recorded conversation I had with my friend and noticed I said *'Ah bon'* a lot and didn't attempt to paraphrase" (p. 461). Thus, the students engaged in a dialogue with themselves, their work, and their instructor, resulting in development and selection of strategies that facilitated their learning within the situated sociocultural framework of the classroom.

The use of appropriate learning strategies often results in increased language proficiency and greater self-confidence (Cohen, 1990; Oxford & Crookall, 1989). Research supports the idea that many learners are relatively unaware of the strategies they use and do not take advantage of the full range of available strategies. As you read about the learners with special needs described in the following section of this chapter, think about how you might help them use the learning strategies described above in a standards-based approach.

 The use of appropriate learning strategies often results in increased language proficiency and greater self-confidence.

Addressing Diverse Learner Needs

In this section, we will explore two groups of learners who have special needs: (1) learners with special physical needs, and (2) learners with special learning needs, such as learners with learning disabilities, at-risk learners, gifted learners, and heritage or home background learners. First, however, we will examine the definition of the term *disabilities* and explore how the federal government has ensured that students with disabilities are part of regular classrooms and receive special accommodations in those classrooms.

The Inclusive Classroom: Accommodating Learners with Disabilities

Teaching foreign languages to all students, as specified in the *SFLL*, requires special attention to the needs of students with disabilities. A *disability* is a mental or physical impairment that limits a major life activity—for example, caring for oneself, performing a manual task, hearing, walking, speaking, thinking, and so forth. Prior to 1975, students with disabilities were placed together in classes often labeled "Special Education." In 1975, Public Law 94-142 (Education for All Handicapped Children Act of 1975) directed public schools to find, enroll, and educate all handicapped children. In addition, Public Law 101-476 (Individuals with Disabilities Education Act of 1990, often referred to by its acronym IDEA), and Public Law 105-17 (Amendments to IDEA, 1997) ensure that persons with disabilities are not denied participation in or benefits from educational programs or activities, and that these persons do not face negative bias or stereotyping associated with a disability. Through a provision called *inclusion*, students who have physical, intellectual, or emotional impairments are now part of regular classrooms and receive special accommodations in those classrooms. IDEA was reauthorized in 2004 as Public Law 108-446 to include updates related to newly identified disabilities, accommodations, access, and teacher preparation. Prior to the 2004 reauthorization, students with learning disabilities were often excluded from foreign language study. The law now stipulates that foreign language is one of the core subject areas that must be accessible by learners with disabilities.

The law defined the following categories of disabilities: autism, deafness, deaf-blindness, development delay, emotional disturbance, hearing impairment, mental retardation, multiple disabilities, orthopedic impairment, other health impairment (e.g., asthma, attention deficit hyperactivity disorder, diabetes, Tourette's syndrome), specific learning disability (e.g., perceptual disabilities, dyslexia, or minimal brain function), speech or language impairment, traumatic brain injury, and visual impairment (National Dissemination Center for Children with Disabilities [NICHCY], 2007). See *Teacher's Handbook* Web site for further details of how a large, well-respected school division[2] provides services and resources.

www.cengagebrain.com

In 2006–2007, 6.7 million children, or 9% of all school-age children, in the U.S. received special support services to address their disabilities (NCES, 2008b). School personnel work with families and learners to outline individualized education programs (IEPs) or individualized family service plans (IFSPs) to ensure that students with disabilities or special needs are provided with a Free Appropriate Public Education (FAPE) throughout their years in school. Of the 100 largest school divisions in the United States, 11.6% of the school population has had an IEP developed by a team consisting of a counselor, principal, teacher, parent, and sometimes the student (NCES, 2006). The IEP includes a statement of the child's current functional performance, annual goals, and which services will be provided when/where and for how long; a statement about how the child will interact with nondisabled children; and a statement about how progress will be measured and the child's role in statewide required tests. In some cases, adjustments, or *accommodations*, are offered in the form of extended time for tests, oral tests for blind students, and tests in the native language for ELLs. In addition to providing an IEP, schools may provide students with a 504 Plan, which explicitly outlines services and accommodations for students who require special assistance but whose disabilities may not fall into one of the categories outlined in the IDEA legislation.

Through a provision called *inclusion*, students who have physical, intellectual, or emotional impairments are now often part of regular classrooms and receive special accommodations in those classrooms.

As you read through the following suggestions for how to work with students with special needs, keep in mind that they bring more to the foreign language classroom than their disability—they bring a different way to learn a language, as shown by the case study of a two-semester project in which a graduate teaching assistant (TA) developed alternative teaching and assessment strategies to accommodate a blind learner (Wilberscheid, 2007/2008). In this study, an "aging, blind, African-American Muslim who neither read Braille nor used computers" (p. 85) was paired with a novice instructor from Mexico who had been taught in traditional ways. The TA used the following teaching strategies: The TA put the language in context during and outside of class, e.g., in meals; used rhythmic repetition in dance, song, authentic conversation; generated vocabulary activities and word lists related to the learner's interests; provided CDs and equipment to play them; required short tape-recorded recitations and longer story-telling sessions; required a tape recording of two learner-created songs; had the learner provide the speech modeling and inspiration for the rest of the class; provided a tutor; consulted with other faculty members in devising alternative assessments and strategies; and involved the learner with other TAs who talked about Mexican music and culture. Their work together produced ripple effects among other students and faculty, who later reported making accommodations for a student in a wheelchair, for students with documented cognitive processing difficulties, and for students with autism and schizophrenia. The TA remarked that "Each of these students has such incredible persistence. To teach them is a learning experience for us." Another replied, "There is so much hope in that—persisting in the face of obstacles that seem so hard . . . and they (the disabled learners) become our teachers. . . no diversity without community. The hope in persistence" (p. 97).

Teaching Foreign Languages to Learners with Special Physical Needs

Accommodating Learners' Physical Needs. Teachers need to be aware of how students' physical limitations will affect their participation in certain types of hands-on activities, such as TPR, and how alternative activities might be provided to accomplish language learning goals. Students who have physical disabilities may require space for a wheelchair, crutches, or a walker. They may also need extra time to move through the halls to the next class and therefore might require early dismissal or a companion to help negotiate the hallways or carry books.

Accommodating Deaf and Hearing-Impaired Learners. Deaf and hearing-impaired students may come from a home where their family members are also deaf or hearing impaired or a home where their family members are hearing. In either case, the students have the benefit of having learned American Sign Language (ASL),[3] Mexican Sign Language (LSM - Lengua de Señas Mexicana)[4] or some other form of manual communication. Teachers should keep in mind that deaf and hearing-impaired students come from a community of people who share or at least deeply understand their special needs in communication. In a foreign language class, deaf students who have learned ASL and English in school could be learning a third or subsequent language (Strong, 1988). Spinelli (1989) describes an approach to language instruction for deaf students in which they are taught to use sign language in the foreign language through the use of videotapes showing target-culture signing. Using the TL signing system is a more effective system for communication than finger spelling the foreign language. Foreign language teachers of deaf students must think visually about their teaching. Students might be given the scripts that often accompany audiocassette or CD programs, and they should be permitted to refer to their textbooks or to other written material during oral presentations. Teachers may need to prepare written scripts of oral activities to assist students with comprehension, and a note taker may be required for discussions. The visual and written modalities might be stressed in combination with comparative study of the deaf culture as opposed to that of the hearing culture.

Students who have hearing impairments may also require preferred seating arrangements, face-to-face talk if they read lips, and perhaps interpreters. Students who are hearing impaired can often tell the teacher how they learn most effectively and can suggest ways for the teacher to aid their learning. Teachers should keep in mind that reading can be difficult and frustrating for a deaf person, depending on the degree of hearing loss. Since a great deal of reading ability is associated with phonological awareness and profoundly deaf children cannot make letter-sound correspondences, reading is a tedious process for most deaf children. The following are suggestions for teaching strategies:

- videotape classes;
- use visuals and audio materials together;
- summarize key points in an introduction and a conclusion;
- use a typed outline of the lesson;
- reduce the number of words in your directions (use key words); and
- don't be afraid to repeat instructions (Moore & Moore, 1997).

Accommodating Visually Impaired Learners. In the case of students with visual impairments, large-type, Braille, and auditory texts or other types of assistive technology are needed; oral examinations, reading services, preferred seating in the classroom, and perhaps space for a guide dog are other accommodations. Teachers can capitalize on oral skills and the use of discussion, especially since students' primary goal may be to develop interpersonal speaking abilities. In addition, students need extra class time to process material that they read in Braille. Partnerships between class members can be arranged for TPR activities that involve manipulatives, which may result in greater use of the TL. For example, in practicing vocabulary dealing with clothing, a student with a visual impairment tells a sighted student where he wants to place a specific item of clothing on a laminated paper doll (B. Kraft, personal communication, April 22, 1992). In exam situations, special considerations can be made, such as giving only oral exams for these students or having each student dictate answers to another student who writes them down (Phillips de Herrera, 1984). Students may also be allowed to tape classes, or to put their responses to assignments on tape (Moore & Moore, 1997). Involving visually impaired or blind students in the class through auditory activities in which they can provide modeling for pronunciation or other speaking practice minimizes the effect of their disability and strengthens their contributions to the classroom climate.

Teaching Foreign Language to Learners with Special Learning Needs

The *SFLL* make it clear that individuals require varied kinds of support to facilitate their learning. Schools deliver a variety of services to assist students who have special learning needs. Some services provide support for learners who lack certain skills or learning conditions; others are for students whose abilities exceed those of their peers. In any case, each learner brings a unique configuration of skills, talents, and knowledge to the foreign language classroom and should be provided with supporting services. According to Fairfax County Public Schools (1992), some of these students have documented learning disabilities while others simply need some adjustments in their class schedules, testing or homework arrangements, or other educational services. Students who are considered *average* or *non-gifted* (the term *gifted* will be discussed later) may also have special cognitive needs. It is paramount that the foreign language teacher understand the characteristics of these groups in order to use specific teaching strategies that will enable them to experience success in the language classroom.

Accommodating Average or Non-Gifted Learners with Special Cognitive Needs. Average students with special cognitive needs are *able* to perform at expected levels, but they may actually perform at a lower level because of emotional, motivational, cultural, or social difficulties; they may also have poor study skills. Specific strategies for the foreign language teacher include the following:

- Communicate specific expectations and monitor student progress constantly.
- Give specific explanations and instructions orally and visually, step by step.
- Provide a variety of activities, some of which require physical movement.
- Get students on task immediately and provide frequent changes of pace.
- Display student work as a form of reinforcement for work done well.
- Choose reading selections, writing assignments, and presentation topics related to student interests.
- Provide choices of activities and higher-level thinking activities as students seem ready.
- Have students repeat the homework assignment instructions and, if time allows, begin the assignment. This provides time to work with students needing assistance (Fairfax County Public Schools, 1992, p. 5).

Accommodating Students with Learning Disabilities. A second group of special needs students are those with *learning disabilities* or *other health impairments*. Public Law 108-446 defines a *learning disability* in this way:

> A disorder in one or more of the basic psychological processes involved in understanding or in using language, spoken or written, that may manifest itself in an imperfect ability to listen, think, speak, read, write, spell, or to do mathematical calculations, including conditions such as perceptual disabilities, brain injury, minimal brain dysfunction, dyslexia, and developmental aphasia. The term does not include learning problems that are primarily the result of visual, hearing, or motor disabilities, of mental retardation, of emotional disturbance, or of environmental, cultural, or economic disadvantage (NCES, 2008c).

Public Law 108-446 describes *other health impairment* as a category of disability in which children have limited strength, vitality, or alertness, including a heightened alertness to environmental stimuli, that results in limited alertness with respect to the educational environment due to chronic or acute health problems such as asthma, attention deficit disorder (ADD) or attention deficit hyperactivity disorder (ADHD),[5] diabetes, epilepsy, a heart condition, hemophilia, lead poisoning, leukemia, nephritis, rheumatic fever, and sickle cell anemia . . . (NCES, 2008c).

A learning disorder interferes with a student's ability to store, process, or produce information. Learning disorders are intrinsic to the individual, are presumed to be due to central nervous system dysfunction, and may occur across the life span. Problems in self-regulatory behaviors, social perception, and social interaction may exist with learning disorders but do not by themselves constitute a learning disorder. Although learning disorders may occur concomitantly with other conditions (e.g., sensory impairment, mental retardation, or serious emotional disturbance) or with extrinsic influences (such as cultural differences and insufficient or inappropriate instruction), they are not the result of those conditions or influences (Brinckerhoff, Shaw, & McGuire, 1993). An impairment can be quite subtle and may go undetected throughout life. Nevertheless, learning disorders create a gap between a person's true capacity and day-to-day productivity and performance (Levine, 1984).

The category of students labeled as having learning disabilities poses a challenge for teachers of all disciplines, partially because there is a lack of agreement among cognition experts concerning the specific criteria that determine whether or not a student has a learning disability, and partially because most of the related assessments are based on memory work, an area in which not all learners excel. State and local agencies have the responsibility to test and diagnose learning disabilities. Once diagnosed, the learners then have access to services provided by federal, state, and local agencies to help them achieve in the least restrictive educational environment. However, Lyon and Moats (1993) point out that these agencies use different testing measures and criteria in classifying learners with learning disabilities, and they are often influenced by the political/social agendas of community groups. For example, one criterion often used in diagnosing a learning disability is the discrepancy between the IQ score and the score on a measure of academic achievement, such as word recognition, reading comprehension, written language, listening comprehension, oral expression, or mathematics.[6] In some states, a 15-point discrepancy would classify a student as having a learning disability while in other states the discrepancy must be 22 points (Sparks & Javorsky, 1998).

Students are often categorized as learning disabled as a result of the type of instruction they receive and not necessarily because of verified learning disorders. For example, Bruck (1978) discovered that students with learning disabilities who learned French by means of a traditional approach actually acquired little knowledge of the language, because the method exploited the areas in which they had the most difficulties: memorization, learning language out of context, and understanding abstract rules. Learning disabilities, particularly in cases of students labeled *mildly disabled*, may be exacerbated by traditional classrooms that emphasize rules and bottom-up processing. Unfortunately, many learners are incorrectly classified as having learning disabilities and carry that label with them throughout their educational experience, while other learners who may require special assistance are never diagnosed with a learning disability.

Although students labeled as having learning disabilities may vary widely in their specific learning problems, Levine (1984) cites the following types of difficulties that are commonly exhibited:

- difficulties in keeping attention focused: tuning in and out, inconsistent performance, impulsive behavior, and a negative self-image;
- language processing difficulties;
- spatial orientation problems: words look different, and reversals in letters and in placement of letters and words are common;
- poor memory;
- difficulty in organizing work; and
- sequencing problems: difficulty in putting a series of items in correct order, difficulty in following instructions, difficulty in organizing work (adapted from Levine; as cited in Spinelli, 1996, pp. 74–75).

Several researchers in the field of special education have studied the relationship between learning disabilities and foreign language learning. These findings consistently support the notion that students identified as having various types of learning disabilities can learn a language, with appropriate accommodations, at least as well as low-achieving students who do not have learning disabilities. Their findings can be summarized as follows:

1. Learners are capable of learning a foreign language with some degree of success (Javorsky, Sparks, & Ganschow, 1992; Sparks & Ganschow, 1993; Sparks, Ganschow, Fluharty, & Little, 1995/1996; Sparks, Ganschow, Javorsky, Pohlman, & Patton, 1992; Sparks, Ganschow, & Pohlman, 1989).
2. Presence of a second disability (such as ADHD) may not result in more severe FL learning problems; these students perform as well as students who are not labeled as having a learning disability (Sparks, Philips, & Javorsky, 2008).
3. The L1 literacy skills that appear to enable adequate L2 performance, such as L1 reading, writing, and L2 aptitude, were already apparent as early as the fourth grade (Sparks, Humbach, & Javorsky, 2003).
4. Phonologic and orthographic difficulties experienced by learners with learning disabilities can be addressed through instruction in which "students simultaneously hear a sound, see the symbol(s) that correspond with that sound and write the symbol(s)" (Sparks et al., 1995/1996, p. 170).

An implication of these findings is related to the university-level practice of waiving foreign language requirements for students who have a documented learning disability. In research examining this issue, the majority of students receiving FL course substitutions failed to meet any LD legal/research criteria (Sparks, Artzer, Javorsky, Patton, Ganschow, Miller, & Hordubay, 1998; Sparks & Javorsky, 1998). In a 1998 legal ruling in *Guckenberg v. Trustees of Boston University*, it was stated that "Universities must provide accommodations, but are not legally required to provide course substitutions for the FL requirement, . . . if the university deems foreign language as an essential part of the curriculum" (as cited in Sparks & Javorsky, p. 11). The implication of this ruling is consistent with the research showing that everyone can learn a language if appropriate accommodations are made.

The research conducted by Sparks, Javorsky, Ganschow, and colleagues has been criticized for not recognizing the ways in which the social context of learning and of the classroom can influence cognitive processes and language learning and the potential effects of affective variables when considering the relation between aptitude and achievement (Arries, 1999; Mabbott, 1994, 1995; MacIntyre, 1995). Nevertheless, the results indicate that students with learning difficulties are able to successfully acquire a second language. Key concepts that are current in the standards-based classroom of the 21st century should be considered in research on learning disabilities. Among these concepts and potential variables are proficiency and student-centered, standards-based, and socioculturally motivated instruction. Arries suggests that teachers take a qualitative approach to analyzing how LD-classified students perform in their classes and make appropriate accommodations as suggested by the students through interviews and self-reports.

There are several implications from the learning disability foreign language research for the language teacher whose students manifest learning difficulties:

1. In a proficiency-oriented, standards-based classroom, a learning disability may not have the confounding influence it might have in a more traditional memory/skills-based classroom.
2. Given the lack of consensus regarding the classification of LD, the language teacher should not assume that learners who are not labeled LD do not have learning disabilities.
3. The language teacher should not assume that students with learning disability labels cannot experience success in foreign language learning (Sparks, Humbach, & Javorsky, 2008). Immersion programs may provide the best environment in which students who have learning disabilities can learn a foreign language, since students are involved in meaningful interaction and hands-on experiences (Curtain, 1986; Mabbott, 1994; Spinelli, 1996).
4. A classroom environment that is rich in sociocultural learning (see Chapter 1) and includes content-based and story-based approaches (see Chapters 3, 4, 7) can provide the type of meaningful instructional support and learning experiences that facilitate language learning for students with learning disabilities.
5. The language teacher should carefully assess why an individual is having a problem in the class and should engage students in self-assessment and conferences (see Chapter 11). The teacher should be familiar with and use a variety of strategies for helping students with specific kinds of difficulties in learning the foreign language.

The following are some general strategies for helping students with learning disabilities in the foreign language classroom:

- Use a well-organized daily classroom routine, with frequent praise and repetition of ideas (McCabe, 1985; Moore & Moore, 1997).
- Develop a communicative-oriented rather than a grammar-oriented class, with as much personal interaction as possible (Mabbott, 1994).
- Use frequent review and repetition, and present small amounts of material at one time (Sparks et al., 1992).
- Provide additional input on phonological sound-symbol systems and syntactic grammar systems of the language for LD as well as low-achieving students (Sparks, Humbach, & Javorsky, 2008).
- When conducting listening and reading activities, give fewer instructions at one time, provide pre-listening/pre-reading discussion, and give comprehension questions prior to and after the reading selection, spending more time focusing on a literal level first before moving to a figurative level (Barnett, 1985; Moore & Moore, 1997).

- Provide opportunities for students to learn through more than one modality, particularly through the tactile (touching, manipulating objects) or kinesthetic (use of movement, gestures) modalities (Spinelli, 1989). One such approach emphasizes the use of the tactile and kinesthetic modalities in teaching reading to dyslexic/learning disabled students (Gillingham & Stillman, 1969; Schneider, 1996; Sparks, Ganschow, Kenneweg, & Miller, 1991). Sparks and Ganschow (1993) showed significant gains in teaching Spanish to learning disabled students using a multisensory, structured language approach for teaching phonological and syntactic elements of a foreign language.[7]
- Have realistic expectations of what students can do, and measure their progress in terms of their own abilities rather than in terms of what the entire class can attain.
- Provide ample opportunities for students to interact with other students in the class by means of cooperative learning activities. Emphasize how important it is for all students to understand, respect, and help one another in the learning process.
- Allow use of tape recorders, keyboards, computers, and other assistive technologies.
- Make special provisions for assignments and testing. Allow students to take a test orally if they have trouble reading; allow students to take a test a second time if they did not do well the first time; give students additional time to complete tests; allow students to use grammar charts and dictionaries during tests. Realize that students with learning disabilities may not perform well on certain test formats such as spelling, memorizing dialogs, reading aloud, and taking notes (Mabbott, 1994).
- Consider integrating dynamic assessment by offering mediation throughout some of the oral interpersonal and interpretive assessments, as described in Chapter 11.
- Provide time for more individualized work with special education students and offer continued feedback on their progress. During this time, work with them on developing effective learning strategies.

As you read through the lists of strategies presented here, you may have recognized that many of them have already been suggested throughout the *Teacher's Handbook* for use with all students. Research suggests that the instructional methods that are effective with students who have learning disabilities tend to be the same as those that are effective with other students, except that students with learning disabilities may need more attention (Evarrs & Knotek, 2005; Larrivee, 1985). Students with physical or learning disabilities may need more individualized instruction and more one-to-one instruction from the teacher (Madden & Slavin, 1983), while students with behavior disorders may require closer supervision (Thompson, White, & Morgan, 1982).

Providing Effective Learning Experiences for *At-Risk* Students

As foreign language teachers face the challenge of teaching special needs students who have been mainstreamed into regular classes, they are also encountering more and more children labeled *at-risk* of educational failure. *At-risk* students are those who "are likely to fail—either in school or in life" (Frymier & Gansneder, 1989, p. 142) due to circumstances beyond their control (Spinelli, 1996, p. 72). In 2000–2001, 613,000 students, or 1.3% of the school population, were considered at-risk, and 39% of schools had programs to assist them in becoming successful learners (NCES, 2003). These students have a high likelihood of dropping out of school, being low achievers, or even committing suicide. They are at-risk because of a wide variety of circumstances they face outside of school: poverty, dysfunctional family life, neglect, abuse, or cultural/ethnic/racial background. The "three strongest social correlates of suicidal behavior in youth are family breakdown, a youth's unemployment, and decreasing religious observance among the young"

(Frymier, 1989, p. 290). *At-riskness* has been described as "a function of what bad things happen to a child, how severe they are, how often they happen, and what else happens in the child's immediate environment" (Frymier & Gansneder, p. 142). At-risk students often display emotional and/or psychological symptoms such as depression, anxiety, difficulty in concentrating, and excessive anger, as well as physical symptoms such as respiratory problems, headaches, and muscle tension (Vanucci, 1991).

 At-risk students are those who are likely to fail due to circumstances beyond their control.

Socioeconomic status, educational level, and poverty are additional factors that may also put a student at risk of failure. Students who are at risk are often from low socioeconomic environments and single-parent families, and from certain heritage groups, such as African American, Hispanic, Asian, or Native American.[8] They frequently experience problems in school because of their loss of identity or ethnic roots, difficulty in integrating themselves into the majority culture, and other students' incorrect perceptions of them. While the educational attainment of Hispanic and Black students has increased in recent years, it is still lower than that of non-Black and non-Hispanic students (NCES, 2007a). Perhaps due to efforts to provide programs for at-risk students, Finn and Owings (2006) reported improvement in the adult lives of at-risk students. They found that, among high school graduates classified as at-risk due to socioeconomic status or race/ethnicity, 61% enter post-secondary school and about half of them finish two-year or four-year programs. However, academic risks such as attaining reasonable test scores, passing grades, and graduating from high school are related to lack of success in employment and further education. Further, behavioral risk factors, such as coming to class on time, attending class regularly, working hard in class, completing assignments, and being involved in extracurricular activities are more likely to result in furthering education in a post-secondary program.

In many cases, the difficulties that minority students face seem insurmountable when the students are placed in classrooms that stress total conformity to the majority culture. Educators have come a long way in the past 20 years in learning to address the needs of at-risk and minority students. Students are sent to alternative schools if their performance indicates a risk of failure as revealed in possession, distribution, or use of alcohol or drugs; physical attacks or fights; chronic truancy; possession or use of a weapon other than a firearm; continual academic failure; disruptive verbal behavior; and possession or use of a firearm. Teen pregnancy/parenthood and mental health needs were least likely to be sole reasons for transfer (Kleiner, Porch, & Farris, 2002). Within alternative schools, the goal is to return students to a regular school as soon as possible, or to enable them to graduate by means of academic counseling, smaller class size than in regular schools, remedial instruction, opportunity for self-paced instruction, crisis/behavioral intervention, and career counseling.

Much of the research in multicultural education for teaching at-risk students has clear implications for classroom instruction. Heining-Boynton (1994) points out that frequent assessment and adaptation of instruction to learners' needs are beneficial for these learners, along with techniques that foreign language teachers have praised for years as good instruction. The following list illustrates possible strategies that foreign language teachers might use as they attempt to provide successful language learning for all students:

www.cengagebrain.com

1. Engage students in activities that encourage social interaction and promote the use of higher-order thinking skills to challenge students' creativity (Kuykendall, 1989). See Appendix 10.4 on the Web site for a chart of strategies to extend student thinking.

2. Relate learning about another language and culture to students' own life experiences (Kuykendall).

3. Offer descriptive instead of evaluative feedback in an effort to encourage progress rather than cause frustration. Also, display each student's work at some time during the academic year (Kuykendall).

4. Maintain direct, sincere eye contact when communicating with individual students (Kuykendall).

5. Make every effort to give all students equal opportunities to participate.

6. Use heterogeneous and cooperative groupings for interactive tasks, as described in Chapter 8 (Kuykendall).

7. Make the language curriculum reflect the individual cultures of the students by including study of key historical/political figures from various cultures, inviting guest speakers from various cultures, engaging students in discussion in the TL about their own cultures, and discussing in the TL current events that involve the students' own cultures (Kuykendall).

8. If there are native speakers of the TL who are students in the language class, encourage their ethnic pride by engaging them in activities such as providing oral input in the TL, helping other students undertake culture projects, offering classmates additional cultural information, and sharing family photographs.

9. When presenting the cultures of the people who speak the TL, include people of different age groups, both male and female, and from as many geographical regions as possible.

10. When sharing opinions or discussing abstract topics, encourage students to express their own ideas concerning values, morals, and religious views, as shaped by their own cultures and religious convictions.

11. Use visuals that portray males and females of diverse racial and ethnic origins.

12. Hold the same achievement expectations for all students in the class, except in cases of physical or intellectual disabilities (Kuykendall).

13. Provide opportunities for students to help one another. Sullivan and McDonald (1990) found that cross-age peer tutoring is an effective strategy that enables students to exercise autonomy, gain self-esteem, achieve at a higher level than normal, and learn more about students who are different from themselves. In Sullivan and McDonald's study, high school Spanish III students in an urban school district taught Spanish to elementary school children. See Case Study Two, "A Play for My Buddies," in Chapter 9 on the *Teacher's Handbook* Web site for an example of cross-age tutoring.

www.cengagebrain.com

14. Maintain positive teacher–parent relationships by inviting parents to see students' work in the foreign language, such as special projects, exhibits, or drama presentations. Talk to parents about their children's individual talents and progress (Kuykendall).

Teaching Gifted Learners

Gifted learners make up another category of special needs students. Challenging and expanding the academic capabilities of gifted learners is neither a more nor a less important charge than developing the academic capabilities of slow learners. Tomlinson (1997) provides a statement of teaching gifted learners that can be applied to teaching all learners well:

> What it takes to teach gifted learners well is actually a little common sense. It begins with the premise that each child should come to school to stretch and grow daily. It includes the expectation that the measure of progress and growth is competition with oneself

rather than competition against others. It resides in the notion that educators understand key concepts, principles and skills of subject domains, and present those in ways that cause highly able students to wonder and grasp, and extend their reach. And it envisions schooling as an escalator on which students continually progress, rather than a series of stairs, with landings on which advanced learners consistently wait. (n.p.)

Defining Giftedness.   A specific definition of the term *gifted* was provided by Congress in Public Law 97-35 (1981), the Omnibus Education Reconciliation Act:

> Children who give evidence of high performance capability in areas such as intellectual, creative, artistic, leadership capacity, or specific academic fields, and who require services or activities not ordinarily provided by the school in order to fully develop such capabilities (Sec. 582[3][A]).

The National Association of Gifted Children (NAGC) in 2008 estimates that there are 3 million (6%) academically gifted students in the U.S. school-age population. In their presentation of the work of 29 researchers, Sternberg and Davidson (1986) conclude that giftedness is viewed most often in terms of cognitive processing capacities. Although identification of gifted learners has been a major focus of much of the literature in the area of gifted education, most measures are unsatisfactory. Researchers agree that multiple measures are preferred over any single achievement test and that efforts should be made to specify alternate types of giftedness (Feldhusen, 1989). The National Council of Supervisors of Foreign Languages describes linguistically gifted students as those who have an IQ, based on a standardized intelligence test, in the top three to five percent of the student population and scores of 500 to 600 on the verbal or math section of the SAT exam (Bartz, 1982). Although functional definitions generally refer to the upper two percent of the population as the *highly gifted* and the top five percent of the population as the *gifted*, to date there are no data to show what portion of the general population and what portion of the gifted population are *linguistically* gifted. Nor is there conclusive evidence to explain why certain students are gifted learners. While practices in the past have been to identify a percentage of the population as gifted, current practice is to identify and nurture the giftedness within each learner (Tomlinson, 1997; Treffinger & Feldhusen, 1996).

Gifted education is often justified on the basis of generally accepted purposes: (1) to provide young people with opportunities for maximum cognitive growth and self-fulfillment through the development and expression of one or a combination of performance areas where superior potential may be present, and (2) to increase our society's reservoir of persons who will help to solve the problems of contemporary civilization by becoming producers of knowledge and creative works rather than mere consumers of existing information (Renzulli, 1999). Thus, programs for the gifted typically include challenging real-world tasks, instruction targeted to the learner's strengths, enabling students to observe and perform in ways consistent with what professionals in a given field might do; e.g., the study of science enables students to conduct experiments as a scientist would; the study of civics gives students practice in behaving as a delegate at a national political convention.

   Try to identify the giftedness in each learner.

Curricular and Instructional Modifications for Gifted Learners.   Program models for gifted learners traditionally involved *acceleration*, which is instruction provided at a level and pace appropriate to the student's level of achievement or readiness (Feldhusen, 1989), and *enrichment*, which is in-depth study of broad topics involving higher-level thinking processes (Renzulli, 1986; Renzulli & Reis, 1985). The best programs include acceleration as well as enrichment and other adjustments according to the learner's needs and abilities, often within, but not limited to, the regular classroom setting. The NAGC has prepared *Pre-K–Grade 12 Gifted Program Standards* (2000) that address gifted education from the perspectives of student identification, professional development, socio-emotional guidance and counseling, program evaluation, program design, program administration and management, and curriculum and instruction. All curricular models for the gifted call for use of varied modes and levels of thinking, grounded in learners' interests and capacities, in order to create meaningful products. Modifications to curriculum and instructional practices should be done so that all learners benefit, not just gifted learners (VanTassel-Baska, 2003). Successful models include the Integrated Curriculum Model (VanTassel-Baska), the Schoolwide Enrichment Model (Reis, Burns, & Renzulli, 1992; Renzulli & Reis, 2003), the Parallel Curriculum Model (Tomlinson, Kaplan, Renzulli, Purcell, Leppien, & Burns, 2002), and *compacting*. According to Renzulli and Reis, curriculum compacting is a way to "(1) adjust the levels of required learning so that all students are challenged, (2) increase the number of in-depth learning experiences, and (3) introduce various types of enrichment into regular curricular experiences" (pp. 190–191). The process of modifying curriculum and instructional practices to benefit specific groups of learners is called *differentiation*.[9]

As with all modifications, the first step is to define the goals and outcomes of a given unit, perhaps using *SFLL* or *ESL Standards*, pre- or post-tests for the unit, or standardized tests. The second step is to identify what the students already know and are able to do, noting what background knowledge they may already have about this unit and where they may be able to progress more quickly or where they may need further in-depth study. In the final stage, students and teacher work together to gather materials to enrich their study, identify small flexible groups for skill instruction, or identify activities to replace others students already know.

Differentiated instruction is often a preferred means of matching a core curriculum to the abilities of learners, gifted or not. Differentiation requires that teachers deepen and widen fields of study, allow for accelerated progress through assigned material, minimize the extent of drill and practice activities, provide for in-depth study and use of critical-thinking skills, assess progress and then modify their instruction, and employ every possible strategy to ensure that instruction and practice are contextualized and meaningful. See further explanation and examples later in this chapter.

Cooperative learning, as described in Chapter 8, allows students to excel in social learning environments where their levels of expertise can be appreciated and used in task-oriented activities. With cooperative learning, as with differentiated instruction and curriculum compacting, educators should employ the program models and instructional strategies that suit the needs of learners, not restricting a particular model or practice to a select group of students.

Strategies for Teaching Gifted Learners in the FL Classroom. The language teacher's task therefore is to organize instruction so that the linguistically gifted can benefit while other learners also benefit (Fenstermacher, 1982). Gifted learners need opportunities to use all of their abilities and to acquire new knowledge and skills. The following are strategies that might be used by the language teacher to teach gifted learners:

- Provide opportunities for students to study and research certain cultural topics in greater depth—for example, through projects in which they investigate the living patterns of the TL group.
- Present recorded and online segments and readings that are appropriately challenging.

- Provide opportunities for students to use their critical thinking skills through debate of controversial societal issues and interpretation of literary works.
- Allow gifted students to choose the topic of their taped segments or readings from time to time, thereby encouraging work in areas of interest.
- Build in some time for gifted students to work with one another on assignments or projects, with you serving as facilitator.
- Allow some opportunities for gifted students to assume leadership roles through activities such as serving as group leaders/facilitators and providing peer help to students who missed class or need extra assistance.
- Involve gifted learners in interaction with other students in the class through cooperative learning tasks, such as those presented in Chapter 8. Research shows that cooperative learning for gifted students may result in (1) higher mastery and retention of material than that achieved in competitive or individual learning; (2) increased opportunities to use critical thinking and higher-level reasoning strategies; (3) acquisition of cognitive restructuring, along with practice gained by explaining tasks and solutions to peers—in other words, learning through teaching; and (4) enhancement of social interaction and self-esteem (Fulghum, 1992; Johnson & Johnson, 1991).

Disproportionality in Special and Gifted Education.   Over the last decade or so, it has become clear that ethnic groups are over- or under-represented in special and gifted education. For example, there are approximately 1.5 to 2 times as many Black students as Whites in programs for children with mild cognitive disabilities and emotional/behavioral disabilities (Donovan & Cross, 2002). See the *Teacher's Handbook* Web site for data maps representing minority groups by disabilities. Similarly, Donovan and Cross report that Black and Hispanic students are less than half as likely to be in a gifted program as whites. Ford and Thomas (1997) and Ford (2003) cite studies showing that, on average, 50% of gifted minority students underachieve. Researchers reporting to the National Center for Culturally Responsive Education Systems (NCCREST) propose that perhaps some of the under- and over-representation problems may originate within the educational system in situations where, for instance, opportunities for early intervention are not readily available, or students referred to special education have not had high-quality reading instruction (Klingner, Artiles, Kozleski, Harry, Zion, Tate, Durán, & Riley, 2005). Perhaps learners have not learned to adapt to the norms of classroom and school codes of conduct. Poverty may be another contributing factor. See the *Teacher's Handbook* Web site for efforts of NCCREST to provide culturally responsive education. Callahan (2005) lists several steps schools and teachers can take to broaden representation in gifted programs, ranging from expanding the conceptions of intelligence and giftedness to providing examples of gifted performance, to early identification, and elimination of policies or practices that limit the number served in a gifted program (pp. 99–102). For the classroom teacher, specific challenges arise when attempting to help such learners. In Appendix 10.5 on the *Teacher's Handbook* Web site, Ford (2003) outlines useful techniques to enhance the achievement of gifted minority students.

www.cengagebrain.com

Heritage Language Learners

Another growing group of students requiring specific types of attention in the classroom is the HL learner group. *HL* learners, sometimes also called home background learners, have learned languages other than English at home in the U.S., as a result of their cultural or ethnic backgrounds; they speak or understand the HL; and they are bilingual to some degree in English and the HL (Valdés, 1999). The term *heritage language* is used to refer to languages of immigrant, refugee, and indigenous groups as well as former colonial languages. The term *heritage* is problematic in that it refers to past realities instead of contemporary or future realities that can be supported and created through the effective use of cultural and linguistic expertise. The term *community language (CL)* has been suggested as an alternative to HL in order to focus on the present and future realities that can be shared by members of the speech community. Whatever the terminology, it is certain that the language learning experience of HL begins in the home rather than the classroom (UCLA Steering Committee, 2000).

Between 1979 and 2006, the number of children ages 5–17 who spoke a language other than English at home increased from 3.8 to 10.8 million, or from 9% to 20% of the U.S. population (NCES, 2008d). Speaking a language other than English varied by race/ethnicity and by poverty status. In 2006, 72% of these students were Hispanic and 18% were poor (p. 2). Home background learners speak many languages in the United States, including Chinese, Spanish, Korean, Hmong, Greek, Armenian, Navajo, Tagalog, and Ukrainian, to name only a few (Wiley, 2005).

The *SFLL* classifies students into four categories, depending on their home language background: (1) those who have no home background other than English; (2) those who are second- and third-generation bilinguals schooled exclusively in English in the U.S.; (3) first-generation immigrant students schooled primarily in the United States; and (4) newly arrived immigrant students. Heritage learners are placed into foreign language classes at the K–12 level for a variety of reasons. Unfortunately, in some cases, school administrators may place heritage learners into foreign language classes where they already know the language, for reasons of convenience and in the absence of clearly defined goals for language study. Sometimes heritage learners take classes in their HL in order to acquire new content knowledge (e.g., culture or literature) and/or to improve their proficiency in the language. For example, as a teacher of Spanish, you may find heritage learners in your class who have fairly well-developed oral interpersonal communication skills in Spanish but limited reading ability and oral and written presentational skills. In other instances, heritage learners wish to study another language. For example, as a teacher of French, you may have Asian or Hispanic heritage learners for whom French is their third language.

 Heritage or home background learners have learned languages other than English at home in the United States, as a result of their cultural or ethnic backgrounds.

Challenges for Teachers of Heritage Learners. Issues surrounding HLs have in some cases become controversial national concerns. The U.S. Constitution does not specify a national language (Thomas, 1996). In fact, documents written by the founding leaders of the Continental Congress as they were shaping the new country were circulated in French, German, and English. Researchers studying language changes among the multiethnic waves of immigrants who came to the United States found that the mother tongue was often displaced by monolingual English by the second, third, or fourth generation (Fishman, 1964, 1994; Veltman, 1983). While it is clear that learning to use English will result in greater access to education and employment opportunities (Valdés, 1999), preservation of the HL and culture helps foster understanding and diversity. Ethnic bilingualism is a midstage in the transition from the mother tongue to English monolingualism in the United States. Schools find themselves in the bizarre position of preparing bilingual speakers of other languages to become monolingual English speakers while at the same time preparing monolingual native speakers of English to become bilingual speakers of a foreign language (Cummins, 2005).

Valdés (1999) issues a strong challenge to language teachers, calling for awareness that "language maintenance efforts are as important a part of our profession as is the teaching of language to monolingual speakers of English" (p. 15). In the 1990s, a group called "U.S. English" attempted to establish English as the national language and later as the language of individual states. Fearing that English in the U.S. was being threatened by immigrant populations, these groups ignored the facts of the U.S. 1990 census, in which the pattern of assimilation of immigrant groups outlined by Fishman in 1964 was affirmed (Valdés); that is, generally by the third generation, English has become the dominant language with near loss of the HL. A rich field for research is to discover ways in which HL is maintained and/or lost, particularly among third- and fourth-generation immigrants in school and in communities (Fishman, 2001; Montrul, 2005). Additionally, Nieto points out that since language is so closely related to identity, which languages are taught, how, and to whom raises complicated questions about power, people, lifestyles, morality, ethics, advantages, and disadvantages (Nieto & Bode, 2008).

Schools have recognized, with the support of the National Association of Secondary School Principals, the American Association of Applied Linguistics, and other professional groups, that maintaining the HL while learning a new language enriches the academic and cultural experience of the learner and the society (Bucholtz, 1995). Simultaneously, the very presence of heritage learners can help schools and educators recognize the community "funds of knowledge" (Moll, 1992, p. 20) that exist in HL students' homes and communities. Just as there are multiple intelligences (Gardner, 2006), there are multiple dimensions and layers in literacy, identity, knowledge, and discourse in both the dominant and HLs and cultures. Although students need to acquire the literacies of the dominant society, educators need to value the literacies that students possess (Wang & García, 2002). The questions surrounding language and identity are many and the answers complex. Valdés (2005b) suggests that an ecological perspective on the maintenance and development of community languages (CLs) begin with advocacy for *all* languages, support for community agencies that teach language, assistance in preparing teachers of HL/CL, a licensure program for teachers of HL/CL, and establishment of HL/CL programs, research, and training in higher education to prepare future scholars and teachers of HL/CL. Later in this chapter you will explore two approaches to teaching diverse learners: differentiated instruction and community-based learning, including service-learning.

 Preservation of the HL and culture enriches the academic and cultural experience of the learner and the society. ■

Figure 10.3 shows the needs of each home background learner group in terms of the development in English and the HL. Home background learners sometimes use their home language and English, a practice that reflects their status as members of a speech community in which a single language does not meet all of their communicative needs (Gutiérrez, 1997). In further describing the language maintenance needs of home background or heritage learners, Valdés (1999) shows that these students already have highly developed interpersonal communicative abilities and perhaps need only to be able to learn ways to establish respect, distance, or friendliness and how to talk with adult strangers and in professional contexts. These are skills that Cummins (1980) refers to as Basic Interpersonal Communication Skills (BICS). However, to accomplish success in academic settings, Cummins claims that heritage learners need Cognitive Academic Language Proficiency (CALP). To gain this kind of academic proficiency, heritage learners require assistance in developing interpretive skills and need to read a wide variety of authentic materials. Perhaps most essential is practice in oral and written presentational communication, since these learners often lack knowledge of formal language use appropriate for a presentation to an audience.

FIGURE 10.3 Characteristics of Students with Background in the Target Language

STUDENT CHARACTERISTICS	ENGLISH LANGUAGE DEVELOPMENT NEEDS	HERITAGE/HOME DEVELOPMENT N
Second- and third-generation "bilinguals" schooled exclusively in English in the United States	Continued development of age-appropriate English language competencies	Maintenance, retrieval, and/or of language competencies (e.g., or ductive abilities) Transfer of literacy skills developed in English to the home language Continued development of age-appropriate competencies in both oral and written modes
First-generation immigrant students schooled primarily in the United States	Continued development of age-appropriate English language competencies	Development of literacy skills in first language Continued development of age-appropriate language competencies in oral mode
Newly arrived immigrant students	Acquisition of oral and written English	Continued development of age-appropriate competencies in both oral and written modes

Source: From *Standards for Foreign Language Learning in the 21st Century* (p. 19), 1999. Used by permission of the American Council of the Teaching of Foreign Languages.

Goals and Strategies for Teaching HL Learners. Valdés (1995, 2005a) acknowledges that few theoretical advances have been made in teaching HL learners and no attempts have been made to analyze the theories underlying existing instruction. Recognizing the scarcity of research on HL learning, Webb and Miller (2000) collected data from experienced HL teachers and their students, which resulted in a statement of shared goals and fundamental beliefs that describe what teachers and learners themselves should do, what a successful HL learning environment looks like, and what is contained in an effective HL curriculum. The following are among the most salient of the shared beliefs. See Appendix 10.6 on the *Teacher's Handbook* Web site for the full statement:

www.cengagebrain.com

- Teachers of HLs should . . . enrich the lives of students by giving them options of variety in register so they can communicate with a variety of audiences in the HL (p. 83).
- Students of HLs should . . . be encouraged to teach their teachers as well as their peers the individual or unique characteristics of their HLs (p. 84).
- A successful HL environment is one in which . . . interaction among the school, the family unit, and the community is ongoing (p. 84).
- An effective HL curriculum is based on . . . recognized standards for both language arts and foreign language (p. 85).

Schools can play an important role in language maintenance and prevention of language loss by addressing the needs of HL learners in classrooms. Attitudes toward language learning and cultural diversity are more positive when students report a home language other than English, and when schools are located in ethnically and racially diverse settings (Cortés, 2002). So far, research on HL learners in schools has attempted to address the following issues from the perspective of the language learner:

and appreciation of the language and culture of the language they speak;
...ent of strategies to overcome embarrassment or anxiety about speaking
...age; and
...of the existence of other varieties of the same language and the relative
...e variety they speak.

...d appreciation of their language was a motivating factor for the learn-
...nd Miller (2000) study. Although learners were initially reluctant to use
...ass or in social settings in school, their most successful teachers found
...showing the value of the language and ways in which it could be used
...e learners might not use the language in foreign language class as of-
...ght expect. Potowski (2004) found only a 56% usage rate, with girls us-
...han boys; students used the language with the teacher 82% of the time
but only used it 32% of the time to talk with peers; Spanish was used for on-task projects
and English was used for more noninstructional, real-world communication. Sometimes
this lack of use is attributed to a mismatch between the HL/CL experience at home and in
communities and the HL/CL taught in schools. In such cases, the HL/CL taught in schools
is a standard variety based on norms of reading and writing, which may differ from the
home/community oral tradition variety (Wiley, 2005).

Potowksi (2004) proposes that students' use or non-use of the HL could be due to
the way they identify themselves with one of two or more cultural groups. Sometimes
the failure of the school to address the needs of the learners can result in abandonment
of the language by potential heritage learners. Kondo (1999), for example, found that
heritage learners of Japanese wanted to improve their oral communication skills but were
unmotivated beyond lower levels of language classes because undergraduate classes did
not match their interests or needs. Awareness of other varieties of the language they
speak and the relative place of their variety in relation to others and to a standard variety
is an important aspect of the knowledge needed by heritage learners. Pérez-Leroux and
Glass (2000) found that teachers sometimes feel threatened by heritage learners when
there is a mismatch between the standard dialect the teacher knows and the regional one
the student knows.

Experienced language teachers who have diverse learners in their classrooms expressed several concerns and found several solutions that are tabulated (Biggins & Givens, 2008) in the following eight instructional approaches, along with an example for
each. Additional examples can be found at the URL listed on the *Teacher's Handbook*
Web site. You will probably find many similarities between this listing and the points you
have been learning throughout *Teacher's Handbook*.

www.cengagebrain.com

1. Understand that the teachers' and students' cultural backgrounds, perspectives, and
   expectations may differ, and look for ways to capitalize on those differences and align
   expectations; e.g., do not assume that all speakers of the same language have the
   same culture.
2. Engage students in meaningful tasks; e.g., provide a context and connect it to what
   students already know.
3. Provide multimodal instruction that considers the learning styles, literacy development, and processing strengths and weaknesses of students; e.g., support oral instruction with vivid visual input.
4. Give new material a context and move from the concrete to the abstract; e.g., help
   students stay organized by providing a step-by-step scope and sequence of your
   instruction.
5. Use cooperative learning groups and other instructional arrangements that allow students to interact and practice; e.g., allow for peer coaching.

6. Incorporate a variety of assessment techniques and allow students to demonstrate content knowledge in multiple ways; e.g., give students a choice of assignments.
7. Collaborate with other professionals; e.g., ask to be advised about meetings of other departments such as ESL or special ed.
8. Involve parents in the educational process; e.g., invite culturally diverse parents to share their expertise as appropriate (pp. 11–13).

In addition to the use of appropriate instructional strategies, program models specifically designed for heritage learners will provide data to help teachers determine whether heritage speakers maximize their potential when included in the regular language sequence, whether special courses or lines of study should be developed for them, and whether self-instructional models are helpful (Mazzocco, 1996). In a recent study, Lynch (2008) found common linguistic ground at the intermediate and advanced level between lower-proficiency heritage learners and second language learners who were not from a heritage background. Also, see the *Teacher's Handbook* Web site for URLs on HL programs.

www.cengagebrain.com

Despite the absence of a solid body of research on HL learning, instructors have reported success in using certain types of teaching strategies to help heritage learners adapt to and work with varieties of languages they speak. Figure 10.4 depicts sample instructional strategies that have been used at both the secondary and post-secondary levels as they address the four goals listed earlier (Valdés, 1995).

FIGURE 10.4 Heritage Learners: Instructional Goals and Frequently Used Pedagogies

INSTRUCTIONAL GOAL	FREQUENTLY USED PEDAGOGY	LESS FREQUENTLY USED PEDAGOGY
Transfer of literacy skills	Instruction in reading and writing Teaching of traditional grammar	
Acquisition of prestige variety	Teaching of prestige variety Teaching of traditional grammar Teaching of strategies helpful in monitoring use of contact features Teaching of strategies designed to monitor use of stigmatized features	Introduction to sociolinguistic principles of language variation and language use
Expansion of bilingual range	Teaching of vocabulary Reading of different types and kinds of texts	Structuring of classwork to provide participation in activities designed to expand linguistic, sociolinguistic, and pragmatic competence
Language maintenance	Instruction in reading and writing Teaching of vocabulary	Consciousness raising around issues of identity and language Reading of texts focusing on issues of race, class, gender, and other sociopolitical topics Carrying out ethnographic projects in language community

Source: From "The Teaching of Minority Languages as Academic Subjects: Pedagogical and Theoretical Challenges," by G. Valdés, 1995, *The Modern Language Journal, 79,* 299–328, p. 309. Used by permission.

www.cengagebrain.com

Cummins (2005) suggests that emphasis on using cognates and developing literacy through books in dual languages will assist heritage learners in making use of their background knowledge in the HL. See the *Teacher's Handbook* Web site for suggested projects.

Rodríguez Pino (1997) suggests that home background language learners be engaged in the following types of classroom activities:

- ethnographic study of the community, such as tracing the genealogy of a family;
- vocabulary expansion activities to identify standardized synonyms and regional words beyond their current usage level;
- interactive diaries in which they write to each other and share ideas about subthemes, such as the future, their culture, society, literature, vices and virtues, values, social relationships, and the arts; a typical assignment appears in Figure 10.5;
- sociolinguistic surveys; for instance, students might collect photos of six different kinds of flowers (or animals or tools or professions, etc.), all representing a specific category; students place them on a card and conduct a survey in their community asking native speakers to speak the words for the photographed items into a tape recorder, then they tabulate their results to make a linguistic map of their neighborhood; and
- reading of the literature of the home background student, especially if it is not yet an integral part of the literary canon; e.g., native speakers of Spanish in the southwestern United States might read Ricardo Aguilar's *Madreselvas en flor*, listen to the tape of the author reading aloud from his work, and complete the following sentences in Spanish:

1. When the author read about _____, I felt _____.
2. I like the way in which the author _____.
3. I didn't like _____.
4. I didn't understand _____.
5. The experiences of this author remind me of _____.
   (adapted from Rodríguez Pino, 1997, pp. 70–75)

FIGURE 10.5 Sample Assignment for Journal Writing for Home Background Learners

EXPERIENCIAS ESCOLARES	SCHOOL EXPERIENCES
Instrucciones: Hable con dos o tres parientes (preferiblemente, su/s abuelos/as, si es posible) y pregúnteles sobre sus experiencias en la escuela. Pregunte sobre las materias, los maestros, la descripción de la escuela y de la sala de clase, los juegos de recreo, sus experiencias con la primera y segunda lengua, las aventuras después de clase, etcétera.	**Instructions:** Talk with two or three of your relatives (preferably your grandparents, if possible) and ask them about their experiences in school. Ask about subjects, teachers, the description of the school and the classroom, games during recess, their experiences with the first and second language, adventures after school, etc.
Escritura: En su diario compare sus propias experiencias con las de sus parientes. ¿En qué se parecen o difieren? ¿Cómo han cambiado las cosas/situaciones escolares? Mencione una o dos cosas del pasado que le hubiera gustado experimentar en la escuela.	**Writing:** In your journal, compare your own experiences with those of your relatives. How are they similar or how are they different? How have things and circumstances in school changed? Mention one or two aspects of the past that you would have liked to experience in your schooling.

Source: From "La reconceptualizacion del programa español para hispanohablantes: Estrategias que reflejan la realidad sociolinguistica de la clase," by C. Rodríguez Pino, in Colombi and Alaracon, eds., *La Ensenanza del Español a Hispanohablantes: Praxis y Teoria* (pp. 65–82), 1997, p. 72. Boston: Houghton-Mifflin. Used by permission.

Hancock (2002) also suggests the following activity that corresponds to the learning strategies described earlier in this chapter. Notice how it draws the learner's attention to developing strategies to use the language in class and other social settings.

> You are a high school student living in New York City with your parents, who are from Puerto Rico. They speak Spanish with you all the time, but you speak to them in English. You are getting ready to leave home to attend college, where you want to study advertising. You also want to study Spanish, because you realize that employers value bilingual employees. You want to practice reading and writing in Spanish before you leave for college. Which language learning strategies could you use to prepare yourself for college Spanish? (p. 2)

To summarize, you have seen that the diversity among learners in your classroom can be as varied as each of the individual students. You will find differences in intelligences, physical and mental abilities, learning styles, strategies, language background, home background, and race and ethnicity. Furthermore, as a teacher you bring your own particular style to the way you choose to teach.

We will now turn our attention to *differentiated instruction* as a strategy for enabling learners to take multiple, but equally valid, paths to reach a common learning goal.

Addressing Diverse Learner Needs Through Differentiated Instruction

The *SFLL* recognize learner diversity and the unique needs of learners, enabling teachers to engage learners on the basis of their background knowledge, interests, needs, goals, and motivation. Differentiated instruction (Tomlinson, 1995, 1999a, 1999b; Tomlinson & Eidson, 2003) has been found to work well for *all* students because it is a systematic approach to planning curriculum and instruction that addresses individual learner variations discussed in this chapter as well as the learner variations pointed out in earlier chapters (e.g., variations in ZPD, background knowledge, educational goals, learning styles, and modalities). This approach suggests that teachers concentrate on two classroom factors: the essential meaning of the curriculum and the nature of the student. Flexibility in *how* we teach is more likely to result if we pay attention to *whom* we teach and *what* we teach them. Of course, Tomlinson and Eidson also recommend that teachers keep these student characteristics in mind as they craft curriculum and instruction: what learners already know and are able to do, what they enjoy doing, and what their learning profiles look like with regard to learning style, intelligence preference, etc., as shown earlier in this chapter. In Chapter 5 of *Teacher's Handbook,* you saw how differentiated instruction was designed for teaching middle school learners. In our discussion for the current chapter, we will show how to integrate backward design, shown in Chapter 3, with differentiated instruction.

Remember that the first step in backward design is to start with your goal, that is, what do you want students to know and be able to do at the end of the instructional unit? Next, you determine what evidence will show you that your students know and have achieved the desired results. And third, you plan the learning experiences and instruction needed to enable your students to reach those goals. Refer to Figure 10.6 as you read the following section about which aspects of the template should not be differentiated and which may or should be differentiated. You might also want to review backward design as described in Appendix 3.2 on the *Teacher's Handbook* Web site and Figure 3.5. The point of differentiated instruction is to enable learners to reach a common high-level learning goal via activities that are qualitatively different and appropriate to the learners' interests, readiness, and capacity for performance. Remember from Chapter 5

www.cengagebrain.com

FIGURE 10.6 Differentiation Based On Backward Design

STAGE 1 – DESIRED RESULTS

Box G
Established Goals:
Community Standard 5.1: All students should use the language within and beyond the school setting (NSFLEP, 2006, p. 64)

Should **not** be differentiated

Box U
Understandings:
Use of the "language as a tool for communication with speakers of the language through life: in schools, in the community, and abroad" (NSFLEP, 2006, p. 64)

Box Q
Essential question:
How can students relate to heritage speakers of Russian in their school and community?

Box K
Knowledge:
Customs, origins, life histories and interests of heritage speakers of Russian in their school, in their community, e.g. veterans, gulag survivors, recent immigrants, graduate students (NSFLEP, 2006, p. 457)

Box S
Skills:
Identify and locate heritage speakers; interviewing skills; assisting in adjustments to local community by giving directions, helping in after-school or church or temple functions (NSFLEP, 2006, p. 457)

STAGE 2 – ASSESSMENT EVIDENCE

May be differentiated

Box T
Performance tasks:
Students watch Russian webcasts and view teen interviews through URLs at the National Capital Language Resource Center site; students and teacher co-construct a rubric for interpretive, interpersonal, and presentational communication (See Chapters 6, 8, 9, and 11)

Box OE
Other evidence:
Quizzes on asking questions and vocabulary for nationalities and home background; related chapters from the student's textbook; reports on findings from Web research to locate heritage speakers and describe their experiences

Box KC
Key criteria:
Identify appropriate Web sites; interpret authentic materials orally and in writing at the intermediate proficiency level; conduct interpersonal communications using appropriate conversational language; present findings to real audiences in local community and in Russian community abroad

Should **not** be differentiated

STAGE 3 – LEARNING PLAN

www.cengagebrain.com

Box L
Learning Activities:
WHERETO
See Activity C in **View and Reflect** on the *Teacher's Handbook* Web site for ideas to include here.

Where the instruction is going, what is expected, where students are coming from
Hook and hold student interest
Equip students, help them experience and explore issues
Students rethink and revise understandings
Student evaluate own work
Activities are tailored (personalized) to the needs, interests, and abilities of learners
Activities are organized

Should be differentiated

Source: Shrum & Glisan, 2010, original material, adapted from Tomlinson & McTighe, 2006, p. 36.

that Strickland (2003) uses *tiering* as a way to match performance tasks to learners' needs while keeping the key criteria the same; some tasks are more difficult, others are related to interpersonal skills or to auditory learning, etc. Figure 10.6 shows that differentiation is *not* appropriate for the following areas:

- *established goals* in Box G, because these are the content standards, Five Cs or TESOL student standards
- essential questions in Box U
- basic understandings in Box Q
- key criteria in Box KC of Stage 2

Differentiation may be appropriate for the following areas in which learners begin at different points, practice different skills based on what they already know, and end with different knowledge as a result:

- *Knowledge* in Box K
- *Skills* in Box S
- Performance tasks in Box T
- Other Evidence in Box OE

Differentiation is strongly encouraged in these areas:

- *Learning activities* in the learning plan in Box L.

Within the learning plan (Stage 3, Box L) in Figure 10.6, instruction becomes differentiated if teachers vary five aspects of their teaching:

- content
- process
- products
- affective elements
- learning environment (Tomlinson & Eidson, 2003)

Differentiating *content* means varying what students will know and will be able to do as a result of instruction. Differentiating *process* means asking students to make sense of the content in varied ways, resulting in *products* that are also differentiated. Ways to differentiate *affective elements* in the classroom may include helping learners to feel safe and validated, and differentiated use of the *learning environment* or classroom space could entail moving the furniture into multiple configurations that facilitate whole-class, small-group, or individual work. See Strickland (2003) for an example of a differentiated unit for French I.

Tomlinson (1999b) describes *undifferentiated, slightly differentiated*, and *fully differentiated* classrooms. See Case Study One in this chapter for examples. Here we highlight the ways in which one teacher fully differentiates the content, process, product, affect, and classroom environment of a seventh-grade social studies class or exploratory Latin class.

Ms. Cassell, the teacher of this fully differentiated Latin class, focused her instruction around *key questions* for herself and for her students. First, she asked herself what she wanted students to know and be able to do upon completion of instruction, and she wrote these down in broad terms: why they should study ancient times, how cultures vary and share themes, etc. She began with learners' needs, and provided differentiated tasks, flexible grouping, and ongoing assessment and adjustment. She asked students to assume the role of a member of Roman society and to conduct research to answer the core questions she provided. According to the students' interests, she adjusted *content* (e.g., whether they described a farmer's life or a soldier's), *process* (e.g., what kinds of skills they had in researching history), and *product* (e.g., whether they produced a first-person personal data sheet describing what their life in ancient Rome would have been like or developed a videotape describing what life would have been like).

Ms. Cassell also expected students to answer questions about their lives that were similar to the Roman culture questions they had just answered. The questions were consistent with student interests and appealed to their *affective* involvement in the class and in their communities: e.g., How is what you eat shaped by the economics of your family and by your location? What is your level of education and how is that affected by your status in society?

Ms. Cassell adjusted the learning environment by creating opportunities for the students to work in whole class or in small groups coupled with individual work. As students worked alone or in groups to conduct their research, the above questions led to other questions that were also differentiated based on:

- their *readiness* to build on what they knew already (e.g., small or large groupings, reading or writing goals with specific kinds of materials at varied levels of complexity and difficulty);
- their *interests* (e.g., What games did Roman children play? What was the practice of science like then? What was the purpose and style of art?); and
- their *learning profiles* (e.g., whether students used a diary journal, or a monologue).

Ms. Cassell's differentiated instruction culminated in a final, *complex question*, tailored to the students' accomplishments in the lesson: "Now that you have seen how the lives and language of several generations of Romans varied, how will your life differ from that of the previous generation in your family, and how will your grandchildren's lives compare with yours?" This question's complexity lies in its requirement that the learner compare and contrast multiple aspects of the lives of members of two generations. By contrast, a less-complex question might be "How will language change from the generation before you to two generations after you, and why will those changes take place?" (Tomlinson, 1999b). This question requires only that the learner process knowledge about the changes in languages and project what is likely to happen.

As you read this example provided by Tomlinson, you probably thought about how similar this lesson is to those you have been designing throughout *Teacher's Handbook*. Indeed, this lesson is an example of the kind of standards-based, learner-centered instruction you have been studying. By contrast, the other two examples described by Tomlinson and elaborated in Case Study One are teacher-fronted: in one, the teacher explains and tests facts; in the other, the teacher offers multiple assignments for students to choose from, but does not facilitate engagement with her academic discipline. Although more work is needed in this area, differentiated instruction offers an effective and interesting way for teachers to address the varied needs of learners in the language classroom.

Another way to address the various needs of learners and to recognize and validate their diverse backgrounds is to engage them in using the foreign language to interact in TL communities. The *SFLL* Communities goal area offers an avenue for bringing students together with the common goal of exploring TL communities and interacting with members of these communities.

STANDARDS HIGHLIGHT: Bringing Diverse Student Groups Together Through Participation in Multilingual COMMUNITIES

The Communities Goal Area

As you read through the previous sections of this chapter, you probably noticed that lists of strategies for teaching diverse learners are often similar, and you may have wondered how these can be pulled together in a unifying way. The Communities goal area of the *SFLL* can be a vehicle for engaging diverse groups of learners in using the language both within and beyond the school setting. The Communities standards, which combine elements from each of the other goal areas, integrate meaningful language use; application of cultural practices, products, and perspectives; connections to other discipline areas; and development of insights into one's own language and culture. The two Communities standards are

- Students use the language both within and beyond the school setting.
- Students show evidence of becoming life-long learners by using the language for personal enjoyment and enrichment (NSFLEP, 2006, pp. 64, 66).

The first standard focuses on language as a tool for communication with speakers in a variety of communities: the classroom, the school, the local community, TL communities within the United States, and TL communities abroad. The second standard relates to the use of the TL for continued learning and for personal entertainment and enjoyment. As students gain confidence in the second language, they might use the language to access various entertainment and information sources, read a novel, travel abroad, or participate in a service-learning experience. Be sure to watch the video clip in the View and Reflect section (Activity A) for this chapter on the *Teacher's Handbook* Web site for an example addressing this standard.

www.cengagebrain.com

The Communities goal area focuses on language use within and beyond the school setting and for personal enrichment and enjoyment.

Linking Language Learning Experiences to Communities

Having read about diverse kinds of students who may be in your foreign language class, you may begin to see that developing communities among learners in the classroom can complement learners' work within the larger school community and in communities beyond the school. Over the past decade, colleges and universities have incorporated *community-based learning (CBL)* into their curricula in an attempt to engage students in responsible and challenging projects both inside and outside the classroom.

Kolb's (1984) model of CBL, shown in Figure 10.7, is a useful way to think about making learning real in communities. It is a student-centered model that uses learners'

FIGURE 10.7 Kolb's Model of Community-Based Learning

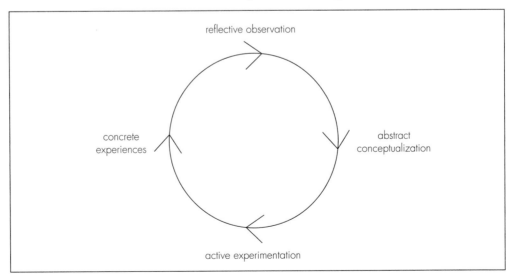

Source: From "From the margins to the mainstream: Foreign language education and community-based learning," by D. M. Overfield, 1997, *Foreign Language Annals, 30,* 485–491, p. 486. Used by permission of the American Council of the Teaching of Foreign Languages.

experiences as a basis for learning. Using concrete experiences with members of a community, learners participate in guided reflection (e.g., class journal or group discussion), think about the hypotheses they formed prior to the experience, and formulate abstract concepts that are then put into practice in communicative situations outside the classroom (Overfield, 1997, p. 486).

Overfield describes an example of CBL in which students used language to connect with a community by responding to a call from a local agency to help refugees and recent immigrants learn about their new community (pp. 488–489). Spanish I students socialized with Cuban refugees through various activities, such as visiting an art gallery. The two groups learned about each other by asking and answering questions and comparing their cultures. Language learning was mediated through classroom reflection, written journal entries and portfolio documents, and generating comments like the following about the value of the learning experience:

> As an African American, I didn't think I'd have anything in common with these Cuban refugees. My Spanish isn't very good, and what do they know about my culture? When one asked me what I like to eat, I told her she wouldn't understand. She told me to tell her. So I tried to tell her what I eat, and I told her about Sunday dinners with my family. She said she does the same things with her family! We talked for an hour. On Saturday we [another student and herself] are going to the mall with her and her mother (p. 489).

This type of mediated learning is the result of "building bridges between classrooms and communities" (Cone & Harris, 1996, p. 39). As seen in Kolb's (1984) model, the abstract conceptualization of not having anything in common with the refugees was changed by active experimentation and concrete experiences, leading to reflective observation and more concrete experiences.

 How does the type of mediated learning described in this Communities project relate to the sociocultural theory of learning presented in Chapter 1?

Among the manifestations of CBL in recent years is a concept called *service-learning,* which involves an engagement in community action using knowledge and reflection gained in academic learning (Tilley-Lubbs, 2007, p. 299-300). Research has shown that service-learning increases civic responsibility and facilitates academic objectives (Roquemore & Schaffer, 2000). Among the benefits of service-learning experiences in communities are a reciprocity of understanding between learners and community members, the development of an "insider" perspective, the questioning of traditional stereotypes, and the improved use of the TL in real settings (Boyle-Baise & Kilbaine, 2000; Long, 2003; Tilley-Lubbs, 2003, 2007). In a study of 22,000 college students, using quantitative and qualitative measures, Astin, Vogelgesang, Ikeda, and Yee (2000) found significant positive effects of service-learning on academic performance (e.g., GPA, writing skills, critical thinking skills), values (e.g., commitment to activism and to promoting racial understanding), self-efficacy, leadership (e.g., leadership activities, self-rated leadership ability, interpersonal skills), choice of a service career, and plans to participate in service after college.

An example of a service-learning project is the study conducted by Tilley-Lubbs (2003, 2007) in which post-secondary students learning Spanish were paired with members of the Hispanic community who had recently immigrated to the United States. The students helped the immigrants with getting a driver's license, renting an apartment, making doctor's appointments, etc. Collaborating with local high and middle school teachers, the post-secondary students and their Hispanic partners visited local schools to teach ESL and Spanish and to offer models of cross-cultural understanding.

The special emphasis of service-learning within CBL is the role played by academic learning. Students in the above study read more than 50 articles about multicultural education, educational theory, social justice, and immigration/migration issues. They then incorporated this academic knowledge into their reflections to understand their actions within the community. The academic learning separates service-learning from community service by providing a theoretical base for interpreting experiences in the community and offers a basis for scholarly work on matters of social justice and power relationships in society. Results of the qualitative analysis of this project showed that students were transformed to become agents of change in the Hispanic families with which they worked and in their own families. Transformation was reciprocal for the immigrant families, as one group of students provided the legal and entrepreneurial expertise to enable the family to establish a Hispanic bakery; another helped families understand the impact of domestic violence; another helped teens improve self-esteem. See Hellenbrandt, Arries, and Varona (2003) and Caldwell (2007) for other examples of service-learning projects; see the Haas and Reardon (1997) video segment in View and Reflect Activity A on the *Teacher's Handbook* Web site for a description of a project in which students connected with the local Chilean community in New York by means of engaging in e-mail communications with key pals in Chile and interacting in Spanish in a local New York Chilean bakery. See also View and Reflect Activity A, Case Study One in Chapter 11, for a project in which students engaged with a community of fans and family of the late singer Carole Fredericks to study the impact of the African heritage community on her songs and the effects of her performances on worldwide communities.

www.cengagebrain.com

In sum, in this chapter you have reflected on the various types of needs that learners bring to the foreign language classroom. You have explored specific strategies for addressing those needs and for validating the diversity of learner backgrounds so that students experience success in their language learning. This chapter has presented ideas for differentiating instruction, all of which support the approach of *Teacher's Handbook* throughout the chapters. Finally, you have seen how the Communities goal area of *SFLL* offers ideas for developing communities among learners in the classroom and engaging them in interaction with members of TL communities.

TEACH AND REFLECT ·

EPISODE ONE
Designing a Language Lesson Appropriate for Diverse Learning Styles

ACTFL/NCATE 3.a. Understanding Language Acquisition and Creating a Supportive Classroom; 3.b. Developing Instructional Practices that Reflect Language Outcomes and Learner Diversity; 4.a. Understanding and Integrating Standards in Planning; 4.b. Integrating Standards in Instruction; 4.c. Selecting and Designing Instructional Materials; 5.a. Knowing Assessment Models and Using Them Appropriately

TESOL/NCATE 3.a. Planning for Standards-Based ESL and Content Instruction; 3.b. Managing and Implementing Standards-Based ESL and Content Instruction; 3.c. Using Resources Effectively in ESL and Content Instruction; and 4.c. Classroom-Based Assessment for ESL

For this activity, use a lesson you created during earlier chapters of *Teacher's Handbook* or design a new one. Using the template in Figure 10.6 , expand this lesson into a fully differentiated backward designed lesson. Your lesson can focus on any of the elements previously discussed—for example, a presentation of grammar using the PACE model (Chapter 7) or work with an authentic listening or a reading appropriate for students at the elementary school, middle school, or high school level and beyond (Chapter 6). Within your lesson, design at least three activities that appeal to different learning styles. Refer to the elements of learning styles described earlier in this chapter (Oxford, 1990b; Scarcella & Oxford, 1992), and to the suggestions made by Gahala (1993) and Tomlinson (1999a) on how to differentiate instruction.

EPISODE TWO
Working Within Communities

ACTFL/NCATE 1.c. Identifying Language Comparisons; 2.a. Demonstrating Cultural Understandings; 3.b. Developing Instructional Practices that Reflect Language Outcomes and Learner Diversity; 4.a. Understanding and Integrating Standards in Planning; 4.b. Integrating Standards in Instruction; 4.c. Selecting and Designing Instructional Materials

TESOL/NCATE 2.a. Understand and Apply Knowledge about Cultural Values and Beliefs in the Context of Teaching and Learning; 3.a. Planning for Standards-Based ESL and Content Instruction; 3.b. Managing and Implementing Standards-Based ESL and Content Instruction; 3.c. Using Resources Effectively in ESL and Content Instruction; and 4.c. Classroom-Based Assessment for ESL

Task one:

www.cengagebrain.com

Identify a community near your school where the TL is spoken at home or at work. Interview a selection of community members about how they learned the language and what it means to them. Identify a way in which students in your school can interact with members of the community in a focused project, perhaps by reading some poems, writing a play with native speakers, helping with child care, or helping teach literacy. Design the project so that it addresses the Communities goal area of *SFLL*. Read Hellenbrandt, Arries, and Varona (2003) for ideas on how to involve academic learning in communities. Read Overfield (1997) for insights into how to combine a model of communicative competence with Kolb's (1984) model of community-based learning and incorporate some of the aspects of her work into your project. See Case Study Three on the *Teacher's Handbook* Web site for a description of diversity in a small rural community. If your interest is in post-secondary instruction, see Overfield (2002) for similar insights.

Task two:

At the post-secondary level, the study of literature becomes a primary focus for language learning. In "Beyond orality: Investigating literacy and the literary in second and foreign language instruction" by Kern and Schultz, (2005), the issues related to learning oral language and accomplishing literacy are discussed and elaborated. Pay particular attention to the appendix of the article that describes a course using multiple modes of media as well as multiple literary selections. The theme of the course is *croisements,* which can be interpreted as "crossroads" or "intersections" as well as "crossbreeding" or "hybridization." Through reading novels, viewing films, and studying art, students explore the injustices of racial discrimination, the history of the French Revolution, reverse stereotypes, and social issues for Muslim women in a polygamist society.

1. Read the article and identify how each of the literary selections and their corresponding multimodal selections will address diverse learners' needs.

2. Design an overview of a similar course for the language you teach.

TECHNO FOCUS: *Quería expresar lo que siento através de esa película* [I wanted to express what I feel through this movie] (Hugo,[10] 10th grade)

Esa clase me levanta el espíritu. [That class lifts up my spirit.] (Rosalinda, 10th grade)

These are the words used by two recently immigrated English language learners (ELLs) in a large urban high school in the southeastern U.S. who participated in an iMovie™ project as part of their ESL class. Mrs. Garvin's work using this technology is an easily replicable model of technology integration that enables and empowers learners to communicate in English. In their iMovies™ the students described with music, images, and narration what their home countries and families were like. They described how and why they came to the U.S. and what life here has been for them. They interviewed their parents and other family members who are here in the U.S., and described their aspirations for the future. The movies represent the communities to which they belong, but more than that, the students prepared the movies so that they could be viewed by real audiences, such as school boards, parent/teacher groups, and other community groups.

1. Read Travieso-Parker, Shrum, and White (2007) for a description of the project and these topics: Hispanic presence in the U.S., in Virginia, and in the high school where this project took place; an exploration of the relevant theoretical frameworks of language learning in a social and collaborative setting; the placement of iMovie™ and storytelling within the context of critical and transformative pedagogy; and the implications of learner-created iMovies™ in the preparation of language teachers, particularly related to national standards for students and teachers in ESL and foreign language. The project is placed on the backdrop of the No Child Left Behind Act (2001)[11] and the U.S. Department of Education's (USDOE) National Technology Plan (2004).
    a. List the steps the students participated in to develop their project. Describe how the work on the project transformed them.
    b. Brainstorm ways in which a project such as this could be presented to real audiences. Look at http://www.apple.com/ilife/imovie to learn how to create an iMovie™.

DISCUSS AND REFLECT ·

www.cengagebrain.com See the *Teacher's Handbook* Web site for additional case studies:
Case Study Two: Facing Challenges in Planning as a Beginning Language Teacher
Case Study Three: Cultural Diversity in a Small Rural Community

NCATE_____

CASE STUDY ONE
Differentiating Instruction: Three Classrooms

ACTFL/NCATE 2.a. Demonstrating Cultural Understandings; 2.c. Integrating Other Disciplines in Instruction; 3.a. Understanding Language Acquisition and Creating a Supportive Classroom; 3.b. Developing Instructional Practices that Reflect Language Outcomes and Learner Diversity; 4.a. Understanding and Integrating Standards in Planning; 4.b. Integrating Standards in Instruction; 4.c. Selecting and Designing Instructional Materials

TESOL/NCATE 3.a. Planning for Standards-Based ESL and Content Instruction; 3.b. Managing and Implementing Standards-Based ESL and Content Instruction; and 3.c. Using Resources Effectively in ESL and Content Instruction

As mentioned earlier in the chapter, Tomlinson (1999b) describes an undifferentiated, a moderately differentiated, and a fully differentiated classroom for a unit on Rome for seventh grade social studies; the topic is also appropriate for a Latin class at the same grade level.

The "just the facts" classroom. It is not just the facts that make Mr. Appleton's classroom undifferentiated. Rather, it is undifferentiated because all of the students do the same thing, without any variation of tasks according to student readiness or interest. Mr. Appleton teaches ancient Rome by having his students read the textbook in class and take notes on important details. Then they answer the questions at the end of the chapter. Students who don't finish must do so at home. The next day they answer the questions together in class.

Mr. Appleton likes to lecture on ancient Rome and works hard to prepare his lectures. He expects students to take notes. After his lecture, he gives a quiz on both the notes and the text. He gives students a study sheet before the test, clearly spelling out what will be on the test.

Mr. Appleton may have a sense of what he wants his students to know at the end of the lesson, but not about what his students should understand and be able to do. He teaches the facts of the content, but no key concepts, guiding principles, or essential questions.

The "students like it" classroom. In the moderately differentiated classroom, Ms. Baker teaches about ancient Rome by giving her students graphic organizers to use as they read the textbook chapter; she later explains the organizers to the class so that anyone who missed details can fill them in. She brings in pictures of the art and the architecture of the period and tells students how important the Romans were in shaping our architecture, language, and laws. Among the class activities are a toga day and a Roman banquet day, a word-search puzzle of vocabulary words about Rome, a movie clip that shows gladiators and the Colosseum, and group study for the exam. The options for student projects include creating a poster that lists important Roman gods and goddesses, their roles, and their symbols; developing a travel brochure for ancient Rome that a Roman of the day might have used; writing a poem about life in Rome; dressing dolls like citizens of Rome or drawing the fashions of the time; building a model of an important ancient Roman building or a Roman villa; and making a map of the Holy Roman Empire. Students can also propose their own topic.

Although Ms. Baker's class is clearly more engaging and interesting than Mr. Appleton's, it still lacks definitive purpose. Without a clear vision of the meaning of her subject or of the nature of her discipline and what it adds to human understanding, there is little clarity about facts, concepts, guiding principles, or essential questions. "Because there is no instructional clarity, there is no basis for defensible differentiation" (Tomlinson, 1999a, p. 16).

The differentiated classroom. As you saw earlier, in the fully differentiated classroom, Ms. Cassell introduces some major themes that will help her students understand why it's important for young people to study ancient times: varied cultures share common elements; cultures are shaped by beliefs and values, customs, geography, and resources; people are shaped by and shape their cultures; societies and cultures change for both internal and external reasons; and elements of a society and its cultures are interdependent. She groups facts and vocabulary terms around these themes and develops essential questions to intrigue her students and to cause them to engage with her in a quest for understanding.

Ms. Cassell continually assesses the way students are operating in their ZPDs, their interests, and their learning profiles; she involves them in goal setting and decision making about their learning, and she modifies her instructional framework and her instruction as needed. To answer the question, "How would your life and culture be different if you lived in a different time and place?", students assume the role of someone from ancient Rome, such as a soldier, a teacher, a healer, a farmer, a slave, or a farmer's wife, basing their choice solely on their own interests. In this task, heritage learners might decide to take the role of the soldier who conquers new territories to understand political and cultural dominance and oppression; students with disabilities might select the role of the healer to explore medical issues of the time. Working alone and in groups, students investigate print, video, computer, and human resources to understand what their life in ancient Rome would have been like, and to create a first-person data sheet that provides accurate, interesting, and detailed information about daily schedule, food, clothing, home, and interactions with societal systems of the time.

Ms. Cassell plans for what students should know, understand, and be able to do at the end of a sequence of learning and, as they work through these tasks, she differentiates the questions she poses to them, the kinds of research assignments she gives them, and the evaluation of their work in consultation with her (Tomlinson, 1999b).

Ask yourself these questions:

1. How does Mr. Appleton treat content, process, product, affect, and learning environment?
2. Using Figure 10.6, describe how Ms. Cassell differentiated instruction.
3. What aspects of differentiated instruction do you see in Ms. Cassell's class?
4. What advantage is there to starting a new unit with a question? Use the examples in this case study to support your position.

To prepare for class discussion:

1. Identify reasons why teachers might prefer an undifferentiated fact-based curriculum and develop a list of circumstances in which such an approach might suit special needs learners.
2. Review the videotaped lessons in Activities A and B in the View and Reflect section for this chapter on the *Teacher's Handbook* Web site. Make a list of the ways in which the teachers differentiate instruction to facilitate learning.

www.cengagebrain.com

REFERENCES

Alatis, J., & Barnhardt, S. (Eds.). (1998). *Portfolio assessment in the modern language classroom.* Washington, DC: National Capital Language Resource Center.

American Council on the Teaching of Foreign Languages (ACTFL). (2007). *Diversity and inclusion in language programs.* Retrieved August 5, 2008, from http://www.actfl.org/i4a/pages/index.cfm?pageid=4743.

Arries, J. F. (1999). Learning disabilities and foreign languages: A curriculum approach to the design of inclusive courses. *The Modern Language Journal, 83,* 98–110.

Astin, A. W., Vogelgesang, L. J., Ikeda, E. K., & Yee, J. A. (2000). *How service learning affects students. Executive summary.* Higher Education Research Institute, Los Angeles, UCLA Graduate School of Education & Information Studies.

August, D., & Hakuta, K. (Eds.). (1997). *Improving schooling for language-minority children: A research agenda.* Washington, DC: National Academy Press.

Bailey, K. M. (1983). Competitiveness and anxiety in adult second language learning: Looking at and through the diary studies. In H. W. Seliger & M. H. Long (Eds.), *Classroom-oriented research in second language acquisition* (pp. 67–103). Rowley, MA: Newbury House.

Barnett, H. (1985). Foreign languages for the learning disabled: A reading teacher's perspective. *New York State Association of Foreign Language Teachers Bulletin, 36,* 7–9.

Bartz, W. (1982). The role of foreign language education for gifted and talented students. *Foreign Language Annals, 15,* 329–334.

Biggins, A. R., & Givens, S. M. (2008). *Teaching to diversity in the foreign language classroom.* Retrieved August 11, 2008, from http://www.nclrc.org/about_teaching/topics/learner_diversity.html#teaching_to_diversity.

Boyle-Baise, M., & Kilbaine, J. (2000). What really happens? A look inside service-learning for multicultural teacher education. *Michigan Journal of Community Service Learning, 7,* 54–64.

Brinckerhoff, L. C., Shaw, S. F., & McGuire, J. M. (1993). *Promoting postsecondary education for students with learning disabilities: A handbook for practitioners.* Austin, TX: Pro-Ed.

Bruck, M. (1978). The suitability of early French immersion programs for the language disabled child. *The Canadian Modern Language Review, 34,* 884–887.

Bucholtz, M. (1995). From Mulatta to Mestiza: Passing and the linguistic reshaping of ethnic identity. In K. Hall and M. Bucholtz (Eds.), *Gender articulated, language and the socially constructed self* (pp. 351–373). New York: Routledge.

Caldwell, W. (2007). Taking Spanish outside the box: A model for integrating service learning into foreign language study. *Foreign Language Annals, 40,* 463–469.

Callahan, C. M. (2005). Identifying gifted students from underrepresented populations. *Theory into practice, 44*(2), 98–104.

Carroll, J. B., & Sapon, S. M. (1959). *Modern Language Aptitude Test.* San Antonio, TX: The Psychological Corporation.

Cassady, J. C., Neumeister, K. L. S., Adams, C. M., Cross, T. L., Dixon, F. A., & Pierce, R. L. (2004). On gifted students in school: The Differentiated Classroom Observation Scale. *Roeper Review, 26,* 139–146.

Castro, O. (2006). Learning styles – how making too many "wrong mistakes" is the right thing to do: A response to Sparks. *Foreign Language Annals, 39,* 529–535.

Castro, O., & Peck, V. (2005). Learning styles and foreign language learning difficulties. *Foreign Language Annals, 38,* 401–410.

Cohen, A. D. (1990). *Language learning: Insights for learners, teachers, and researchers.* New York: Newbury House/Harper.

Cone, D., & Harris, S. (1996). Service-learning practice: Developing a theoretical framework. *Michigan Journal of Community Service Learning, 3,* 31–43.

Cooper, T. (2001). Foreign language teaching style and personality. *Foreign Language Annals, 34,* 301–317.

Cortés, K. H. (2002). Youth and the study of foreign language: An investigation of attitudes. *Foreign Language Annals, 35,* 320–332.

Cummins, J. (1980). The construct of language proficiency in bilingual education. In J. E. Alatis (Ed.), *Georgetown University roundtable on languages and linguistics* (pp. 76–93). Washington, DC: Georgetown University Press.

Cummins, J. (2005). A proposal for action: Strategies for recognizing heritage language competence as a learning resource within the mainstream classroom. *The Modern Language Journal, 89,* 585–592.

Curtain, H. (1986). The immersion approach: Principle and practice. In B. Snyder (Ed.), *Second language acquisition: Preparing for tomorrow* (pp. 1–14). Central States Conference Proceedings. Lincolnwood, IL: NTC/Contemporary Publishing Group.

Díaz, L., & Heining-Boynton, A. L. (1995). Multiple intelligences, multiculturalism, the teaching of culture. *International Journal of Educational Research, 23,* 607–617.

Donato, R., & McCormick, D. (1994). A sociocultural perspective on learning strategies: The role of mediation. *The Modern Language Journal, 78,* 453–464.

Donovan, M. S., & Cross, C. T. (Eds.) (2002) Minority students in special and gifted education. Washington, DC: National Academy Press.

Education for All Handicapped Children Act, Public Law No. 94-142. 20 U.S.C. §§1400 et seq. (1975).

Ehrman, M. E., & Oxford, R. L. (1989). Effects of sex differences, career choice, and psychological type on adults' language learning strategies. *The Modern Language Journal, 73,* 1–13.

Evarrs, S. B., & Knotek, S. E. (2005). Foreign language and special education. In A. L. Heining-Boynton, (Ed.), *2005-2015 Realizing our vision of foreign languages for all* (pp. 117–134). Upper Saddle River, NK: Pearson/Prentice Hall.

Fairfax County Public Schools. (1992). *Strategies for learners with special needs in the foreign language classroom: A teacher's guide.* Fairfax, VA: Fairfax County School Board.

Feldhusen, J. F. (1989). Synthesis of research on gifted youth. *Educational Leadership, 46*(6), 6–11.

Fenstermacher, G. (1982). To be or not to be gifted: What is the question? *Elementary School Journal, 82,* 299–303.

Finn, J. D., & Owings, J. (2006). *The adult lives of at-risk students (NCES 2008-328).* Washington, DC: National Center for Education Statistics, U.S. Department of Education.

Fishman, J. (1964). Language maintenance and language shift as a field of inquiry. *Linguistics, 9,* 32–70.

Fishman, J. (1994). Critiques of language planning: A minority languages perspective. *Journal of Multilingual and Multicultural Development, 15,* 91–99.

Fishman, J. (2001). 300-plus years of heritage language education in the United States. In J. K. Peyton, D. A. Ranard, & S. McGinnis (Eds.), *Heritage Languages in America: Preserving a national resource* (pp. 81–97). Washington, DC: Center for Applied Linguistics/Delta Systems.

Ford, D. (2003). Equity and excellence: Culturally diverse students in gifted education. In N. Colangelo & G. A. Davis (Eds.), *Handbook on gifted education* (3rd ed.) (pp. 506–520). Boston: Pearson Education.

Ford, D. Y., & Thomas, A. (1997). Underachievement among gifted minority students: Problems and promises. *Council for Exceptional Children.* Retrieved October 29, 1998, from http://www.cec.sped.org/digests/e544.htm.

Frymier, J. (1989). Understanding and preventing teen suicide. *Phi Delta Kappan, 70,* 290–293.

Frymier, J., & Gansneder, B. (1989). The Phi Delta Kappa study of students at risk. *Phi Delta Kappan, 70,* 142–146.

Fulghum, R. (1992). A bag of possibles and other matters of the mind. *Newsweek, 88,* 90, 92.

Gahala, E. (1993). Differentiating instruction: Teaching all your students. *Foreign Language News/Notes 9,* 1–3.

Gahala, E., & Lange, D. L. (1997). Multiple intelligences: Multiple ways to help students learn foreign languages. *Northeast Conference Newsletter, 41,* 29–34.

Gardner, H. (2006). *Multiple intelligences: New horizons.* New York: Basic Books.

Gillingham, A., & Stillman, B. W. (1969). *Remedial training for children with specific disability in reading, spelling, and penmanship.* Cambridge, MA: Educators Publishing Service.

Gutiérrez, J. R. (1997). Teaching Spanish as a heritage language: A case for language awareness. *ADFL Bulletin, 29,* 33–36.

Haas, M., & Reardon, M. (1997). Communities of learners: From New York to Chile. In J. K. Phillips (Ed.), *Collaborations: Meeting new goals, new realities, Northeast Conference Reports* (pp. 213–241). Lincolnwood, IL: NTC/Contemporary Publishing Group.

Haley, M. H. (2001). Learner-centered instruction and the theory of multiple intelligences with second language learners. *Teachers College Record, 106,* 163–180.

Haley, M. H. (2004). Understanding learner-centered instruction from the perspective of multiple intelligences. *Foreign Language Annals, 34,* 355–367.

Haley, M. H., & Hancock, C. R. (2007/2008). The many views of diversity: Understanding multiple realities. *NECTFL Review, 61,* 5–20.

Hancock, Z. (2002). Heritage Spanish speakers' language learning strategies. *ERIC Digest* EDO-FL-02-06. Washington, DC: Center for Applied Linguistics.

Heining-Boynton, A. (1994). The at-risk student in the foreign language classroom. In B. Wing (Ed.), *Meeting new challenges in the foreign language classroom, Northeast Conference Reports* (pp. 21–38). Lincolnwood, IL: NTC/Contemporary Publishing Group.

Heining-Boynton, A. L., & Heining-Boynton, D. B. (1994). Learning styles, personality, and the foreign language teacher. In R. M. Terry (Ed.), *Dimension '94: Changing images in foreign languages* (pp. 53–65). Valdosta, GA: Southern Conference on Language Teaching.

Hellenbrandt, J., Arries, J., & Varona, L. (Eds.). (2003). *Juntos: Community Partnerships in Spanish and Portuguese: The AATSP professional development series handbook,* Vol. 5. Boston: Heinle & Heinle.

Hunt, M. (1986). Teachers: Foreign language in junior and senior high school. In G. P. Macdaid, N. G. McCaulley, & R. I. Kainz (Eds.), *Atlas of types tables* (p. 240). Gainesville, FL: Center for Application of Psychological Types.

Individuals with Disabilities Education Act (IDEA), Public Law 105-17, 105-20, U.S.C. §§1400 (1997).

Individuals with Disabilities Education Act (IDEA), Public Law 108-446, 105-20, U.S.C. §§300 (2004).

Javorsky, J., Sparks, R. L., & Ganschow, L. (1992). Perceptions of college students with and without learning disabilities about foreign language courses. *Learning Disabilities: Research and Practice, 7,* 31–44.

Johnson, D. W., & Johnson, R T. (1991). What cooperative learning has to offer the gifted. *Cooperative Learning, 11,* 24–27.

Kern, R., & Schultz, J. M. (2005). Beyond orality: Investigating literacy and the literary in second and foreign language instruction. *The Modern Language Journal, 89,* 381–392.

Khalil, A. (2005). Assessment of language learning strategies used by Palestinian EFL learners. *Foreign Language Annals, 38,* 108–117.

Kleiner, B., Porch, R., & Farris, E. (2002). Public alternative schools and programs for students at risk of education failure: 2000–01. In National Center for Education Statistics, *Education Statistics Quarterly.* Retrieved April 7, 2004, from http://nces.ed.gov.

Klingner, J. K., Artiles, A. J., Kozleski, E., Harry, B., Zion, S., Tate, W., Durán, G. Z., & Riley, D. (2005). Addressing the disproportionate representation of culturally and linguistically diverse students in special education through culturally responsive educational systems. *Education Policy Analysis Archives, 12*(38). Retrieved August 28, 2008, from http://epaa.asu.edu/epaa/v13n38/.

Kolb, D. A. (1984). *Experiential learning: Experience as the source of learning and development.* Englewood Cliffs, NJ: Prentice Hall.

Kondo, K., (1999). Motivating bilingual and semibilingual university students of Japanese: An analysis of language learning persistence and intensity among students from immigrant backgrounds. *Foreign Language Annals, 32,* 77–88.

Kuykendall, C. (1989). *Improving Black student achievement by enhancing students' self image.* Washington, DC: Mid-Atlantic Equity Center.

Lange, D. (1999). Planning for and using the new national culture standards. In J. K. Phillips & R. M. Terry (Eds.), *Foreign language standards: Linking research, theories, and practices. The ACTFL Foreign Language Education Series* (pp. 57–135). Lincolnwood, IL: NTC/Contemporary Publishing Group.

Larrivee, B. (1985). *Effective teaching for successful mainstreaming.* New York: Longman.

Lawrence, G. (1996). *People types and tiger stripes.* Gainesville, FL: Center for Applications of Psychological Type.

Lawrence, G. (1997). *Looking at type and learning styles.* Gainesville, FL: Center for Applications of Psychological Type.

Levine, M. (1984). Learning abilities and disabilities. The Harvard Medical School Health Letter: *Medical Forum, 9,* 1–3.

Long, D. R. (2003). Spanish in the community: Students reflect on Hispanic cultures in the United States. *Foreign Language Annals, 35,* 223–252.

Lynch, A. (2008). The linguistic similarities of Spanish heritage and second language learners. *Foreign Language Annals, 41,* 252–281.

Lyon, R., & Moats, L. C. (1993). An examination of research in learning disabilities: Past practices and future directions. In G. R. Lyon, D. Gray, J. Kavanagh, & N. Krasnegor (Eds.), *Better understanding of learning disabilities: New views from research and their implications for education and public policies* (pp. 1–15). Baltimore, MD: Brookes Publishing.

Mabbott, A. S. (1994). An exploration of reading comprehension, oral reading errors, and written errors by subjects labeled learning disabled. *Foreign Language Annals, 27,* 293–324.

Mabbott, A. S. (1995). Arguing for multiple perspectives on the issue of learning disabilities and foreign language acquisition: A response to Sparks, Ganschow, and Javorsky. *Foreign Language Annals, 28,* 488–494.

MacIntyre, P. (1995). How does anxiety affect second language learning? A reply to Sparks and Ganschow. *The Modern Language Journal, 79,* 90–99.

MacIntyre, P., & Noels, K. A. (1996). Using social-psychological variables to predict the use of language learning strategies. *Foreign Language Annals, 29,* 373–386.

Madden, N., & Slavin, R. (1983). Mainstreaming students with mild handicaps: Academic and social outcomes. *Review of Educational Research, 53,* 519–569.

Mazzocco, E. H. D. (1996). The heritage versus the non-heritage language learner: The Five-Colleges' Self-Instructional Language Program's solutions to the problem of separation or unification. *ADFL Bulletin, 28,* 20–23.

McCabe, L. (1985). Teaching the slower student. *New York State Association of Foreign Language Teachers Bulletin, 36,* 5–6.

Moll, L. (1992). Bilingual classroom studies and community analyses: Some recent trends. *Educational Researcher, 21,* 20–24.

Montrul, S. (2005). Second language acquisition and first language loss in adult early bilinguals: Exploring some differences and similarities. *Second Language Research, 21,* 199–249.

Moore, S., & Moore, F. X. (1997). Conference handouts. Retrieved April 6, 2004, from http://www.fln.vcu.edu/ld/conf.html.

Myers, I. B., & McCaulley, M. H. (1985). *A guide to the development and use of the Myers-Briggs Type Indicator.* Palo Alto, CA: Consulting Psychologists Press.

Myers, I. B., McCaulley, M. H., Quenk, N. L., & Hammer, A. L. (1998). *MBTI manual: A guide to the development and use of the Myers-Briggs Type Indicator* (3rd ed.). Palo Alto, CA: Consulting Psychologists Press.

National Association for Gifted Children (NAGC). (2000). *Pre–K–grade 12 gifted program standards.* Washington, DC: Author.

National Association of Gifted Children (NAGC). (2008). *Frequently Asked Questions.* Retrieved August 11, 2008, from http://www.nagc.org /index2.aspx?id=548.

National Center for Educational Statistics (NCES). (2003). *Contexts of elementary and secondary education: Special programs, public alternative schools for at-risk students.* Retrieved August 10, 2008, from http://nces.ed.gov/programs/coe/2003/section4/indicator27.asp.

National Center for Educational Statistics (NCES). (2006). *Characteristics of the 100 largest public elementary and secondary school districts in the United States, 2003-2004.* Retrieved July 31, 2008, from http://nces.ed.gov/pubs2006/100_largest/tables/table_a10.asp.

National Center for Educational Statistics (NCES). (2007a). *Status and trends in the education of racial and ethnic minorities.* Retrieved July 31, 2008, from http://nces.ed.gov/pubs2007/minoritytrends/ind_1_1.asp.

National Center for Educational Statistics (NCES). (2007b). *Characteristics of schools, districts, teachers, principals, and school libraries in the United States: 2003-2004 Schools and Staffing Survey.* Retrieved July 31, 2008, from http://nces.ed.gov/pubsearch/pubsinfo.asp?pubid=2006313.

National Center for Educational Statistics (NCES). (2008a). *Participation in education: Elementary/Secondary education.* Retrieved July 31, 2008, from http://nces.ed.gov/programs/coe/2008/section1/indicator07.asp.

National Center for Educational Statistics (NCES). (2008b). *Participation in education 2002-2008. Elementary/Secondary education: Children and youth with disabilities in public schools.* Retrieved July 31, 2008, from http://nces.ed.gov/programs/coe/2008/section1/indicator08.asp.

National Center for Educational Statistics (NCES). (2008c). *Condition of education 2008: Supplemental notes.* Retrieved August 10, 2008, from http://nces.ed.gov/programs/coe/2008/supnotes/n08.asp.

National Center for Educational Statistics (NCES). (2008d). *Participation in education 2002-2008. Elementary/Secondary education: Language minority school-age children.* Retrieved August 13, 2008, from http://nces.ed.gov/[rpgrams/coe/2008/section1/indicator07.asp.

National Dissemination Center for Children with Disabilities (NICHCY). (2007). Building the legacy: Individuals with Disabilities Education Act Amendments of 2004. Retrieved August 4, 2008, from http://www.nichcy.org/training/contents.asp#description.

National Institute of Mental Health (NIMH). (2008). Attention Deficit Hyperactivity Disorder. Retrieved August 11, 2008, from http://www.nimh.nih.gov/health/topics/attention-deficit-hyperactivity-disorder-adhd/index.shtml.

National Standards in Foreign Language Education Project (NSFLEP). (2006). *Standards for foreign language learning in the 21st century (SFLL).* Lawrence, KS: Allen Press.

Nieto, S., & Bode, P. (2008). *Affirming diversity: The sociopolitical context of multicultural education* (5th ed). Boston: Pearson.

Nisbet, D. L., Tindall, E. R., & Arroyo, A. A. (2005). Language learning strategies and English proficiency of Chinese university students. *Foreign Language Annals, 38,* 100–107.

No Child Left Behind Act of 2001, Pub. I No. 107-110, 115 Stat. 1425 (2002).

Omnibus Budget Reconciliation Act, Public Law 97-35, Congressional Information Services §8582 (1981).

Overfield, D. M. (1997). From the margins to the mainstream: Foreign language education and community-based learning. *Foreign Language Annals, 30,* 485–491.

Overfield, D. M. (2002). The foreign language learning community: Content and collaboration in the university. *NECTFL Review, 50,* 32–35.

Oxford, R. L. (1990a). *Language learning strategies: What every teacher should know.* Boston: Heinle & Heinle.

Oxford, R. L. (1990b). Language learning strategies and beyond: A look at strategies in the context of styles. In S. Magnan (Ed.), *Shifting the instructional focus to the learner, Northeast Conference Reports* (pp. 35–55). Lincolnwood, IL: NTC/Contemporary Publishing Group.

Oxford, R. L., & Crookall, D. (1989). Research on language learning strategies: Methods, findings and instructional issues. *The Modern Language Journal, 73,* 404–419.

Oxford, R. L., & Lavine, R. Z. (1992). Teacher-student style wars in the language classroom: Research insights and suggestions. *ADFL Bulletin, 23,* 38–45.

Pérez-Leroux, A. T., & Glass, W. R. (2000). Linguistic diversity and inclusion in the foreign language classroom. *Foreign Language Annals, 33,* 58–62.

Phillips de Herrera, B. (1984). *Teaching English as a foreign language to the visually handicapped.* Paper presented at the annual convention of Teachers of English to Speakers of Other Languages, Houston, TX.

Potowski, K. (2004). Student Spanish use and investment in a dual immersion classroom: Implications for second language acquisition and heritage language maintenance. *The Modern Language Journal, 88,* 75–101.

Reid, J. M. (1987). The learning style preferences of ESL students. *TESOL Quarterly, 21,* 87–111.

Reis, S. M., Burns, D. E., & Renzulli, J. S. (1992). *Curriculum compacting.* Mansfield Center, CT: Creative Learning Press.

Renzulli, J. S. (1986). The three-ring conception of giftedness: A developmental model for creative productivity. In R. J. Sternberg & J. E. Davidson (Eds.), *Conceptions of giftedness* (pp. 53–92). New York: Cambridge University Press.

Renzulli, J. S. (1999). What is this thing called giftedness, and how do we develop it? A twenty-five year perspective. *Journal for the Education of the Gifted, 23,* 3–54.

Renzulli, J. S., & Reis, S. M. (1985). *The schoolwide enrichment model: A comprehensive plan for educational excellence.* Mansfield Center, CT: Creative Learning Press.

Renzulli, J. S., & Reis, S. M. (2003). The Schoolwide Enrichment Model: Developing creative & productive giftedness. In N. Colangelo & G. A. Davis (Eds.), *Handbook on Gifted Education* (3rd ed.) (pp. 184–203). Boston: Pearson Education.

Rodríguez Pino, C. (1997). La reconceptualización del programa español para hispanohablantes: Estrategias que reflejan la realidad sociolingüística de la clase. In M. C. Colombi & F. X. Alarcón (Eds.), *La enseñanza del español a hispanohablantes: Praxis y teoría* (pp. 65–82). Boston: Houghton Mifflin.

Roquemore, K. A., & Schaffer, R. H. (2000). Toward a theory of engagement: A cognitive mapping of service-learning experiences. *Michigan Journal of Community Service Learning, 7,* 14–24.

Scarcella, R. C., & Oxford, R. L. (1992). *The tapestry of language learning.* Boston: Heinle & Heinle.

Schmidt, R., & Watanabe, Y. (2001). Motivation, strategy use, and pedagogical preferences. In Z. Dörnyei & R. Schmidt (Eds.), *Motivational and second language acquisition* (pp. 313–352). Honolulu: University of Hawaii.

Schneider, E. (1996). Teaching foreign languages to at-risk learners. *ERIC Digest* EDO-FL-97-03. Washington, DC: Center for Applied Linguistics.

Sparks, R. L. (2006). Learning styles – Making too many "wrong mistakes": A response to Castro and Peck. *Foreign Language Annals, 39,* 520–528.

Sparks, R. L., Artzer, M. L., Javorsky, J., Patton, J., Ganchow, L., Miller, K., & Hordubay, D. (1998). Students classified as learning disabled and non-learning disabled: Two comparison studies of native language skill, foreign language aptitude, and foreign language proficiency. *Foreign Language Annals, 31,* 535–551.

Sparks, R. L., & Ganschow, L. (1993). The effects of a multisensory, structured language approach to teaching Spanish on the native language and foreign language aptitude skills of at-risk learners: A follow-up and replication study. *Annals of Dyslexia, 43,* 194–216.

Sparks, R. L., Ganschow, L., Fluharty, K., & Little, S. (1995/1996). Exploratory study on the effects of Latin on the native language skills and foreign language aptitude of students with and without learning disabilities. *The Classical Journal, 91* (2), 165–184.

Sparks, R. L., Ganschow, L., Javorsky, J., Pohlman, J., & Patton, J. (1992). Test comparisons among students identified as high-risk, low-risk, and learning disabled in high school foreign language courses. *The Modern Language Journal, 76,* 42–159.

Sparks, R. L., Ganschow, L., Kenneweg, S., & Miller, K. (1991). Use of an Orton-Gillingham approach to teach a foreign language to dyslexic/learning disabled students: Explicit teaching of phonology in a second language. *Annals of Dyslexia, 41,* 96–118.

Sparks, R. L., Ganschow, L., & Pohlman, J. (1989). Linguistic coding deficits in foreign language learners. *Annals of Dyslexia, 39,* 179–195.

Sparks, R., Humbach, N., & Javorsky, J. (2008). Longitudinal and individual differences among high and low-achieving, LD, and ADHD foreign language learners. *Learning and Individual Differences, 18,* 29–43.

Sparks, R. L., & Javorsky, J. (1998). *Learning disabilities, foreign language learning, and the foreign language requirement.* Paper presented at the annual meeting of American Council on the Teaching of Foreign Languages. Chicago, IL.

Sparks, R. L., Philips, L., & Javorsky, J. (2003). College students classified as having learning disabilities and attention deficit hyperactivity disorder and the foreign language requirement. *Foreign Language Annals, 36,* 325–338.

Spinelli, E. L. (1989). Beyond the traditional classroom. In H. S. Lepke (Ed.), *Shaping the future: Challenges and opportunities, Northeast Conference Reports* (pp. 139–158). Burlington, VT: Northeast Conference on the Teaching of Foreign Languages.

Spinelli, E. L. (1996). Meeting the challenges of the diverse secondary school population. In B. Wing (Ed.), *Foreign languages for all: Challenges and choices, Northeast Conference Reports* (pp. 57–90). Lincolnwood, IL: NTC/Contemporary Publishing Group.

Sternberg, R., & Davidson, J. (Eds.). (1986). *Conceptions of giftedness*. New York: Cambridge University Press.

Strickland, C. A. (2003). There's a pattern here folks! In C. A. Tomlinson & C. C. Eidson (Eds.), *Differentiation in practice: A resource guide for differentiating curriculum, grades 5–9*. Alexandria, VA: Association for Supervision and Curriculum Development.

Strong, M. (1988). *Language learning and deafness*. Cambridge, UK: Cambridge University Press.

Sullivan, V. J., & McDonald, W. E. (1990). Cross-age tutoring in Spanish: One motivating method. *The Pennsylvania State Modern Language Association Bulletin, 63*(2), 13–17.

Teachers of English to Speakers of Other Languages (TESOL). (2008). *TESOL values*. Retrieved August 15, 2008, from http://www.tesol.org.

Thomas, L. (1996). Language as power: A linguistic critique of U. S. English. *The Modern Language Journal, 80*, 129–140.

Thompson, R. H., White, K. R., & Morgan, D. P. (1982). Teacher-student interaction patterns in classrooms with mainstreamed mildly handicapped students. *American Educational Research Journal, 19*, 220–236.

Tilley-Lubbs, G. A. (2003). *Crossing the border through service-learning: A study of cross-cultural relationships*. Unpublished doctoral dissertation, Virginia Polytechnic Institute and State University, Blacksburg, VA.

Tilley-Lubbs, G. A. (2007). The intersection of the academy and the community: Researching relationships through community-based education. In A. Wurr & J. Hellenbrandt (Eds.), *Learning the language of global citizenship: Service-learning in applied linguistics* (pp. 297–323). Boston: Anker.

Tomlinson, C. A. (1995). *How to differentiate instruction in mixed-ability classrooms*. Alexandria, VA: Association for Supervision and Curriculum Development.

Tomlinson, C. A. (1997). *The dos and don'ts of instruction: What it takes to teach gifted learners well*. Retrieved August 13, 2008, from http://www.nagc.org/index.aspx?id=659.

Tomlinson, C. A. (1999a). *The differentiated classroom: Responding to the needs of all learners*. Alexandria, VA: Association for Supervision and Curriculum Development.

Tomlinson, C. A. (1999b). Mapping a route toward differentiated instruction. *Educational Leadership, 57*(1), 12–16.

Tomlinson, C. A., & Eidson, C. C. (Eds.) (2003). *Differentiation in practice: A resource guide for differentiating curriculum, grades 5–9*. Alexandria, VA: Association for Supervision and Curriculum Development.

Tomlinson, C. A., Kaplan, S. N., Renzulli, J. S., Purcell, J., Leppien, J., & Burns, D. (2002). *The parallel curriculum*. Thousand Oaks, CA: Corwin Press.

Tomlinson, C. A., & McTighe, J. (2006). *Integrating differentiated instruction & understanding by design*.
Alexandria, VA: Association for Supervision and Curriculum Development.

Travieso-Parker, L., Shrum, J. L., & White, D. F. (2007). Stories students tell: I-movies in an ESL class. In K. Murphy-Judy, M. Kassen, & M. Peters (Eds.), *Technology and Teacher Education*. Miami, OH: CALICO Monograph Series.

Treffinger, D. J., & Feldhusen, J. F. (1996). Talent recognition and development: Successor to gifted education. *Journal for the Education of the Gifted, 19,* 181–193.

UCLA Steering Committee. (2000). Heritage Language research priorities conference report. *Bilingual Research Journal, 24,* 333–346.

U.S. Department of Education. (2004). *Toward a new Golden Age in American education: How the Internet, the law, and today's students are revolutionizing expectations. National education technology plan*. Washington, DC: Office of Educational Technology.

Valdés, G. (1995). The teaching of minority languages as academic subjects: Pedagogical and theoretical challenges. *The Modern Language Journal, 79,* 299–328.

Valdés, G. (1999). Introduction. In L. A. Sandstedt (Project Director), *The AATSP professional development handbook series for teachers: Vol. 1. Spanish for native speakers* (pp. 1–20). Greeley, CO: American Association of Teachers of Spanish and Portuguese.

Valdés, G. (2005a). Bilingualism, heritage language learners, and SLA research: Opportunities lost or seized? *The Modern Language Journal, 89,* 410–426.

Valdés, G. (2005b). Toward an ecological view of languages for all. In A. L. Heining-Boynton (Ed.), *2005-2015 Realizing our vision of foreign languages for all* (pp. 117–134). Upper Saddle River, NK: Pearson/Prentice Hall.

VanTassel-Baska, J. (2003). What matters in curriculum for gifted learners: Reflections on theory, research, and practice. In N. Colangelo & G. A. Davis (Eds.), *Handbook on Gifted Education* (3rd ed.) (pp. 174–183). Boston: Pearson Education.

Vanucci, S. R. (1991). *Understanding dysfunctional systems*. Unpublished manuscript.

Veltman, C. (1983). *Language shift in the United States*. Berlin, Germany: Mouton de Gruyter.

Von Károlyi, C., Ramos-Ford, V., & Gardner, H. (2003). Multiple intelligences: A perspective on giftedness. In N. Colangelo & G. A. Davis (Eds.), *Handbook on Gifted Education* (3rd ed.) (pp. 100–112). Boston: Pearson Education.

Wang, S., & García, M. I. (2002). *Heritage Language learners*. White paper for the National Council of School Supervisors of Foreign Languages. Retrieved April 11, 2004, from http://www.ncssfl.org.

Webb, J. B., & Miller, B. L. (Eds.). (2000). *Teaching heritage language learners: Voices from the classroom*. ACTFL Foreign Language Education Series. Yonkers, NY: American Council on the Teaching of Foreign Languages.

Wilberscheid, L. (2007/2008). The transformative power of diverse realities: A case study of accommodation and teamwork. *NECTFL Review, 61,* 84–98.

Wiley, T. (2005). The reemergence of heritage and community language policy in the US national spotlight. *The Modern Language Journal, 89,* 594–601.

Woodrow, L. (2005). The challenge of measuring language learning strategies. *Foreign Language Annals, 38,* 90–99.

NOTES

1. It is important to note that the minority groups named in the census are defined in this way: American Indian includes Alaskan Native; Black includes African American; Pacific Islander includes Native Hawaiian; and Hispanic includes Latino. Race categories exclude Hispanic origin unless specified since Hispanic is generally viewed as a culture rather than a race.

2. See the *Teacher's Handbook* Web site for the link to handbooks produced by Fairfax County Public Schools for definitions, services, and resources for parents, for blind and visually impaired students, and for deaf or hard-of-hearing students.

3. In some states, instruction in American ASL for hearing students parallels the Five Cs of the *SFLL*. For example, in the *Virginia Framework for Instruction in ASL (FASL)* a sample progress indicator for the Communication standard in the presentational mode for students in their third year of study of ASL is: "Students perform cultural arts events commonly enjoyed by members of the Deaf community; e.g., scenes from plays, poetry, excerpts from short stories" (1998, p. 8). See the *Teacher's Handbook* Web site for the link to *Virginia FASL*.

4. See the *Teacher's Handbook* Web site for a recent research study comparing LSM and ASL in border regions of the United States and Mexico. You will also find information about how to make signs in LSM and a URL for an amusing but poignant play in Spanish by Mexican dramatist Alberto Lomnitz that you might use to sensitize students to deafness and deaf culture.

5. ADD (attention deficit disorder) and ADHD (attention deficit hyperactivity disorder) are conditions in which a child has impaired relationships at home, school, or work as a result of the following symptoms: ADD is characterized by impulsiveness—a child who acts quickly without thinking first; and inattention—a child who daydreams or seems to be in another world and is sidetracked by what is going on around him or her. ADHD differs from ADD in that an additional symptom occurs: hyperactivity, characterized by a child who can't sit still, walks, runs, or climbs around when others are seated, and talks when others are talking (National Institute of Mental Health, 2008).

6. In determining the discrepancy between an IQ score and a measure of achievement, the *Modern Language Aptitude Test* (MLAT) by Carroll and Sapon (1959) should not be used, as it is a measure of aptitude, not achievement. The test does, however, predict moderately well the likelihood of success in college-level foreign language classes (Castro & Peck, 2005; Sparks, 2006; Sparks, Philips, & Javorsky, 2003).

7. Because of its emphasis on drills, this approach contradicts the position taken in *Teacher's Handbook*. It may nevertheless be effective for certain learners. Readers who would like more information on the approach should see Schneider (1996) or use the link on the *Teacher's Handbook* Web site to the Orton-Gillingham Academy Web site.

8. There is a larger percentage of students from African American, Hispanic, Asian, or Native American heritage groups within the at-risk population. The acronym to refer to these groups is AHANA. There are students, of course, within the heritage groups who excel as well.

9. To see what differentiation looks like in a classroom, refer to Cassady, Neumeister, Adams, Cross, Dixon, and Pierce (2004), who developed a Differentiated Classroom Observation Scale.

10. Hugo, Rosalinda, and Mrs. Garvin are all pseudonyms.

11. The Elementary and Secondary Education Act of 2001. Public Law 107-110, became known as "No Child Left Behind (NCLB)." See *Teacher's Handbook* Web site for links to this legislation and to a study critical of the effects of the law. This law shapes reform in education, placing emphasis on stronger accountability, more local freedom, proven methods, and more choices for parents. Each state sets challenging academic standards to be met by all students by 2013. Each state also decides which assessment measures it will use to determine whether or not student performance meets the goals, and sets a timeline by which it will accomplish its goals with Adequate Yearly Progress (AYP) reports. Furthermore, each state indicates what steps will be taken if the goals are not met. Federal funding is provided for state and local projects related to the law. As of this writing, the assessments being emphasized are those for mathematics, science, and language arts (reading and writing in English).

CHAPTER

11

Assessing Standards-Based Language Performance in Context

In this chapter, you will learn about:

- the paradigm shift in assessment practices
- the washback effect of tests
- purposes of tests
- summative vs. formative assessments
- the continuum of test item types
- assessment formats: prochievement, performance-based, and PALS
- an interactive model for assessing interpretive communication
- authentic assessments

- developing and using scoring rubrics
- standards-based Integrated Performance Assessments (IPAs)
- empowering students through assessment
- portfolios and self-assessments
- interactive homework
- classroom assessment techniques (CATs)
- implications of the OPI for oral assessment
- dynamic assessment

Teach and Reflect: Analyzing and Adapting a Traditional Test; Adding An Authentic Dimension to a Performance-Based Assessment Task; Designing an Integrated Performance Assessment (K-16)

Discuss and Reflect: Developing Authentic Assessment Tasks and Rubrics

CONCEPTUAL ORIENTATION

Assess: to gather information about and measure a learner's level of knowledge or skills
Test: a vehicle for determining a learner's level of knowledge or skills
Evaluate: to interpret and/or assign a value to information about a learner

Grade: to convert assessment information about a learner into a form that is understandable to the learner, such as a letter grade, points on a rubric, numerical score, or written feedback

All of the terms defined above are related to gathering information, interpreting it, reporting it, and making decisions in a systematic way based on learners' performances of a given task, written or oral. Educators have typically associated the term *assessment* with describing and reporting a learner's performance and the term *evaluation* with assigning a value judgment to that performance. In the last decade, the term *assessment* has been used to refer to "the act of determining the extent to which the desired results are on the way to being achieved and to what extent they have been achieved" (Wiggins & McTighe, 2005, p. 6). Current understanding of assessment, therefore, encompasses much more than just administration of tests and assignment of grades. Assessment in today's foreign language classes is carried out for a variety of reasons, such as understanding the language learning process, determining the difficulties students may experience and misconceptions that they may have, and documenting students' language development over time. In short, the information gathered during assessment provides a window into student learning, thinking, and performance. Equipped with this knowledge, teachers can improve instruction and student performance.

We test, evaluate, and assess to make informed decisions. Sometimes we want to determine what a learner knows already, sometimes we want to sample a learner's knowledge about something that was taught, and sometimes we want to determine how to structure a lesson for a learner. The people who will make informed decisions are the "audience" for the test. Sometimes they are within the school, close to the instruction, such as teachers and learners. Sometimes they are parents, school board members, or administrative personnel. Sometimes the audience is outside the school and consists of legislators, college admissions officials, scholarship agencies, accreditation agencies, or funding agencies. Shohamy (2001) reminds us that tests can hold great power in the hands of bureaucrats who may use them to make predictions about the future, engage in decision-making that may impact a great of people, or even exercise power or control.

From the perspective of the learner and the teacher, the historical purpose of testing was to evaluate learner achievement and assign grades. In recent years, however, assessment has been given more prominence as a vehicle for providing feedback to learners, improving learner performance, and assessing and informing instruction. In fact, Wiggins (1993) has traced the word *assessment* to its Latin root *assidere,* which means "to sit with," and he suggests that we consider assessment as something we do *with* students rather than *to* them (as cited in Phillips, 2006, p. 83). Throughout this chapter, you will see the recurring theme of the value of assessment in assisting and improving learner performance and in therefore having a seamless connection to instruction.

Planning for Assessment in a New Paradigm

In Chapter 3, you explored a paradigm for instructional planning that has occurred as a result of current SLA research, *Standards for Foreign Language Learning in the 21st Century (SFLL)* (National Standards in Foreign Langue Education Project [NSFLEP], 2006), and experiences in classrooms. This way of envisioning planning and instruction has also affected the way we conceive of and conduct learner assessment. Figure 11.1 depicts the paradigm shift in assessment that has occurred in recent years, and is still new for many educators. Planning begins with a consideration of what learners should be able to do by the end of a period of instruction and what assessments would best serve to assess

FIGURE 11.1 Paradigm Shift in Assessment Practices

	OLD PARADIGM	NEW PARADIGM
Purpose of Assessment	To evaluate learners and assign grades	To assess learner progress in proficiency and attainment of standards; to guide and improve student performance; to evaluate and inform instruction and program design; seamless connection between instruction and assessment
Place of Assessment in Planning and Instruction	Assessment occurs at the end of instruction	Identification of assessment evidence before learning experiences are planned so that targeted goals and performances guide classroom practices (backward design)
Types of Assessment	Focus on *either* formative or summative assessment; limited number of assessments; largely paper-and-pencil and textbook tests	Balance of formative and summative assessments; multiple measures; focus on performance in authentic tasks; integration of technology
Assessment Content & Formats	Testing of grammatical knowledge and vocabulary; contexts devoid of meaning; discrete-point items, often with one right answer	Integrated assessment of 3 modes of communication and goal areas of standards; meaningful contexts; open-ended formats, allowing for divergent responses and creativity; oral assessments, TPR, observation checklists
Role of Learner	Has limited opportunities to demonstrate knowledge and skills; must provide "right" answers; receives little feedback about how to improve performance; has few opportunities to learn as a result of assessment; has no role in assessment planning or decision-making	Has multiple opportunities to demonstrate knowledge and skills; encouraged to be creative in language use; receives rubrics before assessment; receives regular feedback and coaching on how to improve performance; learns as a result of assessment; participates in assessment planning and decision-making
Role of Teacher	Provides grades and corrective feedback	Describes targeted performance prior to administering assessments; reports on student progress; provides feedback and coaching for improvement; uses assessment results to improve program and teaching
Grading System/ Feedback	Points/grades given for correct responses; corrective feedback	Rubrics to describe range of performance possible[1]; points/grades given for both accuracy and creativity in language use; rich feedback that describes how performance could improve

Source: Shrum & Glisan, 2008, original material.

achievement and track progress; you explored this type of *backward design* planning process in Chapter 3, in which assessment plays a pivotal role. Within backward design, you anticipate and even plan your assessments as part of designing a thematic unit, *before* instruction begins. This approach precludes having to think of how you might assess students after you have already taught a unit, as was the practice in the old paradigm.

FIGURE 11.2 Curricular Priorities and Assessment Methods

In effective assessments, we see a match between the type or format of the assessment and the needed evidence of achieving the desired results. If the goal is for students to learn basic facts and skills, then paper-and-pencil tests and quizzes generally provide adequate and efficient measures. However, when the goal is deep understanding, we rely on more complex performances to determine whether our goal has been reached. The graphic below reveals the general relationship between assessment types and the evidence they provide for different curriculum targets.

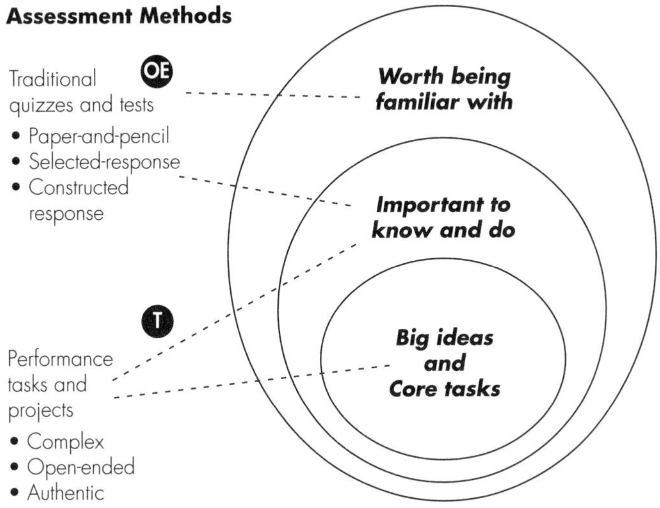

Assessment Methods

Traditional quizzes and tests
- Paper-and-pencil
- Selected-response
- Constructed response

Worth being familiar with

Important to know and do

Big ideas and Core tasks

Performance tasks and projects
- Complex
- Open-ended
- Authentic

Note: OE = Other Evidence; T = Performance Task.

Source: From *Understanding by Design* (p. 170), by G. Wiggins and J. McTighe, 2005, Alexandria, VA: Association for Supervision and Curriculum Development. Reprinted by permission. Copyright © 2005 by ASCD. Reprinted by permission. Learn more about ASCD at www.ascd.org.

An important concept in the new assessment paradigm is the emphasis on the use of multiple measures in assessing student progress in order to provide ongoing opportunities for students to show what they know and can do with the language. Figure 11.2 depicts curricular priorities and sample assessment methods; note that while paper-and-pencil tests and quizzes may be adequate for assessing basic facts and skills, performance tasks are necessary for assessing deep understanding and big ideas. Furthermore, in order for broader program evaluation to occur, assessment should be done from the standpoint of multiple perspectives (Donato, Antonek, & Tucker, 1994). For example, you may recall that Chapter 4 reported a study by these researchers in which they assessed a Japanese FLES program through a multiple perspectives analysis that included oral interviews with learners, observations of classroom lessons, and questionnaires completed by learners, parents, foreign language teachers, and other teachers in the school. These types of assessment data provide the basis for a comprehensive assessment not only of learner progress but also of program effectiveness.

The new vision for assessment highlights the need for both formative and summative measures (see Chapter 4), assessment within meaningful and authentic (i.e., real-world) contexts, and opportunities for students to exhibit creativity and divergent responses. Phillips notes that a great deal of classroom assessment still consists of the "decades-old testing in the form of quizzes and chapter tests with single written right answers" (2006, p. 79). In the new assessment paradigm, there is no place for decontextualized testing of discrete language elements such as translation of vocabulary words and fill-in-the-blank verb conjugations within disconnected sentences. In a standards-based language program, assessments feature a series of interrelated tasks that reflect the three modes of communication, more than one goal area, and technology. It is important to note that in the new paradigm, a *task* is a performance-based, communicative activity that reflects how we use language in the world outside of the classroom.

The new assessment paradigm also features expanded roles for both teacher and learners. Teachers inform students of how they will be assessed prior to an assessment, and they show students samples of performance that would meet and exceed expectations. Additionally, they provide rich feedback that describes how students could improve their performances. Learners have multiple opportunities to demonstrate growth in language development and progress in attaining the standards; they learn as a result of assessment; and they participate in the assessment planning process, through means such as portfolio development, in which they are empowered to make decisions about how they illustrate their own progress. Of course, the entire assessment process also serves to inform and improve classroom instruction and curricular development.

 In the new assessment paradigm, there is no place for decontextualized testing of discrete language elements such as translation of vocabulary words and fill-in-the-blank conjugations within disconnected sentences.

Current research in assessment argues for "alternative approaches to assessment" that attempt to bring about a more direct connection between teaching and assessment (McNamara, 2001, p. 343). In this chapter you will explore several types of assessments that accomplish this goal. Additionally, it should be noted that the same kinds of activities designed for classroom interaction can serve as valid assessment formats, with instruction and assessment more closely integrated. "Teaching to the test" is no longer viewed with disdain, but rather as a logical procedure that connects goal setting with goal accomplishment (Oller, 1991; Wiggins, 1989). Further, as teachers and learners work toward standards-driven goals using authentic materials from real-world contexts, assessment takes a more realistic form. A cutting-edge approach to blending instruction and assessment that is currently being researched is *dynamic assessment*, in which the teacher takes on the role of joint problem solver/mediator with the learner instead of serving as an observer of learner behavior (Poehner, 2007). This innovative approach will be presented later in the chapter; however, it bears mentioning at this point that it represents a reconceptualization of how assessment has traditionally been viewed since it targets what learners are able to do in cooperation with others rather than what they can do alone. In this way, it is similar to how the classroom teacher interacts with learners in their individual ZPDs as you learned in Chapter 1 (Lantolf & Poehner, 2007; Poehner & Lantolf, 2003; Sternberg & Grigorenko, 2002).

One of the ways in which assessment can be linked more closely to instruction is in the type of "washback effect" that it has on instruction; i.e., the impact of tests and assessment on the curriculum and on teaching and learning practices (Poehner & Lantolf, 2003; Shohamy, 2001; Swain, 1984). Tests have negative washback when they constrain teaching and learning practices, and positive washback when they promote learning that extends beyond the test (Messick, 1996). For example, preparing students for a high-stakes standardized test (i.e., a test upon which important decisions affecting a student's future may be based, such as entrance to a university, teacher certification, graduation) that consists largely of discrete point, multiple-choice grammatical items may have negative washback because it often forces the teacher to focus on decontextualized grammatical practice in place of meaningful communication. Additionally, these types of tests do not provide feedback to the test taker about his/her progress. On the contrary, preparing students for a performance-based or standards-based assessment is likely to have positive washback because instruction can include opportunities for language acquisition, exploration of authentic materials, and development of learning strategies.

Four basic principles that can guide foreign language teachers in the development of classroom tests are: (1) test what was taught; (2) test it in a manner that reflects the way in which it was taught; (3) focus the test on what students can do rather than what they cannot do; and (4) capture creative use of language by learners (Donato, Antonek, & Tucker, 1996). For example, if learners spend their class time developing oral interpersonal communication, then testing formats should include assessment of oral language output. Similarly, students who learn in class how to narrate in the past by writing paragraphs about events that occurred during their childhood should be tested by being asked to write paragraphs about past events in their lives. Walz (1989) reminds us that the same criticisms of foreign language textbooks, with respect to contextualization of activities, apply to classroom tests as well: Test items should be designed so that students must understand the meaning being conveyed in order to complete the tasks. Furthermore, since a large portion of classroom time is spent in learning language for communication in real-life contexts, testing should also reflect language used for communication within realistic contexts (Adair-Hauck, 1996; Harper, Lively, & Williams, 1998; Shrum, 1991).

Working Toward Standards-Based Authentic Assessment

Throughout this book you have explored ways to integrate *SFLL* into planning and instruction. The proof of the effectiveness of standards-based instruction is in the results of assessment of student learning. *Teacher's Handbook* proposes that teachers work toward designing and implementing authentic assessments that measure student progress in attaining the standards. Although the term *authentic assessment* will be explored in detail later in this chapter, we provide an explanation at this point. The term *authentic* has been used to describe the type of assessment that mirrors the tasks and challenges faced by individuals in the real world (Wiggins, 1998). If student progress in attaining the standards is to be effectively assessed, teachers must adopt an approach to assessment that includes authentic assessment as one type of measure. Since implementation of authentic assessment is still a new endeavor for many teachers, a worthwhile goal is for teachers to work toward implementing more of these assessment tasks for both formative and summative purposes.

The reality of the classroom setting and instructional goals is that teachers make use of a wide variety of assessments, which may vary according to the degree to which they are authentic, given the definition provided above. In recognition of the value of multiple measures in assessing language performance, this chapter presents a variety of assessment formats that have a place in a standards-based curriculum. The latter part of the chapter deals with purely authentic and summative standards-based assessments and strategies for scoring or grading them. Although there are differences in the various test formats presented throughout the chapter in terms of their purpose, implementation, and the degree of authenticity that they reflect, they all share the following characteristics:

- They are contextualized, i.e., they are placed in interesting, meaningful contexts.
- They engage students in meaning-making and in meaningful communication with others.
- They elicit a performance of some type.
- They encourage divergent responses and creativity.
- They can be adapted to serve as either formative or summative assessments.
- They address at least one mode of communication.
- They can be used or adapted to address goal areas and standards.

 What concepts about assessment do you recall from Chapters 4 and 5?

Purposes of Tests: A Definition of Terms

Figure 11.3 categorizes key types of tests according to the purposes they serve. Administrative assessments often include *standardized tests* and *proficiency tests*. *Standardized tests*, also referred to as *norm-referenced tests*, measure learners' progress against that of other learners in a large population; examples are the SAT, the TOEFL, Advanced Placement Tests, and PRAXIS exams. Norm-referenced tests, for instance, might tell us that a student obtained a score that placed him or her in the top 10% of students who took the test, or that he or she did better than 60% of those who took the test (Hughes, 2003). Standardized tests typically follow a uniform procedure for administration and scoring. On the other hand, *proficiency tests* are also called *criterion-referenced tests* because they measure learner performance against a criterion. For example, the ACTFL Oral Proficiency Interview uses the educated native speaker as the criterion against which to judge oral performance; one of the criteria used to judge speaking at the intermediate level is the ability to create with the language. Criterion-referenced tests, therefore, classify individuals according to whether or not they are able to perform a task or sets of tasks in a satisfactory manner (Hughes). Proficiency tests might also be given for instructional purposes, in order to provide feedback regarding the learner's progress in reaching a specific proficiency level.

Instructional tests include *commercially prepared achievement tests*, such as textbook publishers' tests, which examine the extent to which students have learned a body of material taught, as well as *teacher-made classroom assessments*, which cover a wide range

FIGURE 11.3 The Purpose of the Assessment

The Purpose of the Assessment

General purpose of the assessment

Specific reason for the assessment

Administrative
- general assessment
- placement
- exemption
- certification
- promotion

Instructional
- diagnosis
- evidence of progress
- feedback to the respondent
- evaluation of teaching or curriculum

Research
- evaluation
- experimentation
- knowledge about language learning and language use

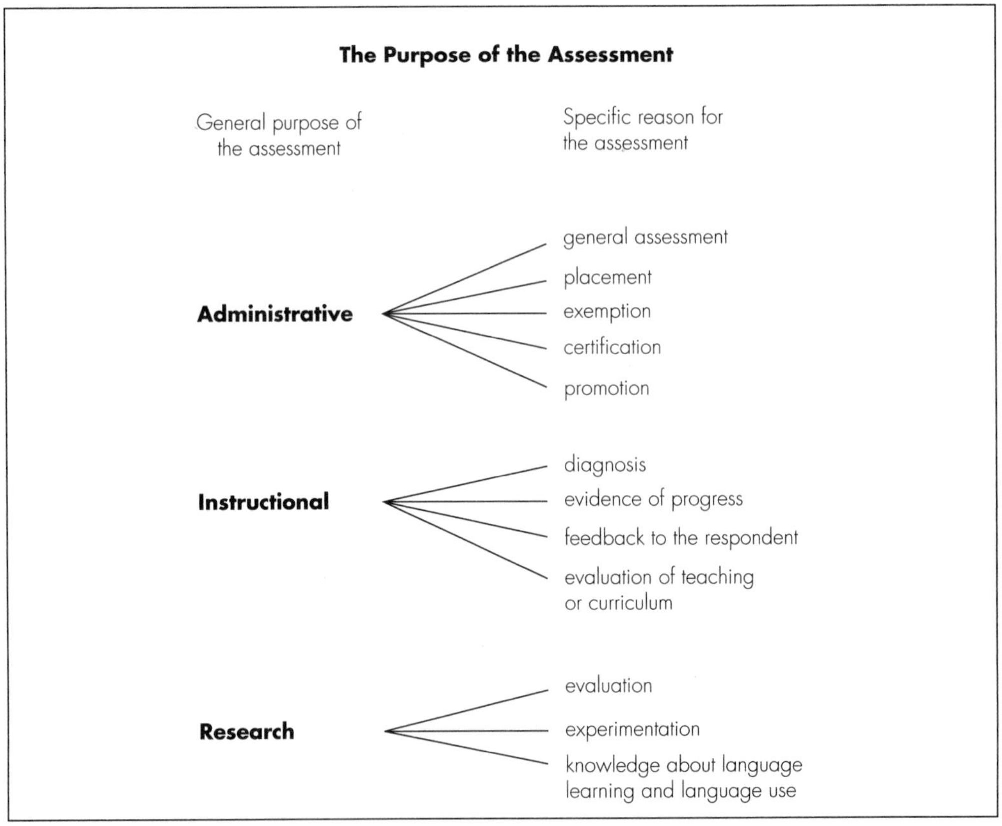

Source: From *Assessing Language Ability in the Classroom,* 2nd ed. (p. 23), by A. D. Cohen. Copyright © 1994 Heinle, ELT, a part of Cengage Learning, Inc. Reproduced with permission. www.cengage.com/permissions.

of strategies to assess achievement of instructional objectives and learner progress in attaining the standards and in meeting proficiency-based goals. In this chapter our focus is on instructional assessment—specifically, teacher-made classroom assessments—the purposes of which, as noted in Figure 11.3, are to diagnose learning difficulties, demonstrate evidence of learner progress, provide feedback to the learner, and use assessment results to evaluate teaching and the curriculum. As illustrated in Figure 11.3, tests may also be administered for *research* purposes, such as to learn more about language acquisition. A research question might prompt the use of an interpersonal performance task in which students' oral interactions are recorded and analyzed to learn more about how they communicate with one another (Brooks, Donato, & McGlone, 1997; Phillips, 2006). Many of the empirical studies cited in *Teacher's Handbook* used research-based tests.

Summative vs. Formative Assessments

All assessments have some characteristics in common, related to what learners can expect from them. Learners have the reasonable right to expect that their scores should be the same regardless of who is doing the scoring; i.e., learners can expect that scorers will view the responses objectively. Furthermore, learners can expect that the test consistently measures whatever it measures. This is called *reliability* (Gay, 1987). Learners should also be able to expect that the test measures what it is supposed to measure and that this measurement is appropriate for this group of learners. This is referred to as *validity*. A test is considered to have *face validity* if it looks as if it measures what it is intended to measure, especially to the test taker (Hughes, 2003). For example, a multiple-choice grammar test that pretends to measure oral proficiency lacks face validity. As you will see later in the chapter, authentic and standards-based assessments are considered to have face validity because they mirror performance in the world.

As you learned in Chapter 4, assessments can be classified as either *summative* or *formative*. *Summative assessment* often occurs at the end of a course and is designed to determine what the learner can do with the language at that point. Opportunities for further input or performance after the test is administered usually occur in the next language learning experience or course. The most common summative form of assessment is a final exam. *Formative assessments* are designed to help form or shape learners' ongoing understanding or skills while the teacher and learners still have opportunities to interact for the purposes of repair and improvement within the instructional setting. Specific types of summative and formative assessments will be presented later in the chapter.

Shohamy (1990) suggests that language teachers make extensive use of formative testing that is integrated into the teaching and learning process. Examples include quizzes of 5 to 15 minutes duration, class interaction activities such as paired interviews, and chapter or unit tests. A sufficient amount of formative testing must be done in the classroom in order to enable learners to revisit and review the material in a variety of ways, and formative feedback must enable the learner to improve without penalty. In this regard, teachers find it helpful to distinguish between ungraded assessment, which gives objective and formative information to the learner, and graded assessment or evaluation, which places value judgments on performance. In addition, programs should include summative assessment that focuses not only on achievement of unit and course objectives, but also addresses students' development of oral proficiency and progress in attaining standards-based goals.

Although summative and formative assessments differ in their purpose and in the nature of the evaluation designed for each, they also share similarities. Both types of assessments are systematic, planned, and connected to the curriculum. Also, many of the assessment tasks are similar. For example, a role-play situation may serve as both a formative assessment task designed to check learner progress within a unit and as a summative assessment at the end of the year or course to assess oral proficiency and learners' ability to perform global linguistic tasks. Consequently, planning a year-end summative assessment does not need to be overwhelming, since it should reflect the types of formative tasks that students have experienced throughout the instructional experience (Donato & Todhunter, 2001).

Teachers should be advised that the results of summative assessments may be compared across grade levels, classes, and even schools; proficiency results are often used in this way. Additionally, the results of summative assessments may be used to justify the existence of programs and support advocacy, as in the case of early language programs (Donato & Todhunter, 2001).

 Formative assessments are designed to help form or shape learners' ongoing understanding or skills while the teacher and learners still have opportunities to interact for the purposes of repair and improvement within the instructional setting. *Summative assessment* often occurs at the end of a course and is designed to determine what the learner can do with the language at that point. ▄

Continuum of Test Item Types

Natural-situational 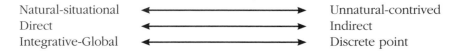 Unnatural-contrived
Direct Indirect
Integrative-Global Discrete point

"Most language tests can be viewed as lying somewhere on a continuum from natural-situational to unnatural-contrived" (Henning, 1987). With this statement, Henning posited a continuum with the point on either end representing a specific type of test item.

Natural-situational assessments present tasks that learners might encounter in the world outside of the classroom, such as writing a response to a letter received from a pen pal or key pal from the target culture. In comparison, *unnatural-contrived assessments* feature traditional test items that often focus on isolated grammatical structures and vocabulary within contexts that do not reflect the world beyond the classroom, such as a fill-in-the-blank exercise for verb manipulation.

Cohen (1994) further explains the extreme points on this continuum by describing two types of contrasts: *direct* versus *indirect* assessments and *integrative-global* versus *discrete-point* test formats. *Direct assessments* are those that "incorporate the contexts, problems, and solution strategies that students would use in real life," while *indirect assessments* "'represent competence' by extracting knowledge and skills out of their real-life contexts" (Liskin-Gasparro, 1996, p. 171). For example, having students deliver a talk to an audience of their peers is a direct test of their ability to engage in oral presentational communication because it incorporates a context and communicative strategies found in real life. A multiple-choice grammar test is considered an indirect test of grammatical competence because, although not performed in real life, it provides a window into the learner's competence. However, indirect measures often lack face validity, as defined earlier.

Discrete-point assessments test one point at a time, such as a grammatical structure or one skill area, and include formats such as multiple-choice, true-false, matching, and completion; an example of this is a quiz on verb endings. Although discrete-point items are most often associated with assessment of one isolated grammar or vocabulary point, they can also be used to assess interpretive listening/reading/viewing or sociocultural knowledge, e.g., a multiple-choice item in which students read a brief description of a dinner invitation and must choose the appropriate form of refusal from among four options (Cohen, 1994).

Unlike discrete-point assessments, *integrative-global assessments* assess the learner's ability to use various components of the language at the same time, often requiring multiple modes or skills as well. For example, an integrative test might ask learners to listen to a taped segment, identify main ideas, and then use the information as the topic for discussion, as the theme of a composition, or to compare the segment to a reading on the same topic; learners could be graded on the basis of several criteria including their ability to interpret the text, interact interpersonally with a classmate, and produce a written product. Cohen (1994) describes the continuum of test items as featuring the most discrete-point items on one end, the most integrative items on the other end, and the majority of test items falling somewhere in between (pp. 161–162). Discrete-point and integrative test formats may be either direct or indirect assessments, depending on the degree to which the tasks address problems and strategies that learners would be likely to encounter in the world outside of the classroom.

What implications does the discussion of the continuum of test item types have for foreign language teachers? First, the selection of assessments and test types should always depend on the teacher's objectives and what is intended to be assessed. For example, if literal comprehension of a reading is being assessed, perhaps a discrete-point, multiple-choice test would be appropriate, while on the other hand, if interpersonal speaking is being assessed, an integrative assessment that engages students in real-life communication would be in order. Secondly, test types that directly address the knowledge, modes, or skills that they are intended to assess may be more valid measures than their indirect counterparts. Although at first students may seem to prefer "one-right-answer" types of tests because that is what they are most accustomed to, recent findings indicate that students may acquire a more positive attitude toward direct tests because they have face validity and allow them to show what they are able to do with the language in real-life contexts. Furthermore, students tend to be more enthusiastic about direct tests if they reflect the type of classroom instruction and practice that they have experienced. For example, in the Integrated Performance Assessment (IPA), about which you will learn later in this chapter, students overwhelmingly commented on how they were able to apply what they had learned to "real" tasks, how they had freedom to express themselves by using what they already knew, and how they felt a sense of accomplishment in being able to use what they had learned in real communicative tasks (Glisan, Adair-Hauck, Koda, Sandrock, & Swender, 2003). Thirdly, teachers should understand the limitations of discrete-point testing in terms of its role in assessing learner performance. As mentioned above, discrete-point items may be used appropriately to assess the interpretive mode of communication and sociocultural knowledge. However, when these items are used to assess grammar and vocabulary, teachers must understand that what is being assessed is recognition—not production or performance. To illustrate, if a learner accurately completes a fill-in-the-blank exercise that requires verb conjugation, the teacher cannot assume that the learner will be able to use these verbs appropriately and accurately in a real-life oral interpersonal task.

Assessment Formats: A Definition of Terms

Figure 11.4 lists the key characteristics that are often used to describe attributes of foreign language assessments in the new assessment paradigm; you will see these terms in the descriptions of the assessment formats that follow in this chapter. You may notice that there is considerable overlap in the assessment formats and characteristics. For example, all authentic tests are also performance-based and interactive; standards-based tests are performance-based and may also be proficiency-based.[2] All of these formats are also *integrative*, since learners attend to many linguistic elements, various types of knowledge, and/or more than one mode of communication at once.

FIGURE 11.4 Characteristics of Foreign Language Assessments

Proficiency-based/Prochievement	Learners perform tasks designed for a particular level of proficiency in order to determine their ability to perform specific language functions within contexts and content areas, using a particular text type and level of accuracy.
Performance-based	Learners use their repertoire of knowledge and skills to create a product or a response, either individually or collaboratively.
Interactive	Learners interact or are engaged in listening, reading, or viewing an authentic text, and they use that knowledge to communicate their opinions or to perform a related task.
Authentic	Learners perform tasks that mirror the tasks and challenges faced by individuals in the real world.
Standards-based	Learners perform tasks that require them to address one or more goal areas and standards in *SFLL*.

Source: Shrum & Glisan, 2005, original material.

Assessment Formats: Prochievement, Performance-Based, Interactive Model

This section presents several assessment formats that may be effectively implemented within a standards-based foreign language program. Although each format serves specific assessment purposes, they all feature contextualized test formats and focus on the creative use of the target language. Suggestions are provided for how each format can be adapted to assess learner progress in attaining specific standards of *SFLL*.

Prochievement Format: Assessing Achievement and Proficiency

Prochievement (**pro**ficiency + **achievement**) tests are classroom tests designed to assess the degree to which students have achieved the objectives of a particular lesson or thematic unit while at the same time assessing their ability to function along a proficiency-based continuum (Gonzalez Pino, 1989). Prochievement tests, which may be oral or written, were born out of the desire to blend proficiency-based performance with grammatical structures and vocabulary being taught in classrooms and to enable learners to use the target language in life-like situations. Since the late 1980s, prochievement tests have offered foreign language teachers an appealing alternative to the classroom tests that traditionally had been mechanical and decontextualized. Formats include role-plays, paired interviews, picture descriptions, task-based discussions, and writing activities such as the one illustrated in Figure 11.5 that assesses grammar/vocabulary as well as intermediate-level writing proficiency. This test item could be adapted to address the written interpersonal mode of communication of *SFLL* (Standard 1.1) by adding a more authentic context and a potential audience of readers for the written product; e.g., students write an e-mail message to a new Spanish-speaking student in which they give their classmate directions for getting around the new school.

Figure 11.6 shows a sample oral prochievement task designed to assess use of grammatical structures such as reflexive verbs and expressions of time, as well as intermediate-level speaking functions. This task could be adapted to reflect the oral interpersonal mode of communication by making it a role-play or interactive discussion in which students are required to ask questions, exchange information, and negotiate meaning.

FIGURE 11.5 Prochievement Test Item in Writing

Thematic Unit: Which Way Do I Go?
Setting: Students give and respond to directions to find locations on a city map and within the school.
Assessment Task: Students write directions to get from one site to another in the school, choosing sites that require at least five or six directions in the target language.

Rubric: Writing directions

	4	**3**	**2**	**1**
Directions	able to direct precisely from point A to point B	mostly clear directions; reader arrives at correct destination	confusion resulting from directions	inaccurate; incomplete
Appropriate number of directions	uses 6 or more sentences to give direction	uses 4 or 5 sentences to give direction	uses 2 or 3 sentences to give direction	uses 1 sentence to give direction
Language structures	0 to 2 errors	3 or 4 errors	more than 4 errors	shows no understanding of grammatical structure

Source: Nebraska Department of Education, 1996, p. 46.

FIGURE 11.6 Prochievement Speaking Task

Monologue. Describe your daily routine for a typical day during the school week. Tell what you do in the morning, during the day at school, and at home in the evening, and at what times. Then describe how this routine may be different on the weekend. Be sure to include interesting details!

Source: Shrum & Glisan, 2005, original material.

 Prochievement test items evaluate achievement of course content and assess performance along a proficiency continuum.

Performance-Based Format: Assessing Global Communication

Performance-based assessments require learners to use their repertoire of knowledge and skills to create a product or a response, either individually or collaboratively (Liskin-Gasparro, 1996). This format includes the use of prompts, which are complex questions or situations requiring the learner to make connections among concepts and develop a strategy for addressing the question or situation. There can be more than one right answer. In comparison to prochievement tests, which usually focus on a narrow area of knowledge and skills (e.g., a specific grammar point), performance-based tests require greater integration of accumulated knowledge and skills. The task-based instruction activities that you explored in Chapters 8 and 9 are performance-based strategies that could also be used for assessment. Figure 11.7 illustrates a sample performance-based assessment task for presentational speaking as used to address Standard 1.3.

FIGURE 11.7 Sample Performance-Based Assessment Task (Presentational Speaking)

> **A Past Event.** Describe a past event that you remember vividly. It should be something memorable because it was particularly funny, unusual, or sad. Talk for at least two minutes, describing the event using past tenses. Be as descriptive as possible so that the listener can picture the event.
>
> You will be evaluated on your ability to:
>
> • talk for at least two minutes;
> • narrate and describe in the past;
> • give details; and
> • use appropriate grammar, vocabulary, pronunciation, and fluency in completing the task.

Source: Glisan & Shrum, 1996, p. 140.

 Performance-based assessments require learners to use their repertoire of knowledge and skills to create a product or a response, either individually or collaboratively.

PALS Project.   An effective example of performance-based assessment is the Performance Assessment for Language Students (PALS) project in Fairfax County, Virginia, the purpose of which is to design and implement performance tasks and evaluate the abilities of language learners (Tulou & Pettigrew, 1999). In order to design assessments that focus on what students know and can do in the foreign language, a task force of Fairfax County language teachers created a variety of performance tasks that place students in real-life situations in which they need to use the language. The tasks, together with scoring criteria, were developed and used for both formative and summative assessment purposes. Tasks were designed so that they would "engage students in simulated real-world tasks; have more than one right answer; reward skill development, creativity, and linguistic accuracy; promote problem-solving skills and tap higher-level thinking skills (especially in upper levels); and let the students know how their performance will be evaluated before they perform the tasks" (pp. 191–192). The decision was made to create assessments that would assess the presentational mode of communication (both speaking and writing) because teachers felt that this mode offered students the opportunity to perform to the best of their ability without relying on a peer's performance as is often the case in a face-to-face interpersonal task.

PALS tasks were designed for formative assessment according to the following template:

- Theme and topic (as determined by the school curriculum)
- A statement of the task objective
- The task description
- The minimal descriptions for completing the task
- Suggestions
- Directions (Tulou & Pettigrew, pp. 192–193)

Figure 11.8 illustrates a sample PALS writing task for Level 1 French/German/Spanish.[3]

The Fairfax County School Division also used PALS to design summative assessment tasks to measure speaking and writing performance at the mid-year and end-year points. The purpose of these summative assessments was to chart the progress of each student on a proficiency continuum based on the *ACTFL Performance Guidelines for K–12 Learners* (1998). Figure 11.9 illustrates a series of end-of-year speaking tasks for Level 3; students respond spontaneously without prior preparation, and their responses are audiotaped.

FIGURE 11.8 PALS Writing Task for Level 1: French/German/Spanish

---

Figure 1. PALS Writing Task I
Level 1: French/German/Spanish

Theme: Student Life
Topic: School, Leisure Time
Task Objective: To write about your busiest day
Task Description: Your school is planning to create a web page on the Internet. On that page, the designers would like to let students of other countries know about the life of teenage students at your school.
Choose your busiest day and write a paragraph about what you do in the morning, afternoon, and evening.

Minimum requirements:
Write about:
a. one activity you do in the morning
b. two activities you do in the afternoon
c. two activities you do in the evening
Write 12 sentences (100 words or ½ page).

Suggestions: You may use a graphic organizer such as a day planner, as given below; choose your busiest day and jot down your activities.

Directions: You may not use a dictionary.

Scoring Criteria: Level-1 writing rubric
Write as much as you can. Show what you can do.

✳✳✳

Choose your busiest day . . .

day of the week: _____

morning	
afternoon	
evening	

Source: From "Performance assessment for language students," By G. Tulou and F. Pettigrew. In M.A. Kassen, ed., *Language Learners of Tomorrow: Process and Promise* (pp. 193–194), 1999, National Textbook Company. Used by permission of the McGraw-Hill Companies.

See Appendix 11.1 on *Teacher's Handbook* Web site for an example of the end-of-year writing tasks for Level 3.

See the *Teacher's Handbook* Web site for a link to the Fairfax County School Division site where you can find more information on the PALS project.

Design of Performance Assessment Tasks. In designing performance assessment tasks within a backward design model, keep in mind the following steps:

1. Identify the outcomes or objectives to be assessed.
2. Create a meaningful task context.
3. Identify a product or performance to be created by learners.
4. Consider options in task design—e.g., To what extent will the task allow for student choice? Will students work individually and/or in pairs/groups? To whom will students present their products and performances? How long will students be involved in this task?
5. Plan task activities.

www.cengagebrain.com

FIGURE 11.9 PALS End-of-Year Speaking Tasks for Level 3

Scenario: As part of a program to promote global understanding, you have entered a contest to win a free trip to France/Germany/Spain. For the application you must submit three speaking samples on tape to share some of your ideas and show your linguistic ability.

Prompt #1 (60 seconds to prepare, 60 seconds to speak)
Describe the person you most admire and explain why. You may want to include a description of him/her and his/her influence on you.

Prompt #2 (60 seconds to prepare, 60 seconds to speak)
Describe your plans for the future. You may want to include summer, college, or career plans.

Prompt #3 (60 seconds to prepare, 60 seconds to speak)
Describe the best class you ever remember taking and tell why it was the best. You may want to include what you learned and how and why it affected you.

Source: From "Performance assessment for language students," by G. Tulou and F. Pettigrew. In M.A. Kassen, ed., *Language Learners of Tomorrow: Process and Promise* (p. 218), 1999, Lincolnwood, IL: National Textbook Company. Used by permission of the McGraw-Hill Companies.

6. Identify evaluative criteria.
7. Generate an exemplary response—i.e., create a sample product or performance; the characteristics of this sample will be used to develop scoring criteria and as a possible model for students to see prior to the assessment.
8. Make decisions about scoring—e.g., Is the purpose of the assessment formative or summative? What scoring tool will be used to grade the assessment? (Prince George's County Public Schools, MD, 2008).

An Interactive Model for Assessing Interpretive Communication

A strategy for assessing interpretive reading, listening, and viewing is the interactive format proposed by Swaffar, Arens, and Byrnes (1991). Their interactive model for testing reading parallels their approach to teaching reading, as well as that of the Interactive Model for Integrating the Three Modes of Communication presented in Chapter 6, both of which consider the following key processing factors:

- informational background: the reader's context
- metacognition: How does the reader structure comprehension?
- intent: Why is the text being read?
- the learner's language ability

This test design, which can also be applied to the testing of interpretive listening and viewing, diagnoses not only text-based products, but also reader-based processing. An example of *text-based products* is finding factual answers to specific questions using information from the text; an example of *reader-based processing* is the ability to infer or formulate a main idea or to evaluate the text. Accordingly, the model features three components to verify whether the learner can:

1. account for a text's pragmatic as well as its informational and formal features (i.e., can the learner demonstrate literal comprehension and "read between the lines" to infer meaning?);
2. link comprehension of the text to L2 production or self-expression; and
3. provide an individual interpretation of the text (Swaffar, Arens, & Byrnes, 1991, pp. 157–159).

Several aspects of this interactive testing format are similar to specific phases of the interactive model that you explored in Chapter 6—learners demonstrate literal comprehension of key information in the text, develop inferences, and share their personal points of view. This type of approach to testing interpretive communication is far different from the simple plot summaries or single factual questions that often appear on tests of reading or listening.

The design illustrated below is an adaptation of a five-step model proposed by Swaffar, Arens, and Byrnes (1991). Sample items from their text are included to exemplify each step.

1. Students listen to, read, or view an authentic text.
2. *Focus on situational context:* Students identify main ideas by focusing on content or text schema.

Instructions: Identify and write down key words from the text that provide the following information about the main idea of the text:

Who: _____   What: _____

When: _____   Where: _____

Using these words, write a sentence expressing the main idea of the text.

---

3. *Focus on information:* Students identify details (vocabulary development).

Instructions: Find synonyms or references from the text for the following words:

---

4. *Focus on grammatical competence:* Students use the grammatical structures in the text to further explore text ideas.

Instructions: In the story, events and their timing are of major importance. Write two sentences about major events in the story. Use past tenses.

---

5. *Focus on intent of text:* Students develop their points of view.

Instructions: What do you think would have happened if the story had continued? Write a three- to five-sentence description of another ending to the story. [This section could also attract learners' attention to particular cultural points.]

As illustrated above, the interactive format can test learners on their interpretive listening/reading/viewing abilities; grammatical, lexical, and cultural knowledge; ability to interact with the text; and presentational writing, all within the framework of a real context. See Appendix 11.2 on *Teacher's Handbook* Web site for an example of a German reading used as a test within this framework.

What additional kinds of tasks does the Interactive Model for Integrating the Three Modes of Communication (Chapter 6) feature that are not found in this interactive testing format?

Authentic and Standards-Based Assessment

You have already explored several assessment formats that involve learners in using the target language for specific purposes within contextualized tasks, and you saw how these assessments could be adapted to address various goal areas of the standards. In this section, you will learn about newer approaches to assessment: the *authentic* and *standards-based* approaches. You may recall the earlier suggestion that teachers should work toward developing authentic and standards-based assessments to include in their repertoire of assessments. An important issue concerning these types of assessments is how to score and grade them. To this end, you will also explore how to design and use scoring rubrics to be used with performance-based, authentic, and standards-based assessments.

Authentic Assessment

We have seen earlier that test results are often used by various groups of individuals in order to make decisions about instruction and about learners. Wiggins (1998) proposes that assessment also be educative in two ways: (1) it should be designed to teach by improving the performance of both teacher and learner, and (2) it should evoke exemplary pedagogy (p. 12). Educative tests must include credible tasks from which performance is assessed, reflecting a performance-based classroom and challenges learners will face in the real world.

As you learned earlier in this chapter, the term *authentic* is used to describe the type of assessment that mirrors the tasks and challenges faced by individuals in the real world (Wiggins, 1998). An assessment task, problem, or project is authentic if it:

- is realistic in that it tests the learner's knowledge and abilities in real-world situations;
- requires judgment and innovation;
- asks the student to "do" the [academic] subject rather than reciting information so that the student carries out a task using the language in a meaningful way;
- replicates or simulates the contexts in which adults are "tested" in the workplace, in civic life, and in personal life so that students address an actual audience, not just their teacher;
- assesses the student's ability to use a repertoire of knowledge and skill efficiently and effectively to negotiate a complex task; and
- allows appropriate opportunities to rehearse, practice, consult resources, and get feedback, and refine performances and products (Wiggins & McTighe, 2005, p. 154).

Authentic tasks, which may be used for either formative or summative purposes, engage learners in nonroutine and multistage tasks, real problems, or problems that require a repertoire of knowledge (Wiggins, 1994). According to Wiggins and McTighe, authentic assessments should teach students "what the 'doing' of a subject looks like and what kinds of performance challenges are actually considered most important in a field or profession" (2005, p. 337). In foreign language classes, e.g., these assessments should engage learners in using the target language to perform tasks that they are likely to encounter outside of the classroom (e.g., obtaining information from a Spanish Web site or discussing an issue with a Spanish-speaking friend). Authentic assessments also require learners to produce a quality product and/or performance, and they involve "transparent or demystified criteria and standards" so that learners understand exactly what is expected of them and how their performance will be rated (see the next discussion on scoring rubrics). Furthermore, these assessments allow for thorough preparation, self-assessment, and clarifications and modifications through discussion with the assessor and/or one's peers (Wiggins, pp. 75–76).

Authentic assessments enable teachers to "assess what we value so that we value what we assess" (Center on Learning, Assessment, and School Structure [CLASS], 1998). Often learners are engaged in proficiency-based or standards-driven activities in the classroom but are then still tested on their knowledge of linguistic details by means of paper-and-pencil, discrete-point formats; in this case, there is a gap between the communication we value and the linguistic forms we assess. Authentic assessments provide a way to reduce this gap, and they aim to improve performance. They involve challenges and roles that help students rehearse for complex tasks that face adults and professionals, while focusing on whether students can create polished, thorough, and justifiable responses, performances, or products (Liskin-Gasparro, 1997; Wiggins, 1990). In this regard, authentic tests share the characteristics of performance-based tests except that they add the dimension of a real context and audience. For example, compare the performance-based task in Figure 11.7 with the authentic formative task shown in Figure 11.10. In Figure 11.7, the learner is performing with the language in a meaningful task, but the only audience is the classroom teacher. In Figure 11.10, the learner is also performing in the same way, but the audience is now a consumer who needs a particular service, which the learner will provide. (It is important to note that this task was designed so that students prepared a real itinerary for a real Spanish teacher, who is taking a real trip to Spain; this is not an imaginary situation.) The task will require multistaged research and interaction on the part of the learner, but the end result is meaningful use of language for real audiences.

In Case Study One in the Discuss and Reflect section of this chapter, you will find a Performance Task Template (CLASS, 1998) that includes the steps that might be followed in designing an authentic assessment task.

FIGURE 11.10 Authentic Assessment Task

Un viaje por España *(A Trip through Spain)*

You and your partner are Spanish travel agents who have decided to market your services to American school groups. You know there is intensive competition for this business. You have received a memo from Señorita Surprenant, one of New England's most traveled Spanish language teachers. She is heading back to Spain this spring with a group of her students. She is not committed to any specific regions, cities, or sites. She is looking for the following: a good price, great art museums, famous settings in literature, rare cultural opportunities (e.g., dance, sport, food), and all within a 7–10-day time frame.

You know Spain and its opportunities, but you are not really sure what will please Señorita Surprenant. You draw up a list of options that could be included in a trip and then call Señorita Surprenant. You talk with her about the options and use this chance to decide what will be the kinds of things that will most convince her that you are the agency to handle the trip.

Using your knowledge and your impression of what Señorita Surprenant is looking for in the trip, you submit a written proposal, including an itinerary and your rationale for the itinerary, a map setting out the route to be followed, and a price list for students and chaperones.

Source: Adapted from Center on Learning, Assessment, and School Structure, "Developing authentic performance assessments," 1998. Paper presented at meeting of ACTFL Beyond the OPI Assessment Group. Used with permission. Contributed by J. Surprenant, teacher.

Authentic tasks require learners to address an actual audience and mirror challenges faced by real individuals in real-world settings. ▪

 The teacher is not the only audience in authentic tests. ▪

Evaluating Authentic and Performance-Based Tasks: Scoring Rubrics

Authentic and performance-based tasks can be assigned a grade with the use of a rubric,[4] a set of scoring guidelines for evaluating student work (Wiggins, 1998, p. 154). Rubrics answer the following questions:

- By what criteria should performance be judged?
- Where should we look and what should we look for to judge performance success?
- What does the range in the quality of performance look like?
- How do we determine what score should be given and what that score means?
- How should the different levels of quality be described and distinguished from one another? (Relearning by Design, Inc., 2000[5])

Rubrics provide the means for teachers to provide feedback to learners about their progress as well as to evaluate performance and even assign grades. Because rubrics contain rich descriptions of performance, teachers can use them effectively to provide feedback that focuses on the quality of learner performance and specifies how performance can be improved. However, perhaps of more importance, *rubrics show learners what good performance "looks like" even before they perform an assessment task*. Therefore, learners should see and discuss the rubrics for a particular assessment task before they begin the task.

Although rubrics can be created in a variety of formats, they all contain three common features:

1. They focus on measuring a stated **objective** (performance, behavior, or quality).
2. They use a **range** to rate performance.
3. They contain specific performance characteristics, arranged in levels indicating the **degree** to which a standard of performance has been met (San Diego State University, 2001b).

It is important to note that teachers sometimes use the term *rubric* to refer to any type of scoring guide. However, according to the strict definition of the term, *rubric* should only be used to describe a set of scoring criteria that reflect the three characteristics above and include a rich description of performance across a range of performance levels. Figure 11.11 illustrates a rubric that might be used to assess the authentic task in Figure 11.10. Examine Figure 11.11 as you continue to read about the features of rubrics. A typical rubric:

1. Contains a *scale* of possible points to be assigned in scoring work, on a continuum of quality. High numbers are assigned to the best performances: Scales typically use 4, 5, or 6 as the top score, down to 1 for the lowest score. The highest number on a rubric usually represents performance that is exemplary or exceeds expectations. Teachers often use an even number of total points (e.g., 4 or 6) to avoid the tendency to assign the middle score automatically.
2. Provides *descriptors* for each level of performance to enable more reliable and unbiased scoring.

FIGURE 11.11 Sample Scoring Rubric for the Authentic Task in Figure 11.10

	EXCEEDS EXPECTATIONS 4 POINTS	MEETS EXPECTATIONS 3 POINTS	PROGRESSING 2 POINTS	DOES NOT MEET EXPECTATIONS 1 POINT
Quality of Research	Evidence of thorough research in preparation for proposal design; main facts and wealth of details about sites, museums, culture	Evidence of effective research in preparation for proposal design; main facts with a few details about sites, museums, culture	Evidence of some research; main facts with few or no details about sites, museums, culture	Little evidence of research; incomplete facts and details
Quality of Written Proposal	Well-written, clear, easy to understand; uses own words; few errors in grammar, vocabulary, spelling	Well-written, mostly clear with a few unclear parts or easy to understand except for a few places; uses primarily own words and some language from sources; some patterns of errors in grammar and/or vocabulary and/or spelling	Approximately half of writing is clear; quality of writing interferes with understanding in some places; uses much language directly from sources; when using own language, patterns of errors in grammar, and/or vocabulary, and/or spelling	Poorly written; hard to understand; uses primarily language directly from sources; or if using own language, many patterns of errors in grammar, vocabulary, and spelling
Degree to Which Proposal Is Convincing	Very persuasive; addresses the requested information of client; convinces client to take the trip	Gives some reasons that are convincing; addresses most of the requested information of client; seriously persuades client to consider the trip	Gives only a partial rationale for taking the trip; addresses many though not all of the requested details and/or is not very convincing	Not persuasive; fails to address most of the client's requested information; language used does not convince client to take trip
Justification of Prices of Trip	Includes complete breakdown of prices with clear justification for costs	Includes some breakdown of prices and/or some justification for costs, although more clarity required	Either price breakdown or cost justification is incomplete; client still has questions	Incomplete breakdown of prices and incomplete justification of costs

Source: Adapted from Glisan, 1998, original material. (based on task from the Center on Learning, Assessment, and School Structure [CLASS], 1998).

3. Is either *generic* or *task-specific*. Generic rubrics are often used within a specific mode of communication, such as interpersonal speaking, and can be applied to a number of different tasks. The criteria in a generic rubric typically describe characteristics of language production or proficiency without specifying particular content or task details (Center for Advanced Research in Language Acquisition [CARLA], 2008b). Appendix 11.3.a on the *Teacher's Handbook* Web site is an example of a generic rubric for presentational speaking at the intermediate level of proficiency adapted from the *ACTFL Performance Guidelines for K–12 Learners* (American Council on the Teaching of Foreign Languages [ACTFL], 1998). Appendix 11.3.b is an adaptation of the generic presentational speaking

www.cengagebrain.com

rubric using more learner-friendly language. Task-specific rubrics are used to assess specific performance tasks, and their descriptors combine elements of language production with task requirements. The rubric in Figure 11.11 is task-specific. Rubrics that combine characteristics of generic and task-specific are useful to learners since they provide feedback on both broader language development and elements specific to the task.

www.cengagebrain.com

4. Is either *holistic* or *analytic*. If holistic, each band on the rubric describes performance based on several criteria to enable the rater to judge performance based on an overall impression (CARLA, 2008b). See Appendix 11.3.c on the *Teacher's Handbook* Web site for a holistic, generic rubric for speaking tasks. An analytic rubric is divided into a series of criteria, with a range of descriptions for each. Examples of criteria for interpersonal speaking might be "use of text type," "communication strategies," and "comprehensibility." On the *Teacher's Handbook* Web site you will find three analytic rubrics: Appendices 11.3.a. and 11.3.b. are for oral presentations and Appendix 11.3.d. is for interpersonal speaking.

Note that a rubric may be *longitudinal* when it measures progress over time toward mastery of educational objectives and enables us to assess developmental change. The ACTFL Proficiency Guidelines represent longitudinal, developmental rubrics. You will see other examples of rubrics later in the chapter.

Rubrics show learners what good performance "looks like" even before they perform an assessment task.

According to Relearning by Design, Inc. (2000, p. 8), there are different types of criteria that can be addressed in a rubric, and they relate to different aspects of performance:

"impact of performance"	the success of performance, given the purposes, goals, and desired results
"work quality and craftsmanship"	the overall polish, organization, and rigor of the work
"adequacy of methods and behaviors"	the quality of the procedures and manner of presentation, prior to and during performance
"validity of content"	the correctness of the ideas, skills, or materials used
"sophistication of knowledge employed"	the relative complexity or maturity of the knowledge employed

Can you identify each of the criteria from above in the rubrics shown in Figure 11.11?

www.cengagebrain.com

Many assessments make the mistake of overemphasizing content while underemphasizing the impact of performance and adequacy of methods and performance (Relearning by Design, Inc., 2000). See Appendix 11.4 on the *Teacher's Handbook* Web site for a fuller description of each of these criteria types.

Designing Rubrics. How does a teacher design a rubric? The following steps represent one approach to creating a rubric:

Step 1: Look at the performance task and decide what the dimensions or criteria for performance should be. Appendix 11.5 on the *Teacher's Handbook* Web site lists sample performance dimensions possible for particular types of assessment tasks. Of the potential criteria that you may have selected, narrow down the list to between three and five of the most important criteria (CARLA, 2008a). If samples of student work from similar tasks are available, they should be used to determine the criteria for performance.

Step 2: Decide how many levels of performance you wish to include and how they should be defined. Four levels is an ideal number. Possible labels for the levels are "Exceeds Expectations, Meets Expectations, Progressing, Does Not Meet Expectations," or "Exemplary, Accomplished, Developing, Beginning."

Step 3: Write the performance descriptions for each level of the rubric. The descriptors should include the most salient and defining characteristics of performance and should stem from an accurate analysis of many student work samples. Keeping in mind that the audience for the assessment is another individual in a real-world or simulated setting, first ask the question: What would an excellent performance look like if that person were the judge? Create a performance description that such a person would judge as excellent. Next, describe what unacceptable task completion would look like; then develop the levels in between. See Figure 11.12 for a sample format for rubric design. Appendix 11.6 on the *Teacher's Handbook* Web site illustrates a template for designing an analytic rubric across four levels of performance. While creating performance descriptions, teachers should keep in mind the following:

- Rubrics that rely on comparative or evaluative language will sacrifice validity. For example, overly comparative language such as *fewer, more/less than,* as well as numbers (of words, sentences, etc.) place undue emphasis on the quantity of student work instead of rewarding students appropriately for the quality of their work. In addition, descriptors should be written in simple, concise terms that are understandable to learners.
- Since rubrics are meant to be criterion-referenced (not norm-referenced), the highest point on the scale should describe genuinely excellent performance, as derived from student samples of genuine excellence. The standards or performance criteria described in the rubrics are not the same as expectations: The scoring should alert students to their real levels of performance. Consequently, on a given task, it may happen that no one gets the highest score, and many students may get low scores. Therefore, scores do not automatically translate into letter grades, since the meaning of a score on a rubric represents attainment of a standard of performance rather than a ranking of the performance of the test taker relative to the performance of others who have taken the test. This does not mean, however, that scores on rubrics cannot be converted to letter grades, as will be discussed below.
- Teachers are faced with the decision of whether to create generic or task-specific rubrics. The more task specific the rubric, the more specific the performance descriptions, as shown in Figure 11.11, for example. However, teachers often design generic rubrics for issues of feasibility, i.e., they can be used to score multiple authentic tasks (CLASS, 1994, pp. 1–6).

Step 4: Present each rubric to students to help them understand the expectations of the assessment before they engage in the task.

FIGURE 11.12 Format for Rubric Design

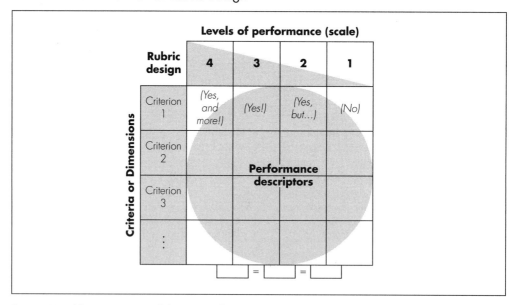

Source: Used by permission of the Center for Advanced Research on Language Acquisition (CARLA) at the University of Minnesota. "Rubric Design," Virtual Assessment Center, available on the CARLA website at http://www.carla.umn.edu/assessment/vac/Evaluation/p_7.html.

Step 5: Pilot rubrics extensively with learners and revise them accordingly. As you become familiar with learner performance, change rubrics as necessary in order to describe performance more effectively. In other words, rubrics should always be a work in progress.

www.cengagebrain.com

See the *Teacher's Handbook* Web site for a link to Rubristar, a tool that teachers can use to develop rubrics when they do not wish to start from scratch.

Converting Rubric Scores to Grades. An important issue when using rubrics is how to convert the rubric scores to gradebook scores. There are several considerations to keep in mind. First, since the level that **"meets expectations" is not the highest level attainable on a rubric,** teachers often do not assign the highest grade to it. For example, a teacher may decide that a student who meets the expectations of the task receives a grade in the "B/B+" range and that the student who "exceeds expectations" merits an "A." In this case, the student who "almost meets expectations" earns a grade in the "C/C+" range, and one who "does not meet expectations" receives a grade in the "F/D+" range. However, it is ultimately the teacher who decides the match between the level of performance on the rubric and a letter grade. Secondly, **different methods for making score conversions are used for holistic rubrics and for analytic rubrics** (see details below).

Holistic Rubrics: The Fairfax County (VA) Public Schools developed a system for scoring the PALS tasks in which they convert holistic scores to grades. See Appendix 11.7 on the *Teacher's Handbook* Web site for an example of their holistic rubric and conversion to grades for the Level 1 speaking tasks. It is important to note that the Fairfax County system is based on a four-point range of performance: exceeds expectations, meets expectations, almost meets expectations, and does not meet expectations. According to the

Fairfax County system, holistic ratings using the four-point range of performance can be converted to percentages and letter grades in one of two ways:

1. Assign a specific percentage to each performance rating, using percentage ranges such as the following:

Exceeds expectations	A = 95%
Meets expectations	B = 85%
Almost meets expectations	C = 75%
Does not meet expectations	D = 65% or F = 55%
	(depending on quality of performance)

2. Assign a range of percentages for each level on the rubric, as in the example below, which is used in the Fairfax County Public Schools (1999):

Exceeds expectations	93.5–100%
Meets expectations	84–93%
Almost meets expectations	74–83%
Does not meet expectations	54–73%

Then assign a letter grade, depending on where the student performed within the specific level. For example, the following percentage ranges for the performance levels were determined based on the grading scale of Fairfax County Public Schools:

A	94–100%
B+	90–93%
B	84–89%
C+	80–83%
C	74–79%
D+	70–73%
D	64–69%
F	0–63%

Analytic Rubrics: Converting scores from analytic rubrics to grades is a much more complicated matter. It is critical that teachers remember that, for analytic scoring rubrics, **raw scores cannot be converted directly to percentages.** For example, if a student receives threes on each of the six criteria on the scoring rubric (meets expectations), he or she earns 18 out of 24. In a straight-percentage system, this is 75%, which on most school districts' grading scales is a "C". However, assigning a "C" to a student who has met the expectations of the task would be unfair. Therefore a conversion system must be used to align the points earned with the school division's philosophy of a "B" for "meets expectations" (Fairfax County Public Schools, 1996). Points must be adjusted mathematically to convert rubric scores to grades. Since it is not possible for a student to score a zero on a rubric, teachers must first decide what the minimum passing grade would be—e.g., a 60%. A mathematical equation then converts rubric points to a range of percentages between the highest possible—100% and the lowest possible—e.g., 60%.

www.cengagebrain.com

As of the writing of this fourth edition of *Teacher's Handbook,* there are several avenues that teachers may pursue in order to accomplish this score conversion. First, there is presently a Web site called Roobrix (see Figure 11.13), which calculates a custom-made

FIGURE 11.13 Roobrix Web Site

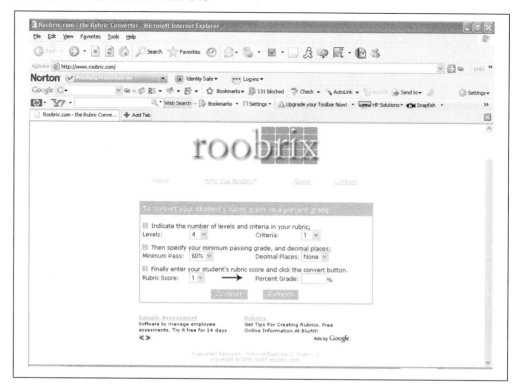

Source: Makkai, C., 2006–2007, http://www.roobrix.com.

conversion based on the lowest passing percentage as entered by the teacher; see the *Teacher's Handbook* Web site for the link to this site. Secondly, teachers who are interested in custom-making their own conversions—and who are adept at algebra!—may use the following two-step formula, which yields similar results as the Roobrix program:

Step 1: $\dfrac{\text{(Lowest Raw Score)}}{\text{(Maximum Raw Score)}} \times (100 - y) + y = $ (Minimum Passing %) (Solve for y value)

Step 2: $\dfrac{\text{(Student Raw Score)}}{\text{(Maximum Raw Score)}} \times (100 - y) + y = $ Actual Percentage using y value from equation 1

(Source of formula description: R. Glisan, personal communication, August 10, 2008.)

www.cengagebrain.com

Thirdly, many school districts have developed their own rubric score conversion systems. For example, a popular system is the one used by the Fairfax County Public Schools. On the *Teacher's Handbook* Web site is a link to the conversion chart for converting raw rubric scores to percentage scores and the chart for converting percentage scores to points. This system may be helpful for teachers who have a similar grading procedure.

For analytic scoring rubrics, raw scores cannot be converted directly to percentages. ▪

Standards-Based Integrated Performance Assessments (IPAs)

As you read earlier in the chapter, authentic assessments offer an exciting means of engaging students in tasks that reflect the challenges faced by individuals in the world beyond the classroom. Since a focus of *SFLL* is to weave foreign language more closely into the total educational experience and to enable learners to use L2 for a variety of real-life purposes, authentic assessments have a place in assessing student progress in attaining the standards. The *Integrated Performance Assessments (IPAs)* were designed by ACTFL to address a national need for measuring student progress in attaining the competencies described in both the national standards and the *ACTFL Performance Guidelines for K–12 Learners* (ACTFL, 1998) within authentic contexts (Adair-Hauck, Glisan, Koda, Swender, & Sandrock, 2006; Glisan, Adair-Hauck, Koda, Sandrock, & Swender, 2003). The design of the IPA is based on the following principles regarding assessment, instruction, and the nature of guidance and feedback to learners:

- Performance is effectively assessed within tasks that test learners' knowledge and skills in real-world situations, i.e., in "authentic" contexts in which students use the language in their lives both within and outside of the classroom.
- Performance-based tasks require students to "do something with the language" (complete a task) and not merely recite from memory.
- Performance-based situations provide opportunities for students to use a repertoire of skills, areas of knowledge, and modes of communication in order to negotiate tasks; therefore the IPA features an integrated sequence of tasks reflecting the interpretive, interpersonal, and presentational modes of communication within a specific area of content (e.g., health).
- In order for students to be successful in performance assessment, they need to be aware of what their performance should look like; students should be given models of the standards we expect them to achieve.
- Performance-based assessment blends classroom instruction and experiences; it features a cyclical approach in which learners receive modeling, engage in practice, perform the assessment task, receive feedback from the teacher, engage in additional practice, perform another task, etc.
- Assessment can improve performance if students receive feedback in their attempts to complete tasks.
- Teacher feedback of high quality is that which provides learners with information regarding their performance as compared to model performance. Based on clearly defined criteria, teacher comments address whether the student performance "meets" the expectations for the level, "exceeds" the expectations, or "is not there yet." Comments do not consist of judgmental statements such as, "That was good" (Glisan et al., 2003, pp. 9–10).
- Performance-based assessment requires more time than traditional testing, but the time is justified since this type of assessment is linked closely to instruction and leads to improvement in student performance.

Reflecting the interconnected nature of communication as proposed in the standards, IPAs provide opportunities for students to demonstrate the ability to communicate within a specific content area across the three modes of communication. Since IPAs can be used to assess the content of a specific unit of instruction, they may also be considered prochievement assessments: the *achievement* part is the vocabulary, grammar, and content knowledge (cultural, for example), while the *proficiency* part relates to the global functions or tasks and text types characteristic of each proficiency level. IPAs were developed to meet the need for valid and reliable assessments that "determine the level at which students comprehend and interpret authentic texts in the foreign language, interact with others in the target language in oral and written form, and present oral and written messages to audiences of listeners and readers" (Glisan et al., 2003, p. 8). The IPA prototype consists of a series of tasks at each of three levels—Novice Learner, Intermediate Learner, and Pre-Advanced Learner—as defined in the *ACTFL Performance Guidelines*

FIGURE 11.14 Integrated Performance Assessment: A Cyclical Approach

I. Interpretive Communication Phase
Students listen to or read an authentic text (e.g., newspaper article, radio broadcast, etc.) and answer information as well as interpretive questions to assess comprehension. Teacher provides students with feedback on performance.

III. Presentational Communication Phase
Students engage in presentational communication by sharing their research/ideas/opinions. Sample presentational formats: speeches, drama skits, radio broadcasts, posters, brochures, essays, Web sites, etc.

II. Interpersonal Communication Phase
After receiving feedback regarding interpretive phase, students engage in interpersonal oral communication about a particular topic which relates to the interpretive text. This phase should be either audio- or videotaped.

Source: From *ACTFL Integrated Performance Assessment* (p. 18) by E. W. Glisan, B. Adair-Hauck, K. Koda, S. P. Sandrock, & E. Swender, 2003. Yonkers, NY: ACTFL. Used by permission of the American Council of the Teaching of Foreign Languages.

for K–12 Learners (1998). As illustrated in Figure 11.14, the IPA series features three interrelated tasks, each of which reflects one of the three modes of communication, and integrates another goal area of the standards (e.g., Connections or Cultures). Each task provides the information and elicits the L2 interaction necessary for students to complete the subsequent task.

Figure 11.15 illustrates an overview of the Intermediate-Level task for the context "Famous Person."

 Which goal areas and standards are reflected in this IPA series of tasks?

FIGURE 11.15 Overview of Intermediate-Level IPA Task for "Famous Person"

You are a member of the language club at your school. The club members have decided to name the club in honor of a famous person from the _____ culture. All members will vote soon in order to select a famous person in whose honor the club will be named. However, you all need to do some research in order to make a good decision! After locating some interesting descriptions of famous people from the _____ culture, you decide to read an article about _____, a famous _____, that has recently appeared in the popular magazine _____. After reading the article, you discuss this famous person as a possible candidate with a classmate, as well as discussing the classmate's choice from the article s/he has just read. Finally, you make a decision and write a letter of nomination for the famous person of your choice. Your letter must be convincing to the other members of the language club!

Source: From "The Integrated Performance Assessment (IPA): Connecting assessment to instruction and learning," by B. Adair-Hauck, E. W. Glisan, K. Koda, E. Swender, & P. Sandrock, 2006, *Foreign Language Annals, 39,* p. 366; original from *ACTFL Integrated Performance Assessment* (p. 22) by E. W. Glisan, B. Adair-Hauck, K. Koda, S. P. Sandrock, & E. Swender, 2003, p. 22. Used by permission of the American Council of the Teaching of Foreign Languages.

FIGURE 11.16 A Cyclical Approach to Second Language Learning and Development

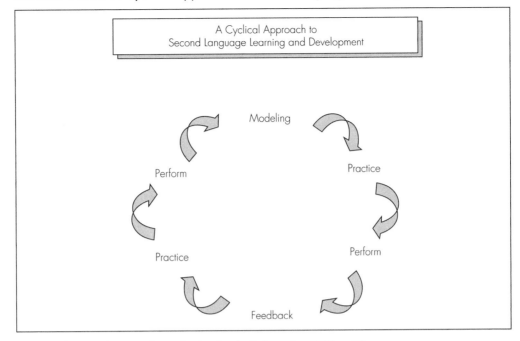

A Cyclical Approach to
Second Language Learning and Development

Modeling

Practice

Perform

Perform

Practice

Feedback

Source: Glisan, Adair-Hauck, Koda, Sandrock, & Swender, 2003, p. 23.

A unique feature of the IPA prototype is its cyclical approach to language instruction, which includes modeling, practicing, performing, and feedback phases (see Figure 11.16):

1. Modeling of expected student performance is an important feature of the IPA framework. Before students begin a task, teacher and students view samples of exemplary student work in the target language and discuss the criteria presented in the IPA rubrics that determine what constitutes performance at each level: exceeds expectations, meets expectations, does not meet expectations. The IPA rubrics for interpretive, interpersonal, and presentational communication for novice, intermediate, and pre-advanced levels appear in Appendix 11.8 on the *Teacher's Handbook* Web site. It is important to note that these rubrics are analytic and generic across IPA tasks, and that they address the criteria for the various modes of communication described in the *ACTFL Performance Guidelines for K–12 Learners* (ACTFL, 1998). Teachers can easily assign points to each level of the rubric in order to convert rubric scores to grades, as described earlier; the rubrics would have three points except for the Interpersonal and Presentational Intermediate-Level rubric, which would have four points.

2. Teachers provide ample practice of the types of tasks that students will be asked to perform on the IPA. For example, classroom activities that take place during the year can be focused on students being able to interpret authentic texts and use L2 in meaningful contexts with one another.

3. Students begin the IPA by exploring a printed, audio, or video text and performing a series of interpretive tasks depicted on the *Comprehension Guide Template* designed for their particular level of proficiency (as shown in Appendix 11.9 on the *Teacher's Handbook* Web site), and the teacher rates individual student performance using the interpretive rubrics. In the feedback phase, the teacher provides quality feedback by discussing with students why their interpretive skills are rated *exceeds, meets,* or *does not meet expectations.* Through the use of assisting questions and collaborative dialogue (in the ZPD), the teacher assists students in understanding the strengths and

weaknesses of their performance as well as how to improve their performance. This feedback loop not only serves to inform students of their progress, but it also enables all learners to gain the same level of comprehension of the authentic text before they proceed to the interpersonal and presentational tasks. This is important because, if a learner is not able to interpret the authentic text successfully, this will prohibit him/her from performing the interpersonal and presentational tasks.

4. Students then perform the interpersonal task, which requires that they use the information they learned from the interpretive task to discuss a particular issue or question with a classmate.[6] The teacher uses the interpersonal rubrics to rate performance and provide feedback. It is critical to note that feedback in an IPA does not mean saying "Good job" but rather providing helpful comments about how to improve, such as "You are able to communicate autobiographical information. You are able to ask only one question. You have difficulty asking most questions. You need to work on the various types of asking questions in German" (Glisan et al., 2003, p. 35). Students use this specific type of feedback to focus on areas that need attention in order to improve future performances.

5. Finally, students perform the presentational task, and the teacher rates performance using the presentation rubrics. The feedback phase follows.

It is interesting to note that an IPA can be used as either a formative or summative tool. As can be seen in the description of the cyclical process, it is clearly a formative assessment that directly informs instruction and improves learning and performance. The IPA can also be used as a summative tool in assessing student progress at the end of a course or sequence of instruction. In this case, however, teachers need to administer four or five IPAs in order to have enough data to confirm a learner's ability to function within the contexts of several goal areas of *SFLL* and his/her ability to perform at a given proficiency level. As illustrated in Figure 11.16, the IPA framework supports the seamless connection between instruction and assessment. Furthermore, the feedback loop distinguishes the IPA from other types of assessment—the teacher intervenes after each phase of the IPA to provide feedback, improve student performance, and equip the students with the background knowledge necessary to engage in the subsequent task.

 What is the role of the ZPD in the IPA feedback phase?

 In what way does the IPA framework illustrate a seamless connection between instruction and assessment?

Research on the IPA. The IPA has been field tested at both the secondary and postsecondary levels. The field testing that occurred in six pilot site K–12 school districts across the country confirmed the washback effect of the IPA on teachers' perceptions of their teaching practices. For example, 83% of teachers reported that implementation of the IPA had a positive impact on their teaching, while 91% indicated that the project had a positive effect on their creation of future assessments (Adair-Hauck et al., 2006). It was apparent that IPA training raised teachers' awareness regarding ways to improve some of their instructional practices. As a result of using an IPA, many teachers found that their students experienced difficulty in performing an oral interpersonal task because they needed strategies for negotiating meaning and practice in communicating spontaneously without having recourse to a printed script. Teachers reported that implementing the IPA made them more aware of the need to integrate into their teaching the three modes of communication, standards-based interpretive tasks with authentic texts, more interpersonal speaking tasks, and rubrics to help students improve their performance (Adair-Hauck et al.). On the student questionnaire, a frequent student comment was that, during the IPA, it was "difficult to tell what was classroom practice and what was assessment"; this comment revealed the degree to which the IPA succeeded in making the connection between instruction and assessment seamless (Glisan, Adair-Hauck, Koda, Sandrock, & Swender, 2003).

The IPA was also field tested at the U.S. Air Force Academy in an advanced Spanish course on Latin American Culture and Civilization, where students were exposed to tasks across the three modes and a practice IPA as a part of the course. As a final IPA featuring the theme of *illegal immigration*, cadets watched a video segment from *Espejo Enterrado* ("The Buried Mirror"), from the videodisc program based on the book by Carlos Fuentes and used throughout the course; this was the first time that a video text had been used in the IPA interpretive phase. In the interpersonal phase, cadets debated the issues of illegal immigration, and they completed two presentational tasks—a paper describing their opinions about illegal immigration in the U.S. and a two- to three-minute oral presentation in which they discussed their opinions (Glisan, Uribe, & Adair-Hauck, 2007). Results of the assessment revealed that the cadets performed better in the oral presentational mode than in the interpersonal mode, which confirmed the findings of the initial IPA study conducted at the secondary level, indicating that spontaneous, face-to-face interaction is more challenging and requires extensive classroom practice in which students "are placed in communicative situations where they must negotiate meaning and think on their feet" (Glisan et al., pp. 52–53). In this project, the interpretive mode was the only mode in which some students did not meet expectations, which the course instructors attribute to the fact that cadets needed more exposure to interpretive strategies such as inferencing and guessing in context.

Beyond the information obtained regarding cadet performance across the modes, this post-secondary IPA project yielded additional findings of interest. First, cadets who had studied Spanish in the middle school grades performed significantly better in the interpersonal task, which lends further support for extended sequences of language study. Secondly, there was a negative correlation between the numbers of years of high school Spanish and the cadets' performance across the modes; i.e., as the number of high school years of language study increased, performance on the modes of communication decreased. The authors attribute this finding to the fact that cadets reported having had traditional high school language experiences that focused on form and grammar rather than on communicative interaction. Third, pre- and post-survey data confirm that the IPA had a significant positive effect on cadets' motivation for and perceptions about language learning and their attitudes about the IPA type of assessment (Glisan, Uribe, & Adair-Hauck, 2006). More specifically, findings revealed that students preferred the IPA assessment format to that of more traditional exams and that they perceived that the IPA was a better measure of their communication abilities. In sum, if foreign language instruction does not integrate the three modes of communication, students will not develop the ability to engage in these forms of communication. The research on the IPA conducted thus far confirms that, in order for this form of assessment to be a valid measure of proficiency across the modes of communication, instruction must be aligned with the IPA format of assessment—i.e., it must engage learners in communicating in the three modes.

The IPA has the potential to serve as an effective research tool as the profession examines ways to assess progress in meeting the standards and proficiency-based goals. Currently, the IPA is the only standards-based model that assesses progress made in attaining the goal areas of *SFLL* plus progress along the proficiency continuum. As more work is done in developing and refining the IPA, this assessment prototype has tremendous potential for helping the profession come to a better understanding of what standards-based assessment is and how such assessment can inform and improve classroom instruction.[7]

See the *Teacher's Handbook* Web site for a link to the CARLA Virtual Assessment Center (VAC) of the Center for Advanced Research in Language Acquisition (CARLA) for ideas on developing performance assessments that are based on the backward design concept, integration of the three modes of communication, and the IPA framework. Also see the link to New Jersey's "Thematically Organized Assessments" (TOAs), which feature performance-based assessment tasks that target a specific proficiency level and assess communication across the three modes of communication.

In sum, authentic assessment, the use of scoring rubrics, providing rich feedback to learners about their performance, and standards-based assessment such as the IPA provide exciting options for teachers as they work toward linking instruction more closely to assessment, improving learner performance, and assessing learner progress toward attaining the standards within tasks that they are likely to encounter in their lives outside the classroom.

Empowering Students Through Assessment

As you have seen in this chapter, current approaches to assessment emphasize the role of the learner in using L2 to accomplish a variety of communicative tasks, acquire information about C2 and other content areas through exploration of authentic texts, and create products and performances in L2. The discussion thus far in this chapter has echoed the pivotal role that modeling, feedback, and interaction play in guiding learners in language classrooms. In performance-based, authentic, and standards-based tasks, learners are given more responsibility for their learning than they were in the traditional assessment paradigm. In other words, they are able to interact with and help their peers, obtain feedback and guidance from the teacher, make decisions about how they will prove that they have acquired knowledge and skills, and formulate individual responses to open-ended questions, problems, and/or projects. In this regard, the new assessment paradigm has *empowered* learners to play more of an active role in the assessment and improvement of their learning. When students are empowered, they are better able to set personal goals for learning, self-assess accurately, seek out assistance when necessary, monitor their own progress, make improvements in their performances, and participate in learning communities.

Another way through which we empower learners is to give them responsibility for assessing their own progress, making decisions about which work samples best illustrate their progress in attaining the standards, using the foreign language outside of the classroom setting, and providing feedback to teachers about instruction. This section presents several assessment strategies that empower the learner in these ways. These strategies also enable the teacher to assess learners and instruction by means of multiple perspectives, as was discussed at the beginning of this chapter. In addition, each of these strategies may be used as an *informal* means of assessment, a way to obtain data and feedback concerning student progress and effectiveness of instruction without necessarily assigning formal grades.

Portfolio Assessment: Collection, Selection, Reflection

A *portfolio* is a "collection of evidence used by the teacher and learner to monitor the growth of the learner's knowledge of content, use of strategies, and attitudes toward the accomplishment of goals in an organized and systematic way" (Tierney, Carter, & Desai, 1991, p. 41). For example, a portfolio may contain learner goal-setting worksheets, tape-recorded interpersonal tasks, journal entries, written responses to interpretive tasks, cultural investigations, self-assessments, etc. A portfolio documents the growth and development of students *over a period of time*; it is a rich description of a learner's work and offers perspectives that tests do not provide.

The portfolio collection must include "student participation in selecting contents, the criteria for selection, the criteria for judging merit, and evidence of student self-reflection"

(Paulson, Paulson, & Meyer, 1991, p. 60). In a portfolio, learners have an opportunity to select evidence of their learning, reflect on it, and make it part of the assessment of their learning.[8] In this way, they become empowered to participate in their own assessment.

 In a portfolio, learners have an opportunity to select evidence of their learning, reflect on it, and make it part of the assessment of their learning.

Figure 11.17 compares traditional assessment and portfolio assessment. The following are reasons for implementing portfolio assessment:

- Portfolios can include evidence of language development *at a specific time* and also evidence of language performance and progress *over time.*
- Since portfolio assessment is closely linked to instruction, teachers can be certain that they are measuring what they have taught, and they can give feedback on the effectiveness of instruction.
- Since portfolio assessment is incorporated fully into instruction, it does not require additional time spent specifically on assessment.
- Portfolios promote positive student involvement, which has a positive impact on students' self-confidence, facilitates student use of learning strategies, and increases students' ability to assess and revise their work.
- Portfolios offer the teacher and student an in-depth knowledge of the student as a learner, which enables the teacher to individualize instruction for the student.
- Using portfolios introduces students to an assessment format with which they may need to become familiar—more and more schools and districts are adopting portfolio assessment for both students and teacher professional development.
- Using assessment portfolios gives teachers opportunities to involve parents in their children's language learning (National Capital Language Resource Center [NCLRC], 2004b).

There are various types of portfolios. Hammadou (1998) identifies several types of portfolios: showcase, documentation, evaluation, and process. Portfolios at the K–12 level are most often used to document students' progress and to engage learners in reflecting on their own learning process. Evaluation and showcase portfolios are frequently compiled by teachers and other school professionals in order to (1) demonstrate accountability to their students, parents, school administrators, and governmental

FIGURE 11.17 Traditional Assessment vs. Portfolio Assessment

TRADITIONAL ASSESSMENT	PORTFOLIO ASSESSMENT
Measures student's ability at one time	Measures student's ability over time
Done by teacher alone; student often unaware of criteria	Done by teacher and student; student aware of criteria
Conducted outside instruction	Embedded in instruction
Assigns student a grade	Involves student in own assessment
Does not capture the range of student's language ability	Captures many facets of language learning performance
Does not include the teacher's knowledge of student as a learner	Allows for expression of teacher's knowledge of student as learner
Does not give student responsibility	Student learns how to take responsibility

Source: From *Portfolio Assessment in the Foreign Language Classroom,* 2004, National Capital Language Resource Center, Washington, DC. Used by permission.

agencies by showcasing their abilities and the performance of their students; and/or (2) demonstrate required skills necessary to achieve licensure or certification (i.e., National Board Certification).[9] Such a portfolio might include a teacher's certificate of rating on the Oral Proficiency Interview, a statement of philosophy about teaching, videotaped teaching scenarios, lesson plans addressing national standards with self-reflections on lessons taught, standards-based performance assessments, a professional development plan, and samples of student work.

Contents of the Portfolio.   The contents of the portfolio are generally determined by the two principal players in the creation of a portfolio. First is the portfolio designer, who sets the guidelines for what it should contain. This person is either the audience for the portfolio or knows what the audience will expect to see. The portfolio developer is the person whose work is featured in the portfolio. Usually this person selects items to be included as documents based on his/her judgment and the stipulations of the portfolio designer. The size and format of the portfolio are determined by decisions the designer or developer of the portfolio makes about the purpose of the portfolio, the selection of type and number of documents, and the type of self-reflective narrative that highlights the importance of the contents of the portfolio.

The items to be included in the portfolio are called *artifacts*. These include student products, student goals, and self-reflections: Student products document what students have learned, and the self-reflections and goals show how students are learning and how progress is being made (NCLRC, 2004b). In a standards-based program, learners must demonstrate their progress in each of the five goal areas of *SFLL*.

The self-reflections are usually prepared in the form of a narrative and justify why each piece of work was selected and what it means in the student's personal growth as a language learner. Sample artifacts include goal-setting worksheets; self-assessment records; tape-recorded oral proficiency interviews; videotaped interpersonal discussions and oral presentations/speeches; journal entries; letters to pen pals/key pals; compositions; written responses to interpretive tasks; analyses of cultural products, practices, perspectives; and ratings on performance assessments. Appendix 11.10.a on the *Teacher's Handbook* Web site features a sample portfolio template and Appendix 11.10.b presents a sample portfolio table of contents.

Important features in the presentation of artifacts are the goal-setting and self-reflection components, which encourage students to be involved as active learners in their learning and self-assessment. Teachers should provide learners with the opportunity to set their own personal goals and thus reflect on their reasons for learning a second language. Goals can be short term (What do I want to be able to do by the end of this thematic unit?) or long term (What do I want to be able to do by the end of this year/semester?). Students need assistance in setting appropriate, reachable goals; a goal that would not be appropriate would be "I want to understand everything my French-speaking friends say." See the *Teacher's Handbook* Web site for a link to the NCLRC Web site that contains a sample lesson for setting reasonable goals for a middle school class and a student goal-setting worksheet. Appendix 11.11 on the *Teacher's Handbook* Web site provides a goal-setting and self-assessment form.

www.cengagebrain.com

In the self-reflection component, students describe why they selected each artifact for inclusion in the portfolio, what they learned from the artifact, and what the artifact illustrates about their performance. This is a pivotal feature of the portfolio because it holds students accountable for their selections and verifies the degree of learning that has taken place. Self-reflections should address the goals that students set initially and the learning objectives that they were attempting to achieve (i.e., standards-based objectives). The self-reflection could also address implications for future learning needed

(Campbell, Melenyzer, Nettles, & Wyman, 2000). The following is an example of a self-reflection:

> *I included this composition because it shows that I understand the perspectives behind the practice of the "Quinceañera" in Spanish-speaking countries. My goal in this unit was to understand why this custom is so important and whether we have anything like it in the U.S. I learned from our readings and my e-mail discussions with my Mexican key pal that there is a lot of religious importance connected to this custom and also a history of traditions. I was able to compare this custom to some customs that we have in the U.S. such as "sweet sixteen" celebrations. This paper also shows how many new words I learned in Spanish for many products and practices associated with the Quinceañera. In the future, I would be interested in learning about other typical customs in the life of young Hispanics and what perspectives they represent.*

Portfolios may also include *attestations*, evidence of a student's progress that comes from teachers, peers, parents, or other adults; examples include records from a parent–teacher conference, teacher observation notes, and peer-assessment forms (NCLRC, 2004b).

 Portfolio artifacts include student products, student goals, and self-reflections.

Steps in Designing and Implementing Portfolio Assessment. The Portfolio Assessment Project, conducted through the NCLRC, identifies the following steps for designing and implementing foreign language portfolio assessment:

1. *Set assessment purpose:* Determine the purpose in order to have a focus and direction for the assessment. What aspect of language learning will the portfolio be used to assess? Who will use the portfolio? Why are you making the assessment?
2. *Identify instructional objectives:* Identify portfolio objectives or standards-based goals for students to work toward in the area specified by the assessment purpose. What exactly do you want students to achieve? Consider the goal areas of *SFLL*.
3. *Match tasks to objectives:* Identify language learning tasks that match the objectives and through which students will obtain artifacts to be used in the portfolios. What can students do to show evidence of their progress toward the objective? Plan language tasks that will allow students to systematically practice and reflect on their learning.
4. *Describe student reflection:* Describe how students will reflect on their work. What self-assessment, goal-setting, and metacognitive tasks will you include?
5. *Set criteria:* Establish criteria by which the individual artifacts and the portfolio will be assessed. How will you determine the degree of student progress toward the goals?
6. *Determine organization and logistics:* Determine how the portfolio will be managed, considering the purpose of the assessment and the audience. Where will the portfolio

be stored? How often will artifacts be submitted? Who will select the artifacts? Remember that it takes more than one artifact to reliably show progress toward a goal and that artifacts should be selected in a systematic manner. Will parents participate as an audience, and if so, how?

7. *Monitor progress:* Continually monitor the portfolio for validity and reliability and make adjustments as necessary. Is the portfolio assessing the specified areas consistently? Are you receiving useful information about your students to inform instruction?

8. *Evaluate the portfolio process:* After you have completed the portfolio semester or year, reflect on the entire process and evaluate your success with the portfolio. What worked well that you will include next time? What changes will you make for the next time? (NCLRC, 2004b)

Barrett (2000) suggests that students share their portfolios with their peers in the final presentation stage of portfolio development, which is when appropriate public comments can be made to encourage collaboration and commitment to professional development and lifelong learning.

www.cengagebrain.com

Since the main purpose of a portfolio is to track progress and empower learners to assess their own learning, the issue of assigning grades to a portfolio can be a challenging one. Given the realities of the classroom and school policies, foreign language teachers may find it necessary to score or grade their students' portfolios. When teachers score classroom portfolios, the experience should be constructive and positive. Criteria for grading should include the degree to which the artifacts illustrate progress in attaining the various standards of *SFLL* and other learning objectives (i.e., proficiency development), quality of self-reflections, organization, presentation, etc. Appendix 11.12 on the *Teacher's Handbook* Web site provides an example of a rubric that could be used for assessing and grading the portfolio. Teachers are encouraged to develop rubrics for evaluating portfolios and to present these to students prior to beginning the portfolio process. Appendix 11.13 illustrates a sample end-of-year portfolio assessment in which students are given a choice of three performance tasks; a rubric for scoring this assessment is also included in this appendix.

Whether or not portfolios are graded, it is critical that teachers provide feedback to learners, as illustrated in Appendix 11.14 on the *Teacher's Handbook* Web site, which contains a feedback sheet that could be used in a formative conference with students. In addition, students may be asked to present their portfolios formally to the teacher, peers, parents, or other outside audiences.[10]

Electronic Portfolio Formats. Recently, there has been much attention paid to electronic portfolios, which involve "the use of electronic technologies to enable students and teachers to collect and organize artifacts in various media types (texts, graphs, audio, video, etc.) and establish hypertext links to organize that material and connect it across artifacts as well as to appropriate standards, especially in the case of standards-based portfolios" (Egéa-Kuehne, 2004, pp. 21–22).[11] The advantages of electronic portfolios are that they:

- increase students' technological and multimedia skills and knowledge;
- provide hyperlinks to foreign language content standards and educational technology standards (see Chapter 12), thus enabling students to effectively show evidence of having met standards;
- use minimal storage space;
- are more portable;
- have a long shelf life;
- are more easily and widely accessible and distributed; and
- enable the projection of artifacts and performances anytime and anywhere (Egéa-Kuehne, 2004; Kilbane & Milman, 2003).

The process of compiling an electronic portfolio is similar to that of a traditional paper portfolio except that students need to select and use appropriate technological tools and strategies in order to digitize images, audio recordings, video artifacts, etc., and to individualize their portfolios. It is important to remember that the primary goals of the electronic portfolio are the same as those of paper portfolios. In other words, teachers must be cautious to not allow the "glitz" of an electronic portfolio to become the focus. The primary focus should be the degree to which artifacts and self-reflections illustrate learner progress in attaining learner goals and standards. As Barrett (2000) reminds us, an electronic portfolio without goals, standards, and/or reflections is just a multimedia presentation, a fancy electronic resume, or a digital scrapbook.

www.cengagebrain.com

Barrett (2000) suggests that students develop the electronic portfolio by defining the portfolio context, collecting digital portfolio artifacts, selecting and reflecting on the artifacts, connecting the artifacts in digital form, presenting the portfolio to an audience, and evaluating its effectiveness in light of its purpose. See the *Teacher's Handbook* Web site for a link to Barrett's detailed site that deals with how to develop electronic portfolios; this site contains information concerning the specific technology tools and rubrics for evaluating electronic portfolios. Also, for assistance in managing the portfolio development process, see the links provided to the Grady Portfolio and the Open Source Portfolio Initiative.

Learner Self-Assessment

In addition to engaging students in selecting and reflecting on work samples that illustrate their progress, another strategy for empowering students is to have them perform self-assessments. These assessments might be done as part of a review for a test on a thematic unit, in order to prompt students to review and assess what they are able to do and what areas still need attention. For example, at the end of a "Making Social Plans" unit, students might be given a list with statements such as:

	YES	ALMOST	NOT YET
I can call and invite someone to go to a party.			
I can convince a friend to go out even if he or she doesn't want to.			
I can accept an invitation.			
I can decline an invitation and give a reason.			
I can write an e-mail message to a Spanish-speaking friend and discuss plans for the weekend.			
I can read the movie listing in an authentic Spanish newspaper and identify movies of interest and times they are playing.			
I can describe social events that an Hispanic teenager typically enjoys.			

Following this self-assessment, students would have the opportunity to collaborate with the teacher and/or peers to work on the objectives that had not yet been attained.

Self-assessments can also be implemented as a summative way to have students evaluate their progress. Figure 11.18 illustrates a summative self-assessment checklist for a third-grade

FIGURE 11.18 Summative Self-Assessment Checklist for Third-Grade Japanese Students

Name _____   December 3rd grade

Things I Can Do in Japanese

Think about what you can do in Japanese. Make a checkmark under the appropriate column for each sentence. After our testing, Jessica-sensei will write a red "O" in the correct column according to how you do on the test.

	Yes!	With help	Not yet
Communication Skills			
I can say whether I have something using "_ ga aru."	○	✓	
I can ask for things using "kudasai."	⊘		
I can say "here you are" and "thank you."	⊘		
I can count to 100 by tens.		○	✓
I can count to 1,000 by hundreds.	✓		○
I can read all the hiragana we learned so far (35).	All ✓	Many ○	Few ___
Culture Skills			
I can recognize three kinds of Japanese writing: Kanji, hiragana, and katakana.	✓	○	
I can recognize different Japanese coins.	⊘		
I can play rock-paper-scissors in Japanese.	⊘		
Connections to Other Subject Areas			
I can find Japan and the U.S. on a globe and a map (geography).	⊘		
If you give me a price, I can "draw" the correct amount of money I need using 1, 5, 10, 50, 100, and 500 yen coins (math).		⊘	
Comparisons (of Language and Culture)			
I know the difference between Japanese and American money and I can tell you about how much each Japanese coin is worth in American dollars.	⊘		
Communities (Japanese Beyond the School)			
I have done at least two homeworks for Japanese so far this year.	Yes! ⊘	No ___	
I have told someone outside of school about the things I learned in Japanese class.	Yes! ✓	No ___	

Source: From *Languages and Children – Making the Match,* 4th ed., by H. Curtain and C. A. Dahlberg, 2010. Boston: Allyn & Bacon. Reprinted by permission of Jessica Haxhi.

Japanese class that experienced standards-based instruction. Note that, prior to completing the summative assessment, the student self-assesses using a checkmark placed in the appropriate column for each item. After the actual assessment, the teacher indicates with circles what the student was actually able to do on the assessment. This type of system enables the teacher and students to determine how accurate students' self-assessments are in terms of actual assessment results. A worthwhile goal would be for the teacher to help learners acquire more skill in self-assessing, and hence, in improving their learning and performances.

Interactive Homework

Another aspect of empowering students is providing them with interesting opportunities to use the foreign language outside of class and thereby to assess their learning at home. Although there is inconclusive evidence that more time spent on homework necessarily leads to higher achievement, studies overall point to a positive relationship between the time spent on homework and achievement, particularly at the secondary level (Sharp, Keys, & Benefield, 2001).[12]

According to Antonek, Tucker, and Donato, homework functions on three interrelated levels:

1. Homework communicates to the parent what and how well the child is learning in the classroom.
2. Homework facilitates classroom learning if it is linked to what the child can realistically perform without the assistance of the teacher and other students.
3. Homework mediates the relationship of school and home by serving as a public awareness tool that informs parents about the curriculum and encourages their support for programs (1997, p. 65).

The principles of teaching language in context for meaningful communication found throughout *Teacher's Handbook* apply to homework tasks as well. Specifically, *Teacher's Handbook* suggests that foreign language homework assignments:

- consist of more than mechanical, decontextualized workbook exercises;
- be clear enough so that students can understand instructions at home;
- be related to activities done in class;
- provide the basis for activities to be done in class the next day (e.g., students might prepare interview questions that they will use the next day in a pair activity);
- be meaningful and interesting to students;
- evaluate the extent to which learners can use language independently (their actual level of development);
- if possible, engage students in interaction with others (peers, parents);
- enable students to self-assess their progress;
- provide the teacher with feedback regarding the effectiveness of instruction (e.g., if many students are experiencing difficulty with an assignment, it may point to specific work that needs to be done in class); and
- empower student learning.

The professional literature as revealed in research articles and methodology textbooks has failed to consider fully the role of homework. However, one study suggests the concept of "interactive foreign language homework" as a way to involve parents/caretakers in schoolwork. Antonek, Tucker, and Donato (1997) based their work on that done by the Center on Families, Communities, Schools, and Children's Learning at the Johns Hopkins University, where interactive homework in various subject areas was piloted. Through a process called Teachers Involve Parents in Schoolwork (TIPS), students talk about homework in the classroom, describe the types of homework they like best, explain how their parents help them with homework at home, and solicit parents' active involvement in completing assignment at home (Epstein, 1993).

 Interactive foreign language homework is a way to involve parents/caretakers in schoolwork.

In the study by Antonek et al. (1997), interactive homework assignments were developed and piloted in a K–5 Japanese program in an effort to involve parents in helping students with Japanese vocabulary and cultural information. The majority of parents reported having enjoyed completing the assignments with their children and having the

FIGURE 11.19 Interactive Homework Assignment

Source: From "Interactive homework: Creating connections between home and school," by J. L. Antonek, G. R. Tucker, and R. Donato, in A. Mollica, ed., *Teaching Languages – Selected Readings from Mosaic* (pp. 169–184), 1997, p. 175. Lewiston, NY: Soleil Publishing, Inc. Used by permission.

opportunity to learn more about the Japanese program. Figure 11.19 illustrates a sample interactive homework assignment, which consists of six parts:

1. title introducing the topic of the homework, a statement indicating the connection between the assignment and classwork, the date, and student signature;
2. a list of FL phrases with English translations;
3. instructions for students to carry out three to five language functions (e.g., expressing thanks and greeting someone);
4. instructions for students to teach their parents how to carry out language functions;
5. ways for students and parents to interact in the foreign language (e.g., exchange greetings and courtesy expressions); and
6. cultural information relevant to the lesson.

Space is also provided for parents to sign and give feedback on the child's performance (Antonek et al., pp. 67–68).

The researchers suggest that 10 minute assignments work best and that they be kept to one page and be reproduced on colored paper for easy identification by parent and child. Although the example in Figure 11.19 focuses on verbal language, the assignments could also guide students and parents in producing a short written product, such as a note, letter, or creative paragraph. It is important to note that these assignments must be carefully designed since parents may not know the target language; parents become learners along with their children. Appendix 11.15 on the *Teacher's Handbook* Web site contains a checklist for constructing an interactive homework assignment.

www.cengagebrain.com

Spanish teachers in Pinellas County, Florida, designed a similar approach using tasks that elementary school students do at home with their parents (Kucerik, 2000). Through this endeavor, a home assessment system was developed that makes parents and classroom teachers partners in assessment. Parents are introduced to the program by way of a letter that explains the goals of the program and the role of the parent. This assessment process uses a pocket chart in each classroom; assessment cards (held in the pocket chart), which contain written language tasks reflecting the goals of the program; name cards for each student in the program; and a profile sheet for recording the long-range achievement of each student. The profile sheet is kept in the student's portfolio and is updated regularly. As the school year begins, each student receives the first assessment card (see Appendix 11.16 on the *Teacher's Handbook* Web site), which contains 10 tasks or skills, written in the native language. Below each skill is also printed a place for the student's name, the date, and parent signature. Students are instructed to take the assessment card home and practice the skills with a family member until they feel ready to present them in class. The goals are consistent practice and increasing confidence in using the language, not rapid completion of the cards. Once a child is ready to return a card to school, he or she places it in the pocket chart in the classroom. The teacher uses the completed cards placed in the pocket chart to review and assess students. When a student demonstrates the ability to successfully complete the task, the teacher initials the card and records it on the student's profile sheet. Students receive the next level card once all of the skills on the previous card have been successfully demonstrated in class. The goals of this home assessment program "empower students to set learning objectives and direct their own achievement" (Kucerik, pp. 4–5).

Designed in these innovative ways, homework assignments can play a new role in engaging learners in interesting language use outside of the classroom, in setting their own learning goals, and in directing their own achievement.

Classroom Assessment Techniques (CATs)

This final assessment strategy is different from those previously described in that its purpose is to engage learners in providing feedback on instruction, and indirectly, on their learning. *Classroom Assessment Techniques (CATs)* are informal, formative assessment strategies that are aimed at improving instruction, rather than assigning grades or points (Angelo & Cross, 1993). According to Angelo and Cross, the function of CATs is to "improve the quality of student learning, not to provide evidence for evaluating or grading students" (p. 6). The goal of these strategies is therefore to better understand students' learning and how to improve one's teaching. Consequently, CATs are both a set of assessment strategies and a teaching approach, based on the principle that the more teachers know about what and how their students are learning, the better equipped they are to improve their teaching.

CATs are largely simple, non-graded, anonymous, in-class activities that give both the teacher and learners useful feedback on the teaching-learning process (ACTFL/Weber State University, 2003). The following is an example of the Minute Paper CAT, which is one of the most commonly used strategies.[13] It should take a minute to do, usually at the end of a class period, and its purpose is to provide rapid feedback on whether the teacher's objective for the lesson matched what learners actually learned:

The One-Minute Paper

During the last few minutes of class period, ask students to use a half-sheet of paper and write "The most important thing I learned today and what I understood the least."

Source: Iowa State University Center for Excellence in Learning and Teaching, 2008; adapted from Angelo & Cross, 1993.

www.cengagebrain.com

The questions posed can be made specific to the content of the foreign language class, as Carduner (2002) did in her third-year college Spanish composition course. See Appendix 11.17 on the *Teacher's Handbook* Web site.

A sample CAT that addresses higher-level thinking skills is the RSQC2, an acronym for Recall, Summarize, Question, Comment, and Connect (Angelo & Cross, 1993, pp. 344–348). Students take two minutes to *recall* and list in rank order the most important ideas from a previous day's class. Then they take another two minutes to *summarize* those points in a single sentence in order to "chunk" the information. Next, students are asked to write one major *question* that they want to be answered. Finally, students identify a thread or theme to connect this material to the course's major goal. Another option is for students to be invited to leave a suggestion about any class issue in a suggestion box (Iowa State University Center for Excellence in Learning and Teaching, 2008). Spanos, Hansen, and Daines (2001) reported on their use of the RSQC2 CAT in an advanced-level German culture course, in which students posted their feedback anonymously through an online bulletin board. The German instructor found that several students were missing key ideas and connections on a particular topic, and she was able to modify instruction accordingly.

Iowa State University has a Web site that features a list of sample CATs, a description of each, and a course example (see the *Teacher's Handbook* Web site for the link). You may also find it helpful to consult Angelo and Cross (1993) for additional examples.

The function of CATs is to "improve the quality of student learning, not to provide evidence for evaluating or grading students."

A number of research studies have cited the merits of CATs (Angelo, 1991, 1998; Angelo & Cross, 1993; Carduner, 2002; Steadman, 1998), particularly in terms of affect. The most frequently cited advantage to using CATs reported by faculty in Steadman's study was "an increase in student satisfaction as a result of having a voice in their learning" (Carduner, p. 544). Faculty in multiple research studies indicated that the use of CATs served as a catalyst for (1) promoting a greater sense of the classroom as a learning community (Angelo & Cross); (2) encouraging reflective practice, and thus positive change, on the part of the instructor (Steadman); and (3) raising students' metacognitive awareness (Angelo & Cross; Carduner).

CATs have been used effectively in an electronic format for students in upper-level foreign language courses. Spanos, Hansen, and Daines (2001) found that having students engage in CATs by using an online bulletin board, portfolios, and online discussions instead of using the traditional paper-and-pencil format had unique advantages: students provided more reflective responses because they had more time to plan and submit their responses; the voices of more introverted students were heard more often since they had additional time to plan what they wanted to say; and students were actively engaged with the course material outside of class.

In conclusion, for teachers, frequent use of CATs can (1) provide ongoing feedback about the day-to-day learning and teaching process at a point when it is still possible to make instructional changes, (2) provide useful information about student learning with a much lower investment of time compared to other means of formal assessment, (3) help foster good rapport with students and increase the efficacy of teaching and learning, and (4) encourage the view that teaching is a formative process that evolves with time and feedback (ACTFL/Weber State University, 2003). For students, frequent use of CATs can (1) help them to become better monitors of their own learning, (2) point out the need to alter study skills, (3) provide concrete evidence that the instructor cares about learning, and (4) help them to feel that their opinions about instruction are valuable (ACTFL/Weber State University).

As illustrated in this section, students can play a greater role and be more empowered in their learning through assessment strategies, such as portfolios, self-assessment, interactive homework, and classroom assessment techniques.

The Oral Proficiency Interview: Implications for Classroom and Program Assessment

In Chapter 8, you learned about the impact that the ACTFL Oral Proficiency Interview (OPI) has had on language instruction over the past two decades. Here we revisit the OPI for the purpose of exploring its implications for classroom and program assessment, particularly as it relates to oral interpersonal communication.

As you learned in earlier chapters, the OPI is a standardized procedure for the global assessment of oral proficiency. It measures language production holistically by identifying patterns of strengths and weaknesses within the assessment criteria of global tasks or functions, contexts/content areas, accuracy, and text type. An official OPI is a face-to-face, tape-recorded interview lasting from five to thirty minutes and conducted by a certified proficiency tester. The following is a brief description of how the interview is conducted. As pointed out in Chapter 8, an understanding of the scale and/or the interview procedure does not imply an ability to rate oral speech samples. Furthermore, the OPI is not designed to be used as a classroom test. The ACTFL OPI Testing Program is administered by Language Testing International (LTI). For more information about the OPI or to schedule an OPI, see the link to LTI on the *Teacher's Handbook* Web site.

www.cengagebrain.com

The interview begins with a brief warm-up in order to help the interviewee feel comfortable and confident. Next, the interviewer moves the conversation forward through one or more level checks to establish the floor of performance or to determine at what level the interviewee can consistently perform the tasks for a given level. This phase demonstrates the tasks/contexts that the interviewee can perform with confidence and accuracy. Once the interviewer has determined that the speaker can handle the tasks and topics of a particular level, he or she raises the interview to the next major level by means of probes to establish the ceiling of the performance. The interaction in this phase illustrates the limitations of the interviewee's proficiency. The level check and probe phases may need to be repeated as each level is verified and the next level is examined. After the level checks and probes have been conducted and the interviewer believes that the evidence points to a particular level, the interviewee is asked to participate in a role-play, which serves as a final level check or probe. The role-play checks the functions that cannot easily be elicited by means of the conversation itself. Finally, the interview is brought to a close in the wind-down, at which time the discussion returns to a comfortable linguistic level for the interviewee and ends on a positive note (Swender, 1999).[14]

A modified version of the OPI, called the Simulated Oral Proficiency Interview (SOPI), was developed at the Center for Applied Linguistics (CAL) and uses taped responses as a cost-effective alternative to the face-to-face OPI (Stansfield & Kenyon, 1992, 1996). The SOPI consists of a master tape with test directions and questions, a printed booklet with pictures and other materials used for responding, and an audiotape for recording the interviewee's responses (Hadley, 2001, p. 438). Stansfield and Kenyon (1996) describe the SOPI as consisting of the following phases: (1) personalized questions simulating an initial encounter with a native speaker; (2) performance-based tasks such as those based on a visual to elicit questions, directions, descriptions, or narrations; and (3) topic- and situation-based tasks that elicit functions such as supporting an opinion, describing advantages and disadvantages, apologizing, or giving an information talk (p. 1; as cited in Hadley, p. 438). Interviewees' oral responses are recorded individually and evaluated by a tester. Stansfield and Kenyon (1992) report high correlations between the proficiency ratings given in the OPI and those given in the SOPI. For more information on the SOPI, consult the Center for Applied Linguistics Web site (link provided on the *Teacher's Handbook* Web site).

www.cengagebrain.com

Implications for Classroom Assessment. That the OPI has had an impact on assessment over the past two decades would be an understatement. The descriptions of performance that characterize each of the OPI levels now provide a common frame of reference to describe achievement in terms that have become meaningful to the vast majority of educators and students (e.g., *functions, text types*) (Liskin-Gasparro, 2003; North, 1993). As Liskin-Gasparro noted in her historical description of the OPI in celebration of its twentieth anniversary, testing formats such as prochievement tests and oral performance tests were inspired by the "emphasis in the OPI on formats and techniques that maximize student language production, along with its focus on tasks rather than linguistic accuracy alone" (p. 487).

The format of the OPI has provided many ideas for classroom assessment of oral interpersonal speaking:

1. The OPI has illustrated to teachers that they can use similar formats in assessing interactive speaking in the classroom: paired interviews, spontaneous role-plays, individual interviews. Note that the OPI format has most applicability for assessing interpersonal communication that is two-way and interactive. As explained in Chapter 8, teachers should be careful not to confuse interpersonal and presentational communication. Formats for assessing oral presentational communication include oral presentations, skits, multimedia presentations, and demonstrations.

2. The structure of the OPI offers a guide for how individual interviews with students might be structured: a warm-up, tasks to check for the level, probes to push for language at a higher level, possibly additional level checks, and a wind-down.

3. OPI interviewers must leave their traditional teacher behaviors behind during the assessment (e.g., correction, repetition of interviewee's responses). This is also advisable during classroom assessment, since traditional teacher behavior—such as overt correction—will often undermine attempts to obtain a ratable speech sample (i.e., students will be too anxious to talk).

4. The role of questions asked during an OPI is pivotal. Yes/no questions should be reserved for finding topics of interest to discuss, making novice speakers confident about their performance, and obtaining permission to pursue a topic. In classroom

oral interview situations, an abundance of yes/no questions will result in a lot of talking on the part of the teacher and little speech on the part of the student.

5. Listening and responding to the interviewee is essential in an OPI, and this principle should also be followed in classroom assessments. If active negotiation of meaning is the goal in an oral interview, then the teacher must listen to the content of the interviewee's message and respond accordingly.

6. In an OPI, interviewers generally stay with the same topic and spiral the function up to the next level. For example, if the topic is "work" and the discussion is occurring at the intermediate level, the interviewer might probe to the advanced level by asking how the interviewee obtained a job. It is more natural and less demanding on the interviewee to probe within the same topic rather than changing both the topic and the proficiency level. This same principle applies to individual classroom interviews in order to keep the natural flow of conversation and minimize anxiety on the part of the interviewee.

7. As in an OPI, interviewees need sufficient time to think in assessment situations, and teachers should not expect rapid-fire answers to questions. Pauses to think do not necessarily indicate a performance deficit.

The *ACTFL Proficiency Guidelines—Speaking* (ACTFL, 1999) offer ideas for how to construct rubrics at the various proficiency levels. You might examine the IPA rubrics for the interpersonal mode of communication to see the proficiency-based criteria for rating performances: language function, text type, communication strategies (quality of engagement and interactivity and clarification strategies), comprehensibility, and language control.

As teachers prepare for assessing oral interpersonal communication, they will want to plan multiple opportunities for formative assessment, such as paired interviews, information-gap and jigsaw activities, and role-plays. An effective means of grading these activities is using the "TALK Scores," a method for monitoring and evaluating group speaking activities, presented in Appendix 8.9. Conducting oral assessment in the classroom poses feasibility challenges, particularly in cases of larger classes. In planning for oral assessment, the teacher might consider the following alternatives: (1) assess pairs of learners using audiotape; (2) assess groups of four or five learners using videotape; (3) manipulate the scheduling of the assessment—e.g., assess only part of the class orally on each thematic unit, making sure that at the end of the grading period every learner has the same number of oral test grades, or conduct oral assessment over the course of several days so that part of the class is assessed each day; or (4) while a group of learners is being assessed orally, engage the rest of the class in an interesting reading or writing task.

Implications for Program Assessment. Teachers should also plan for summative assessments to track students' progress in achieving proficiency levels; an OPI-like format for individual interviews would work well in this regard. Rubrics similar to those used for an IPA are effective in assessing the skills that are required for satisfactory performance at each level of proficiency. An example of a summative assessment based on the OPI and the SOPI is the Pittsburgh Public Schools Oral Ratings Assessment for Language Students (PPS ORALS), an online testing program that makes large-scale oral testing feasible, as well as easy to create, administer, and rate (Fall, Adair-Hauck, & Glisan, 2007). The impetus for this type of assessment was to determine whether students were reaching the district-wide goal of *Intermediate-Low* (labeled *Proficient* on their scale) in speaking and to track their progress in oral proficiency through the grade levels. This assessment is a semi-direct and computer-mediated speaking test that mirrors the format of both the ACTFL OPI and CAL's SOPI: warm-up, level checks, probes at a higher level, and a winddown. Students complete 10 tasks so that a large enough speech sample is obtained while still enabling the test to be administered during a typical 40-minute class period. District world language teachers have created a bank of open-ended tasks for the test bank, and they are trained to rate the speech samples of students from their colleagues' classes. The PPS ORALS feature two levels of the test: The Proficient Level Test assesses Novice through Intermediate-Low levels and the Distinguished Level Test assesses through the Intermediate-High level (Fall et al.). Between 2003 and 2006, over 6,000 students were assessed using the PPS ORALS, illustrating that large-scale oral testing is feasible as a summative assessment. In Chapter 8, you learned that the PPS ORALS have yielded proficiency results that are similar to those reported in other studies using the OPI—i.e., that students with four years of language study generally demonstrate Intermediate-Low to Intermediate-Mid oral proficiency. On the *Teacher's Handbook* Web site, see Appendix 11.18 for the PPS Speaking Rubric and a link to more information regarding the PPS ORALS.

www.cengagebrain.com

Teachers should remember that, in a standards-based program, oral interpersonal and presentational communication do not occur in a vacuum, but rather are linked to communication in other modes (as in the IPA and the Interactive Model for Integrating the Three Modes of Communication), as well as to exploration of content in the other goal areas of *SFLL*. The OPI offers many effective ideas for assessing oral communication, and connecting these ideas to the broader issues of standards-based instruction and authentic assessment is likely to result in more effective assessment of learners and of instruction.

Mediating Performance: An Introduction to Dynamic Assessment

In our earlier discussion of a new paradigm for assessment, you were introduced to the term *dynamic assessment*, a form of assessment through which teachers function as mediators in assisting learner performance rather than as independent observers of learner behavior (Lantolf & Poehner, 2004; Poehner, 2008). Since this type of assessment has only recently begun to be explained within the context of foreign language assessment, an introduction to it is provided here and teachers are encouraged to explore additional information as it continues to appear in published SLA research.

The term *dynamic assessment (DA)* was coined by Luria (1961), a colleague of Vygotsky, and was made popular by Feuerstein, Israeli researcher and special educator (Poehner, 2007). However, as Poehner has pointed out, the term *assessment* in DA is understood quite differently from how it is used in traditional assessment in the fields of education and psychology. Whereas traditional assessment entails observing and recording learners' behaviors in order to make generalizations about their abilities (i.e., learners' past linguistic development), assessment in a dynamic context "involves transformation of those abilities through dialogic collaboration between learners and assessor-teachers, or *mediators*," i.e., it contributes to learners' ongoing linguistic development (Poehner, p. 324). Further, it focuses on how the learner responds to assistance, or *intervention*, by the teacher/mediator (Center for Advanced Language Proficiency and Educational Research [CALPER], 2008).

There are two approaches to DA: *interactionist* and *interventionist*. In the *interactionist* approach, the interaction between the teacher/mediator's assistance evolves as the situation demands and is not determined in advance; thus, interactions and types of assistance "vary from person to person, as well as for the same person over time, because individuals have different ZPDs" (Lantolf & Poehner, 2007, p. 49). Additionally, not all learners require assistance on the same feature of the assessment. In the *interventionist* approach, a limited number of prompts is established in advance. Reminders, hints, and leading questions are given point values according to how explicit or implicit they are. The more explicit the mediation, the further the learner is from achieving independent performance; on the other hand, the less help a learner needs, the closer he or she is to being able to self-regulate and perform without a mediator's support.

In comparing these two approaches to DA, Lantolf and Poehner (2007) note that the interventionist approach is particularly useful for assessment of large numbers of students since the assessment can be scored and results compared. Interactionist DA may be a better alternative for classroom-based formative assessment, for example during group work or individual tasks where teachers can provide individualized assistance. What needs to be remembered is that both forms of DA must be conducted in interesting contexts where the goal is for students to actively create meaning with language, rather than just "get the right answer." Additionally, although all of the current work on DA deals mainly with assisting students with grammatical forms, it can also be applied to many other aspects of language learning, such as interpreting text, exploring cultural comparisons, and developing deeper understandings of academic content in content-based lessons. The *Teacher's Handbook* Web site contains links to two Web sites that feature information regarding DA.[15]

www.cengagebrain.com

Implications for FL Assessment.   For foreign language teachers who want to move beyond simply assessing what students can do alone and are interested in the potential of assessment to support the ongoing linguistic development of their students, DA has a place in their approach to assessment. Given that all assessments must have clearly defined goals, dynamic assessment should be used as a supplement to other forms of assessment rather than as a substitute for existing procedures (CALPER, 2008). Although work on DA for foreign language classroom contexts is still in its infancy, the following are several implications for how teachers might begin to incorporate it into their assessment practices:

1. Teachers could compare the amount of assistance needed on an initial DA test to determine progress made as a result of the mediation.
2. Teachers could use DA in individual oral testing in order to provide mediation when needed as a student performs an oral task. The score on the assessment could take into account the number of mediation moves required and the degree of implicitness or explicitness.
3. Teachers could use DA to assist individual learners while they cooperatively carry out presentational writing tasks such as essays, brochures, and letters.
4. Teachers could implement DA within the IPA format, particularly with the interpretive and interpersonal tasks.

In sum, dynamic assessment holds much promise for bringing instruction and assessment together. Hopefully, future research on DA will shed light on how this form of assessment can support and contribute to learners' L2 communicative language abilities.

Assessment in a dynamic context contributes to learners' ongoing language development.

Planning for Classroom Assessment

The following are guiding principles that should assist foreign language teachers as they plan for assessment in a standards-based classroom.[16] Each principle is further exemplified by a listing of sample assessments that were presented in this chapter. This listing of principles and sample assessments also serves as a summary of the key points presented in this chapter.

1. Instruction and assessment should be mirror images of each other. (formative assessments, IPAs, CATs)
2. Assess learner progress by means of multiple measures that encompass both formative and summative assessments. (self-assessments, portfolios, IPAs)
3. All assessments must be contextualized and feature meaningful use of language. (IPAs, authentic assessments, performance-based assessments)
4. Performance-based assessment should have a central place in the assessment plan. (IPAs, authentic assessments, performance-based assessments)
5. Use the *ACTFL Proficiency Guidelines* and the *ACTFL Performance Guidelines for K–12 Learners* to frame descriptions of performance and set expectations. (IPAs)
6. Consider working toward more authentic and standards-based assessment formats. (IPAs)
7. Consider the value of rubrics to measure student performance when performance-based, authentic, and/or standards-based assessments are used. (IPAs, authentic assessments, performance-based assessments)
8. Consider the importance of empowering students in tracking their own progress, selecting and reflecting on their own work samples, making improvements in performance, and providing feedback about the instruction they are receiving. (self-assessments, portfolios, interactive homework, CATs) (adapted from Duncan, 2000)
9. Experiment with ways to layer dynamic assessment over some of the existing assessments in order to continue to foster learners' development into the future and more effectively merge instruction and assessment. (DA, IPAs)

TEACH AND REFLECT ·

NCATE

EPISODE ONE
Analyzing and Adapting a Traditional Test

ACTFL/NCATE 5.a. Knowing Assessment Models and Using Them Appropriately

TESOL/NCATE 4.a. Issues of Assessment for English Language Learners; and 4.c. Classroom-Based Assessment for ESL

Task One: Analyze the following traditional test given to a French I class. Why is it considered "traditional"? Explain, using the following questions as a guide:

1. Is there a context? If there is none, what context could be applied?
2. What knowledge and/or skills are being evaluated?
3. How is the learner asked to use the target language?
4. Does the test address standards-based competencies? Explain.
5. Why is this test not considered performance-based, authentic, integrative, or interactive?
6. What might this test reflect concerning the classroom practices of the test designer?

Chapter 6 Test: French I

Name _____

I. Write the French equivalents for the following numbers:

1. 23 _____
2. 46 _____
3. 69 _____
4. 72 _____
5. 95 _____

II. Complete the following sentences with the present tense of the infinitives:

1. (descendre) Nous _____ en ville.
2. (attendre) La famille _____ un autobus.
3. (vendre) Un homme _____ des sandwiches.

III. Change the present-tense sentences below to the near future using _aller_ + infinitive.

1. Nous arrivons de France. _____
2. Il va de Paris à Chicago. _____

IV. Give the French translations for the words and expressions below.

1. tomorrow _____   3. next week _____
2. next Wednesday _____   4. tonight _____

Task Two: Now, on a separate sheet of paper, adapt this test to make it contextualized and performance-based. Explain how each section will be scored.

NC&TE_____

EPISODE TWO
Adding an Authentic Dimension to a Performance-Based Assessment Task

ACTFL/NCATE 5.a. Knowing Assessment Models and Using Them Appropriately

TESOL/NCATE 4.a. Issues of Assessment for English Language Learners; and 4.c. Classroom-Based Assessment for ESL

1. Analyze the following oral performance-based assessment task in which learners are asked to use the target language in order to communicate meaningful information. Make a list of the global functions, information, vocabulary, and grammatical points learners would have to use to complete the following task:

Describe yourself orally: tell your name, age, where you're from, and where you live now. Describe your academic major and career plans, as well as your interests or hobbies. Tell about any job that you currently have and/or other activities on which you spend your time.

2. Now adapt this task to make it authentic according to the criteria for task authenticity presented earlier in the chapter (Wiggins, 1998; Wiggins & McTighe, 2005). Think of which elements you need to add to the task in order to make it reflect a real-world situation. You might start by asking yourself, "In what settings do people find themselves having to provide autobiographical information?"

www.cengagebrain.com

TECHNO FOCUS: In this chapter you read about the use of PPS ORALS in the Pittsburgh Public Schools to assess the effectiveness of the district's world languages program. Teachers who participated in this program used PowerPoint to develop proficiency-based tasks for their students to practice. To see a sample of these tasks in French, German, Hebrew, Italian, Japanese, and Spanish, go to the Web site http://www.pps.k12. pa.us. Then type "World Languages" in the search box; this will take you to a Google search results page where you should then click on "Pittsburgh Public Schools / World Languages." Then click on "proficiency practice," select your language, and look at the tasks for various levels of proficiency.

a. Select one level of proficiency and compare the tasks the students are asked to engage in as they develop their proficiency.

b. The Pittsburgh world language teachers also developed situations for communication, called sit-comms, to be used in daily practice to prepare students for the PPS ORALS. To see how to use the sit-comms, go to http://www.pps.k12.pa.us. Then search for "World Languages"; then click on "FLAP dissemination," then click on "oral proficiency practice – situations for communication"; then on the PDF file entitled "Sit-comms: When? Why? How?" Look at some of the sample sit-comms in the other links on that page. Keeping in mind the process of backward design, how do you think the sit-comms relate to the assessment tasks for the level you selected in **a.** above?

c. Now go back through the site until you find the button for "course syllabi" on the left menu; select from high school, middle school, or elementary school, and then the course level you think most likely matches the proficiency level you selected for tasks a and b above. Examine the syllabus in these areas: goals, performance benchmarks, student assessment, and the rubric for the PPS Proficiency Scale. What evidence of backward design do you see? How is it reflected in the assessment instruments, in the tasks the students perform to practice, in the performance benchmarks, and in the course goals?[17]

NCATE_____

EPISODE THREE
Designing an Integrated Performance Assessment (K–16)

ACTFL/NCATE 4.a. Understanding and Integrating Standards in Planning; 4.c. Selecting and Designing Instructional Materials; 5.a. Knowing Assessment Models and Using Them Appropriately

TESOL/NCATE 3.a. Planning for Standards-Based ESL and Content Instruction; 3.b. Managing and Implementing Standards-Based ESL and Content Instruction; 4.a. Issues of Assessment for English Language Learners; 4.b. Language Proficiency Assessment; and 4.c. Classroom-Based Assessment for ESL

Create an IPA for a class that you are currently teaching or plan to teach. Follow these steps:

1. Select a level for the IPA depending on the approximate proficiency level of your class: Novice, Intermediate, Pre-Advanced, Advanced.

2. Find an authentic text that relates to a possible thematic unit (see Chapter 3). Your text could be a printed text, audio text, or video text. Your text should lend itself to addressing the Cultures and/or Connections Goal Area.

3. Design a series of comprehension tasks using the corresponding Comprehension Guide Template found in Appendix 11.9 on the *Teacher's Handbook* Web site.

4. Create an oral interpersonal task that uses some of the information from the interpretive phase. This task must be one in which two students converse to exchange information or complete a task.

5. Design a presentational task (oral or written) as the culminating activity. Be sure that students are asked to use information from both the interpretive and interpersonal phases as they complete the presentational task.

You may find it helpful to examine the IPA Rubrics found in Appendix 11.8 on the *Teacher's Handbook* Web site as you design these three tasks for your IPA.

Now describe two ways in which you might layer DA over specific IPA tasks. How might you account for DA results in your scoring/grading of the tasks you selected?

DISCUSS AND REFLECT ·

www.cengagebrain.com

See the *Teacher's Handbook* Web site for an additional case study:
Case Study Two: Planning for Portfolio Assessment

NCATE_____

CASE STUDY ONE
Developing Authentic Assessment Tasks and Rubrics

ACTFL/NCATE 4.a. Understanding and Integrating Standards in Planning; 5.a. Knowing Assessment Models and Using Them Appropriately

TESOL/NCATE 3.a. Planning for Standards-Based ESL and Content Instruction; 3.b. Managing and Implementing Standards-Based ESL and Content Instruction; 4.a. Issues of Assessment for English Language Learners; and 4.c. Classroom-Based Assessment for ESL

Mr. Alma teaches Spanish at Bustamante High School in La Plata City. This year he has three Spanish II classes and two Spanish III classes. A teacher for eight years, he has kept abreast of innovations in teaching foreign languages by reading journal articles and attending workshops and conferences. He is active in his local foreign language collaborative and the state foreign language association. Mr. Alma uses the principles of proficiency-oriented instruction when he plans and designs activities, and recently he has experimented with standards-based learning scenarios.

For the past year, Mr. Alma has been trying to develop more effective means of assessing learners' functional use of the language. Last week, he attended a full-day workshop on authentic assessment sponsored by the state foreign language association. Mr. Alma had been integrating performance-based testing into his assessment plan by designing situations in which learners would use the language orally in order to complete a communicative task successfully. However, as he learned at the workshop, while his performance-based tasks were effective in eliciting oral performance, they tended to measure speaking alone, with no integration of other skills; they were seldom designed to include more than two learners; and they did not address standards-based goals. With his new knowledge of and motivation for authentic assessment, Mr. Alma attempts the design of an authentic assessment task to evaluate learner performance in Unit 4 for Spanish II. He uses the authentic performance task template presented at the workshop (CLASS, 1998) in his task design (see Figure 11.20). Here is the task he designs:

Task: You are a writer for your school newspaper, and the editorial team is planning an issue of the paper for the Hispanic community nearest your school. You have been assigned a feature story dealing with a popular Hispanic singer, actor/actress, or sports figure. Your end product will be a magazine story describing the life of the person and will include some photographs. In order to write the story, you need to do the following:

1. Working with two co-writers (classmates), investigate popular magazines to find some popular Hispanic singers, actors/actresses, or sports figures. Use the Internet to access this information quickly. Choose a Hispanic figure of interest to you and your co-writers. (Note: A variation on this assignment would be to have students interview a Hispanic individual who lives in the community and treat him/her as a "famous person.")
2. Find out everything you can about the Hispanic figure through research, using the Internet and other sources. Decide what information each co-writer will be responsible for finding.
3. Have a discussion with your co-writers in order to obtain the information that they found in their research. Decide what details you want to include in your story. Young readers will undoubtedly want to know how the person got started in his/her career and became so famous.
4. Together with your co-writers, write the newspaper story. Make it exciting enough to attract the attention of youth who will want to buy the issue just to read your article!

Mr. Alma's task is a multistage activity that requires various subtasks and opportunities for students to engage in discussion, research, and work together. On the next page is the template distributed during the workshop Mr. Alma attended. He plans to build his scoring rubrics from it.

Ask yourself these questions:

1. What makes this an authentic task according to the criteria set forth by Wiggins and McTighe (2005)?
2. Were opportunities provided for students to practice carrying out a range of tasks likely to be necessary in the real world? Explain.
3. Was there concern for the development of linguistic accuracy? Explain.
4. How does this task address standards-based goals?

To prepare for class discussion:

1. Design a timeline for this task in order to project how much class time will be needed, which parts will be completed out of class, and which aspects will be done individually and collaboratively. What will students submit to Mr. Alma in addition to the final magazine article?
2. Develop a scoring rubric to assess learner performance on this task. Remember to use the criteria on the template. Begin by developing the description of what exemplary task completion would look like for each criterion. Then describe what unacceptable or poor task completion would look like, and then develop the levels in between. Refer to the rubric presented in Figure 11.11 as an example.
3. Now design your own authentic task related to the same thematic unit that you designed in Episode One, Task C, of Teach and Reflect for Chapter 3. Be sure that the task reflects a real-world activity and has a real audience. You may find it helpful to examine the authentic task presented in Figure 11.10 and the one given in this case study. You may also wish to use the authentic performance task template presented in this case study in Figure 11.20. Design a scoring rubric similar to the one presented in Figure 11.11.

FIGURE 11.20 Authentic Performance Task Template

AUTHENTIC PERFORMANCE TASK TEMPLATE

Spanish II: Unit 4 (The World of Work), Grade 10

Achievement Target(s):

Performance Competencies: Discuss work and career; narrate and describe in the past; obtain information.
Content Standards: Communication (1.1, 1.2, 1.3); Cultures (2.1); Connections (3.2): Communities (5.1)

Criteria to Be Used in Assessing Performance:

Impact of Performance: Is the article informative and engaging?
Work Quality and Craftsmanship: Is the article well-designed, effectively written, clear?
Adequacy of Methods and Behavior: Was the student methodological in the process of producing the product? Did s/he conduct appropriate research and keep in mind the audience?
Validity of Content: Is the article accurate? Does it reflect correct information?

Mode(s) and Genre(s) of Performance:

Modes: oral, written, displayed (presentational)
Genres: oral interview, discussion; written interview questions, article; displayed article with photographs

---

Source: Adapted from Center on Learning, Assessment, and School Structure, "Developing authentic performance assessments," 1998. Paper presented at meeting of ACTFL Beyond the OPI Assessment Group. Used with permission.

REFERENCES

Adair-Hauck, B. (1996). Authentic assessment in second language learning. *Pennsylvania Language Forum, 68,* 10–30.

Adair-Hauck, B., Glisan, E. G., Koda, K., Swender, E. B., & Sandrock, P. (2006). The Integrated Performance Assessment (IPA): Connecting assessment to instruction and learning. *Foreign Language Annals, 39,* 359–382.

American Council on the Teaching of Foreign Languages (ACTFL). (1998). *ACTFL performance guidelines for K–12 learners.* Yonkers, NY: Author.

American Council on the Teaching of Foreign Languages (ACTFL). (1999). *ACTFL proficiency guidelines—Speaking.* Yonkers, NY: Author.

American Council on the Teaching of Foreign Languages (ACTFL)/ Weber State University. (2003). *Foreign Language Methods On-Line.* Ogden, UT. Funded by the U.S. Department of Education. Module 10, Theme 3.

Angelo, T. A. (Ed.). (1991). *Classroom research: Early lessons from success. New Directions for Teaching and Learning, No. 46.* San Francisco, CA: Jossey-Bass.

Angelo, T. A. (Ed.). (1998). *Classroom assessment and research: An update on uses, approaches, and research findings. New Directions for Teaching and Learning, No. 75.* San Francisco, CA: Jossey-Bass.

Angelo, T. A., & Cross, K. P. (1993). *Classroom assessment techniques: A handbook for college teachers* (2nd ed.). San Francisco, CA: Jossey-Bass.

Antonek, J. L., Tucker, G. R., & Donato, R. (1997). Interactive homework: Creating connections between home and school. In A. Mollica (Ed.), *Teaching languages—Selected readings from Mosaic* (pp. 169–184). Lewiston, NY: Soleil Publishing.

Barrett, H. C. (1999). *Electronic teaching portfolios.* Retrieved April 12, 2004, from http://www.electronic-portfolios.com/portfolios/site2000.html.

Barrett, H. C. (2000). *The electronic portfolio development process.* Retrieved April 11, 2004, from http://www.electronicportfolios.com/portfolios/EPDevProcess.html#epdev.

Brooks, F. B., Donato, R., & McGlone, V. (1997). When are they going to say "it" right? Understanding learner talk during pair-work activity. *Foreign Language Annals, 30,* 524–541.

Cahalan, M., Ingels, S., Burns, L., Planty, M., & Daniel, B. (2006). *United States high school sophomores: A twenty-two year comparison, 1980–2002* (NCES 2006–327). National Center for Education Statistics, Institute of Education Sciences. Washington, DC: U.S. Department of Education.

Campbell, D. M., Melenyzer, B. J., Nettles, D. H., & Wyman, R. M. (2000). *Portfolio and performance assessment in teacher education.* Boston: Allyn & Bacon.

Carduner, J. (2002). Using classroom assessment techniques to improve foreign language composition courses. *Foreign Language Annals, 35,* 543–553.

Center for Advanced Language Proficiency and Educational Research (CALPER). (2008). *Dynamic Assessment.* Retrieved August 14, 2008, from http://www.dynamicassessment.com.

Center for Advanced Research in Language Acquisition (CARLA) Virtual Assessment Center (VAC). (2008a). *Creating rubrics.* Retrieved August 14, 2008, from http://www.carla.umn.edu/assessment/VAC/Evaluation/p_7.html.

Center for Advanced Research in Language Acquisition (CARLA) Virtual Assessment Center (VAC). (2008b). *Types of rubrics.* Retrieved August 14, 2008, from http://www.carla.umn.edu/assessment/vac/Evaluation/p_6.html.

Center on Learning, Assessment, and School Structure (CLASS). (1994). *Rubrics and scoring criteria: Guidelines and examples.* Paper presented at the meeting of the ACTFL Beyond the OPI Assessment Group. Yonkers, NY: ACTFL.

Center on Learning, Assessment, and School Structure (CLASS). (1998). *Developing authentic performance assessments.* Paper presented at the annual meeting of the ACTFL Beyond the OPI Assessment Group. Yonkers, NY: ACTFL.

Cohen, A. D. (1994). *Assessing language ability in the classroom* (2nd ed.). Boston: Heinle & Heinle.

Curtain, H., & Dahlberg, C. A. (2010). *Languages and children—Making the match* (4th ed.). Boston: Pearson Allyn & Bacon.

Donato, R. (1995). Original unpublished material.

Donato, R., Antonek, J. L., & Tucker, G. R. (1994). A multiple perspectives analysis of a Japanese FLES program. *Foreign Language Annals, 27,* 365–378.

Donato, R., Antonek, J. L., & Tucker, G. R. (1996). Documenting a Japanese FLES program: Ambiance and achievement. *Language Learning, 46,* 497–528.

Donato, R., & Todhunter, S. (2001). *Creating and conducting year-end assessment interviews in a Spanish FLES program.* Presentation at the IUP Spring Methodology conference. Indiana, PA.

Duncan, G. (2000). The standards-based classroom and assessment: The proof is in the pudding. In G. Guntermann (Ed.), *Teaching Spanish with the Five C's: A blueprint for success* (pp. 71–90). Fort Worth, TX: Harcourt College.

Egéa-Kuehne, D. (2004). Student electronic portfolio assessment. In C. Cherry & L. Bradley (Eds.), *Assessment practices in foreign language education* (pp. 19–28). Southern Conference on Language Teaching Dimension 2004. Valdosta, GA: Valdosta State University.

Epstein, J. (1993). School and family partnerships. *Instructor, 103*(2), 73–76.

Fairfax County Public Schools. (1996). *A.S.A.P. Alternative strategies for assessing performance. Foreign Language Program.* Fairfax County, VA.

Fairfax County Public Schools. (1999). *PALS: Performance Assessment for Language Students. Scoring the level one speaking task*. Retrieved April 27, 2004, from http://www.fcps.edu/DIS/OHSICS/forlang/PALS/rubrics/1spk_hol.htm.

Fairfax County Public Schools. (2004). *PALS: Performance Assessment for Language Students. Level one speaking tasks holistic rubric*. Retrieved August 10, 2008, from http://www.fcps.edu/DIS/OHSICS/forlang/PALS/rubrics/pdfs/Level%201%20Speaking%20Tasks%20Holistic%20Rubric.pdf.

Fall, T., Adair-Hauck, B., & Glisan, E. W. (2007). Assessing students' oral proficiency: A case for online testing. *Foreign Language Annals, 40,* 377–406.

Feuerstein, R., Rand., Y., & Hoffman, M. B. (1979). *The dynamic assessment of retarded performers: The learning potential assessment device, theory, instruments, and techniques*. Baltimore: University Park Press.

Gay, L. R. (1987). *Educational research: Competencies for analysis and application*. Columbus, OH: Merrill Publishing.

Glisan, E. W., Adair-Hauck, B., Koda, K., Sandrock, S. P., & Swender, E. (2003). *ACTFL integrated performance assessment*. Yonkers, NY: ACTFL.

Glisan, E. W., & Shrum, J. L. (1996). *Enlaces testing program* (2nd ed.). Boston: Heinle & Heinle.

Glisan, E. W., Uribe, D., & Adair-Hauck, B. (2006). *The Integrated Performance Assessment: Linking learning, instruction, and assessment*. Presentation at the Northeast Conference on the Teaching of Foreign Languages. New York, NY.

Glisan, E. W., Uribe, D., & Adair-Hauck, B. (2007). Research on Integrated Performance Assessment at the post-secondary level: Student performance across the modes of communication. *The Canadian Modern Language Review, 64,* 39–68.

Gonzalez Pino, B. (1989). Prochievement testing of speaking. *Foreign Language Annals, 22,* 487–496.

Hadley, A. O. (2001). *Teaching language in context* (3rd ed.). Boston: Heinle & Heinle.

Hammadou, J. A. (1998). A blueprint for teacher portfolios. In J. Harper, M. G. Lively, & M. K. Williams (Eds.), *The coming of age of the profession: Issues and emerging ideas for the teaching of foreign languages* (pp. 291–305). Boston: Heinle & Heinle.

Harper, J., Lively, M. G., & Williams, M. K. (1998). Testing the way we teach. In J. Harper, M. Lively, & M. K. Williams (Eds.), *The coming of age of the profession: Issues and emerging ideas for the teaching of foreign languages* (pp. 263–276). Boston: Heinle & Heinle.

Henning, G. (1987). *A guide to language testing*. Rowley, MA: Newbury House.

Hughes, A. (2003). *Testing for language teachers*. Cambridge, UK: Cambridge University Press.

Indiana University of Pennsylvania. (2008). *Rubric for final oral interview for Spanish 220 Intermediate Conversation and Grammar*. Retrieved August 11, 2008, from http://www.iup.edu/WorkArea/showcontent.aspx?id=45475.

Iowa State University Center for Excellence in Learning and Teaching (2008). *Classroom assessment techniques (CATs)*. Retrieved January 5, 2008, from http://www.celt.iastate.edu/teaching/cat.html.

Kilbane, C. R., & Milman, N. B. (2003). *What every teacher should know about creating digital teaching portfolios*. Boston: Allyn & Bacon.

Kucerik, J. (2000). Let's assess: Connecting students, parents, and teachers. *Learning Languages, 5,* 4–9.

Lantolf, J. P., & Poehner, M. E. (2004). *Dynamic assessment in the language classroom*. CALPER Professional Development Document (CPDD) 0411. University Park, PA: CALPER Publications.

Lantolf, J. P., & Poehner, M. E. (2007). *Dynamic assessment in the foreign language classroom: A teacher's guide*. University Park, PA: CALPER Publications.

Liskin-Gasparro, J. E. (1996). Assessment: From content standards to student performance. In R. C. Lafayette (Ed.), *National standards: A catalyst for reform. The ACTFL Foreign Language Education Series* (pp. 169–196). Lincolnwood, IL: NTC/Contemporary Publishing Group.

Liskin-Gasparro, J. E. (1997, August). *Authentic assessment: Promises, possibilities and processes*. Presentation made at University of Wisconsin-Eau Claire.

Liskin-Gasparro, J. E. (2003). The ACTFL Proficiency Guidelines and the Oral Proficiency Interview: A brief history and analysis of their survival. *Foreign Language Annals, 36,* 483–490.

Luria, A. R. (1961). Study of the abnormal child. *American Journal of Orthopsychiatry: A Journal of Human Behavior, 31,* 1–16.

McNamara, T. (2001). Language assessment as social practice: Challenges for research. *Language Testing, 18,* 334–399.

Messick, S. (1996). Validity and washback in language testing. *Language Testing, 13,* 241–257.

National Capital Language Resource Center (NCLRC). (2004a). *Portfolio assessment in the foreign language classroom*. Washington, DC: NCLRC.

National Capital Language Resource Center (NCLRC). (2004b). *Portfolio assessment in the foreign language classroom*. Washington, DC: NCLRC. Retrieved August 11, 2008, from: http://www.nclrc.org/portfolio/intro.html.

National Standards in Foreign Language Education Project (NSFLEP). (1999). *Standards for foreign language learning in the 21st century*. Lawrence, KS: Allen Press.

Nebraska Department of Education. (1996). *Assessments*. Retrieved August 6, 2008, from http://www.nde.state.ne.us/FORLG/Frameworks/FLFAsses.pdf, p. 46.

North, B. (1993). *The development of descriptors on scales of language proficiency*. Washington, DC: National Foreign Language Resource Center.

Oller, J. (1991). Foreign language testing: Its breadth (Part 1). *ADFL Bulletin, 22*(3), 33–38.

Padilla, A. M., Silva, D. M., & Nomachi, T. (1996). *Portfolio assessment for secondary school foreign language classes.* Paper presented at the meeting of the American Council on the Teaching of Foreign Languages, Philadelphia, PA.

Paulson, F. L., Paulson, P. R., & Meyer, C. A. (1991). What makes a portfolio a portfolio? *Educational Leadership, 48,* 60–63.

Pennsylvania State Modern Language Association (PSMLA). (2003). *PSMLA standards and guide to assessment: What to teach and how to test it!* PSMLA.

Phillips, J. K. (2006). Assessment now and into the future. In A. L. Heining-Boynton (Ed.), *2005–2015: Realizing our vision of languages for all* (pp. 75–103). Upper Saddle River, NJ: Pearson Education, Inc.

Poehner, M. E. (2005). *Dynamic assessment of oral proficiency among advanced L2 learners of French.* Unpublished doctoral dissertation, Pennsylvania State University, University Park, PA.

Poehner, M. E. (2007). Beyond the test: L2 dynamic assessment and the transcendence of mediated learning. *The Modern Language Journal, 91,* 323–340.

Poehner, M. E. (2008). *Dynamic assessment: A Vygotskian approach to understanding and promoting second language development.* Berlin: Springer Publishing.

Poehner, M. E., & Lantolf, J. P. (2003). *Dynamic assessment of L2 development: Bringing the past into the future.* CALPER Working Papers Series, No. 1. The Pennsylvania State University, Center for Advanced Language Proficiency, Education and Research.

Prince George's County Public Schools, MD. (2008). *A process for designing performance assessment tasks.* Retrieved on August 7, 2008, from http://www.pgcps.pg.k12.md.us/%7Eelc/designsteps.html.

Relearning by Design, Inc. (2000). *Rubric sampler.* Retrieved April 5, 2004, from: http://www.relearning.org/resources/PDF/rubric_sampler.pdf.

San Diego State University. (2001a). *Creating a rubric for a given task.* Retrieved August 8, 2008, from http://webquest.sdsu.edu/rubrics/rubrics.html.

San Diego State University. (2001b). *Rubrics for Web lessons.* Retrieved April 5, 2004, from http://webquest.sdsu.edu/rubrics/weblessons.htm.

Sharp, C., Keys, W., & Benefield, P. (2001). *Homework: A review of recent research.* Slough, UK: National Foundation for Educational Research.

Shohamy, E. (1990). Language testing priorities: A different perspective. *Foreign Language Annals, 23,* 385–394.

Shohamy, E. (2001). *The power of tests.* London, England: Pearson Education Limited.

Shrum, J. L. (1991). Testing in context: A lesson from foreign language learning. *Vision, 1,* 3, 7–8.

Spanos, T., Hansen, C. M., & Daines, E. (2001). Integrating technology and classroom assessment. *Foreign Language Annals, 34,* 318–324.

Stansfield, C. W., & Kenyon, D. M. (1992). The development and validation of a simulated oral proficiency interview. *The Modern Language Journal, 76,* 129–141.

Stansfield, C. W., & Kenyon, D. M. (1996). Simulated oral proficiency interviews: An update. *ERIC Digest.* Washington, DC: Center for Applied Linguistics.

Steadman, M. (1998). Using classroom assessment to change both teaching and learning. In T. A. Angelo (Ed.), *Classroom assessment and research: An update on uses, approaches, and research findings* (pp. 23–35). New Directions for Teaching and Learning, No. 75. San Francisco, CA: Jossey-Bass.

Sternberg, R. J., & Grigorenko, E. L. (2002). *Dynamic testing: The nature and measurement of learning potential.* Cambridge, MA: Cambridge University Press.

Surprenant, J. (1998). Un viaje por España. Test item developed for a workshop with CLASS.

Swaffar, J., Arens, K., & Byrnes, H. (1991). *Reading for meaning.* Englewood Cliffs, NJ: Prentice Hall.

Swain, M. (1984). Large-scale communicative language testing: Case study. In S. J. Savignon & M. S. Berns (Eds.), *Initiatives in communicative language teaching: A book of readings.* Reading, MA: Addison-Wesley.

Swender, E. (1999). *The ACTFL oral proficiency interview tester training manual.* Yonkers, NY: ACTFL.

Tierney, R. J., Carter, M. A., & Desai, L. E. (1991). *Portfolio assessment in the reading-writing classroom.* Norwood, MA: Christopher-Gordon.

Tulou, G., & Pettigrew, F. (1999). Performance assessment for language students. In M. A. Kassen (Ed.), *Language learners of tomorrow: Process and promise* (pp. 188–231). Lincolnwood, IL: National Textbook Company.

Vygotsky, L. S. (1986). *Thought and language.* Cambridge: MIT Press.

Wallinger, L. M. (1997). *Foreign language homework from beginning to end: A case study of homework practices in foreign language classes.* Unpublished manuscript. College of William and Mary, Williamsburg, VA.

Wallinger, L. M. (2000). The role of homework in foreign language learning. *Foreign Language Annals, 33,* 483–497.

Walz, J. (1989). Context and contextualized language practice in foreign language teaching. *The Modern Language Journal, 73,* 160–168.

Wiggins, G. (1989). Teaching to the (authentic) test. *Educational Leadership, 46,* 41–47.

Wiggins, G. (1990). The case for authentic assessment. Washington, DC: ERIC Clearinghouse on Tests, Measurement, and Evaluation.

Wiggins, G. (1993). *Assessing student performance.* San Francisco: Jossey-Bass.

Wiggins, G. (1994). Toward more authentic assessment of language performances. In C. Hancock (Ed.), *Teaching, testing, and assessment: Making the connection* (pp. 69–85). Lincolnwood, IL: National Textbook Company.

Wiggins, G. (1998). *Educative assessment.* San Francisco: Jossey-Bass.

Wiggins, G., & McTighe, J. (2005). *Understanding by design.* Alexandria, VA: Association for Supervision and Curriculum Development.

NOTES

1. The term *rubrics* will be defined and described later in this chapter.

2. The term *alternative assessment* is also used to refer to assessment formats that focus on student-generated responses, on performance, and/or communicative language use in authentic contexts.

3. See Tulou and Pettigrew (1999) for models of student performance on the formative writing tasks in French, German, and Spanish. Detailed descriptions of the scoring criteria are included.

4. The word *rubric* comes from the Latin word *ruber* meaning "red." In medieval times, a rubric was a set of instructions or a commentary attached to a law or liturgical service and was usually written in red ink. Rubric came to mean a guideline or something that instructs people (Wiggins, 1998, p. 154).

5. Relearning by Design, Inc. was formerly the Center on Learning, Assessment, and School Structure and was established in 1991 as a not-for-profit corporation in Rochester, New York. Relearning by Design moved to Geneseo, New York, in 1991 and to the Princeton, New Jersey, area in 1994.

6. In the project conducted by ACTFL to develop and field test the IPA, teachers videotaped the interpersonal phase in order to be able to analyze the interpersonal communication for rating purposes and to examine the strategies that students used to communicate with one another. We encourage teachers to videotape at least once or twice during the school year in order to have a record of student progress and to gather student work samples that can be used as exemplars.

7. ACTFL conducts IPA workshops that train teachers in how to design and implement IPAs. Also, individuals may purchase the *ACTFL Integrated Performance Assessment Manual*, available through ACTFL, which has a detailed explanation of the IPA and how to implement it.

8. The Center on Learning, Assessment, and School Structure (1998) coined the term "anthology" to describe an "assessment portfolio" that contains a valid sample of student work, including performance on authentic performance tasks, traditional classroom test results, and scores from standardized testing. An anthology can be used "to base important decisions about student competence, promotion, and graduation on a collection of credible work . . ." (Wiggins, 1998, p. 197).

9. See Campbell, Melenyzer, Nettles, and Wyman (2000) and Barrett (1999) for ideas on how portfolios are used in teacher education programs to document growth in teaching.

10. For additional information about portfolio assessments and worksheets to guide in planning, compiling, and evaluating a portfolio, see Portfolio Assessment in the Foreign Language Classroom, available from the National Capital Language Resource Center (http://www.nclrc.org.).

11. Some researchers make a distinction between electronic and digital formats. Technically, electronic portfolios contain artifacts that may be displayed in analog form (e.g., videotapes) or computer-readable form (e.g., word processing document files). Digital portfolios contain artifacts that have been converted to computer-readable forms (e.g., scanned documents) (Egéa-Kuehne, 2004, p. 22). In *Teacher's Handbook*, the term electronic portfolio is used to refer to either type of digital integration.

12. According to a 2002 study conducted by the National Center for Education Statistics (NCES), 37% of 10th graders surveyed reported spending more than 10 hours weekly on homework, which increased from only 7% in 1980 (Cahalan, Ingels, Burns, Planty, & Daniel, 2006). Wallinger (1997) reports that writing is the primary skill practiced in homework assignments, and that beginning-level assignments tend to be rote practice. Assignments requiring higher-order thinking and allowing for individual expression are reserved primarily for advanced learners. Wallinger (2000) also reports that in her study of 66 schools offering French I in grade 9, students were expected to complete 1 to 1.25 hours of homework in French per week.

13. Other names used for the Minute Paper CAT are "Ticket Out the Door" and "Exit Slips."

14. An online version of the OPI, called the ACTFL Oral Proficiency Interview by Computer (OPIc), was developed in order to deliver electronically and on-demand a test of oral proficiency. The OPIc, delivered via the Internet, is a semi-direct test individualized to the test taker and designed to elicit a 20- to 30-minute sample of ratable speech. For a description of other forms of the ACTFL OPI, see the link to Language Testing International on the *Teacher's Handbook* Web site.

15. Contact the Center for Advanced Language Proficiency Education and Research (CALPER) for a training DVD that provides a printed narrative of the history and practice of DA as well as video examples of mediated interactions and an oral analysis of them. See the *Teacher's Handbook* Web site for a link to CALPER.

16. See the *Teacher's Handbook* Web site for a link to information regarding the National Assessment of Educational Progress (NAEP) in Foreign Languages, which is projected to be administered in Spanish beginning in 2012.

17. Thanks to the members of FR/SPAN 5984 Second Language Acquisition and Pedagogy at Virginia Tech, Fall, 2008, for their suggestions for tasks a, b, and c in this technology focus.

CHAPTER 12

Using Technology to Contextualize and Integrate Language Instruction

In this chapter, you will learn about:

- digital natives and digital immigrants
- new literacies
- Technology-Enhanced Language Learning (TELL)
- using technology to support standards-based instruction
- International Society for Technology in Education (ISTE) standards for students and teachers
- classroom technologies
- multimedia technology in the three modes of communication

- Computer-Mediated Communication (CMC)
- synchronous and asynchronous communication
- simulations
- messaging technologies
- social networks, wikis, blogs
- telecollaboration
- speech recognition
- podcasting/vodcasting
- WebQuests
- distance learning
- proper use of Web sites

Teach and Reflect: Are Your Students Technologically Literate? Helping Students Address the *National Educational Technology Standards;* Examining the Potential Use of a TELL Exercise; Creating a WebQuest

Discuss and Reflect: Teaching Culture Through Photos

CONCEPTUAL ORIENTATION

Perhaps the most convincing reason to use technology in teaching languages is the nature of 21st century students, who are sometimes called *digital natives* (Prensky, 2001) because they have grown up using the Internet and other technological devices;

they are native speakers of the language of computers, video games, and the Internet. Their teachers, on the other hand, are called *digital immigrants* because they did not grow up with such tools, although some have acquired an understanding of them. By the time they graduate from college, today's students will have spent 5,000–10,000 hours viewing video games; 10,000 hours on cell phones; and 20,000 hours watching TV, including YouTube online. They will watch 500,000 commercials and will send 250,000 e-mails and Instant Messages (Prensky, 2008). By contrast, they will spend 5,000 hours reading books. Prensky's terms, digital natives and immigrants, have provided a useful metaphor for talking about those who are comfortable with new technologies and those who are not. However, the difference is not wholly generational, and as any language teacher knows, making distinctions between natives and immigrants may limit the fullness of understanding and richness of experience for both cultures. We may well ask ourselves, "What is so engaging about the media and networked informal learning sites that youth willingly devote hours to participate in them, even . . . where participation involves school-based literacy practices such as compositions, editing, and peer review?" (Black, 2008, p. 600).

The scope of this chapter includes a description of what technology has come to mean for foreign language learners and teachers, information about the standards so that teachers can make good decisions about selecting and using technology, and brief descriptions of some of the research on various technological projects of interest to foreign language teachers. Technology brings new challenges and opportunities more rapidly than *Teacher's Handbook* can keep up with them in print. We have incorporated discussion of technology into the Conceptual Orientation of each chapter, and to show language teachers' use of technology, each chapter contains a Techno Focus in the Teach and Reflect or the Discuss and Reflect section. In this chapter, we will explore the connections between three sets of standards: the *Standards for Foreign Language Learning in the 21st Century (SFLL)* (NSFLEP, 2006), the *PreK–12 Standards for English Language Proficiency* (Teachers of English to Speakers of Other Languages [TESOL], 2006), and the *National Educational Technology Standards (NETS)*, which were developed by the International Society for Technology Education (ISTE) in 2007 and 2008. We will provide examples of successful integration of technology in second language classrooms, a template for building a WebQuest, and a template for a Web-enhanced unit, based on the integrative model described in Chapter 6. We encourage you to explore new technologies and information available on the *Teacher's Handbook* Web site and to incorporate them into your teaching if they enrich the language learning experience you can provide for your students. For detailed support, see the *Teacher's Handbook* Web site for a link to several editorials in the journal *Language Learning and Technology* describing emerging technologies.

www.cengagebrain.com

New literacies. You have seen that *Teacher's Handbook* embraces a sociocultural understanding of language teaching and learning. Being careful to note that literacy is not simply reading and writing, Lankshear and Knobel (2006) offer a sociocultural definition of literacy as "socially recognized ways of generating, communicating, and negotiating meaningful content through the medium of encoded text within contexts of participation in Discourses" with others (p. 64). When we use language in reading, writing, speaking, and listening, we encode oral and written text as members of a socially meaningful group, or as playing a socially meaningful role (Gee, 1996). With this definition, such activities as writing letters, keeping inventories, reading novels, making phone calls, and posting e-mails are considered familiar literacies. Encoded text in these familiar literacies includes handwritten and typed alphanumeric symbols as well as audio texts that we move from one person to another, from place to place. Encoded texts are those that have been rendered in a form that allows them to be retrieved, worked with, and made available independently of the person and context of their origins (Knobel & Lankshear, 2007).

New technologies have enabled us to generate and share communication in encoded texts with others in varied cultural contexts. While we may have thought of text, author, authority, and place as static, now we find they are fluid and can change easily with the advent of Web-enhanced tools. Web 1.0 was the first such venture to be used in schools, with online capabilities such as Ofoto, Britannica Online, personal Web sites, publishing, content management systems, directories and hierarchical taxonomies, and Netscape. In 2001, Web 2.0 became available, with options that enable multiple contributions to materials posted on a Web site. It changed the interaction from a model of passing information in a linear, two-dimensional plane to a model of forming relationships as users invite others to contribute to their Web presence in a three-dimensional space. This enables users to shape and define a fictional personality that can move and function in the virtual world as easily as in the real world. Thus, in Web 2.0, products and activities that result in networks among users have emerged: e.g., Flickr to store photos; Wikipedia for free online encyclopedia information; blogging for sharing ideas; wikis to share ideas and create projects; and Tagging, such as RSS feeds to track interest in Web sites and connect people with similar interests. Multiple persons in interaction with each other using these new technologies can pose intelligent problems, contribute creatively to solutions, and provide authoritative information better than any single communicator.

Thus, among the new conduits of meaning for foreign language learners we find several technological activities that can be managed in order to maximize communication in reading, writing, speaking, and listening among varied cultural contexts. New literacies required to negotiate these activities include being able to find key information in electronically and visually busy pages, knowing how to navigate among Web sites, validating information, selecting and contributing to a blog, authoring a definition on Wikipedia, and remixing music and video with voice to create new meanings.

Despite the mandates and the ever-increasing presence of technology in everyday life, technology use in the language classroom should be embraced only if there are substantial benefits to learners. Martínez-Lage and Herren (1998) caution that "technology is not the panacea for magically improved language learning" (p. 162), but the authors also offer three benefits of planned and purposeful use of technology:

1. Better and more effective use of class time, i.e., some activities can be moved outside the classroom, thus extending contact time with the target language (TL) and reserving classroom time for interpersonal face-to-face interaction between teachers and learners;
2. Individualized learning, i.e., technology enables learners to work at their own pace and level; and
3. Empowerment, i.e., teachers can provide more authentic, current, and culturally rich materials to the learners, and learners can gain new control over their own learning.

Raby (2007) reports that five learner conditions need to be present in order to derive benefits from working in technological environments: "desire to acquire a foreign language, take and keep the initiative for work, maintain one's effort until the work is completed, regulate and evaluate one's work through interactions with electronic tools and interactions with peers and tutors, [and] renew the learning experience" (Raby, 2007, p. 185).

In recognition of these potential benefits, recent standards movements have incorporated the use of technology. The *SFLL* include technology as one of the elements in the weave of foreign language learning, and the International Society for Technology Education (ISTE) provides standards for technologically literate students and teachers in the *National Educational Technology Standards for Students (NETS-S)* (ISTE, 2007) and the *National Educational Technology Standards for Teachers (NETS-T)* (ISTE, 2008). Technology helps us reach our goals for teaching and learning languages in ways that we cannot do otherwise. It provides interesting and unique ways to connect language learners to the TL and culture, building communities of language learners around the world. It enables learners to establish interaction with peers who are learning the language and with experts and native speakers of the TL they are studying. It helps improve student motivation and enthusiasm for language learning. It brings the world into contact with the learner, transforming a teacher-centered classroom into a learner-centered one (Maxwell, 1998). As a professional, you will find technology useful if you apply the basic principles of good language instruction to the selection of technology tools and materials for your students.

In the related literature, you will see the term *Computer-Assisted Language Learning (CALL)* used to refer to the application of computers in teaching and learning languages. Although much of the use of technology in teaching and learning involves a computer, not all technological applications require a computer. We will use the term *Technology-Enhanced Language Learning (TELL)* to refer to all uses of technology in language education. Subsumed within *TELL*, then, are the terms *CALL* and *Computer-Mediated Communication (CMC)*, referring to those applications in which a computer is involved. We will use the term *Computer-Assisted Autonomous Language Learning (CAALL)* to refer to settings in which learners work with technologies on their own, apart from a classroom setting, albeit on tasks that may be related to their class assignments. We will also use the term *Information Communication Technology (ICT)* to refer to those technologies that assist in sharing information for purposes of communication, a use of technology that is particularly relevant to language learning. Examples of ICT are cell phones, instant messaging services, testing, podcasting, YouTube, blogs, wikis, and others.

 TELL is Technology-Enhanced Language Learning. ▬

Technology Connects the Standards

Using technology in the language classroom provides a unique way to connect the goals for language learning as described in the *SFLL*. In earlier chapters of *Teacher's Handbook*, you learned about an important goal of language learning: to know how, when, and why to say what to whom. You also learned about the motivation that students may have for reaching this goal, and about how the Five Cs represent the content goal areas in broad terms. You saw how sample performance indicators can measure learners' progress in what they know and are able to do with the TL.

Learning scenarios that accompany the standards show how teachers might address the *SFLL* in their instruction. These scenarios contain a broad richness of circumstances specific to each instructional setting that goes beyond the standards, and, indeed, forms a backdrop, or a fabric, on which the standards may operate. This fabric has been called the *weave* of curricular elements, and appears in Figure 2.3 in Chapter 2 of *Teacher's Handbook* (NSFLEP, 2006, p. 33).

The elements of this weave are unique to each instructional setting, yet each setting contains all of them: the language system, cultural knowledge, communication strategies, critical-thinking skills, learning strategies, other subject areas, and technology. All of these elements of the weave can be brought together through the use of technology to thread rich curricular experiences through the language learning process. Through the use of online chats and electronic pen pals (key pals), teachers can present students with living, vibrant people who use the TL for daily communication. Cultural elements, from daily table manners to world-famous paintings and literature, can be represented on the Web in authentic visual and print dimensions. Authentic audio or video can be delivered in person by the teacher, by classroom guests, by the students themselves, or via technology with video/audio tape recordings, DVDs, CD-ROMs, and the Internet. Technology mediates language learning by forming a bridge between the authentic world and the language learner. Through the purposeful use of technology, teachers can connect all five of the goal areas for productive language learning experiences.

 Through the purposeful use of technology, teachers can connect all five of the goal areas for productive language learning experiences. ▪

Using Technology to Support Standards-Based Instruction

As you saw in Chapter 1, learners use tools such as language and social interaction as mediation between themselves and their environments. Learners can also use technological tools to mediate their interactions with a body of content knowledge, e.g., French culture and literature, and their interactions with native speakers of French. For example, imagine that native English-speaking students of French have been assigned a task to engage with members of an online discussion forum facilitated through the French magazine *Le Monde*. Two students post requests for help with their use of French and receive responses politely asking them to post statements that contribute to the political and cultural issues debate, which is the topic of the forum. They do not post anything of this sort and, as a result, they receive no further responses. By contrast, another student opens his posting by apologizing for his French, saying that he is a learner of the language. He then posts comments on racism and cultural imperialism. Using a mix of English and French, he is able to maintain a presence on the forum, and receives a number of supportive responses from members of the forum, who assist him as he improves his French. Furthermore, his teacher monitors his participation in the archives of the forum and provides additional support when needed. This scenario, based on a study by Hanna and de Nooy (2003), presents an example of more capable peers who assist a learner in his Zone of Proximal Development (ZPD), working in real communicative situations. It illustrates that "participation in open and thematically oriented Internet communities supports the very process L2 education ostensibly seeks to provide, such as the use of language as a resource for ongoing identity formation and personally meaningful communication in the service of goals that extend beyond 'practice' or 'learning' in the restrictive senses associated with institutional settings" (Thorne, 2008, p. 434). Technology is a mediational tool that enables learners to expand their oral expression, acquire new language, learn about cross-cultural perspectives, and explore new content.

 What is the role of mediation in language learning? Refer to Chapter 1. ▪

 Technology is a mediational tool that enables learners to expand their oral expression, acquire new language, learn about cross-cultural perspectives, and explore new content. ▪

Research on TELL in Language Classrooms

"Why do we still know so little about the efficacy of the technologies into which we have invested much energy, time, and money in our teaching and learning endeavors?" (Felix, 2005, p. 269). This question summarizes the frustration felt by researchers and teachers alike in the search for definitive answers to the ways in which technology works in L2 classes. There are many reasons why we don't have more concrete answers and why the picture is fragmented (Arnold, 2007). First, most studies are individual, based on a single software program and one researcher's study of the variables of interest for a specific location. Technology continues to expand and refine in ways that can affect learner use and learning outcomes before studies can be mounted and results reported. There are often design flaws in studies that need to be worked out in subsequent studies. There are few meta-analyses that look across studies aimed at similar variables, and there are virtually no mega studies using large populations. Grgurovic and Chapelle (2007) are currently developing a database for studies on L2 learning and technology, but to date the most we can say is that technology enhances the face-to-face experience by providing additional exposure to the language at times other than the class hour, and in different environments than the class setting. Since early research focused on reading and writing, at this time we have enough research to confirm that the use of technology has a small but positive effect on L2 reading, writing, and vocabulary development. There is also evidence of positive effects on student perceptions of CALL, motivation, computer literacy, target culture awareness, and classroom climate in terms of enjoyment and comfort (Felix, 2005).

Research on the use of technology in language classrooms has focused primarily on the potential for improved learning of language skills and the appeal technology holds for students. Products designed for language learning in the 1980s and early 1990s were of the drill/practice type, and language educators quickly moved beyond them to embrace more interactive approaches to technology in such programs as those described later in this chapter. Use of the Internet and other interactive tools captured the attention of language teachers and researchers alike. Teachers felt assured that their students would not be disadvantaged by the use of technology in tandem with class activities, or even by replacement of some of their classroom time with technologically enhanced activities (Adair-Hauck, Youngs, & Willingham-McLain, 1998).

Researchers now study the ways in which technology can be used to help learners acquire aspects of language, such as vocabulary, or skills, such as reading or writing. Much of the research is analysis of specific software and its effectiveness for learners. However, studies have shown that technology in general has been used effectively to:

- facilitate the acquisition of vocabulary (Beauvois, 1997; Chun & Plass, 1996; Davis & Lyman-Hager, 1997; Grace, 1998; Jones & Plass, 2002; Pennington, 1996);
- support input-rich activities through use of reading assistant software, integrated video, and the Internet (Cononelos & Oliva, 1993; Davis & Lyman-Hager; Garza, 1991);
- facilitate increased writing through use of writing assistant software, e-mail, and chat rooms (Chikamatsu, 2003; Oliva & Pollastrini, 1995; Suh, 2002);
- provide intelligent computer-mediated feedback (Cononelos & Oliva; Kern, 1995; Nagata, 1993, 1999; Nagata & Swisher, 1995; Smith, 2003);
- enhance listening comprehension and retention (Jones & Plass; Murphy & Youngs, 2004);
- facilitate exploration of authentic language use through e-mail or the Internet (Oliva & Pollastrini; Sotillo, 2005); and
- enhance student motivation (Borrás & Lafayette, 1994; González-Bueno & Pérez, 2000; Lee, 2002; Masters-Wicks, Postlewate, & Lewental, 1996) (adapted from Cubillos, 1998).

In addition, Internet-mediated technologies have contributed to the enhancement of use of authentic materials in two ways. First, they have encouraged dialogue among individuals and partner classes across the globe, allowing learners to interact with expert and native speakers of the languages they are studying (Belz, 2007; Belz & Thorne, 2006; Furstenberg, Levet, English, & Maillet, 2001; Johnson & English, 2003; Kramsch & Thorne, 2002). Second, researchers have shown that computer-mediated tools have enabled learners to develop meaningful use of language in social interactions (Belz) by helping them to notice aspects of the TL and their native language that communicate politeness and to negotiate sociocultural significance and expectations. For example, Ishihara (2007) studied the benefits of a Web-based program with authentic video viewing, explanatory prose, input boxes for student response, feedback, and comparison of their responses to correct responses. Results showed that students who experienced the Web-based program were more aware of differences in how to appropriately apologize, e.g, giving many repetitions of the apology in Japanese; and in giving and receiving compliments, e.g., using expressions appropriate to the interlocutor and shifting the credit to others in Japanese.

As teachers decide to deliver instruction with the assistance of a technological tool, they use their knowledge of the Five Cs and the weave of other curricular elements particular to their circumstances to select suitable technological products and techniques. These questions might be used as a guide when considering inclusion of technological tools in instruction:

1. How will the use of technology help students learn aspects of the language in meaningful contexts?
2. What can students presently do with the language in each of the five *SFLL* goal areas?
3. What standards within the goal areas will this tool help students address?
4. How will the tool help students use language in response to those standards?
5. What process will learners experience in using the technology and associated materials? What elements of the weave will be included?
6. What will this tool cost in terms of time, planning, supplies, and equipment? List costs.
7. What are the alternatives? Is there a high school, college, university, library, or other agency nearby that could help by providing services or resources?
8. Is this the best way to accomplish the objectives of instruction and to meet the needs of students?

Implementing Technology Standards in the Classroom

The International Society for Technology Education (ISTE) (2002) developed the *National Educational Technology Standards (NETS)* to describe what students, teachers, and administrators should know and be able to do with technology in the service of instruction, available on the *Teacher's Handbook* Web site in Appendices 12.1 and 12.2. According to Terry (2000) and ISTE, approximately 90–92% of state education agencies have used the *NETS* to help teachers and students develop competency in using technology. An indication of the importance of technology for language learning is the inclusion of it in the *SFLL* as part of the weave, and TESOL (2007) has developed draft versions of technology standards, available in Appendix 12.3 on the *Teacher's Handbook* Web site.

The *National Educational Technology Standards for Students* (*NETS-S*) (ISTE, 2007) describe what students need to know and be able to do with technology as shown in Appendix 12.1 on the *Teacher's Handbook* Web site. Standards for teachers (*NETS-T*) (ISTE, 2008) then build on the student standards, and standards for administrators and school technologists are derived from the teacher and student standards. In this chapter we focus our attention on technology standards as they relate to student performance.

To help us understand what good standards-based instruction using technology looks like, the student standards are the foundation for the teacher standards, which describe what teachers need to know and be able to do in order to enable learners to use technology. The teacher standards provide profiles of technologically literate students, examples, and conditions for learning. The *NETS-S* state that students need to know how to use technology for these purposes:

1. creativity and innovation
2. communication and collaboration
3. research and information fluency
4. critical thinking, problem solving, decision making
5. digital citizenship
6. technology operations and concepts (ISTE/*NETS*, 2007).

Relative to the above list of ISTE/*NETS* standards, an illustrative example is Project *Fresa* (Spanish for *strawberry*) involving students in a fifth-grade class in an elementary school in California who decided to explore the lives of workers in the strawberry fields that surrounded their school (Warschauer & Ware, 2008).[1] The students were 80% Latino and spoke Spanish and English with varying degrees of proficiency. They examined the local and state standards of learning for their grade level so they would know what they were supposed to learn in that grade and formulated their research questions about strawberry field workers based on what they had observed in their families and friends who worked in the strawberry fields. They conducted interviews in Spanish and English, then translated them; learned how to construct graphs and how to display data; and built PowerPoint presentations accompanied by photos and their own poetry in Spanish and English. They invited guest speakers to their classroom to learn about environmental issues and workers' rights; they began an e-mail exchange with students in Puerto Rico who lived in a coffee-growing area to make comparisons in conditions for workers in coffee- and strawberry-growing regions; and they invited parents and government officials to view their multimedia presentations. In this year-long project, the students addressed all six *NETS-S* standards. They addressed the first standard, creativity and innovation, by working together in a group to create original works, such as their poetry and their multimedia presentations. They demonstrated that they understood the second standard of communication and collaboration by working in project teams to solve problems and by interviewing workers and their families in multiple languages. They addressed the third standard, research and information fluency, by locating, evaluating, and synthesizing information from digital sources on the Internet and by processing data in graphs and charts. They addressed the fourth standard, critical thinking/problem solving/decision making, as they planned and managed their activities to complete the project. They addressed the fifth standard, digital citizenship, by continuing their project beyond their fifth-grade year in collaboration with students in a coffee-growing region. They demonstrated that they understood the sixth standard, technology operations and concepts, by selecting and using applications effectively and productively as they showed their project on the Web and to real audiences in their community. Teachers, administrators, and researchers can reflect upon a project like this one to see how it enables language students (ELLs or learners of Spanish) to integrate the technology standards with the Five Cs, specifically Communication in the presentational mode, Connections, and Communities (NSFLEP, 2006).

Multimedia Technology in the Three Modes of Communication

Multimedia involves the convergence of text, audio, sound, still pictures, animation, and video into a single presentation. Opportunities abound for integration of multimedia instruction with the three modes of communication outlined in the *SFLL*. In the next section, we will explore additional uses of multimedia and use of computers for communication. Use of technologies should be guided by the principles for teaching as outlined in *Teacher's Handbook*—that is, clear goals for tasks, use of writing/reading/listening/speaking process, authentic materials, and constructivist approaches to learning. Teachers who recognize the ways in which technology can address individual student needs will then guide their students in how to use and benefit from technologies.

Figure 12.1 provides an overview of various types of technologies and how each type of technology might be used to address one or more of the *SFLL* modes of communication. As you explore this chapter, you might also consider how each type of technology can also address the Cultures, Connections, Comparisons, and Communities *SFLL* goal areas.[2] We have not attempted to include every possible technology or every possible use in this chapter. We have selected those technologies that offer the greatest potential for addressing standards-based goals in the foreign language classroom. The charts in Figures 12.1 and 12.2 are designed to help you organize your

FIGURE 12.1 Types of Technologies at a Glance

TECHNOLOGY	INTERPRETIVE COMMUNICATION	INTERPERSONAL COMMUNICATION	PRESENTATIONAL COMMUNICATION
Overhead projector, document cameras, whiteboards, smartboards	x		x
Multimedia centers	x	x	x
YouTube and other video	x		x
Reading and listening assistants	x	x	
Writing assistants	x	x	x
Simulations and games such as Second Life	x	x	
Courseware such as Blackboard, Scholar, Moodle	x	x	x
VoiceThread, chat rooms, threaded discussions	x	x	x
Listservs	x	x	x
E-mail, UserNets, bulletin boards, blogs, wikis	x	x	x
Facebook, MySpace, Ning	x	x	x
PowerPoint			x
WebQuests	x		x
Distance learning	x	x	x

Source: Shrum & Glisan, 2010, original material.

FIGURE 12.2 Pedagogical Principles and TELL

PEDAGOGICAL PRINCIPLE	L2 IMPLEMENTATION	TECHNOLOGY-ENHANCED IMPLEMENTATION
1. Use authentic materials; edit the task not the text, and provide scaffolding (Chapters 3, 6)	Task-based language teaching, target tasks, sequencing of tasks	Simulations, tutorials, personal computers, word processors, spreadsheets
2. Elaborate and enrich input	Exposure to varied sources	Web sites, communication via Web searching, Skype, YouTube
3. Promote learning by doing	Negotiation of meaning, interactional modification	Blogging, Instant Messenger, video conferencing
4. Encourage inductive (chunk) learning	Implicit instruction (Chapters 6, 7)	WebQuests
5. Focus on form, error correction	Learners notice and adjust their interlanguage (Chapters 2, 8)	Quia, ilrn, Eduspace, Tell Me More, other commercially available programs
6. Respect learner's individual developmental processes	Timing pedagogical intervention to learner's ZPD	Branching and adaptivity in programming
7. Promote cooperative/ collaborative learning	Negotiation of meaning, interactional modification	Problem solving, computer-mediated communication with tasks designed to foster interaction
8. Individualize/differentiate instruction (Chapters 5, 10)	Analyze needs of learners and provide differential strategies and tasks	Branching, adaptivity in programming; autonomous learning

Source: Based on "Optimal psycholinguistic environments for distance foreign language learning," by C. Doughty and M. H. Long, 2003, *Language Learning and Technology*, 7(3), 50–80, pp. 52, 53. Reprinted by permission.

thinking about types of technologies and to consider how teachers can use them to encourage communication between students, between students and the teacher, and between students and expert speakers of the language in the classroom and beyond.

Replacing or Supplementing the Chalkboard/Blackboard

Chalkboards, blackboards, whiteboards, and overhead projectors are examples of low-level technology that teachers and students use every day. Some teachers use clipboard-sized whiteboards so that individuals or groups of students can write simultaneously while whole-class focus is on the larger whiteboard on the wall. Next-generation chalkboard replacements are digital and include document cameras and touch-sensitive smartboards connected to a computer that projects materials onto a screen, a television monitor, or a whiteboard. Images projected in these ways also can be broadcast as part of a distance-learning class. See View and Reflect on the *Teacher's Handbook* Web site for a description of how an EFL elementary school teacher used Activboard®, a commercially available smartboard.[3]

www.cengagebrain.com

Multimedia Center

Formerly called language laboratories, modern multimedia centers are places where several types of technologies are centrally located to allow students to use them in tandem or separately, as individual learners or in pairs or groups. In these centers, clusters of four to eight computers in a circular arrangement with workstation tables allow students to work individually or in pairs at each computer. The computers are networked via a wireless or a physical wiring system to each other and to a central computer or console controlled by the teacher or a laboratory assistant. The console may be mobile so that teachers can move it from classroom to classroom. Wireless communication unleashes the possibilities of a multimedia center, freeing students and teacher from a central location, allowing them to become satellites that can access the central information from a handheld or laptop computer in the center or beyond its walls.

As an alternative to a lab or multimedia center, some schools have equipped "smart" classrooms with technology that includes access to the Internet, an LCD projector, a document camera, and a VCR/DVD player. Many teachers use one or more small cassettes, CD players, or iPods/MP3 players in their classrooms. One can be used for listening as a whole class, or several can be placed around the classroom as listening stations with individualized directions for singles, pairs, or small groups of learners. Students who have their own CD/portable cassette players or iPods/MP3 players can practice at home. Many publishers provide packaged or downloadable materials with each textbook for use at home. Several publishers make available online learning programs to accompany their textbooks. See Chapter 6 for ways to use authentic taped materials to enhance listening practice for students, and Chapters 8, 9, and 11 for ideas about using these materials in written and/or oral form.

Multimedia centers allow access to authentic speech and video recorded live in the target country, with follow-up tasks in which students engage in contextualized two- or three-way communication with other students, the teacher, or native speakers. Use of a multimedia center can assist in the development of auditory literacy through listening and using tapes; visual literacy through pictures and use of presentational software as described in Chapter 9; verbal literacy through use of language; and computer literacy through use of computers, VCRs, DVD players, and other equipment in the center.

There are a number of programs available for language learning that can be delivered online, downloaded, or installed via CD-ROM. These programs can be useful for professionals in business, for home schooling, for additional practice, or for adding less commonly taught languages to a curriculum. See the *Teacher's Handbook* Web site for links to programs developed by Transparent Language®, Auralog's Tell Me More®, and Berlitz®. Each of these products has adopted an approach to language learning compatible with its products.

www.cengagebrain.com

The following sections of this chapter describe materials that can be incorporated into a multimedia center. On the *Teacher's Handbook* Web site, see Appendix 12.4 for a rubric to evaluate multimedia projects (see also Chapter 9) and Appendix 12.5 for a software evaluation rubric.

Video

Videotext as a contextualized segment can be in the form of film, videotapes, laser disks, CD-ROMs, DVDs, or YouTube. These are texts in the sense that they provide an authentic piece of language and culture that can be presented in written form as well as visual form. The videotext may contain elements of language use and cultural authenticity; it is possible to access all Five Cs of language learning through videotext. As we elect to use videotext, we should apply the same criteria and careful judgment in selection and use as we apply to reading or listening texts. See Chapter 6 for a thorough treatment of the use of videotexts. Also, see Appendix 12.6 on the *Teacher's Handbook* Web site for ways to use a videotext for language learning. Appendix 12.7 on the *Teacher's Handbook* Web site provides clues to give students help in their comprehension as they watch a videotext.

Computer-Mediated Communication (CMC)

Computer-mediated instruction is when the computer serves to facilitate or enhance communication between the learner and the source of authentic material, between learners, or between machines. A product of computer-mediated instruction is CMC. Like other forms of communication, CMC involves use of all three modes of communication: interpretive, interpersonal, and presentational. CMC offers several widely acclaimed benefits:

1. more equal and increased participation than in regular face-to-face classroom-based activities (Blake, 2000, 2005, 2006); Bump, 1990; Cahill & Catanzaro, 1997; Chun, 1994; Kelm, 1992; Kern, 1995; Sullivan & Pratt, 1996; Warschauer, 1996);
2. positive attitudes (Beauvois, 1994);
3. greater student empowerment with decreased teacher control and dominance (Kern; Sullivan & Pratt);
4. wider variety of discourse functions and interactional modifications (Chun; Liu, Moore, Graham, & Lee, 2002; Sotillo, 2000); and
5. opportunities for intracultural communication (Abrams, 2003, 2006).

Two forms of CMC have been developed: synchronous and asynchronous. In synchronous CMC, people communicate with each other in real time and simultaneously, e.g., Instant Messenger, online chat rooms, Skype. In contrast to synchronous CMC, *asynchronous* CMC is carried out by participants at different times, e.g., bulletin boards, forums, e-mail, threaded discussions, and blogs. In the following sections, we will briefly discuss specific formats of synchronous CMC (a task-based project among native and nonnative speakers, and simulations) and asynchronous CMC (e-mail, listservs, UserNets, newsgroups, blogs or Weblogs, telecollaboration, bulletin boards, forums, and threaded discussions). Some forms of CMC may be synchronous or asynchronous, depending on the use made of them, e.g., chat rooms.

 In *synchronous* communication, people communicate with each other in real time and simultaneously. *Asynchronous* CMC is carried out by participants at different times.

Synchronous CMC

Chun and Wade (2004) point out that synchronous CMC has been shown to be an effective tool for improving speaking and communication (Abrams, 2006; Beauvois, 1998; Blake, 2005, 2006; Lee, 2002, 2004), for developing grammatical competence (Pellettieri, 2000), and for developing discourse competence (Chun, 1994). In 2004, Lee described a study designed to explore the sociocultural aspects of synchronous communication. Well-designed online discussion activities were used by native-speaker and nonnative-speaker students at two U.S. universities. One of these online discussions included questions about how information technologies influence students' personal, family, and community life, and affect the exchange of ideas. Through questionnaires, oral interviews, and analysis of the online discussions, Lee (2004) found that the online format provided a kind of ZPD through which native speakers and more capable peer students provided scaffolding that facilitated the use of correct forms, the negotiation of meaning, and the development of ideas. The research is clear that benefits from CMC are not presumed to come from the tools and programs themselves, but rather from how CMC is used to promote meaningful interaction and real cultural reflection (Blake, 2007), thus placing primary importance on the teacher's role as designer of appropriate tasks and feedback.

Benefits from CMC are not presumed to come from the tools and programs themselves, but rather from how CMC is used to promote meaningful interaction and real cultural reflection.

What benefits of synchronous electronic communication do you recall from Chapter 8?

www.cengagebrain.com

There is evidence to indicate that students who use synchronous CMC engage in negotiation of meaning in ways similar to that of oral interpersonal communication (Beauvois, 1997; Blake 2000; Warschauer, 1996). Smith (2003) studied the chatscripts of 14 nonnative students studying intensive English. Students were given two types of tasks, jigsaw (cleaning up a garage) and decision-making (shopping for a gift), and were expected to participate actively in solving the problems presented to them. On the *Teacher's Handbook* Web site, see Appendix 12.8, "Jigsaw Task: Messy Garage," and Appendix 12.9, "Decision-Making Task: Gift." Results showed that 34% of the turns taken by the participants were used to negotiate meaning, while the other turns were used to complete the various tasks the students had been given. Smith mapped the CMC interaction in ways similar to those found in face-to-face communication. Undoubtedly, the negotiation of meaning that takes place in CMC has the potential to help students in their spoken, face-to-face negotiations as well.

In addition to showing that students do negotiate meaning in CMC, some research has compared the quality of the increased output that students create in synchronous CMC vs asynchronous CMC. Abrams (2003, 2006) studied how students used synchronous and asynchronous CMC in preparation for subsequent face-to-face communication. In the 2003 study, students who used synchronous CMC did produce more language, but there was no difference in the quality of the language as measured in richness of vocabulary and in the variety and complexity of sentences compared to use of asynchronous CMC. In the 2006 study, Abrams documented how task-based CMC in this format of *intracultural communication* can produce benefits similar to those found in face-to-face communication. Recall the Hanna and de Nooy (2003) study cited earlier in this chapter, in which the learner of French was able to negotiate meaning using his interlanguage of French and English to make statements about racism and cultural imperialism and to continue to participate in an asynchronous manner with peers in France.

In sum, learners use synchronous CMC to communicate in a written interpersonal mode with others. Learners negotiate meaning and complete interactive tasks in ways similar to face-to-face communication despite the absence of body language. As you read the next section on asynchronous CMC, keep in mind the elements of synchronous CMC.

How does the important concept of negotiation of meaning function in synchronous and asynchronous CMC?

Simulations. As teachers help students to develop interpretive and interpersonal communication using computer software, they may find that the next step in creating presentational communication lies in the use of the scaffolding features built into simulations, where the technology provides a "scaffold of a situation and enough information to function within it ... participants make decisions and negotiate their way through the simulation as they might if it were real" (Levine & Morse, 2004, p. 139). Jones (1982) identifies the necessary elements of a simulation as (1) a simulated environment or a representation of the real world; (2) structure, created by rules of conversational interaction; and (3) reality of function or the learner's "reality" perspective of the event. Students are often familiar with simulations because many computer games are simulations.

The computer appears to understand language and produces it meaningfully, thus supporting the learner's "reality" perspective of their interactions with the simulation and others involved in the situation (Crookall & Oxford, 1990). For example, a murder is committed in a small town in the target country. Students see a map of the town with salient buildings and descriptions of key characters who knew the victim. Students are given roles to follow, such as reporter, detective, family members, and town citizens. As they participate in the investigation, students make decisions about whom to interview, what to say, and how to respond. The computer then incorporates their input, resulting in varied consequences and opportunities for further use of language to solve the murder.

Several programs have been developed that respond to selections and choices that students make as they solve daily problems; for example, renting an apartment in *A la rencontre de Philippe* (Furstenberg & Malone, 1993); moving about on site in foreign countries in *Montevidisco* (Larson & Bush, 1992); and relating TL literature to their own lives in *Ciberteca: Una carta a Dios* (Chun & Plass, 1999). Other examples along the lines of solving a murder mystery include *Un Muertre à Cinet* (Oliver & Nelson, 1998), *Un Misterio en Toluca* (Oliver & Nelson, 1997), and *Mord in Mainz Murder Mystery* (Goulding & Jorth, 2004).

The idea of living in virtual communities finds expression in the 3D virtual world of Second Life (Rosedale, 2003), where users become residents who build the community itself. For foreign language learners, it provides an alternative immersion world in which authentic language and materials can be used while learners practice real-life situations. Sweley (2008a) describes the work of Gloria Clark, a faculty member at Penn State who developed a virtual world on Second Life for her Spanish students, who were able to conduct daily life interactive communicative activities such as making a purchase, asking directions, or taking a cab—all from the comfort of their classroom, dorm room, or anywhere else they could get on the Internet. Benefits include the use of authentic materials; opportunities to interact in real time or asynchronously with real people; the ability to create a new identity, an avatar; and obvious appeal to students who enjoy such 3D gaming technology. At this time, Second Life is far from universal acceptance, and may be more suitable for post-secondary applications since participants must be over 18. Participation is mostly free, but there is a charge for certain kinds of participation and for owning "land" in which to create the virtual world. There is also a considerable time investment in setting up the virtual world and linking it to course goals and assignments.

Cohen and Sykes (2007) are exploring the use of 3D virtual worlds by using *simulated immersive environments* in which learners adopt an avatar, adopt gestures, and perform communicative speech acts. Other players can enter the spaces, as can the teacher, and the interactions are individualized and use multiple modes of visual and auditory presentation.

Asynchronous CMC

E-mail and Other Messaging Technologies. The first type of asynchronous CMC was e-mail. Chun and Wade (2004) report that e-mail is an effective means of promoting L2 linguistic development (González-Bueno, 1998; González-Bueno & Pérez, 2000), for promoting C2 learning (Cononelos & Oliva, 1993; Jogan, Heredia, & Aguilera,

2001), and for exploring linguistic and cultural learning within constructivist and social contexts. The *SFLL* make numerous suggestions for use of e-mail; a sample progress indicator for grade 4 regarding presentational communication is: "Students give short oral notes and messages or write reports about people and things in their school environment and exchange the information with another language class either locally or via e-mail" (NSFLEP, p. 45).

These technologies are a form of written interpersonal communication. The tone and register used is like that of spoken language, with the added advantages reported by students that they have time to look at their messages, to think about how their correspondence will be understood, and to make revisions. The rapid-fire turn-taking of speaking face-to-face that intimidates slow or timid learners is modified by the "window" on the screen in which learners can type their comments, taking the time to monitor them and make them as correct as possible.

E-mail, IM, and text messaging can be incorporated into real tasks that teachers ask learners to perform. For example, to practice realistic communication, a student can write the instructor an e-mail message explaining an absence from school, justifying the seriousness of the excuse, requesting information about the assignment for the next class day, and apologizing for being absent. Many teachers report that students find that these modes of communication offer an accessible means of gaining the floor and making conversational gambits, thus creating more opportunities to practice the TL.

Listservs. An outgrowth of e-mail is the use of teacher listservs, which enable teachers to communicate with a group and allow the group members to communicate with each other to share information about assignments or class progress. Many professional listservs are available to teachers, as shown in the Preliminary Chapter. Two popular international listservs are FLTEACH, administered by LeLoup and Ponterio (2004) at SUNY Buffalo, and LLTI (Language Learning and Technology International), a listserv maintained at Dartmouth University. On these listservs, teachers exchange information about texts, materials, teaching techniques, learner difficulties and successes, and sources of new information. Some listservs allow members to receive a compilation of e-mail messages, called a *digest,* instead of receiving each message individually. See the *Teacher's Handbook* Web site for information on how to subscribe and access information from these listservs.

www.cengagebrain.com

UserNets, Newsgroups, Electronic Bulletin Boards, Weblogs (Blogs), and Wikis. These forms of communication are extensions of listservs that operate on the Internet and are usually established around a topic of common interest. These resources can be effective when teachers monitor them, as reported by Cononelos and Oliva (1993), who successfully used Italian UserNet groups and e-mail to enable learners to access Italian news broadcasts and write to each other via e-mail about the weather and news in their areas.

Blogs, originally called Weblogs, are Web sites on which participants post asynchronous commentaries that often take the form of brief essays or expository writing and that allow visitors to post comments. The sites are usually maintained and monitored by the individual. Cooke-Plagwitz (2004) reports successful use of blogs in learning German. Because comments on a blog are archived in chronological order, users can see how the discussion develops. Precursors to blogs were chat rooms and threaded discussions that were used successfully to enable students to reach deeper levels of intercultural understanding and to make more use of negotiation of meaning (Chun & Wade, 2004; Weasenforth, Biesenbach-Lucas, & Meloni, 2002). See the *Teacher's Handbook* Web site for links to information on how to set up a blog and to the *Raison d'Être Project,* which makes effective use of a monitored blog. See also an example of a teacher's use of a blog in Chapter 6, Teach and Reflect.

Wikis are social networks in which many users can contribute to or edit the content of the site. A wiki is a collection of interlinked Web sites in which a community of users posts information and edits each other's and their own work. The largest wiki is Wikipedia, which according to its Web site has over 7 million articles in 200 languages. In this wiki, students can look up in the TL definitions and explanations of terms and concepts. Wikipedia has established guidelines for posting and editing work. Use of wikis has begun to change our views of authority, authorship, and information exchange. As in all cases of Web use, teachers should caution students to verify information by seeking multiple sources, using trusted sites, and blending online materials with published refereed sources. Teachers and students can set up their own wikis using a source such as PBworks, a Web-based company that believes that setting up a wiki should be "as easy as making a peanut butter sandwich" (Weekly, 2005).

Telecollaboration. Some researchers have developed an intercultural approach to CMC, describing it as "online communication used to bring together language learners in different countries in order to carry out collaborative projects or undertake intercultural exchanges" (O'Dowd & Ritter, 2006). Two projects, *Cultura* (Bauer, deBenedette, Furstenberg, Levet, & Waryn, 2006) and the Images, Myths, and Realities Across Cultures (IMRAC) by Johnson and English (2003), continue to provide insights into how French-as-foreign-language learners in the U.S. and ESL learners in France communicate synchronously and asynchronously via e-mail, chat rooms, and videoconferencing. In these projects, which have had considerable longevity in the world of technological projects, teachers draw attention to the ways in which language reflects deeply ingrained values. Ongoing interaction among the students enables them to use humor and irony and to see how their own use of language is received by others. Belz (2002) describes a project in which German students preparing to become teachers of ESL and American students of German language read parallel texts and viewed films and interacted via e-mail, synchronous chat, and Web site development. For example, one topic was intercultural/interracial first love, and the groups developed Web sites to represent the terms *beauty, love,* and *racism* in each of their cultures. Belz found that the groups held varying valuation of the language they were learning, perceptions of their proficiency, and of work ethics. For example, the German students held a perception that the American students would not be proficient in German, and the Americans held the perception that the German students were lazy or not very attentive to their electronic tasks. Belz shows how the project developed intercultural awareness in students and suggested ways to prepare students for the experience.

Social networks. With the advent of multiple-user domains, students have found it very appealing to connect with peers through social networks such as Facebook, MySpace, Ning, and Friendster. These mediated networks allow for creation of fictional personalities as well as display of real information. The pedagogical value of these mediated social networks remains unexamined, and students and teachers should be cautious about revealing real identities on the Web (Cohen & Sykes, 2007).

Translation devices/services. Translation programs and online dictionaries are available for free and for purchase online, but to use them effectively, students need the guidance of their teachers. Translator programs operate by analyzing the structure of a sentence in the source language and then generating a sentence based on the rules of the TL. The difference between learning a language and using a translation is in the complexity of language and its ability to express human thought with precision.

Translation programs are intended to provide the general idea, or "gist," of an article or document, or the most common use of a given word or expression. Students may use these programs inappropriately for their homework or their compositions. The translation may lack cultural knowledge and the application of higher-level thinking that students would normally apply to creating their own expression. Students should be cautious in using a translation program because such programs do not help them learn how to interpret and communicate in the TL. Similarly, use of an online dictionary should be limited to consulting the meaning and proper use of a word, while also verifying that the correct meaning or connotation of the word is selected, e.g., *fly*—the insect or the verb. Teachers can maximize student learning in the use of translation programs by illustrating selected errors in a brief lesson (Sweley, 2008b). See the *Teacher's Handbook* Web site for suggested sources for online dictionaries.

www.cengagebrain.com

In sum, both synchronous and asynchronous CMC offer rich environments in which learners negotiate meaning and explore new ways to learn language. As technologies develop, learners and teachers are likely to continue to make effective use of them to develop interpersonal and presentational communication.

Empowering Learners Through Web-Enhanced Technologies

Among the types of multimedia instruction, we will discuss here a commercially available product that tracks speech and two teacher-created products: podcasts and WebQuests.

Speech recognition. There are several commercially available products that assist learners in mastering linguistic forms at the phoneme, word, or sentence level. One flexible program that features a speech recognition tracking device as one of its many features is Tell Me More® by Auralog. Figure 12.3 shows the screen that learners see when they record their spoken phonemes, words, and sentences following a native speaker prompt. Learners see the waveform of the native pronunciation, followed by the waveform of their own speech, with a blue indicator line that draws their attention to the intonation of the native speaker. Red indicates where the learner's speech does not conform to that of the native speaker. The bar at the right shows on a scale of 1–7 how closely the learner's speech matches the native speaker's. The teacher can set the level of tolerance in the scale to allow for more variation for beginners than for more advanced learners. The bar displays an unlimited number of repetitions and enables learners to review all of their attempts. Through the tracking device, both the learner and the teacher can see what progress is being made. A 3D animation of the lips, teeth, and tongue also assists learners in mimicking the model.

This software also provides learners with a conversational stimulus, offers several possible correct responses, and branches to alternative rejoinders depending on which response the learner selects. Then the learner views a video in which the actors' utterances are replaced by those made by the learner so that the learners can see themselves in the scenario of the video action. To date, no software exists to allow learners to create their own utterances without having to follow a model, but the future for speech recognition software holds great promise in this area.

Language learning solutions like the one described above are sometimes designed for Computer Assisted Autonomous Language Learning (CAALL), and others are designed to work within a classroom setting in a blended, or hybrid, learning environment, with or without distance-learning components. Most programs of this type have made use of

FIGURE 12.3 Speech Recognition Tracking Device

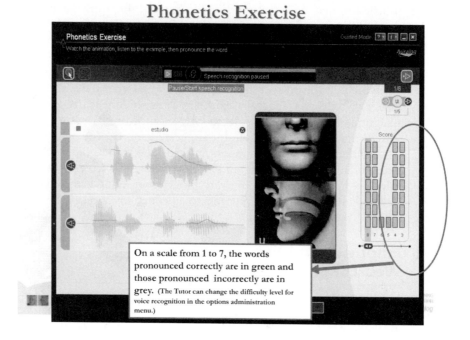

Phonetics Exercise

Source: Tell Me More® Version 9, 2007. Auralog, Inc. Used with permission from Tell Me More, www.tellmemore.com.

artificial intelligence and include a speech recognition device that aids in pronunciation improvement, e.g., DynEd® and Tell Me More®.

Blake (2007) reports that the use of such autonomous language learning solutions holds promise, perhaps because, as Raby (2007) pointed out, they increase learner motivation to complete a task by providing a "hook" to interest the students, an alternative solution when the learner gets "stuck," and evidence of success that increases the learner's self-esteem. Barr, Leakey, and Ranchoux (2005) studied the effects of the use of Tell Me More® and found that there was no difference between the group using the technology and those not using it. However, they attributed this lack of difference to the time it took to accustom learners to the technology, time that was not spent learning language in those groups. The authors speculated that other differences may emerge once learners are more familiar with the program. Shrum (2007) reported that 95% of students improved when the use of Tell Me More® was implemented for 20 hours outside the classroom but in conjunction with class assignments. Part of the problem in assessing the value of CMC is that studies tend to compare CMC with face-to-face instruction, when in reality, and as pointed out by Prensky (2008), the learning process itself may be very different when accomplished through CMC or through face-to-face instruction, making comparison less meaningful. For example, in a face-to-face classroom, a given learner has a limited number of opportunities to speak during a 50-minute class period, even if the class is organized in a highly communicative manner, making use of pair and group work. In a 50-minute period of work on a software program, the learner has an opportunity to respond every time there is an interaction with the software. Additional research on CAALL language learning solutions will help inform teachers and learners about how to use them most beneficially.

Podcasting/Vodcasting. By using an iPod or an MP3 player, teachers can create multimedia lessons using video, audio, music, and voice. This form of practice is popular with students because they can use it any time or any place, whenever they use their iPod or MP3 player. Teachers can create their own materials at http://www.boxpopuli.com, by using iTunesU at http://www.apple.com/itunesu, or by using a number of sites mentioned on the *Teacher's Handbook* Web site. See the Teach and Reflect section of Chapter 2 for a podcast created by a teacher. In another example, using iWeb, iTunes, and her iPod, Miller (2007) composed a podcast that combined photos of student work created around a cultural unit, added music, and students' own voices talking about the project. She posted the podcast on her Web site so that students can download it for listening and speaking practice.

www.cengagebrain.com

Rich Internet Applications. The Center for Language Education and Research (CLEAR) at the University of Michigan provides a "toolkit" to assist teachers in creating their own Web-enhanced materials. At its Web site, http://clear.msu.edu/clear/store/, teachers can create a *mashup*, that is, the site provides space and instructions so that teachers can combine many sources from several Web pages into one. They can also create their own "better than YouTube" videos, develop and post podcasts, create worksheets to match their textbooks, embed conversations into their Web pages, and create their own interactive language practice exercises. The site contains video tutorials to show how to use all of the tools in the Rich Internet Applications.

MERLOT. Another location that teachers can trust for peer-reviewed materials is the Multimedia Educational Resource for Learning and Online Teaching (MERLOT) at http://www.merlot.org. Their World Languages site is supported by ACTFL and contains recommendations and reviews of software and other technologies, assignments for students, as well as links to other sites and ways to connect with colleagues and other experts.

WebQuests

March (2003) defines a WebQuest as "a scaffolded learning structure that uses links to essential resources on the Web and an authentic task to motivate students' investigation of a central, open-ended question, development of individual expertise and participation in a final group process that transforms newly acquired information into a sophisticated understanding" (p. 1). WebQuests are based on principles espoused in *Teacher's Handbook:* constructivist approaches to learning, cooperative learning activities, and scaffolding within a sociocultural learning environment. After completing a WebQuest, a learner will have deeply analyzed a body of knowledge, transformed it in some way, and demonstrated an understanding of the material by creating something that others can respond to, online or offline (Dodge, 1997). WebQuests in foreign languages have been documented as a set of systematic inquiry-based tasks that can enhance learner autonomy (Luke, 2006) and engagement in class. Levi Altstaedter, and Jones (2008) showed that WebQuests enhanced student motivation, particularly with regard to the cultural values they learned and their expectations for learning. According to these researchers, WebQuests improved students' use of language and their understanding of the Comparisons and Cultures goals of the *SFLL*. There are six parts to a good WebQuest:

1. an *introduction* that sets the stage and provides some background information; it may also capture the learners' interest;
2. a *task* that is doable and interesting;

3. a set of *information sources* needed to accomplish the task;

4. a description of the *process* or strategies students should use to complete the task;

5. some *guidance* on how to organize the information acquired, e.g., guiding questions, concept maps, timelines, cause-and-effect diagrams, flow charts; and

6. a *conclusion* that brings closure to the quest, reminds students of what they have learned, and encourages them to reflect on the experience and to extend it into other domains (adapted from Dodge, 1997).

Students typically respond well to WebQuests that assign them (1) a role to play, e.g., scientist, detective, reporter; (2) persons with whom to interact, e.g., classmates, key pals, fictitious personalities; and (3) a scenario in which to work, e.g., "You've been asked by the Roman Senate to brief them on the recent conquests of General Caesar" (adapted from Dodge, 1997). Students can be asked to synthesize conflicting opinions and put multiple sources of data together to discover the non-relevant and the relevant factual information, take a stance and defend it (Dodge, 1998). A short-term WebQuest can be accomplished in one or two class periods, whereas a long-term WebQuest may last a month or two. You will find examples of WebQuests for all subject areas as well as help in designing them at http://webquest.sdsu.edu, a site managed by Bernie Dodge, originator of the concept.

www.cengagebrain.com

In this section, we will help you set up a WebQuest. See Figure 12.4 for the WebQuest Design Process in a flow chart, and visit http://webquest.org/index.php, where you can click on "create WebQuests" for additional guidance. On the *Teacher's Handbook* Web site, you will also find links to the *"Idea Machine"* to help generate ideas for a WebQuest, and *"WebQuest Taskonomy"* to generate tasks for inclusion in a WebQuest.

In the first phase of creating your WebQuest, you will *explore the possibilities* by brainstorming ideas for a topic and by drawing a web much like those you used in Chapters 4 and 5. Use March's (2004) *"Idea Machine,"* and then chunk or cluster similar ideas together by looking for relationships among topics or people involved in the topics. Brainstorming about survival, for instance, produced the results found in Figure 12.5. Identify what your students may already know about this topic, and identify the learning gaps in which they need help. Consult the *Teacher's Handbook* Web site to see what other information and WebQuests are available. After you have found a topic, identified the learning gaps, and inventoried the resources, you are ready to uncover the questions. This box in the flow chart in Figure 12.4 is in a different shape because here you must decide whether or not you have enough information to create a WebQuest, and whether or not the topic lends itself to this strategy.

The second phase in creating your WebQuest is *designing for success*; you will shape, outline, and draft your WebQuest. Establish the learning outcomes and identify the transformations you want to happen as your students work with information they learn as input. By working through the tasks you designate, the learners are transformed, the material is transformed, and perhaps you are transformed. To ensure this transformation, identify tasks that students will perform in the WebQuest by coordinating your goals in the *SFLL* or the *PreK–12 English language proficiency standards* with the *"WebQuest Taskonomy"* (see Dodge, 2004). For instance, in the "Survival" topic in Figure 12.5, students who investigate the social studies aspects of earthquakes might hypothesize that government has provided inadequate help to people dealing with the psychological stress of rebuilding after an earthquake. They could then write the hypothesis, along with their justification of it, in a short e-mail or videotape sent to an expert, asking for verification or feedback. Here they use their skills in written or oral presentational communication, seeking real-world feedback.

FIGURE 12.4 The WebQuest Design Process

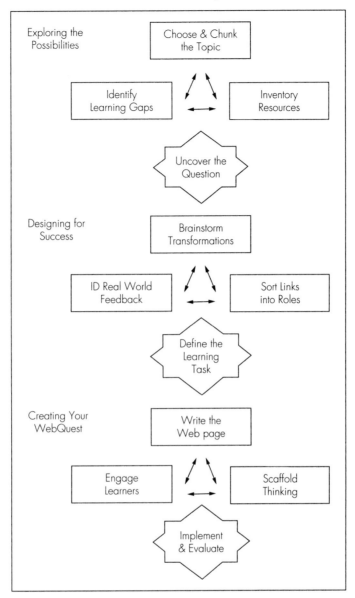

Source: From March, T. (1998). The WebQuest design process.
Retrieved on October 2, 2008, from http://www.tommarch.com/
writings/wq_design.php. Used by permission.

Also in the second phase, you determine the roles students will play. The roles should be real-world jobs that students can learn about from the links you give them so that they can speak and behave like a person who holds that job. For instance, in earthquake survival, one student role might be the public health officer who designs educational pamphlets or gives interviews with news media about the dangers of disease after an earthquake. Another real-world role would be that of a news reporter, in which students ask questions, probe, and summarize. In these roles, students use interpretive, interpersonal, and presentational communication. The WebQuest could be designed to address the Communities standard by setting up a student role in which a public health

FIGURE 12.5 Web for "Survival"

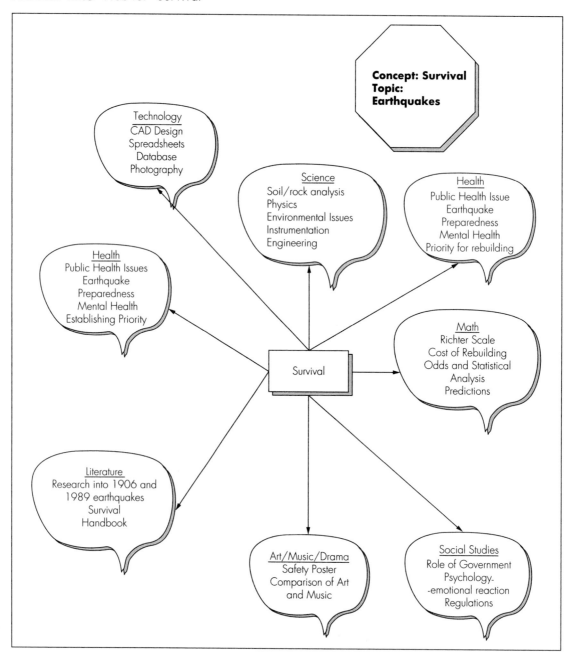

Source: March, T. (2004). The idea machine. Retrieved October 15, 2008 from http://tommarch.com/learning/idea_machine.php. Used by permission.

worker brings cautionary information in the TL for a community of recent immigrants who live in the earthquake region. To encourage more negotiation, you might impose some conditions on the roles, e.g., the newspaper reporter's home has been destroyed in the earthquake, and he/she may use intonation, vocabulary, and language structures to show empathy when interviewing victims of the quake.

Having worked through these aspects of the second phase, you are at another decision point: defining the learning task. Here you must ask yourself questions about whether the available resources on the Web address learning gaps and support the roles, whether you have identified the kinds of higher-level thinking in which you want students to engage, and whether the activities in the WebQuest mirror the real world.

In the third phase, you use all of the resources you have gathered to *create your WebQuest's* main Web page and write an introduction that *hooks* the students into the activities and sends them to the Web pages you have already found for them. You create activities for students to do using the TL, and they create a final product or products to show what they have learned.

In creating a WebQuest, keep in mind the standards-based goals you have for student learning and provide appropriate grouping activities as well as motivational elements. Make sure that you provide supportive scaffolded instructions and write a conclusion that wraps up the WebQuest. Also be sure to include a measure of evaluation of students' performance (see Chapter 11) and an evaluation of or feedback on the WebQuest itself. See Teach and Reflect, Episode Three in this chapter for a WebQuest design assignment. Also see the *Teacher's Handbook* Web site for a listing of sample WebQuests in a variety of languages and for Web sites that provide additional resources and templates.

www.cengagebrain.com

Proper Use of Web Sites. When teachers direct their students to Web sites for projects, they should have confidence in the accuracy of what is contained on those sites. In Appendix 12.10 on the *Teacher's Handbook* Web site, Alexander and Tate (1999–2005) offer a set of questions that can act as guidelines in evaluating Web sites to be used in instruction. They focus on these aspects of a Web site: authority, accuracy, objectivity, currency, and coverage.

Teachers should be aware that students often use materials from Web pages without proper citation. Teachers can avoid these issues by teaching students proper citation format, making them aware of how to take notes and incorporate reference material, asking for an annotated bibliography, and structuring assignments so that students must apply their own higher-level thinking skills as described in Bloom's taxonomy (see Chapter 3). See the *Teacher's Handbook* Web site for recommended Web sites on citation formats and strategies to avoid inappropriate use of information.

Distance Learning

The technological applications discussed previously in this chapter refer to settings in which teachers make use of the technology within their classrooms, or for assignments students can complete outside of class. *Distance learning* refers to classroom situations in which the teacher and the students are in different classrooms. Students could be learning foreign languages from a teacher in another school, town, state, or country via a computer network or a telephone system National Council on State School Supervisors for Languages (NCSSFL, 2002). Distance learning offers a solution for the limited availability of foreign language teachers, especially for students in remote locations, for school districts wishing to expand their offerings to include elementary school programming or advanced placement/upper-level offerings, and for school systems wishing to offer language classes with small enrollments. Distance learning may be delivered via several means. The longest-standing form of distance learning is *teleconferencing*—teacher-to-class, student-to-student, or class-to-class. Teleconferencing requires instructors and learners to be in specific places on a consistent basis, much like a regular classroom, only they are not in the same room. *Hybrid* or *blended* courses are those in which teacher and students meet face-to-face once or twice a week with additional work on the computer during the rest of the week. In some cases, the independent work is *drill and kill* used for mechanical practice, reserving class face-to-face time for communicative practice. In other cases, the computer projects include online monitoring, teacher-led conversations, and native-speaker interviews. Results of a study of distance-learning programs indicate that the online group had higher scores than the traditional classroom group on grammatical accuracy and syntactic complexity in writing assignments (Chenoweth, Jones, & Tucker, 2006). In addition, students in the online group in this study spent one hour less per week studying, presumably because the online portion of the class was more efficient, enabling students to reach goals more quickly. In another study, Blake and Delforge (2007) found that there were no differences in student outcomes for discrete grammatical knowledge between online and regular classroom groups. To date, research on the effectiveness of distance learning in foreign languages is specific to sites, programs, and software used, which makes it difficult to make generalizable conclusions. Nevertheless, administrators view it as a cost-effective way to reach larger or formerly inaccessible audiences. This is an area that promises to draw researchers' attention in the future.

www.cengagebrain.com

Successful distance-learning programs are based on development of proficiency, within standards-based approaches to language instruction. Decisions about use of distance-learning technology generally do not rest with the classroom teacher, but rather with school boards, or institutions of higher education. See the *Teacher's Handbook* Web site for additional sources and Appendix 4.2 for the NCSSFL "Position Paper on Distance Learning in Foreign Languages," which approaches the impact of distance learning on students from the decision-maker's perspective.

What the Future of Technology Holds for Language Learning

Among the technologies we might expect in the future are better speech-recognition programs that can understand what language learners say despite their imperfect use of language; additional user-friendly ways of merging text, video, and sound; faster response times in CMC; and development of authentic speech that can be incorporated into teacher-created materials. As we study the kinds of communication produced through technology, we will perhaps expand our understanding of virtual space and human communication, e.g., how to signal and understand emotions or gestures in online communication (Warner, 2004).

Each year, Educause,[4] a leading source of vision, information, and resources related to education and technology, publishes a report called the *Horizon Report* (Johnson, Levine, & Smith, 2009) that describes which technologies will emerge in the next year, in the next two to three years, and in the next four to five years. In 2009, two of the report's critical challenges to the education community as a whole were that (1) "There is a growing need for formal instruction in key new skills, including information literacy, visual literacy, and technological literacy" (p. 5); and (2) "Students are different, but a lot of educational material is not" (p. 5). These challenges are particularly relevant to teachers of language who would do well to keep in mind Levy's seminal study on technology and foreign language learning (1997), which suggests that there should be a fit between teachers' philosophies of language teaching and learning, and what they see as the capabilities of technology to facilitate language learning in their classrooms. Throughout *Teacher's Handbook*, you have seen that the use of authentic texts helps students as they learn how to communicate, to make connections and comparisons, and to understand cultures and communities. As teachers shape language learning and cultural content around the five goal areas outlined in the *SFLL* and the goals of the *PreK–12 English language proficiency standards*, they often find that technology helps them make the TL and its texts more real and accessible to learners. Not only are students the receivers of the language and culture, but they are also now capable of direct interaction with peers and experts who use the language daily. Because learners are already active users of communicative technologies, they can easily use these technologies to negotiate meaning in the TL. Teachers have at their fingertips the language learning standards to guide them and the technology to connect the real world to the classroom in ways never before possible.

Whatever the future may hold, two things are certain: Technologies and technologists have much to offer language teachers, and language teachers are eager to find new ways to put technology to work in the service of instruction.

TEACH AND REFLECT ···

NCATE____

EPISODE ONE
Are Your Students Technologically Literate? Helping Students Address the *National Educational Technology Standards*

ACTFL/NCATE 2.b. Demonstrating Understanding of Literary/Cultural Texts and Traditions; 3.b. Developing Instructional Practices that Reflect Language Outcomes and Learner Diversity; 4.a. Understanding and Integrating Standards in Planning; 4.b. Integrating Standards in Instruction; 4.c. Selecting and Designing Instructional Materials

TESOL/NCATE 3.a. Planning for Standards-Based ESL and Content Instruction; 3.b. Managing and Implementing Standards-Based ESL and Content Instruction; and 3.c. Using Resources Effectively in ESL and Content Instruction

This episode is designed to enable you to showcase your technological skills in helping your students address the National Educational Technology Standards.

First, re-examine Appendices 12.1, 12.2, and 12.3, to become more familiar with the *NETS-S* for students and *NETS-T* for teachers. Second, refer to the *SFLL*, TESOL's *Technology Standards* (2007) and TESOL's *PreK–12 English Language Proficiency Standards* (2006) to find profiles, learning scenarios, and appropriate standards for the students you teach. Third, compile a list of five Web sites written in the language you teach. The sites should focus on a topic of your choice and can serve as the basis for a lesson you might teach. Include the name of each site, its URL, and the reasons why you chose it. Fourth, apply the guidelines provided by Alexander and Tate (1999–2005) in Appendix 12.10 on the *Teacher's Handbook* Web site to evaluate the quality of the Web sites. Fifth, brainstorm a list of ways in which you might use each site in your lessons. Sixth, show which of the technology standards for students you will address with the sites you have selected and the ways in which you will use them.

www.cengagebrain.com

NCATE____

EPISODE TWO
Examining the Potential Use of a TELL Exercise

ACTFL/NCATE 3.a. Understanding Language Acquisition and Creating a Supportive Classroom; 3.b. Developing Instructional Practices That Reflect Language Outcomes and Learner Diversity; 4.b. Integrating Standards in Instruction; 4.c. Selecting and Designing Instructional Materials

TESOL/NCATE 3.a. Planning for Standards-Based ESL and Content Instruction; 3.b. Managing and Implementing Standards-Based ESL and Content Instruction; 3.c. Using Resources Effectively in ESL and Content Instruction; and 4.c. Classroom-Based Assessment for ESL

www.cengagebrain.com

Appendix 12.11 on the *Teacher's Handbook* Web site is an example of a TELL meaning-enhancing communicative information-gap exercise presented by Chun and Brandl (1992, pp. 260–262). Using what you learned about information-gap activities in earlier chapters, analyze this activity for its communicative potential. Use Appendices 12.10 and 12.12 on the *Teacher's Handbook* Web site to assist you in your analysis. Then answer the following questions:

1. How do you think students will communicate with the computer in this exercise?
2. At what point in a lesson would this exercise be used?
3. What kind of grouping circumstances do you envision when using this kind of exercise with a class?
4. How will students communicate in the three modes, as a result of using this exercise, when they communicate with peers?
5. How would you revise this activity for your language? Consult preview opportunities at the Web sites of various textbook publishers (such as QUIA at http://heinle.com) to see examples of exercises or consult various textbooks or software packages, and apply Appendices 12.10 and 12.12 for guidance.

*NCATE*_____

EPISODE THREE
Creating a WebQuest

ACTFL/NCATE 3.b. Developing Instructional Practices that Reflect Language Outcomes and Learner Diversity; 4.a. Understanding and Integrating Standards in Planning; 4.b. Integrating Standards in Instruction; 4.c. Selecting and Designing Instructional Materials; 5.a. Knowing Assessment Models and Using Them Appropriately

TESOL/NCATE 3.a. Planning for Standards-Based ESL and Content Instruction; 3.b. Managing and Implementing Standards-Based ESL and Content Instruction; 3.c. Using Resources Effectively in ESL and Content Instruction; and 4.c. Classroom-Based Assessment for ESL

TECHNO FOCUS: Create your own WebQuest. Start by reviewing Figures 12.3 and 12.4 online at http://www.ozline.com/webquests/design.html; and http://webquest.org/index.php where you will find ideas, rubrics, and a taskonomy for additional guidance. See also Dodge's (1997) recommendations for the content of a WebQuest and view several sample WebQuests linked to from the *Teacher's Handbook* Web site. Next, use March's (2004) "Idea Machine" tool to brainstorm a planning web, and use Dodge's (2004) "WebQuest Taskonomy" to decide which tasks to include (again, see the *Teacher's Handbook* Web site). Use Alexander and Tate's (1999–2005) guidelines in Appendix 12.10 to evaluate the Web sites you select. Share your WebQuest with your classmates and use it with your students. Reflect on how you might improve it.

DISCUSS AND REFLECT ·

www.cengagebrain.com

See the *Teacher's Handbook* Web site for additional case studies:
    Case Study Two: Creating a Template for Web-Enhanced Materials
    Case Study Three: My WebQuest Became a Research Project

CASE STUDY ONE
Teaching Culture Through Photos

ACTFL/NCATE 2.b. Demonstrating Understanding of Literary/Cultural Texts and Traditions; 3.a. Understanding Language Acquisition and Creating a Supportive Classroom; 3.b. Developing Instructional Practices that Reflect Language Outcomes and Learner Diversity; 4.a. Understanding and Integrating Standards in Planning; 4.b. Integrating Standards in Instruction; 4.c. Selecting and Designing Instructional Materials; 5.a. Knowing Assessment Models and Using Them Appropriately

FIGURE 12.6 Instructional Uses of Digital Cameras

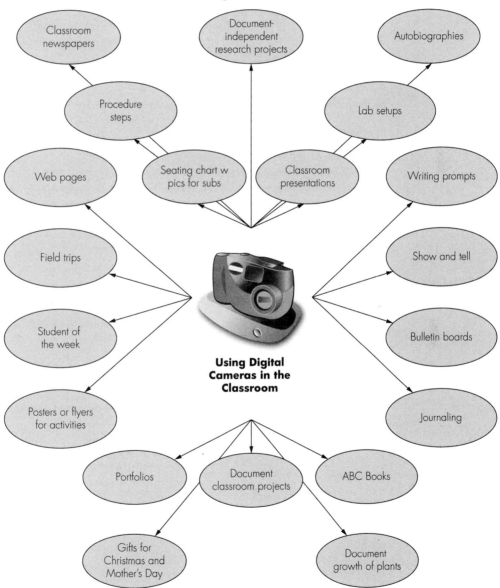

Source: Concept map developed by Judith Griffin for the University of Wisconsin Department of Education. Reprinted by permission of Judith Griffin.

TESOL/NCATE 3.a. Planning for Standards-Based ESL and Content Instruction; 3.b. Managing and Implementing Standards-Based ESL and Content Instruction; 3.c. Using Resources Effectively in ESL and Content Instruction; and 4.c. Classroom-Based Assessment for ESL

Madame Verité,[5] a French teacher, attended a summer workshop on using digital cameras in teaching culture. She was thrilled to see the variety of ways photography could be used in her classroom. One of the visuals used in the workshop appears in Figure 12.6. She decided to create a five-day unit in which her French III students would develop their photography skills while using content-based instruction to understand French daily culture and create descriptions of themselves.

Ask yourself these questions:

1. What insights have you gained from looking at the various ways in which digital cameras can be used in teaching languages?
2. What are the benefits and disadvantages of using this technology?
3. Look at Madame's lesson plan at the following Web site: www.carla.umn.edu/technology/modules/examples-camera.html; click on *La culture par les photos*. How does her lesson plan support the Five Cs?
4. How are authentic materials used?
5. How does Madame plan to assess student learning and performance?

To prepare for class discussion:

1. How would you use digital cameras in your lessons?
2. How would you modify this lesson for a post-secondary class?
3. How can photography be used to promote the knowledge and skills *(savoirs)* of Intercultural Communicative Competence (Byram, 1997; Byram & Risager, 1999; Deardorff, 2006) as described in Chapter 5?

REFERENCES

Abrams, Z. (2003). The effect of synchronous and asynchronous CMC on oral performance in German. *The Modern Language Journal, 87,* 157–167.

Abrams, Z. (2006). From theory to practice: Intracultural CMC in the L2 classroom. In L. Ducate & N. Arnold (Eds.), *Calling on CALL: From theory and research to new directions in foreign language teaching* (CALICO Monograph Series, Vol. 5, pp. 181–209). San Marcos, TX: CALICO.

Adair-Hauck, B., Youngs, B. E., & Willingham-McLain, L. (1998). *Assessing the integration of technology and second language learning.* Paper presented at ACTFL meeting, Chicago, IL.

Alexander, J., & Tate, M. A. (1999–2005). Evaluating Web resources. Retrieved October 9, 2008, from http://www3.widener.edu/Academics/Libraries/Wolfgram_Memorial_Library/Evaluate_Web_Pages/659/.

Arnold, N. (2007). Technology-mediated learning 10 years later: Emphasizing pedagogical or utilitarian applications? *Foreign Language Annals, 40,* 161–177.

Barr, D., Leakey, J., & Ranchoux, A. (2005). Told like it is. An evaluation of an oral development pilot project.

Language Learning and Technology, 9(3), 55–78. Retrieved September 22, 2008, from http://llt.msu.edu/vol9num3/barr/default.html.

Bauer, B., deBenedette, L., Furstenberg, G., Levet, S., & Waryn, S. (2006). The *Cultura* project. In J. A. Belz & S. L. Thorne (Eds.), *Internet–mediated intercultural foreign language education* (pp. 31–62). Boston: Heinle.

Beauvois, M. H. (1994). E-talk: Attitudes and motivation in computer-assisted classroom discussion. *Computers and the Humanities, 28,* 177–190.

Beauvois, M. H. (1997). Computer-mediated communication (CMC): Technology for improving speaking and writing. In M. D. Bush & R. M. Terry (Eds.), *Technology-enhanced language learning* (pp. 165–184). Lincolnwood, IL: NTC/Contemporary Publishing Group.

Beauvois, M. (1998). Write to speak: The effects of electronic communication on the oral achievement of fourth semester French students. In J. A. Muyskens (Ed.), *New ways of learning and teaching: Focus on technology and foreign language education* (pp. 165–183). Boston: Heinle & Heinle.

Belz, J. A. (2002). Social dimensions of telecollaborative foreign language study. *Language Learning and Technology, 6*(1), 60–81. Retrieved September 29, 2008 from http://llt.msu.edu/vol6num1/belz/.

Belz, J.A. (2007). The role of computer mediation in the instruction and development of L2 pragmatic competence. *Annual Review of Applied Linguistics, 27*, 45–75.

Belz, J. A., & Thorne, S. L. (Eds.). (2006). *Internet-mediated intercultural foreign language education.* Boston: Heinle & Heinle.

Berlitz. [Computer software] (2009). Retrieved January 4, 2009, from http://www.berlitz.us/web/html/default.aspx.

Black, R. W. (2008). Just don't call them cartoons: The new literacy spaces of anime, manga, and fanfiction. In J. Coiro, M. Knobel, C. Lankshear, & D. J. Leu (Eds.), *Handbook of research on new literacies* (pp. 538–561). New York: Lawrence Erlbaum Associates.

Blake, R. (2000). Computer-mediated communication: A window on L2 Spanish interlanguage. *Language Learning & Technology, 4*(1), 120–136. Retrieved September 27, 2008, from http://llt.msu.edu/vol4num1/blake/default.html.

Blake, R. (2005). Bimodal chatting: The glue of a distance language learning course. *CALICO Journal, 22*(3), 497–511.

Blake, R. (2006). Two heads are better than one: C(omputer) M(ediated) C(ommunication) for the L2 curriculum. In R. P. Donaldson & M. A. Haggstrom (Eds.), *Changing language education through CALL* (pp. 229–249). New York: Routledge.

Blake, R. (2007). New trends in using technology in the language classroom. *Annual Review of Applied Linguistics, 27*, 76–97. Cambridge, UK: Cambridge University Press.

Blake, R., & Delforge, A. (2007). Online language learning: The case of *Spanish without walls*. In B. Lafford & R. Salaberry (Eds.), *The art of teaching Spanish: Second language acquisition from research to praxis* (pp. 127–147). Washington, DC: Georgetown University Press.

Borrás, I., & Lafayette, R. C. (1994). Effects of multimedia courseware subtitling on the speaking performance of college students of French. *The Modern Language Journal, 78*, 61–75.

Bump, J. (1990). Radical changes in class discussion using networked computers. *Computers and the Humanities, 24*, 49–65.

Byram, M. (1997). *Teaching and assessing intercultural communicative competence.* Clevedon, UK: Multilingual Matters, Ltd.

Byram, M., & Risager, K. (1999). *Language teachers, politics and cultures.* Clevedon, UK: Multilingual Matters, Ltd.

Cahill, D., & Catanzaro, D. (1997). Teaching first-year Spanish online. *CALICO Journal, 14*(2–4), 97–114.

Chenoweth, N. A., Jones, C. M., & Tucker, G. R. (2006). Language online: Principles of design and methods of assessment. In R. P. Donaldson & M. A. Haggstrom (Eds.), *Changing language education through CALL* (pp. 146–167). New York: Routledge.

Chikamatsu, N. (2003). The effects of computer use on L2 Japanese writing. *Foreign Language Annals, 36*, 114–127.

Chun, D. (1994). Using computer networking to facilitate the acquisition of interactive competence. *System, 22*, 17–31.

Chun, D. M., & Brandl, K. K. (1992). Beyond form-based drill and practice: Meaning-enhanced CALL on the Macintosh. *Foreign Language Annals, 25*, 255–267.

Chun, D., & Plass, J. (1996). Effects of multimedia annotations on vocabulary acquisition. *The Modern Language Journal, 80*, 183–198.

Chun, D., & Plass, J. (1999). Ciberteca: Una carta a Dios [Computer software]. New York: Nonce Publishing Consultants, Ltd.

Chun, D. M., & Wade, E. R. (2004). Collaborative cultural exchanges with asynchronous CMC. In R. M. Terry (Series Ed.), L. Lomicka & J. Cooke-Plagwitz (Vol. Eds.), *The Heinle professional series in language instruction: Vol. 1. Teaching with technology* (pp. 220–247). Boston: Heinle & Heinle.

Cohen, A. D., & Sykes, J. M. (2007). *Strategies, CMC, and learning pragmatics.* Paper presented at the 17th International Conference on Pragmatics and Language Learning. Honolulu, HI, March 26–28, 2007.

Cononelos, T., & Oliva, M. (1993). Using computer networks to enhance foreign language/culture education. *Foreign Language Annals, 26*, 527–534.

Cooke-Plagwitz, J. (2004). Using the Internet to train language teachers to use the Internet: A special topics course for teachers of German. In R. M. Terry (Series Ed.), L. Lomicka & J. Cooke-Plagwitz (Vol. Eds.), *The Heinle professional series in language instruction: Vol. 1. Teaching with technology* (pp. 220–247). Boston: Heinle & Heinle.

Crookall, D., & Oxford, R. L. (1990). *Simulation, gaming, and language learning.* New York: Newbury House.

Cubillos, J. (1998). Technology: A step forward in the teaching of foreign languages. In J. Harper, M. G. Lively, & M. K. Williams (Eds.), *The coming of age of the profession: Issues and emerging ideas for the teaching of foreign languages* (pp. 37–52). Boston: Heinle & Heinle.

Davis, J. N., & Lyman-Hager, M. A. (1997). Computers and L2 reading: Student performance, student attitudes. *Foreign Language Annals, 30*, 58–72.

Deardorff, D. K. (2006). A model of intercultural competence and its implications for the foreign language curriculum. In S. Wilkinson (Ed.), *Insights from study abroad for language programs* (pp. 86–98). Boston: American Association of University Supervisors, Coordinators, and Directors of Foreign Language Programs, Thomson Heinle.

Dodge, B. (1997). Some thoughts about WebQuests. Retrieved April 14, 2004, from http://edweb.sdsu.edu/courses/edtec596/about_webquests.html.

Dodge, B. (1998). *WebQuests: A strategy for scaffolding higher level learning.* Paper presented at National Educational Computing Conference. San Diego, CA.

Retrieved April 15, 2004, from http://webquest.sdsu.edu/necc98.htm.

Dodge, B. (2004). WebQuest taskonomy: A taxonomy of tasks. Retrieved October 15, 2008, from http://webquest.Sdsu.edu/taskonomy.html.

Doughty, C., & Long, M. H. (2003). Optimal psycholinguistic environments for distance foreign language learning. *Language Learning and Technology, 7*(3), 50–80.

DynEd. (2008). [Computer Software]. Burliingame, CA: DynEd International.

Felix, U. (2005). What do meta-analyses tell us about CALL effectiveness? *ReCALL, 17*, 269–288.

Furstenberg, G., Levet, S., English, K., & Maillet, K. (2001). Giving a virtual voice to the silent language of culture: The CULTURA Project. *Language Learning and Technology, 5*(1), 55–102.

Furstenberg, G., & Malone, S. A. (1993). A la rencontre de Philippe [Computer software]. New Haven: Yale University Press.

Garza, T. J. (1991). Evaluating the use of captioned video material in advanced foreign language learning. *Foreign Language Annals, 24*, 239–258.

Gee, J. P. (1996). *Social linguistics and literacies: Ideology in discourses* (2nd ed.). London: Taylor and Francis.

González-Bueno, M. (1998). The effect of electronic mail on Spanish L2 discourse. *Language Learning & Technology, 1*(2), 55–70. Retrieved March 17, 2004, from http://www.polyglot.cal.msu/llt/num1vol2/article3.

González-Bueno, M., & Pérez, L. C. (2000). Electronic mail in foreign language writing: A study of grammatical and lexical accuracy, and quantity of language. *Foreign Language Annals, 33*, 189–198.

Goulding, C, & Jorth, C. (2004). Mord in Mainz murder mystery. [Computer software]. Boston: Heinle & Heinle.

Grace, C. A. (1998). Retention of word meanings inferred from context and sentence-level translations: Implications for the design of beginning-level CALL software. *The Modern Language Journal, 82*, 533–544.

Grgurovic, M., & Chapelle, C. (2007). Database of comparison studies: Computer-assisted vs classroom second/foreign language instruction. Retrieved September 29, 2008, from http://tesl.engl.iastate.edu:591/comparison/main.htm.

Hanna, B., & de Nooy, J. (2003). A funny thing happened on the way to the forum: Electronic discussion and foreign language learning. *Language Learning & Technology, 7*(1), 71–85.

International Society for Technology Education (ISTE)/National Educational Technology Standards (*NETS*) Project. (2002). National Educational Technology Standards. Retrieved October 10, 2008, from http://cnets.iste.org.

International Society for Technology Education (ISTE)/National Educational Technology Standards Project (*NETS*). (2007). National Educational Technology Standards for Students (*NETS-S*). Retrieved September 22, 2008, from http://www.iste.org/AM/Template.cfm?Section=NETS.

International Society for Technology Education (ISTE)/National Educational Technology Standards Project (*NETS*). (2008). National Educational Technology Standards for Teachers (*NETS-T*). Retrieved September 22, 2008, from http://www.iste.org/AM/Template.cfm?Section=NETS.

Ishihara, N. (2007). Web-based curriculum for pragmatics instruction in Japanese as a foreign language: An explicit awareness-raising approach. *Language Awareness, 16*(1), 21–40.

Jogan, M. K., Heredia, H. A., & Aguilera, M. G. (2001). Cross-cultural e-mail: Providing cultural input for the advanced foreign language students. *Foreign Language Annals, 34*, 341–346.

Johnson, K. (2009). La culture par les photos. Retrieved January 3, 2009, from http://db.carla.umn.edu/cobaltt/lessonplans/FMPro?-db=lessonplans.fp6&-format=detail-LP.html&-lay=fullinfo&-recID=32838&-find.

Johnson, L., Levine, A., & Smith, R. (2009). *The 2009 horizon report*. Austin, TX: The New Media Consortium.

Johnson, S. P., & English, K. (2003). Society and culture: Images, myths, and realities across cultures. *The French Review, 76*, 492–507.

Jones, K. (1982). *Simulations in language teaching*. Cambridge, UK: Cambridge University Press.

Jones, L. C., & Plass, J. L. (2002). Supporting listening comprehension and vocabulary acquisition in French with multimedia annotations. *The Modern Language Journal, 86*, 546–561.

Kelm, O. R. (1992). The use of synchronous computer networks in second language instruction: A preliminary report. *Foreign Language Annals, 25*, 441–453.

Kern, R. G. (1995). Restructuring classroom interaction with networked computers: Effects on quantity and characteristics of language production. *The Modern Language Journal, 79*, 457–476.

Knobel, M., & Lankshear, C. (2007). *A new literacies sampler*. New York: Peter Lang.

Kramsch, C., & Thorne, S. L. (2002). Foreign language learning as global communicative practice. In D. Block & D. Cameron (Eds.), *Globalization and language teaching* (pp. 83–100). London: Routledge.

Lankshear, C., & Knobel, M. (2006). *New literacies: Everyday practices and classroom learning* (2nd ed.). New York: Open University Press.

Larson, J., & Bush, C. (1992). Montevidisco [Computer software]. Provo, UT: Brigham Young University.

Lee, L. (2002). Enhancing learners' communication skills through synchronous electronic interaction and task-based instruction. *Foreign Language Annals, 35*, 16–24.

Lee, L. (2004). Perspectives of nonnative speakers of Spanish on two types of online collaborative exchanges: Promises and challenges. In R. M. Terry (Series Ed.), L. Lomicka & J. Cooke-Plagwitz (Vol. Eds.), *The Heinle professional series in language instruction: Vol. 1. Teaching with technology* (pp. 248–265). Boston: Heinle & Heinle.

LeLoup, J., & Ponterio, R. (2004). FLTEACH: Online professional development for preservice and inservice foreign language teachers. In R. M. Terry (Series Ed.), L. Lomicka & J. Cooke-Plagwitz (Vol. Eds.), *The Heinle professional series in language instruction: Vol. 1. Teaching with technology* (pp. 26–44). Boston: Heinle & Heinle.

Levi Altstaedter, L., & Jones, B. (2008). *Motivating students' foreign language and culture acquisition through web-based inquiry.* Unpublished manuscript. Blacksburg, VA: Virginia Polytechnic Institute and State University.

Levine, G., & Morse, S. (2004). Integrating diverse digital media in a global simulation German course. In R. M. Terry (Series Ed.), L. Lomicka & J. Cooke-Plagwitz (Vol. Eds.), *The Heinle professional series in language instruction: Vol. 1. Teaching with technology* (pp. 248–265). Boston: Heinle & Heinle.

Levy, M. (1997). *Computer assisted language learning: Context and conceptualization.* Oxford, UK: Clarendon Press.

Liu, M., Moore, Z., Graham, L., & Lee, S. (2002). A look at the research on computer-based technology use in second language learning: A review of the literature from 1990–2000. *Journal of Research on Technology in Education, 34,* 250–273.

Luke, C. (2006). Fostering learner autonomy in a technology-enhanced, inquiry-based foreign language classroom. *Foreign Language Annals, 39*(1), 71–86.

March, T. (1998). The WebQuest design process. Retrieved October 2, 2008, from http://www.tommarch.com/writings/wq_design.php.

March, T. (2003). What WebQuests are (really). Retrieved September 10, 2008, from http://bestwebquests.com/what_webquests_are.asp.

March, T. (2004). The idea machine. Retrieved October 15, 2008, from http://tommarch.com/learning/idea_machine.php.

Martínez-Lage, A., & Herren, D. (1998). Challenges and opportunities: Curriculum pressures in the technological present. In J. Harper, M. Lively, & M. Williams (Eds.), *The coming of age of the profession: Issues and emerging ideas for the teaching of foreign languages* (pp. 141–167). Boston: Heinle & Heinle.

Masters-Wicks, K., Postlewate, L., & Lewental, M. (1996). Developing interactive instructional software for language acquisition. *Foreign Language Annals, 29,* 217–222.

Maxwell, D. (1998). *Technology and foreign language learning. A report to the Charles E. Culpeper Foundation.* Washington, DC: National Foreign Language Center.

Miller, K. M. (2007). Using iPod with your language students. *The Language Educator, 2*(5), 50–21.

Murphy, D., & Youngs, B. (2004). From the classroom to the Web: Applying best practices from foreign language education in the development of Web-based listening materials. In R. M. Terry (Series Ed.), L. Lomick, & J. Cooke-Plagwitz (Vol. Eds.), *The Heinle professional series in language instruction: Vol. 1. Teaching with technology* (pp. 121–128). Boston: Heinle & Heinle.

Nagata, N. (1993). Intelligent computer feedback for second language instruction. *The Modern Language Journal, 77,* 330–339.

Nagata, N. (1999). The effectiveness of computer-assisted interactive glosses. *Foreign Language Annals, 32,* 469–479.

Nagata, N., & Swisher, M. V. (1995). A study of consciousness-raising by computer: The effect of metalinguistic feedback on second language learning. *Foreign Language Annals, 28,* 337–347.

National Council of State Supervisors for Languages (NCSSFL). (2002). Position statement on distance learning in foreign languages. Retrieved April 21, 2004, from http://www.ncssfl.org/position.htm.

National Standards in Foreign Language Education Project (NSFLEP). (2006). *Standards for foreign language learning in the 21st century (SFLL).* Lawrence, KS: Allen Press.

O'Dowd, R., & Ritter, M. (2006). Understanding and working with "failed communication" in telecollaborative exchanges. *CALICO Journal, 23*(3), 623–642.

Oliva, M., & Pollastrini, Y. (1995). Internet resources and second language acquisition: An evaluation of virtual immersion. *Foreign Language Annals, 28,* 551–563.

Oliver, W., & Nelson, T. (1997). Un Misterio en Toluca [Computer software]. Boston: Heinle & Heinle.

Oliver, W., & Nelson, T. (1998). Un Muertre à Cinet [Computer software]. Boston: Heinle & Heinle.

Pellettieri, J. (2000). Negotiation in cyberspace: The role of chatting in the development of grammatical competence. In M. Warschauer & R. Kern (Eds.), *Network-based language teaching: Concepts and practice* (pp. 59–86). Cambridge, UK: Cambridge University Press.

Pennington, M. (1996). *The computer and the non-native writer: A natural partnership.* Cresskill, NJ: Hampton Press.

Prensky, M. (2001). Digital natives, digital immigrants, part 1. *On the Horizon, 9*(5), 1–6. Retrieved September 21, 2008, from http://www.marcprensky.com.

Prensky, M. (2008, March 28). *Engage me or enrage me.* Keynote address delivered at the Northeast Conference on the Teaching of Foreign Languages, New York.

QUIA. [Computer software] (1998–2008). Quia corporation. Retrieved October 10, 2008, from http://www.quia.com.

Raby, F. (2007). A triangular approach to motivation in Computer Assisted Autonomous Language Learning (*CAALL*). *ReCALL, 19*(2), 181–201.

Rosedale, P. (2003). Second Life [Computer software]. San Francisco: Linden Labs.

Shrum, J. L. (2007, October). *Language teaching in the 21st century*. Plenary session presented at the Mountain Interstate Foreign Language Conference, Roanoke, VA.

Skype. [Computer software] (2008). Retrieved October 10, 2008, from http://www.skype.com/welcomeback/.

Smith, B. (2003). Computer-mediated negotiated interaction: An expanded model. *The Modern Language Journal, 87*, 38–57.

Sotillo, S. (2000). Discourse functions and syntactic complexity in synchronous and asynchronous communication. *Language Learning & Technology, 4*(1), 82–119. Retrieved May 26, 2004, from http://llt.msu.edu/vol4num1/sotillo/default.html.

Sotillo, S. (2005). Corrective feedback via instant messenger learning activities in NS-NNS and NNS-NNS dyads. *CALICO Journal, 22*(3), 467–496.

Spartanburg School District III. *Creating a WebQuest: Survival*. Retrieved April 15, 2004, from http://www.spa3.k12.sc.us/survival.htm.

Suh, J-S. (2002). Effectiveness of CALL Writing Instruction: The voices of Korean EFL learners. *Foreign Language Annals, 35*, 669–679.

Sullivan, N., & Pratt, E. (1996). A comparative study of two ESL writing environments: A computer-assisted classroom and a traditional oral classroom. *System, 24*(4), 491–501.

Sweley, M. H. (2008a). Unreal world: Second Life adds new dimensions to second language study. *Language Educator, 3*(2), 22–25.

Sweley, M. H. (2008b). No substitute for the real thing. *Language Educator, 3*(1), 42–43.

Teachers of English to Speakers of Other Languages. (2006). *PreK–12 English language proficiency standards*. Alexandria, VA: Author.

Teachers of English to Speakers of Other Languages. (2007). *TESOL technology standards*. Alexandria, VA: Author.

Tell Me More® Version 9 [Computer software] (2007). Auralog, Inc. Retrieved September 29, 2008, from http://www.tellmemore.com.

Terry, R. M. (2000). *Technology competencies for teacher certification: A survey of the states*. Retrieved April 14, 2004, from https://facultystaff.richmond.edu/~rterry/Survey/start.html.

Thorne, S. (2008). Mediating technologies and second language learning. In J. Coiro, M. Knobel, C. Lankshear, & D. J. Leu (Eds.), *Handbook of research on new literacies* (pp. 415–447). New York: Lawrence Erlbaum Associates.

Transparent Language® [Computer software]. (2007). Transparent Language, Inc. Retrieved October 10, 2008, from http://www.transparent.com.

Warner, C. (2004). It's just a game, right? Types of play in foreign language CMC. *Language Learning & Technology 8*(2), 69–87. Retrieved May 25, 2004, from http://llt.msu.edu/vol8num2/warner/default.html.

Warschauer, M. (1996). Comparing face-to-face and electronic communication in the second language classroom. *CALICO Journal, 12*, 7–26.

Warschauer, M., & Ware, P. (2008). Learning, change, and power: Competing frames of technology and literacy. In J. Coiro, M. Knobel, C. Lankshear, & D. J. Leu (Eds.), *Handbook of research on new literacies* (pp. 215–240). New York: Lawrence Erlbaum Associates.

Weasenforth, D., Biesenbach-Lucas, S., & Meloni, C. (2002). Realizing constructivist objectives through collaborative technologies: Threaded discussions. *Language Learning & Technology, 6*(3), 58–86. Retrieved May 15, 2004, from http://llt.msu.edu/vol6num3/weasenforth/default.html.

Weekly, D. (2005). Why PB Works. Retrieved June 28, 2009, from http://www.pbworks.com.

NOTES

1. See the *Teacher's Handbook* Web site created for Project *Fresa* at http://eden.clmer.csulb.edu/netshare/cti/%20FOR%20PSRTEC%20WEBSITE/Amada%20and%20Michelle/lessons.html.

2. Keep in mind that teachers may adapt and apply technologies in tandem and for multiple purposes, and that those technologies listed in this chapter often require an infrastructure of several other technologies in order to operate in the form we have listed them. In recent years, teachers and students have increasingly used the types of technologies that appear in Figure 12.1 in both their academic and everyday lives.

3. Many thanks to Susan Neate for her lesson on Activboard®.

4. See the Educause web page at http://www.educause.org for the annual *Horizon Report*, and for additional resources. The Educause Learning Initiative provides informative summaries on technological topics. The titles of the summaries all begin with *7 things you should know about...* and then topics include such items as blogs, Voice thread, Web 2.0, etc.

5. This lesson plan was developed by Johnson (2009) during a CARLA workshop.

Appendices

APPENDIX 2.1 THE CHRONOLOGICAL DEVELOPMENT OF LANGUAGE TEACHING

What is the role of context in each method described below?

ERA	TIME PERIOD	APPROACH	METHOD	TECHNIQUES	PROPONENT(S)
I. Influence of Teaching of Latin and Greek	until late 19th century	The mind needs to be trained by analysis of the language, memorization of rules, paradigms; application of these rules in translation exercises (Chastain, 1988).	Grammar-translation	translation; learning of grammar rules; memorization of bilingual word lists; little or no emphasis on oral skills	No one person; German scholar Karl Ploz (late 1800s) very influential
II. Reaction to Grammar-Translation Method	late 19th–early 20th century	Learners should acquire rules of grammar inductively through imitation, repetition, speaking, and reading. The best way to teach meaning is to use visual perception (Chastain, 1988).	Direct	exclusive use of L2; use of visuals; grammar rules taught through inductive teaching; emphasis on correct pronunciation	Comenius, Gouin, Jespersen, de Sauzé
III. Result of Structural Linguistics and Behavioral Psychology/ National Emphasis on Oral Skills	1940–1950	L2 should be taught without reference to L1. Students learn through stimulus-response (S-R) techniques. Pattern drills should precede any explanation of grammar. The natural sequence LSRW should be followed in learning the language (Chastain, 1988).	Audiolingual (ALM)	stimulus-response pattern drills; memorization of dialogues; correction a must; comparison of L1 and L2; exclusive use of L2; grammar rules learned through induction; skills learned in the sequence of listening, speaking, reading, writing; focus on culture	Fries, Skinner, Bloomfield, N. Brooks

IV. Reaction to ALM	1960s	Learners must attain control over the rules of the target language so they can generate their own utterances. The teacher should move from known to new information. Creative use of the language should be promoted. Grammar should be explained so that students understand the rules. Language practice should always be meaningful (Chastain, 1988).	Cognitive (Code)	meaningful language use; deductive teaching of grammar in native language; grammar practice follows mechanical, meaningful, communicative sequence	Chomsky, Ausubel
V. Result of Studies in First Language Acquisition	1974	Comprehension must be developed before speaking. Speech will emerge naturally as students internalize language. Learners learn to understand best through physical movement in response to commands (Asher, Kusudo, & de la Torre, 1974).	Total Physical Response	listening and responding physically to oral commands for first ten hours of instruction; exclusive use of target language; creative language use	Asher
	late 1970s, early 1980s	Learners should acquire language before being forced to learn it. Affective factors merit much attention in language instruction. Communicative competence should be the goal in beginning language instruction. Learners need to acquire a great deal of vocabulary to understand and to speak (Terrell, 1982).	Natural (Approach)	creative, communicative practice; limited error correction; "foreigner talk"; acquisition activities: comprehension, early speech production, speech emergence; inductive teaching of grammar	Terrell
VI. Focus on Effective Development of Individual: Humanistic Methods	1972–1973	Teachers can help students most by allowing them to take more responsibility for their own learning. Learning is not relegated to imitation and drill. Learners learn from trial and error and are capable of making their own corrections (Gattegno, 1976).	Silent Way	use of Cuisenaire rods to denote words and structures; students more responsible for learning; self and peer correction; early writing practice	Gattegno

	1976	Community Language Learning	The teacher, in the role as "knower" or "counselor," should remain passive in order to reduce anxiety among students. Learners learn when working in community with others who are trying to achieve similar goals (Curran, 1976).	translation by teacher from native language to target language in early lessons; theme of each class determined by learners; analysis of group conversations from tape	Curran
	1978–1979	Suggestopedia	Relaxation techniques and concentration assist learners in releasing the subconscious and in retaining large amounts of language (Lozanov, 1978).	"suggestive" atmosphere (living room setting, soft lights, baroque music, dramatic techniques by teacher); dialogues accompanied by music in background; role-play and activities to "activate" the material in dialogues; grammatical explanations given in native language	Lozanov
VII. Effects of Drama on Language Teaching	1972–1980	Dartmouth Intensive Language Model (DILM)	The teacher must help learners to overcome their inhibitions so that they can live the language experience more fully. The teacher should be an actor and possess vitality in the classroom. The target language should be spoken exclusively, and all errors should be corrected. The language must come to life in the classroom (Rassias, 1983).	drama and action by teacher; immediate correction of grammar and pronunciation errors; skits and games; "micrologue" for teaching culture; master teacher and apprentice teachers (who conduct drill sessions); inductive teaching by master teacher	Rassias

VIII. Proficiency	1980s–1990s	Knowing a language means being able to use it in communication. Learners use the language to perform functions in a range of contexts and with a level of accuracy in grammar, vocabulary, pronunciation, fluency and pragmatic competence, and sociolinguistic competence.	No particular method	opportunities for self-expression and creativity; use of language in a variety of contexts; exposure to authentic texts; interaction with others; integration of culture and language	Proficiency Guidelines established by ACTFL/ETS
IX. Standards	1996–present	Foreign language has a central role in the learning experience of every learner. Competence in a language and culture enables the learner to communicate with others in a variety of settings, gain an understanding of self and other cultures, acquire new bodies of knowledge, develop insight into his or her own language and culture, and participate in the global community. Language and culture education enhances communication skills and higher-order thinking skills.	No particular method	opportunities to use the language as a vehicle for learning content; integration of skills and culture; interaction with others by means of technology; exploration of cultural products and practices and their relationships to cultural perspectives	Standards developed by ACTFL (in collaboration with other professional foreign language organizations) and TESOL

Approach = a set of theoretical principles or basic assumptions that are the foundation of a method.

Method = a procedural plan for presenting and teaching language, based on the approach adopted

Technique = a particular strategy—one of many—for implementing a method (Anthony, 1963)

Source: Adapted from Shrum & Glisan (1994).

APPENDIX 3.1 FOREIGN LANGUAGE PLANNING MODEL USING BLOOM'S REVISED TAXONOMY

	Bloom's Level	Definition of Level	Learning Actions	Sample Foreign Language Activities*
Higher-order Thinking	**Create**	Putting information and ideas together to develop an original idea or engage in critical thinking	Compose, construct, create, design, devise, estimate, forecast, generate, hypothesize, imagine, infer, invent, make, plan, produce, role play, rearrange parts, present, propose, transform, write	Creating stories, advertisements, charts, surveys, paintings, pamphlets, posters, presentations, songs, productions (presentational mode); writing essays, poems, new endings to stories, reports, recipes, news articles; designing games, lessons, cartoons, inventions, models of cultural products; responding to hypothetical situations, open-ended role-plays, culturally authentic situations (interpersonal mode); providing alternative interpretations of a text based on cultural, historical, personal perspectives (interpretive mode)
	Evaluate	Judge the value of ideas and materials by developing and applying specific criteria and/or standards	Appraise, assess, consider, check, criticize, critique, debate, discuss, experiment, evaluate, give opinion, judge, prioritize, recommend, relate, summarize, test, weigh	Conducting debates, trials, discussions, arguments, panel discussions (interpersonal mode); writing letters, recommendations, summaries of surveys, editorials, persuasive speeches, evaluations and self-evaluations (presentational mode); designing and conducting content-based experiments; evaluating a character's actions in a story (interpretive mode)
	Analyze	Break information into smaller segments so that it can be understood	Analyze, classify, compare, contrast, deconstruct, deduce, differentiate, distinguish, dissect, infer, integrate, investigate, organize, outline, paint, report, research, survey, select, separate, solve, structure, subdivide	Defining words and expressions; creating diagrams, charts, graphs, illustrations, spreadsheets, outlines; developing surveys and questionnaires; conducting cultural investigations; comparing and contrasting features of L1 and L2; comparing and contrasting products, practices, perspectives in L1 and L2; inferring ideas from an authentic text (interpretive mode)

Lower-level Thinking	**Apply**	Use learned information, concepts, and principles in completing new tasks	Execute, practice, calculate, apply, build, carry out, change, demonstrate, modify, implement, interview, record, report, solve, sketch, teach, use guides/charts/maps, prepare	Conducting interviews and discussions following a model (interpersonal mode); designing models, visuals, paintings, brochures, illustrations, projects, performances that follow outline or criteria (presentational mode); following maps, verbal directions/instructions, recipes, or experiments; developing lessons to teach material/skills; completing puzzles; continuing a story that was heard or read (interpretive mode)
	Understand	Make sense of material	Summarize, discuss, explain, outline, demonstrate an understanding of, interpret, paraphrase, relate, predict, restate, show, distinguish, illustrate, rewrite	Summarizing the gist of an audio, video, or printed authentic segment (interpretive mode); creating predictions/illustrations for an authentic text; writing conclusions/implications based on data (presentational mode); giving examples of cultural products, practices, perspectives; explaining the significance of a cultural artifact or object in one's personal world
	Remember	Recall and recognize learned material	Identify, label, recall, define, describe, find, group, recognize, list, locate, match, name, recite, repeat, retrieve, select, sort, state, locate, discover	Labeling drawings, visuals; making lists of words and expressions for a given theme; naming words in a given category (e.g., months of year, foods, seasons); reciting numbers, alphabet, days/months, etc.; completing worksheets and workbook pages that elicit recall; naming facts about TL culture; matching cultural products and practices to perspectives; locating on a map countries in which TL is spoken

*Note: These activities would be done using the target language.

Source: Shrum & Glisan, 2010 (based on Bloom's Revised Taxonomy Planning Framework, http://www.kurwongbss. qld.edu.au/thinking/Bloom/blooms.htm).

Note: Several examples are given in the chart of how the three modes of communication might be used across the levels of the taxonomy. This chart is not meant to be inclusive, and there are many other possibilities for how the modes might be applied to the various levels of thinking.

APPENDIX 3.2 PLANNING TEMPLATE ILLUSTRATING BACKWARD DESIGN

<table>
<tr><td colspan="2">Stage 1—Desired Results</td></tr>
<tr><td colspan="2">Established Goals: G

• What relevant goals (e.g., content standards, course or program objectives, learning outcomes) will this design address?</td></tr>
<tr>
<td>Understandings: U
Students will understand that. . .

• What are the big ideas?
• What specific understandings about them are desired?
• What misunderstandings are predictable?</td>
<td>Essential Questions: Q

• What provocative questions will foster inquiry, understanding, and transfer of learning?</td>
</tr>
<tr>
<td>Students will know. . .   K

• What key knowledge and skills will students acquire as a result of this unit?
• What should they eventually be able to do as a result of such knowledge and skills?</td>
<td>Students will be able to . . .   S</td>
</tr>
<tr><td colspan="2">Stage 2—Assessment Evidence</td></tr>
<tr>
<td>Performance Tasks: T

• Through what authentic performance tasks will students demonstrate the desired understandings?
• By what criteria will performances of understanding be judged?</td>
<td>Other Evidence: OE

• Through what other evidence (e.g., quizzes, tests, academic prompts, observations, homework, journals) will students demonstrate achievement of the desired results?
• How will students reflect upon and self-assess their learning?</td>
</tr>
<tr><td colspan="2">Stage 3—Learning Plan</td></tr>
<tr><td colspan="2">Learning Activities: L
What learning experiences and instruction will enable students to achieve the desired results? How will the design

W = Help the students know Where the unit is going and What is expected? Help the teacher know Where the students are coming from (prior knowledge, interests)?
H = Hook all students and Hold their interest?
E = Equip students, help them Experience the key ideas and Explore the issues?
R = Provide opportunities to Rethink and Revise their understandings and work?
E = All students to Evaluate their work and its implications?
T = Be Tailored (personalized) to the different needs, interests, and abilities of learners?
O = Be Organized to maximize initial and sustained engagement as well as effective learning?</td></tr>
</table>

Source: From *Understanding by Design* (p. 22), by G. Wiggins and J. McTighe, 2005. Alexandria, VA: Association for Supervision and Curriculum Development. Copyright © 2005 by ASCD. Reprinted by permission. Learn more about ASCD at www.ascd.org.

APPENDIX 3.3 EXCERPT FROM NEBRASKA K–12 FOREIGN LANGUAGE FRAMEWORKS

Goal One: **Communicate in Languages Other than English**

Standard 1.1   *Students engage in conversations, provide and obtain information, express feelings and emotions, and exchange opinions.*

Students are able to:	Beginning	Developing	Expanding
A	Express basic needs.	▶ Elaborate on needs. ▶ Interact in basic survival situations.	▶ Manage unforeseen circumstances and complicated situations.
B	Express basic courtesies.	▶ Incorporate appropriate gestures into conversations.	▶ Converse using language and behaviors that are appropriate to the setting.
C	Express state of being.	▶ Create simple descriptions within a context.	▶ Create detailed oral descriptions within a context.
D	Express likes and dislikes.	▶ Qualify likes and dislikes.	▶ Exchange personal feelings and ideas for the purpose of persuading others.
E	Express agreement and disagreement.	▶ Support opinions. ▶ Describe a problem. ▶ Make suggestions and recommendations.	▶ Express individual perspectives and defend opinions. ▶ Collaborate to develop and propose solutions to problems. ▶ Negotiate a compromise.

▶▶▶

Goal Two: **Gain Knowledge and Understanding of Other Cultures**

Standard 2.1   *Students demonstrate an understanding of the relationship between the perspectives and practices of cultures studied and use this knowledge to interact effectively in cultural contexts*

Students are able to:	Beginning	Developing	Expanding
A	Identify and react to cultural perspectives and practices in the culture studied.	▶ Describe and analyze cultural characteristics and behaviors of everyday life. ▶ Identify differences in cultural practices among same-language cultures.	▶ Analyze the development of different cultural practices. ▶ Compare and contrast cultural practices among same-language cultures.
B	Recognize and interpret language and behaviors that are appropriate to the target culture.	▶ Produce language and behaviors that are appropriate to the target culture.	▶ Apply language and behaviors that are appropriate to the target culture in an authentic situation.
C	Identify some commonly-held generalizations about the culture studied.	▶ Analyze some commonly held generalizations about the culture studied.	▶ Evaluate some commonly held generalizations about the culture studied.
D	Identify social and geographic factors that affect cultural practices.	▶ Discuss social and geographic factors that affect cultural practices.	▶ Analyze social and geographic factors that affect cultural practices.
E	Identify common words, phrases, and idioms that reflect the culture.	▶ Interpret the cultural connotations of common words, phrases, and idioms.	▶ Integrate culturally embedded words, phrases, and idioms into everyday communication.

▲▲▲

Source: Nebraska Department of Education. (1996a). *Nebraska K–12 foreign language frameworks.* Retrieved June 3, 2008, from http://www.nde.state.ne.us/FORLG/Frameworks/Frameworks.pdf, pp. 23 & 43. Used by permission of the Nebraska Department of Education.

Class: Level 1 Language Class

Year Planner—Example A

Goals	Goal 1: COMMUNICATION	Goal 2: CULTURES	Goal 3: CONNECTIONS	Goal 4: COMPARISONS	Goal 5: COMMUNITIES
Standards	1.1 Students engage in conversations…	2.1 Students … perspectives and practices of cultures	3.1 Students reinforce … their knowledge through other disciplines	4.1 Students … use different patterns to communicate and apply to own language	5.1 Students apply language skills beyond school setting
Contexts/ Outcomes	Students engage in conversations about typical school situations	Students demonstrate an understanding of the relationship between the perspectives and practices of greetings and leave-takings in Germany	Students reinforce and further knowledge of art by studying German artists	Students recognize that the German language uses different sound patterns from English	Students apply language skills beyond the school setting by using the Internet to converse in German with German teenagers.
Progress Indicators	1.1.A Express basic needs 1.1.B Express basic courtesies	2.1. A Identify cultural perspectives and practices	3.1.B Identify information for use in other disciplines	4.1.A Identify sound patterns and compare to own language	5.1.A Identify the target language in daily lives
Essential Skills/ Knowledge	• Verbs—want, need • Vocabulary for school items, clothes, gift suggestions • Phrases for polite requests	• Descriptions of greetings • Leave-taking customs	• Accessing information from computer and library • Listing of resources for the information desired • Information on artists—their lives and times	• Vowel sounds • Consonant sounds	• How-to log-skills • Conversation skills • Writing skills
Assessments	• Situation cards—role-plays of losing school supplies and borrowing from friends • Quizzes • Letter to pen-pal on Internet	• Role-play greetings and leave-taking situations	• Student log/notes • Projects on various perspectives on relationships of art to society	• Listening identification • Pronunciation test	• Student logs of language use • Internet chat paper copies
Resources	• Chapter 2 • Chapter 9 • Video • Internet pen-pals	• Chapter 1 • Video	• Library • WWW	• Tapes • Videos	• Logbook • Computer-Internet account • Addresses for Internet

Source: Nebraska Department of Education. (1996b). *Nebraska K–12 foreign language frameworks*. Retrieved June 3, 2008, from http://www.nde.state.ne.us/FORLG/Frameworks/FLFCurric.pdf, p. 212. Used by permission of the Nebraska Department of Education.

APPENDIX 3.5 SAMPLE UNIT PLAN ("SHOPPING AT THE MARKET") FROM NEBRASKA'S FOREIGN LANGUAGE FRAMEWORKS SAMPLE UNITS

Unit: Shopping at the Market
A unit integrating the five Frameworks goals

Goals:
Goal 1: Communicate in Languages other than English
Goal 2: Gain Knowledge and Understanding of Other Cultures
Goal 3: Connect with Other Disciplines and Acquire Information
Goal 4: Develop Insight into the Nature of Language and Culture
Goal 5: Participate in Multilingual Communities at Home and Around the World

Standards: Students...

1.1 Engage in conversations...exchange opinions.
1.2 Understand...written and spoken language...
1.3 Convey information...
2.1 Demonstrate an understanding of the relationship between the perspectives and practices of cultures studied and use this knowledge to interact effectively in cultural contexts.
3.2 Acquire information and perspectives through authentic materials ... within the cultures.
4.2 Recognize that cultures use different patterns of interaction and can apply this knowledge to their own culture.
5.1 Apply language skills and cultural knowledge within and beyond the school setting.

Contexts/Outcomes:

Students engage in conversation and convey information in a market using correct cultural practices.

Progress Indicators: *Students are able to...*

1.1.A Express basic needs.
1.1.C Create simple descriptions.
1.1.D Express likes and dislikes.
1.1.F Respond to one-on-one interactions.
1.1.G Ask and answer simple questions.
1.2.A Respond appropriately to directions....
1.2.E Identify aural, visual and context clues.
1.3.A Give directions....
1.3.B Give a description orally....

2.1.A Identify and react to cultural perspectives and practices in the culture studied.
2.1.B Recognize and interpret language and behaviors that are appropriate to the target culture.

3.2.A Extract information from sources intended for native speakers....

3.2.B Use authentic sources to identify the perspectives of the target culture.

4.2.A Identify similarities/differences between the target culture and the students own culture using evidence from authentic sources.

4.2.B Identify similar and different behavioral patterns between the target culture and the student's own culture.

5.1.B Locate connections with the target culture through the use of technology, media, and authentic sources.

Essential Skills/Knowledge:

- Vocabulary for foods and daily needs
- Common phrases for shopping
- Use of the verb *gustar*
- Question formation
- Simple commands
- Adjectives
- Cultural information for do's and don'ts of shopping at Mexican markets
- Use of the World Wide Web

Assessments:

- Quizzes on the vocabulary and simple commands
- Review quiz on *gustar* and adjective agreement
- Listening check from video
- Role play of shopping at the market (culminating assessment*)

Instructional Strategies:

- TPR for foods
- Video practice of market situations in Mexico
- Role-play situations
- Description of pictures of markets
- Interviews with native speakers
- Practice with commands

Resources:

- WWW search for Mexican markets
- Hyperstudio lesson on markets in Cuernavaca
- Photos of Mexican markets
- Textbook

*Performance task:

Students will role-play a shopping experience in a Mexican market using appropriate cultural behavior. The student will go to the market stall owner (the teacher) and, with a list of three items to purchase, will select the three items from the ones displayed and bargain for the best price for each.

Rubric

	4 Exceeds expectations	3 Excellent	2 Good	1 Not yet
Expresses likes/ dislikes	no errors	almost all correctly expressed	some errors, majority correctly stated	few or none correctly stated
Is comprehensible (pronunciation, structures, vocabulary usage) (x 2)	near-native pronunciation, use of structures beyond expected proficiency	easily understood, infrequent errors	comprehensible with noticeable errors in pronunciation, structures and/ or vocabulary usage	nearly or completely incomprehensible
Asks and answers questions accurately	no errors	almost all correctly stated	some errors, majority correctly stated	few or none correctly stated
Demonstrates appropriate cultural practices	near-native use of practices	almost all demonstrated and appropriate	some demonstrated and appropriate	inappropriate or none demonstrated
Follows Instructions	bought more items than required	followed instruction completely	mostly followed instructions	little evidence of following instructions

Source: Nebraska Department of Education. (1996b). *Nebraska K–12 foreign language frameworks*. Retrieved June 3, 2008, from http://www.nde.state.ne.us/FORLG/Frameworks/FLFCurric.pdf, p. 227–228. Used by permission of the Nebraska Department of Education.

APPENDIX 4.5 THEMATIC PLANNING WEB

Source: Curtain, H., & Dahlberg, C. A. (2004). *Languages and children – Making the match* (3rd ed.). Boston: Allyn & Bacon, p. 203. Copyright © 2004 Pearson Education. Adapted by permission of the publisher.

APPENDIX 4.7 SEMANTIC MAP

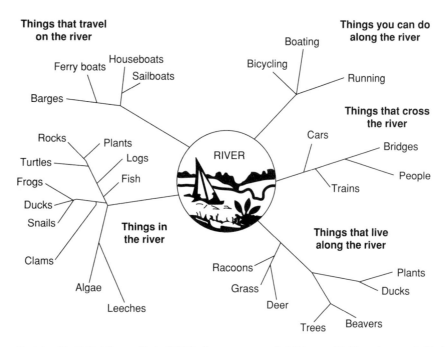

Source: Curtain, H., & Dahlberg, C. A. (2004). *Languages and children – Making the match* (3rd ed.). Boston: Allyn & Bacon, p. 167. Copyright © 2004 Pearson Education. Adapted by permission of the publisher.

APPENDIX 4.8 TREE MAP

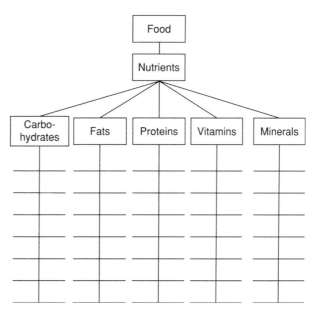

Source: Curtain, H., & Dahlberg, C. A. (2004). *Languages and children – Making the match* (3rd ed.). Boston: Allyn & Bacon, p. 265. Copyright © 2004 Pearson Education. Adapted by permission of the publisher.

APPENDIX 6.2 INTERACTIVE MODEL USED WITH AN AUTHENTIC SPANISH READING

Interpretive Mode:

Preparation Phase:

You will read a magazine article about a popular Hispanic singer, Shakira. In preparation for reading this article, explore the following questions.

1. What do you know about Shakira?
2. Have you listened to her music? Which songs? Do you like her music? Explain.
3. Glance at the article for 30 seconds. What type of information do you expect to find in this type of article?
4. Why might you be interested in reading this article?
5. Brainstorm some words and expressions you might encounter in this article.

Comprehension Phase:

Main Ideas. Skim the article for one minute and select the subtitle that would best describe it.

_____ **1.** Corazón y cerebro

_____ **2.** Sus preocupaciones

_____ **3.** Su nueva vida como actriz

Important Details. Work with a classmate to find the following details from the article in Spanish.

1. Cómo aprendió inglés: _____
2. Lo que expresa en español: _____
3. Un premio que había ganado: _____
4. Cómo es ella, según ella misma: _____
5. El origen y significado de su nombre _____
6. Dónde nació: _____
7. Lo que dice sobre Colombia: _____
8. Algún detalle sobre su familia: _____

Vocabulary work: Identify the following words or expressions found in the text:

1. 5 words/expressions that deal with singing, song producing, artist awards.
2. 5 words/expressions that deal with faith and/or religion.
3. 5 adjectives that describe people.
4. 2 nationalities.
5. 3 words/expressions that deal with careers/aspirations/dreams.

¡Qué caña! famosos

Música, deporte, películas, libros, juegos para consola y ordenador, Internet...

Shakira

Sólo los chicos de Operación Triunfo han podido con ella en las listas de ventas. Y, por si fuera poco, su "Servicio de lavandería", su primer disco con canciones en inglés, ya está "centrifugando" a mil revoluciones en EE UU.

Érase una vez...: "Oré y le pedí a Dios que me enviara una buena canción, y recuerdo que, unas horas después, empecé a componer 'Objection', el primer tema de *Servicio de lavandería*".

"My taylor is rich": "Tenía que buscar una manera de expresar mis ideas y mis sentimientos, mis historias del día a día en inglés. Así que compré un par de diccionarios de rima, leí poesía y también a autores como Leonard Cohen y Walt Whitman".

Bilingüe: "Puedo hablar de negocios en inglés, pero lloro, grito y amo en español".

¡Ay, el amor!: "Es imposible no hablar del amor en mis canciones. Es el gran misterio de la vida. Hace que me haga nuevas preguntas todos los días".

Ritmo en el cuerpo: "Soy roquera, pero nadie me gana a bailar salsa, cumbia y vallenato" (ritmos latinos muy populares en Colombia).

Un ritual: "Antes de un concierto, rezo el Salmo 91 de la *Biblia*, ese que habla de acogerse a la sombra del Todopoderoso y evitar al león, a la víbora, al cazador".

Se define como... "apasionada y obstinada, pero racional y analítica; o sea, una mujer con corazón, cerebro y coraje".

¡A sus órdenes!: "A mí nadie me obliga a hacer absolutamente nada con lo que no esté de acuerdo. Al menos, en este momento de mi vida..."

Tras el 11 de septiembre... "me preocupa que surjan brotes de xenofobia. Porque yo digo que no todos los árabes son musulmanes, y no todos los musulmanes árabes son terroristas, ni mucho menos. Por ejemplo, yo vengo de una familia libanesa católica, que no es terrorista".

Llanto por Colombia: "Somos una nación con gente pujante, creativa, trabajadora, soñadora, alegre. Sin embargo, cada día tenemos que enterrar a nuestros muertos y procurar mantener la esperanza".

Sueños cumplidos: "Llevo 11 años de carrera y he logrado muchos sueños. No me podía imaginar cuando empezaba, y era una cantante para adolescentes, que terminaría grabando un *MTV Unplugged* (disco acústico grabado en directo)".

¿Y mañana...? "El día que hacer música deje de producirme placer, pues dejaré de compone[r]

AQUELLOS MARAVILLOSOS AÑOS

1985: Empieza a componer sus primeras canciones. Poco después, con sólo 13 años, comienza a cantar profesionalmente.

1991: Firma su primer contrato con Sony Music y graba su primer álbum: *Magia*.

1993: Alcanza el tercer puesto en el Festival de Viña del Mar (Chile) con la canción "Eres".

1996: Su tercer disco, *Pies descalzos*, vende más de cuatro millones de copias y logra 25 discos de oro y 55 de platino.

1998: Su álbum *¿Dónde están los ladrones?* supera los diez millones de copias vendidas.

2000: Premio "Lo Nuestro" a la Mejor Artista Femenina; premio MTV, y dos Grammy Latino en las categorías de Mejor Interpretación Femenina de Pop y de Rock.

2001: Premio Grammy al Mejor Álbum Pop Latino, y dos premios "Lo Nuestro" en las categorías de Mejor Interpretación Rock y Mejor Álbum Rock. La revista británica Teen People la elige entre las 25 personas más bellas del mundo menores de 25 años.

2002: Su último disco, *Servicio de lavandería (Laundry Service)* vende más de medio millón de copias en España y supera ya los dos millones en Estados Unidos.

Okapi, mayo 2002
8

La foto del mes

okapi
es más

DNI

Nombre: Shakira Isabel Mebarak Ripoll. Shakira, en árabe, significa "diosa de la luz".

Nacimiento: Barranquilla (Colombia), 2 de febrero de 1977.

"Grupo sanguíneo": Sangre libanesa, por parte de padre, y colombiana, por parte de madre.

Estado civil: Soltera con compromiso. Su novio, Antonio de la Rúa, de 26 años, es hijo del ex presidente de Argentina, Fernando de la Rúa.

Profesión: Artista, de toda la vida. A los cuatro años de edad ya bailaba la "danza del vientre", rezaba cantando y escribía poemas.

Discos: *Magia* (1991), *Peligro* (1993), *Pies descalzos* (1996), *The Remixes* (1997), *¿Dónde están los ladrones?* (1998), *Shakira MTV Unplugged* (2000) y *Servicio de lavandería* (2001, Columbia).

INTERPRETIVE + INTERPERSONAL MODES:

Interpretation/Discussion Phase:

Guessing Vocabulary in Context. Use the context of the article to guess the meaning of the following words. Check your guesses with a classmate and your teacher.

Page 8
Paragraph 3: negocios _____ lloro _____
grito _____
Paragraph 5: roquera _____
Paragraph 9: brotes de xenofobia _____
Paragraph 10: gente pujante _____ soñadora _____
Paragraph 11: he logrado muchos sueños _____

Page 9
grupo sanguíneo _____

Interpretation. Use the following questions to interpret the article in more detail and to share your reactions. Share your opinions with a small group of classmates.

1. ¿Qué tipo de persona es Shakira? Explique con ejemplos del artículo.
2. ¿De qué se preocupa en cuanto al 11 de septiembre?
3. Describa la etnicidad de Shakira.
4. En su opinión, ¿qué influencia ha tenido su origen hispano en su carrera y en el éxito que ha tenido?
5. ¿Qué otra información le gustaría saber sobre Shakira?

INTERPERSONAL + PRESENTATIONAL MODES:

Creativity Phase:

Role Play

> Student A: You are a reporter for a popular Hispanic teen magazine (your Spanish study has paid off!) and have pulled some strings to get an exclusive interview with Shakira!! Ask her 6 questions (3 might be questions taken from the article, but 3 should be new ones). Be sure to obtain information that would be of interest to your teenage readers!

> Student B: You are Shakira's public relations manager. Shakira was scheduled to be interviewed by a Hispanic teen magazine today, but unfortunately she is sick. Shakira has asked you to participate in the interview in her place, since you also speak Spanish and know Shakira so well. Give details that you think Shakira's teenage fans will enjoy!

Oral: Answering Machine Message. Leave a 3-minute message in Spanish in which you tell your best friend about your exciting interview with Shakira! Share the most exciting information that you learned about her. Ask your friend to return the call so that you can tell him/her the rest of the story.

Written: Magazine Article.   Using some information from the article you read and the additional information from your exclusive interview, write a feature article about Shakira for your Hispanic teen magazine. Pay attention to the layout of the article: use subtitles and perhaps some photos. Write at least 200 words in Spanish and use 5 new words/ expressions (that you learned in the original article). Ask a classmate to read your first draft and respond to the content and accuracy.

INTERPRETIVE MODE (REVISITED):

Extension Phase: (Exploring intertextuality)

Access the Web site http://www.mtv.es and find out more information about Shakira. You could also listen to some of her songs! Share with a group of classmates additional details about her and her life.

Source of lesson: Glisan, 2010, original material.
Source of reading: *Okapi es más*. Mayo 2002. Bayard Revistas. Madrid, España, pp. 8–9.

APPENDIX 8.2 INSTRUCTIONAL CONVERSATION DISCOURSE IN A FOREIGN LANGUAGE CLASS: FEATURE DESCRIPTION

TF	Thematic Focus	A topic is initiated by a question or comment, and developed with related subtopics throughout the discourse.
C	Connected Discourse	Multiple, interactive, connected turns Balanced turn taking & coherent topic development
DT	Direct Teaching	Provision or confirmation of linguistic or other factual information when necessary, in response to 1. student request or use of English 2. student stopping before completing idea 3. student correction of form 4. incomprehensible or inappropriate utterance
QU	Questions with Unpredictable Answers	Questions are open-ended or have unpredictable answers
PL	Promotion of Language and Expression	The teacher extends the quantity and quality of student production 1. open-ended invitation for information or opinion 2. repeating, rephrasing, or expanding her own utterance to elicit a response 3. suggesting an answer in an invitation to speak 4. prompting self-correction by repeating part of a student utterance 5. prompting use of Spanish

R	Responsiveness	The teacher responds to content
		1. confirmation of the student's prior contribution without reformulating
		2. follow-up question that elicits new information
		3. follow-up comment that contributes new information or teacher opinion
RPL	Responsiveness + Promotion of Language	The teacher responds to content, while extending the quantity and quality of production
		1. confirmation of content while reformulating
		2. follow-up question or making a follow-up comment that incorporates a reformulation
		3. follow-up question that suggests new information

Source: Todhunter, S. (2007). Instructional conversations in a high school Spanish class. *Foreign Language Annals, 40,* p. 621. Reprinted by permission of John Wiley & Sons, Inc.

APPENDIX 8.3 A SAMPLE INSTRUCTIONAL CONVERSATION (IC)

Christmas Lights (Segment from Weekend)

Note: The teacher has posed warm-up questions: *¿Qué tal pasaron el fin de semana? ¿Qué bicieron ustedes?* [How did you spend your weekend? What did you do?]

T = Teacher

XXX = unintelligible speech

Features from Appendix 8.2 appear in brackets after each Teacher utterance.

Eduardo:	uh *Yo uh . . .¿Yo uh . . . uh poní?* [uh I uh . . . I uh . . . uh put?]
T:	*¿Puse?* [Put – CORRECT PAST FORM] [DT]
Eduardo:	*Yo puse I knew it XXX ¿Yo puse uh las luces de Navidad?* [I put – I knew it XXX I put uh Christmas lights?]
T:	*¿Sí?* [Yes?] [R]
Eduardo:	*y . . . Mi uh yard* [And . . . my uh yard]
T:	*Sí, ¿En tu patio?* [Yes, in your yard?] [RPL]
Eduardo:	*En mi patio uh, ¿es un lightbulb grande?* [In my yard uh is a big light bulb?]
T:	*Es un grande ¿Una bombilla así?* (DRAWS ON BOARD) [It's a big—a big lightbulb like this?] [DT]
Eduardo:	*Sí.* [Yes.]
T:	*¿Sí?* [Yes?] EXPRESSION OF INTEREST) [R]
Eduardo:	*Sí. Muchos luces.* [Yes. A lot of lights.]
T:	*Much—Muchísimas luces de Navidad, ¿si?* [Very many Christmas lights, yes?] [RPL]
Eduardo:	*Sí.* [Yes.]
T:	*¿De colores o todas en blanco?* [Colored or all white?] [QU/RPL]
Eduardo:	*. . . Todas en blanco.* [. . . All white.]
T:	*Todas en blanco. Aah.* [All white. Aah.] [R]

T: *¡Qué elegante! ¿Verdad?* [How elegant, right?]   [R]

T: *¿Quién más tiene luces en sus—*(MANY HANDS RAISED) [Who else has lights in their—] [QU/PL]

Source: Todhunter, S. (2007). Instructional conversations in a high school Spanish class. *Foreign Language Annals, 40,* pp. 608–609. Reprinted by permission of John Wiley & Sons, Inc.

APPENDIX 8.9 "TALK SCORES": MONITORING AND EVALUATING GROUP SPEAKING ACTIVITIES

What: An uncomplicated way to assess student performance during small group activities.

When: As often as possible and as much as you can observe during a group activity.

Why: Often we have subjective impressions (often correct!!!) about a student's level of participation, cooperation, performance. The TALK SCORES allow you to compare your impressions with real classroom performance.

How: Each letter of the word *TALK* represents one PERFORMANCE OBJECTIVE to be observed during small group activity. During an activity, the teacher should select only ONE objective to observe. The goal should be that at the end of one or two weeks, students have been observed for ALL FOUR performance objectives (a "round").

PERFORMANCE OBJECTIVES:

T = TALKING IN THE TARGET LANGUAGE
Is the student TALKING in the target language?
Is the student TRYING to communicate?
Is the talk TASK RELEVANT?

A = ACCURATE
Is the student performing at an ACCEPTABLE level of ACCURACY?
Does the student demonstrate the objective of the lesson that is being used in this activity (i.e., grammar focus, vocabulary, language function)?

NB Total accuracy is not to be expected but you should have a clear idea of what language elements you will observe. For example, in an activity that requires students to use "time," the teacher could observe how accurately students are constructing time expression (It's 2:30, 3:45, etc.).

L = LISTENING
Is the student ON TASK?
Does the student LISTEN to his/her partner or partners?
Does the student LISTEN to directions?

K = KIND
Is the student KIND and COOPERATIVE?
Does the student KILL the activity by his/her lack of cooperation?
Does the student work with his/her group?

PROCEDURES:

During an activity, circulate around the room observing for ONE performance objective for each activity (T, A, L, or K). Record in your grade book the objective you are observing, the date, and the activity:

EXAMPLE:
Obj. – T
date – 9/18
Act. – ex. c page 12—partner practice

In other words, on September 18, you decided that this activity was a good one to use for observations on TRYING TO TALK IN THE TARGET LANGUAGE.

You should try to cover all four objectives over a two-week period. Again, covering all four objectives is called a round. As your grade book fills up with scores for students, you *will begin to see* students who need more observation and students whom maybe you should observe less often. For example, if at the end of the week Mary Leech has been observed for three objectives while John Arnold has been observed for only one, that will indicate that John needs more of your attention. The goal is that when it is time to compute scores you have an equal number of rounds for each student (e.g., two T scores, two A scores, two L scores, two K scores).

SCORING:

For each objective, score with either a "+", "✓", or "−"

Example

T+	A−	L✓	K+

Plus ("+") scores are worth 2 points   → EXCELLENT
Check ("✓") scores are worth 1 point   → GOOD TO FAIR
Minus ("−") scores are worth 0 points   → NEEDS WORK

For *one round of scoring* (one T, A, L, K) the following grade conversions can be used:

POINTS

7–8	=	A
5–6	=	B
3–4	=	C
1–2	=	D
0	=	F

At the end of a round you will have a PROFILE of a student's activity during pair or group work (see sample grade book page). You may want to experiment with observing more than one objective per activity or per student.

Class: Spanish						
	T	A	L	K		
NAMES					Round one	Grade
Jason	T✔	A−	L−	K+	3	C
Ann	T−	A−	L✔	K+	3	C
John	T+	A+	L+	K−	6	B+
Kelly	T+	A−	L+	K✔	5	B
Mark	T−	A−	L+	K+	4	C+
Kelly	T+	A+	L+	K+	8	A+
Jen	T✔	A+	L+	K+	7	A
Robert	T+	A−	L−	K✔	3	C
Sharon	T✔	A+	L+	K+	7	A
	Ex. C p.12 partner practices	Time activity	Info-gap activity	Peer correction of HW assign.		

Source: Donato, 2004. Used by permission of Richard Donato.

APPENDIX 9.18 MULTIMEDIA RUBRIC

Presenter _____ Place a checkmark in the box that best describes each topic wziegler@stewireless.com rziegler@esu8.org

Topic/Content	Learning	Progressing	Proficient	Excelling
Idea Development	Student selects a topic unrelated to the unit theme.	The student's topic is related to the unit theme. Topic is too narrow or too broad for the level or time provided for the project.	Student selects topic or theme consistent with unit theme. There is a clear understanding of appropriate depth.	Student selects topic or theme consistent with unit theme and clearly identifies the theme to the reader.
Audience	Consideration for the audience appears to be missing.	The students developed the presentation without a theme or audience in mind.	The project is at the correct level of learning for this audience. The demonstration of learning is appropriate for the audience.	The information speaks clearly to the presentation audience. The presentation stretches the audience's knowledge or imagination.
Organization	The information sequences appear to be out of order with details missing the beginning, middle, and end. The presentation appears confused.	The information sequences and details have some order. The beginning, middle, and end of the presentation have some structure.	The information sequencing, details, and summary encourage the viewer to continue learning from the presentation. There is clear development of beginning, middle, and end.	The information sequence, introduction, summary, and closing invite the audience to continue learning through the presentation.
Content	The information is inaccurate and/or has no cited reference as to source.	The information may be accurate; information sources may be referenced.	The content meets the learning goals. Accuracy is apparent in the presentation of the information. Sources cited identify location of the information used to develop the presentation.	The content presented meets the intended learning goals with the information clearly documented as to accuracy and source. Appropriate and consistent voice.
Media Selection	The media selected for the presentation interferes with learning about the topic.	The media selected limits learning about the topic.	The media selected helps the student share his/her information, knowledge, or opinions in a pleasing, appropriate, and purposeful manner.	The media selected enhances the content presented in the presentation.
Design	The media elements limit and/or confuse learning about the topic.	The media elements are more important than the content of the presentation.	The media elements (colors, balance, animation, font, graphics, and/or special effects) contribute to the presentation of the content	The media elements included in the presentation accent the media information presented.
Media Manipulation	The media takes center stage with little focus on the content. The media becomes a distraction.	The audience focuses on the media and the media transitions, making focus on the content difficult.	The focus of the presentation centers on the content rather than on the media used to present the information.	The audience focuses on the content. The media are seamless and invisible, thus allowing the viewers to learn and enjoy the presentation.
Assessment	The learner missed the unit learning goals. The learner's understanding of his/her performance is missing.	The learner mastered few of the unit learning goals. The learner's understanding of his/her performance is beginning to develop.	The student demonstrates understanding, applies content and skills appropriately, and measures the learning gained in this unit by using a rubric.	The learner's presentation meets the unit learning goals The learner can identify, analyze, and defend why his/her presentation received the ranking.

Source: Ziegler, R., & Ziegler, W. (2000). *Multimedia rubric.* Waco, NE: Learning for the Future. Used by permission.

Index